Overview

Management and Performance

Second Edition

Andrew D. Szilagyi, Jr.
University of Houston

Scott, Foresman and Company
Glenview, Illinois
London, England

The Scott, Foresman Series in Management and Organizations
Lyman W. Porter and Joseph W. McGuire, Editors

This book is dedicated to my children, Darin, Dana, and Drew

Credits appear on the last page of the book, which is an extension of the copyright page.

Library of Congress Cataloging in Publication Data
Szilagyi, Andrew D.
  Management and performance.
  Includes bibliographical references and index.
    1. Management.   2. Organizational effectiveness.
I. Title.
HD31.S94   1984   658   83-20029
ISBN 0-673-16604-X

Preface

The link between the activities of managers and the level of effectiveness of the organization is the theme and title of this book—*Management and Performance*/Second Edition.

Focus of the Book

As a look at any management professor's bookshelf will attest, there are many ways of presenting management in an introductory course. Some texts take a behavioral or situational approach, others believe that a quantitative orientation is necessary given today's computer technology, while still others focus on the different schools of management thought. While each of these approaches has merit, this text takes the approach that there is no one best way to manage or to present the topic of management. Rather than build on any single approach, the focus of this book is on what the manager actually does—in other words, *the manager's job*. By learning what managers do, future managers will be able to develop a personal style that works best.

This book emphasizes *the manager's job* in five distinctive ways:

- First, managers perform specific functions. They plan what needs to be done and organize work flows, communication, and people. In addition, they lead employees toward goal accomplishment and attempt to control the resources of an organization efficiently and effectively.

- In performing their functions, managers act within certain roles. They are superiors to groups of employees; they are themselves subordinates to other superiors; information flows through them from sources internal and external to the organization; they represent the organization to other organizations, and they make decisions that influence how well the organization achieves its goals.

- Success as a manager depends largely upon acquiring important managerial skills. These include how well managers know their work, whether they have proper relationships with other employees, the degree to which they perceive how the different components of the organization fit together, and their ability to pinpoint opportunities and problems.

- Because management takes place on many organizational levels, we have stressed the *strategic activities* of the manager's job—strategy formulation, implementation, and evaluation.

- Finally, managers are judged on the basis of performance. It is important for managers to understand that performance cannot be simply measured in dollars and cents. It is many-sided and includes such factors as cost control, sales revenue, adherence to laws, product quality, satisfied employees, and good corporate citizenship.

We present the manager's job in six parts. Part One defines the manager's job, with special emphasis on the development of the field of management and the important historical foundations of management thought. Part Two, Planning, discusses how managers develop the framework for performance, highlighting organizational environments, goals, strategic planning, and decision making. In Part Three, Organizing, establishing order, function, and design is the main subject. Part Four, Leading, discusses the ways managers direct performance, focusing on motivation, leadership, and group behavior. Part Five, Control, presents the important process of evaluating and controlling performance. Finally, Part Six, Change, covers trends and issues that are important to the process of management, managerial careers, and change in management and organizations.

Unique Features

In addition to a strong orientation toward *the manager's job*, this book differs from other management texts in four ways:

▪ *Realism.* It is essential to present real-life situations that managers face daily. Research from current management periodicals such as *Business Week* and *Fortune*, special chapter-opening sections called *The Practice of Management*, and boxed textual illustrations entitled *The Manager's Job* add a sense of realism throughout.

▪ *Involvement.* The best way to get students involved is to have them come as close as possible to experiencing management situations. While this cannot be accomplished solely in a textbook, a good way to achieve involvement is by introducing situations faced by managers through the use of cases and exercises. *A Case for Analysis* is found at the end of every chapter; *Experiential Exercises* are added to ten of twenty chapters.

▪ *International perspective.* Management is not something practiced only in the fifty states. And today, as more and more organizations become multinational, future managers must be prepared to work in foreign cultures, where customs and resources demand adaptive management approaches. This has been recognized by integrating an international perspective throughout the book.

▪ *Organizational focus.* Management is crucial to the success of *all types* of organizations, not just profit-making enterprises. We have included many illustrations from the health-care, governmental, and service sector. In addition, operations management and production is thoroughly covered (chapter 18).

New Features

We have updated, added applications, and strengthened the integrated treatment of the manager's job in this Second Edition. Major aspects of the revision include:

▪ Stressing the *managerial skills* portion of our manager's job framework. At whatever level and in whatever industry or organization a manager works, development of critical skills (technical; human; conceptual; and diagnostic) is essential to his or her success.

▪ New chapters on *Strategic Planning* (chapter 5) and *Management Information Systems* (chapter 17) have been added. Ten other chapters have been extensively revised.

▪ New or expanded treatments of such topics as automation and robotics, special management groups (venture groups, quality circles), the Japanese/American relationship in management, the current increased emphasis on quality, the new matrix organizational design, and the influence of culture, which is critical to our understanding of management in the international realm, are given.

■ Nearly one-half of the more-than-30 cases and experiential exercises in the book are new. Most are drawn from current practitioner literature and deal with the manager in real-life situations.

■ *The Manager's Job* inserts in each chapter have not only doubled in number, but most portray situations which have occurred during the last two years.

■ In addition to the popular *Summary for the Manager,* most chapters end with a section entitled *Points to Consider: An Emphasis on Managerial Skills.* This short section highlights the relationship between the chapter's content and the development of managerial skills.

■ Finally, each of the book's six main parts begins with an interview with a practicing manager. These interviews introduce the chapter's content through the words of a real manager, tying together theoretical and applied approaches.

Acknowledgments

I am indebted to my colleagues, many of whom improved this book in numerous ways. I am especially grateful to the following individuals who took valuable time to offer comments and reviews: Peter J. Frost, University of British Columbia; David A. Gray, University of Texas, Arlington; Ricky W. Griffin, University of Missouri, Columbia; Lawrence R. Jauch, Southern Illinois University; Marvin Karlins, University of South Florida; William R. LaFollette, Ball State University; Harry N. Mills, East Texas State University; William L. Moore, California State University, Hayward; W. Alan Randolph, University of South Carolina; Celeste M. Sichenze, Northern Virginia Community College; Mary S. Thibodeaux, North Texas State University. I would also like to recognize the students at the University of Houston for patiently undergoing classroom testing of many of the book's concepts, cases, and exercises.

My special thanks go to a group of individuals whose time, commitment, and support of my work were extensive. First, appreciation is given to Lyman W. Porter and Joseph W. McGuire, University of California-Irvine, who, in their role as consulting editors to Scott, Foresman, made significant contributions to the text. Second, Jim Sitlington, John Nolan, Trisha Nealon, and Barbara Schneider of Scott, Foresman are singled out for their support, commitment, and contributions to this second edition. It is not often that an author can say that he or she has had the opportunity to work with true professionals. Even though we have been through some rough times, I can call them friends. Finally, I would like to acknowledge A. Benton Cocanougher, dean of the College of Business Administration, University of Houston, for his support.

Of course, the individuals who receive my greatest thanks are my wife, Sandy, and my children, Darin, Dana, and Drew. Many times the need to meet deadlines took precedence over recreational activities, and ''vacation'' has been a word seldom used in our home. To my family, I can only express my love and appreciation, for without their help, *Management and Performance*/Second Edition would only be an idea.

Andrew D. Szilagyi, Jr.
Houston, Texas

Contents

PART TWO

Developing the Framework for Performance: Planning

7   Managerial Decision Making   208

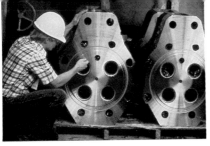

14   Managing Groups   464

PART FIVE

Evaluating Performance: Control

INTERVIEW:

Elizabeth Calderon
Associate Hospital Director
Hermann Hospital, Houston   502

17 Management Information Systems   578

18 Production and Operations Control   604

The Adaptive Organization and Manager: Change

Management and Performance

INTERVIEW

Michael Lombardo

Behavioral Scientist and Project Manager, Research Division Center for Creative Leadership Greensboro, North Carolina (The Center for Creative Leadership is a nonprofit educational institution that aims to provide research-based tools for recognizing and developing creative leadership potential in management.)

Q: As you see it in your work as a researcher in the field of management, what does a manager need for success in his or her profession?

A: Although I can just scratch the surface, I am going to tick off six points that illustrate some critical managerial skills. Most reflect an *understanding* of the particulars of the individual manager's job.

First, understand your organization. Every organization has a culture that is unique. The kinds of people who make up the organization give it its character.

Second, you need to understand your organization's major agenda. The elements of an agenda include the problems, priorities, and processes that face a manager in his or her particular role. A manager spends a lot of time figuring out the external environment and then learns to focus on one or two major issues.

Third, use your time as a manager wisely. The nature of managerial work is just too complex for the well-known but simplistic time-management formulas.

Make yourself *available* to others.

Fourth, managers must develop ways of assimilating and using information. People have natural limits when it comes to information processing. A manager must learn to chunk up information into categories and themes and to follow a focusing strategy. Also a manager must remember that others are needed to help process information. *Groups* of people, entire departments, work on truly complex problems; a manager must learn to depend upon his or her staff for support.

Fifth, managers must learn to distinguish between the kinds of problems they face. Some problems are straightforward, but most problems, 90% I'd say, are more complex, often ill-structured, and frequently ambiguous. Problems can develop over the course of several years, and their nature can change as they develop. Perhaps suddenly, perhaps gradually, managers find that they are not dealing with what they thought they were.

Sixth, and perhaps most critical, managers must develop the ability to *take aim* on a problem. They must ask "what questions do we have to answer?" Is it a matter of analysis of competition? Production processes? R & D possibilities? Can our action on a problem be coordinated with other areas of our organization? Should it be? How does this problem impact on the overarching strategy and planning for the entire organization?

Q: Do the key managerial skills vary in importance by level?

A: Very clearly. Managerial skills vary by level because managerial jobs vary by level.

Lower-level managers spend their time on details—minor problems, breakdowns in the system; they actually have a good deal of variety on the job, but in only one content area. Higher-level managers have fewer problems, but in more content areas. Content

Defining the Manager's Job

areas would be defined as research and development, accounting and wages, recruitment and personnel, policy and strategy, sales and commercial matters, general management, and the like.

Higher-level managers tend to engage in fragmented decision making. The pace of life for lower-level managers may be hectic, but their decision-making tends to be straightforward. The pace of life for upper-level managers tends to be relatively calm, but their decision-making tends to be complex—calling for uncommon diagnostic and conceptual skills.

Q: In what ways has the manager's job changed in the last decade? Are there any unique problems?

A: There has been a dramatic increase in the last 10 years in the organizational ambiguity managers have to deal with. Governmental deregulation has had a major impact on entire industries.

There have also been major changes in demography. The post-WWII baby boom has produced a surplus of junior managers, and there are not enough senior managers to train them. Time frames for careers have changed as a result.

Furthermore, there has been a decrease in the number of levels of management as organizations have become more decentralized. Managers are frequently making lateral moves.

An increasing number of managers today are specialists. More power is accorded to those people responsible for financial and legal questions. There is more tension between line management and specialized staff management than there ever was in the past. Many decisions hinge now on the regulatory environment—what's legally right and what's legally wrong.

Although financial, legal, and strategic aspects of management have become increasingly important, many businesses are, in spite of this, going back to basics. Organizations are rethinking why they are in business, and many are answering with the original statements that defined their enterprises—their aims to produce a specific, high-quality product, to provide a special service, etc.

Q: From your experience, what are the major challenges facing managers of today and future managers?

A: Managing the problems of size—the magnitude, coordination, scope of what must be done—is one of the major challenges facing managers and future managers today. The challenge is in combining efficiencies and economies of scale with uniform procedures; it is a question of *control*.

Q: How may future managers be better prepared to face these challenges?

A: Preparation for managerial jobs has an important place in colleges and universities; and now there is a trend for training to be somewhat less analytic and more experiential. In the past, there was a tendency to present organizations as if they were rational creations—they are not. One well-known management maxim states that knowing the "right" answer is 10% of a problem's solution, and getting the job done through people is the other 90%. Organizational politics is really a term for how decisions are made. The important things to remember is that the real skills are *implementation* skills.

On-the-job preparation is most important of all. Many things contribute to learning on the job. An organization's effort to help people gain varied experience, or job enrichment (rather than rotating job content, which is not always possible), is a primary way. In addition, managers frequently find themselves in new situations in their existing jobs. Starting from scratch on a project, working from a position of suddenly new responsibilities or a with jump in scope, or moving from line management to staff or vice versa are typical challenges that provide on-the-job preparation. It's only common sense for management to develop people by systematically rotating their experience.

1

The Manager's Job

Chapter Outline

Key Points

1. Management deals with resources, tasks, and goals.
2. The manager's job concerns the integration of functions, skills, and roles to achieve performance goals.
3. Three types of managers exist: executive, middle level, and first line.
4. Four managerial functions are identified: planning, organizing, leading, and controlling.
5. Effective managers acquire important technical, human, conceptual, and diagnostic skills.
6. Applying managerial skills in the different functions requires behavior in at least three roles: interpersonal, informational, and decisional.
7. In defining managerial performance, one must be concerned with standards of performance, level of analysis, time frame, and measurement components.
8. Success in the future for managers may depend heavily on the ability to understand the importance of international organizations and on the ability to manage in different countries and cultures.
9. Management cannot be reduced to a simple checklist of activities; it requires a high degree of flexibility in adapting to many complex situations.

Walt Disney

To people around the globe, Walt Disney was known for his creative genius and his contributions to the world of entertainment. Yet, in none of the separate arts that made his company famous—drawing, painting, photography, writing, music, acting, and architecture—did he himself excel. What Walt Disney did do well was inspire, stimulate, restrain, plan, and coordinate hundreds of talents brighter than his own into producing at levels of quality that could not have been accomplished without him. In essence, he was an excellent manager.

Born into a working-class family in the Midwest, Disney quickly exhibited skills for hard work, perseverance, and use of new technologies in work. To his credit, he built an organization around these same skills and principles so effectively that the company continued to prosper after his death in 1974.

Each success forced him toward more difficult goals. Mickey Mouse was succeeded by the Silly Symphonies, which broke new technical ground in the coordination of sound and color. In 1938, he gambled with the first feature-length cartoon, *Snow White and the Seven Dwarfs.* He then produced *Fantasia,* which blended color, shape, and motion with classical music. In the fifties the studio produced an ambitious program of cartoons (*Cinderella, Peter Pan*) and live-action movies (*20,000 Leagues Under the Sea*).

With the introduction of television, most people in the movie industry trembled. Disney did not. He set out to master the new entertainment medium with his *True-Life Adventure* features and, eventually, the highly successful *Disney's Wonderful World of Color* weekly series. His movie ventures did not stop during this time, as the success of the Davy Crockett epics attests. When he turned his attention to the design of Disneyland, he achieved effects of structural coordination that amazed even the most skilled city planners.

Out of the public's eye, Disney established a well-run organization that could produce his entertainment products. He set up different departments to concentrate on ventures for the various markets (e.g., tv, movies). In this way, he kept his finger on the pulse of the viewing public. He also maintained a separate technical and idea development unit to ensure that the creative skills that made his organization so successful were not impeded. His skills at management even made an impact in the financial area when he established formal financial controls systems.

Disney's biggest contribution, however, was instilling in his people ideals of hard work, creativity, teamwork, and attention to detail. This style of management cascaded through the organization and into every job. Overall, Walt Disney made a profound impact not only on twentieth century culture, but also on management in the creative industries.

Suggested from Max Ways, "The Business Hall of Fame," *Fortune* (January 1976): 121.

1

What do Robert Crandall, Mary Kay Ash, James McIlhenny, John Nevin, and Tom Landry have in common with Walt Disney? Beyond the possibility that all have at one time visited Disneyland, the similarity does not concern age, sex, or industry affiliation (i.e., air travel, cosmetics, publishing, manufacturing, or professional sports). What each of these persons has in common is that they are in some way concerned with the integration of resources, tasks, and goals—in other words, they are managers. They happen to be high-level managers: Robert Crandall is president of American Airlines, Mary Kay Ash is founder and chairman of Mary Kay Cosmetics, Inc., James McIlhenny is president of *U.S. News & World Report,* John Nevin is chairman of Firestone Tire and Rubber, and Tom Landry is the coach of the Dallas Cowboys professional football team.

The three characteristics—resources, tasks, and goals—are basic to what organizations are all about. Consider, for example, a major league baseball team such as the Chicago Cubs. It consists of players and equipment and performs on a field (resources). Players are assigned particular positions (tasks) and attempt to perform at a level that will win as many games as possible (goal). Similarly, a hospital involves employees, equipment, buildings, and finances (resources), functioning through the work of individual specialists such as physicians, nurses, and therapists (tasks), whose objective is to improve the health of the patients (goal). The job of integrating resources and tasks for goal attainment is a key function of *management*. While the responsibilities of managers vary greatly—from choir director and baseball manager to corporation president—we can say that without some form of management, organizations could not exist.

This text has two major objectives: (1) to focus on the manager's job by examining how managerial performance at every level affects the performance of individual workers, departments, and entire organizations; and (2) to present concepts and techniques for improving managerial performance. These objectives apply to every organization we will study. All organizations strive to accomplish goals, be they oil companies (return on investment, profit margin), hospitals (patient health, cost control), police departments (crime prevention), or a local chamber of commerce (drawing new industry to the area).

The Field of Management

A careful examination of the writings of management scholars and practicing managers reveals a number of definitions of management. While some give lengthy definitions, others simply define it as the process of getting things done through people. For our purposes, we will define management as: *The process of integrating resources and tasks toward the achievement of stated organizational goals.*

Managers—those who practice management—are responsible for giving directions to the organizations they manage. They must translate organizational goals into unit objectives, organize resources (people, finances, and equipment) in a manner to achieve results, and see to it that the stated goals are met.

Although this definition may be simple, the manager's job rarely is, because problems must be faced continually, and new, different situations crop up constantly. Equipment shortages, employee motivation problems, rising costs, consumer and community reactions, and the like confront managers daily. Getting everything to work smoothly is the challenge that makes management such an interesting field.

The Process of Management

Management is concerned with resources, tasks, and goals. More importantly, however, management involves a *process;* in other words, a systematic and organized way of doing things.[1] All managers, regardless of their particular organizational affiliations, engage in a systematic, interrelated set of activities designed to achieve an objective. Understanding this process is the key to successful management.

In exhibit 1-1, we have identified the major managerial activities that form the foundation for our discussion. First, managers focus on *deciding what to do*. This involves establishing the framework for performance, or *planning* the work to be done. At this stage, for example, the product manager of household detergents at Procter & Gamble is concerned with such external factors as consumer attitudes toward household products, personal disposable income levels, recent innovations in product development, and the source and strength of the competition. Integrating the

Exhibit 1-1
The Manager's
Job Simplified

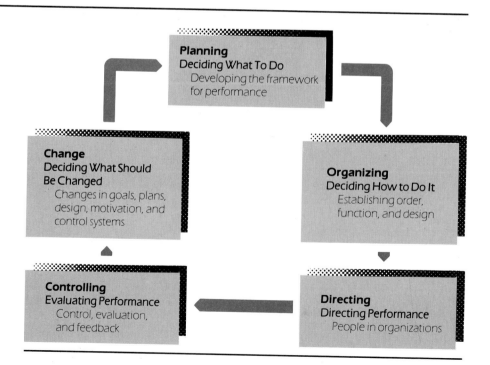

influences of the external environment with the resources and goals of the organization (e.g., market share, profit margin) leads to the achievement of these goals.

Second, managers *decide how to do it;* in other words, *organizing* to establish order and function and to design their unit to achieve the stated goals. At this stage, the product manager focuses on selecting people to make up the team; training them to do their respective jobs; establishing authority, responsibility, and accountability relationships; and acquiring and allocating the necessary financial and physical resources.

Third, a concern for *directing performance* becomes dominant. In essence, the focus is on *leading* employees in the most effective manner possible. At this stage, the hospital administrator, for example, concentrates on improving worker motivation and cooperation between groups and on examining his or her own leadership style as it relates to goal achievement.

Fourth, managers become involved in *evaluating performance*. This is the *control* function, which, for the hospital administrator, involves evaluating individual and group performance, examining financial indicators of effectiveness and efficiency, and investigating any problems that may have developed in communication, resource allocation, and interpersonal relationships.

Finally, the manager looks at *what needs to be changed*. This emphasis on adaptability concerns evaluating all previous activities—plans, goals, employee selection and training, motivation, group behavior, and control systems—to determine what factors or activities may or may not need *change* so that goals are achieved.

It should be pointed out that the four activities of planning, organizing, leading, and controlling—what we will term the management *functions*—are unique activities. The change component, however, generally occurs *within* each of the four management functions and is not considered as a separate activity. Given the rapidly changing environment of management, we will highlight the impact of change throughout the book and particularly in the last two chapters.

Art, Science, and Profession

The best response to the question of whether management is an art or a science is that it is both.[2] If we define *art* as a personal aptitude or skill, then management has certain artistic components. To manage effectively, individuals must have not only the necessary abilities to lead but also a set of critical skills acquired through time, experience, and practice.[3] On the other hand, management involves certain aspects that have a strong scientific orientation to them. To perform at high levels in a variety of situations, managers must be able to draw on the sciences—particularly economics, political science, mathematics, psychology, sociology, and cultural anthropology—for assistance and guidance.

For our purposes, it seems more appropriate to present management as being a *field of knowledge* that is heavily *applications and practitioner* oriented and *situationally* based. This presentation recognizes the necessity of systematically studying why and how people work together to accomplish specific goals. In other words, management is more accurately defined as a field than as a science, because its foundations are built with components of several sciences rather than with self-contained theories and laws.

Similar to the physician, lawyer, or engineer, the manager is a practitioner. As the physician draws on the basic sciences of chemistry, biology, and physiology, the manager draws on the sciences of mathematics, psychology, and sociology to solve some practical problems. But, like the physician or lawyer, the manager frequently is confronted with problems that cannot be answered by science. These problems cannot stand the time of careful scientific research, but must be solved in a short period of time.

This *situational* nature of management concerns two important facts about managing.[4] First, not all problems faced by managers can be solved with an equation or theory. For example, solving the problem of low motivation for two subordinates may mean additional training for one and more challenging tasks for the other. Each situation is different and requires correspondingly different corrective strategy. Second, no matter how often we hear about the "behavioral sciences," "management science," and "scientific management," in planning activities, leading people, and controlling performance, the manager will find intuition, subjective beliefs, or just pure common sense to be very important.

For example, Delta Airlines, unlike many of its competitors during the late 1960s and early 1970s, resisted the stampede to replace their fleet of first generation jets with the new, more expensive jumbo jets. Their decision on aircraft needs was based on a combination of analysis and common sense. Delta's detailed analysis indicated that most of their routes were relatively short (less than 500 miles on an average), making the larger jets uneconomical. Intuition and common sense told them that their main aircraft—the Boeing 727—was far from being obsolete. They felt that the plane was well built and ideally suited for short- to medium-distance routes. More than anything, however, Delta's management believed that the plane was adaptable to changes that could make a good plane a better one, such as improved engines, navigation equipment, and cabin design. Along with Braniff and Continental airlines, Delta convinced Boeing not to give up on the 727.

Delta eventually ordered only enough jumbo jets to cover some of their longer routes. In addition, they were able to purchase a new series of 727s with key modifications such as a fuel-efficient engine. As a result, they not only have a modern, new fleet of efficient planes, they are not overly burdened by a large debt as are their competitors who purchased many jumbo jets.[5]

One area in which the common-sense manager has had some success has been in figuring out the fickle American appetite. Confronted in 1960 with what his lawyer called a bad deal—$2.7 million for the McDonald's name—Ray Kroc said, "I closed my office door, cussed up and down, threw things out the window, called my lawyer back, and said, 'Take it!' I felt in my funny bone it was a sure thing."[6] Kroc's feelings proved correct, as systemwide sales from the McDonald's fast food chain are nearing $3 billion.

Some individuals state that "knowledge (science) without skill (art) is useless" and "skill (art) without knowledge (science) means stagnation"; we may add that "managing without common sense spells trouble."

Perhaps the key to management success is the ability to tie together knowledge, skill, and common sense into a workable framework.

Is the field of management a true profession? When one looks at the three characteristics (principles, performance, and ethics) of a profession, the answer is no stronger than a *maybe*. First, are managerial decisions based on a generally accepted set of *principles*? Principles exist—such as steps in planning, the control process, and the like—but few are generally accepted by all as involved in or perfectly applicable to each situation.[7]

Second, are the achievements of managers recognized through *performance* as opposed to such factors as favoritism, nepotism, accident, the Peter Principle, and so on? It is the rule rather than the exception that competence determines the good name of a manager. Many people, however, can point to managers who have achieved their positions through reasons not related to work, such as family or personal relationships.

Finally, are managers directed by a clearly stated code of ethics? Here again, most managers have a good understanding of what is right and wrong. However, as we will discuss in a later chapter, a clearly delinated code of ethics does not exist. As a result, management is forming its own code of ethics as certain questionable practices are tried in the public eye.

What this all means is that a manager's job is part art and part science, performed in a manner approaching that of a profession. In a later section of this chapter, we will redefine what the manager does in terms of functions, skills, and roles.

Types of Managers

As you are aware, there are many different types of managers in organizations with varying tasks and responsibilities. In this section, we broadly classify managers into two categories: (1) level, and (2) responsibilities.

Levels of Management

In order to illustrate the different levels of managers, exhibit 1-2 depicts the organizational chart of a medium-sized chemical company, and exhibit 1-3 isolates the manufacturing function of the company.

In exhibit 1-3, three levels of management are shown. These levels usually are called executive, middle, and first-line management.[8]

Executive Managers Sometimes termed "top management," this small group of individuals makes up the highest level of management. Managers in these positions are responsible for interacting with representatives of the external environment (e.g., financial institutions, governmental and political figures, important suppliers and customers) and establishing organizational goals, plans, strategies, and broad operating policies and guidelines. While there is a great variety across different organizations, typical titles include president, chief executive officer (CEO or COO for chief operating officer), executive vice president, senior vice president, and vice president.

Exhibit 1-2
A Typical Organizational Chart

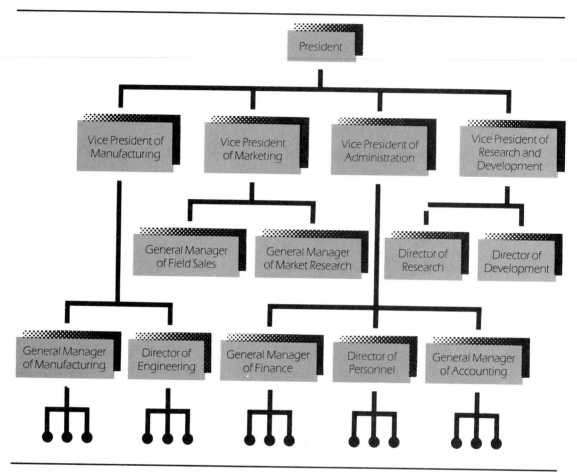

Middle-Level Managers   A number of management levels are included within this category, such as the positions of general manager, plant manager, and operations superintendent shown in exhibit 1-3. The responsibilities of middle-level managers include translating executive orders into operation, implementing plans, and directly supervising lower-level managers. This is probably one of the most important management levels, because it is a prime training ground for future executives, and it is at the center of the organization's activities.

First-Line Managers   Characterized by such titles as sales manager, clerical supervisor, and lab supervisor, these managers are responsible for directing first-line, nonsupervisory employees. Additional duties include evaluations of day-to-day performance indicators such as volume produced, quality control, inventory, and preventive maintenance. The majority of management graduates will be on this level within the first three to five years of full-time employment.

Exhibit 1-3
Levels of Management in a Manufacturing Company

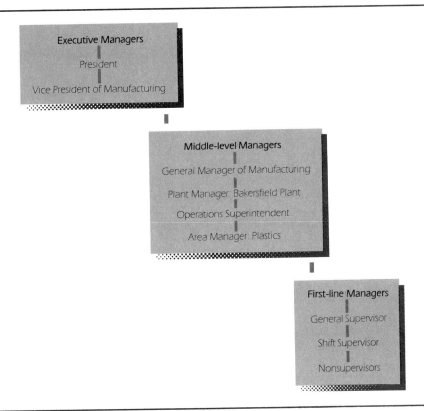

Responsibilities

A second way of describing types of managers is to distinguish between *line* and *staff* responsibilities. A line manager's responsibilities and activities have a *direct impact* on the products or services of the organization. In the company depicted in exhibit 1-2, the marketing and sales managers are considered line managers. A plant manager is also a line manager.

A staff manager's responsibilities and duties *support* the activities of line managers. Examples are managers of personnel, finance, research and development, and accounting. The personnel manager of a chemical plant, for example, is responsible for the human resources of the facility, including: (1) identification of plant staffing needs; (2) selection, placement, and training of newly hired employees; (3) company compliance with federal guidelines on safety, antidiscrimination, and pay policies; (4) development and implementation of a performance evaluation system; and (5) maintenance of the plant's compensation, employee benefit, and employee relations functions. We will discuss in more detail the differences and similarities between line and staff managers in later chapters.

Managerial Functions

We have presented the process of management as involving planning, organizing, leading, and controlling. This process—what we will term managerial functions—is outlined in detail in exhibit 1-4. Managerial functions will be examined as the first of the three components that make up the manager's job: functions, skills, and roles. The boxed insert above illustrates these components in that Ninfa Laurenzo included them all in her definition of what makes her a successful manager. Functions, skills, and roles will not only be discussed at length in this chapter, but our study of them will also serve as the basic foundation for this book.

Developing the Framework for Performance: Planning

Planning is probably one of the most important managerial functions because it sets the pattern for the other activities to follow. Planning encompasses four elements:

- Evaluating environmental forces and organizational resources
- Establishing a set of organizational goals
- Developing strategies and plans to achieve the stated goals
- Formulating a decision-making process.

Consider a large petroleum corporation during the early 1970s. The oil embargo and the influence of OPEC countries had drawn attention to the corporation's vulnerability to environmental forces. The majority of the company's crude-oil supplies were controlled by the foreign governments, and top management believed that the

Exhibit 1-4
Managerial Functions

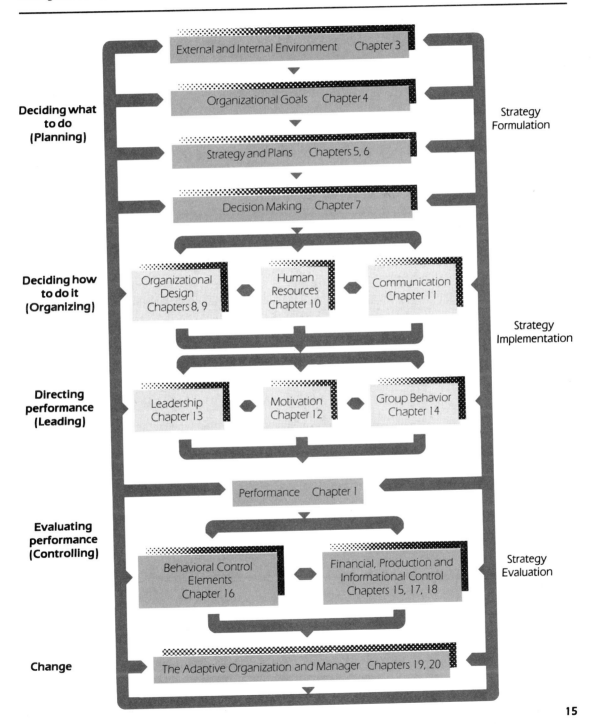

Deciding what
to do
(Planning)

External and Internal Environment   Chapter 3

Organizational Goals   Chapter 4

Strategy and Plans   Chapters 5, 6

Decision Making   Chapter 7

Strategy
Formulation

Deciding how
to do it
(Organizing)

Organizational
Design
Chapters 8, 9

Human
Resources
Chapter 10

Communication
Chapter 11

Strategy
Implementation

Directing
performance
(Leading)

Leadership
Chapter 13

Motivation
Chapter 12

Group Behavior
Chapter 14

Performance   Chapter 1

Evaluating
performance
(Controlling)

Behavioral Control
Elements
Chapter 16

Financial, Production and
Informational Control
Chapters 15, 17, 18

Strategy
Evaluation

Change

The Adaptive Organization and Manager   Chapters 19, 20

long-term impact of uncertain raw materials would be detrimental to the organization's survival (evaluating environmental forces). An evaluation of the strengths of the corporation concluded that the organization: (1) was really an energy company with untapped resources in coal reserves; and (2) the refining division had developed skills that could be easily transferred from the manufacture of oil products to industrial chemicals (evaluating organizational resources).

Therefore, top management strongly believed that the future stability of the company rested on the expansion of activities related to the manufacture (mining) and distribution of coal and industrial chemicals. A corporate goal was established: by the year 1990, at least 50 percent of the company's revenues will come from coal and chemical products (establishing organizational goals). Formal five- and ten-year plans were developed to meet the stated goal. Included in the plans were allocation of resources (financial, human, and physical), statements of responsibility for all levels of management regarding implementation, and a timetable of expected events (developing plans and the formulation of a decision-making process).

Establishing Order, Function, and Design: Organizing

As shown in exhibit 1-4, once management has established goals and developed plans to achieve these goals, the emphasis moves to designing and developing an organization that can successfully implement the stated plans. It is important to recognize that various goals require different kinds of organizations. For example, in the oil company, the type of organization developed in the petroleum division may not be effective in the coal or chemical divisions.

Three elements are essential to organizing:

- Developing the structure of the organization
- Acquiring and training human resources
- Establishing communication patterns and networks.

As an example, assume that you are the administrator of a soon-to-be-opened medical diagnostic clinic in Seattle. The clinic will employ physicians, nurses, technicians, and a maintenance staff and function primarily as an outpatient clinic specializing in comprehensive physical examinations. Although it will serve the general public, the clinic will rely on contracts to perform physicals on the employees of local firms and institutions.

Once the planning phase has been completed, your concern switches to internal organization. First, you formulate elements of the clinic's structure. You establish policies and procedures for authority relationships, reporting patterns, the chain of command, departmentalization, and various administrative responsibilities (designing the structure of the organization). Second, you take steps to hire a competent work force. Where required, you establish programs for training new employees in skills necessary to their jobs (acquiring and training personnel). Finally, you build formal communication and information networks, emphasizing communication on all levels, the types of information to be communicated, how communication is to flow, and reduction of barriers to effective communication (establishing communication networks).

Directing Employee Performance: Leading

After the organization's goals and plans have been formulated and the issues of structure and staffing have been resolved, the next step is directing the employees toward attaining the stated goals. The essential function of *leading, directing,* or *motivating* is getting the organization's employees to perform in ways that will assist in achieving the defined goals.

Three components make up the leading function:

- Motivating employees
- Influencing employees
- Forming effective groups.

As can be seen, the focus of the leading function is on the individual employee as well as on the interrelationships between employees in groups.

Returning to the example, your attention as clinic administrator is first directed toward establishing conditions that will result in high employee motivation, such as providing a performance-based pay and promotion program and jobs that are designed to offer challenge, variety, and career growth. As a newly appointed manager, you next must evolve your own most effective leadership style and learn reinforcing behaviors that will hopefully influence employees to high performance (influencing employees). Third, you must give attention to how groups will be formed; i.e., to which composition and structural characteristics of the groups can yield high levels of performance (forming effective groups).

Evaluating Performance: Controlling

The major objective of the control function is ensuring that the organization is in fact moving toward achieving the formulated goals.

Three basic components constitute the control function:

- Elements of a control system
- Evaluating and rewarding employee performance
- Controlling financial, informational, and physical resources.

An effective control function allows the manager to know whether the organization's performance is on target or if he or she must take corrective actions to meet performance standards.

To accomplish this, the overall organizational goal is translated into performance standards (control system elements) by establishing individual goals and a formal performance evaluation system to rate the extent to which the goals have been accomplished. Depending on their performance, employees are given rewards such as pay increases and promotions. If performance is consistently below standard, a decision to terminate employment may have to be made (evaluating and rewarding employee performance). Next, a formalized—usually computer-based—reporting system is developed. Frequently called a management information system (MIS), it is used to

"To my mind, the secret of executive performance is the ability to delegate authority. For instance, nothing ever reaches this desk."

Drawing by Whitney Darrow, Jr.; © 1969 The New Yorker Magazine, Inc.

collect data and report organizational performance in such terms as financial indicators, adherence to scheduled deadlines, and the degree of utilization of the organization's resources. Attention is given to the important nonbehavioral aspects of organizational performance, such as cost analysis, budgeting, production, inventory, or quality control (controlling resources).

The Adaptive Organization

One of the most important points managers need to understand is that organizations are rarely static creations. More often than not, there are major changes in the internal or external environment that force the organization to change.

For example, any of the following situations would cause a radical change in the functions of management in our oil company example:

- A Mideast oil-producing country is overthrown, and a communist government takes over.

- Workers at a newly opened chemical plant join a militant union and go out on three wildcat strikes over a nine-month period.

- Congress passes a law requiring divestiture of assets (i.e., oil companies can no longer control the flow of gasoline from the ground to the service station pump).

Similarly, what reaction would our clinic's management have in any of the following situations?

- A national health insurance law is enacted.

- Insurance companies refuse to cover medical malpractice suits.

- Federal and state governments pass laws that limit hospital cost increases.

Reading daily newspapers reveals that these situations are not unrealistic. They can—and do—occur!

These examples suggest that managers must not only be able to adapt to changing conditions but, whenever possible, must develop methods to forecast changes and their impact. It is also important to recognize that adaptation and change involve how the organization is managed as well as the skills, duties, and career development of the manager.

Strategic Activities of the Manager's Job

Exhibit 1-4 also indicates that the functions involved in the process of management can be broken down into three broad *strategic activities:* (1) strategy formulation; (2) implementation; and (3) evaluation. *Strategy formulation* is planning to achieve organizational goals, stated in a way that defines what business the organization is in or is to be in, as well as the kind of organization it is or is to be. This process asks what the organization *might do,* in terms of environmental opportunities; what it *can do,* relating to present and future organizational resources; what it *wants to do,* reflecting the aspirations of top management; what it *ought to do,* bringing ethical and societal issues to the forefront. It integrates these decisions into a statement of what it *should do.*[9] *Implementation* and *evaluation* deal with mobilizing organizational resources and are critical steps in accomplishing goals.

Consider the case of Scripto, a familiar name in writing instruments. The company had planned to be the world's foremost producer of pens and pencils. But in implementing this plan in the mid-1970s, Scripto initially ignored the market for cheap, disposable ballpoint pens (18-25 cents), preferring instead to concentrate its efforts in the market for higher priced writing instruments. This error allowed Bic Pen the opening they needed to introduce a line of less expensive pens and felt-tip instruments. As a result, Bic has overtaken Scripto in sales and market share and far exceeds Scripto in almost all the important financial measures of performance.

Realities of Managerial Functions

From a functional orientation, management is a systematic way of getting things done in organizations. However, we cannot relegate managerial functions to a checklist of things to do, how to do them, and when they should be done. On the contrary, the process of management is best seen as the basic framework for performance, not a universal, all-encompassing theory or set of procedures. We must look at reality on at least three points.

First, the functional approach to management is not a rigid, step-by-step system. In other words, if we think that on Monday, managers plan; on Tuesday, they restructure the department; on Wednesday, they motivate, we are wrong. Managers do all these things *every day* they work. Planning may follow goal setting, but motivation, leadership, communication, and control are daily occurrences. For example, the project manager who is responsible for the construction of a warehouse may systematically go from planning through to control on one project before it has been completed. However, if this manager is overseeing the construction of three warehouses at the same time, he or she must make all the management functions part of each day. This overlapping of management functions indicates the need for a flexible approach to the manager's job.

Second, levels of proficiency in each function differ for individual managers. That is, one manager may feel most skilled in planning, another's strength may be in motivating subordinates, and a third may feel most comfortable with the quantitative aspects of the control function. This does not mean that the corporate planner does only planning, the construction supervisor only supervises, or the manager of internal audit only works with figures. Managers must be skilled in all the management functions to be effective in their work. As we will see, managers at different levels in the organization allocate proportionately different amounts of time to planning, organizing, leading, and controlling. However, although the individual may be most proficient in one managerial function, the need to develop skills in the other functions cannot be overlooked.

Finally, we must all recognize that there is no "one best way" to manage an organization. The process of management is a basic framework, not the source of solutions to organizational problems. Each situation faced by managers may require a slightly different application of the framework. This *situational* approach to management has been termed the *contingency* approach, and it is directed toward developing managerial actions that are most appropriate for the specific situation and the people involved.[10] By considering the important variables in a situation, the manager can take the most appropriate actions needed to achieve organizational goals. In other words, an effective manager can *recognize, diagnose,* and *adapt* to the situation.

Established situational or contingency approaches will be covered throughout this book. The manager who applies these approaches knows very well that pat answers to organizational problems do not exist. If they did, all we would need to do is list them and refer to them at the appropriate time. Predicting performance is certainly much more elusive than this. Even the best manager just cannot find simple answers to complex problems, and this is why the field of management is so challenging.

 ## How Managers Spend Their Time

Our discussion to this point has focused primarily on the types of managers and what functions they perform. While most managers are concerned with each function, the time devoted to each varies by management level in the organization.

Exhibit 1-5 is a suggested profile of the amount of time that the three levels of management—executive, middle, and first line—devote to the main functions. Some interesting differences evolve from an analysis of this exhibit.[11] Executive management spends the most time on issues of planning and change. This is in line with the duties and responsibilities of chief executives, which concern overall policy and *strategy formulation.* The main function of a chief executive, such as in major retailers Sears, J.C. Penney, and Montgomery Ward, is to chart out, plan and direct the company's progress, along with keeping a sharp eye out for possible important

Exhibit 1-5
Distribution of the Manager's Time

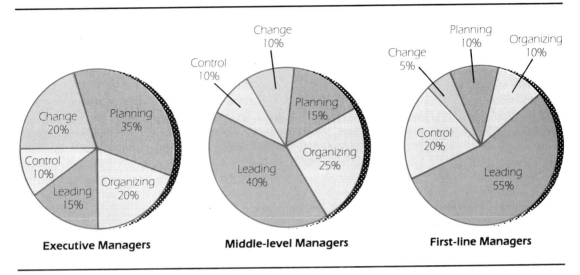

Change 10%
Control 10%
Planning 15%
Organizing 25%
Leading 40%

Change 20%
Planning 35%
Control 10%
Leading 15%
Organizing 20%

Planning 10%
Organizing 10%
Change 5%
Control 20%
Leading 55%

Executive Managers   **Middle-level Managers**   **First-line Managers**

changes. For example, top management in these three merchandising firms would be concerned with overall pricing strategies and the location of new stores, and they would frequently analyze changes in consumer preferences, mobility, and disposable income.

At the middle manager level, the time allocation switches to an emphasis on organizing and leading. This is what we call *strategy implementation*. In other words, these managers are primarily responsible for putting into action the plans and strategies of the executive management team. For example, store managers at Sears devote most of their time to organizing their stores and directing subordinate department managers in implementing the company's new product and pricing policies.

Finally, leading and controlling performance are the prime duties of first-line managers and where they spend most of their time. In essence, the focus is on *implementation* and *evaluation* of the organization's plans to achieve goals. In our Sears example, the department manager of women's fashion goods is responsible for seeing that the new product line and pricing policies are carried out, as well as for evaluating the consumer's response to the new policies (e.g., sales revenue, inventory, etc.). He or she sends the data up through organizational channels to top management, which then considers if any change is needed in these policies.

As this simplified example illustrates, the level in the organization has a strong impact on where managers spend their time. Although most executive managers spend the majority of their time on long-range issues, they more than likely draw on a wealth of experience gained when they were "down on the firing line" during the early part of their careers. As individuals progress up the management ladder, the different amounts of time they spend on the various functions lets them acquire the skills needed to be a high performer.

 # Managerial Skills

Our approach to management suggests that the manager's job can be studied from at least three perspectives. We have just discussed the *management function* approach. The second approach deals with *managerial skills*.

Most successful managers have acquired a certain set of skills during their working lives that has had a strong impact on their levels of achievement. All managers need four specific managerial skills: (1) technical; (2) human; (3) conceptual; and (4) diagnostic.[12] A summary of these skills is shown in exhibit 1-6.

Technical Skills The ability to use tools, techniques, procedures, or approaches in a specialized manner is referred to as a technical skill. Examples of people with technical skills are the civil engineer, heart surgeon, accountant, or patent attorney—all are recognized as experts at what they do. For the manager, the nature of technical skills is twofold. First, the manager has usually developed some expertise in the work being done. The project manager in a research and development (R&D) laboratory normally has made some scientific contribution to the particular field. Second, the

Exhibit 1-6 Managerial Skills	Skill	Description	Example Activities
	Technical	Use of tools, techniques, and procedures in a specialized manner.	1. Pathologist analyzing a blood sample. 2. Engineer designing a bridge.
	Human	Interpersonal relationships dealing with selecting, motivating, and leading other employees.	1. Accounting manager supervising a group of audit accountants. 2. Manufacturing manager resolving conflict between an inventory supervisor and a loading supervisor.
	Conceptual	Ability to see the total organizational picture by integrating and coordinating a large number of activities.	1. Executive vice president analyzing the potential effects of a merger with another firm. 2. Personnel vice president examining the total impact of a proposed labor contract in the firm.
	Diagnostic	Ability to quickly get at the true cause of a certain situation through a maze of data, observations, and facts.	1. Human resources manager analyzing the causes of employee turnover. 2. Marketing manager anticipating changes in consumer buying habits.

manager uses skills in managing the work being done. To successfully run an R&D group, the project manager needs to know how to plan scientific studies, how to organize the group, how to evaluate scientific performance, and so on.

Human Skills   The second skill needed relates to the ability to select, motivate, work with, and lead employees, either individually or in groups. To be effective, the R&D project manager needs to know the qualifications of other scientists in order to select members of the team properly, as well as have a knowledge of what motivates these scientists, how to structure communication networks, and the degree of direction need to get the work done.

Conceptual Skills   This third managerial skill relates to the ability to integrate and coordinate the organization's activities. In a sense, it concerns the ability to see the "total picture," how the different parts of the organization fit together and depend on each other, and how a change in one part of the organization can cause a change in another part. The director of the R&D lab must be able to see how the most theoretical of research activities (those dealing with new discoveries and innovations) fit with applied research efforts (specific projects designed to solve a particular consumer problem) into the overall purpose of research and development. And he or she must be able to link the work of different groups together when the greatest impact of their efforts comes from their joint effort. For example, until recently most chemical plants used an expensive, time-consuming procedure to test air pollution levels around their facilities. Upon observing this procedure, a sharp-eyed R&D manager recalled a much simpler test, which had been developed in a research effort on a different problem, that could easily be adapted for this use. Using this simplified, faster method has resulted in a savings of thousands of dollars.

Diagnostic Skills   Diagnostic skills include the ability to determine, by analysis and examination, the nature of a particular condition. In other words, it is not only the ability to specify *why* something has occurred, but also the ability to develop certain speculations in a *what if* situation. Individuals who have developed diagnostic skills have the ability to cut through unimportant aspects and quickly get to the heart of the problem. For example, high employee turnover is a serious management problem, usually meaning the increased costs of hiring, placement, training, and the intangible costs related to not having the right people around to do the work. After a number of unsuccessful attempts to reduce the turnover of clerical personnel in an insurance claims department (e.g., changing the office layout, replacing supervisors, and so on), the department manager used a questionnaire and a series of employee interviews to find out about the concerns of the employees. Both the survey and interview data confirmed that the main problems concerning departmental employees were issues of low pay raises and a lack of proper job training. A revised compensation system coupled with an increased emphasis on employee training resulted in a 40 percent drop in turnover in one year. Diagnostic skills are probably the most difficult skills to develop because they require the proper blend of analytic ability and common sense to be effective.

Managerial Skills and Management Levels

The four managerial skills essential to performance also vary in importance according to level in the organization. As shown in exhibit 1-7, technical skills increase in importance as one goes down the organizational structure. A head nurse in a pediatric ward, for example, is likely to have greater technical skills with patients than the director of nursing, because these skills are needed to deal with everyday activities and problems. Similarly, because first-line managers spend most of their time in leading (see exhibit 1-5), we would expect that human skills are most important at the lower levels. This does not mean that top management should not be concerned with human skills; on the contrary, human skills are very important to executive management. It does mean that executives are required to do more than lead subordinates.

Conceptual and diagnostic skills are most important at the higher levels of management because executives are responsible for broad-based, long-term decisions that have a significant impact on the survival and performance of the total organization. These skills have some importance at the lower levels of management, but they are usually related to specific problems for specific situations.

How Managerial Skills Are Acquired

Managerial skills, besides having differing importance to various levels of management, differ also in the ease or difficulty with which they can be acquired. Technical skills appear to be the easiest to acquire because they can be taught through education and training. Human skills, on the other hand, are much more difficult to acquire because interpersonal relationships involve consideration of the differences in attitudes, emotions, and cultural characteristics of peers, subordinates, and superiors. These characteristics of course vary with different employees, and their impact on performance is hard to predict. The entire field of organizational behavior has devel-

Exhibit 1-7
Skills Needed
for Effectiveness
at Different
Managerial Levels

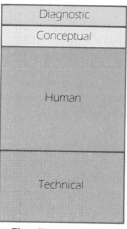

First-line Managers

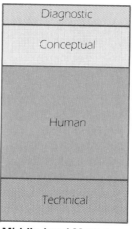

Middle-level Managers

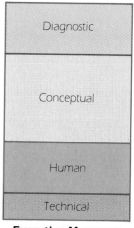

Executive Managers

oped in response to the problem of describing and predicting the behavior of people in organizations.

Finally, conceptual and diagnostic skills are the most difficult to acquire, mainly because they involve time to acquire and a certain level of intellectual ability. In addition, development of conceptual and diagnostic skills depends, to a certain extent, on the degree to which technical skills and human skills have been mastered. In essence, conceptual and diagnostic skills are *mature* skills that require a capacity to learn and a level of experience in observing and practicing acceptable behaviors.

There are at least three mechanisms that facilitate the acquisition of managerial skills. These are: (1) education; (2) experience; and (3) a mentor relationship.

The fast growth in MBA degrees and executive development programs across the country stresses the importance now being placed on *education* as a skill developer. Some individuals, however, argue that management courses neglect to teach people the realities of becoming effective managers. Livingston maintains that what is stressed in business schools is analytical ability—an emphasis on problem solving and decision making.[13] What is missing, he states, are the crucial elements of problem finding and opportunity finding. Analytical skills are important, but a manager's success will ultimately depend on his or her ability to anticipate problems and opportunities long before they arise. In our terminology, educational programs are effective in developing technical skills; other mechanisms are required to develop human, conceptual, and diagnostic skills.

"*Experience* is the best teacher" is an old saying that contains much truth for managerial success. Experience in management generally refers to three facets. First, experience is the *exposure* to a variety of situations, problems, and demands. For example, a project manager in a large engineering design and construction company may have held positions in design, contract administration, and construction before advancing to this important post. Exposure is "learning the ropes" by being an integral part of various organizational activities. Second, gaining experience involves *time,* which is necessary to allow enough exposure to various managerial situations. Finally, experience is a level of *maturity,* which is a philosophical attitude or belief about the individual at work. It is the ability to resist panic in crisis situations and replace it with calm, analytical reasoning; the ability to look beyond trivial matters to the cause of the problem; and a crucial managerial quality that comes from exposure to a variety of situations over a length of time.

Consider the case of John James, the president of Dresser Industries, a diversified organization specializing in the manufacture of high-technology products for the energy industry:

> If I were to give an ambitious, young person advice about getting ahead today, I'd tell them first of all that they must undergo a continual learning process. Someone, for example, who starts out in finance should be willing to cross-train or learn all they can about, say, engineering, manufacturing or marketing, and so on. In other words, don't let yourself get stuck in some specialized niche. . . . You can never stop learning or growing, you have to keep improving your ability to listen—to be open to other people's ideas—you must be able to take criticism. You can't be a know-it-all. As the old saying goes, if you can't take the heat, stay out of the kitchen![14]

Mentor relationships, a topic coming up recently in management literature, is a long-standing activity in management practice. In simple terms, it is a situation where a young manager learns a set of managerial skills from observing, working with, and relating to a more seasoned manager. Mentorship can be a formal activity; for example, Hughes Aircraft and the Jewell Company have programs in which each aspiring manager has a higher level executive as an organizational sponsor. Or it can be an informal activity, such as a developing friendship between a young and older manager. A recent survey of top management in a variety of companies revealed that: (1) over two-thirds of the surveyed executives had developed a mentor relationship with an older executive during the first fifteen years of their careers; (2) those with mentors were more likely to follow a career path, had learned more about the business they were in, and were more satisfied with their work and careers; and (3) executives who have had a mentor in turn sponsor more proteges than executives who have not had a mentor.[15]

What is gained from a mentor relationship? For the protege, it not only is an opportunity to learn the business from an experienced manager (technical skills), but it also affords a learning experience on how to relate to people (human skills) and how to approach various problems faced by the organization (conceptual and diagnostic skills). More than this, however, it is an opportunity for the protege to acquire some career *direction,* and it is a means to develop a personal *philosophy of management* and the invaluable quality of *self-confidence* in managerial ability.

For example, consider the case of Susan Swan, a vice president at Morgan Guaranty Trust. At the ripe old age of 30, she became responsible for managing the $1 billion pension fund for this fifth largest of U.S. banks:

> "I have earned the success I now enjoy. However, I have not forgotten that I received a little help along the way—a mentor," Susan notes. "A mentor is someone who smooths the edges, who helps you along the road to success. If you attract someone to play that role, you have to demonstrate that you're worth it. I earned my stripes when I became a vice president."[16]

Mentoring is not solely an American phenomenon. Joachim Zahn, head of Daimler-Benz (maker of Mercedes-Benz automobiles) credits Dr. Fritz Brinckmann, a noted German accountant and industrialist, for being a mentor, or *meister,* when he worked for Brinckmann's accounting firm early in his career. Brinckmann not only supported Zahn and gave him invaluable advice, he also introduced Zahn to the top influential people in German industry. These acquaintances proved to be significant in Zahn's later career with the automaker. For the mentor, working with a protege provides a feeling of satisfaction—a sense of pride and accomplishment in developing a capable manager.

The important conclusion to be drawn from this discussion is that acquiring the skills necessary to be a successful manager is a complex activity. It is more than just reading a book, listening to lectures, or on-the-job experience. The successful manager has acquired technical, human, conceptual, and diagnostic skills through a continual education process, extensive exposure to a variety of organizational conditions, and hopefully a relationship with an individual who acts as a mentor. The end product is a manager who has the skills, maturity, and confidence to perform at high levels.

Managerial Roles

We have so far drawn attention to two important aspects that define the manager's job: (1) to manage involves a systematic way of doing things consisting of a set of managerial *functions*—planning, organizing, leading, and controlling; and (2) successful achievement as a manager is dependent on acquiring a set of crucial management *skills*—technical, human, conceptual, and diagnostic. The last perspective on the manager's job we will look at is the set of behaviors, or roles, that are required.

The concept of a *role* is drawn from the behavioral sciences and is defined as an organized set of observable behaviors that are attributed to a specific office or position. A role for the manager is the *capacity* in which he or she acts. For example, a manager may act as a leader of subordinates, a spokesperson of the organization, a source of information, or one who makes decisions. In a simple way, we may say that managers "wear many hats" while performing their jobs.

In a detailed study of managerial activities, Mintzberg identified a series of roles relating to *interpersonal, informational,* and *decisional* activities.[17] Mintzberg argued that all managers have formal authority and status given to them by the organization. Authority and status give rise to interpersonal relations with subordinates, peers, and superiors, who in turn provide managers with information to make decisions.

Consider the position of a regional sales manager of a medium-size electronics company. The sales manager supervises eight sales representatives and three office workers in the Detroit office, which is responsible for the sales and service of the company's products in the states of Ohio, Indiana, and Michigan. A summary of managerial roles is shown in exhibit 1-8.

Interpersonal Roles

Three interpersonal roles characterize managerial activities. First is the *figurehead*, which for the sales manager involves ceremonial work, such as receiving visitors and signing documents, and hierarchical duties, such as requesting a subordinate to follow up on a specific job. Second, the sales manager in a *leader* role hires, trains, and motivates field and office personnel. Third, in a *liaison* role the sales manager interacts with other managers outside of the organization. For example, in establishing a contract with a customer, the sales manager is acting as a liaison for or representative of the organization.

Informational Roles

In performing the interpersonal roles, the manager is involved in a number of interactions that allow the flow of information. The result is that many managers act as focal points for information exchange in organizations. In other words, the manager becomes the "person to talk to." Three individual informational roles are prominent. First, as a *monitor,* the sales manager is a receiver and collector of information, and thus often becomes well informed on what's actually going on in the organization. This role involves such activities as gathering information on changes in consumer

Exhibit 1-8
Description
and Examples
of Managerial
Roles

Role	Description	Examples
Interpersonal Roles		
Figurehead	Symbolic head; performs routine duties of a legal or social nature.	Greeting visitors; signing legal documents (university president signing diplomas); usually at executive manager level.
Leader	Responsible for motivation of subordinates and for staffing and training.	Most activities involving subordinates: formal authority position.
Liaison	Maintains network of outside contacts to obtain favors and information.	"Keeping in touch" with the external community through phone calls, meetings, etc.
Informational Roles		
Monitor	Seeks and receives information to obtain thorough understanding of organization and environment.	Reading periodicals and reports, conversations, and other activities related to changes in consumer activities, competitors' plans, etc.; "keeping one's ear to the ground."
Disseminator	Transmits information received from outsiders or insiders to other organization members.	Formal reports, memos, or phone calls to other company managers regarding activities in the business or local community.
Spokesperson	Transmits information to outsiders on organization plans, policies, actions.	Conversations with suppliers, customers, speeches to local groups.
Decisional Roles		
Entrepreneur	Initiates and supervises design of organizational improvement projects as opportunities arise.	Realigning subordinates' jobs and responsibilities; new product or promotional ideas.
Disturbance handler	Responsible for corrective action when organization faces unexpected crises.	Resolving employee conflicts; adjusting to strikes at suppliers; reacting to a bankrupt customer.
Resource allocator	Responsible for allocation of human, monetary, and material resources.	Scheduling time for projects; awarding bonuses and pay raises.
Negotiator	Responsible for representing the organization in bargaining and negotiations.	Negotiating shipping rates and schedules with transportation companies; labor-management contracts.

Adapted from H. Mintzberg, *The Nature of Managerial Work* (New York: Harper & Row, 1973).

attitudes toward the product, learning of competitors' plans, and setting the future marketing plans of his or her own firm. The *disseminator* role involves transmitting information to peers, subordinates, and superiors *within* the organization. Finally, as a *spokesperson,* the sales manager transmits information to individuals *outside* the organization by such means as a meeting with a customer on an upcoming product price change, a call to a trucking company to discuss problems of product delivery time, or a speech to a local chamber of commerce on the company's plans to build a new warehouse in their community.

Decisional Roles

Managers' unique access to information and their interpersonal relationships put them at a central place in the organization where important decisions are made. Four specific decisional roles can be usually adopted. First, the *entrepreneurial* role has the manager initiating some change or improvement. For example, the sales manager may realign the responsibilities of the sales representatives so they specialize in certain products rather than handle all products for a set of customers. This decision may be based on the recognition that the company's product line has grown too complex for each sales representative to become an expert. Specialization may permit better service to customers. Second, as a *disturbance handler,* the manager takes charge when the organization is put in a difficult position. Responses to a bankrupt customer, to conflicts between sales representatives, or to a strike by trucking companies that affects delivery of the product are examples. In the *resource allocator* role, the manager decides how the resources of the organization are to be divided. In this role, the sales manager decides how much money to spend on training and supplies, how much time to spend structuring the work of subordinates, and whether or not to bid on a contract with a new customer. Finally, as a *negotiator,* the manager enters into negotiations with internal or external parties on behalf of the organization. For the sales manager, this would involve such situations as negotiating shipping schedules with customers, establishing a lease on office space, and coming to an agreement with transportation companies on the shipping rates.

Mintzberg's work has not only highlighted the various functions of management, it also calls attention to the dynamic environment in which managers frequently operate. The realities of organizational life usually interrupt the systematic and rational functions of planning, organizing, leading, and controlling that serve as the foundation of what managers do. Managers must constantly adapt to changes, react to crises, and be able to wear a variety of hats.

An Emphasis on Performance

Our definition of *management* says, in effect, that a manager's major objective is to achieve organizational goals; in other words, there is a strong emphasis on performance. Typically, managerial performance has been discussed in terms of *efficiency* and *effectiveness*. As noted management scholar Peter Drucker has stated, efficiency means "doing things right," and effectiveness means "doing the right things."[18]

Efficiency is a concept based on the physical and engineering sciences and concerns the relationship between "inputs" and "outputs." For example, the efficiency of an automobile engine is based on the energy value of the fuel necessary to generate a given level of power output. In organizations, the inputs are the human, physical, and financial resources available to the manager. Efficient managers achieve high levels of output (goal accomplishment) with a given base of inputs. When managers are able to minimize the cost of the resources used to attain goals, and still attain the goals, they are functioning efficiently. In sports, we are speaking of efficiency when we say that "this team went further than we could ever imagine, given the talent the manager has to work with." Casey Stengel and the 1969 New York Mets baseball team and the U.S. hockey team in the 1980 Winter Olympics are classic examples.

Effectiveness is the degree to which the goals of an organization are met. In essence, effective managers have selected the correct approaches and therefore have achieved their goals. For example, Procter & Gamble, IBM, and Federated Department Stores have consistently outperformed other organizations within their industries according to such measures as return on investments, sales margin, growth in earnings, and so on.

Although few people would disagree with the statement that a manager must be both effective and efficient, it is too broad and ambiguous for our purposes. We need a more concise framework.

A Framework for Performance

The term *performance* will be used as a somewhat global concept that represents the results of organizational activities. Effectiveness and efficiency will be viewed as subcomponents of performance.[19]

Here is a framework for performance for managers to carefully consider in attempting to achieve organizational goals:

- Performance is not a single standard, but consists of *multiple criteria.*
- The *level of analysis* of performance ranges from the individual employee to the user of the organization's products and services, and on to society in general.
- The *focus* of performance can concern maintenance, improvement, and developmental goals.
- The *time frame* for performance, from short term to long term, must be established.
- How performance will be *measured,* ranging from quantitative/objective to qualitative/subjective measures, should be considered.

Performance Criteria   As shown in exhibit 1-9, the concept of performance involves many different standards. This part of the performance framework suggests that managers must judge performance with multiple criteria. For example, a dean of a university business school could identify teaching, research publications, and community service as performance criteria to evaluate faculty.

Exhibit 1-9
A Framework
for Managerial
Performance

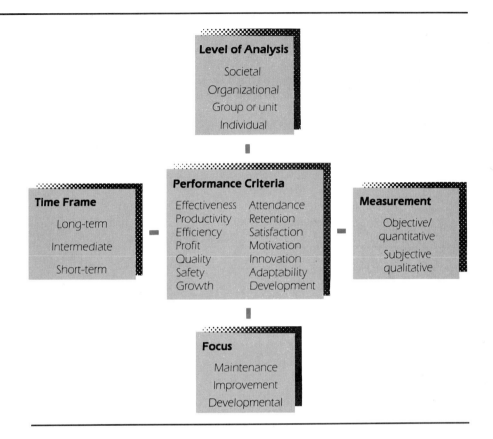

Level of Analysis This factor concerns whether performance criteria apply to the individual, group, department, or society. For example, the manager of an audit group in an accounting firm could be interested in the morale of individual employees, the productivity of the group, or the client's satisfaction with the group's activities and would apply different criteria in evaluating each.

Performance Focus A frequently overlooked aspect concerns the focus or kind of performance desired. Three distinctions can be made: (1) *maintenance,* or performance designed to maintain a specific level of activity; (2) *improvement,* or performance usually described with an action verb such as increase/decrease or add/reduce, which implies some change is desired; and (3) *developmental* performance activities, which are related to growth, learning, or advancement. For example, the quality control manager in a steel pipe manufacturing company could be interested in maintaining daily product inspection rates at 50 percent of production (maintenance), reducing quality rejects by 25 percent (improvement), and training subordinates in the use of laser technology in quality control (developmental).

Time Frame   The time frame component of our performance framework relates to when goals are to be achieved. Putting performance activities in some time frame (scheduling) stresses the need to consider goal attainment in short-term, intermediate, and long-term perspectives. The manager of a data processing department, for example, may want to immediately reduce, from three days to one, the turnaround time on financial reports, to decrease employee turnover in the department by 40 percent within one year, or to have a new computer installed and employees trained to use it within four to five years.

Performance Measurement   Finally, the manager needs to be concerned with how performance will be measured. Performance measurement usually involves the use of objective/quantifiable and/or subjective/qualitative data. Objective measurement concerns data to which some hard number can be assigned as a value, such as sales dollars, percentage reduction in costs, or the number of days allotted for project completion. Subjective measurement, on the other hand, usually involves obtaining an opinion or evaluation through perceptual means. Job satisfaction measurement, questionnaires, or supervisory evaluations of subordinate performance are examples.

In summary, organizational performance is a complex dimension that is more than "doing things right" or "doing the right things." The manager carefully considers who or what is performing, what performance is to be measured, how performance is to be measured, and when it is to be measured. Another concern is the ethics behind a manager's performance. We will discuss this in chapter 3.

The Manager's Job: An Integrative View

In this chapter, we provided a contemporary definition and description of the manager's job. Our view of the manager's job focuses on four elements: (1) functions; (2) skills; (3) roles; and (4) performance. A summary of this presentation—the foundation for this book—is illustrated in exhibit 1-10.

First, what the manager's job all leads up to is performance, the ultimate test. Second, at the core of the manager's job are the *functions* of planning, organizing, leading, and controlling. They serve as the basic framework for managerial activities. Third, how the individual performs the managerial functions depends both on the manager's skills and what behavioral role he or she has taken on. Finally, managerial behavior differs by the particular *level* in the organization. Executive, middle, and first-line managers differ in the time they devote to specific functions, the nature of the skills each function requires and the role in which they perform.

Exhibit 1-10
The Manager's Job

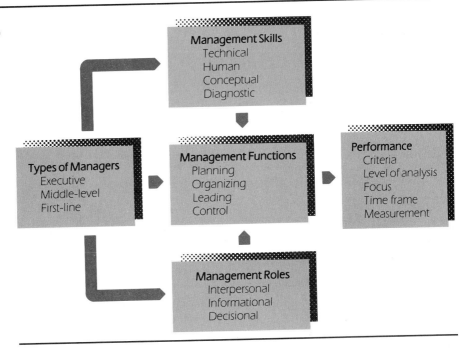

The Need for Managers

We frequently have heard the comment that most large corporations are impersonal, self-perpetuating, machinelike entities in which the efforts of individuals are neither valued nor felt. Granted, some organizations are large and ponderous. The people *within,* however, are the ones who make the decisions and chart the future directions of the organization. Managers make such organizations as Exxon, IBM, the Mayo Clinic, and Stanford University successful.

Managers also contribute to corporate disasters and embarrassments. Firestone Tire and Rubber's self-destructing 500 radial, Lockheed's political kickbacks, and the bankruptcies of Penn-Central and Braniff Airlines are classic examples of the impact of management on the total organization. We hope that, by studying the field of management, future managers will contribute to the *success* of organizations and apply management techniques to bring errant institutions under control.

The Forces Affecting Managerial Performance

In some respects, the need for managers in the 1980s, the 1990s, and beyond will be greater than at any time during this century. Consider the following list of articles taken from *Fortune, Business Week, Forbes,* and *The Wall Street Journal:*

- "U.S. Auto Makers Reshape for World Competition"
- "Revlon: A Painful Case of Slow Growth and Fading Glamour"
- "Kodak Fights Back: Everybody Wants a Piece of its Markets"
- "Europe's New Managers"
- "Du Pont: Straining to Pay the Price of its Conoco Victory"
- "Esquire: Finding Profits in Fields Beyond Magazines"
- "Humana's Hard-Sell Hospitals"
- "Scripto Erases its Past"
- "Women: The New Stars in Banking"

To some respected scholars and practicing managers, articles such as these highlight the crisis managers will face for the remainder of this century. There are four specific issues that are most frequently discussed. First, many organizations are becoming increasingly more *internally complex*. Many of the traditional ways of running an organization are giving way to new methods such as free-form designs, flextime, dual authority systems, computerized information systems, self-governing teams, behavior modification programs, and the growing use of management and technical specialists. As one would expect, the greater the internal complexity, the greater and more varied the demands on management.

Second, the *external environment* affecting most organizations is also becoming increasingly *complex* and *dynamic*. Organizations are finding they must monitor constantly not only the competitive market environment but the political, social, and technological environments as well. Consider the following examples: (1) One of IBM's major competitors in the business typewriter market is a division of Exxon, an energy company; (2) the majority of Gillette's sales revenue comes from products that were introduced since 1972; (3) Honda is now assembling its cars in the United States, a competitive factor no auto manufacturer would have considered even ten years ago; (4) administrative paperwork associated with governmental rules and requirements costs organizations as much money as they contribute to employee pension plans; and (5) the impact of OPEC is felt in the daily lives of every American.

Third, the complexities of the internal and external environments will challenge *management talent*. The cold, hard fact is that due to population and demographics, there will be an extreme shortage of experienced managers to train young future managers who climb onto the organization's career ladder during the 1980s.[20] As a result, management faces three crucial problems: (1) how to design jobs so the young manager can gain valuable experience without the constant supervision of an experienced manager; (2) how to identify and train "high risers" so they can perform effectively in top management positions early; and (3) what to do in the late 1980s and early 1990s when these young managers are ready to fight for the small number of top management jobs.

Finally, one of the greatest needs for managers will be in the international sphere, including both profit and not-for-profit organizations. Managers in the U.S. must recognize that their profession should not have a limited geographic perspective. The need for managers in the international realm means that managers must understand international and cross-cultural differences, as well as how to manage on foreign soils.

Managers can no longer believe that the impact of what they do and help produce is limited to their immediate environment. On the contrary, the products and services produced in this country, as well as products and services produced in other countries, must be considered within an international arena of influence. American managers help produce computers that are sold overseas, for example, and we also import oil, automobiles, and other goods from other countries. Knowledge of this integration of management among many countries is an important part of the manager's job.

Some people view today's situation as a challenge to management rather than a crisis. And, in fact, developing and participating in a teaching and learning process geared to meet the needs of management in the future can be a challenging proposition. Yet the rewards are worth the effort.

SUMMARY FOR THE MANAGER

1. Our definition of *management*—the process of integrating resources and tasks toward the achievement of stated organizational goals—clearly suggests that management is results, or *performance,* oriented. For the manager, this performance approach requires a knowledge base and proficiency in the managerial functions, skills, and important roles.

2. A way of classifying managers is by their level in the organization. Such terms as *executive manager, middle-level manager,* and *first-line manager* have been used to distinguish between different types of managers.

3. Four managerial functions are identified: planning, organizing, leading, and controlling. These functions do not present a rigid, checklist approach to management. On the contrary, most managers probably perform these functions daily, allotting different amounts of time to each depending on the level in the organization that the managers occupy.

4. Effectiveness as a manager requires that the individual develop a set of skills that can be applied to most managerial situations. The four identified skills—technical, human, conceptual, and diagnostic—vary in importance with levels in the organization. We want to emphasize that these skills cannot be acquired solely from textbooks. Beyond education, the two most important mechanisms for acquiring these skills are experience and developing a mentor relationship with a senior manager.

5. In addition to functions and skills, the third important aspect of the manager's job is the set of roles he or she performs. The three broad role categories—interpersonal, informational, and decisional—not only cut across the main managerial functions, but require the development and use of the important types of managerial skills. This orientation to the managerial functions, skills, and roles serves as our foundation for defining the manager's job.

6. Performance in the manager's job is complex and requires more than a discussion of the differences between the terms *effectiveness* and *efficiency.* In particular, a definition of *managerial performance* considers at least five different aspects: multiple criteria; level of analysis; focus; time; and measurement characteristics. Each manager defines performance criteria, who or what is performing, how performance is measured, and when performance is measured.

7. There is no one best way to manage; there are no hard rules, laws, or equations. The key to managerial success is the manager's ability to analyze and understand each situation and to perform the necessary functions, skills, and roles that lead to effectiveness.

REVIEW AND DISCUSSION QUESTIONS

1. What is your definition of management?
2. How does management draw from both art and science?
3. Why do we suggest that management cannot be reduced to a simple checklist?
4. Describe the differences between a first-line supervisor and a middle-level manager in terms of functions, skills, and roles.
5. How does a mentor function in an organization?
6. What are the major differences between interpersonal and decisional roles?
7. How may an individual acquire human skills? Diagnostic skills?
8. Identify a number of objective and subjective performance criteria for (1) a postmaster of a suburban post office and (2) a head nurse in a hospital.

NOTES

1. See P. F. Drucker, *Management: Tasks, Responsibilites, and Practices* (New York: Harper & Row, 1974); and J. F. Mee, *Management Thought in a Dynamic Economy* (New York: New York University Press, 1963).
2. L. Gulick, "Management is a Science," *Academy of Management Journal* (March 1965): 7-13.
3. P. F. Drucker, *The Practice of Management* (New York: Harper & Row, 1954).
4. J. W. Lorsch, "Making Behavioral Science More Useful," *Harvard Business Review* (March-April 1979): 171-81.
5. "Flying High at Delta Airlines," *Duns' Review* (December 1977): 60-61.
6. R. Rowan, "Those Business Hunches Are More Than Blind Faith," *Fortune* (April 23, 1979): 114.
7. E. H. Schein, "Organizational Socialization and the Profession of Management," *Industrial Management Review* (Winter 1968): 1-16.
8. See L. Sayles, *Leadership: What Effective Managers Really Do . . . and How They Do It* (Englewood Cliffs, N. J.: Prentice-Hall, 1979); and R. Stewart, *Managers and Their Jobs* (London: Macmillian & Company, 1967).
9. C. R. Christensen, K. R. Andrews, and J. L. Bower, *Business Policy* (Homewood, Ill.: Richard D. Irwin, 1978).
10. F. E. Kast and J. E. Rosenzweig, *Organization and Management* (New York: McGraw-Hill, 1974).
11. T. A. Mahoney, T. H. Jerdee, and S. J. Carroll, "The Job(s) of Management," *Industrial Relations* (February 1965): 97-110.
12. R. L. Katz, "Skills of an Effective Administrator," *Harvard Business Review* (September-October 1974): 90-102.
13. J. S. Livingston, "Myths of the Well-Educated Manager," *Harvard Business Review* (January-February 1971): 79-89.
14. W. G. Smith, "John James: Don't Get Stuck in Some Specialized Niche," *Texas Business* (December 1979): 36.
15. See A. Zaleznik, "Managers and Leaders; Are They Different?" *Harvard Business Review* (May-June 1977): 67-68; E. Collins and P. Scott, "Everyone Who Makes It Has a Mentor," *Harvard Business Review* (July-August 1978): 89-101; G. R. Roche, "Much Ado About Mentors," *Harvard Business Review* (January-February 1979): 14-31; and J. Stuller, "Should You Be A Mentor?" *Success* (May 1983): 21-23.
16. K. White, "The Woman Executive," *Sky* (August 1979): 51.
17. H. Mintzberg, *The Nature of Managerial Work* (New York: Harper & Row, 1973).

18.   P. F. Drucker, *Managing for Results* (New York: Harper & Row, 1964), p. 5.

19.   See J. Ghorpade, *Assessment of Organizational Effectiveness* (Glenview, Ill.: Scott, Foresman, 1971); P. S. Goodman, J. M. Pennings, and Associates, *New Perspectives on Organizational Effectiveness* (San Francisco: Jossey-Bass, 1977); and R. Steers, "Problems in the Measurement of Organizational Effectiveness," *Administrative Science Quarterly* (December 1975): 546-58.

20.   See E. C. Gottschalk, "Promotions Grow Few as Baby Boom Group Eyes Managers' Jobs," *The Wall Street Journal* (October 22, 1981); and "An Uneven Flow of Management Talent," *Business Week* (February 20, 1978): 51.

A CASE FOR ANALYSIS

The Manager's Job
Lee Iacocca of Chrysler

He has hired Frank Sinatra, John Houseman, and Ricardo Montalban. He was the prime mover behind one of the auto industry's most successful models, the Mustang. He can be found as much in Washington, D.C., in the newspaper, or on tv plugging his company's products as in Detroit behind his desk. Only Lido Anthony (Lee) Iacocca, chairman of Chrysler, could convince thousands of Americans with the phrase, "You can go with Chrysler, or you can go with someone else—and take your chances."

Iacocca, the son of Italian immigrants, has been fighting for his corporation's life. In early 1978, Iacocca was sitting comfortably as president of Ford Motor Company as Chrysler's profits were about to fall off a cliff. In November of that same year, Iacocca, recently fired from Ford, joined Chrysler as their new president. During the next three years, the company lost nearly $3.5 billion, saw its stock price drop to below $5 per share, and, to stave off bankruptcy, received a multiple-billion dollar bailout from the U.S. Congress.

Chrysler is on the road to recovery. Whether it will survive is still an unanswered question—no one, however, can fault Iacocca for giving it

his all. He has used a combination of brains, bluster, bravado, and a good degree of management ability. For example:

- When the company needed money and the banks delayed, he threatened to go into bankruptcy—the banks came through.
- When the company couldn't pay its bills, he convinced suppliers to be patient.
- When he needed pay cuts and the union protested, he gave them a choice—a pay cut or their jobs.
- When he became dissatisfied with the company's advertising campaign, he went on tv as Chrysler's main salesperson.
- With his extensive knowledge of the industry, he personally took charge of designing the company's new front wheel drive products.
- He reduced Chrysler's breakeven point from 2.3 to 1.2 million autos by cutting operations and functions everywhere.

To some people, it is easy to dismiss Iacocca as just another "supersalesperson" because he is so good at it. He exudes confidence and conviction—well-tailored clothes, big cigar, self-satisfied smile. But Iacocca has proven he is also a remarkable manager. He has a knack for getting the most out of all employees, for making them do more than they think they can.

Of his subordinate managers, he can be quite demanding. One of his tools is a black book he always carries around. In it are itemized each manager's quarterly goals and targets. Those who do not achieve their goals are in for a chewing out. To improve overall management, Iacocca brought in proven executives from other firms (primarily Ford), and installed sophisticated financial tools and production equipment.

Lee Iacocca always wanted a challenge—at Chrysler, he got his wish.

Adapted from "Iacocca's Tightrope Act," *Time* (March 21, 1983): 50-61.

Questions for Discussion

1. What managerial skills, roles, and functions are illustrated in this case?
2. How valuable was Iacocca's experience at Ford to his Chrysler position?
3. Is Iacocca "the right person at the right time," or could any good executive have achieved the same results?

EXPERIENTIAL EXERCISE
Defining the Manager's Job

Purpose

1. To examine the key components of a manager's job.

2. To gain an understanding of the variety of demands on a manager.

Required Understanding
The functions, skills, and roles of a manager's job.

How to Set Up the Exercise
Set up groups of four to eight students for the forty-five minute exercise. The groups should be separated from each other and students asked to converse only with members of their own group.

Instructions for the Exercise
Consider the job of a divisional sales manager in a large suburban branch store of a major national retail organization. This manager's area of responsibility includes women's fashions, teen sportswear, children's clothing, and women's accessories. Each of these four areas is headed by a department manager who reports directly to the divisional manager. The branch store employees, approximately 600 people, recorded sales last year exceeding $5 million. Of this, the divisional manager was responsible for 185 employees and sales of $2 million. The divisional manager reports directly to the assistant store manager.

Exhibit 1-11 presents a list of activities in which the divisional sales manager has engaged during the last year. Individually and as a group, rank in order these ten activities in terms of the amount of time the divisional manager has spent on each.

		Ranking	
Exhibit 1-11 Allocation of Time for a Divisional Sales Manager	**Managerial Activity**	**Individual**	**Group**
	1. Evaluating employee training programs		
	2. Conducting employee performance evaluations		
	3. Training new department managers		
	4. Evaluating sales and cost data		
	5. Planning future personnel needs		
	6. Defining limits of authority for department managers		
	7. Developing department and employee performance goals		
	8. Discussing sales and cost performance with the assistant store manager		
	9. Planning for sales and introduction of new fashions		
	10. Identifying promotional ladders for employees		

1. *Individually,* each of the group members should rank in order the ten activities on the basis of the amount of time devoted to each activity, from number 1, the activity that demanded the most time by the divisional manager, to number 10, the activity that demanded the least time (*no* ties, please). Mark your responses on exhibit 1-11.

2. *As a group,* repeat the instructions presented in step 1 above.

3. Display group rankings and appoint a spokesperson from each group to present and discuss the group decision with the class.

2

Foundations of Management Thought and Practice

Chapter Outline

Key Points

1. At least three different schools make up the study of management: Classical, behavioral, and management science. The contingency approach emerges as an alternative viewpoint.
2. The classical school of management involves two separate branches: the scientific management branch, which introduced the scientific method to management; and the administrative theory branch, which stressed the managerial functions of planning, organizing, and controlling.
3. The behavioral school focused on the need for managers to consider the psychological reactions of employees to work. It served as the foundation of the contemporary field of organizational behavior.
4. The management science school was oriented toward a quantitative analysis of managerial problems through mathematical models and use of the computer.
5. A contingency view stresses the need for managers to adapt their managerial activities to the external and internal environmental components of the organization.
6. Contributions to management thought originated not only from scholars and scientists but also from practicing managers.
7. The schools of management differ in their orientation to the functions, skills, and roles that define the manager's job.
8. Although management has a rich and significant history, a single, universally accepted approach to effective management does not exist.

Olive Ann Beech

Beech Aircraft Corporation

Walter Beech was a daredevil pilot with a genius for designing and selling airplanes, but he was short on management skills. If it weren't for Olive Beech, his wife—shrewd, ambitious, tough—the Beech Aircraft Corporation probably never would have made its mark in the business community.

A native of Kansas, Olive Ann Mellor had a bank account at the age of 7 and was helping pay the family bills by age 11. A business course in grade school led to a job as a bookkeeper and, in 1924, she joined the newly formed Travel Air Manufacturing Company in Wichita as secretary to Walter Beech, the founder and president. When no one came forward to handle financial matters, she took charge of accounts receivable and payable. "Business fascinated me," she claims.

Walter merged the company with Curtiss-Wright in 1929 and moved to New York as a vice president of the parent company. Olive moved too—as Walter's bride. Four years later, the couple returned to Wichita and started Beech Aircraft in a factory shut down by the depression. Their first plane, the Model 17, was a single-engine biplane that was destined to become a general aviation classic. This was followed by the twin-engine Model 18, which was chosen as the chief training plane for the Army and Navy during World War II. In 1940, when both the Beeches were hospitalized, a group of executives attempted to take over the company. Returning to work first, Mrs. Beech became de facto company head and crushed the coup by firing several executives.

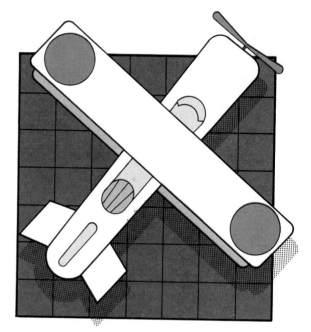

After the war, Beech Aircraft became an important defense contractor, and its president became an expert in finance, especially in acquiring loans to increase production capacity. "You have to be honest to pry large amounts of money out of skeptical banks," she says, "and you have to believe in what you're trying to borrow for."

When neither her two daughters nor their husbands wanted active roles in the company, Beech sold out to Raytheon Company in 1980. Not only were revenues at that time at a solid $600 million, but Raytheon's management found the corporation in excellent shape. In her five decades with Beech, Olive never learned to fly a plane. "I had no reason to," she explains. "I always had plenty of pilots."

Adapted from A.M. Louis, "The Hall of Fame of U.S. Business Leadership," *Fortune* (April 4, 1983): 145.

2 The field of management, as we know it today, has a history of development that cuts across many centuries. Since people first grouped together, they have tried to organize their activities in order to achieve some mode of effectiveness and efficiency. While many of these different ways of organizing have remained, there is yet no single, unified theory of management that can be applied successfully to all situations.

Managers have at their disposal many ways of looking at the activities, authority, responsibilities, and behavior of people in organizations. Each of these ways may be more useful for some problems than for others. For example, the manner in which Texaco approaches the energy exploration problem is different from the way General Motors looks at the energy consumption of its cars. Similarly, the manner in which a head nurse solves a motivation problem among subordinates is different from the way a merchandising vice president approaches the issue of managerial turnover. Because there is no universal theory of management, managers must be able to integrate theory with insight and common sense to solve a problem.

Analyzing and understanding the development of management thought goes beyond taking a history lesson. Much can be learned about management today and tomorrow by investigating how historical counterparts approached their problems.

The foundations of management thought will be presented here in three parts. First, we will provide an overview of the three major schools of management—classical, behavioral, and management science. An emerging view of management—the contingency approach—will also be discussed. Second, we will provide a more detailed theoretical discussion on each approach. Because the discussion in the second part will concentrate on the contribution of management scholars, the last section will focus on the contributions of practitioners to the foundations of management thought.

Schools of Management Thought

The literature on management includes a variety both of topics and writers. Early contributors were management practitioners who wrote about their experiences and attempted to generalize to some basic principles. Later, many of the contributions came from writers who could be classified as more scientific and scholarly in orientation. These scholarly writers attempted to build the emerging field of management on a foundation of the known sciences and disciplines—primarily in the fields of engineering, psychology, political science, mathematics, economics, and philosophy.

As a result of these two perspectives—the practitioner and the scholar—numerous classification schemes have been presented as schools of management thought; some count as few as three approaches, others as many as seven.[1] In order to present the essence of the management movement, we have chosen to discuss three schools.

The *classical school* of management evolved in the early part of this century and to some extent is accepted and practiced by many managers even today. Over time, two separate branches of the classical school have developed: the emphasis on the *man-*

agement of jobs (scientific management); and the emphasis on *management of organizations* (administrative theory).

The first to develop was the *management of jobs* branch. At the most basic level, the writers and practitioners in this area were engineers and scientists who were concerned with issues of *efficiency* (or, getting the most performance out of a certain amount of resources). The concern for improvement in efficiency led to the development of many methods related to machine design, plant layout, tools, work methods, and material flow.

With the emergence of large, complex organizations, managers became more concerned with managing these organizations than with improving the efficiency of individual jobs. The literature in this era sought to describe management in terms of the functions performed by the manager, with particular emphasis on coordinating the resources of the organization (e.g., people, tasks, finances, and equipment) toward achieving stated goals. Although many variations or descriptions of managerial functions have been presented, the three major functions most frequently mentioned are *planning, organizing,* and *controlling.*

The *behavioral school* of management offered a somewhat different perspective. Whereas the classical school gave attention to the efficiency of job activities, the behavioral school of management sought to understand the psychological and sociological processes—attitudes, motivation, group structure—that affected employee performance. In simple terms, the classical approach focused on the *jobs of workers,* and the behavioral school focused on the *workers in jobs.*

The *management science* school emphasized the quantitative aspects of the manager's job. Evolving out of World War II research on the application of quantitative methods to military and logistical problems, this approach features highly sophisticated use of mathematics and statistics. Because of the technical nature of the approach, management science is more closely aligned with the classical approach, particularly in quantitative applications to planning and control problems. The popularity of the management science approach owes a great deal to the development of the computer, because it can generate previously impossible solutions to complex problems.

Although not recognized as a separate school, a contemporary view of management called the *contingency* or *situational* school is emerging. In its most basic formulation, the contingency approach is concerned with the relationship between an organization and its environment, both *internal* and *external.* This approach is more *eclectic* than the other three schools. It borrows the managerial functions (planning, organizing, and controlling) from the classical approach, the cooperation and humanism of the behaviorists, and the competitive strategies of the management science approach. In other words, it does not teach ''one best way'' to manage, preferring to emphasize flexibility, adaptability, and survival as its goals.

The short but dynamic existence of formal management thought has seen the emergence of many concepts and contributors, as we will discuss in more detail throughout this chapter. A brief summary of these contributions and contributors is presented in exhibit 2-1.

Possibly one of the most important features of exhibit 2-1 is the ''Environment'' column. As we discussed in chapter 1, one of the crucial factors in becoming a

Exhibit 2-1
Summary of Concepts and Contributors to Management Thought

	Selected Contributions	Selected Contributors	Environment
Classical School	Scientific management Control systems Time & motion studies Management functions Administrative theory	Gantt (1908) Taylor (1911) Gilbreth (1911) Church (1914) Fayol (1916) Mooney & Reiley (1931) Davis (1935) Urwick (1943)	Expanding size of organizations Market growth for goods & services World War I Depression Post-Industrial Revolution Decline of owner/manager Rise of professional manager
Behavioral School	Participation Motivation applications Professional managers Hawthorne studies M.B.O.	Roethlisberger (1939) Mayo (1945) Barnard (1938) Drucker (1954) McGregor (1960)	World War II Unionization Need for trained managers Federal regulations Worker unrest
Management Science School	Operations research Simulation Game theory Decision theory Mathematical models	Churchman (1957) March & Simon (1958) Forrester (1961) Raiffa (1968)	Growth in corporation size Conglomerates Cold War Recession Military/Industrial complex
Contingency View	Dynamic environment Organic-mechanistic Technology Matrix designs Social responsibility Organizational change Information systems	Burns & Stalker (1961) Woodward (1965) Thompson (1967) Lawrence & Lorsch (1967)	Expanding economy Space race High technology products Vietnam War Civil rights International trade increase Social discontent Growth of skilled professions Computers

successful manager is the ability to learn and apply managerial skills.[2] We suggest that the skills needed for effective managerial performance are, to some extent, dependent on the external environment at any given time. In other words, the environment makes demands on the organization and the manager, and successful adaptation to the environment will facilitate attaining high performance levels.

For example, during the time of the development of the classical school, the environment helped create a need for managers who were proficient in technical skills. What was required for success was the ability to change businesses effectively from the informal owner/manager-operated establishment to the more formal organization needed in post-Industrial Revolution society. Use of engineering practices coupled with effective planning, organizing, and controlling provided the means to achieve levels of success. Toward the middle of this century, the changing work force and diverging population demanded that more attention be given to the individual worker's needs and growth. This required the ability to learn and use behavioral or human skills.

Finally, in the second half of this century, the environment of most organizations became much more complex and changeable. The competitive market became more dynamic, technological innovations increased at a rapid pace, the economy was subject to fluctuations, governmental influence increased, and foreign markets and competitors grew in importance. The complexity of the environment required equally complex conceptual and diagnostic skills.

Seeds of Management Thought

We often refer to the development of formal management thought as having its origins in the early part of the twentieth century with the formulation of the classical school. Many of the ideas that formed the foundations of formal management thought, however, originated much earlier than this century.[3] Some of the most prominent contributions include the following:

Sumerian Priests   The Sumerian civilization, which dates back to about 3000 B.C., put priests in charge of the formal tax system. Recognizing a need for better control of that society's resources, the priests developed one of the first reporting or auditing procedures.

The Egyptians   The obvious contribution by Egyptians to management thought was the construction of the pyramids. The planning and organization of resources, both physical and human, is impressive even by today's standards.

Chinese Civil Service   Among the wondrous tales brought from the Far East in the late sixteenth century were accounts of government rationally administered by an elite corps of scholars/decision makers.[4] Chosen through competitive examination, these Chinese civil servants were the ablest and most learned members of their society. Later it was determined that the Chinese imperial bureaucracy was subject to extensive manipulation and corruption by clerical subordinates. Higher officials, although required to demonstrate competence in classical scholarship, were lacking in practical administrative knowledge and unable to deal with everyday problems.

Karl von Clausewitz   In his book, *The Principles of War,* von Clausewitz discussed the management of war.[5] His basic principles are still used today: (1) decentralize command; (2) use entire force with all energy; (3) concentrate power at the enemy's weakest point; (4) never waste time; and (5) follow up success with utmost energy.

The Industrial Revolution   The development of the steam engine and other mechanized equipment helped establish the foundation of modern society and organizations. The result, the Industrial Revolution, involved both economic and social changes. It brought about the mechanization of production, caused a major shift in emphasis from the craftsworker to large-scale manufacturing, and finally facilitated the development of the professional manager. What emerged was a society that encouraged business and profit and an increased need for more capably trained and skilled individuals to serve as managers.

Classical School of Management

The Industrial Revolution gave rise to the need for a more sophisticated approach to administration. The development of new manufacturing technologies concentrated great quantities of raw materials and large numbers of workers in the emerging factories. Since it was apparent that it would be difficult to coordinate all resources into a smoothly running process, people began to pay more attention to the problems of management. Our presentation of the classical approach will cover the two perspectives mentioned earlier.

Scientific Management

Scientific management arose during the first decades of this century out of a need to improve manufacturing productivity through more efficient use of physical and human resources. Factories at that time had problems formulating proper work procedures, establishing the boundaries of jobs, and coordinating the flow of raw materials. A breakthrough occurred when certain members of the engineering profession became interested in the process of work flow. One engineer in particular, Frederick Taylor (1856–1915), became known as the father of scientific management.[6]

Taylor's Scientific Management   Taylor's ideas about management of jobs grew out of his years of experience in three companies—Midvale Steel, Simonds Rolling Machine, and Bethlehem Steel. His basic approach was to observe the separate functions and the motions each worker performed in his job. After careful analysis of his observations, he would redesign the job in a more efficient manner, or the "one best way."

Taylor's approach to management was influenced by his basic philosophy of work. First, he believed that prosperity for the employer and the employee could be achieved only through *maximizing* productivity. Productivity improvements, however, could come only from developing more *efficient* jobs. Second, there was too much "soldiering" among factory workers. The term *soldiering* came from his observations of military personnel. Today we call this "goofing off." Third, the continued growth of industry could come only from a complete revolution in the *mental attitudes* of employers and employees toward work. The future economic well-being of the worker would come from more efficient work methods and habits. Finally, the heart of scientific management is in the *cooperation* between management and the worker. Through cooperative effort of all concerned, the betterment of society would result.

In his work at Midvale Steel, Taylor began his studies with an analysis of the job of a lathe operator. He was concerned with a number of factors. For example, there were no work standards that specified daily work output for the operator, nor was there a relationship between output and the wage system. He was particularly concerned that there was no standard for a "fair day's work for a fair day's pay." He also blamed management's practice of making decisions based on hunch and "rules of thumb" as the primary contributor to a large amount of waste.

In his studies of lathe operators, pig iron handlers, and shovelers, Taylor developed a process of fact gathering and objective analysis that focused *exactly* on what the worker *did* to perform his task. He identified each element of the worker's job and measured every factor that was adaptable to measurement. From these studies, a set of "scientific management" principles evolved.[7] Some of the more important principles are:

- *Develop a science for each element of a worker's job to replace rules of thumb.* Use the scientific method rather than intuition and experience to determine the workers' activities. Ensure that each motion and movement is the most efficient possible. For example, Taylor's analysis of the process of loading pig iron onto a flatcar resulted in a 400 percent increase in the tonnage loaded per worker.

- *Job specialization should be a part of each job.* Taylor believed that each worker should know his job well and become a *specialist* in what he did. This specialization also included management, which he termed "functional foremanship." Taylor's foremanship concept held that each employee should be supervised by several foremen, each with distinct responsibilities. One foreman would be responsible for machine speeds, another for repair, still another would be an inspector, a disciplinarian, a cost-and-time foreman, etc.

- *Ensure the proper selection, training, and development of workers.* Taylor believed that it was important to properly identify the person for the right job. Proper selection of people with the appropriate abilities, coupled with specific training, would facilitate good performance. Taylor suggested that tests be used to determine whether or not a person had the necessary attributes for a particular job. For example, he developed a speed and reaction test for quality control inspectors.

- *Planning and scheduling of the work are essential.* Everything in the organization had to be done by plan, from yearly plans for the total organization to daily plans for the individual worker. Planning and scheduling involved getting the people and the materials at the right place, right time, and ready to work or in the proper condition to be used.

- *Standards with respect to methods and time for each task should be established.* Taylor observed the workers' movements along with the time needed to complete a particular movement. He redesigned the job, giving it highly efficient motions with specific times required for each step. This was the forerunner of contemporary time and motion studies.

- *Wage incentives should be an integral part of each job.* Taylor instituted a program whereby workers were paid for what they did, which meant different wage rates for different jobs. In addition, workers were paid a bonus if they bettered the standard time established for the task.

Consider Taylor's shoveling experiments. Through his analysis of the job, Taylor determined that the optimum size shovel for handling materials carried about twelve and a half pounds. This meant that small shovels should be used for heavy materials, such as sand, and larger shovels should be used for lighter materials, such as cinders. Combining shovel size with worker training and incentive wages enabled Taylor to increase the productivity of the workers from 16 to 59 tons shoveled per day. This productivity increase per worker decreased the number of shovelers needed per day from 500 to 140.

Although Taylor's scientific management approach led to significant increases in productivity and higher wages for workers, workers and unions became increasingly uncomfortable. They feared that working harder or faster would exhaust the available work and would bring about more layoffs. Thus, as Taylor's ideas spread and were accepted by management, resistance was growing among frontline workers to scientific management because it endangered their jobs.[8] In a sense, this awareness laid the groundwork for a rising interest in human needs and behavior.

In the long run, however, Taylor made a lasting contribution to making jobs and the management of these jobs more efficient and productive. His observational methods of analysis led not only to the development of time and motion study but also stimulated others to continue the formulation of management thought.

Other Contributors to Scientific Management   Further development of scientific management principles continued to expand as more managers accepted Taylor's ideas. Three of the more prominent contributions were made by the Gilbreths, Gantt, and Emerson with their studies in work simplification, scheduling and control, and principles of efficiency.

Frank B. and Lillian M. Gilbreth (1869–1924 and 1878–1972, respectively) produced significant contributions in motion study and *work simplification*.[9] During his early work experience as an apprentice bricklayer, Frank Gilbreth recognized that his work could be improved greatly through studies of fatigue and motion. His analysis of the job convinced him that many of the body movements could be combined or eliminated so that the bricklaying procedure could be simplified and production increased. Craftsmen who adopted Gilbreth's methods were able to increase their productivity by 200 percent.

Gilbreth's contributions were based on the principle that motion and fatigue were closely related, and that every motion that was eliminated would reduce fatigue. With the use of motion picture cameras, the Gilbreths found the most efficient and economical motions for each task, thus reducing fatigue and upgrading production. This improved worker morale not only because of its obvious physical benefits, but because it showed management's concern for the welfare of the worker.

An important, but little-known factor in their work was the three-position promotion plan for workers. According to the plan, the three positions included the worker doing his present job, training his successor, and learning new skills for movement to the next highest job. This contributed significantly to morale because workers could look ahead to promotion and avoid dead-end jobs.

Contributions toward *work scheduling and control* were made by Harry L. Gantt (1861–1919), who was an associate of Taylor at Midvale and Bethlehem Steel.[10] Gantt's most famous contribution was the Gantt chart, a system of control and scheduling we still use today. A typical chart (shown in exhibit 2-2) depicted the relationship between the work planned and completed on one axis and the time elapsed on the other axis.

Gantt's contributions, however, go beyond just the chart. For example, he developed a task bonus system different from Taylor's in that it provided fair renumeration regardless of output. Unlike Taylor's system, which was a pure incentive system, Gantt set a standard wage for each job, but work over and above the standard was rewarded with a bonus. He also recognized the importance workers placed on job security and proper training procedures. Above all, Gantt believed that improved efficiency in organizations resulted from the work methods of the manager, not solely the worker.

The *principles of efficiency* were further developed by Harrington Emerson in 1913 with his book, *The Twelve Principles of Efficiency*.[11] His basic principles of efficient use of organizational resources are summarized as follows: (1) use of jobs clearly defined by objective and fact-based analysis; (2) the need for standard operations, conditions of work, and schedules; (3) the fair use of discipline; (4) the need for

Exhibit 2-2
An Example of a Gantt Chart*

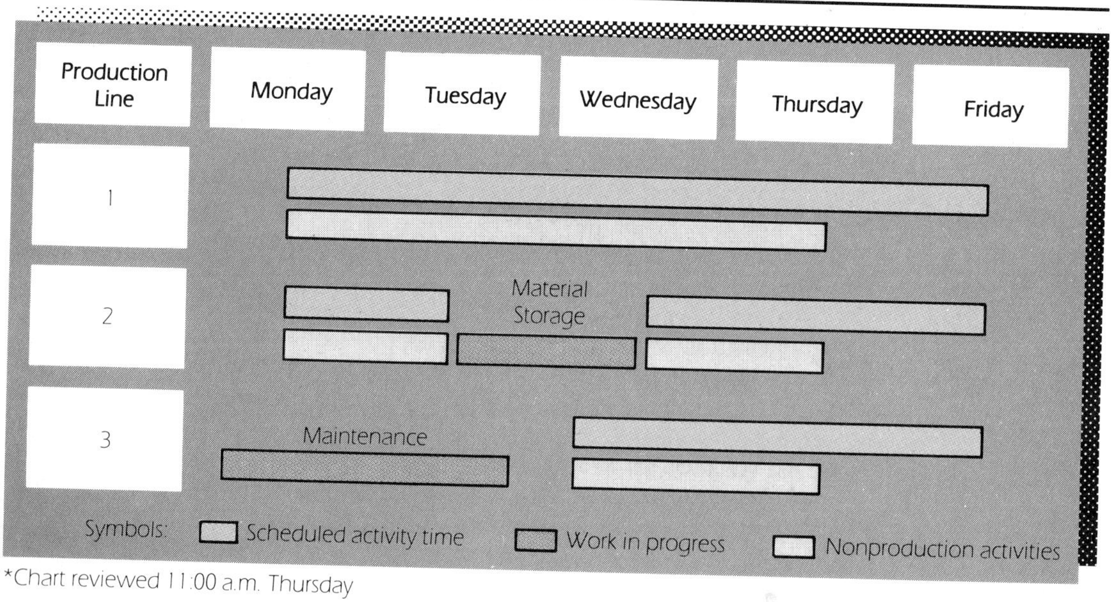

Production Line	Monday	Tuesday	Wednesday	Thursday	Friday
1					
2		Material Storage			
3	Maintenance				

Symbols: ☐ Scheduled activity time   ☐ Work in progress   ☐ Nonproduction activities

*Chart reviewed 11:00 a.m. Thursday

accurate records and job-related instructions; (5) the necessity of integrating all jobs into a whole; and (6) rewards for workers for performing jobs efficiently.

In his work as one of the first management consultants, Emerson presented two concepts that today can be found in most organizations. First, he believed that the most efficient organizational design had strict distinctions between line and staff functions; that is, certain individuals were responsible for the production and marketing of the organization's goods and services, and others acted in support of the line managers. For example, a line manager would be a manufacturing superintendent, and a staff manager would be the personnel manager. Second, Emerson strongly advocated the use of clear statements of goals and objectives for the total organization. In some respects, these two concepts identified Emerson with those who later contributed to management thought along the lines of administrative theory, or management of the total organization.

Administrative Theory

Scientific management, with its emphasis on efficient production, was quite limited in scope. While efficiency of production certainly was of great importance, of equal or greater concern were issues related to the *management of the total organization*. Organizations and the management of organizations had become much more complex than could be handled by scientific management principles.

From this situation emerged a body of ideas known as *administrative theory*. As we will see, there have been many individual contributors to this approach. They all had in common their concern with the development of the basic *functions* of management. We will briefly discuss the contributions of Fayol, Urwick, and Davis.

Henri Fayol: Principles and Functions of Management   Similar to many of the management contributors of the time, Henri Fayol (1841–1925) was an engineer with extensive business experience. Working as the managing director of a large coal-mining organization in France gave Fayol his particular perspective on the management process. His book, *Administratim Industrielle et Generale* (later translated as *General and Industrial Management*), had a major impact on the emerging field of management.[12]

Fayol's contributions to management thought were fourfold. First, as shown in exhibit 2-3, he made the distinction between *operating* and *managerial* activities of an organization. This was a subtle but important influence in elevating the work of managers.

Second, Fayol elaborated on managerial activities by being one of the first to clearly identify specific *management functions*. His five major functions included the following:

- *Planning*. The activity that attempts to forecast future actions and directions of the firm. It is used to develop operating procedures and assists in the decision-making process.

- *Organizing*. This management function is concerned with establishing the organization's structure of authority, responsibility, and tasks.

Exhibit 2-3

Fayol's Business
Activities

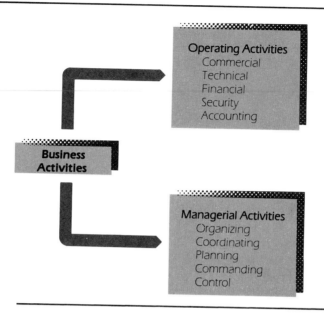

- *Commanding.* Closely related to the function of leading, this activity is concerned with the *direction* of subordinates. Fayol also included in this activity concepts related to communications, managerial behavior, and reward and punishment.
- *Coordinating.* This function concerns all activities and efforts needed to bind the organization together to achieve a common goal.
- *Controlling.* This function concerns the evaluation of organizational activities as they relate to stated goals and plans.

While some have criticized Fayol's management functions as lacking in priorities and clarity, they comprised one of the first such statements and have laid important groundwork.

Third, Fayol proposed fourteen *principles of management* to guide managers in resolving concrete problems. These principles are shown in exhibit 2-4. Managers of his time likely used the thought behind many of these principles. It was Fayol, however, who first presented these principles in a coherent form, making it possible for all managers to learn from them. While some scholars have criticized Fayol's lack of specificity, he did make it clear that the principles would not relieve management of the responsibility for determining "the appropriate balance" of behaviors.

Fayol was also a leader in recognizing the need for managers to acquire and learn certain abilities and skills. He noted that skills and abilities varied not only by the manager's level in the organization (types of managers as we discussed in chapter 1), but also by the size of the organization. Fayol also strongly urged that managerial training be introduced in schools, rather than taught only on the job, and he was one of the early promoters of formal, "in-house" management training programs. He felt that such training would go far beyond the manager's job to affect family, church, military and political activities of the manager.

Fayol's contributions to management thought were significant. Above all, he established the foundation for further work in managerial functions.

Other Contributors to Administrative Theory   Many others have contributed to the administrative theory branch of the classical approach by building on the man-

Exhibit 2-4
Fayol's Principles of Management

---

1. **Division of labor.**   Specialization of labor results in increased productivity through the reduction of job elements required of each worker. Specialization of labor permits large-scale production at minimum cost.

2. **Authority.**   Fayol defined *authority* as the "right to give orders and the power to exact obedience." He distinguished between the official authority that derives from holding a given position and the informal authority that derives from the officeholder's own personality, experience, values (morals), and other personal characteristics that enable the manager to influence the efforts of subordinates.

3. **Discipline.**   The basis of discipline is obedience to rules and procedures reached between parties in the firm. Fayol believed that clear statements of agreements are necessary and that the state of discipline of any group of people depends on the worthiness of its leaders.

4. **Unity of command.**   Fayol believed that an employee should receive orders from only one superior. Recognition and observance of this principle eliminates conflict and breakdown in authority and discipline.

5. **Unity of direction.**   Each group of activities with the same goal is properly managed under one head and one plan.

6. **Subordination of individual interest to the common goal.**   This principle states that the whole is greater than the *sum* of its parts, and that the overall objectives the organization seeks to achieve take precedence over the objectives of individuals.

7. **Remuneration.**   The compensation of all employees for services rendered should be based on a systematic attempt to reward good performance.

8. **Centralization.**   Centralization is the degree to which the importance of subordinates' roles is reduced. He stated that managers should retain final responsibility but give subordinates enough authority to do the task successfully.

9. **Scalar chain.**   Fayol defined the hierarchy from top to bottom through which all communications flow. This chain implements the unity-of-command principle and allows the orderly flow of information.

10. **Order.**   Fayol applied the principle of order to the material and human resources of the firm. This principle states that materials and people must be in the right place at the right time.

11. **Equity.**   Fayol defined equity as the use of established rules tempered by a sense of kindliness and justice. Employees respond to equitable treatment by carrying out their tasks with a sense of loyalty.

12. **Stability of personnel.**   Fayol noted that successful firms usually had a stable group of managers. As a general principle, top management implements practices that encourage the long-term commitment of employees, particularly of managers, to the organization.

13. **Initiative.**   Employees should be given the freedom to develop and implement a plan of action.

14. **Esprit de corps.**   Fayol defined *esprit de corps* as unity of effort through harmony of interests. The most effective means for achieving esprit de corps is through unity of command and through oral rather than written communication.

Exhibit 2-5
Various Descriptions of Management Functions

Contributor	Planning	Organizing	Control	Others
Dale	X	X	X	Staffing, innovation
Davis	X	X	X	
Drucker	Set objectives	X	Evaluation	Motivation
Fayol	X	X	X	Commanding, coordination
Koontz, O'Donnell	X	X	X	Direction, staffing
McFarland	X	X	X	
Mee	X	X	X	Motivation, innovation
Newman	X	X	X	Resource assembling, direction
Terry	X	X	X	Coordination, direction
Urwick	X	X	X	Forecasting, coordination, command
American Management Association	X	X	Execution	
Air Force	X	X	X	Commanding, coordination
Chrysler	X	X	Appraisal	Guiding
Firestone	X	X	Evaluation	Direction
General Electric	X	X	Measuring	Integration
Texaco	X	X	X	Motivation, innovation

X indicates function included

agement functions first presented by Fayol. Some of these contributors are shown in exhibit 2-5.

Lyndall Urwick's book, *The Elements of Administration,* was a landmark contribution to management thought for two reasons.[13] First, he attempted to blend scientific managment and administrative theory into a more comprehensive package. The book provided scholars and practitioners with a broad understanding of the management of the total organization. Its discussion ranged from the job level to the organizational level but was specific enough to provide insights into how principles of the managerial functions could be generalized.

Second, like Fayol, Urwick noted that the management process consisted of three functions—planning, organizing, and controlling. He added further insight by stating that the three functions were guided by the subfunctions of forecasting, coordination, and command. More importantly, he expanded on the controlling function to include three subfunctions: staffing, selecting, and placing. Urwick's expansion of the control function not only founded the personnel aspect of organizations, but it served as the forerunner of the behavioral approach.

Ralph C. Davis, in *The Principles of Business Organization and Operation,* provided a significant synthesis of the basic factors involved in organization and the operation of a business.[14] Similar to Urwick's concept, he founded his approach on the functions of planning, organizing, and an expanded control activity. His discussion of the concept and classification of business objectives was a unique contribution. Davis identified *primary* and *secondary* objectives of a business. Primary objectives were called *service* objectives of the firm, including social objectives and personal objectives of individuals and groups. The secondary objectives related to the economy and effectiveness of operations. In a sense, Davis was ahead of his time in identifying social objectives and survival above profitability as prime objectives of an organization (see chapter 4).

Summary of the Classical School

At least three aspects should be noted concerning the classical approach to management thought. First, the focus on managerial activities has moved from a concern for the management of jobs to management of the total organization. This is an important developmental process. Second, the expansion of management thought within this approach strongly suggests the need for different *skills* in order to achieve high levels of managerial performance. The need for technical skills is foremost in the scientific management approach. In the administrative theory approach, the management of the organization requires a growing awareness of human skills and conceptual skills. Finally, the *roles* that managers perform is distinctly different in Taylor's scientific management than it is in Fayol's approach. Taylor's manager is very much an occupant of interpersonal *roles,* particularly the figurehead and leader roles. Fayol's manager, however, must be proficient in operating in all three major role categories—interpersonal, informational, and decisional. Overall, by looking at the classical approach to management, we can better evaluate the importance of the three key factors in a manager's job—functions, skills, and roles.

Behavioral School of Management

The practice of management, as suggested by the contributors to the classical approach, was built on the thoughts and experiences of engineers and professional managers. They proposed that, with efficiently designed jobs, the right kind of incentives, and the proper use of managerial functions, productivity would increase. It is not surprising that this formal, impersonal approach to management would meet with some resistance from the workers.

This resistance, along with other challenges to the classical approach, gave rise to the development of the *behavioral school of management.* Two branches contributed to the behavioral school—the human relations movement and the development of organizational behavior. These approaches were concerned with a better understanding of how psychological processes interacted with the activities and jobs in the organization. Whereas the classical approach focused on the *jobs of workers,* the behavioral approach was concerned with the *people in these jobs.* Several individuals made significant contributions to this approach.

The Human Relations Movement: Elton Mayo

A group of Harvard researchers, headed by Elton Mayo (along with his associates, including Fritz J. Roethlisberger), conducted a landmark study of human behavior in the Hawthorne plant (Cicero, Illinois) of Western Electric from 1927 to 1932. Since then, this research has been known as the *Hawthorne studies*.[15]

Mayo and his associates were called in by Western Electric after an experiment carried out by the company engineers between 1924 and 1927 with work-area lighting produced confusing results. The engineers, true to the scientific management tradition of seeking answers to industrial problems through research, studied two groups of workers to determine the effects, if any, of different levels of lighting on worker performance. In one group (test group) the level of illumination was changed, while the other (referred to as the control group) experienced no change.

In their initial tests, the engineers found that productivity improved in the test group when the lighting conditions increased. But what concerned the engineers was that productivity also increased in the test group when illumination was decreased! To add to the confusion, the control group's productivity kept increasing even though this group experienced no changes in work-area illumination. Mayo's subsequent entry into the lighting experiment formally ushered in the behavioral approach to management.

Mayo conducted a series of experiments over the next few years to further investigate the Western Electric situation. He conducted research in four distinct phases:

- Experiments to determine the effects on worker productivity of changes in illumination.

- Experiments to determine the effects on worker productivity of other work-related factors. These factors included salary increases, introducing varying lengths of rest periods and coffee breaks, shortened workdays and workweeks, and other changes in working conditions (the relay assembly room experiments).

- An extensive employee interview program to determine worker attitudes.

- An analysis of the various social factors at work (the bank wiring observation room experiment).

As in the original experiments, productivity increased in both the test and control groups in the new tests. After a thorough analysis of the total results, Mayo and his associates concluded that what caused the productivity changes was a series of *psychological reactions* of the participants. Briefly, it appeared that because the test and control groups had been singled out for special attention, they had developed a sense of group pride that motivated them to increase performance levels. The change in supervisory styles from a directive to a more sympathetic style further reinforced their better performance.

The Harvard researchers suggested that the way people were treated had an important impact on performance. In other words, the workers in the tests were not reacting to changes in illumination but to the experiment itself and to their involvement in it. They acted in a way that they thought the experimenters wanted and because they were the center of attention. Since that time, this phenomenon is known as the *Hawthorne effect*.

Mayo further concluded that the social environment of work, particularly the effect of the informal work group, had a great influence on productivity. From this conclusion the researchers suggested that management must recognize the importance of the worker's needs for recognition and social satisfaction. Management should make an effort to turn the informal group into a positive, productive force by providing workers with a new sense of dignity and well-being. Mayo termed this the concept of the *social man*—individuals are motivated by social needs and good on-the-job relationships and respond better to work-group pressure than to management control activities. What was needed was a totally new approach to the human in the workplace—a view that people are motivated to work not solely by economic concerns, but by complex needs.

The Hawthorne studies had a significant impact on management thought. The teachings and practices of the classical school were being seriously questioned, especially the dehumanizing nature of scientific management. As a result of this and other studies, both practitioners and scholars began to take a second look at the importance of human resources in organizations. Training programs were begun to teach supervisors to better understand how people and groups behave in work situations. Improved selection, placement, and incentive systems evolved. In the workplace, the worker, rather than the job, became the focal point for managerial activities. The impact on scholarly research is felt even today with the behavioral science emphasis in management theory.

Other Contributors to the Human Relations Movement

The contributors who followed the Hawthorne studies were as numerous as those who built on Fayol's work. We will discuss many of these contributions in detail in our chapters on motivation, leadership, and group behavior. Two contributors, however, deserve specific mention: Chester Barnard and Douglas McGregor.

Chester Barnard   As president of New Jersey Bell, Chester I. Barnard (1886–1961) combined his work experience and extensive readings in sociology and philosophy into an analysis of the executive's job in an organization. The result was *The Functions of the Executive,* one of management's few classic texts.[16]

According to Barnard, people form organizations in order to achieve goals they could not achieve working alone. This "cooperative effort" is the basis of his definition that, "An organization is a system of consciously coordinated activities or forces of two or more persons." His major point was that an organization can operate efficiently and survive only when both the organization's goals and the goals and needs of the individuals working for it are kept in balance. This formed his basic elements of organizations: (1) a system of cooperation; (2) common purpose; and (3) an emphasis on efficiency and effectiveness.

Barnard also stimulated interest in the areas of motivation, decision making, communications, and the importance of objectives. For example, he proposed that

"In his mysterious way, God has given each of us different talents, Ridgeway. It just so happens that mine is intimidating people."

From the *Wall Street Journal*-Permission, Cartoon Features Syndicate.

worker cooperation and motivation were related to the balance between *inducements* and *contributions*. Inducements were the sum total of financial and nonfinancial rewards employees received in exchange for their efforts (i.e., contributions). The nature of the communications system provided employees with the information they needed to evaluate the balance between inducements and contributions. Finally, he set forth an approach that was later called the *acceptance theory of authority*. This theory stated that employees will determine whether an order is legitimate and whether or not they will accept it. In other words, employees will accept an executive order only if what they are asked to do agrees with how they view the goals of the organization and their own personal interests.

Douglas McGregor: Theory X and Theory Y   One of the main contributors to the behavioral science movement was Douglas McGregor.[17] In his major work, *The Human Side of Enterprise*, McGregor advanced two beliefs for managers about human behavior—Theory X and Theory Y.

Theory X represented the traditional approach to management as defined by Taylor's scientific management principles. From the Hawthorne studies and other behavioral research efforts, many practicing managers recognized the need to adopt a totally different set of assumptions about people at work. The acceptance of the Theory Y approach, with its tenets of participation and a concern for employee morale, encouraged managers to begin practicing their profession in a radically different way. Theory Y encouraged the following: (1) delegating authority for many decisions to lower level workers; (2) attempting to make workers' jobs less routine and boring; (3) increasing the level of responsibility in each worker's job; (4) improving the free flow of information and communications within the organization; and (5) recognizing that people are motivated by a complex set of psychological needs, not just by money.

In a sense, McGregor's contribution may be more significant than Mayo's. Whereas Mayo's work was a data-based research study in one organization, McGregor's work represented a major philosophical change for managers. Though some have criticized the approach because it lacks specific details on *how* to manage, it suggested that a major reorientation in managerial thinking was necessary.

From Human Relations to Organizational Behavior

Mayo, McGregor, and others pioneered the movement toward a better understanding of people at work in organizations. Later researchers, who were more rigorously trained in the social sciences (such as psychology, sociology, political science, and anthropology), began investigating the human resources issue in management with more sophisticated research techniques. The work of these later researchers helped found the field called "organizational behavior."[18]

The field of organizational behavior is identified by five distinguishing characteristics: (1) a foundation built on the scientific method; (2) an interdisciplinary orientation taken from the social sciences; (3) a level of analysis that includes a focus on the individual, groups, and the organization; (4) a contingency orientation, suggesting that there is no universally accepted theory or approach to the study of people in organizations; and (5) an important concern for applications. Researchers in the field have contributed a tremendous amount of literature on such topics as motivation, leadership, group and intergroup behavior, and the design of work. We will discuss each of these topics in later chapters.

Summary of the Behavioral School of Management

The human relations movement and the growth of the contemporary field of organizational behavior made significant contributions to our understanding of people at work, people in groups, and people in organizations. Through courses in higher education and continuing education programs, in-house training classes, published articles, and on-the-job experiences, the behavioral school of management has motivated managers to become more aware and sophisticated in dealing with subordinates.

If you, as future managers, are considering adopting the behaviorial approach, you'll need to recognize certain key points. First, the potential contribution of the behavioral approach has not been fully realized, since many managers have been reluctant to accept behavioral principles. As we noted in chapter 1, managers acquire certain attitudes and skills through several mechanisms (e.g., education, experience, mentor relationships). Once these attitudes have developed, it is difficult to change them. In other words, managers with many years of experience will not readily admit that they cannot handle people or that their ways have become outdated. This situation, hopefully, will change as more new and future managers are trained in behaviorial principles.

Second, behavioral scientists are equally responsible for the unrealized potential of the behavioral approach. Too often, behavioral scientists communicate their findings in academic journals that are neither appealing nor accessible. When these researchers attempt to write for the practitioner, many times they use language the manager cannot understand. This further inhibits understanding and acceptance of their ideas. Third, because the study of human behavior in organizations is both relatively new and complex, behavioral scientists often differ in their recommendations on a particular problem, making it difficult for managers to decide whose advice to follow.

Finally, as we noted in chapter 1, the behavioral approach is strongly oriented to human skills. And, although human skills are important, effectiveness as a manager requires proficiency in many skills.

The Management Science School

During the 1940s, an approach to management emerged that attempted to solve people and work problems in organizations using a more sophisticated, mathematically based scientific approach. This is known as the *management science school*.

Foundations

During World War II, a significant research program was begun to investigate the applicability of quantitative methods to military and logistical problems. Some of the projects included methods of increasing bombing accuracy, development of search procedures to locate enemy submarines, and the transportation of supplies and equipment. Most of the research projects were conducted with the use of interdisciplinary teams, culled from fields such as engineering, mathematics, statistics, economics, psychology, and political science. After the war, many people saw great potential for the newly developed methods in the industrial world.

The application of management science principles followed a two-step sequence. Initially, since many of the new methods were oriented toward the manufacturing function, applications in *production management* quickly emerged. Applying the principles to such problems as the flow of raw materials, quality control, inventory control, and new manufacturing processes achieved significant results. Later, both management science scholars and practitioners recognized that the principles being applied to the manufacturing function could be applied to other organizational functions (see chapter 18). This change to a much broader focus created the second stage of development in the management science approach—the *operations management focus*. Management science principles were now being applied to personnel scheduling, business planning models, simulated decision-making activities, and so on.

The management science approach differs from the classical and behavioral schools of thought in a number of important ways. The distinguishing characteristics include:[19]

■ *Managerial decision making.* Management science differs from scientific management primarily in focus. Scientific management is concerned with production tasks and the efficiency of workers and machines. Management science stresses that efficiency comes from proper planning and making the right decisions. (In other words, improper decisions can be implemented in an efficient manner.) Management science principles and techniques provide the format to make proper decisions.

■ *Mathematical models.* A model is a simplified representation of a real situation. In management science, a mathematical model attempts to reduce a managerial decision to a mathematical form so that the decision-making process can be simulated and evaluated *before* the actual decision is made. For example, a manager may be concerned with the relationship between production rates and inventory requirements for customer orders. By reducing such variables as production rates, inventory storage space, available manpower, and the frequency and quantity of customer orders into a mathematical model, the manager can test different values of each variable until he or she finds an acceptable solution.

■ *Computer applications.* More than any one factor, the use of the computer has been the driving force behind the emergence of the management science approach.[20] With its speed, the computer in minutes can handle extremely complex problems with an immense volume of data and calculate numerous variations on a solution that would take a team of experts many months using manual calculations.

■ *Evaluation criteria.* Because the main focus of the management science approach is on proper decision making, models have been evaluated against a set of effectiveness criteria. Examples include cost savings, revenue, return on investment, improved scheduling and the meeting of deadlines.

As management science and operations management began making inroads into many organizational applications, the term *operations research* came to represent the various models and techniques in use. This term identified the desire to use scientific analysis in the solution of managerial problems in all types of organizations.

In exhibit 2-6, we have summarized some of the main operations research techniques. The seven techniques identified—break-even analysis, linear programming, queuing (waiting in line) theory, network models, simulation, probability analysis, and regression analysis—by no means include all the techniques that are being applied today. They are meant to give the reader an overview of current uses.

Summary of Management Science

With its emphasis on decision-making, models, and the computer, the management science school has become an integral part of the problem-solving framework in many organizations. Its techniques are used in many settings, not just in manufacturing.

The management science school has made a significant impact on the practice of management; however, it still does not have a high level of acceptance by many managers. First, using our managerial *skills* theme, management science techniques have helped in the acquisition of technical and conceptual skills (and maybe, to a certain extent, some diagnostic skills). However, management science has not yet

Exhibit 2-6
Examples of Operations Research Techniques

Technique	Description	Example
Break-Even Analysis	Determining the particular point of operations at which total revenue equals total cost and profit is zero.	With the use of price, quantity, and cost data, finding the level of sales that will result in a profit for the firm.
Linear Programming	A model that determines the best way to allocate limited resources to reach an optimum solution.	With a given number of warehouses, customers, and shipping costs, determining the routes that will minimize transportation costs.
Queuing Theory	Investigating the relationship between waiting time (of people, materials, or equipment) and the cost of additional facilities.	Deciding whether to add new bank tellers given the number of customers waiting in line.
Network Models	Planning the activities of a project so that it can be completed on schedule.	Constructing a new plant.
Simulation	Simulating a process with the use of a mathematical model and the computer.	Aircraft trainers that simulate landings and takeoffs.
Probability Analysis	Attempting to predict the decisions of people using probabilities.	Deciding whether or not to expand a retail store size with probabilities associated with an increase, decrease, or no change in area population size.
Regression Analysis	Attempting to predict the effects on one variable of changes in other variables.	Predicting the effects of changes in price and advertising on sales.

reached the state where it can help managers develop effective human skills. Most applications have been found in planning and control activities; its contributions have been only modest in such areas as organizing, motivating, staffing, and leadership. Second, from a managerial *role* framework, the management science school leans heavily toward decisional roles at the expense of interpersonal and informational roles. Thus, its contributions to date have only covered a portion of the manager's job.

Finally, there is a growing resistance to the management science school on the basis that "experts" are trained to the teeth in the *techniques,* but not in the *practice* of management.[21] In other words, some practitioners and scholars point out that mathematical models are no substitute for native shrewdness, sound common sense, and abundant energy. In their zeal to solve more and more so-called complex problems, management scientists develop models that are far from the realities of the management situation. This bridge between theory and practice must be overcome before management science can continue to contribute to management thought.

The Contingency View of Management

The contingency view of management emerged from the real-life experience of managers, researchers, and consultants. More often than not, these individuals found that the methods, techniques, and prescriptions suggested by the three management schools—classical, behavioral, and management science—did not consistently work in every situation. Why, for example, would strict adherence to the managerial functions of the classical approach result in high performance in one situation, but not another? Why would workers in one group respond well to a Theory Y approach, while those in another did not? Why would a mathematical planning model perform effectively for one product, but less effectively for another product in the same organization? In response to these and other questions, a contingency view began to emerge.

The contingency view suggests that the effectiveness of various managerial practices, styles, techniques, and functions will vary according to the *particular* circumstances of the situation.[22] This approach also recognizes that the state of management thought has not advanced to the point at which definitive prescriptions for the best way to manage in every situation are available. In fact, there are some who believe that because of the complexities of the environment, organizations, and humans in these organizations, we may never reach a point where we have answers or approaches for solving most problems. For this reason, the contingency approach is not recognized as a formal management school.

Components of the Contingency View

As shown in exhibit 2-7 on the following page, we can best understand the contingency approach by analyzing the determinants of contingency thought and the managerial questions that arise from adopting this view of management. Gaining knowledge about the facts surrounding various situations is the only way to improve our effectiveness as managers.

The main determinants of the contingency view relate to the external and internal environments of the organization. The *external environment* concerns the state of the economic, social, political, and technological areas and their impact on or relationship to the organization. For example, consider the following illustrations: (1) Mideast oil problems have significantly changed the thinking of many energy company executives about the future of crude oil as a fuel; (2) the development of miniature electronic components has totally reoriented the business machine industry; (3) federal laws and enforcement policies on equal opportunity and safety have elevated the importance of the personnel function in most organizations; and (4) national concerns over the environment have forced automobile manufacturers to radically change their new cars to be more fuel efficient.

The *internal environment* is more commonly referred to as the state of the organization with respect to the various constraints and resources that are available. At least three components are used to describe the internal environment:

Exhibit 2-7
Summary of Contingency Management

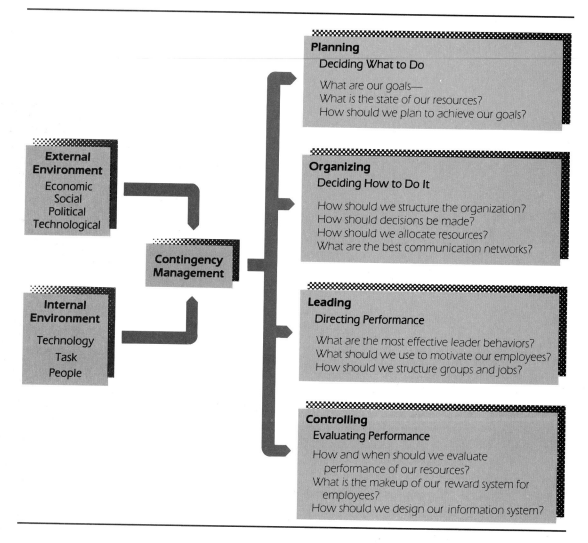

Planning

Deciding What to Do

What are our goals—
What is the state of our resources?
How should we plan to achieve our goals?

Organizing

Deciding How to Do It

How should we structure the organization?
How should decisions be made?
How should we allocate resources?
What are the best communication networks?

Leading

Directing Performance

What are the most effective leader behaviors?
What should we use to motivate our employees?
How should we structure groups and jobs?

Controlling

Evaluating Performance

How and when should we evaluate
performance of our resources?
What is the makeup of our reward system for
employees?
How should we design our information system?

External Environment
Economic
Social
Political
Technological

Contingency Management

Internal Environment
Technology
Task
People

Technology Constraints   Technology refers to the type and nature of the processes used to produce the organization's goods or services. For example, the technology used to manufacture plastics is different from the technology of banking. Two constraints, or limiting factors, are most important. First, how *flexible* is the technology to changes the external environmental demands? In the manufacture of steel, large capital investments in machinery and equipment are necessary to produce the product. As such, steel companies cannot change their processes around very quickly to meet new consumer demands. The impact of the Japanese steel industry on U.S. companies, with its new equipment and technology, is well documented. On the other hand, the retailing industry, with its emphasis on human resources rather than on physical plant and equipment (i.e., it is labor intensive), can adapt readily to changes in consumer demands and taste. In other words, every industry is constrained by its technology, some more than others.

Second, the type of technology that is used in an organization determines the nature of the *interdependence* between different units. Interdependence concerns the degree to which one individual, group, or organization is dependent on another for materials or services to perform the task. For example, workers on an automobile assembly line are highly dependent on one another. The tire mounters cannot do their job until the brakes have been installed; the bumpers cannot be installed until the car has been painted, and so on. The key factor with technology constraints is that the greater the level of dependence, the greater the need for *coordination* and, hence, managerial attention and decisions.[23]

Task Constraints   The nature of the tasks performed by individual workers is also a contingency factor. Employees who work on *routine* tasks perform their work in a repetitive fashion. Such jobs require a more precise set of instructions, training, directing, and control than do nonroutine, *complex* jobs. For example, newspaper press operators perform their jobs according to a set of procedures and guidelines that dictates their responsibilities, quantity and quality requirements, and scheduling. On the other hand, the manager of product planning for a company such as General Foods or Procter & Gamble follows only a minimum of procedures because the job contains many uncertainties with respect to consumer acceptance, production requirements, and product specifications.

The important contingency aspect is that the task dictates how a manager acts in various situations. A manager supervising a group of workers in routine jobs is heavily concerned with the control functions because much of the subordinates' job is described by rules, policies, and procedures. The manager of a group of subordinates who perform complex tasks is less concerned with the control aspects than with the planning and change aspects.

Individual or People Constraints   This third contingency factor relates to the types of individuals employed in the organization and their levels of competence. First, the manager must be concerned with the dominant psychological needs of the work force. Do workers seek high wages and job security, or are the needs for advancement, learning, and personal development more important? The Chevrolet Lordstown plant taught a valuable lesson in the mismatch between the workers and their jobs. It was not until after a rash of strikes that management of this assembly line plant recognized that many of the employee-relations problems could be traced to the fact that the workers—who were more highly educated than employees at other plants—were reacting negatively to both the boredom of the assembly line and the lack of any opportunity for advancement.

Second, the abilities, skills, and levels of competence of the organization's work force must be carefully analyzed before any major decisions affecting the survival of the firm are made. In essence, the question is how good is the managerial and non-managerial work force? In the 1950s and 1960s, American Motors' decision to compete head-on with Ford and GM resulted in failure because they did not have the necessary personnel to compete effectively. In other words, they went in over their heads!

As shown in exhibit 2-7, the focus of a contingency orientation to management is a series of questions (or problems) that managers must face. These questions stress two points. First, no one specific management approach answers the questions—there just is no "one best way" to handle all possible contingencies and constraints. Second, these questions should make you keenly aware of the need to consider the importance of functions, skills, and roles in performing the manager's job. These three characteristics must be integrated in order to attain high levels of achievement.

Summary of the Contingency View

The contingency view approaches management from a totally different perspective than do the formal schools of management. Rather than apply a universal technique to each situation, it suggests that different situations require different approaches.

The contingency view supports the use of classical, behavioral, or management science ideas in various situations, depending on the state of the external and internal environments. The basic managerial functions of planning, organizing, and control are the important elements of any management approach. They must, however, be adapted to the situation. Planning is always important, but it is only as effective as the quality and quantity of information used. Organizations must set goals, but these goals must recognize the capabilities and resources of the firm. One must emphasize structural design, but what *type* of design? Concern for people in the workplace is without question an important consideration. Yet, managers must recognize that a Theory X approach may be more effective in a particular situation than a Theory Y approach. Finally, operations research techniques can be of tremendous value only when we have some confidence in the quality of the assumptions and of the input data. No matter how complex and sophisticated our mathematical model, unreliable input results in an unreliable solution.

More than any approach to management, the contingency view provides a clear look at the realities of the manager's job. There is a constant emphasis on managerial functions, skills, and roles. It recognizes the importance of the management functions of planning, organizing, and control as a key to effective performance. It focuses attention on acquiring proficiency in all four of the major managerial skills—technical, human, conceptual, and diagnostic. With its emphasis on investigation, observation, and analysis of various managerial problems and the possible courses of action, it highlights the conceptual and diagnostic skills, a focus the other approaches lack. Finally, the contingency view recognizes that the manager is more than just a leader or a decision maker or an information handler. In reality, the manager is all three.

The contingency view is not without its critics and thus should not be portrayed or accepted as the best or only way to manage. There is criticism that stressing the "it all depends" view adds more *confusion* than *order* to the practice of management. By accepting contingency approaches, the practitioner is swamped with more "what ifs" and "what happens when" ideas than he or she can deal with, allowing the manager to sink or swim without the use of tested and proven prescriptions, techniques, or methods. Others point out that the contingency view is without a theoretical foundation, making it near impossible to research, gain valuable information, or develop a knowledge base. Whether management is an art, a science, or a field of study and practice, certain elements should serve as a foundation for continued growth and development.[24]

These criticisms, and those directed at the other management schools, certainly have some validity and should, therefore, be carefully considered by the manager. Our approach to management is neither based, nor limited, by adherence to a particular popular school. It is our view that a manager's job revolves around certain basic but broad *functions* that require different *skills* and performs a variety of *roles*. The ultimate test is *performance*, no matter what approach is used.

Management Thought: A Summary

In this chapter, we have attempted to provide an overview of approaches to management thought. A summary of our presentation is shown in exhibit 2-8. This exhibit has been developed around our belief that a manager's job is best described in terms of *functions, skills*, and *roles*. There are at least three important points for the manager to consider.

First, the description of the managerial *functions* has grown significantly from the classical school to the contingency orientation. We have seen how the functions performed by the manager have developed from a concern for efficiency and the basic ideas about planning, organizing, and control to an emphasis on human factors, mathematical models, and finally to a recognition that what the manager does is determined to a great extent by the state of the environment, both internal and external to the organization.

Second, the different schools of management each stress the importance of acquiring certain managerial *skills*. The differences involve not only priority but also complexity. Scientific management and the human relations views each stress the importance of a primary skill—technical for the former, human skills for the latter. On the other hand, the organizational behavior branch of the behavioral school and the contingency view each stress the need to acquire proficiency in multiple skills.

Finally, the scope of managerial activities is represented by the different *roles* that the management schools emphasize. The classical approach looks at the manager's roles as being primarily interpersonal, but the behavioral school and contingency view present the manager's job in much broader scope.

The differences in functions, skills, and roles are an important distinguishing characteristic of the four management schools. More than any one factor, however, this summary exhibit should remind the manager of the importance of the growth of management as a profession—one that is not only becoming more and more complex, but one that can afford a highly rewarding career as well.

Exhibit 2-8
Summary of Management Schools

	Basic Functions	Skills Required	Roles Stressed
Classical			
1. Scientific Management	1. Developing more efficient jobs through job specialization, planning, motion, and time standards.	Technical	Interpersonal
2. Administrative Theory	2. Planning, organizing, and controlling.	Technical Human Conceptual	Interpersonal Informational
Behavioral			
1. Human Relations	1. Emphasis on the person's psychological reactions to a job.	Human	Interpersonal
2. Organizational Behavior	2. Exploring the effects on employee behavior of the job, supervisory relations, group structure, and organizational practices.	Human Conceptual Diagnostic	Interpersonal Informational Decisional
Management Science	Developing mathematical models to assist managerial decision making.	Technical Conceptual Diagnostic	Informational Decisional
Contingency	There is no "one best way" to manage. Managerial activities and behavior are determined by the state of the situation.	Technical Human Conceptual Diagnostic	Interpersonal Informational Decisional

 # Contributions by Practicing Managers

Throughout the twentieth century, practicing managers have made many contributions to the development of management. Taylor, Fayol, and Barnard, for example, all held managerial positions when they presented their views and approaches to management. Being an applied field of study, we should expect significant contributions from practicing professionals today. We have singled out four additional practicing managers who have each made a unique contribution to management thought—Charles P. McCormick, James F. Lincoln, Pierre Du Pont, and Alfred P. Sloan.

Charles P. McCormick: Employee Participation

Employee participation in management became an important concept for the McCormick Company, a food products firm, during the 1930s. Developed by the company's president, Charles P. McCormick, the plan stressed how employees in the headquarters, factory, and sales force could share both the responsibilities and opportunities of company management. "Multiple management," as it became known, was the fore-runner of many of today's participative management approaches.[25]

McCormick's first venture into participative management was on the company's junior board of directors. The junior board consisted of seventeen promising young employees who were given free access to many company records, including detailed financial data. They were instructed to review various parts of the business and make recommendations that would supplement (or oppose) the judgments of the senior members of the main board of directors. The junior board was highly successful and made a number of suggestions that helped the company through the Great Depression. The concept was expanded later in the development of two other boards: (1) the factory board, which included supervisors and nonsupervisory workers; and (2) the sales board, made up of members of the sales and distribution staff.

McCormick's participative management plan involved a number of important points:

- *Involvement.* It permitted workers and lower level managers to get involved in the company's major decision making.
- *Communications.* Both vertical and horizontal communications networks were opened up in the company.
- *Management development.* The various boards could be used to identify and evaluate the special talents of employees and attempt to put them in more challenging jobs.
- *Sponsorship.* Each board member was sponsored by a higher level executive (see the discussion of mentors in chapter 1). This helped the lower level employee become socialized more quickly in the organization and gain valuable experience.
- *Evaluation.* With the use of a senior board and a junior board, the company benefitted from having a variety of points of view about its programs.

McCormick's vision of future management was also early for its time. He noted that the primary purpose of management was to build people. It should place the human factor above profit, knowing that if its human organization is constructed of the right kind of material, the profit will take care of itself.

James F. Lincoln: Incentive Management

At Lincoln Electric, a Cleveland-based firm, James F. Lincoln became known for his approach to individual motivation through the use of incentives and profit sharing.[26] During the late 1930s, Lincoln was concerned that pride in one's work, self-reliance, and other time-tested virtues were being replaced by a greater dependence on someone else—principally the government. He felt that it was time to return to the days when individual ambition was dominant. In other words, he believed that people were not primarily motivated by money, nor by security, but by recognition of their skills and performance.

Lincoln's incentive plan sought to develop all employees to their highest abilities and then reward them with a "bonus" based on their contribution to the firm's profits. This bonus, which could double individuals' annual wages, was given over and above regular compensation, which was already comparable to area wages. At Lincoln

Electric, there were no work stoppages or strikes, turnover for all types of employees was almost nonexistent (there was, and still is, a waiting list for new jobs), worker productivity was five times as great as for other manufacturing companies, and profits were rising along with bonuses. The incentive plan at Lincoln is still as successful as ever today, and is being copied by many other small- to medium-size organizations.

Beyond Lincoln's contribution to motivation by incentives, the basic philosophy of management is both interesting and adaptable even by today's standards. Some of his more important points are as follows:

- Occasionally give workers jobs over their heads; challenge brings out the best in people.
- Personal advancement is based solely on the individual's performance and contribution to the firm.
- Stress teamwork; every worker must feel responsible to a team.
- You are a leader, not a boss.

Lincoln's emphasis on motivation, teamwork, and leadership were to serve as the foundation of many contemporary organizational programs in the management of human resources.

Pierre Du Pont: Modern Top Management

When Pierre Du Pont took over as chief executive of the family firm, E.I. Du Pont de Nemours, the company was already a century old. He knew Frederick Taylor; in fact, he hired him as a consultant on a number of occasions. However, Du Pont was more concerned with higher level management problems. While Taylor worked on problems at the job and factory level, it was Du Pont who introduced modern top management thought and practice.

During Du Pont's early tenure, most industrial companies were one-man shows, such as Carnegie and Ford. Du Pont revolutionized the executive office, setting up the procedures for forecasting, long-range planning, budgeting and allocating resources that are taken for granted today. He created functional departments for manufacturing, sales, purchasing, finance, and transportation. On top of the functional arrangement, Du Pont set up a tightly centralized general office for the total company. The company's governing body was the *executive committee,* composed of the president and the heads of the major functional departments. To enable the executive committee to make resource allocation decisions, Du Pont set up a system to provide it with information about departmental expenditures, including data on expenses, rates of return, and proposed spending plans.[27] The executive committee also coordinated the flow of materials through the company, attempting to control inventory, the physical movement of goods at all stages, and the fluctuating demands of working capital. While some students of management consider John D. Rockefeller the founder of top management thinking, the committee system he established at Standard Oil was scrapped almost entirely in favor of the Du Pont system.

The Du Pont system, however, was not without its problems. When the company diversified into paints, dyes, chemicals, and fibers, the complexities created by massive diversification coupled with a severe economic recession brought about big losses. As a result, the company separated top management from day-to-day decisions about resource allocation. This move was the beginning of management decentralization, to which Du Pont also contributed.

Alfred P. Sloan: Management Decentralization

Du Pont's organizational expertise carried over to an emerging firm in the 1920s, General Motors. In order to save the young company from financial failure, the Du Pont family invested millions of dollars along with many of its management ideas. Influenced by the emerging decentralized structure at Du Pont, GM's new president, Alfred P. Sloan, formalized the system of decentralized operations and centralized control and review.[28] Essentially, the system enabled top management to control the various parts of the company in a more efficient and rational manner. Each division, or department, was considered as an *individual operating company,* with its own functional departments (e.g., manufacturing, sales, and purchasing). But each division would have to operate according to a set of guidelines—from personnel to finance—established by top management. Under the system, the divisions were required to develop detailed data on costs, sales, purchases, and profits so that top management could then authorize production levels. While the divisions made day-to-day decisions, it was ultimately top management that made the major policy decisions on how resources would be deployed and the direction of the company.

The idea of decentralized product divisions enabled each division to react much more quickly to the ever-changing environment. In the late 1920s, GM recognized the changing trends in consumer tastes for automobiles. Consumers no longer wanted the bland-looking but reliable car. They were beginning to express a desire for variety of products based on style, not just low cost and engineering. By 1927, GM was offering a full line of cars that covered a wide price and style range. The decentralized structure not only permitted GM to react to the market faster but also enabled them to pass Ford in size and sales—a lead they have not relinquished today. Sloan's decentralization idea, later revised as "profit-center" management, is still a dominant force.

 SUMMARY FOR THE MANAGER

1. Each of the management schools of thought developed during different parts of this century. The important point is that the particular management school was appropriate for the environment at that time—management thought adapted to the conditions of the organization's environment. Because of this, the schools of management differed in their emphasis on the functions, skills, and roles of the manager's job.

2. The classical school of management consisted of two branches. The scientific management approach stressed the use of the scientific method toward developing a better understanding of the management of jobs. This orientation resulted in emphasizing control aspects, technical

skills, and interpersonal roles of the manager's job. The administrative theory branch, with its focus on the management of the total organization, first noted the importance of the managerial functions of planning, organizing, and controlling. This branch also expanded the view of the manager's job in terms of needed skills and required roles.

3. Employee reactions to certain features of the classical school, coupled with changes in the environment of many organizations, created a need to refine the manager's job. This need resulted in the development of the behavioral school of management. Managerial functions, skills, and roles were changed to emphasize the importance of managing an organization's people.

4. Two major events gave momentum to the development of the management science school. First, World War II created a need for more sophisticated methods of handling and solving complex managerial problems. Second, the advent of the computer enabled managers to solve these problems with great speed and accuracy. These two factors helped redefine the manager's job to stress the technical and conceptual skills applied to informational and decisional roles.

5. The complex and dynamic environment of the 1960s and 1970s clearly revealed that there was no universal approach to management. The contingency view of management emphasized adaptation to the organization's external and internal environment. The manager's job became as complex and dynamic as the world around it. The focus of managerial activities was on all functions (planning, organizing, leading, controlling, and change), skills (technical, human, conceptual, and diagnostic), and roles (interpersonal, informational, and decisional). To be successful, the manager was required to carefully analyze each particular situation and apply the needed functions, skills, and roles.

6. Throughout the history of management thought, major contributions came from both scholars and practitioners of management, stressing the need for management scholars and practitioners to interact frequently to exchange ideas and thoughts.

 # REVIEW AND DISCUSSION QUESTIONS

1. What can today's managers find interesting about the history of management thought?
2. Why were the two branches of the classical school termed the management of jobs and the management of the organization?
3. What were Taylor's major contributions to management?
4. How are Fayol's principles of management different from those of the contingency approach?
5. What were the key factors in the development of the behavioral school of management?
6. What is the "Hawthorne effect"?
7. What are the factors or events behind the management science school?
8. What are some of the problems with the management science school?
9. What major skills and roles does the contingency school of management stress?
10. Why have the contributors to management thought come from both the academic and practitioner orientation?

NOTES

1. H. Koontz and C. O'Donnell, *Management: A Systems and Contingency Analysis of Managerial Functions* (New York: McGraw-Hill, 1976).

2. J. D. Thompson, *Organizations in Action* (New York: McGraw-Hill, 1967), p. 147.

3. D. A. Wren, *The Evolution of Management Thought* (Englewood Cliffs, N.J.: Prentice-Hall, 1968).

4. R. L. A. Sterba, "Clandestine Management in the Imperial Chinese Bureaucracy," *Academy of Management Review* (January 1978): 69-78.

5. K. von Clausewitz, *Principles of War* (Harrisburg, Pa.: Military Service Publishing, 1942).

6. F. W. Taylor, *Principles of Scientific Management* (New York: Harper and Brothers, 1911).

7. Ibid., pp. 36-37.

8. L. E. Davis and J. C. Taylor, eds., *Design of Jobs* (Santa Monica, Calif.: Goodyear Publishing, 1979).

9. F. B. Gilbreth, *Bricklaying System* (New York: Clark Publishing, 1909).

10. H. L. Gantt, *Work, Wages, and Profits* (New York: Engineering Magazine Co., 1911).

11. H. Emerson, *The Twelve Principles of Efficiency* (New York: Engineering Magazine, 1913).

12. H. Fayol, *General and Industrial Management*, trans. J. A. Conbrough (Geneva: International Management Institute, 1929).

13. L. Urwick, *The Elements of Administration* (London: Sir Isaac Pitman, 1943).

14. R. C. Davis, *The Principles of Business Organization and Operation* (Columbus: H. L. Hedrick, 1935).

15. F. J. Roethlisberger and W. J. Dickson, *Management and the Worker* (Boston: Harvard University Press, 1939).

16. C. I. Barnard, *The Functions of the Executive* (Boston: Harvard University Press, 1938).

17. D. McGregor, *The Human Side of Enterprise* (New York: McGraw-Hill, 1960).

18. L. L. Cummings, "Towards Organizational Behavior," *Academy of Management Review* (January 1978): 90-98.

19. H. M. Wagner, *Principle of Management Science* (Englewood Cliffs, N.J.: Prentice-Hall, 1976), p. 5.

20. J. W. Forrester, *Industrial Dynamics* (Cambridge, Mass.: M.I.T. Press, 1961).

21. T. Levitt, "A Heretical View of Management Science," *Fortune* (December 18, 1978): 50-52.

22. P. Lawrence and J. W. Lorsch, *Organization and Environment: Managing Differentiation and Integration* (Homewood, Ill.: Richard D. Irwin, 1967).

23. Thompson, *Organizations in Action*, p. 54-55.

24. See J. W. Lorsch, "Making Behavioral Science More Useful," *Harvard Business Review* (March-April 1979): 171-81.

25. C. P. McCormick, *Multiple Management* (New York: Harper and Brothers, 1938).

26. J. F. Lincoln, *Incentive Management* (Cleveland, Ohio: Lincoln Electric Company, 1951).

27. P. Smith, "The Masterminds of Management," *Dun's Review* (July 1976): 17-19.

28. A. P. Sloan, *My Years with General Motors* (Garden City, N.Y.: Doubleday, 1964).

A CASE FOR ANALYSIS

Management Foundations

Harry Cunningham of K-Mart and Joyce Hall of Hallmark Cards

Among the more fascinating questions that can be asked about managers are those concerning motive. What makes managers tick? What drives them on? Why does each approach management differently? Simple, universal answers cannot be found—because motives differ from person to person, from one manager to another. This point is well illustrated by a look at the careers of Harry Cunningham, the man credited with the innovation called K-Mart, and Joyce C. Hall, who built Hallmark Cards into a multimillion dollar company.

Harry Cunningham had not set out to be a retailer. He studied journalism at Miami University, Ohio, and then got a job on a newspaper in Harrisburg, Pennsylvania, not far from his birthplace. After World War II, he met an S. S. Kresge executive and saw a chance for advancement with that company. Starting at the bottom as a stock boy in a Virginia store, he worked as many as ninety hours a week. Promotions came fast. In 1957 he was given the new title of "general vice president" with no specified duties. He seemed to be in line for a top job, but the incumbent, who didn't want a crown prince around the Detroit headquarters, suggested he travel.

And travel he did. After two years, he had visited all except fourteen of Kresge's 725 stores. What Cunningham found was that while the company still was viewed highly by its customers, many had been moving to the suburbs, stranding inner city stores. Cunningham, searching for new directions, studied the discount stores that were booming. Here was an idea that Kresge, with its strong national organization, could carry further than discounters. Because the company had traditionally looked down on discounters, he did not trumpet this conclusion. Advocating this new strategy, he felt, would adversely affect his career at Kresge.

After he became president, Cunningham tried to get his company behind the discount store idea. Wanting a broad management consensus, he set up an executive level task force to study why and how Kresge should make such a major shift. Before the first K-Mart opened in 1962, management was so confident of the idea that it had already made a commitment for thirty-three K-Marts. In a few years, Kresge's sales and profits passed those of Woolworth, which had moved slowly into discounting with Woolco stores. In 1979, the company's name was changed to K-Mart corporation.

In a business that many people would consider unglamorous, Joyce Hall found a lifetime of excitement with greeting cards—in the pursuit of excellence, or, as he calls it, "quality." Hall says he learned about quality from a Kansas City grocer whose stores sold nothing but the best. People were glad to shop in them even if they had to pay more.

Hall's innovations were many. The first, which helped Hallmark rise from a small regional business to national leadership, was a display case built around 1930. Up until then, cards had been kept under store counters, usually in a mess. Working with an architect, Hall designed an open case which displayed cards in slots. The retailer replenished the slot from a box in a drawer below. And this led to a second innovation, a method of inventory control. At the bottom of each storage box, Hallmark put a reorder card for the retailer to mail. This inventory system is now computerized, and Hallmark's warehousing operations are a marvel of modern management.

In the human resource area, Hall changed the jobs of artists, which had traditionally been repetitive tasks. As designs became more numerous and more sophisticated, the artists' work was reintegrated: now a single artist does the entire design for a card. He also sent his artists to New York and Europe to absorb new ideas by perusing art galleries, clothing store windows, and theaters. No new design, however, went into production without his "O.K.J.C." on it.

In the 1930s, Hall thought the company was ready for national advertising. He approached a number of agencies who told him to forget the idea, because, supposedly, a brand name could not be established in greeting cards. He proved that prophesy completely wrong. As tv became popular, his "Hallmark Hall of Fame" was first turned down by the networks because of a strict rule that time could be sold only in thirteen week blocks. Finally, NBC agreed to let him buy time when he wanted it—an exception that led to the TV "spectaculars" and then to the "specials" sponsored by other companies.

Adapted from Max Ways, "The Business Hall of Fame," *Fortune* (January 1977: 123; and January 30, 1978: 94).

Questions for Discussion

1. What was Cunningham's philosophy of management? Hall's? In what ways were they similar and different?
2. Discuss Cunningham's and Hall's performance as managers in terms of functions, skills, and roles.
3. What effect did the external environment have on the success of Cunningham and Hall?

PART TWO

INTERVIEW

Norman G. Schuld

*Manager of Industry
Outlook and Energy Policy
Exxon Corporation
New York, New York*

Q: How important is an external environmental analysis to Exxon's planning process?

A: The external environmental analysis is what we at Exxon call our Business Climate and Energy Outlook. It is extensive in scope and forms the backdrop for virtually every key decision.

Our Business Climate and Energy Outlook (BCEO) is developed annually on a grassroots basis. We have affiliates operating in 81 countries throughout the world, and it is the responsibility of our management in these countries to develop their view of the business climate or operating environment for their country. This would include an assessment of economic viability and political stability. They also develop an industry energy outlook for their country, which focuses not only on oil demand and supply, but also on the make-up of total energy demand and supply, including the utilization of gas, coal, nuclear, hydro, and renewable energy resources.

In those countries where Exxon does not operate, we periodically (every other year or so) develop a grassroots outlook using staff from either one of our affiliates or one of our regional offices.

These affiliate outlooks are consolidated by region (Canada, U.S.A., Latin America, Europe, Middle East, Far East) and submitted to Exxon's Corporate Planning Department in New York. It is the responsibility of the New York staff in conjunction with the regions through well-established communication channels to develop a consolidated worldwide view of energy markets.

Heavy concentration is given to oil supply/demand balances, since oil is still Exxon's key business line (albeit we are in the coal, gas, and nuclear lines as well). We attempt to evaluate oil demand trends after taking into account oil's competition with other fuels and supply trends, based on geological prospects. Obviously, both supply and demand are affected by price, and it is only through development of a set of bases that are consistent worldwide that we can develop an equilibrium supply/demand/price scenario.

It is probably the long-range oil price trend that emerges from our BCEO that is used most by the corporation in all facets of decision making.

Q: What general sources of information are used?

A: Each affiliate and region is free to use whatever data are at their disposal. These sources would include supply/demand data published by the government in industrial trade groups, information gathered from personal discussion with government officials, and market intelligence developed internally at Exxon.

Q: To what extent do broad organizational goals guide the planning process?

A: In the broadest sense, Exxon's organizational goal is to remain a viable company within the energy business, particularly in those facets of energy we know best. These, of course, include conventional oil and gas. Of significant interest on a smaller scale is the development of synthetic fuels and coal, and continued participation in the petrochemical business.

As such, most of the planning process eventually focuses on the viability of these industries and an evaluation of how Exxon can profitably participate in

Developing the Framework for Performance: Planning

them. The Business Climate Outlook developed by Exxon could ostensibly be used as the backdrop for evaluating a company's participation in steel or agriculture or high-tech industry, but the focus would be different. We tailor this background information to our own business lines.

Q: How much emphasis does Exxon place on contingency planning?

A: The answer to this question is *more and more*. Back in the 1960s, oil markets were relatively stable, and long-range price, demand, and supply projections were easy to develop based on extrapolation of historical information. Business planning revolved around risk analysis and cash-flow management.

The two oil price shocks of 1973 and 1979 have dramatically changed the oil market environment. Fundamental relationships between oil-consuming nations and oil-producing countries have changed, and the fundamental relationships between energy oil consumption as related to economic activity have also changed. No longer is the development of a single reference case outlook satisfactory for planning purposes. Alternative scenarios are continually developed as the backdrop for specific Exxon capital investment plans and key strategies.

This is not to say we have abandoned the development of a reference case within Exxon. We are a large organization and need to have a common basis for communication. Our reference case includes such things as energy supply/demand projections for various fuels, and price and cost projections for them as well. It allows us to evaluate a gas project in North Europe against a coal project in Colombia against an oil prospect in Alaska under a consistent set of assumptions.

Exxon does not develop three or four internally consistent BCEO's for the evaluation of all of our plans and strategies. What we do is tailor contingency planning to specific key issues. For example, we might develop two or three scenarios to help us evaluate where to place our research dollars or two or three scenarios to help us evaluate a multi-billion dollar investment project in a gas field in the North Sea. Contingency planning that relates to specific projects seems more useful in the allocation of capital than the broader concept of alternative general scenario planning.

Q: What important skills should future managers develop to become effective planners?

A: Planning is not an end in itself; I have found it to be useful only when the ideas and perceptions generated by the planning process can be translated into useful decision-making tools for our company. For example, the development of three or four political scenarios around the future of the Middle East oil-producing countries is interesting but may do little to help us decide whether to proceed with a multibillion dollar synthetics development project in the U.S.

Somehow, scenario planners must develop better ways to communicate with those who decide on capital allocation. Likewise, the decision-making bodies within large corporations must continue to be more flexible in their view on specific project economics. There is no single right answer.

Future managers should develop a sensitivity to listening to plausible outcomes for their projects based on conditions different from a given base reference case. From an understanding of the myriad assumptions planners make to eventually recommend proceeding with a project, one can also begin to understand key areas of vulnerability and monitor these as projects develop and resources are committed. Flexibility to change direction as the environment changes or as new light is shed on key issues will be quite an important management skill in the future.

Organizational Environments

Chapter Outline

Key Points

1. An analysis of an organization's external and internal environments is the beginning of the planning process.
2. The main components of the external environment—economic, political, social, and technological factors—vary in importance to different organizations.
3. The internal environment is defined in terms of organizational resources—financial, physical, human, system, and technological.
4. A special issue in the area of human resources is the analysis of managerial values, which are important determinants of managerial behavior.
5. Managerial ethics or codes of conduct play an important role in how managers perform their jobs.
6. Forecasting concerns the prediction of future events of importance to the organization.

The U.S. Auto Industry

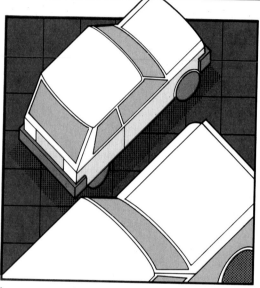

Forced by foreign competition, U.S. automakers are, for the first time in decades, undergoing a major restructuring of the way they do business. For example:

- The breakeven point—the level at which they start making profits on sales of cars and trucks—has been lowered by nearly 3 million vehicles.
- Overhead costs have been trimmed by over $9 billion.
- New contracts have been signed with the unions that will conserve at least $4 billion in labor expenses.
- Plant work rules are being eased, which could save automakers millions.

Whether this is enough to stem the foreign tide is an unanswered question.

The automakers' major objective is to regain profitability while maintaining production flexibility so they can adjust more quickly to a rapidly changing car market. Yet realizing this objective may not solve the basic problems that caused them to lose more than $7 billion in operating profits over the past few years. The reason: the belief, still strongly held by the industry, that an increase in car sales alone, without significant internal changes, is the only road to recovery.

Progress is being made. Years of depressed sales, coupled with fierce competition from the Japanese, have convinced U.S. automakers that they must change, or at least reexamine their basic business practices. Management now realizes that simply shrinking the size of cars is not enough. They must also make major changes that will permit production efficiencies to match or surpass those of its foreign rivals. And so managers are looking for new ways to improve productivity in their plants—from management reorganization and labor relations to product development and supplier relations.

While the need for major shifts in operating procedures is obvious, management is worried about other factors. Particularly, Detroit believes that it will be faced with an uncertain market in the U.S. for years, thanks to the likelihood of uncertainties in world oil supplies and the lack of clear-cut policies on energy, trade, and the economy from Washington. In response, the industry is planning products within broad ranges to accommodate almost any shift in consumer demand.

New inventory policies, reorganized management, and advanced manufacturing and product development procedures have proven successful. Such changes are impressive for an industry that has long resisted change. That stubbornness to change allowed sloppy practices to develop, masked by strong market growth. But when foreign competition exposed U.S. automakers to the harsh realities of the need for improved productivity, the message was clear: measure up or wither away.

Adapted from "U.S. Auto Makers Reshape for World Competition," *Business Week* (June 21, 1982): 82-92.

3

With this chapter, we begin a five-part section on the important managerial function of *planning*. As illustrated by *The Practice of Management* on the U.S. automakers and depicted in exhibit 3-1, at least six key activities make up the planning function: (1) analyzing the organization's external environment (foreign competition, changing markets, governmental actions); (2) determining the state of the organization's internal resources (human resources, plant and equipment, financial resources); (3) establishing goals and objectives (regain profitability while retaining production flexibility); (4) formulating a strategic plan (downsizing cars); (5) putting plans into action/the operating plan (new inventory policies, restructuring the organization); and (6) affecting all planning activities is the process of managerial decision making.

In this chapter we will focus on the relationship between the organization's environment and management with a three-part presentation. First, we will provide a detailed discussion of the components and dimensions of an organization's *external environment*. Second, we will stress the importance of considering the organization's *internal environment*—its resources—in the planning function. Finally, we will turn to a brief discussion of the various forecasting techniques used by organizations in the planning process.

 **The External Environment**

Organizations of every type are in constant interaction with the external environment. The important components of the environment that have a direct impact on the organization include suppliers, customers, competitors, government agencies, and society

Exhibit 3-1
The Planning Process

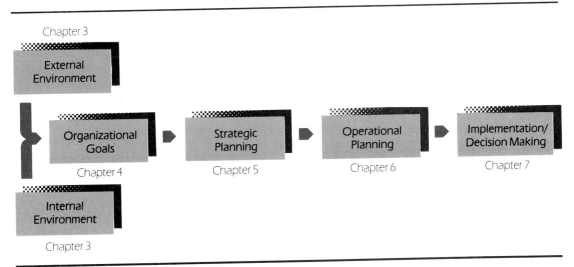

in general. The interaction is both wide and varied, depending on the particular organization. For example, Eli Lilly, the pharmaceutical company, is concerned about raw material supplies from chemical companies, approval of new drugs from the Food and Drug Administration (FDA), the knowledge of its products by physicians, and the purchase decisions of pharmacists. On the other hand, the Newport News Shipbuilding Company requires orders for new ships by the Navy and private companies, metal plates from numerous firms, a good working relationship with the union representing the employees, and approval of its hiring and placement policies by the Equal Employment Opportunity Commission (EEOC). In order to cover this topic adequately, our discussion of the external environment will focus on two issues: (1) environmental components, and (2) environmental dimensions.

Environmental Components: Domestic and International

Many external forces affect the daily operations of an organization. These forces, representing the external environment, are shown in exhibit 3-2. At least three conditions apply to the environment of an organization. First, while many groups in the environment interact with an organization, it is helpful to categorize them into four separate *components*. These break down into economic, political, and social, and technological components. Second, the individual environmental components will affect particular organizations in *different* ways. For example, the technological environment is of key importance to the computer industry, but of lesser importance to furniture manufacturers. Third, at any one point in time, *changes* in certain environmental components will have a more significant effect on an organization than would changes in others. Changes in consumer demand for automobiles, for example, can result in revisions to production schedules and layoffs of workers in a rather short period of time. On the other hand, a governmentally imposed mile-per-gallon standard for cars will have its effect on the same companies over a longer time period.

As an illustration, the four environmental components for a state-supported university and an energy company are presented in exhibit 3-3. This exhibit and the following discussion illustrate how the external environment interacts with and affects the functions of managers and organizations.

Economic Environment   Most organizations transform raw materials and resources to produce goods and/or services for consumption in a competitive economy. Thus, the economic environment involves the state of the economy, as well as suppliers, customers, and competitors.

The Economy   The general state of the economy can have a significant impact on the organization and the manager's job. The U.S. automakers' plight is a good example. Facing strong foreign competition is a significant challenge in itself, but when confronted with high interest rates, high inflation, and increasing unemployment, the task of a turnaround may be overwhelming. For automakers and other industries, the lesson is clear—the planning process must give great consideration to economic trends.

Exhibit 3-2
Environmental Components

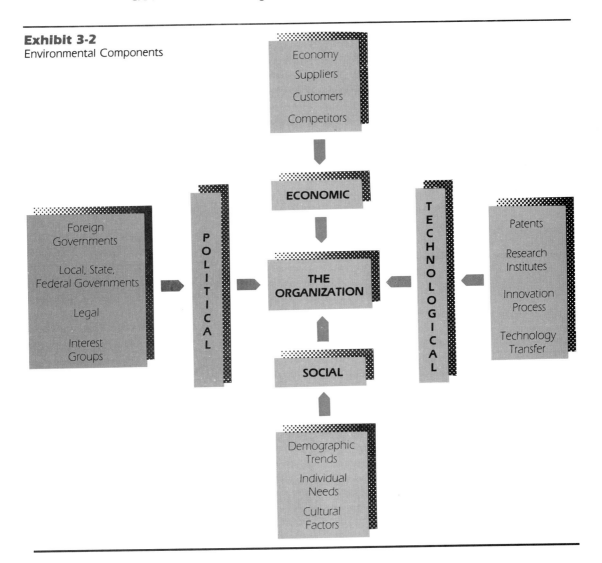

Suppliers   Organizations must acquire raw materials, labor, equipment, and financial support from the environment in order to produce products and services. Physical, human, and financial resources are raw material supplies for most organizations.

In the case of *physical* raw materials, consider the environment of an electric utility company that uses coal to generate power. The purchasing agent for the utility is faced with a threefold responsibility: (1) obtain a steady supply of high-quality coal; (2) purchase the coal at minimum price; and (3) avoid becoming overly dependent on a single supplier. The usual procedure is to take bids from suppliers on price, quality, and amount and accept those from the one or two lowest bidders.

Organizations also need *human* resources to produce goods and services. In some cases the labor contract between management and a labor union provides the firm with

Exhibit 3-3
Environmental Components

Components	Environment	
	State-Supported University	**Energy Company**
Economic The state of the economy of different nations; relationships with customers, suppliers, and competitors.	Increasing education cost; declining enrollments; relationships with private foundations and other universities.	Increasing production costs; fluctuating demand; varying customer needs.
Political The general political climate of society; public image and attitudes toward product and services.	Funding levels from the state; tenure restrictions; faculty unionization.	Divestiture and regulation; oil embargo; nationalization by foreign countries; OPEC.
Social The general sociological and cultural changes in society.	Questions concerning the value of a college degree; continuing education programs; internal personnel policies.	Attitudes toward high gas prices, conservation; concerns over pollution and destruction of natural resources; eliminating employment discrimination.
Technological The availability of resources and constraints facing organizations; the level of technology.	Availability of quality instructors; teaching innovations such as computers, videotape, etc.	Declining raw material sources (e.g., crude oil); availability of alternative sources (e.g., solar, nuclear, coal, etc.).

a great portion of the needed human resources. In the absence of a union, getting the right people often depends on variations in labor market supply and demand. For example, during the late 1970s, there was a strong demand for computer systems specialists, petroleum exploration engineers, and certain skilled craftsworkers in the building trades. We saw a similar strong demand for specialized scientists, engineers, and technicians during the space race era of the 1960s. To hire and retain these employees, the organization must provide competitive wages, working conditions, and employee benefits.

On the other hand, during the same period, an excess supply of applicants existed for teaching positions in elementary and secondary schools. Many qualified individuals competed for a few open positions. The organizations thus had the opportunity to choose the best candidates.

Financial resources can be provided to the organization from such investor sources as stocks, bonds, and from banks that give a line of credit for daily operations. Like human resources, financial resources are subject to the forces of environmental supply and demand. An expanding economy coupled with a past record of good financial performance enable an organization to sell equity and debt issues usually with a minimum of effort. On the other hand, a recession-prone economy and/or poor past financial performance creates a difficult situation for the organization in acquiring financial support.

Customers and Competitors We may look at the organization-customer-competitor relationship from at least two environmental viewpoints. First, using *economic* terms, we may classify external relationships as being competitive, oligopolistic, or monopolistic. A *competitive* environment exists when there are a large number of buyers and sellers (producers) of goods and services. For example, restaurants and clothing stores in an urban area can be put into this classification. In such cases emphasis is placed on price, quality, product characteristics, and advertising claims. An organization may operate in an *oligopolistic* environment, in which there are few sellers or producers but many buyers. The tire, automobile, and gasoline industries would be examples. In such environments price and product differentiation become quite important. Finally, a *monopolistic* environment may exist where there is only one seller but many customers. Utility companies—telephone, electric, natural gas, and so on—would fall into this category, though deregulation may change this.

The second way of looking at the organization-customer-competitor relationship is by considering the availability of *substitute* products and services. For example, with vacation traffic, airlines face competition not only from other airlines, but from Amtrak, various bus lines, and auto rental agencies. A family looking for a residence may pick from a regular house, a townhouse, or a condominium. In the not too distant future, our choices for fuel sources will include oil, gas, coal, solar, nuclear, and such exotic substitute sources as geothermal energy and harnessing ocean currents.

Political Environment Organizations of every type operate within and through various political systems. In a broad sense, the interaction between the organization and the political environment is one of mutual influence. On one hand, organizations try to influence the political system in order to enhance their opportunities and chances of survival. The most visible of these are the extensive *lobbying* efforts by organizations at all levels of government. On the other hand, certain elements of the political system, such as regulatory agencies, attempt to influence the activities of organizations in order to promote environmental protection, avoid unfair competition, and so on.

Sources of political influence. The major sources of political influence originate from governmental bodies at the national, state, and local levels. With the emergence of such groups as OPEC (Organization of Petroleum-Exporting Countries), we have seen the governmental sphere of influence expand to include foreign governments .[1]

An organization's political environment also extends beyond governmental bodies to the whole complex set of groups and individuals possessing power to influence the activities of organizations. These *interest groups* include in their membership trade associations, consumer protection groups, and unions. Many interest groups have exerted a great deal of pressure and influence on organizations, particularly in recent times. The Ralph Nader organization on automobile safety, the Sierra Club on land and wildlife conservation, and the AFL-CIO on worker interests are just three of many examples. Others are the National Organization of Manufacturing and local chambers of commerce.

The Manager's Job

Daniel Sharp
of Xerox

Over the past decade, American corporation managers have been discovering one supposedly rich foreign market after another, only to have their hopes dashed or diminished by unexpected political changes or upheavals. Because of this situation, these managers are gradually acknowledging that they need both new skills and fresh insights to thrive overseas.

Analyzing the foreign political environment is one of the main responsibilities of Mr. Daniel Sharp, director of international relations for Xerox. Rather than hire political analysts to diagnose the international environment, Mr. Sharp relies primarily on a well-placed group of foreign "agents." Two years ago, Xerox's Latin American managing directors were made formally responsible for both anticipating and planning how to deal with local political risks. Now their annual raises partly depend on their political savvy. Sharp insists on quarterly reports from the local managers to keep U.S. executives informed about foreseeable moves that may affect their business in each country.

Xerox consults outside authorities on some major issues, but Sharp says that "our best sources" are the local managers. As he explains: "They are better educated and informed about their environments than anyone here at staff headquarters. Often they went to school with those who run the government and other important institutions in their countries."

Adapted from L. Kraar, "The Multinationals Get Smarter About Political Risks," *Fortune* (March 24, 1980): 92.

Activities of Political Sources   The interaction between organizations and the federal government has become more involved and extensive during the last thirty years. Sometimes a part of the federal government such as the defense department acts as a consumer of goods and services. In most cases, however, the interaction concerns the relationship between an organization and a growing number of regulatory agencies. These agencies establish certain rules and procedures under which organizations must operate and act to police the industry to ensure that those rules are obeyed.

These regulatory agencies may focus on a specific industry or some specific organizational activities.[2] For example, the Civil Aeronautics Board (CAB) and the Federal Aviation Agency (FAA) oversee airlines and aircraft, the Securities and Exchange Commission (SEC) oversees the securities industry, the Federal Drug Administration (FDA) regulates drugs, and the Federal Communications Commission (FCC) regulates telecommunications organizations.

Other agencies have a broader focus. The EPA looks after environmental affairs, OSHA is concerned with the safety and health of workers, and the EEOC attempts to eliminate work-related discrimination. Organizations are also concerned with the acts of congress. Legislation has an impact on merger possibilities, tax laws, and foreign trade activities.

In addition to these federal activities, managers must interact in numerous ways with state and local governments. These can include state and local corporate income taxes, zoning laws, governmental services (fire and police), and so on.

Interest groups also become involved in organizational influence activities. Consumer boycotts of goods and services, independent trucker slowdowns due to lower speed limits and rising diesel prices, demonstrations against nuclear power, and class action suits against utility companies because of high rates are just a few examples that we see in daily headlines.

The effects of these political sources on the organization, particularly federal regulatory agencies, can be looked at from three perspectives. First, there are certain *gains* for the organization in being influenced by these forces. Most people would agree, for example, that workers have benefited from certain actions of OSHA, society in general is better off because of the scrutiny given to new drugs by the FDA, and the air we breathe and the water we drink are protected because of EPA decisions.

While there are certain gains, there are heavy *costs* to the organization in adhering to federal guidelines. These costs can take the form of added research and development on a new product, "opportunity costs" associated with delaying the introduction of a new product whose earlier outbreak could result in a significant competitive advantage to the organization, and the ever-present costs related to completing the enormous amount of paperwork required by federal agencies.[3]

Finally, and most important to our discussion, elements of the political environment can act as *constraints* to limit a manager's freedom of action. In a sense, coping with these elements adds a degree of uncertainty to the manager's job that some believe may result in lower levels of efficiency and effectiveness. Whether the political environment is detrimental to the performance of many organizations is beyond the scope of this book; it is also not usually within the domain of responsibility for most managers. What is important is that the influence of the political environment exists now and probably always will.

Social Environment   The social environment, involving informal guidelines associated with the customs, culture, and trends in population, can influence how most organizations and managers function. Such guidelines may vary by country or region and may be quite different when compared with the "home" country of the organization. Understanding the social environment is an extremely important element of the manager's job. Our discussion will focus on three factors related to the social environment: (1) demographic trends; (2) individual needs; and (3) cultural differences. These factors are illustrated in exhibit 3-4.

Demographic Trends   Significant shifts in demographic characteristics of the population affect organizations in terms of the nature of the work force and the profile of the buying public, or customer. For example, many organizations are becoming more and more aware of the changing characteristics of available management talent. Through a trend analysis, it has been suggested that during the 1980s managers in the forty-five to sixty age bracket—traditionally the group of individuals with the most experience—will number only about 75 percent of the managers that will be needed.[4] Twenty-five year olds, on the other hand, will number 4.3 million in 1985—a 35 percent increase from 1970. The key question is not only who will manage the organization, but who will be available to train and supervise the large number of young graduates just climbing onto the first rung of the management ladder. Changes in career planning and personnel acquisition and training may occur (see chapters 19 and 20).

Exhibit 3-4

Forces Shaping the Social Environment

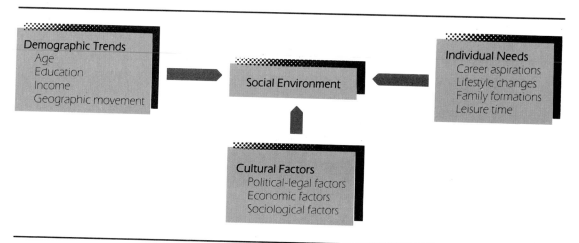

Changes in the behavioral profiles of customers are being felt today. For example, the group of people known for years as making up the post-war baby boom are now themselves starting their own families and tend to be far more well off financially than other population sectors. Organizations are faced with the need to alter their marketing efforts to capture the buying power of this influential and affluent group. Changes in fashion, luxury goods, travel, and home furnishings are part of this marketing effort. Even such fast food outlets as McDonald's are altering their menus to include breakfast and dinners to attract this population sector.

Individual Needs   In some cases changes in demographic patterns will be felt by organizations as individuals begin to express the desire to satisfy different needs through the job. Two major changes currently are being observed. One is the increased emphasis on the satisfaction of personal growth and career development.[5] Many employees want more than just money and security from a job—they see the job as an opportunity for continuing learning and growth, requiring frequent career moves.

A second trend that may be related to demographic patterns is one of changes in lifestyle. Individuals and families are more mobile, and many people wish to express creativity in their personal life, through hobbies, for example. To accomplish this, individuals need more leisure time. Many organizations and labor unions have recognized the growth of this need by adopting shortened or modified workweeks. Organizations have adopted several variations on this concept; for example, individuals must work forty hours, but can do so in four days or four and one-half days.

Cultural Differences   *Culture* has been defined in many different ways. Basically it relates to a society's economic, social, political, educational, and legal attitudes and beliefs. In recent years the study of culture and its effects on management has given rise to the study of comparative management. A significant amount of literature has been devoted to cross-cultural studies in an attempt to investigate the behavioral and performance characteristics of employees all over the globe.

Cultural factors can act to facilitate or constrain the performance of organizations. Managers must be aware of:

Political-Legal Factors   Each country has its own laws that govern the practices of organizations. Many of these laws are consistent with a country's political climate. A Canadian organization may find operating in the United States similar to functioning "at home" but face many differences in South America.

In many cases the multinational corporation can expect such regulations as: (1) constraints on who can be hired by the firm; (2) tax laws that can take a significant part of earned profits; (3) laws that limit foreign operations and ownership in a country; (4) laws or tradition concerning the degree of participation of workers in policy decisions; and (5) regulations that require frequent discussions and approvals of day-to-day decisions by high-level governmental employees.[6] For example, multinational oil companies operating in Central and South America must hire a high percentage of native workers and managers. In addition, layoffs are not permitted, a government employee must be on site to observe daily activities, and products must be shipped in government-owned or approved tankers.

Economic Factors   The competitive motive so dominant in the U.S. economy is frequently not found in other countries. For example, in selling or operating in communist countries, the only buyer may be the government. In addition, many countries prohibit a large percentage of profits earned within their boundaries to leave that country, and they require a certain percentage of profits to be reinvested in their countries. Labor also becomes a significant economic factor. Many times organizations cannot operate as efficiently as they wish due to restrictions or requirements on the number of workers that are to be employed. That is, a company may be forced to use less-efficient workers instead of automating to handle the work. Finally, many foreign countries require a part ownership of the local operation of the multinational company.[7] After a length of time, or when the makeup of the government changes, it is not uncommon to have the organization's holdings in a country "nationalized" by the foreign government.

Sociological Factors   Behavioral patterns of workers in other cultures vary greatly. For example, in some cultures, the drive to work hard may be less than the drive for leisure time or other activities. This is particularly true in some underdeveloped countries. Even in some highly developed societies, such as Sweden, certain laws permit workers to make as much money in unemployment income as they would have had they worked during the same period. The leadership role of the manager, so well established in our own culture, is not so well accepted in others. In some cases, organizations have found it difficult to instill in foreign managers the need to accept responsibility and to use their authority over other workers. In Japan, the cultural philosophy of "lifelong employment" not only limits selection but also how employees are rewarded.[8] Since the Japanese system is so heavily founded on the principle of seniority, the use of the merit system (i.e., rewards based on levels of individual performance) is restricted, limiting management's motivational influence. Finally, managers must be aware that identification with certain groups can be a significant factor. Membership in certain groups—sex, age, class, religion, or political associations—may reflect the degree to which the individual has access to economic resources, social relations, and hence, power. This affects not only who the organinization can hire, but with whom they must interact in order to perform as effectively as possible.

Cultural factors have become and will continue to be important considerations for managers operating in a foreign environment. However, despite what may be drawbacks, managers should not lose sight of two factors. First, many international operations of U.S.-based firms are highly profitable and in some cases, give the companies a higher level of return than do its domestic operations. These organizations *adapt* to the environment—in this case, the cultural environment. Second, some foreign companies have significant holdings in the U.S. For example, Volkswagen has an assembly plant here, Shell is a foreign owned company, and the British Petroleum Company has a majority ownership share of Sohio, one of the largest contributors to the construction of the Alaskan oil pipeline.[9]

Technological Environment   From the point of view of management, developments in the technological environment are not only the fastest to unfold but can have the most far-reaching impact on the organization in extending or constraining its growth. For example, the introduction of microcomputer technology, resulting in the development of the pocket calculator, has proven to be a boon to the business-machine industry. It has, however, nearly eliminated the market for slide rules. In a similar vein, one can imagine the impact of the low-cost digital watch on the wrist-watch industry.

Managers are generally concerned with two components of the technological environment—the process of innovation; and the process of technology transfer. The *process of innovation* refers to the efforts in the basic sciences to develop new technologies, processes, methods, and products.[10] This process is commonly called research and development (R&D). Examples, which are numerous, include laser technology and self-developing film produced by Polaroid and Kodak.

The *process of technology transfer* involves taking the new technology from the laboratory to the market, that is, the transfer of science to useful products and applications.[11] Technology transfer can occur both within and between industries. For example, we have seen the initial use of videotape recorders by the television networks transferred into a commercial product that can be found in many homes today. Similarly, in less than twenty years, technology has decreased the size and increased the efficiency of the computer, making it easily available to small businesses and for personal use. Technologies can cross into other industries. Laser technology, for example, is used not only in medical surgery, but also to find flaws in metal products and to carry sound impulses in telecommunications.

Factors in the technological environment have at least two important implications for managers. First is the knowledge that the primary impact of new technologies will be *increased product obsolescence* and *competition*. The risks, dramatized by rapid technological advances, can be offset by the identification of new opportunities for the organization to market its products and services. Second, there is the need for many organizations to develop sophisticated *monitoring and forecasting* methods. Managers must develop conceptual and diagnostic *skills* in order to monitor new technological developments, both within and outside their industry, and maintain a competitive position for their organization.

Environmental Dimensions

Our description of the individual components of an organization's environment—economic, political, social, and technological—serves as a basis on which to build the *dimensions* of an organization's environment.

As shown in exhibit 3-5, we have identified two key dimensions of the environment: degree of change; and degree of complexity.[12] These dimensions are:

Degree of Change   This dimension is the extent to which components of the environment are stable or dynamic. It therefore describes whether a manager can predict future events, because a given environmental situation recurs frequently through time, or whether changes are so frequent that predictability of events is low. For example, a pottery manufacturer can expect to produce the same type of product year after year. On the other hand, a vice squad in a police department must treat each case differently with many unexpected results.

A variety of factors can make an environment stable or dynamic, including unpredictable shifts in the economy, rapid change in customer preferences and demands, an unstable government, unnoticed changes in population characteristics, growth in the influence of interest groups, and a rapidly changing technology. The term *dynamic* does not refer to environmental factors that are "variable," such as the weather. For example, the demand for heating oil is strongest during the winter months, but this is known and can be forecast by the producer. Rather, a dynamic component is something that is not expected because it cannot be predicted from past patterns.

Degree of Complexity   An organization's environment can range from simple to complex. Two factors contribute to the complexity of an organization's environment.[13] First, the number of units with which interaction is required—that is, the number of customers, suppliers, and competitors—ranges from few in a simple environment to many in a complex environment. The manager of a small dairy may interact with only a few owners of dairy herds and two or three retail outlets. On the other hand, a flight director at NASA may have to interact with a wide variety of individuals and contributing companies. Second, an environment becomes complex to the extent that it requires the organization to have a great deal of *sophisticated knowledge* about products, customers, and so on. In this respect, the dairy manager operates in a simple environment because processing milk from the farm to the grocery refrigerated case is relatively uncomplicated. The flight director at NASA, however, must be knowledgeable in all components of the operation, from propulsion and communications to life-support systems and reentry processes. To perform this role, the individual must acquire a complex mix of knowledge, skills, and information. Hospitals, full-service banks, and computer manufacturers also operate in complex environments.

Environmental Quadrants   A simplified way of studying the dimensions of an organization's environment is to divide each dimension in half, creating four quadrants, as shown in exhibit 3-5. These four quadrants correspond to different environments faced by organizations.

Quadrant I represents an environment that is stable and fairly predictable. Generally there are few products with a limited number of customers, suppliers, and competitors. Such an environment would describe that of a container company specializ-

Exhibit 3-5
Environmental Dimensions

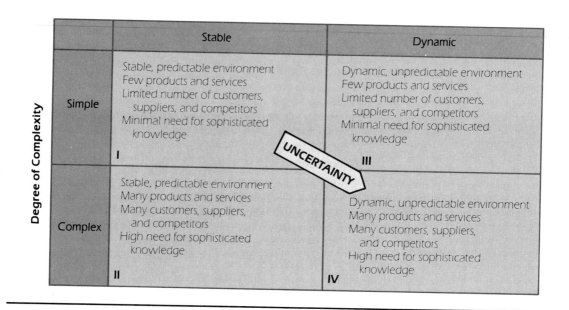

ing in cardboard boxes. The environment has remained relatively unchanged over the years. In addition, the sources of raw materials, the number of competitors, and the major customers are few and easily identifiable.

Quadrant II is similar to the environment of quadrant I with respect to the degree of change, but the environment has become more complex. In other words, the number of customers, suppliers, and competitors and the sophistication of knowledge have increased. Examples include a home appliance manufacturer, such as Whirlpool or Maytag, large accounting firms, and a savings and loan company. In each case, not only is competition increased, but the variety of customers and the degree of knowledge associated with serving these customers is significantly greater than is the case for the cardboard box company.

Quadrant III organizations have a dynamic environment involving a limited number of customers, suppliers, and competitors. This is representative of the environment for a clothing manufacturer that sells its goods to retail outlets. The key to the dynamic nature of the environment is the rapidly changing styles of clothing, particularly men's and women's high-fashion goods.

Finally, *Quadrant IV* presents an environment that is both complex and dynamic. Not only is the environment highly unpredictable with respect to events and trends, but the number of customers, suppliers, and competitors and the degree of knowledge needed to compete are dramatically greater than in other quadrants. Organizations involved in electronics, computer software, and pocket calculators operate in this type of environment. Another example would be a public hospital that is faced with a rapidly changing and unpredictable environment, particularly with respect to new technological innovations (e.g., computer-based diagnostic equipment, microsurgery, and life-support systems) and the political climate (e.g., national health insurance, legislative control over costs). In addition, it must contend with an ever-expanding populace and with competition from the growing number of health maintenance organizations.

Environmental Uncertainty   As exhibit 3-5 also shows, the two environmental dimensions may be combined to determine *environmental uncertainty*.[14] As the environment moves from stable-simple to dynamic-complex, the absence of concrete information about the environment and the lack of knowledge about the effects of specific organizational actions increase to such an extent that managerial decision making becomes a highly uncertain process. In our quadrant I example, decisions made by managers in container firms appear to be influenced by only a few factors and variables. Decisions can therefore be made with some *certainty* about the results. On the other hand, the hospital administrator in quadrant IV faces a quite uncertain state with respect to the attitudes, behavior, and actions of customers, suppliers, and competitors. The decisions are therefore made under conditions of *uncertainty*.

The Internal Environment

Environmental opportunities to produce and market goods and services keep organizations alive and well. In the automobile industry, for example, General Motors recognized opportunities to market diesel-powered cars, Porsche found a niche for itself in expensive sports cars, while Jeep (now a part of American Motors) has profited from market opportunities in off-the-road vehicles.

For an organization to capitalize on environmental opportunities, however, it must have the capacity and ability to accomplish, against many sources of opposition, what it sets out to do. This capacity and ability to achieve stated goals is related to the *resources* of the organization.

Our discussion of the organization's internal environment will consist of three parts. First, we will identify the major resources of an organization. Second, we will look at the special case of managerial values as they relate to organizational resources. Finally, we will discuss the process of identifying resource strategies, weaknesses, and particular competencies.

Organizational Resources

All organizations have at least four types of resources they can use to achieve their goals—financial, physical, human, and system and technological capabilities. These are shown in exhibit 3-6.

	Resource	Description
Exhibit 3-6 Organizational Resources	Financial Resources	The acquisition, allocation, and control of money for financing plant construction, inventory, research and development, receivables, and working capital; involves, for example, cash flow, debt capacity, and new equity available.
	Physical Resources	Include: (1) efficient manufacturing plants and other facilities; (2) location of facilities with respect to markets, suppliers, or utilities; and (3) ownership or contractual access to needed raw materials.
	Human Resources	Include, but are not limited to, *specialized personnel* (engineers, scientists, and skilled labor) and skilled and experienced *management*.
	System and Technological Resources	Expertise and particular competence in *process* elements (quality control systems, information systems, distribution systems, and the like) and *outputs* (patents, brand loyalty, and high-quality product).

Financial Resources   Financial resources are among the most important to all types of organizations, both profit making and not-for-profit. Three activities related to financial resources are important to managers:

Acquisition of Financial Resources   Managers are continually concerned with the *sources* of funds. Three major sources exist: (a) sale of equity on stock; (b) use of debt issues such as bonds; and (c) internal sources, particularly net income.

Allocation of Financial Resources   Commonly referred to as the *budgeting process*, allocating financial resources means providing funds to specific units or departments based on certain criteria. Frequently, most organizations find that the demand for funds is greater than the funds available. Generally speaking, organizations attempt to allocate financial resources where they can get the greatest return or where the survival of the unit is at stake. This poses a dilemma for many organizations. For example, should Ford Motor allocate funds to its highly successful European division in order to maintain high profit levels, or should it give funds to its less successful domestic operations in order to regain a strong profit position? Should B. F. Goodrich continue to support its very profitable chemical and plastics division, or invest a majority of financial resources in the tire division, which has been less profitable in current times? Should the Mayo Clinic use its limited funds for expansion of the hospital, or for the purchase of the latest diagnostic equipment? Each example deals with the problem of allocating scarce financial resources to internal operations.

Controlling Financial Resources   Organizations must know how effectively financial resources are being *utilized*. Many financial tools can be used to assess an organization's short- and long-term financial resource performance, including ratio analysis, cash flow analysis, and computer-based financial models. In addition to these analyses, organizations find it useful to calculate the amount of resources that they will have to reinvest in order to maintain or facilitate their current growth position. Some of the more important control procedures will be discussed in greater depth in chapter 15.

Physical Resources   Physical resources include the ownership and accessibility of physical plants and raw materials. At least three types of physical resources are important to managers:

Physical Plant   This resource relates to the existence and level of *efficiency* of manufacturing plants, research and testing facilities, warehouses, office buildings, and other equipment. For example, the Japanese are known for their highly efficient steel plants, IBM for its research facilities, and Coors for its large brewery. As a physical plant, Walt Disney World in Florida is known for its efficiency as a people mover.

Location of the Physical Plant   Beyond the obvious benefits of efficiency and effectiveness, the *location* of the physical plant can be of great importance. Closeness to customers and suppliers, accessibility to transportation, and availability of skilled labor are all important features. For example, the image of Sears as a retailer is enhanced by the neighborhood location of its major stores and catalog outlets. The proximity of oil refineries to drilling and producing sites along the U.S. Gulf Coast is a benefit to various energy companies, and the center of financial activity in New York is a major reason why many corporations headquarter there.

Raw Material Reserves   Access to natural resources, by *ownership* or *contractual obligations*, can also be considered a physical resource. For example, Boise Cascade, which specializes in wood products, owns vast timberland reserves, and energy firms own coal and uranium deposits. Raw material reserves can also be acquired through long-term contracts. For example, utility companies contract for oil, gas, and coal.

Similar to financial resources, the physical resources of an organization are important not only for continued operation but also for growth of the organization.

Human Resources   Stated simply, human resources make the other resources of an organization work. Two broad categories of human resources can be identified:

Specialized Personnel   Most organizations contain individuals with unique or specialized knowledge in manufacturing, distribution, or scientific fields. Included would be scientists and engineers, sales representatives, computer systems analysts, production and quality control supervisors, and the like.

Managerial Personnel   Certain organizations are known for their excellence in managerial activities. For example, General Motors has been known for its almost endless stream of capable chief executives, Delta and Northwest airlines are recognized in their industry for the professional skill of their managers, and Procter & Gamble and Federated Department Stores have long been identified as sources of well-trained managerial talent in the food processing industry and retail industry, respectively.

System and Technological Resources   The resource elements we just discussed generally concern those factors that organizations have at their disposal *to produce* goods and services. Some organizations, however, have developed certain capabilities in the *manner in which* they produce goods and services. Two such resource elements are system and technological capabilities.

System Capabilities   System capabilities are those *process* aspects that tend to support the main functions of the organization, such as quality control models, reward policies, and distribution systems. For example, Dow Chemical is known for its financial information systems, Lincoln Electric for its profit sharing, and Avon Products for its distribution system.

Technological Capabilities   System capabilities concern certain process elements of an organization; technological capabilities deal more with the particular *output* of the firm. Examples include patents, customer brand loyalty, or a recognized high-quality product. Illustrations of technological capabilities include Polaroid's long-standing patent on its cameras, the fierce brand loyalty given to such beers as Coors and Strohs, and the recognition awarded to automobiles such as Mercedes-Benz, Rolls Royce, Maserati, and Aston-Martin.

Managerial Values and Ethics

During its planning process, an organization is correct to consider its managers and executives an important resource. These managers will analyze the data and make the key decisions that will affect the organization's future. However, the managers are individuals with wants, needs, preferences, likes and dislikes, and inclinations that will influence the way they act. Thus, it is crucial that managerial values and ethics be considered.[15]

Values

Values affect managerial behavior in many ways. For example, managerial values:

- Influence a manager's perception of various situations and problems.
- Influence a manager's decisions and solutions to problems.
- Influence the way a manager looks at other individuals and groups, thus affecting interpersonal relationships.
- Influence the extent to which a manager will be affected by organizational pressures and stress.
- Influence not only the perception of individual and organizational success but the entire definition of achievement.

Of course, value systems are not the sole property of managers. Non-managerial employees as well have value systems that may or may not be similar to those of certain higher level superiors.

The topic of managerial values has received increased attention from behavioral scientists and practicing managers during recent years. The literature has focused on the nature of values, on various classifications of values, and on the value differences among people, professions, and cultures. One of the most useful schemes classifies managerial values into six orientations:[16]

- *Theoretical values.* A person having a strong theoretical value orientation would be primarily interested in the discovery of truth and the systematic ordering of knowledge. Such a person is generally intelligent and shows interests that are empirical, critical, and rational.

- *Economic values.* One who adheres to economic values would be oriented toward practical and useful aspects of work. He or she is interested in the production and consumption of goods and the uses and creation of wealth. The typical stereotype of the American businessperson would fit well into this category.

- *Aesthetic values.* Dominant interests in artistic features of an object, with an emphasis on form, symmetry, grace, and harmony would characterize someone with strong aesthetic values.

- *Social values.* A person with dominant social values would place a primary value on the love of people and the warmth of human relations. They value people as ends, rather than means, and tend to be kind, sympathetic, and unselfish.

- *Political values.* A dominant orientation toward power, influence, and recognition would characterize one who adheres strongly to political values. Competition plays an important role in his or her life, and power is the salient motive.

- *Religious values.* People with an orientation toward unity and creation of satisfying relations with the environment have strong religious values.

There are at least two important points that this and other value classification schemes highlight. First, most values are culturally derived; that is, the various values are *learned* by a person through interactions with parents, teachers, friends, and other individuals. Second, managers can *order* or set priorities for these values differently.

Exhibit 3-7
Ordering of
Values for Three
Occupations

Ministers	Purchasing Managers	R & D Managers
Religious	Economic	Theoretical
Social	Theoretical	Political
Aesthetic	Political	Economic
Political	Religious	Aesthetic
Theoretical	Aesthetic	Religious
Economic	Social	Social

Adapted from R. Tagiuri, "Purchasing Executive: General Manager or Specialist?"
Journal of Purchasing (August 1967): 16-21.

An example of this for ministers, purchasing managers, and R & D managers is shown in exhibit 3-7.

Ethics

As an executive of a large U.S.-based firm, what would you do if . . .

▪ In the process of negotiating a multimillion dollar contract with a foreign nation, a key governmental official asks you for a $250,000 "personal consulting fee." In return, he promises to give your organization special assistance in obtaining the contract from his country. You are aware that not only are such "fees" common practice, but that if it is not paid, the contract would certainly be awarded to one of your major competitors. Would you come up with the money?

▪ During a luncheon meeting, a representative of a major competitor for one of your key product lines suggests that your two companies come to an "informal agreement" on the prices to be set on the competing products. You know that the recent price competition between you has all but eliminated the profitability on the products. The new suggested price would bring profits back to acceptable levels. Should you agree on it?

▪ You have the opportunity to hire a well-known research scientist from a major competitor. This scientist has been involved in the development of a new product that, when introduced to the market later this year, will adversely affect the market share and profitability of your product. By hiring the scientist, you can reduce your reaction time to the new product by two years. Should you hire the scientist?

▪ In preparing a biannual report to the EPA, you come across data that show one of your agricultural products manufacturing plants had been discharging high quantities of a toxic pesticide into a local river. You investigate and find out that the discharging was due to a piece of malfunctioning equipment. The plant manager decided not to repair the equipment because it would have meant a six- to eight-day shutdown of the plant during the busiest season of the year. You are aware that reporting the data will result in a stiff fine from the EPA and in an increase in community opposition to the plant, which is already quite high. What should be in the report?

These situations are all true and represent an important factor in the manager's job—namely, the *ethical* considerations that govern a manager's behavior. In this age of instant information from the media, concerns over the environment, and questions about the role of organizations in our society, the concept of managerial ethics gains significant importance. As is becoming clearer every day, corporate integrity and sound professional ethics are *essential* conditions for managerial effectiveness and even for survival of the organization.

Definition of Managerial Ethics   *Ethics* is derived from the Greek word *ethos,* which refers to a person's fundamental orientation toward life. Initially the word meant a dwelling place, but for Aristotle, it came to mean an inner dwelling place, or what we call *internal character.* Carrying this further, the Latin translation of ethos is *mos, moris,* from which we get our word *moral.* In Latin, the emphasis shifts from internal character to actions—external behavior, acts, habits, and customs.[17] For our purposes, *managerial ethics* refers to internal *and* external standards or codes of conduct used not only to govern the behavior of individuals or groups, but also to determine what is right or wrong, good or evil.

From a managerial point of view, a distinction between illegal and unethical must be made. *Illegal* behaviors are acts that violate a law, or laws, in a particular area or society. *Unethical* behaviors, on the other hand, are acts that are contrary to the moral standards or codes of conduct established by society.

The difference between the two is important to note. While laws that govern legal behaviors are finite and relatively stable, ethical concepts may change over time or between cultures. As the first example indicates, political bribes or payoffs may be acceptable in one culture but not in another. The manager is thus faced with acknowledging (or developing) a complex set of ethical codes.

A definition of unethical behavior can be elusive, due to cultural changes. There are, however, certain practices or categories of behaviors that seem to automatically raise questions of ethics. Some of the most publicized practices are:

- *Political gifts.* Corporate gifts to politicians or their committees are prohibited by U.S. law.[18]
- *Political bribes.* Political gifts are usually indirect contributions; a bribe or payoff is a direct payment that assumes preferential treatment. Some payoffs are illegal under the Foreign Corrupt Practices Act.[19]
- *General business practices.* A global category that can include such practices as Olin selling weapons from its Winchester division to South Africa.[20]
- *Improper reporting procedures.* Refers to internal practices that provide an inaccurate appraisal of the organization's position. Includes, for example, Fruehauf Trailers' improper reporting of excise taxes.[21]
- *Employee privacy.* Subjecting employees to probing interviews, psychological testing, investigative reports, or lie detectors, which can be considered as "loyalty" tests or to help "blacklists."[22]

Some specific, notable examples of reported unethical behavior are shown in exhibit 3-8.

Exhibit 3-8

Examples of Questionable Managerial Ethics

Organization	Description
Ashland Oil, Inc.	Paid more than $300,000 to foreign officials, including $150,000 to President Albert Bernard Bonogo of Gabon to retain mineral and refining rights.
Braniff Airlines	Admitted to the CAB that it had given 21,600 free tickets worth $750,000 to travel agents to promote the company. It also admitted to illegally contributing $40,000 to the Nixon campaign.
Exxon Corporation	Paid $740,000 to government officials and others in three countries. Admits its Italian subsidiary made $27 million in secret but legal contributions to seven Italian political parties.
Fruehauf Trailer	Company top two executives found guilty of conspiring to defraud the government of excise taxes.
Lockheed Aircraft Corporation	Gave $202 million in commissions, payoffs, and bribes to foreign agents and government officials in the Netherlands, Italy, Japan, Turkey, and other countries. Admits that $22 million of this sum went for outright bribes.
Merck & Company, Inc.	Gave $3 million, largely in commission-type payments, to employees of 36 foreign governments between 1968 and 1978.
Northrop Corporation	SEC charged that it paid $30 million in commissions and bribes to government officials and agents in Holland, Iran, France, West Germany, Saudi Arabia, Brazil, Malaysia, and Taiwan.
Olin Corporation	Illegally shipped $1.2 million worth of arms and ammunition to South Africa. Company salesman had lied about the destination of the goods to the U.S. government.
Southwestern Bell	Lost a $1 million suit for illegally tapping the telephone of a Bell manager.
United Brands Company	Paid a $1.25 million bribe to Honduran officials for a reduction in the banana export tax. Admits paying $750,000 to European officials. Investigators say the payment was made to head off proposed Italian restrictions on banana imports.

Adapted from I. Ross, "How Lawless Are Big Companies?" *Fortune* (December 1, 1980): 57-64.

Sources of Ethical and Unethical Behavior   Where do standards of ethical conduct originate; what is the role of society, government, and industry; and why does unethical behavior occur? Answering these questions is just as elusive as attempting to explain cultural differences between nations. A discussion of four factors may help us understand these issues: (1) societal attitudes and beliefs; (2) competitive pressures; (3) the legal environment; and (4) industry codes of conduct.

Societal Attitudes   Exhibit 3-9 presents the results of a survey of over 1,200 managers in a variety of organizations that dealt with the topic of ethical standards.[23] An examination of the factors influencing ethical standards and causing lower standards suggests that there may be at least three contributing factors. First, there may be the perceived decline in certain of society's norms and attitudes, such as a greater emphasis on permissiveness, a decline in the influence of church and family, and an orientation toward quantity as opposed to quality. Second, as already noted, society is increasingly concerned with unethical behavior, with emphasis on public disclosure and media information. This increased awareness may help form ethical standards or at least enforce existing ones.

Finally, there is the important influence of *groups* on our behavior. As some well-known writers have stated, as a society we are becoming less independent as individuals and more oriented to be members of groups. For example, the survey described in exhibit 3-9 asked for a list and ranking of factors that can influence unethical decisions. The responses are as follows:

Factors Influencing Unethical Behavior	*Rank* *On scale of 1 (most influential)* *to 6 (least influential)*
Behavior of superiors	2.15
Formal policy or lack thereof	3.27
Industry ethical climate	3.34
Behavior of one's peers in the company	3.37
Society's moral climate	4.22
One's personal financial needs	4.46

As this survey indicates, the influence of group members, from superiors to peers, can have a significant influence on ethical behavior.

As we will discuss in chapter 14, groups (such as committees, task forces, and interest groups) establish norms that can have a significant impact on individual behavior. This social ethic can vary from across groups and organizations, resulting in conflict and confusion concerning which standard should be followed.

Competitive Pressures Our economic system is built on two fundamental concepts: *effort* (the Protestant work ethic)[24] and *competition*. The essence of these beliefs is that working hard and outperforming others will be rewarded with high levels of success. In recent years, however, we have seen a bigger show of the "winning at all costs" philosophy. Other behaviors, possibly unethical, are thus substituted for hard work and competition. We see examples all around us, such as the increase in cheating on exams, falsifying documents, or making questionable advertising claims. In many organizations in which the managers' pay increases and promotions are based on past performances in contributing to the organization's profits, some managers have devised ways to inflate their profit pictures.

For example, at a truck assembly plant of one of the "Big Three" U.S. automobile companies, managers were given a production goal each week that assumed that everything would go perfectly. The problem was that, on an assembly line, nothing ever does. There are frequent conveyor breakdowns, or high absenteeism, or something else. As a result, production goals were being missed with regularity, and higher level managers were putting pressure on the plant to do something about it.

In response, plant management installed a secret control box in a supervisor's office that overrode the control panel governing the speed of the assembly line. With the device, managers were able to speed up the line and increase production. The use of the secret box, however, violated the labor contract with the United Auto Workers' Union. The workers eventually discovered the deception and later were awarded $1 million in back pay from the courts. Ill feelings between management and labor still

Exhibit 3-9

Factors Influencing Ethical Standards

Factors Causing Higher Standards	Percentage of Respondents Listing Factor	Factors Causing Lower Standards	Percentage of Respondents Listing Factor
Public disclosure; publicity; media coverage; better communication	31%	*Society's standards are lower;* social decay; more permissive society; materialism and hedonism have grown; loss of church and home influence; less quality, more quantity desires	34%
Increased public concern; public awareness, consciousness, and scrutiny; better-informed public; societal pressures	20		
Government regulation, legislation, and intervention; federal courts	10	*Competition;* pace of life; stress to succeed; current economic conditions; costs of doing business; more business competing for less	13
Education of business managers; increase in manager professionalism and education	9	*Political corruption;* loss of confidence in government; Watergate; politics; political ethics and climate	9
New social expectations for the role business is to play in society; young adults' attitudes	5	*People more aware of unethical acts;* constant media coverage; TV; communications create atmosphere for crime	9
Business' greater sense of social responsibility and greater awareness of the implications of its acts; business responsiveness; corporate policy changes; top management emphasis on ethical action	5	*Greed;* desire for gain; worship the dollar as measure of success; selfishness of the individual; lack of personal integrity and moral fiber	8
		Pressure for profit from within the organization from superiors or from stockholders; corporate influences on managers; corporate policies	7
Other	20	*Other*	21

Note: Some respondents listed more than one factor. There were 353 factors in all listed as causing higher standards and 411 in all listed as causing lower ones. Categories may not add up to 100 percent because of rounding errors.

Source: Steven N. Brenner and Earl A. Molander, "Is the Ethic of Business Changing?" *Harvard Business Review* (January–February 1977): 57–71. Copyright 1977 by the President and Fellows of Harvard College; all rights reserved.

plague the plant today. Plant management, when questioned on the matter, claimed that higher level executives had to know about the device, but never asked any questions. So while they knew they were doing something ethically wrong, plant management figured that it must have been okay in the eyes of the company.[25]

The Legal Environment   The legal and legislative environment, contrary to some beliefs, is confusing and full of loopholes when it comes to determining what is or what isn't legally acceptable behavior. Legal interpretations and entanglements often make it difficult for managers to know exactly what course to take.

For example, consider the previously mentioned Foreign Corrupt Practices Act of 1977. The law specifically outlaws "foreign gifts or bribes to any foreign official, political candidate, or party paid by domestic concerns—defined as U.S. corporations, partnerships, or individual representatives of same—for purposes of inducing them to influence their government to assist the giver in obtaining or retaining business.'' Violation of the act costs five years in jail and a $1 million corporate fine.

Sounds simple, right? Wrong. Two significant loopholes exist within the act that may put the manager in a difficult position.[26] For example, the act exempts ''facilitating payments made solely to expedite nondiscretionary official actions.'' Translated into street language, this means that ''grease, dash, or squeeze'' payments are not illegal. In this most important area, the act *excludes* from the definition of *foreign official* (to whom it is a crime to pay bribes and gifts) any foreign employee whose duties are essentially ministerial or clerical. This leads to the startling conclusion that bribes in any amount, for any purpose, are apparently permissible under the anti-bribery law if they are paid to clerical or ministerial employees—regardless of whether the clerk passes the bribe on to the boss!

Second, the law also excludes foreign extortion from its coverage. The Senate Report on the law refers to an example of a ''payment to an official to keep an oil rig from being dynamited'' as being exempted. The loophole here is whether the extortion exemption is limited to threatened physical or property damage or extends to economic damage as well. What if a foreign minister or cabinet official states, ''pay me $100,000 or I'll put you out of business in this country''? Is this asking for a bribe or demanding a permissible extortion payment? Many managers in this situation have gone to the Justice Department to report the demand before any payment is made.

These are a few of the many ambiguities in the manager's legal environment. Since most courts have not ruled on all the implications, the manager is put into a situation where he or she must call upon common sense and good personal ethics.

Industry Code of Ethics   An industry code of ethics is an internally enforced code of conduct that serves as a guide to all members of the profession or industry. Examples of codes of conduct are most noticeable in the medical, legal, and accounting professions. There are, however, few if any professional codes of conduct that serve as guidelines for business or other organizational leaders. There is also some question about whether such an ethical code can be developed. Arguments for it include:

■   It will improve the confidence of customers, suppliers, and others in the quality of goods and services they expect.

■   The complexities of organizational activities demand that some standards of behavior be set and followed.

■   In the long run, adherence to a set of standard ethical codes will increase the quality of management talent reaching the highest levels of organizations.

Arguments against a code of ethical conduct:

■   Codes of conduct will result in a severe restriction of the manager's freedom to act; a code that is too strict can actually restrict some modes of ethical behavior.

■   The environment of any organization is too dynamic for any specific code of conduct. A too-strict code can limit behavior, and a loosely written code may contain meaningless generalities that can be interpreted in an infinite number of ways to suit the particular situation.

■   Enforcement of codes of conduct would be an almost impossible task.

Some form of ethical conduct code is needed. However, until the problems of overly restrictive behaviors, deceptive statements, and enforcement procedures can be overcome, a universally accepted code will be difficult to establish and enforce.

Forecasting

To this point in our discussion we have analyzed the state of an organization's external and internal environments. Our discussion would be incomplete without extending the analysis to predicting future environmental conditions that will influence the organization—this we term forecasting.

We will divide our presentation of forecasting into two parts. First, we will look at information inputs into forecasting, including methods and sources of forecasting information. Then we will discuss the most popular forecasting techniques.

Information Inputs into Forecasting

Forecasting is frequently regarded as one of the main inputs into the organizational planning process. Forecasting, however, is only as good as the quality and validity of the information used to make predictions. Assessing information quality and validity is difficult, because it is usually only through experience or over time that we can judge these factors. Two major issues are related to information inputs into the forecasting process—methods of information and sources of information.

Methods of Forecasting Information   Organizations and managers can acquire information for forecasting in at least three ways. First, there is the manager's *informal monitoring*. It is termed informal because the manager does not actively seek information, but keeps his or her eyes and ears open to all inputs during the normal work schedule. For example, a purchasing agent for a hospital may listen carefully to various presentations by representatives of supply companies to "sniff out" a possible future price increase on the products the hospital purchases.

The second method is termed *formal scanning* because it involves a purposeful effort on the part of the organization to monitor what is happening in the environment. Frequently, organizations set up a formal managerial position that has responsibility for examining all media documents, speeches by politicians, and various reports from external sources for important information.

Finally, there is the *formal search* method, which is a scanning process undertaken by the organization to obtain information for specific forecasting purposes. Such activities are usually performed by formal organizational units, such as market research or one of the fast growing environmental monitoring departments.[27]

Sources of Forecasting Information   A way of classifying the sources of information is by their origin—whether they are external or internal to the organization. *External sources* include suppliers, customers, professional acquaintances, and various media, such as trade publications, newspapers, magazines, and conferences.

Internal sources can focus on contacts with superiors, peers, and subordinates through meetings, reports, and informal conversations.

A study of managers in forecasting roles found that managers show a great preference for personal sources, such as contacts with suppliers, customers, and colleagues, as opposed to impersonal sources, such as conferences and newspapers.[28] In other words, these managers rely heavily on face-to-face communications for the information they need. This strongly supports the need for managers to develop their informational roles and to sharpen their human skills, which are oriented toward interpersonal communications.

Forecasting Techniques

Managers can use a variety of techniques to forecast possible future events. Our discussion will focus on four broad categories of forecasting techniques—qualitative, time-series, causal models, and technological forecasting. This presentation of forecasting techniques is only a brief summary of today's available methods. Other sources provide a more detailed discussion.[29] Exhibit 3-10 presents an evaluation of the techniques.

Qualitative Techniques   Qualitative techniques generally use informed experts when quantitative data are scarce or difficult to use. Three approaches are the most frequently used:

Panel of Executive Opinion   This method consists of combining and averaging top management's views concerning the event to be forecast. The organization generally brings together executives, sometimes at an offsite retreat, from areas such as sales, production, finance, purchasing, and staff. The advantages of this approach are that forecasts can be made easily and quickly without elaborate statistics, and a range of management viewpoints can be considered.

Delphi Technique   Delphi is another type of qualitative or judgmental technique that polls a panel of experts and gathers their opinions on specific topics. In the feedback gained through a succession of anonymous votes, a pattern of response to future events generally emerges.

Historical Analogy   This technique is probably the most commonly used method of forecasting. It takes the form of past trends plotted on a graph or chart, providing a visual curve. It is based on the belief that future trends will develop in the same direction and rate as past trends unless there is a clear indication of change.

Time-Series   The general approach of time-series forecasts is to identify a pattern representing a combination of trend, seasonal, and cyclical factors based on historical data. That pattern is then smoothed to eliminate the effect of random fluctuations and extrapolated into the future to provide a forecast.

Trend Projection   This technique fits a trend line to a mathematical equation and then projects it into the future by means of this equation. Requirements for data vary with the techniques used, but several years of historical data are usually required.

Moving Average   Each point of a moving average of a time-series is the arithmetic or weighted average of a number of points of the variable under study (e.g., sales).

Exhibit 3-10
Summary of Forecasting Techniques

Technique	Example Applications	Accuracy			Time to Develop	Total Cost
		Short Term	Med. Term	Long Term		
Qualitative						
Exec. Opinion	New product development, sales, earnings	Fair	Fair	Poor	3 weeks	Mod. expensive
Delphi	Product and service development, technological breakthroughs	Good	Good	Good	3 months	Mod. expensive
Historical analogy	Sales, earnings	Poor	Fair	Fair	2 months	Inexpensive
Time-Series						
Trend projection	Sales, earnings, new product introduction	Very good	Good	Good	1 day	Inexpensive
Moving average	Sales, inventory control	Fair	Poor	Poor	1 day	Inexpensive
Exponential smoothing	Production and inventory control, sales, earnings	Good	Good	Poor	1 day	Inexpensive
Causal Models						
Regression analysis	Sales, earnings	Very good	Very good	Fair	1 month	Inexpensive
Econometric models	GNP, sales, economy shifts	Very good	Good	Good	3 months or more	Expensive
Economic indicators	Sales, inventory, purchases	Good	Fair	Poor	1 month	Inexpensive
Technological Forecasting						
Cross-impact	Impact of new developments	Good	Good	Fair	1 month	Inexpensive
Morphological analysis	New uses for product developments	Good	Good	Fair	1 month	Inexpensive
Substitution effect	Substitution of new product for old	Poor	Fair	Fair	3 months	Inexpensive

Adapted from J. C. Chambers, S. Mullick, and D. D. Smith, "How to Choose the Right Forecasting Technique," *Harvard Business Review* (July-August 1971): 55-64.

The number of data points is chosen so that the effects of seasonal variations or irregularities are eliminated.

Exponential Smoothing   This technique is similar to the moving average, except that more recent data points are given more weight. The new forecast is equal to the old one plus some proportion of the past forecasting error.

Causal Models When historical data are available and enough analysis has been performed to spell out *explicitly* the relationships between the factor to be forecast (sales) and other factors (price, advertising, and product availability), a causal model can be constructed. It expresses mathematically the relevant causal relationships and takes into account everything known of the dynamics of the variables under study.

Regression Analysis This method assumes that the variable to be forecast can be predicted on the basis of the value of one or more independent variables. For example, if auto sales were the variable to be forecast, they might be dependent on the economy, personal income, price, and time.

Econometric Models This approach uses a system of regression equations that take into account the interaction between various segments of the economy and/or organizational activities. While such models are useful in forecasting, their major use attempts to answer the perennial "what if" questions. These also allow managers to investigate the impact of various changes in the environment and in major segments of the organization's services.

Economic Indicators Economic indicators are data that can forecast the future state of the economy, such as the dollar amounts of sales for raw materials. Each indicator may predict an event or change in the economy (leading indicator), coincide with the event (coincident indicator), or lag behind the event (lagging indicator).

Technological Forecasting Technological forecasting is a special forecasting approach that deals specifically with technological changes that can affect the organization.[30] The rapid pace of technological change has led many firms, hospitals, governments, and other organizations to recognize the importance of predicting future technological developments. Such technological developments as word processors, computerized calculators, lasers, and aerospace technologies have drastically affected the operations of many organizations. While many techniques are incorporated into the classification (including the Delphi technique and trend projection), three are most widely used:

Cross-impact Analysis This technique attempts to identify and determine the significance of relationships and interactions between specific events.[31] A matrix displaying a two- or three-dimensional array of variables, factors, goals, and issues usually is developed. For example, the impact of solar heating is of interest to the housing industry as well as to energy companies and to the management of many commercial buildings.

Morphological Analysis This technique consists of identifying the relevant dimensions of the object, listing all varieties and combinations of those dimensions, and finding practical applications for them.[32] For example, managers have used this technique to find multiple uses for transistors, lasers, and microcircuitry.

Substitution Effect The substitution phenomenon is based on the belief that one product or technology that exhibits a relative improvement in performance over the older product or technology will eventually be substituted for the factor with the lower performance. Mathematical formulations have been developed that indicate that such substitutions occur in a relatively patterned fashion for many technologies. Examples include jet engines over prop engines, microwave over conventional cooking, radial tires over bias-belted tires.

POINTS TO CONSIDER
An Emphasis on Managerial Skills

1. **An accurate external analysis is a must.**
    Ford Motor Company is known for the best and the worst job of analyzing the external environment—the Mustang and the Edsel, respectively. Other examples of good analyses are low-calorie beers and discount department stores. But remember, a poor analysis will probably lead to a costly decision.

2. **An internal analysis is equally important to planning.**
    IBM's entry into the personal computer market fit with its internal resources, but Hewlett-Packard's attempt at marketing low-cost pocket calculators did not fit with its resources. A firm should plan with resources it presently has, or soon will have.

3. **Personal values and aspirations of top management are strong influences.**
    External and internal analyses may present a clear direction for the organization to follow in its planning activities. If this information and data run counter to the aspirations of strong top management personalities, the choice of direction may be surprising. For example, Juan Trippe tried for years to have his company, Pan Am, designated as the ''flag'' airline of the United States, much like Air France, KLM, and BOAC. This aspiration was so strong that he ignored chances to obtain domestic routes for the airline, a situation that adversely affected the company for many years to come.

4. **Take the lead with ethics by setting a good example.**
    If managers feel pressure from superiors to perform (which may lead to unethical behavior), then top management that adopts a strong ethical code can have a significant impact.

5. **Short-term gains from unethical behavior will not pay off in the long-term.**
    Ethics should be evaluated in terms of long-range consequences for the individual *and* the organization. Not only does short-term unethical behavior lead to a poor reputation, continued unethical practices will probably call the type of negative attention to the company that results in stiff governmental regulations.

SUMMARY FOR THE MANAGER

1. The process of analyzing the organization's external and internal environments is one of the most important activities managers perform. It is important not only because such an analysis provides an evaluation of the state of the organization, but also because resulting decisions will have a long-term impact on the organization's performance.

2. An analysis of the external environment highlights three crucial points for managers. First, it forces managers to view the external environment as consisting of economic, political, social, and technological components, each of which may have a different level of importance to and impact on the organization. Second, the external environment creates different degrees of uncertainty for the manager and the organization. Since organizations do not desire high uncertainty, managers will attempt to control the uncertainty through various actions.

3. An analysis of the internal environment focuses on the resources of the organization—financial, physical, human, and system and technological—which establish the competencies and constraints for future activities, or what the organization *can do*. Managerial values play an important part in the activities of an organization.

4. From a viewpoint of managerial *functions*, an external and internal environment analysis provides necessary input for the *planning* function, which in turn guides the other functions.

5. Ethics will continue to play an important part in the manager's job. Although ethics help determine managerial behavior, cultural differences between countries and the lack of a general code of managerial ethics often put added pressures on the manager, resulting in a wide scope of behavior, situation to situation.

6. A variety of techniques are available to the manager to forecast, or predict the occurrence of an event in the future, including qualitative, time-series, technological forecasting, and causal models. It is important for the manager to remember that forecasts, no matter how performed, are only as good as the quality and validity of the input information.

 # REVIEW AND DISCUSSION QUESTIONS

1. Why has it become more important for managers to analyze the external environment carefully before making major policy decisions?
2. What factors contribute to environmental uncertainty for an organization?
3. What are some important demographic trends that managers should recognize?
4. In what types of industries would changes in the technological environment be an important external component?
5. What are the important human resources of an organization?
6. How do managerial values affect organizational decisions?
7. Why have differences in managerial value systems been reported in cross-cultural studies?
8. Can you identify certain products whose image is an important internal resource strength?
9. Why is it important to identify the internal competencies of an organization?
10. What role does forecasting play in the manager's job?

NOTES

1. See E. C. Gottschalk, Jr., ''Firms Hiring New Type of Manager to Study Issues, Emerging Trouble,'' *The Wall Street Journal* (June 10, 1982): 1; and L. Kraar, ''The Multinationals Get Smarter About Political Risks,'' *Fortune* (March 24, 1980): 58-64.
2. T. Alexander, ''Why Bureaucracy Keeps Growing,'' *Fortune* (May 7, 1979): 166.
3. See ''Red Tape Blues,'' *Newsweek* (August 30, 1976): 77.
4. See E. C. Gottschalk, Jr., ''Promotions Grow Few as Baby Boom Group Eyes Managers' Jobs,'' *The Wall Street Journal* (October 22, 1981); and ''An Uneven Flow of Management Talent,'' *Business Week* (February 20, 1976): 87.
5. See D. T. Hall, *Career In Organizations* (Glenview, Ill.: Scott, Foresman, 1976), p. 170; and ''America's New Immobile Society,'' *Business Week* (July 27, 1981): 58-62.
6. R. Azzi, ''The Saudi's Go for Broke,'' *Fortune* (July 31, 1978): 110-19; and R. Ball, ''Why the Europeans Don't Think Like Us,'' *Fortune* (August 9, 1982): 38-40.
7. N. Foy and H. Gordon, ''Worker Participation: Contrasts in Three Countries,'' *Harvard Business Review* (May-June 1966): 358-73.
8. See N. Hatvany and V. Pucik, ''Japanese Management in America: What Does and Doesn't Work,'' *National Productivity Review* (Winter 1981-82): 61-74; and T. Ozawa, ''Japanese Chic,'' *Across the Board* (October 1982): 6-13.
9. A. L. Morner, ''For Sohio, It Was Alaskan Oil—or Bust,'' *Fortune* (April 1977): 172-86.
10. V. J. Baldridge and R. Burnham, ''Organizational Innovation: Individual, Organizational and Environmental Impacts,'' *Administrative Science Quarterly* (June 1975): 165-76.

11. J. M. Utterback, "Innovation in Industry and the Diffusion of Technology," *Science* (February 1974): 620-26; and W. H. Gruber and D. G. Marquis, eds., *Factors in the Transfer of Technology* (Cambridge, Mass.: MIT Press, 1971).

12. H. Mintzberg, *The Structuring of Organizations* (Englewood Cliffs, N.J.: Prentice-Hall, 1979), p. 286.

13. See H. Aldrich, *Organization & Environment* (Englewood Cliffs, N.J.: Prentice-Hall, 1979); and M. W. Meyer, *Environments and Organization* (San Francisco: Jossey-Bass, 1978).

14. R. Duncan, "Characteristics of Organizational Environments and Perceived Environmental Uncertainty," *Administrative Science Quarterly* (September 1972): 313-27.

15. M. Rokeach, *The Nature of Human Values* (New York: Free Press, 1973), p. 5.

16. G. Allport, P. Vernon, and G. Lindzey, *Study of Values* (Boston: Houghton Mifflin, 1960).

17. W. J. Byron, S.J., "The Meaning of Ethics in Business," *Business Horizons* (November 1977): 32.

18. See T. Griffith, "Payoff Is Not Acceptable Practice," *Fortune* (August 1975): 122-25; and W. Robertson, "The Directors Woke Up Too Late at Gulf," *Fortune* (June 1976): 120-25.

19. J. S. Estey and D. W. Marston, "Pitfalls (and Loopholes) in the Foreign Bribery Law," *Fortune* (October 9, 1978): 182-88.

20. H. D. Menzies, "The One-Two Punch That Shook Olin," *Fortune* (June 5, 1978): 120-22.

21. W. Kiechel, "The Crime at the Top in Fruehauf Corp.," *Fortune* (January 29, 1979): 32-35.

22. A. F. Westin, "The Problem of Employee Privacy Still Troubles Management," *Fortune* (June 4, 1979): 120-26.

23. S. N. Brenner and E. A. Molander, "Is the Ethics of Business Changing?" *Harvard Business Review* (January-February 1977): 57-71.

24. J. D. Long, "The Protestant Ethic Reexamined," *Business Horizons* (February 1972): 75-82.

25. G. Getschow, "Overdriven Execs: Some Middle Managers Cut Corners to Achieve High Corporate Goals," *The Wall Street Journal*, (November 8, 1979): 1.

26. Estey and Marston, "Pitfalls," p. 184.

27. P. Lorange and R. F. Vancil, "How to Design a Strategic Planning System," *Harvard Business Review* (September-October 1976): 75-81.

28. F. J. Aguilar, *Scanning the Business Environment* (New York: Macmillan, 1967).

29. S. C. Wheelwright and D. G. Clarke, "Corporate Forecasting: Promise and Reality," *Harvard Business Review* (November-December 1976): 52; and R. O'Connor, *Planning Under Uncertainty* (New York: Conference Board, 1978), pp. 2-3.

30. J. R. Bright, ed., *Technological Forecasting for Industry and Government* (Englewood Cliffs, N.J.: Prentice-Hall, 1968).

31. W. L. Swager, "Technological Forecasting in Planning," *Business Horizons* (February 1973): 37-44.

32. C. R. O'Neal, "New Approaches to Technological Forecasting: Morphological Analysis," *Business Horizons* (December 1970): 47-58.

A CASE FOR ANALYSIS

Organizational Environments
Howard Johnson Company

The orange-roof restaurant of Howard Johnson's has been a landmark for Americans for many years. The company, which once was very much in tune with this country's population, has fallen on hard times.

Companies like McDonald's and Marriott have long since put Howard Johnson's in their shadow with their food and hotel operations. In addition, the company's recent poor financial performance has ignited takeover rumors due to its depressed stock price. How and why has Howard Johnson Company lost its position? Speculations abound from many sources.

Some analysts believe that competition in the food and hotel fields has increased dramatically. There are far more fast food restaurants and motel/hotel complexes located all around the country now than there ever were during the time of the company's late founder, Howard Johnson, Sr. Competitors in these fields have also been more successful in their decisions regarding the location of their facilities than Howard Johnson's has been.

Still others point to the significant change in the eating habits of U.S. citizens. There has been the explosion of fast food outlets, such as McDonald's, Burger King, and the like. In addition, in many young families, both husband and wife work, and working wives tend to be interested more in entertainment in the evening than in cooking a meal. The Howard Johnson's highway restaurants, oriented to mom, dad, and the kiddies, and with bland menus and decor, have been losing out to some of the "theme" restaurants, such as Victoria Station, with more elaborate menus.

During the 1974 oil crisis, the company reacted by stopping nearly all of its expansion plans. Highway travel was way down, resulting in low occupancy rates at many of the Howard Johnson's motels. It took until 1977 for the company finally to regain its momentum for expansion.

Internally, many problems appeared to surface. The company had long adhered to its founder's philosophy of avoiding the use of debt, preferring instead to be as liquid in cash as possible. Expansions were financed primarily through internal funds and equity issues. There also appeared to be some problems within the management ranks at Howard Johnson's. Many managers seemed to sense the changes going on in the United States before the current chief executive, Howard Johnson, Jr., reawakened. It was not until a group of managers confronted the chief executive with their concerns that the company began to move again.

The movement to retain its once-prominent position has been slow but noticeable. First, 103 Ground Round Restaurants have recently opened. With a turn-of-the-century atmosphere, they sell nostalgia and nightly musical entertainment along with a varied menu. Revenues from these new outlets have averaged nearly twice those of the orange-roof restaurants.

The orange roofs are themselves undergoing some renovations. The fast food counters have been replaced by a salad bar, tropical and airy new interiors, and more service. There is concern by management, however, that the company may lose a high percentage of the older clientele who have continued to patronize the traditional restaurants.

Howard Johnson's problems are far from solved. Energy problems continue to be present, and inflation is eating into the income of Americans. Takeover rumors may become fact in the future. The key question is, has Howard Johnson Company awakened too late?

Adapted from "To Be and What to Be—That is the Question," *Forbes* (May 1, 1978): 25.

Questions for Discussion

1. Perform an external environmental analysis on Howard Johnson Company.
2. Perform an internal resource analysis on the company.
3. Do you agree with the current activities of the company? What should they do next?

Management and Goals

Chapter Outline

Key Points

1. Goals generally are formed from an internal and external environmental analysis of the organization and serve as guiding factors for most organizational functions.
2. Certain criteria for good goals apply to each of the different types of goal frameworks.
3. The major characteristics of goals include an emphasis on measurement, multiplicity, and order.
4. Nonmarket goals, or social goals, are important as well as market goals. Rapidly changing societal values dictate an increased concern in management for social issues.
5. An organization's social behavior can take the form of social obligations, social responsibility, and social responsiveness. There are three possible responses to social behavior: tokenism, functional change, and structural change.
6. Activities in pollution control, affirmative action, consumerism, urban development, and philanthropy should be measured. This is the function of the social audit.
7. Achieving organizational and social goals can be hampered by certain internal problems; managers must also recognize a number of contraints involved in acheiving these goals.

Teledyne, Inc.

When interviewed, most corporation executives would probably state with respect to their organization's goals: "We're profit oriented, not product oriented." Fact is, few companies really are that way. Teledyne is a rare exception. "Forget products," says President George Roberts, "here's the key: We create an attitude toward having high margins (i.e., returns on both sales and assets). In our internal system, the company can grow rapidly and its managers can be rewarded richly for that growth if they produce high margins. If they have had low margins, it's hard to get capital from the organization. No one likes to have trouble getting new money for expansion."

Roberts is saying nothing exceptional. What is exceptional is the way Teledyne—a producer of a variety of products including offshore drilling units, auto parts, machine tools, electronic components, unmanned aircraft, and Water Pik home appliances—practices what it preaches. There are very few companies of any size, and certainly none of the billion dollar class, that are as tight with a capital dollar as Teledyne. Many companies spend more for capital projects than they take in as cash. Not so with Teledyne. This is the real secret to the company's ability to grow.

The key is goal discipline: no ego trips, only new investments that will pay off quickly in the form of enhanced cash flow. Says Roberts: "The only way you can make money in some businesses is by not entering them. Internally we hold up high profit margin companies as examples. Our margin on sales is now over 7 percent after taxes, versus a national average for manufacturing 5.4 percent. Since we run a broad cross-section of business, it is clear the rest of American industry can improve, too.

"Take any big old giant company like U.S. Steel. If they really accounted for their business conservatively and line by line in detail as we

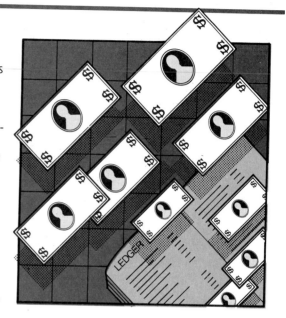

do, they might conclude that they didn't have any margins at all. We make the point that the margin on every product, every project, is important."

The effect of these goals on restricting risk and insisting on a high return on sales and assets, Roberts says, is that he is able to stop preaching. "Now everyone understands that all new projects should return at least 20 percent on total assets. [their goal] . . . This is so ingrained that few lower-returning proposals are ever presented anymore."

As for Chairman Henry Singleton, he is a scientist and an intellectual, but he has an old-fashioned respect for cash. You cannot pay bills with bookkeeping profits. He knows that companies have gone broke after reporting big profits for years—Penn Central, for example, and W.T. Grant. He wants to see the color of some of that money in his companies' reports. Above all, he wants each unit in Teledyne to focus its activities on achieving a high return on sales and assets—returns that can be utilized for overall corporate purposes.

Abridged from R. J. Flaherty, "The Singular Henry Singleton," *Forbes* (July 9, 1979): 45-50.

4

How many times have we heard spokespersons from various organizations make these statements to the media?

"We are planning to increase our market share from 12 to 15 percent this year."

"A 20 percent improvement in sales revenue is what we are aiming for during this fiscal period."

"This administration's objective is to reduce government spending in this city by 25 percent."

"Our goal is to make the Super Bowl this season."

Many company annual reports contain more lengthy statements such as, "We are setting a goal of 15 percent return on invested capital and a 10 percent growth in sales for the upcoming year. These overall corporate goals have been established to motivate our employees to be number one in our industry and to be able to attract capital from the investment community necessary to enhance our continued growth." The Teledyne story in *The Practice of Management* introductory case illustrates how an organization's activities and the behavior of those working within it and in relation to it are influenced by its *goals*. Unless projects at Teledyne can be shown to equal or exceed 20 percent return on total assets, managers are reluctant to even submit them to higher management. In other words, Teledyne's managers *work toward* developing the only projects they *know* can be approved—the ones over the mark.

This chapter looks at how goals serve an important function in the continuing existence of organizations. Realistically developed, stated, and implemented goals can be the guiding principle for increased effectiveness and continued growth.[1] On the other hand, unrealistically developed and/or improperly implemented goals can adversely affect the level of performance or even the survival of the organization.

We will approach the concept of organizational goals in two major parts. First, we will present a general framework of organizational goals. The focus will be on the definition and importance of goals, the criteria for good goals, the various types and characteristics of goals, and certain problems with goals and the manager's job. The second part of our discussion will focus on a special case of organizational goals—the issue of organizational social behavior. As managers, or future managers, we must be concerned with how our actions, and the actions of the organizations we represent, affect our society.

Managers and Organizational Goals

Definition of Organizational Goals

Organizational goals are desired states of affairs or preferred results that organizations attempt to realize and achieve.[2] An acceptance of this definition implies at least two relationships between goals and management. First, goals are influenced by the *aspiration* of an organization's key managers. This was brought out in the last chapter. For example, a goal of McDonald's to "double the number of fast-food restaurants located outside the U.S. by 1985" assumes that: (1) there are sufficient market opportunities in foreign countries; (2) the organization currently has or can easily obtain adequate resources to achieve the goal; and (3) such a goal is desired by the management of the company.

Second, goals reflect a desired *end result* of organizational actions—that which they wish to achieve. McDonald's may want to increase the number of outlets, Delta Airlines may wish to increase sales, the United Auto Workers (UAW) may want to have all their represented workers covered with adequate medical insurance, and General Foods may desire a larger share of the breakfast cereal market. There are a variety of goals that organizations may want to achieve simultaneously.

Some managers and management scholars use the terms goals, objectives, and purposes interchangeably. To some writers, objectives are means for achieving goals, but others reverse the definition.[3] At the outset, we will not differentiate between these concepts. Later in the chapter we will make the distinction.

Importance of Organizational Goals

As we discussed in the last chapter (see exhibit 3-1), goals play an important role in the planning process. At least four reasons stress this level of importance. First, goals help guide the direction of efforts of individuals and groups in an organization. For example, consider two automobile manufacturers, Volvo and Honda. Volvo has stressed the production of a low volume of high-quality and high-priced cars. Honda, on the other hand, is oriented toward a high volume of functional cars at a relatively low price. Even though each of these firms is in the business of providing transportation products, we should expect the two differing goals will lead to different ways of producing and marketing cars.

Second, goals affect how the organization *plans* and *organizes* its activities. Consider two universities—a large, state-supported institution, and a smaller, but growth-oriented, private university. The growth orientation (i.e., the goal) of the private institution may cause its planners to be concerned with more external aspects—seeking outside funds from foundations and other agencies, drawing a wide variety of students to campus, and hiring quality professors. On the other hand, the large, public university may be more oriented toward internal factors in its planning activities, such as control over operating expenses, proper maintenance of the facilities, and support for existing programs.

Third, the use of goals provides the foundation to *motivate* individuals to perform at the highest levels of efficiency and effectiveness. Sometimes it may be better to be number two striving to be number one than to be number one. Many of us have been members of sports teams that are in second or third place, but see a chance to be in first place with the exertion of some additional effort. In a similar manner, we can investigate the competition in the auto rental industry over the past few years. Avis' well known "We try harder" statement has not only been successful as an advertising claim but has proved to be a strong internal motivator of employees. As we will note in later chapters, however, continued high motivation is a function of the level of rewards given to the individuals. If individuals receive rewards (praise, recognition, pay raises, advancement, or a sense of achievement and pride) equal to their levels of performance, they should continue to exert high levels of effort.

Finally, goals form the basis for *evaluating* and *controlling* the activities of the organization. Goals, plans, and motivated workers all work toward the achievement of some end result. Evaluation and control tell us how well we are doing in our attempts to reach these ends, and, if we are not on target, they provide certain guidelines for revising our efforts. Consider again the private university. The university's administration may have set a goal of collecting contributions of $10 million over a three-year fund-raising campaign. When only $2.5 million is collected the first year, an analysis of the contributors may reveal that donations from alumni are far short of what was expected. This may lead administrators to examine why this has occurred and to develop mechanisms to correct the situation—or to revise their goal.

Goals permeate the entire management process by providing the foundations for planning, direction, motivation, and control. Managers must be continually involved in the goal process because without goals organizations could meander in any number of ineffective directions.

Criteria for Good Goals

Certain criteria for goals enable us to classify them as good or poor. Four criteria, examples of which are shown in exhibit 4-1, are most important.

Clarity and Specificity   Goals should be clear and specific concerning the desired outcomes. Clear and specific goals make it known to all employees where their efforts should take them; unclear and/or nonspecific goals create confusion and conflict among workers.

Timing   A particular time or date of anticipated goal accomplishment is an important requirement. With a definite time frame, accurate plans can be developed.

Consistency   Goals must be logically consistent, particularly with respect to the external environment and internal resources, because they indicate whether the organization has taken the right path. For example, General Electric's purchase of a coal

Exhibit 4-1 Criteria for Organizational Goals	**Criteria**	**Example of Poor Goal**	**Example of an Improved Goal**
	Clarity and Specificity	Improve employee communications.	Hold monthly unit meetings to discuss issues and problems and initiate an employee newsletter within three months.
	Timing	Improve production.	Increase production to 95% of capacity within two months.
	Feasibility	Eliminate air pollution from all plants.	Reduce particulate matter venting to the atmosphere by 90% within three years.
	Difficulty and Achievability	Double sales.	Increase yearly sales revenue by at least 20%.

company was logically consistent not only because of its immense resource base, but because the company already was a major manufacturer of power-generation equipment based on coal as a fuel.

Difficulty and Achievability   It is important for goals to be difficult enough to stimulate added effort by workers, but not so difficult that they create frustration. Easily attainable goals may not only be quickly forgotten by employees but may lead to complacency and neglect. For example, using its dominant position in denim pants, Levi-Strauss may set a difficult but achievable goal of being the number one manufacturer of men's and women's *sportswear*. American Motors' claim to outsell GM in auto sales revenue by 1988, however, may be farfetched and unachievable.

These criteria are important to managers in all types of organizations. They provide the direction and momentum needed for improved performance.

Types of Goals

As we suggested in chapter 1, there are many performance criteria or end results that organizations seek to achieve. Among the most frequently stated are the following:[4]

Profitability   Profitability is usually expressed in such terms as net income, earnings-per-share, return on investment, or other similar ratios. Not-for-profit or public-sector organizations are also concerned with this type of goal when we consider their desire to keep costs within specific budget levels.

Productivity   Productivity goals generally concern the levels of output per unit or worker across the organization. Examples include "units produced per day for each employee," "costs per unit of production," or "income generated per employee."

Market   Market goals can be described in a number of different ways. They can relate to a particular penetration of the market, such as "increase the market share for Product A to 20 percent," or an output orientation, such as "sell one hundred thousand units of output this year in the health care industry." Many times, market goals relate to the coverage in a company's product line. An unsatisfactory coverage may prompt management to improve the product line by introducing new products.

Resources   Organizations may establish goals concerning changes in their resource base. Financial resource goals may include "reduce the company's long-term debt by $30 million within three years," "decrease the collection period on accounts receivable to less than thirty days within six months," and so on. Physical resource goals could deal with increases in the number of plants or facilities, production capacity, storage capacity, or maintenance capabilities. Human resource goals may relate to decreases in absenteeism, turnover, and days lost due to accidents. They may also concern improvements in management-development programs, career-planning activities, and executive succession programs.

Innovation   For many organizations, continued growth (or survival) may depend on the development of new products, processes, or services. Sample goals include "development of a new manufacturing process that is more efficient than the existing process within five years," "developing a new automobile engine that will run on a variety of fuels and get 50 mpg. by 1990," or "increase our spending on R&D by 25 percent this year."

Social Responsibility   Most organizations, and managers within these organizations, are becoming keenly aware of their role in society. Concerns over the quality of life, minority employment, pollution, and the deteriorating environment are becoming more important. The last part of this chapter will discuss this topic in depth.

The manager should carefully note that the sample goals above may, in many cases, apply to not-for-profit organizations equally as to those with the profit motive. Hospitals, state and local governments, and social service agencies, for example, are concerned with cost control, output per employee, development and improvement of resources, implementation of innovative practices, and their relationship to society. Any organization that seeks high performance levels needs goals.

Beyond this classification scheme, there are other ways of describing the types of goals that can be found in all organizations. Three categories can be presented: (1) level of analysis; (2) focus; and (3) time frame.

Level of Analysis   A classification scheme for goals may distinguish between official, operative, and operational goals.[5] An official goal is the formal statement of purpose concerning the overall mission of the organization. It is usually a broad statement found in official organizational documents, such as the annual report. Examples include the public utility that "exists to serve the public," the university that is chartered to "disseminate knowledge," and the hospital that is designed to "improve the health of the patients." The official goal is typically vague and aspirational, (maximize profits or contribute to society's welfare), with indefinite time horizons.

The real intentions of organizations are termed *operative* goals—they reflect what an organization is *actually* trying to do. For example, an *officially* stated goal of a telephone company may be to serve customers in a particular geographical area in the most effective manner. *Operationally* this goal may be translated to "courteously handle all requests for information and satisfy 97 percent of requests for assistance."

Finally, *operational* goals are those that have agreed-upon criteria for evaluating the level of achievement. This is where we can make the distinction between goals and objectives. Goals (official and operative) can be considered the ultimate, long-run, end results an organization seeks, while objectives (operational) can be seen as the short- or intermediate-term targets, necessary—but not sufficient—for the accomplishment of official and operative goals.

The key feature is that a goal is said to be operational to the extent that management can precisely state *how* and *when* the goal will be achieved. For example, a farm equipment company may state an *official* goal as, "maximize profits through the sale of farm implements." From an *operative* view, the goal can be stated as, "attaining a level of 15 percent return on invested capital from the sale of the company's product line." Finally, as an *operational* goal or objective, the statement can be made as, "improve return on invested capital to a level of 15 percent by December 1987 through the sale of the company's farm implement products."

Another way of viewing official, operative, and operational goals is by the hierarchical level in the organization that they affect. Exhibit 4-2 illustrates this point. Generally speaking, official and operative goals reflect the concerns of executive and

Exhibit 4-2

The Hierarchial Nature of Goals

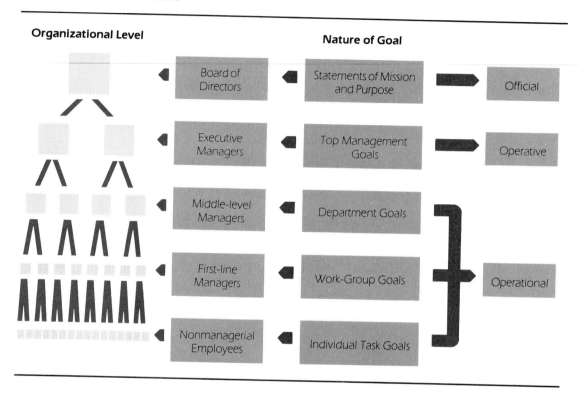

Organizational Level   **Nature of Goal**

Board of Directors	Statements of Mission and Purpose	Official
Executive Managers	Top Management Goals	Operative
Middle-level Managers	Department Goals	
First-line Managers	Work-Group Goals	Operational
Nonmanagerial Employees	Individual Task Goals	

middle-level managers, respectively, and the lower managerial levels are concerned with operational goals.[6]

Focus   Classifying goals by focus describes the *nature of the action* that will be taken. Three categories are most frequently used:

Maintenance Goals   Maintenance goals imply that a specific level of activity is to be maintained over time. Examples include the desire to "operate at 95 percent of manufacturing capacity," and for an airline "to have at least 85 percent of its aircraft in service at one time."

Improvement Goals   Goals that seek improvement often use an *action* verb to indicate a specific change is wanted. "Increasing" market share, "decreasing" customer complaints, and "improving" return on invested capital are examples.

Developmental Goals   Similar to improvement goals, developmental goals refer to a desire for some form of growth, expansion, learning, or advancement. Such goals could include increasing the number of new products introduced, establishing managerial training programs to improve managerial effectiveness, and so on.

Unlike the previous classification schemes, this approach is much simpler in actual use. The important characteristic, however, is how such goals direct the activities and actions of members of organizations.

Time Frame   A dominant classification scheme for goals is based on the time period affected by the goals—either long-term or short-term goals.[7] *Long-term* goals refer to those that usually cover more than a one-year period of time. Examples may include "doubling the number of beds in a hospital within four years," "capturing 30 percent of the market by 1986," or "obtaining a 10 percent growth in sales during the next five years." *Short-term* goals concern those that cover twelve months or less, even though their actual accomplishment may require more than one year. A "reduction in manufacturing costs by $2 million by the end of the year," or "completion of the construction of the warehouse before Christmas," are examples.

Two important aspects of long- and short-term goals should be pointed out. First, many times short-term goals are subdivisions of long-term goals. For example, Colgate may desire an 8 percent market share for a new household detergent within three years of introduction. The first year, a 2 percent market share goal is set, 5 percent for the second year, and 8 percent for the third year.

Second, a high degree of flexibility and adjustment must be part of any long- or short-term goal. As we noted in the previous chapter, changes in the external environment can sometimes turn viable long-term goals into poor ones. Long-term goals must be based on the best possible forecasts available at the time they are made and should not commit the organization to an unretractable position. Similarly, short-term goals should be flexible enough not to endanger the achievement of a long-term goal. An example of the time frame concept is shown in exhibit 4-3.

Exhibit 4-3
Sample Business Goals

Goal	Indices	Year One	Targets and Time Frame Year Two	Year Three
Growth	Sales Revenue	$200M	$200M	$240M
Efficiency	Profits Profits/Sales	$20M 10%	$26.4M 12%	$33.6M 18%
Resource Utilization	Return on Investment Return on Assets	15% 22%	17% 24%	20% 26%
Contributions to Stockholders	Dividends Earnings/Share	$1.00/share $2.00/share	$1.20/share $2.40/share	$1.45/share $2.90/share
Contributions to Customers	Price Quality	Equal or Better than Competition	Equal or Better than Competition	Equal or Better than Competition
Contributions to Employees	Wage Rate Benefits	$4.00/hr Equal or Better than Local Firms	$4.50/hr Equal or Better than Local Firms	$5.00/hr Equal or Better than Local Firms
Contributions to Society	Taxes Scholarships	$ 20M $200K	$ 20M $220K	$ 24M $250K

Adapted from C.W. Hofer and D. Schendel, *Strategy Formulation: Analytical Concepts* (St. Paul, Minn.: West, 1978), p. 21.

Characteristics of Goals

Like any other management concept, organizational goals have certain basic characteristics. Goals should be *measurable; many goals* exist at the *same time;* and, because there are many goals, they are usually somehow *ordered.*

Measurement   Goals of an organization, a department, or of individual managers must be measurable. Unless there are criteria for effectiveness and methods of measuring the criteria, no one will know when a goal has been achieved. As an executive acquaintance has stated, "If you can't count it, measure or describe it, why are you doing it?" Two types of measurement are most frequently presented:

Quantitative measures are those to which some *number* can be assigned. Examples include net income, return on investment, market share, units produced, turnover and absenteeism rate, etc. These are also sometimes referred to as *objective* measures.

Qualitative measures. When managers simply cannot assign a quantitative figure to the achievement of a goal, they may be able to use qualitative or subjective measures to do so. Surprisingly, often qualitative measures are used to evaluate managerial performance. Although quantitative measures are easily adaptable to lower-level jobs (e.g., number of units produced or sold), measuring managerial performance or goal achievement is much more difficult. Many managers alleviate this problem somewhat by creating or attaching a number to the goal. For example, three most frequently mentioned managerial goals and their "qualitative" measures include: (a) "assessing the level of employee morale" through the use of survey questionnaires; (b) "developing future management talent" through participation in training programs or by the number of subordinates who have been promoted; and (c) "being a good corporate citizen" by the number of speeches to local organizations, reduction of customers' complaints, and so forth.

Multiplicity of Goals   Every organization and every manager has more than one goal. On an organizational level, the goals of a hospital may be patient health, control of costs, improvements in service, and reductions in personnel turnover and absenteeism. On a departmental level, the marketing area in a consumer products company can consider unit sales, advertising effectiveness, market coverage, and number of new customers as possible goals. Exhibit 4-4 illustrates the multiplicity and hierarchical nature of goals for three levels and functions within an organization.

Ordering of Goals   In order to remove some of the possible problems associated with the goal concept, managers order their goals. This involves three factors:

Goal Networks   In our discussion of categorizing goals by the level of analysis in the previous section, we noted how a goal is transmitted *vertically* in an organization. In a similar manner, goals must be integrated horizontally in an organization, creating a network of goals. This also is shown in exhibit 4-4. If an organization's goals are not interconnected and mutually supportive, managers may tend to pursue individual goals that can be detrimental to the overall organization. For example, consider two product managers in a marketing department of an electronics firm. The first may react to the global goal of "improving our market performance" by seeking out sales contracts that enhance profit margins, while the second manager may work towards increasing sales revenue. These two behaviors may not be totally congruent with each other. As Sears and W.T. Grant painfully recognized, increased profit margins do not necessarily come with higher sales.[8]

Goal Priorities   With the multiplicity of goals found *across* the entire organization, management must set *priorities* for goals. Goals are generally given a primary or secondary rating. Primary goals are those of the highest importance to the organization. Secondary goals may be more oriented toward short-term considerations. For example, Teledyne has set margins as their primary goal.[9] All other goals—dealing with employee turnover, acquisitions, product development—are secondary but integrated with the primary goal. As an example of goal priorities, consider exhibit 4-5. The exhibit sums up a survey of 1,072 business-oriented managers at various organizational levels that gathered information on what goals managers deemed *important* as well as *essential* to success of the organization.[10] The eight goals are divided into four categories: (1) overall efficiency; (2) growth and status; (3) employee concerns; and (4) social concerns. Two features of this survey data are particularly interesting. First, there is a wide variation in the importance given to efficiency goals, suggesting that cost control and profit-oriented behaviors and values are still dominant among managers. Second, although 65 percent of the managers believed that employee welfare was highly important, only 20 percent felt that it was essential to the success of the organization. This suggests, given the survey's sample, that managerial and behavioral theories are making an impact, but when it comes to a confrontation, profit goals win out over employee welfare goals.

Balancing Goals   In addition to setting priorities, managers find that they must trade off among goals so that an organizationally satisfactory set of goals emerges. Sales goals must be balanced with production goals; product development goals must be balanced with financial goals; short-term goals must be balanced with long-term goals. Stressing one goal to the exclusion of others may lead to suboptimum results.

Exhibit 4-4
The Multiplicity, Hierarchy, and Network Characteristics of Goals

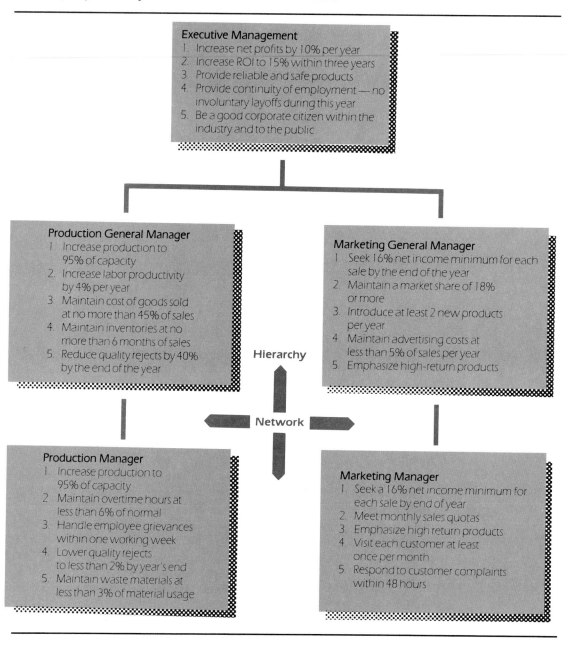

Executive Management
1. Increase net profits by 10% per year
2. Increase ROI to 15% within three years
3. Provide reliable and safe products
4. Provide continuity of employment — no involuntary layoffs during this year
5. Be a good corporate citizen within the industry and to the public

Production General Manager
1. Increase production to 95% of capacity
2. Increase labor productivity by 4% per year
3. Maintain cost of goods sold at no more than 45% of sales
4. Maintain inventories at no more than 6 months of sales
5. Reduce quality rejects by 40% by the end of the year

Marketing General Manager
1. Seek 16% net income minimum for each sale by the end of the year
2. Maintain a market share of 18% or more
3. Introduce at least 2 new products per year
4. Maintain advertising costs at less than 5% of sales per year
5. Emphasize high-return products

Hierarchy

Network

Production Manager
1. Increase production to 95% of capacity
2. Maintain overtime hours at less than 6% of normal
3. Handle employee grievances within one working week
4. Lower quality rejects to less than 2% by year's end
5. Maintain waste materials at less than 3% of material usage

Marketing Manager
1. Seek a 16% net income minimum for each sale by end of year
2. Meet monthly sales quotas
3. Emphasize high return products
4. Visit each customer at least once per month
5. Respond to customer complaints within 48 hours

Exhibit 4-5
The Importance and Essentiality of Goals

Goals of Business Organizations	% Rating High Importance	% Rating as Essential for Success
Overall Efficiency		
Cost efficiency	81%	71%
High productivity	80%	70%
Profit maximization	72%	71%
Growth and Status		
Organizational growth	60%	72%
Industrial leadership	58%	64%
Organizational stability	58%	54%
Employee Concerns		
Employee welfare	65%	20%
Social Concerns		
Social welfare	16%	8%

Source: G. W. England, "Organizational Goals and Expected Behavior of American Managers," *Academy of Management Journal* (June 1967): 108.

Managers and Social Goals

Toward an Awareness of Social Goals

In the previous discussion of organizational goals, we noted how goals such as improving profit levels, increasing market share, and more efficient cost control were influenced by the external and internal environments of the organization. These goals represent responses by the organization to *market* forces; the firm adapts by varying its product line, pricing strategies, promotion, and service to meet changing consumer needs, expectations, and organizational resource strengths.

In the process of working toward market goals, there are many *nonmarket* goals and indirect consequences for society as a whole.[11] As we read and hear frequently from the media, societal elements have put increasing pressure on organizations to minimize adverse nonmarket consequences and maximize the nonmarket benefits of their activities. While many business institutions can justifiably take credit for tremendous strides that have been made in improving living standards, they are also frequently accused of being the cause of many environment-related and sociopolitical problems and for being relatively insensitive to the needs of society. There have been increasing pressures on organizations to take more active roles and assume greater responsibility for correcting the social ills that their work can engender. In other words, there is a growing awareness that nonmarket social goals *as well as* market goals need to be part of an organization's goalset, since each is an important part of what the organization "should do."

Dimensions of Organizational Social Behavior

While the concept of organizational social behavior has generated considerable discussion during recent years, it has remained an elusive concept to define and classify. Frequently, such terms as *social awareness or social responsibility* have been used. For our purposes, we will define and classify *organizational social behavior* as a three-part concept—social obligations, responsibility, and responsiveness.[12]

Social Obligations   This first category concerns the typical activities of an organization directed in response to market forces and/or internal aspirations. According to this framework, an organization meets its social obligations by achieving its goals through its ability to compete for resources and conducting its operations within the legal constraints imposed by society (i.e., obeying the law). An example is an organization that maximizes profits by adherence to economic and legal criteria and constraints. This "normal" behavior by an organization has been criticized by many as being too narrowly defined in that economic and legal factors are insufficient for the long-term success and survival of most organizations. In other words, some believe that satisfaction of the profit motive does not totally ensure the continued survival of the organization. More complex criteria and constraints are needed.

Social Responsibility   This second category is much broader than the first in its definition and scope. Organizational social responsibility suggests that the organization meets the prevailing social norms, values, and performance expectations of society (i.e., meets social demands). At issue are not only the occasions when certain illegalities in organizations occur, but also the criticism that organizations have not done enough to meet societal needs such as minority employment, pollution control, education support, and the like.

Social Responsiveness   Whereas the concept of social responsibility concerns current issues, social responsiveness is anticipatory in nature (i.e., anticipates and creates some demands). That is, the focus is not only on how organizations should respond to current social forces and pressures, but what their long-term position in society is to be. The organization in a socially responsive mode is expected to *anticipate* the changes or the emergence of socially related problems that may be the result of organizational activities.[13] The Alaskan pipeline is an example. In an idealistic sense, those organizations involved in the project were considered socially responsive when they planned for the long-term environmental, social, and economic impact of the pipeline on the land and the people.

Recent surveys have shown that few organizations have gone much beyond the social responsibility stage in their social activities.[14] These same surveys found, however, that business activism will probably increase significantly in the future.

Origins of Organizational Social Behavior

Organizations' concern over social issues has multiple origins. As we will discuss, the origins are historical and come from experienced problems.

The concept of organizational social behavior—social obligations, responsibility, and responsiveness—is not a revolutionary idea of the turbulent 1960s or 1970s. A

"Granted the public has a <u>right</u> to know what's in a hot dog, but does the public really <u>want</u> to know what's in a hot dog?"

Drawing by Richter; © 1978 The New Yorker Magazine, Inc.

close examination of the writings on the history of management thought will reveal many instances of concerns over social issues. Henry Gantt, R. C. Davis, and Chester Barnard each challenged managers to be more active in community affairs.

Practicing managers also have made significant contributions to the social behavior of organizations. For example, Sears, Roebuck instituted the county farm agent concept during the early years of this century. Sears believed that before farm productivity could be improved by new farm technology, the farmer's knowledge needed improvement and some of the ignorance and isolation associated with agricultural work had to be removed. The county farm agent provided the information and assistance that helped farmers to produce more, to produce the right things, and to learn how to get more from their efforts on the land.[15]

Henry Ford I was best known for his radical manufacturing process, yet his social contribution of a guaranteed $5 a day wage to workers was even more radical. Even though the wage was almost triple that of the going standard, the company was convinced that the worker's sufferings were so great that highly visible changes would make an impact on other industries. In a similar fashion, during the Great Depression, IBM pioneered the concept of employment security by putting workers on salary instead of hourly wage. IBM's action was directed at a major social problem of that time—namely, the fear, insecurity, and loss of human dignity that resulted from the Depression. IBM turned a social malady into a business opportunity, and developed a human resource philosophy that is still at work in the corporation. Sears, Ford, and IBM were socially responsive, a historical fact that even the severest critics of American business must accept.[16]

In contrast, we seem to hear about more instances of corporate social irresponsibility, perhaps because of their potential severity.

Some of the more publicized problems:

- 1.4 million *Ford* Pintos and Bobcats recalled due to exploding gas tanks.
- 1.45 million *Firestone* 500 radial tires recalled due to improper tread wear.
- Mercury pollution in the Niagara River from an *Olin* plant.
- 1500 lawsuits filed against *Johns-Manville* by workers who have contracted asbestos-related diseases.
- $20 million fines and settlements against *Allied Chemical* for discharging the toxic pesticide, Kepone, into the Chesapeake Bay.
- *Union Carbide's* air and water polluting plants in West Virginia.

We should note three points on this subject. First, some organizations have not been as socially conscious as they should have been. For example, there is some evidence that Firestone and Union Carbide knew of the existence of their respective problems *before* they became public. Second, as we will discuss shortly, many more organizations have made significant contributions to social issues, but have not received the notoriety that the less successful ones have received. Last, organizations, like individuals, *learn* from their mistakes. The bad experiences of these organizations have no doubt had an effect on other organizations in their social thinking.

Pros and Cons of Organizational Social Behavior

Do today's experts all see socially conscious behavior on the part of organizations in the same category as parenthood, peanut butter, and the flag? Such may not be the case; there are as many equally strong arguments *against* social behavior as there are for it. The major pro and con arguments on the issue are shown in exhibit 4-6.

Two individual points of view may serve to highlight the major differences on this issue. The "against" view is best presented by the well-known economist Milton Friedman, who argues that the only responsibility of business is to *maximize profits* for its owners.[17] Friedman's argument assumes that managers are really agents of the owners and that diverting funds to social activities that do not contribute to profits may be illegal.

The "for" view has been well presented by Keith Davis and his *Iron Law of Responsibility*. The law states that in the long run, those who do not use power in the manner that society considers responsible will tend to lose it.[18] The argument is that since business is a major power in our society, it has an obligation and responsibility to attempt to solve problems of public concern. If business neglects this responsibility, then the only action that society can take is to withdraw some of business' power and give it to institutions that may be better able to solve the problems.

Organizational Responses to Social Issues

When organizations are confronted with issues of a social nature, they may adopt a number of different response patterns or behaviors. As shown in exhibit 4-7, there are

Exhibit 4-6
Arguments For and Against Social Responsibility

Major Arguments for Social Responsibility	Major Arguments Against Social Responsibility
1. It is in the long-run self-interest of the firm to promote and improve the communities where it does business.	1. Violates profit maximization and is, thus, illegal.
2. It improves the public image of the firm.	2. Cost of social responsibility too great and would increase prices too much.
3. It is necessary to avoid government regulation.	3. Business lacks social skills to solve societal problems.
4. Sociocultural norms require it.	4. It would dilute business's primary purposes.
5. Laws cannot be passed for all circumstances. Thus, business must assume responsibility to maintain an orderly, legal society.	5. It would weaken U.S. balance of payments be cause price of goods would have to go up to pay for social programs.
6. It is in the stockholder's best interest. It will improve the price of stock in the long run be cause the stock market will view the company as less risky and open to public attack and, therefore, award it a higher price to earning ratio.	6. Business already has too much power. Such in volvement would make business too powerful.
7. Society should give business a chance to solve social problems that government has failed to solve.	7. Business lacks accountability to the public. Thus the public would have no control over its social involvement.
8. Business is considered by some groups to be the institution with the financial and human re sources to solve social problems.	8. Such business involvement lacks broad public support.
9. Problems can become profitable if firms be come involved.	9. Business plus government creates a monolith.
10. Prevention of problems is better than cures—so let business solve problems before they become too great.	10. Social responsibility cannot be measured.

Adapted from J. R. Monsen, "The Social Attitudes of Management," in *Contemporary Management*, ed. Joseph W. McGuire (Englewood Cliffs, N.J.: Prentice-Hall, 1974), p. 616.

three broad response categories that are most prevalent in organizations today: (1) tokenism; (2) functional change; and (3) structural change.

Tokenism   Tokenism has been the most frequently used response mechanism by organizations for many years. It is the easiest, quickest, and least expensive way to respond to social issues. Examples include membership on local and state commit tees, donation of funds and executive talent to particular causes, and so forth. Token responses, however, are usually short term in nature and can be ineffectual and inef ficient for the organization in the long run.

Exhibit 4-7
Organizational Responses to Social Issues

Response Category	Examples	Positive Features	Negative Features
Tokenism	1. Membership on community committees 2. Donation of funds 3. Donation of management talent	Inexpensive and adaptable	Can be ineffective and inefficient in the long run
Functional Change	1. Ad hoc committees 2 Temporary task forces 3. Permanent committees	Provides support and expertise	Costly in terms of expanding duties; increasing potential for internal conflict
Structural Change	1. Vice president of consumer affairs 2. Environmental affairs department	Visible commitment; developing expertise; meaningful presentation	Costly expansion; value conflicts; makes decision making more complex

Functional Change   This next-highest level of response awareness generally involves a more complex reaction by the organization. The usual procedure is to establish a temporary or permanent committee whose members are responsible for handling specific tasks or for supplying information to management on social affairs. Examples include United Appeal campaigns, employment opportunity review boards, and the like. The drawbacks to functional change responses are expense in terms of staff and manpower and the fact that they can create potential conflicts of interest when individuals must choose between their primary and secondary job duties.

Structural Change   Structural change is the most complex and costly response to social affairs. The typical mechanism is to create a new managerial position, such as vice president of consumer affairs, or a department, such as environmental and social affairs, each of which is formally incorporated into the structure of the organization. By adopting this mechanism, organizations are placing social issues on a relative par with other more traditional organizational concerns such as market share, profit growth, and management development. On the negative side, structural change can further complicate an already complex decision-making process and bring about the potential for major conflicts between the new unit and the other functional areas.

There are three important points that this discussion suggests. First, social responses by organizations generally can be placed in the social obligation and social responsibility categories and, at least partially, in the social responsiveness category. In other words, these responses fall only within a portion of the potential social behavior pattern that we have discussed. Second, there is a varying level of cost, in terms of "real" and "opportunity" costs, to the organization. Tokenism may be the least costly, but it may leave the organization open to accusations of disinterest and insincerity. A major structural change requires more than just appointing a vice president of consumer affairs; it may involve a complete revision of the organization's thinking and decision making. Finally, whatever the response pattern chosen, the organization must carefully examine and diagnose its own particular situation.

Social Issues and Projects

The social issues facing society in general, and business in particular, are difficult and numerous. We have chosen five to discuss not only because of their importance but also because of their relationship to business organizations. As we will see, business organizations (along with not-for-profit organizations) have become involved in many of these issues already, some in a positive manner, some not so positive. The five include: pollution; affirmative action; consumerism; urban development; and philanthropic activities.

Pollution   Perhaps no other issue has gained the level of attention and been the center of so much controversy as that of pollution and its impact on the environment. Because most organizations use some form of natural resources as raw material inputs into their operations, they risk being the leading sources of the significant deterioration of a nation's land, air, and water. Five areas of possible pollution control have been most frequently identified and discussed:

- Reduction of *air pollution* from automobile exhaust emissions, aircraft, and particle discharges from chemical, mining, metals, and other manufacturing processes.
- Reduction of *water pollution* and the destruction of water life from the effluent discharges of industrial plants.
- *Land conservation* and/or proper reclamation by lumber, mining, and petroleum firms along with limitations placed on sports activities (e.g., hunting, dune buggy and motorcycle racing in the deserts of California, snowmobiling in winter lands).
- Reduction of *noise pollution* from industry and aircraft.
- Reduction of *visual pollution* from the billboard industry.

As these issues impinge more and more upon the organization, there are at least three factors to recognize. First, the pollution issue will continue to take up considerable amounts of managerial time and energy. Not only will societal interest continue to grow, but the participation of federal, state, and local governmental agencies will increase. With its regulatory and financial power, the EPA should be able to exert a considerable amount of control over the creation and enforcement of air and water quality standards. In essence, concerns over pollution have or will become an integral part of the manager's *planning* and *control* activities.

Second, despite such highly publicized incidents as the Amoco Cadiz oil spill off the coast of France, Allied Chemical's problems with the pesticide Kepone, Hooker Chemical's Love Canal problems, the Pemex oil spill in Mexico, and the asbestos controversy at Johns-Manville, managers should resist taking a totally defensive position.[19] In many unfortunately unpublicized instances, organizations have taken the lead in trying to solve present and future pollution problems. A good example is the National Coal Policy Project, which is a group of leading conservationists and top executives from the coal-mining and coal-consuming industries who meet to try to devise environmentally safe ways to mine and use coal.[20]

Third, any plan by an organization to reduce or eliminate pollution—particularly air and water—must answer some key questions about technology and cost. For example, some of the technical equipment required to totally eliminate most forms of air pollution is only on the drawing board and not commercially available. Such equipment may be years away from widespread use. As for cost, the amount of money necessary for total pollution elimination is staggering. Businesses are already spending nearly 25 percent of their capital improvement budgets on pollution control and worker safety. In other words, a cost-benefit or trade-off analysis that evaluates the economic and environmental effects must be considered carefully.

There is no doubt that organizations, particularly businesses, are concerned with the pollution issue. Solutions will be found, but it will take time, capital, and the cooperation and commitment of many individuals and groups.

Affirmative Action   Perhaps no two documents have had a more significant impact on the management of human resources in organizations than the Fourteenth Amendment of the Constitution (1868) and the 1972 amendment of Title VII of the Civil Rights Act of 1964. The former promises "equal protection of the law to all persons born or naturalized in the United States," and the latter "prohibits discrimination because of race, color, religion, sex, or natural origin in all employment practices including hiring, firing, promotion, compensation, job classification, and other terms, privileges, and conditions of employment." The result was not only the creation of the Equal Employment Opportunities Commission (EEOC), but an entirely revised way of thinking about people at work.

While we discuss this issue in greater depth in chapter 10, certain implications for organizational goals should be pointed out here. First, any discrimination in the work force is clearly illegal and will not be tolerated. Second, certain executive orders designed to supplement the previous acts require federal contractors (or any organization that receives federal monies) to file a written affirmative action program designed to eliminate any inequities that might exist as a result of past practices. In essence, organizations must supplement their goalset with goals that identify, for example, the percentages of minorities that will be hired or trained by certain future dates. Finally, much the same as McGregor's Theory X and Theory Y, the impact of equal employment opportunity and affirmative action has been to significantly reorient management's thinking about employees. In many cases, concerns over the health and welfare of an organization's people will take as much managerial time as that of capital expansion, mergers, or new product development.

Consumerism   Our lives are touched daily in many ways by the products and services provided by numerous organizations. We have all at one time or another been disappointed by the performance of some product or service we have purchased. On a larger scale, these attitudes may represent a growing movement, termed *consumerism,* which reflects a judgment that organizations have not done their part in protecting the consuming public when they design, promote, sell, and guarantee their products and services.

A recent survey of more than three thousand managers in a variety of organizations, identified the following *business practices* as causes of consumerism's growth.[21] In order of importance, they are: defective products; hazardous or unsafe products; defective repair work; misleading advertising; poor complaint-handling procedures by retailers; advertising that claims too much; deceptive packaging and labeling; poor complaint-handling procedures by manufacturers; failure to deliver merchandise that has been paid for, and inadequate guarantees and warranties.

Important *economic factors* in the growth of consumerism include concern over rising prices, deteriorating product quality, and the impersonal nature of the marketplace.

In response to the needs and desires of consumers, governmental intervention into the manufacture and marketing of products and services has been steadily increasing. Governmental intervention takes the form of various acts and creation of regulatory agencies with a variety of powers. Consumerism, consumer protection, more powerful regulatory agencies, etc., can all be of concern to the manager.

Urban Development   In many areas of the country, because of location and resource potential, organizations have been called upon to give support (and in some cases, take the lead) in community efforts aimed at improving the quality of life within major population centers. This concern over urban development has resulted in a number of significant contributions by organizations.

Typical of some of the programs include the leadership by Ford Motor in the rebuilding of Detroit's downtown area. In addition, Southern Pacific Company helped develop a program for eliminating substandard housing in Watts, and Kodak proposed the establishment of a fund and offered managerial consulting assistance for inner-city business ventures.

Organizations sometimes group together to help solve urban problems. The Allegheny Housing Rehabilitation Corporation, composed of thirty-two large Pittsburgh area companies, was formed to rehabilitate deteriorating inner-city housing. After renovation, the homes are made available to low-income families.

Philanthropic Activities   For many years, organizations have been involved in philanthropic activities. Contributions to the arts, education, hospitals, and a variety of charities have averaged about $2 billion per year. Some of the contributions have been significant. For example: (1) by itself, IBM contributes over $20 million per year to charitable causes; (2) the railroads were instrumental in the formation and development of the Young Men's Christian Association (YMCA); and (3) Texaco has sponsored the Metropolitan Opera radio broadcasts for over forty years.[22]

Some interesting questions develop when one considers philanthropy by private organizations. For example, why do organizations get involved in such activities? Is it to improve profits, is it done to be socially responsible, is it out of the charity of enlightened self-interest, or is it done as a tax write-off?

Let's look at a number of points. First, as an aggregate sum, $2 billion is a large figure, but it represents less than 1 percent of corporate pretax profits. In addition, the federal government has encouraged organizations to make charitable donations, as long as the sum does not exceed 5 percent of net income. In this sense, the tax

The Manager's Job

Cornell Maier of Kaiser Aluminum and Chemical

Although many executives of large corporations are steering their firms increasingly toward social consciousness, Cornell Maier, chairman of Kaiser Aluminum and Chemical, does so with gusto. He goes out of his way to look for ways he and his firm can perform good community deeds. To Mr. Maier, corporate citizenship is a matter of conviction and remarkable personal interest. He feels that business has a clear social responsibility. Business is frequently critical of government involvement, but he believes that if business wants to criticize, it needs to become more involved itself.

To be sure, Kaiser does all the traditional things expected of a leading community employer. In its Oakland, California, headquarters area, for example, it hires disadvantaged workers, donates money to education, supports the local symphony and downtown renovation efforts, and offers financial and personnel backing to the United Way fund.

What sets Kaiser Aluminum and Maier apart, however, is their nontraditional activities. One of the newest is the unique "Summer on the Move" work-learn program developed by Kaiser and the Oakland school district. Some 120 high school students attend morning classes, taught by University of California at Berkeley professors, and work in meaningful jobs in Oakland companies in the afternoon. In a related project, Kaiser has "adopted" Oakland High School, an aging inner-city school with a heavy enrollment of minority students. The company is buying needed facilities for the school and donating the time of its employees to work directly with the students.

In a different vein, Kaiser also has launched a program to educate the families of its employees about the company and its role in society. Mr. Maier believes that executives have done the worst possible job in helping their families understand the world of business and the free enterprise system.

Mr. Maier attributes his crusading interest in social responsibility and free enterprise to his upbringing. Born to poor parents in South Dakota, he was reared by his mother who scratched out a living for her family as a grocery and department store clerk. Following a service stint in World War II, he graduated from UCLA and began his climb up the management ladder at Kaiser.

"I believe I'm one of the luckiest people on earth," he reflects. "I came from a very poor family, more so than most people. I was blessed with a mother who would rather starve than take aid. Also, I was fortunate in going to work for Henry Kaiser, the founder of the company. He was a great inspiration. He believed strongly in community service, and it rubbed off on me."

Suggested from S. Modic, "Maier," *Industry Week* (October 29, 1979): 56-58.

write-off argument appears not to be very valid. Second, while many managers believe that charitable contributions are good for the organization (economically and in a social responsibility sense), the courts have stated that organizations need not show a direct benefit to profits by such contributions. In a stockholders' suit against A.P. Smith Company, the New Jersey Supreme Court ruled that the company's contribution to a university was "essential to public welfare, and therefore, of necessity to corporate welfare." In other words, the court's decision implied that an "indirect benefit" was sufficient justification for such donations.

Organizations differ in the way they handle or manage philanthropic activities. Some make it a board of directors' decision, others place it within the authority of an executive, and many others establish foundations for the sole purpose of being responsible for these activities. Whatever the reasons or ways of managing philanthropic activities, they will continue to be an important function in many organizations.

Social Audit

As the concern over the social behavior of organizations continues to grow, a need to find new methods to measure the performance of organizations in social activities has developed. The makeup of today's society almost ensures that organizations will be held accountable for a much broader range of activities and results than ever before.

This broadened responsibility has led many organizations to develop specific assessment procedures that concern their involvement, support, and contributions to programs that deal with social issues. Several approaches under the heading of a *social audit* have been developed.[23] Four of the most used are the following:

- *Inventory approach.* A descriptive method that lists the organization's social activities for a specific period of time. While it serves the purpose of informing various segments of society of the organization's activities, it provides little information on the extent of involvement or about the effectiveness of the programs.

- *Cost approach.* In addition to a list of activities and programs this approach develops an accounting of the amount spent, in terms of financial outlays, resources utilized, and so on. Since it notes only the "inputs" into social programs, not "results," such an approach gives no indication of the effectiveness of the activities.

- *Program management approach.* Along with a list of programs and costs, this approach requires a statement on whether the organization has met its goals with respect to each program. While it is more detailed than either of the previous two, this approach has been criticized because many of the stated goals can not be measured quantitatively.

- *Cost-benefit analysis.* Incorporating the features of the other three approaches, the cost-benefit method attempts to quantify both the costs and values of each program. Such an analysis commonly follows an accounting procedure in which "assets" and "liabilities" are listed. Here also, the problem of quantifying the benefits and then comparing them with actual costs remains unresolved.

As the concept of organizational social responsibility increases in importance, more and more organizations will attempt to develop methods for overcoming some of the problems of the current social audit approaches. The American Institute of Certified Public Accountants, the American Accounting Association, and the Securities and Exchange Commission have each offered procedures and guidelines for measuring the social performance of organizations.

Organizational Goals and Social Behavior

In the second part of the chapter, we attempted to illustrate the importance of the organization's social behavior within the concept of goals. The relationship may be best summarized in exhibit 4-8, which presents a number of points. First, a thorough analysis of the subject recognizes that a three-way interaction involving the organization, society, and government exists. Second, each of the three main components in the exhibit has its own goals. Goal achievement must not only be measured by the number of interactions (organization-society, organization-government, and so on), but by whose point of view one takes.

Third, establishing social goals, as with setting market goals, implies that detailed policies, plans, and procedures must be developed, as well as information and feedback systems and a commitment to achieve the goals. In other words, a managerial system must be created that plans and controls an organization's social activities.

Exhibit 4-8
Organizational, Societal, and Governmental Goal Action

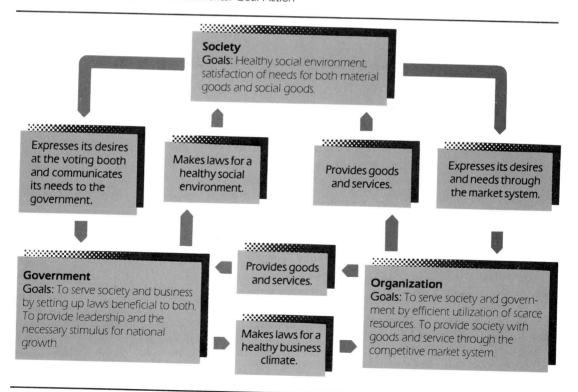

Adapted from C.W. Gross and H.L. Verma, "Marketing and Social Responsibility," *Business Horizons* (October 1977): 80

POINTS TO CONSIDER
An Emphasis on Managerial Skills

1. **Strive for goal acceptance and commitment by employees.**
    Goals do not implement themselves. They need the support and cooperation of the entire organization. To reach high levels of achievement, it is necessary for employees both to accept and be committed to the organization's stated goals.

2. **Emphasize communication of goals.**
    The communication of goals involves at least three aspects: goals that are clearly stated; goals that are "filtered down" to all involved managers; and, the need to give feedback on performance of goal-related activities.

3. **Watch out for goal conflict.**
    A production supervisor who is given goals that include "maintaining a production rate of 95 percent of capacity" and "reduce production costs by 12 percent" quickly becomes aware that the two goals are in conflict. Goals and priorities must be balanced.

4. **Rewards should be clearly tied to goal achievement levels.**
    People join organizations because they seek rewards (pay, advancement, promotion, recognition) for their levels of input. When rewards for goal achievement are not related to employee performance, the person realizing this may draw away from goal achievement.

5. **Economic and social goals must work together.**
    Profit-making organizations survive and grow to the extent that revenues exceed costs; not-for-profit organizations continue to exist by providing services within certain cost constraints. Economic performance and social responsibilities must not negate each other.

SUMMARY FOR THE MANAGER

1. Some form of goal setting is necessary for the organization's proper performance and for the manager's job. Goals, the product of some environmental analysis (internal and external), serve as guiding principles for planning, organizing, leading, controlling, and change. Goals are among the major factors in the management process.

2. Goals can be viewed from a variety of standpoints. They can be short term or long term; the focus can be on maintenance, improvement, or development; and they can vary through the different organizational levels, from corporate goals to individual goals. In addition, no matter what type of organizational goal we are discussing, it must be clearly stated and understood, consistent with the organization's resources, and not too difficult to achieve.

3. Most managers attempt to achieve more than one goal during a particular period of time. This multiplicity places emphasis on how and when goals will be measured. In addition, it affects: (a) how they relate to the goals of other managers; (b) which goals are more important than others; and (c) the necessity for a "give and take" or balancing relationship between goals.

4. Market, profit, and efficiency goals have been the main focus for managers for many years. Non-market or social goals have been increasing in importance as the organization's relationships with society and the environment gain attention. The result is increasing complexity in the manager's job. This situation also creates a dilemma. With rapidly changing societal values, is the manager's real responsibility to the organization, to the stockholders, to the larger com-

munity, or elsewhere? The answer is "all of the above," which requires the manager to set priorities and balance organizational goals.

5. There are at least three frameworks for analyzing social behavior by an organization: (a) social obligations; (b) social responsibility; and (c) social responsiveness. Depending on the dominant framework, organizations will adopt a number of different response patterns when faced with increasing social pressures. Tokenism, functional change, and structural change are the three most used response patterns. Whichever response pattern is chosen, the manager must recognize that each differs in the cost, support, and commitment necessary from the organization, and the acceptance level by society of these responses can also vary greatly.

6. The major issues on which some social goals can be developed are increasing at a rapid pace. Examples include: (a) pollution control; (b) affirmative action; (c) consumerism; (d) urban development; and (e) philanthropic activities. Each requires special knowledge and expertise by the manager.

7. While it is difficult for the manager to be against anything that is for the good of society, a careful analysis of constraints is needed. Above all, the manager must not relegate economic success to secondary importance for fear of jeopardizing the future survival of the organization. Also included in an analysis of constraints are the identification of potential side effects of social actions, the limits of the organization's authority, and the resources that can be allocated.

 REVIEW AND DISCUSSION QUESTIONS

1. Discuss the origins and importance of organizational goals.
2. What are the criteria for organizational goals? Why are they critical for goal achievement?
3. In what jobs would qualitative goals be acceptable?
4. Why is it important for goals to be assigned priority ratings and balanced?
5. What skills and roles are emphasized in organizational goal formation?
6. Can you identify organizations that: (a) meet their social obligations; (b) are socially responsible; and (c) are socially responsive?
7. What are the advantages and disadvantages of the three responses to social pressure?
8. What social issues or projects are important in your community?
9. Can you suggest how an organization's socially conscious behavior can be better measured?
10. Is it possible for organizations to operate with a single overriding goal, or are multiple goals needed? Is there a relationship between the size of the organization and the number of operative goals?

NOTES

1. See M. D. Richards, *Organizational Goal Structures* (St. Paul, Minn.: West, 1978), p. 1.
2. A. Etzioni, *Modern Organizations* (Englewood Cliffs, N.J.: Prentice-Hall, 1964), p. 6.
3. Richards, *Organizational Goal Structures*, p. 5.
4. A. Raia, *Managing by Objectives* (Glenview, Ill.: Scott, Foresman, 1974), p. 38.
5. C. Perrow, "The Analysis of Goals in Complex Organizations," *American Sociological Review* (December 1961): 856.
6. Ibid., p. 857.
7. G. A. Steiner, "Comprehensive Managerial Planning," in Stephen J. Caroll et al., *The Management Process* (New York: Macmillan, 1977), pp. 126-27.

8. See C. J. Loomis, "The Leaning Tower of Sears," *Fortune* (July 2, 1979): 78-85; and R. Loving, Jr., "W.T. Grant's Last Days as Seen from Store 1192," *Fortune* (April 1976): 108-14.
9. R. J. Flaherty, "The Singular Henry Singleton," *Forbes* (July 9, 1979): 48.
10. G. W. England, "Organizational Goals and Expected Behavior of American Managers," *Academy of Management Journal* (June 1967): 108.
11. S. P. Sethi, "A Conceptual Framework for Environmental Analysis of Social Issues and Evaluation of Business Response Patterns," *Academy of Management Review* (January 1979): 64.
12. Ibid., pp. 65-66.
13. M. L. Lovdal, R. A. Bauer, and N. H. Treverton, "Public Responsibility Committees of the Board," *Harvard Business Review* (May-June 1977): 40-54.
14. See D. C. Aker and G. S. Day, "Corporate Responses to Consumerism Pressures," *Harvard Business Review* (November-December 1972): 114-24; and V. M. Buehler and Y. K. Shetty, "Managerial Response to Social Responsibility Challenge," *Academy of Management Journal* (March 1976): 67-78.
15. P. F. Drucker, *Management: Tasks, Responsibilities, Practices* (New York: Harper & Row, 1974), p. 338.
16. E. E. Jennings, "Make Way for the Business Moralist," *Nation's Business* (September 1966): 90.
17. M. Friedman, "Does Business Have a Social Responsibility?" *The Magazine of Bank Administration* (April 1971): 14.
18. K. Davis, "The Meaning and Scope of Social Responsibility," in *Contemporary Management*, ed. J. W. McGuire (Englewood Cliffs, N.J.: Prentice-Hall, 1974), p. 616.
19. See W. Kiechel III, "The Admiralty Case of the Century," *Fortune* (April 23, 1979): 78-89; M. H. Zim, "Allied Chemical's $20 Million Ordeal with Kepone," *Fortune* (September 11, 1978): 82-91; and S. Solomon, "The Asbestos Fallout at Johns-Manville," *Fortune* (May 7, 1979): 196-206.
20. T. Alexander, "A Promising Try at Environmental Detente for Coal," *Fortune* (February 13, 1978): 94-102.
21. S. A. Greyser and S. L. Diamond, "Business Adapting to Consumerism," *Harvard Business Review* (September-October 1974): 38-58.
22. N. K. Barnes, "Rethinking Corporate Charity," *Fortune* (October 1974): 169-82.
23. See R. A. Bauer and D. H. Fenn, Jr., *The Corporate Social Audit* (New York: Russell Sage Foundation, 1972); and D. Fetyko, "The Company Social Audit," *Management Accounting* (April 1975): 135-48.

A CASE FOR ANALYSIS

Social Responsibility
The Beta Oil Company

Troy, Colorado, was a small town of slightly over thirty-five hundred people located at the base of the Rocky Mountains. Since it was founded in the late nineteenth century, the majority of its residents were employed in agricultural work. Much has happened to this town in the last ten years. It has gone from a sleepy little town, to a boom town, to a town in deep trouble.

Everyone knew that the town sat on top of one of the largest shale oil deposits in the world. However, as long as the technology to mine and produce crude oil from the shale rock cost more than normal drilling operations for crude, the town would not gain any economic value from the deposits. This was to change dramatically with the oil crises of the 1970s.

Early in 1975, Beta Oil Company, one of the nation's largest energy producers, announced plans for the construction of a pilot plant to produce crude oil from shale rock in Troy. The pilot plant would be built on a small scale in order to examine the feasibility of a new process that it had leased from a West German firm. When fully operational, the plan would only produce four thousand barrels of oil per day. If the process proved to be economically feasible in line with rising crude prices around the world, Beta had developed plans to expand the plant to produce seventy-five thousand barrels per day. Even though the plant was to be small initially, Beta planned to employ nearly five hundred people during the test plant stage at the facility. With their families, the total influx of new residents working for Beta would be about 1,800, increasing the size of Troy by over 50 percent.

Beta knew from past experience that such a venture would hit Troy like a big shock wave. In order to smooth out any problems and try to make the transition for the residents of Troy as easy as possible, the company established a unit of over thirty employees who were part of the Community Affairs Development Group. Attached to the Personnel Department, the main function of the group was to work with various community leaders and townspeople with regard to employment opportunities, pollution control, community development, and so on. The plant opened in 1977.

The impact of the Beta plant was felt almost immediately by the town. Homes and apartments were built for the transferred employees along with new schools and churches. The company built a new water purification plant for the town. To finance the construction of the new schools and sewer system, it was necessary for the town and district to be bonded: that is, capital improvement bonds were sold and were to be paid off on a yearly basis through a new taxing plan. In addition, the police and fire departments were expanded to handle the

town's growth. In total, slightly over $3 million in bonds were sold.

For the next four years the town of Troy grew tremendously. Beyond the private and public facilities, the state began a program to double the number of miles of paved roads, new snow removal equipment was purchased for the winter months, and various state agencies established regional offices in Troy. The town also drew a significant number of new merchants and other businesses to serve the growth in population. A program was even started to expand and refurbish the small downtown area. By the summer of 1982, the population of Troy had grown to over eight thousand residents.

In the fall of 1982, however, things changed rapidly. Beta announced that it planned to shut down the pilot plant in early 1983. After four years of operation, the company concluded that even with rising crude prices, the present process was still not economically feasible. A skeleton work force of less than thirty employees would continue to maintain the plant, as the company left open the decision to restaff the plant, if and when a new process technology could be developed by the company's scientists or a new license could be obtained.

The impact on the people and businesses of Troy was immediate and disastrous. The town was faced with numerous problems including developing means of paying off the bonds, how to keep the new businesses in town, and what to do about the sudden unemployment of teachers, city employees, and other workers. The high probability of a 25 percent increase in school and sales taxes was particularly distressing to the residents. Private groups would be hit particularly hard. Already committed were two new churches, a new department store, and land had been purchased for a new city park that would include little league facilities and a large swimming pool. One saving feature of the town's rapid growth was the building of a new ski resort five miles from the city limits. However, this was a seasonal business that could not counter the impact of the plant's closing.

The townspeople were extremely bitter and angry with Beta Oil. They felt that the company had lied to them about the plant and its future. They claimed that if they had known that the plant could possibly be closed within five years, the present expansion would never have been contemplated. In defense, Beta pointed to documents and communication that its Community Affairs Development Group had given to the town's leaders which clearly stated the potential temporary nature of the plant. They also pointed to the many facilities, especially the new water works, that the company had donated. Finally, they indicated that a new technology that they were developing in their laboratories in Houston showed great promise and that there was a good chance that the plant could be reopened within three years.

Questions for Discussion

1. Evaluate the social behavior of Beta in this case.
2. Could the company have handled matters any differently so that the current problems could have been alleviated?
3. Does Beta have any obligation to the town of Troy at the present time?
4. Evaluate the role of the leaders of the town in this case.

EXPERIENTIAL EXERCISE
Organizational Goals

Purpose

To study how goals influence managerial decision making.

Required Understanding
The reader should be familiar with the issues and concepts associated with organizational goals.

How to Set Up the Exercise
Set up groups of four to eight persons for the thirty- to forty-five minute exercise. The groups should be separated from each other and asked to converse only with their group members. Before joining the groups, each person is asked to complete the exercise alone, and then the groups should form and reach a consensus.

The Situation
Assume you are a member of the top management team of the Davis Industrial Gas Products Company, a large industrial gas supplier located in St. Louis, Missouri. The firm specializes in packaging and distribution of gas cylinders to industries within a two-hundred mile radius of St. Louis. The firm's main products are oxygen, hydrogen, helium, acetylene, and other gas

mixtures used, for example, in hospitals (oxygen) and manufacturing firms (acetylene for metal cutting). The company purchases the various gases from chemical plants located nearby, processes the gases to improve the levels of purity, and then packages the product in different size cylinders. The firm's financial statement at the end of 1989 is shown in exhibit 4-9.

Exhibit 4-9
Income Statement
of Davis Industrial
Gas Products
Company

Income Statement: 1983

A.

Revenue		$10,000,000
Expenses		
Raw materials	$5,600,000	
Salaries, wages, and benefits	2,850,000	
Depreciation	1,000,000	
Research and development	200,000	
Advertisement	50,000	
Training	40,000	
Public relations	60,000	
Interest expense	300,000	
Total Expenses		10,100,000
Net Loss		($ 100,000)

B. Net profit (loss) and revenues for four years

Year	Revenue	Net Profit (loss)
1983	$10,000,000	($100,000)
1982	9,500,000	380,000
1981	8,000,000	300,000
1980	7,800,000	($ 50,000)

Your top management team will meet shortly to discuss four problems or issues currently facing the company. Decisions on each of the four problems *must be made at this meeting*. The four problems, which are *occurring at the same time*, are:

Problem 1   The local civic club has frequently complained to your company and to the city council about the air pollution originating from your plant. Although this is not proven, the age of your equipment suggests a number of leaks could exist. Your legal advisors have told you that to prove air pollution exists and that Davis is the source would take a minimum of two to three years. Your options are to repair the possible pipe leaks, costing approximately $100,000 (option 1), or to do nothing (option 2).

Problem 2   Your company is pleased with the success in sales of oxygen cylinders to the area hospitals. Your management believes that there is good growth potential in selling other products to hospitals as well as in selling oxygen in smaller cylinders to doctors' offices and nursing homes. You would, however, face increased competition in each of these markets. The new equipment and increase in sales force will cost $300,000. The options are to spend the money (option 1) or to do nothing (option 2).

Problem 3   The relations with the union representing your hourly workers has been tense for years. The three-year union contract will expire in four months. In your initial bargaining, the union has made known its demands for a significant increase in wages and benefits. The cost over the three years of the new contract would be $250,000. Finished inventory at the time of the contract's expiration would last six to eight weeks. Your options are to settle with the union on terms similar to their demands (option 1) or to take a chance on a long and bitter strike (option 2).

Problem 4 Your company has experienced a 35 percent turnover in supervisory and management personnel during the past year. A recent consultant's report indicated that not only are salaries for managerial personnel below the area average, but the company is in need of extensive revisions in its training and development programs. Your options are to spend $100,000 on personnel selection, training, development, and salary upgrading (option 1) or to do nothing (option 2).

Instructions

1. *Individually*, group members should:
   a. Make decisions on each of the four problems discussed above. Remember: (1) decisions on these problems must be made now; (2) the problems are occurring simultaneously; and (3) you have only two options on each problem.
   b. *Rank in order* the underlying goals or objectives that were important in your overall decisions. Mark your responses on exhibit 4-10.
2. As a *group*, repeat the above decisions. Mark group choices, distribution of individual choices, and group ranks on exhibit 4-10.

Exhibit 4-10
Goals in Decision Making

Problems	Individual Decisions		Distribution of Individual Decisions In Group		Group Decision	
	Option 1	Option 2 (circle your choice)	Option 1	Option 2	Option 1	Option 2 (circle group choice)
1. Air pollution	1	2			1	2
2. Improved product line	1	2			1	2
3. Labor relations	1	2			1	2
4. Management development	1	2			1	2

Rank in Order the Underlying Goals in Individual and Group Decisions
(1 = Most important; 6 = Least important)

Goal	Individual Rank	Group Rank
1. Company survival		
2. Improved competitive position		
3. Community image		
4. Stability		
5. Employee relations and development		
6. Internal cost control		

Strategic Planning

Chapter Outline

Key Points

1. Strategy involves choice, direction, and integration.
2. Strategic planning is the process of identifying, selecting, implementing, and evaluating basic courses of action for the organization.
3. The evolution of strategic planning involves the phases of financial planning, forecast-based planning, externally oriented planning, and strategic planning.
4. Stage I of the strategic planning process (foundations) involves the consideration of mission, culture, and performance.
5. Stage II, analysis, concerns an environmental analysis, an internal resource analysis, and a matching analysis.
6. Stage III, decision, concentrates on selecting a strategic option, implementing it, and evaluating it.
7. Small businesses, not-for-profit enterprises, regulated organizations, and European firms can all put strategic planning to good use.

Texaco, Inc.

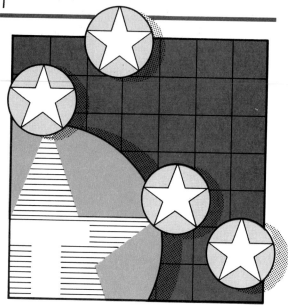

During the 1950s, Texaco, Inc. adopted a long-range strategy centered on a key assumption—that crude oil supplies would remain cheap and readily available for years to come. From that strategy came a number of important plans. Oil exploration was minimized, while significant efforts went into establishing strong market positions in all fifty states. To service those markets, Texaco built an expensive network of regional refineries across the U.S. and invested in a huge central refinery in Trinidad to process its foreign crude oil and service foreign and domestic markets. For twenty years, this strategy worked well—that is, until the effects of OPEC were felt.

Texaco, more so than any other large oil company, was ill prepared for the upheaval of the 1970s, when crude oil surpluses quickly became shortages, producing countries expropriated supplies, prices soared, and oil became a political weapon. When the foundations of its earlier strategy collapsed with the oil embargo of 1973, Texaco faced this turbulent environment with one of the weakest exploration programs, one of the largest—and least efficient—refining and marketing systems, and with little in the way of diversification to balance out the oil shock. To make things worse, Texaco's management was highly centralized and inward looking, making it the least responsive and most inflexible of its competitors.

Led by its new chairman, John K. McKinley, Texaco is beginning to respond from this crisis. Interestingly, its new strategy is based on the inverse of the 1950s strategy—the fact that oil is in short supply and increasingly expensive, forcing it to look to new ventures.

Strategically, Texaco will remain solidly in the energy business. While the traditional oil business will supply needed cash, the new strategic plan counts heavily on synthetic fuels and other alternative energy products to provide the earnings base for the company in the 1990s. This calls for a gradual, but steady shifting of capital investments away from conventional oil operations and into coal gasification, shale oil, and tar sands projects. So as not to be caught as it was in the 1970s, Texaco's new strategic planning system calls for a yearly evaluation, identifying revisions or adjustments where needed.

Organizationally, McKinley restructured the company to be more decentralized. More importantly, he altered its internal culture. Where once secrecy, parochialism and a militarylike hierarchy ruled, now is found decentralized decision making, openness, and a new innovative outlook. New management, it is hoped, and a new strategy will bring Texaco back to its once-dominant position in energy.

Adapted from C. E. Curtis, "Texaco's Single-Minded Boss," *Forbes* (May 9, 1983): 61-67; and "Texaco—Restoring Luster to the Star," *Business Week* (December 22, 1980): 54-61.

5

As the opening case on Texaco, Inc. illustrates, managers frequently face situations in which the direction of the organization must be altered or revised. The momentum for this change may originate from a number of sources, including a dynamic external environment, a revised set of goals, or new management. Whatever the source, how managers approach this situation involves the use of strategic planning.

Our approach to the study of strategic planning involves a discussion of three main parts. First, we will highlight the meaning of strategy and strategic planning—the purposes and evolution of strategic planning. The second part of the chapter will discuss the steps in the strategic planning process. Finally, we will point out how strategic planning has been used in a variety of businesses and enterprises.

# Strategy: A Foundational Concept

Observing and studying organizations frequently offers a paradoxical view. On one hand, organizations are based on belief that order will overcome chaos. This will become clearer in our discussion of organizational design in chapters 8 and 9. On the other hand, organizations are rarely stagnant entities—they are constantly changing products, services, policies, and markets. Planning is the function that transcends both order and change.

For our purposes, we will define *planning* as the set of policies, procedures, methods and decisions used by managers to achieve stated organizational goals and which are intended to affect the future. This definition incorporates two key concepts—goals and strategies.

Goals, as we discussed in the last chapter, are essentially desired end results the organization wishes to achieve. *Strategy*, on the other hand, is a comprehensive and integrated framework that guides organizational choices and decisions that determine the nature and direction of organizational activities.[1]

Strategy is an important concept to an organization, for its selection determines the organization's success and, possibly, its survival. Examples of strategies are all around us: Goodyear chose to expand its tire business while Goodrich decided to concentrate its resources on its chemical operations; Westinghouse decided to exit from the consumer appliance market while General Electric chose to increase its investment; until its merger with National Air Lines, Pan Am chose to ignore domestic routes in favor of international travel while TWA built its international traffic on a strong domestic route system, and so on. Characteristics of strategy include:

- Strategy involves a *choice* of particular actions or activities. These choices involve products and services, the groups to be served, and the allocation of resources.

- Strategy is a function of *direction*. Choice implies what is to be done—direction concerns how it will be done.

- If more than one strategy has been chosen by an organization, they must be *integrated* into a strategic framework, much the same as goals are ordered. If choices are made without the benefit of a framework, the manager abdicates the control over the direction to whoever happens to be making decisions. Tying all these concepts together is something we call *strategic planning,* the subject of this chapter.

What Is Strategic Planning?

Since planning has emerged as a key managerial function, it has been described as long-range planning, corporate planning, comprehensive managerial planning, integrated planning, and of late, strategic planning. For our purposes, we will use the term strategic planning.

We will define *strategic planning* as: The process of identifying, selecting, implementing, and evaluating basic courses of action for the organization. Involved are analyses of the external and internal environment, strategic alternatives and choice, implementation, and evaluation.[2]

What Strategic Planning Is

Strategic planning is a process.[3] This means that there is a rational sequencing of activities. Among its activities are the analysis of the external environment and the organization's internal resources (chapter 3), formulating and/or revising corporate goals (chapter 4), and strategy selection, implementation, and evaluation.

Strategic planning deals with the future impact of current decisions. This means that it tries to identify a series of cause-and-effect relationships that may result from a particular set of decisions. If the results of the planning effort are not to the liking of the managers, they can change the decision and develop alternative plans.

Strategic planning is made up of a *series* of plans, each of which differ in such characteristics as time frame, focus, and level of management involved. Strategic planning is more accurately viewed as an integrated structure of goals, strategies, policies, and procedures of the organization.

"Gentlemen, I have an uneasy feeling that this is more than just an ordinary slack period."

From the *Wall Street Journal*-Permission, Cartoon Features Syndicate.

What Strategic Planning Is Not

Strategic planning is not forecasting. As we discussed in chapter 3, forecasting is an attempt to predict the value of some particular variable (i.e., sales or market share) based on current data, information, or trends. In reality, forecasting is a pre-activity, or premise, of strategic planning.

Strategic planning does not attempt to make future decisions. Quite the opposite, it concerns the impact of current decisions on future events and the alternatives that are open to the manager.

The end product of a strategic planning effort is not inflexible doctrine. Rather than be set in concrete, a strategic plan should be an open, flexible document that adjusts to changes in the external and internal environments. Strategic planning attempts to invent the future for the manager; but when changes do occur during the period of the plan, certain alternatives can be chosen to keep the organization on track. This is what we will refer to in the next chapter as contingency planning.

Purposes of Strategic Planning

When managers engage in strategic planning, they may have a number of different purposes in mind. Some of these purposes are shown in exhibit 5-1.

IBM's entry into consumer markets (personal computers) and A&P's revitalization of its grocery stores indicate a change of direction for the companies. Weeding out poor performers is a tag given to Westinghouse (home appliances), RCA (computers), and PPG-Industries (soda ash) for eliminating unprofitable product lines.

We may see Anheuser-Busch (attempting to control manufacturing costs in a changing beer market) and Nestlé (centralizing international operations) as examples using strategic planning to gain control of operations. Procter & Gamble and 3M Company are interested in the strategic planning process for identifying and training competent managers. Adapting to a changing environment could have been the purpose for Hewlett-Packard in their entry into the micro-computer market and Sears' decision to offer financial services in their stores. Finally, we can count Allied Corporation (formerly Allied Chemical Company) as an organization that used strategic planning to pick up the pace of a tired company.

The many uses of strategic planning just add validity to its importance in management. Before we discuss the actual steps in the process, let's discuss its evolution.

Exhibit 5-1
Some Examples of
Strategic Planning
Purposes

1. Change the direction of the company
2. Accelerate growth and improve profitability
3. Weed out poor performers among divisions or units
4. Concentrate resources on important things
5. Gain control of operations
6. Train and develop managers
7. Better adapt to a changing environment
8. Develop better internal coordination of activities
9. Generate options for consideration
10. Pick up the pace of a tired company

 # Evolution of Strategic Planning

Strategic planning, similar to other management concepts, appears to have evolved over time in certain distinct stages or phases. As shown in exhibit 5-2, we have identified four sequential phases—financial planning, forecast-based planning, externally oriented planning, and strategic planning.

This evolutionary pattern can fit two different levels of analysis. First, it can represent the overall development of strategic planning across many industries. In essence, it represents the evolution of the concept itself. Second, it can apply to sequential development for the individual company. That is, as organizations and managers begin to see the benefits of a planning effort, they would expect to see their financial planning activities evolve into more complex forecast-based planning, followed by externally oriented planning, and so on.[4]

Phases of Evolution

Financial planning is a rudimentary form of planning that is usually practiced by most large organizations. Imbedded in the organization's annual budgeting, this process helps develop procedures and policies to forecast revenue, costs, and capital needs for the upcoming year. The organization's strategy is generally an implicit one—that is, the top management team probably knows the capabilities of their competition, what products and markets they wish to enter, the strengths and weaknesses of their internal resources, etc. The strategy is rarely written down, but its effect is felt in how the budget is developed and implemented.

When the complexities of management increase (i.e., number of products, services, and markets served, sophistication of technological development, dynamic and turbulent economic swings), providing direction to the organization may move beyond the capabilities of the most skilled top management team. This situation generally gives rise to the second phase, *forecast-based planning*. This phase is recognized by the establishment of formal planning staffs whose responsibility it is to extend the time horizon for planning beyond the annual budgeting cycle.

Most large organizations are in, or have passed through, this phase of strategic planning. Characterized by the use of more sophisticated forecasting tools (i.e., trend analysis, regression models, and simulation programs), such an approach can be a significant aid to the organization's planning effectiveness. When managers are forced to analyze long-term trends, they can develop more appropriate goals, along with a better appreciation of the long-range implications of certain decisions.

Forecast-based planning is not without its limitations. Managers easily can get bogged down with reams and reams of data and computer output; the separation of planning staff and line managers can give rise to conflict when the people who put the plan together are not the same people who are responsible for putting it into operation; and finally, planning can become an empty exercise when the plan is put in a desk drawer after it has been accepted or when managers are not rewarded for using it.

The above issues have led many organizations to move to phase three, *externally oriented planning*. As exhibit 5-2 indicates, this phase is a quantum jump above the

Exhibit 5-2
The Evolution of Strategic Planning

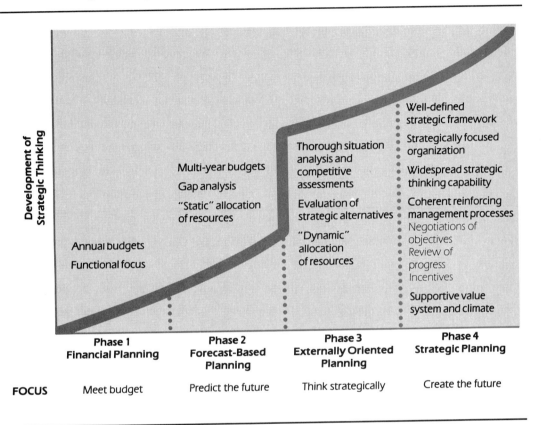

Adapted from F. Gluck, S. Kaufman, and A.S. Walleck, "The Four Phases of Strategic Management," *The Journal of Business Strategy* (Winter 1982): 11.

previous phase in approach and orientation. There are a number of distinguishing characteristics of externally oriented planning:

- The plan begins with a thorough analysis of the environment, including industry and competitor analysis.

- Resources are considered dynamic, not static. That is, an organization's resource profile (chapter 3) can be changed.

- Closely related to the above, plans are viewed in a dynamic rather than a deterministic mode. A strategy need not be only a slight extension of what has been done in the past. More creativity is shown.

- Finally, the key characteristic is that phase-three plans often present not one, but several courses of action. Some are more risky than others—but, more than anything, such an exercise forces managers to think through all their options and the advantages and disadvantages of each.

Externally oriented planning is not without its detractors and problems. Many firms still use an expanded planning staff to develop plans, which can give rise to friction between planners and line managers. As the organization increases its product/service line, there is the problem of increased complexity. Finally, the alternatives generated by the planners may overwhelm many managers. In essence, the combination of the two may lead to information overload for management teams.

The last phase of development is what has been called true *strategic planning*. This phase attempts to incorporate many of the planning benefits noted in previous phases along with some important modifications. These include:

- Establishment of strategic business units (SBU). This means actual strategic planning goes beyond the sole responsibility of top management and is given to lower-level managers, for example product managers, divisional managers, and department managers. Simply, an SBU is a division, department, or unit that has an external market and competitors; its performance is measured in profit and loss; and management has some control over its destiny.[5]

- Instead of putting the plan away once it has been developed, this phase emphasizes total strategic thinking. Strategic planning becomes part of the daily routine as managers are forced to continually think through their actions and decisions.

- Strategic planning performance is built into the organization's reward system (see chapters 12 and 16). The use of the plan cannot be ignored since the manager's merit pay increases and promotions may be heavily based on planning performance.

- Strategic plans should be flexible. Plans are reviewed regularly in light of changes in the environment and adjustments are made if necessary.

As you may have noted, this pattern shows an evolution in the way an organization operates. From a simple budget development process, we have progressed to the use of sophisticated planning tools, a greater concern about the external environment, and to a new way of thinking.

Strategic Planning and Operational Planning

The evolution of the strategic planning concept has given rise to some confusion about what is done, by whom, and when. Frequently, this confusion focuses on the differences between strategic planning and operational planning.

Many people prefer to define strategic planning as activities oriented toward the development and initial communication of corporate (or SBU) plans. On the other hand, activities directed toward implementing plans—those concerned with establishing policies, procedures and emphasizing coordination and the allocation of resources—have been called operational planning. In other words, putting the plan together is strategic planning, while putting it into effect is operational planning.

To avoid confusion, we will consider both these definitions strategic planning. We prefer to call the former the *formulation* part of strategic planning, and the latter the *implementation* part. The implementation function will be covered briefly in the next chapter and in more detail throughout this entire book.

Given this discussion as a foundation, we will now look at what actually is a strategic plan. The next section will highlight the stages and steps involved in strategic planning.

The Process of Strategic Planning

As we discussed earlier, strategic planning is a rational process engaged in by managers. This process, as we will present it, is described in exhibit 5-3. While there may be some disagreement among managers and academicians as to their individual preferences, we believe this model captures the key steps. We also believe that, with minor modifications, the model applies to many different types of organizations, be they small or large, profit or not-for-profit.

Stage I: Foundations

When going through the foundational steps in strategic planning, the manager is really setting the stage for the major parts of the process. In essence, he or she asks the

Exhibit 5-3
The Process of Strategic Planning

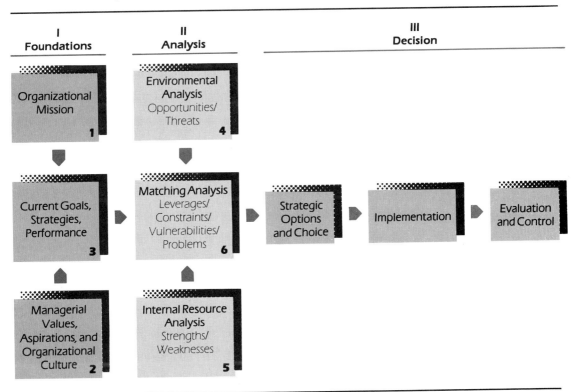

questions: "Where are we?" and "Where have we been?" Issues related to the mission of the organization are at stake, including managerial aspirations, values, and culture, along with the identification of current goals, strategies, and performance.

Step 1: Organizational Mission   The first step in the strategic planning process, possibly the most difficult, is to identify and examine the organizational mission. A mission is usually a general statement of the philosophy of the firm and the direction of its efforts.[6] This statement can include a fairly clear, sometimes written, listing of goals and product/service offerings, and an explicit, or sometimes ambiguous, inference of managerial intentions.

Essentially, a mission statement addresses such questions as, "What business are we in?" and "What business do we want to be in?" For example, United Airlines' original mission may have used the words "Movement of the populace by air with the most efficient and comfortable aircraft available." Over the years, especially with the acquisition of a car rental company and a series of hotels, their mission statement could be revised with the use of the word "travel." When a corporation's mission has changed, its name may also need changing. In this case, United Airlines became UAL, Inc.

Good mission statements are distinguished by certain key characteristics. First, simple statements regarding profit maximization are insufficient. Since organizations impact people, both outside and inside, concern for individual welfare along with social responsibilities to those impacted by the organization's products and services should be mentioned.

Second, mission statements should not be limited to descriptions of current products. Concern should be given to issues related to consumer needs, pricing structure, distribution systems, promotional processes, and manufacturing activities. Finally, the mission statement should not be written so ambiguously that few people can understand it. Being a "good corporate citizen" or "increasing the wealth of the stockholder" are parenthood, peanut butter, and flag statements, but they offer little in the way of what the firm is doing or about to do. In other words, mission statements should be objective and clearly written. Remember—employees and managers in the organization will be reading this statement and using it in their planning activities—a clear meaning is a necessity.

Step 2: Managerial Aspirations, Values, and Organizational Culture   In chapter 3, we pointed out how managerial values can have a significant effect on a person's perceptions, decisions, and general behavior. In the specific case of preparing a strategic plan, the effects of values are no less important.

In addition to managerial values, we would add managerial aspirations and the "culture" of the organization to the list of factors important for preparing the strategic plan.[7] Aspirations—the needs and desires of top management—are crucial elements, for they determine, very simply, what management "wants to do." Even when organizations allow lower-level managers to prepare the major part of a strategic plan, they are affected by certain guidelines and ideas given them by top management.

The influence of top management on strategic planning cannot be underestimated. Examples include Henry Ford II's influence over Ford Motor Company, James

McDonnell's desire for McDonnell-Douglas to minimize its investment in commercial aircraft, Eddie Rickenbacker's tight-fisted cost-control effects on Eastern Airlines, Howard Head's entrepreneurial philosophy on Head Ski Company, William Hewlett and David Packard's desire for teamwork and open communication and its effects on their organization, Hewlett-Packard, Walt Disney's creative thrust, and so on. The lesson is clear—what top management wants must be given strong consideration in any planning efforts.

On a larger scale, strategic planning managers must also recognize the influence of the guiding values and philosophy of the organization—what we call *culture*.[8] Over time, organizations develop certain ways of doing business. These ways become embedded in just about all facets of organizational life and guide most of their activities, in an almost religious way. For example:

- At Delta Airlines, teamwork is threaded throughout all levels. To insure the maintenance of a strong team, no employee has ever been laid off at Delta even in the worst of economic times. Pilots may unload baggage, ticket counter personnel may clean aircraft during slow periods, but everyone has a job. In appreciation of this policy, Delta employees recently banded together and helped purchase a new airplane for the company.

- 3M believes strongly in the creative potential of their people. Not only do they insure that good ideas are given fair hearings, but their belief that large size is a barrier to creativity has resulted in the policy of building small-sized plants. Of their 90 plants, few have more than 250 employees.

- PepsiCo maintains a belief in strong competition, be it external or internal—the key is to win! Managers are rewarded for the degree to which they beat out competition. Pepsi's attack on Coca-Cola (i.e., well-known ''Pepsi Challenge'' taste tests) has become legendary.

- Why do all McDonald's restaurants look the same? One reason is that the values of quality, service, and cleanliness are drilled into all employees throughout their employment period. Spot checks, even by Chairman Ray Kroc, insure adherence to this culture.[9]

- J.C. Penney's may not be as top a financial performer as Sears or Federated Stores, but one thing it stresses above the rest—long-term customer loyalty. Satisfying customer needs comes before all other considerations.

These examples and others are illustrations of the strong influence of organizational culture on various activities and behaviors. Strategic planning documents must recognize the guiding thrust provided by a culture, along with the constraints it provides. A plan which requires a significant cultural change must be looked at carefully. Not that culture does not change; it does, but not overnight.

Step 3: Current Goals, Strategies, and Performance   This last step of the foundation stage concerns an evaluation of what the organization set out to do (goals), how it went about it (strategies), and how well it did (performance). Discrepancies between performance and goals indicate the need for change. This change could involve the mission of the organization, its stated goals, the current strategy or strategies, its method of operation, or its competitive stance.

At minimum, this evaluation should consider all the major functional areas of the business. For example:

Marketing   Such elements as market share and industry position, product-line offerings, effective advertising and distribution channels, etc., are important.

Operations   Aspects to be looked at include cost structure (internal trends and position against competition), plant capacity, employee relations, and so on.

Finance   The indicators here are numerous and easily quantified. The performance and position of the organization can be evaluated with the use of liquidity, profitability, debt, utilization, and equity ratios, together with recent trends in these ratios internally and externally.

Development   This measure can concern at least two factors. First relates to research and development, such as number of new products developed, cost of operation, and future trends. The second concerns the development of people. Human resources, as we stressed in an earlier chapter, must be given strong consideration. Accomplishments in employee training, manpower planning, and management succession should be evaluated.

The examination of these three steps provides management with a good look at the company's foundation—where it is and what it has done. Again, we have termed this the foundation stage because it serves as the basis for the analysis stage.

Stage II: Analysis

With information collected and reviewed from the foundation stage, the next stage of strategic planning for managers to consider is the analysis stage. In this stage, management is concerned with putting together a thorough examination—both external and internal—of the firm's position and possible future directions. As noted in exhibit 5-3, three steps are involved—environmental analysis, internal resource analysis, and an integrated matching (or gap) analysis.

Step 4: Environmental Analysis   An environmental analysis for a strategic plan involves many of the ideas and concepts we discussed in chapter 3. That is, management analyzes the key trends and factors in the economic, social, political, and technological environments. This is also a good time for important inputs from forecasting efforts.

In addition to an analysis of the general environment, at least three other factors need to be reviewed. First, a good understanding of the industry should be developed. In essence, an industry analysis ideally provides a much more detailed look at the specific environment in which the firm competes. Industry structure can have a strong influence in determining the competitive rules of the game as well as the strategies potentially available to the firm.[10] An industry analysis should include the following (see exhibit 5-4):

Bargaining Power of Buyers   The people or organizations that consume the firm's products and services, be they consumers or industrial, need careful attention. How

Exhibit 5-4
Industry Analysis

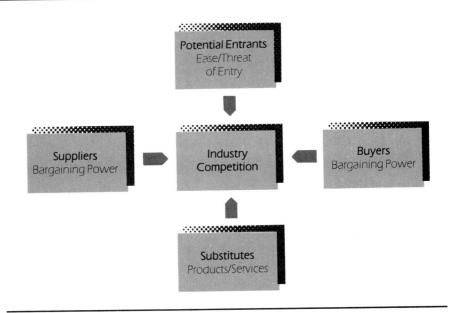

powerful are they, are there few or many, are products from competition differentiated from each other? For example, metal cans for beer and soft drinks make up a
large part of the cost of the products they contain. Such companies as American Can,
the Continental Group, and Crown Cork & Seal would be concerned if their major can
consumers decide to make their own cans.

Bargaining Power of Suppliers   At the other end of the product cycle, trends and
activities associated with raw material suppliers should be carefully analyzed. How
many suppliers exist, how big and powerful are they, are there threats to sudden shifts
in price, quality, and quantity? No doubt, during the oil embargos of the 1970s,
plastic manufacturers were concerned, since petroleum products are one of their key
raw materials.

Substitutes   Rarely are products or services sold without the existence of some
substitutes that are similar in price and performance. Examples include different types
of cord (i.e., steel, rayon, and synthetics) used in tires, cellulose and styrofoam as
substitutes for fiberglass insulation, checking accounts from banks as well as savings
and loans, and the like.

Potential Entrants   History has painfully shown that management needs to look
beyond current competition in analyzing what the future will hold. While entry barriers (i.e., capital equipment in steel manufacturing, technological knowledge in computers) may exist to sufficiently scare future competitors away, this is not always
guaranteed. For example, a major new competitor in word processors is Exxon, an
energy company, with its Quip and Qyx systems; in financial services, major investment companies are faced with competition from Sears; and in the not-too-distant
future, newspaper companies will be faced with stiff competition from cable tv.

The best approach is to follow an industry analysis with a more detailed analysis of key competitors. This competitor analysis should include, for example, some knowledge of competition's goals. If a major competitor establishes a sales growth goal over one oriented toward profitability, management may anticipate strong price competition. Knowing such goals provides an idea of what is driving the competitor.

Identifying the competition's strategies—knowing what the competitor is doing and can do—is equally useful. For example, it took Anheuser-Busch some months before it recognized that Miller Brewing (now owned by marketing-conscious Phillip Morris) would be competing in newly created market segments (i.e., Lite Beer). Or to counter IBM's entry into the personal computer market, Apple Computer began discounting some of its units and offering free software with purchases.[11]

Finally, through analysis, management can develop a good idea of competition's capabilities—what they can and cannot do. General Motors, during the 1950s, probably was not too concerned with overwhelming competition from American Motors, but now it is very concerned with Japanese automakers, because of their strong resource base. Using previous examples, IBM's resource strength and experience and the large number of Sears stores surely was noticed by existing competition in home computers and personal financial services.

Pulling this information together, the end result is the identification of environmental *opportunities* and *threats*. Opportunities give management an idea of what the organization *might do*, while threats indicate some possible barriers to future strategies, something the company *may not do*. Polaroid, for example, may identify opportunities for diversification, upgraded film, and technological innovations, but feel some threats from the growth of 35 mm cameras, videotape products, and the entry of Kodak into the instant camera market.[12]

Step 5: Internal Resource Analysis   Whereas an environmental analysis comes down to identifying what an organization might do, an internal resource analysis focuses on what the organization *can do*. Again, we can go back to chapter 3 for a more detailed discussion of this issue. Exhibit 5-5 also provides examples of key internal resource factors.

Before managers can move ahead to possibly capitalize on environmental opportunities, they must know what, if any, competencies or competitive advantages and disadvantages the organization possesses. These competencies or advantages/disadvantages may originate from any resource base. For example, on the positive side, one can identify Xerox's brand name, Toyota's quality, McDonald's location and service, Maytag's dependability, the image of Mercedes-Benz, DuPont's large, cost-efficient chemical plants, and so on. On the other side, one can point to problems with International Harvester's cash flow, Scripto's poor distribution system in comparison with Bic's, Hooker Chemical's waste dump problems, Firestone's quality problems with its 500 radial tire, and the like.

Similar to the reduction of an environmental analysis to opportunities and threats, the main outcome of an internal resource analysis is the identification of the company's own internal *strengths* and *weaknesses* (see exhibit 5-3). Strengths and weaknesses provide management with an easy-to-grasp idea of which available, or quickly obtainable, resources can support a strategy and which may act as an impediment. Using Polaroid again as an example, we could identify market leadership in instant cameras, strong R&D and marketing functions, and quality products as strengths, while declining sales, product failures (i.e., Polavision), and management turmoil (with the retirement of founder, Edward Land) as possibly weaknesses.

Step 6: Gap or Matching Analysis   A gap or matching analysis is, in its simplest form, the process of integrating the results of environmental and internal resource analyses.[13] The name comes from the identified gap or match between external opportunities/threats and internal strengths/weaknesses.

A gap or matching analysis is an important input into the selection of a strategy. Exhibit 5-6 illustrates this point. Four major elements emerge from a gap or matching analysis—leverages, constraints, vulnerabilities, and problems.

Exhibit 5-5

Resource Profile by Functional Area

	R & D Engineering	Manufacturing	Marketing	Finance	Management
Financial Resources	$ for basic research, new product development, product improvements, and process improvements	$ for plant $ for equipment $ for inventory $ for labor	$ for sales and promotion $ for distribution $ for service $ for market research	Credit rating Credit availability Leverage Price/earnings ratio	$ for planning system $ for control system $ for management development
Physical Resources	Size, age, and location of R&D facilities Size, age, and location of development facilities	No., location, size, and age of plants Degree of automation Type of equipment	No. and location of sales offices, warehouses and service facilities	No. of major lenders Dispersion of stock ownership No. and types of computers	Location of corporate headquarters
Human Resources	Nos., types, and ages of key scientists and engineers Turnover of key personnel	Nos., types, and ages of key staff personnel and supervisors Turnover of key personnel	Nos., types, and ages of key salespeople Marketing staff Turnover of key personnel	Nos., types, and ages of key financial and accounting personnel Turnover of key personnel	Nos., types, and ages of key managers and corporate staff Turnover of key personnel Quality of corporate staff
Systems and Technological Resources	System to monitor technological developments No. patients No. new products % new product sales Relative product quality	Nature and sophistication of: Purchasing Quality control Raw materials Per-unit costs for: Raw materials Direct labor and equipment Productivity Capacity utilization Unionization	Nature and sophistication of: Distribution Pricing Market research Per-unit costs: Sales Distribution and service Key accounts Breadth of product line Brand loyalty Service	Type and sophistication of: Cash management system Corporate financial models Accounting system	Sophistication of planning and control systems Delegation of authority Measurement of reward system Corporate image prestige Influence with regulatory and governmental agencies

Adapted from C. W. Hofer and D. Schendel, *Strategy Formulation: Analytical Concepts* (St. Paul, Minn.: West, 1978): 149.

A *leverage* comes into play when an external opportunity matches an internal strength. In essence, an internal resource appears to support a move (or a strategy) to capitalize on an environmental opportunity. For Polaroid, we could say a leverage exists in upgrading film or further camera innovations because of the support given from market leadership and strong R&D and marketing functions.

A *constraint* exists when capitalizing on an external opportunity may be blocked, or constrained, by an internal resource weakness. In other words, resources may need to be built up before an opportunity can be approached. For example, Polaroid will have to form a strong management team in the wake of Land's retirement before moving toward diversification. Or, the Polavision failure must be carefully analyzed before new product innovation or ventures are contemplated.

Exhibit 5-6
Gap or Matching
Analysis

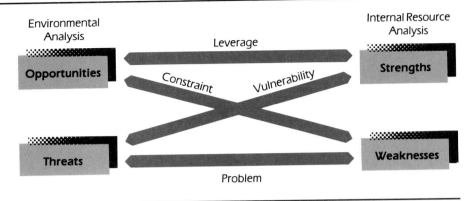

A *vulnerability* is the first use of an environmental threat in our analysis. It represents a situation in which an external force or factor threatens a key internal strength. In other words, an outside element has been identified that poses a problem to an asset of the firm; something the company is doing well is still endangered by something on the outside. In Polaroid's case, one can easily see that Kodak's entry into the instant camera market (or the growth in popularity of 35 mm cameras and home videotape equipment) can threaten Polaroid's strong market leadership.

Finally, a *problem* in gap or matching analysis is seen when an environmental factor hits one of the organization's weak points. The threat may be so severe, it seriously questions the survival of the organization, or, at minimum, its presence puts off plans to capitalize on certain opportunities until the problem is resolved. For Polaroid, the threat from new and strong competition aims right at the heart of its weaknesses associated with declining sales, recent product failures, and management transition.

Our Polaroid example is obviously simplified. Actual matching analyses would be more complex and detailed. What can management do with this information? In essence, an analysis like ours can provide management with certain alternatives from which to choose. The selection of a strategic alternative is the subject of the next stage of strategic planning.

Stage III: Decision

As you may have surmised, the first two stages of strategic planning can involve a great deal of time and effort. And this is as it should be, since making the proper decision is a function of a good foundation and an accurate analysis. With what we have accomplished so far, it is now time to pull it all together and actually select a strategy (or strategies) for an organization.

Stage III consists of three important steps. First, we will identify, evaluate, and choose from among many strategic options available. Second, a crucial step, is to put into effect, or implement, the strategic option we have selected. Finally, we will give attention to the control and evaluation of the effects of our chosen strategy.

Step 7: Strategic Alternatives and Choice   What can be done with the information collected and analyzed in step 6, the gap or matching analysis? This is a question that perplexes many managers and academicians. As a result, a number of different approaches or models have been developed that claim to offer an accurate way of identifying, evaluating, and selecting strategic options.

It is not the purpose of this text to present a lengthy evaluation of each of these models. Other sources and advanced courses are available to satisfy this need.[14] For our purposes, we have selected a model that appears to be the most general and widely used of approaches. Shown in exhibit 5-7, the model is known as the GE (for General Electric) Stoplight Strategy Matrix. Like many other strategic options models, the GE Matrix presents a two-dimensional approach to this problem.[15] The two dimensions should sound familiar:

- *Industry attractiveness* represents our step 4, the result of an environmental analysis. High industry attractiveness may indicate the existence of certain external opportunities, while low industry attractiveness may be the result of external threats.

- *Competitive position* is similar to our external resource analysis, step 5 in the strategic planning process. A weak competitive position could represent significant internal weaknesses, while a strong competitive position is indicative of certain internal resource strengths.

Where a firm's product/product line is located in the matrix depends on what is learned from the matching analysis: leverages in the upper left-hand corner (growth), constraints and vulnerabilities on the diagonal (borderline), and problems (no growth) in the lower left-hand corner.

Consider a hypothetical food products company with three main product lines: fruit juices, breakfast cereals, and soybean products. An analysis of these three product lines indicates that each would be placed in different parts of the matrix: a leverage situation for fruit juices, constraints with breakfast cereals, and problems with soybean products. After placing these product lines (or SBUs) on the matrix, the next step is to identify and evaluate the available strategic options.

For fruit juices, the available options include the strategies of growth, and defense and hold. *Growth* indicates continued investment in the product line to further strengthen its position. Another example could be the situation of Target Stores in their discount store expansion across the country. A *defense and hold* strategy involves maintaining one's strong position in a market. Management may feel comfortable with the current strategy and, thus, wish to hold that position. Other examples include Air Products Inc. with their industrial gases, Wang Labs with word processors, and Motorola with their communication equipment.

Our company's breakfast cereal product line was found to be in a constrained state. Since children are major consumers, this could be due to declining birth rates (external threat) or the availability of substitute breakfast products. The GE model suggests three possible alternatives—shrink, harvest, or rebuild. A *shrink* strategy indicates that the company wishes to maintain a strong position, but the data suggest that the long-term outlook for the product may not be promising. So the company chooses to keep its hand in a smaller, but still visible, product line. This could be the situation

Exhibit 5-7
General Electric's
Stoplight
Strategy Matrix

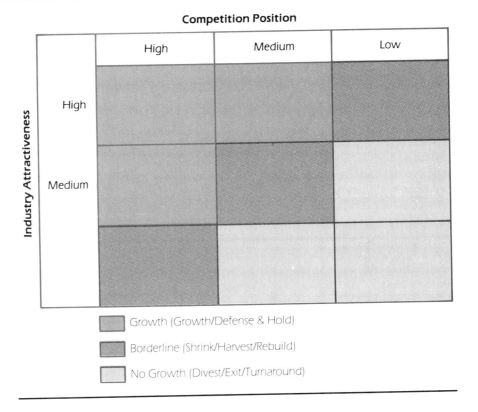

Competition Position

Growth (Growth/Defense & Hold)

Borderline (Shrink/Harvest/Rebuild)

No Growth (Divest/Exit/Turnaround)

faced by Mead-Johnson in baby foods, General Electric with electric coffee percolators, and Celanese with rayon and acetate.[16]

When an organization decides to use a *harvest* strategy, it has chosen to accelerate the shrinking process. In other words, it has taken what it could, or harvested, and has trimmed down its product line. Westinghouse with electronic receiving tubes and Gerber with rubber baby pants are examples. Finally, a *rebuild* strategy indicates that management believes a somewhat bright future exists for the product, but not at levels experienced in the past. The company renews its effort but simply expects less return. A&P's grocery stores and Volkswagen automobiles are illustrations.

The third set of strategies represents those cases where problems exist, as in the soybean product line of our hypothetical firm. This situation could be the result of growing external threats (i.e., many competitors, substitute products) or internal problems such as uncontrolled costs, poor management, or distribution system inadequacies. For this case, management can choose a *divest* or *exit* strategy. The company believes that further competition in the market may result in continuing losses, or worse. A timed exit is, therefore, the proper path. Examples include Woolco's exit from discount retailing, DuPont's from rayon, and RCA's from computers.

If the poor situation can possibly be remedied with work, we can consider a *turnaround* strategy.[17] A turnaround strategy generally involves a combination of two approaches—redefining the market and concentrating on improving operating costs. The first may involve the decision that the company no longer wishes to compete across the total market for a product, concentrating instead on a smaller segment. Crown Cork & Seal's decision to focus on aerosol cans instead of all types of cans and closures, Texaco's decision to sell gasoline in select parts of the country in mostly self-service stations, and American Motors' early strategy to concentrate on small, fuel-efficient cars are examples.

The Manager's Job

C. Edward Acker of Pan American World Airways

There is no in-between for Pan Am—the company either loses big or earns big money, usually in successive years. Faced with this situation, C. Edward Acker, Pan Am's chairman, says he won't accept a salary for 1983 until the carrier returns to continued profitability.

While the entire airline industry is experiencing hard times, Pan Am has special problems. About 75 percent of its revenue comes from international flights. Its major competition is government-owned carriers, which have easier access to new funds and lower labor costs.

The company's strategy, like its financial performance, has been a contradiction. Early in 1980, it won a 10 percent wage cut from its five unions, increased its routes, increased the number of miles flown by 12 percent, and cut fares. In 1982, faced with increased competition and an economic downswing, Acker is forcing another strategy change. Pan Am has sold off much of its real estate holdings to raise cash, plans to reduce its workforce from 30,000 to 25,000, cut flight miles by 8 percent and expenses by 4 percent, while attempting to keep average fares unchanged.

Will this turnaround strategy work? Its success will depend on the cooperation of others. Travel agents, who sell 80 percent of Pan Am tickets, must be convinced that the airline will keep flying; financial institutions want to make sure that the company will be solvent enough to lend it money; and the unions, which have experienced enough labor turmoil to last a lifetime, must go along with additional concessions and no strikes for the company to make it through.

Adapted from John D. Williams, "Pan Am Hopes That a Smaller Work Force and Fewer Flights Will Bring Back Profits," *Wall Street Journal* (October 26, 1982): 31.

In the second part of a turnaround strategy, usually combined with a market re-orientation, management attempts to regain control over operating costs. Two of the most popular approaches are *cost cutting* (i.e., reducing the size of the work force, cutting advertising expenses, reducing inventories) and *asset reduction,* in which certain assets, such as plants, equipment, or total divisions, are sold off. Chrysler's cost cutting and concentration on smaller cars and Firestone's sale of old, costly tire plants are examples. Exhibit 5-8 shows a summary of the strategies.

The exact alternative selected by the organization depends on a number of factors. The quality of information, the severity of the situation, the makeup of the management team, and the resources readily available are all important elements. One of the

Exhibit 5-8
Summary of Strategies

	Growth	Defense/Hold	Shrink/Harvest	Turnaround	Divest/Exit
Objective	Build position for long-term profit	Maintain position for long-term profit	Use position for short-term profit	Short term: Survival Long term: Protected position	Use assets for short term cash flow
Competitive Position	Medium to high	Medium to high	Low to high	Medium to low	Medium to low
Industry Attractiveness	Medium to high	Medium to high	Low to high	Medium to low	Medium to low
Market Share	Build share and diversify markets	Hold share	Protect share and concentrate	Segment market and concentrate	Forego share to increase cash flow
Investment	Maximum possible	Adequate to maintain position	Selected investment for adequate returns	*Short term:* Minimum—focus on cost cutting *Long term:* Minimum in select areas	Minimum

Adapted from L.T. Hosmer, *Strategic Management* (Englewood Cliffs, N.J.: Prentice Hall, 1982): 315.

most important is the particular decision-making style used by the manager. This is the subject of chapter 7.

Step 8: Implementation   Deciding on a strategy is only half the battle. Management must also decide how to put the chosen strategy to work.

Implementation involves a number of important factors, usually associated with the organization's resources. Implementation may require having sufficient financial resources available, insuring that key personnel are trained and in place, that the organization's structure is appropriate for the new strategic direction, that key functions such as marketing and production are properly organized, and that new or revised policies and procedures are written and communicated to employees.

Since this subject area is so detailed, we have chosen to cover it in subsequent chapters, beginning with chapter 6. Later chapters will cover key aspects of organizational design, human resources, production management, and the like.

Step 9: Evaluation and Control   A strategy, as we have discussed, is a direction the organization chooses to take. That direction is one through which a goal, hopefully, will be achieved. Thus, approaches should be developed and put in place that insure that the strategy is achieving the desired results. This is the function of strategic evaluation and control.

Evaluation of a strategy, the process of determining whether a strategic choice as implemented is meeting the goals of the organization, can include a number of different criteria. According to Tilles and Rumelt, some of the criteria to consider are:[18]

External Consistency   Does the current strategy fit with the demands of the external environment? Holiday Inn hit the nail on the head with roadside motels, as did 3M with Scotch Tape, and McDonald's with its breakfast menu.

Internal Consistency   Does the strategy fit with stated goals and internal resource capabilities? What the organization wants to do (goals) and what they can do (resources) must be consistent with what they plan to do (strategy). Hewlett-Packard saw this when deciding not to compete in the low-price pocket calculator market—they were more oriented to high technology applications, not consumer products. Braniff Airlines did not—they attempted to expand their route structure beyond the capabilities of their resources.

Competitive Advantage   Does the strategy provide for the creation and/or maintenance of a competitive advantage in a select area or product? Ideally, an organization should be able to do something better than anybody else, which is a competitive advantage. Coleman lanterns (features), Mercedes-Benz autos (quality), Coca-Cola (brand name), and DuPont chemicals and fibers (cost leadership) are examples.

Acceptable Degree of Risk   Does the strategy fit with the risk preferences of the organization? Is the chosen strategy more or less risky than experienced by the organization in the past? Boeing's 757 and 767 aircraft represent an investment that exceeds the net worth of the company. While risky, the decision is not unlike other projects (i.e., 747) previously implemented. On the other hand, the result of Chrysler's restructuring will indicate whether the organization will actually survive.

Contribution to Society   Is the strategy consistent with a desired contribution to society? As we discussed in the last chapter, social goals (and the strategies developed to achieve these goals) are integral to an organization's goalset.

Stimulus   Does the strategy constitute a clear stimulus to organizational effort and commitment? A strategy not only provides direction to the organization, it should be an energizing factor that enhances employee motivation, effort, and commitment. Delta's teamwork stimulus, Procter & Gamble's commitment to product quality, 3M's innovative orientation, and Bechtel's involvement in international project development are examples. Without the commitment and backing of the firm's employees, a strategic plan could simply be filed away in a desk.

Organizations conduct strategic control—the actual monitoring of performance—in a variety of methods.[19] Among the most popular are:

- Management control, which is based on past organizational performance, historical data, or performance measurement.

- Performance management, which focuses on behavioral aspects of control.

- Real-time control, which emphasizes the use of computers to provide management with current and timely information.

- Adaptive control, which sets into action a program that will respond to unexpected changes.

- Strategic control, which provides for mechanisms to alter a strategy when deviations in performance are noted. We will discuss this type of control in the next chapter as contingency planning.

These control methods are always used in an integrative manner; that is, more than a single method is used at any one time. Part 5 of the text is devoted to the very important topic of control.

Strategic Planning in Other Businesses

As you may have recognized, our previous discussion was primarily oriented to the uses of strategic planning in large, profit-making enterprises. Strategic planning, however, can be used in many types of organizations. As the following discussion will show, strategic planning can be used in small businesses, not-for-profit organizations, regulated businesses, and foreign organizations.

Strategic Planning and Small Businesses

The use of strategic planning in small businesses offers some unique advantages and disadvantages.[20] On the positive side, an organization's small size may not present the complexity and detail faced by strategic planners in larger firms. In fact, the small business may be considered simply a strategic business unit (SBU). Other advantages include limited products, services, and markets served, the relatively small resource base, and a limited number of options.

On the disadvantage side, some equally significant issues exist. First and foremost, the executive team is usually small, sometimes only one person. This executive, or entrepreneur, may have always operated the firm from his or her own instincts and sees little use in a more formalized procedure. Second, information and data to prepare an external and internal analysis may be limited, if they exist. Third, key employees usually have gained their skills through experience rather than with the use of systematic procedures, and resistance to change may develop. Other problems may include the constraint of limited resources and the issue of company ownership.

Small business managers' experiences with strategic planning point to the need for possible modifications in the process we introduced earlier in this chapter. First, the process need not be as detailed or lengthy as practiced by large organizations. It could involve simply responding to the questions:

- Where are we?
- Where do we want to go?
- Can we get there?
- How can we get there?
- What decisions must be made to get there? How do we monitor performance?

Second, because of an organization's small size, most if not all key employees can make inputs into the process. This allows the company to use important expertise and contribute to the development of employee commitment and communication. In essence, it becomes a valuable learning experience for all involved.

Finally, top management (or the top manager) must be willing to give strategic planning a chance. The manager must recognize that his or her company has become a growing enterprise, no longer a ''mom-and-pop'' store. There is a need for taking the planning out of the mind of a single person and spreading the responsibility around. The benefit of this is that the process of transforming a company into a formal organization is enhanced.

Strategic Planning and Not-for-Profit Organizations

Many experts in strategic planning agree that the use of this important managerial tool is increasing in small businesses. But in the not-for-profit area (educational institutions, social service agencies, religious organizations, and various governmental units), the use of strategic planning is not so pronounced.

We can best understand the reasons for this situation by identifying the key differences between the corporate planning model and the not-for-profit model.[21] As we have pointed out, the corporate model stresses clear goals, a detailed strategy formulation process, and a strong emphasis on implementation and control. Various systems are in place to support the strategic planning effort. These include structural, reward, informational, and authority systems.

In the not-for-profit model, some key differences constrain the application of a traditional strategic planning effort. First, rarely are the goals and objectives of not-for-profit enterprises clearly delineated, communicated, and put in measurable terms. Phrases like market share, return on investment, and sales margin just do not apply here. Only in financial survival is there some similarity.

Second, the consumers of not-for-profit services and products are frequently dispersed and not readily identified. This is compounded by the third factor, namely that not-for-profit organizations usually do not have the resource capabilities to conduct or accurately interpret data from strategic planning analysis. Finally, from a human resource point of view, not only are many members of such organizations part-time or volunteer, they also may have a stronger commitment to the profession or clientele than to the organization itself.

Those not-for-profit organizations using strategic planning have successfully done so with some important modifications. First, the planning model is simplified to incorporate three steps: (a) a strategic profile, keyed to identifying what the organization is doing, has done, and how well; (b) testing for the consistency of the match between strategy, environment, resources, and values; and (c) strengthening the evaluation process.

One promising development may help bring about more use of strategic planning in not-for-profit organizations. This is the decision of corporations to ''lend'' key managers to these enterprises for a period of time. United Appeal, the Girl Scouts, and various government agencies have borrowed managers. These managers frequently bring with them a great deal of corporate experience in planning activities. When they leave, there is a high probability that the organizations will incorporate some of their helpful practices into their daily routines.

Strategic Planning and Regulated Businesses

Similar to the situation with not-for-profit organizations, there is a dearth of strategic planning literature for regulated companies. This is surprising, because outside influences, including regulation, are important factors in management for many organizations. As a consequence of the influence of these external ''stakeholders,'' managers will have to invest more time, money, and effort in working outside the organization to develop more sympathetic audiences who are more closely attuned to corporate goals and priorities.[22]

As more firms are involved in some form of regulation, the nature and scope of strategic planning will have to adapt. Some issues that have confronted regulated businesses in their strategic planning exercises are:

Environment The units and constituencies of the firm's external environment become fewer and more easily identified. As a result, planning efforts become more directed toward anticipating the actions and decisions of these particular outside elements.

Focus The focus for strategic planning shifts from emphasis on the consumer to emphasis on the regulatory agency. This is because the agency holds the greatest influence over the organization.

Time Under regulated conditions, the planning time horizon is lengthened. Decisions impacting such industries as banking, insurance, and utility companies rarely are made quickly, and, when made, usually are in effect for a longer time.

Strategies Given the restricted environment, focus, and lengthened time frame, regulated firms have tended to adopt more programmed-type strategies. That is, since their environment is limited, so is their list of strategic options.

In a regulated environment, because of the inherent restrictions, experts believe that organizations will achieve more success when their managers begin to adopt strategies that are more political and social in orientation over those that are solely derived from economic issues. This does not mean that capital, cash flow, and the cost structure of operating a regulated business are not important. What it does mean is that the strategic planning manager must develop new managerial skills to effectively deal with an influential regulatory body.

Strategic Planning in European Businesses

Strategic planning in foreign organizations appears to take two forms—those conducted by the state or a state-supported agency and those conducted by individual firms. Of the few reported studies on strategic planning in foreign countries, the vast majority have focused on European organizations, particularly in England, France, Holland, and Germany.[23]

In general, the findings reveal that European firms recognize the importance of strategic planning, but they are behind the U.S. in using and developing it. In particular, it was found that:

- Of the firms studied, the usage ranged from 40 percent in England to less than 20 percent in France. Similar findings in the U.S. indicate usage approaching 80 percent in large enterprises.

- All studies agree on the lack of clarity and precision in goals. Profitability goals, for example, were mentioned by 100 percent of British firms, 70 percent from German, and 50 percent from French. In France, growth was mentioned on a par with profitability.

- Similar to U.S. firms, the time frame for strategic plans ranged from three to five years.

- Few European organizations were actively involved in environmental scanning.

■ The introduction of strategic planning seems to have followed this sequence: U.S. firms to European subsidiaries of U.S. firms to European firms.

The reasons behind these findings are complex and beyond the scope of this book. Suffice it to say that they probably involve culture, types of markets, differing consumer needs, and state of the economy. The application of strategic planning in European firms appears to offer a number of opportunities for managers.

 ## POINTS TO CONSIDER
An Emphasis on Managerial Skills

1. **Strategic planning is more than predicting the future by extrapolating from the present.**
    When an organization depends too much on forecasting as its planning method, or projects solely from current activities, products, and markets, it may be putting a straitjacket on the future.

2. **Make sure that line managers are involved in the planning process.**
    One of the early problems faced by organizations in using strategic planning occurs when a planning staff alone develops the plans. The problem is that line managers are asked to implement a plan which they have had little say in developing.

3. **A completed strategic plan is not an end in itself.**
    Formulating the strategic plan (i.e., steps 1 through 7) takes time and effort. Don't let the enthusiasm decline—remember, a well-developed plan that is poorly implemented is not going to work.

4. **Strategic plans don't necessarily cope with change—managers do!**
    A strategic plan should serve as a guideline for action. When new problems develop, managers must be allowed to deviate from the plan. Flexibility, not rigidity, is a key word for planning.

5. **Make sure you have identified the proper focus for strategic planning.**
    This is the important strategic business unit concept (SBU). It appears to be beneficial to have people involved with products, markets, and service they know best.

 ## SUMMARY FOR THE MANAGER

1. Strategy involves choice, direction, and integration. It is a comprehensive and integrated framework that guides organizational choices and decisions, which in turn determine the direction of goal achievement activities.

2. Strategic planning is the process of identifying, selecting, implementing, and evaluating basic courses of action for the organization. It is not solely forecasting; it does not attempt to make future decisions; and the end result is not an inflexible document.

3. The many purposes of strategic planning include changing the direction of the organization, weeding out poor performers, gaining control over operations, identifying and training managers, and picking up the pace of a firm.

4. The evolution of strategic planning, as a concept and as used in an organization, generally involves four phases: financial planning, forecast-based planning, externally oriented planning, and formal strategic planning.

5. Stage I of the strategic planning process, foundations, involves establishing the organization's mission, recognizing the importance of managerial aspirations, values, and culture, and evaluating current goals, strategies, and performance.

6. Analysis, the second stage, concerns the preparation of an environmental analysis, evaluating internal resources, and performing a matching analysis.

7. Stage III, the decision sequence, focuses on identifying and evaluating strategic alternatives and choices, implementing the strategic plan, and evaluating and controlling performance.

8. The application of strategic planning is not limited to large, profit-making enterprises. Strategic planning has potential for effective use in small businesses, not-for-profit organizations, regulated firms, and foreign companies.

 # REVIEW AND DISCUSSION QUESTIONS

1. Why has strategic planning become so popular with managers?
2. What effect do managerial values and organizational culture have on the strategic planning process?
3. What managerial skills do you believe are acquired through involvement in strategic planning activities?
4. Why is an environmental analysis stressed so heavily in strategic planning?
5. What is meant by a matching analysis?
6. What is the difference between a harvest and a turnaround strategy?
7. What is a competitive advantage and why is it important to organizations?
8. What is a strategic business unit?
9. Why is it important to have line managers involved in formulating strategic plans?
10. What problems face managers in not-for-profit organizations in using strategic planning?

NOTES

1. K. A. Andrews, *The Concept of Corporate Strategy* (Dow Jones-Irwin: Homewood Ill., 1971), p. 26.
2. G. A. Steiner and J. B. Miner, *Management Policy and Strategy* (New York: Macmillan, 1982), p. 8.
3. G. A. Steiner, *Strategic Planning* (New York: The Free Press, 1979), pp. 13-16.
4. F. Gluck, S. Kaufman, and A. S. Walleck, "The Four Phases of Strategic Management," *The Journal of Business Strategy* (Winter 1982): 9-21.
5. W. E. Rothschild, "How to Ensure the Continued Growth of Strategic Planning," *The Journal of Business Strategy* (Summer 1980): 11-18.
6. D. F. Harvey, *Business Policy and Strategic Management* (Columbus, Ohio: Merrill, 1982), p. 16.
7. Andrews, *The Concept of Corporate Strategy*, pp. 103-17.
8. See T. E. Deal and A. A. Kennedy, *Corporate Cultures* (Reading, Mass.: Addison-Wesley, 1982).
9. T. J. Peters and R. H. Waterman, *In Search of Excellence* (New York: Harper and Row, 1982), p. 15.

10. M. E. Porter, *Competitive Strategy* (New York: The Free Press, 1980), pp. 3-33.

11. "The King of Beers Still Rules," *Business Week* (July 12, 1982): 50-54.

12. P. W. Bernstein, "Polaroid Struggles to Get Back in Focus," *Fortune* (April 7, 1980).

13. See C. Hofer and D. Schendel, *Strategy Formulation: Analytical Concepts* (St. Paul, Minn.: West, 1978).

14. Porter, *Competitive Strategy*, pp. 361-67.

15. "General Electric's Stoplight Strategy for Planning," *Business Week* (April 28, 1975): 49.

16. K. R. Harrigan, "Strategies for Declining Industries," *The Journal of Business Strategy* (Fall 1980): 20-34.

17. C. W. Hofer, "Turnaround Strategies," *The Journal of Business Strategy* (Summer 1980): 19-31.

18. R. Rumelt, "The Evaluation of Business Strategy," in W. F. Glueck, *Strategic Management and Business Policy* (New York: McGraw-Hill, 1980), pp. 359-67; and S. Tilles, "How to Evaluate Corporate Strategy," *Harvard Business Review* (July-August 1963): 111-21.

19. Harvey, *Business Policy and Strategic Management*, pp. 312-30.

20. F. F. Gilmore, "Formulating Strategies for Smaller Companies," *Harvard Business Review* (May-June 1971): 70-84.

21. M. L. Hatten, "Strategic Management in Not-For-Profit Organizations," *Strategic Management Journal* (April-June 1982): 89-104.

22. J. F. Mahon and E. A. Murray, Jr., "Strategic Planning for Regulated Companies," *Strategic Management Journal* (July-September 1981): 251-62.

23. M. A. Salas and M. Montebello, "Strategic Management in Western Europe" in W. F. Glueck, *Strategic Management and Business Policy* (New York: McGraw-Hill, 1980), pp. 339-47.

A CASE FOR ANALYSIS

Strategic Planning
Winnebago Industries

When John K. Hanson retired in the mid-1970s, he felt comfortable that the company he had founded and served as chairman, Winnebago Industries, had a bright future. Then the energy crisis hit, and the firm's gas-guzzling, lumbering recreational vehicles looked like they were driving Hanson's enterprise to the end of the road. Not willing to allow this to happen, Mr. Hanson came out of retirement in 1979 to rescue the company.

He wasted little time in making changes. Immediately, he took over the jobs of president (from his son John V. Hanson) and chairman (from J. H. Bragg). Both men left the company. Then he initiated a large-scale cost-cutting program, which involved selling two RV assembly plants and reducing the work force from 4,000 to 1,400. The cost-cutting paid off in reducing the company's breakeven point by one-half, enabling it to report a significant profit in 1982.

With the company's short-term future no longer in doubt, Hanson turned his attention to more long-term strategic issues. Today, his main thrust is the development and sale of two RVs radically different from Winnebago's traditional highway giants. The new models will be small, vanlike hybrids some 20 feet long and powered by front-wheel-drive diesel engines. Given the names Centauri and LeSharo, they will retail from $20,000 to $25,000, depending on optional equipment. In Hanson's opinion, the buyers of his new models will be "baby-boomers" (now approaching middle age) who will appreciate the van's 6-foot standing space and 22-24 mpg. Hanson states, "We're concentrating on what no one else has or will have."

Not everyone is buying into Hanson's new strategic plan. Many analysts have raised questions not only concerning the strategy itself, but about how it will be implemented. For example, some are concerned that the 2-liter engine powering the new vans will provide little passing power for such a large body. In addition, since the engine is being built by France's Renault, RV mechanics will have to journey to Winnebago's headquarters in Forest City, Iowa, for costly training programs to learn how to service the unfamiliar engine. Apparently dealers also recognize these problems—less than 10 percent of Winnebago's 350 dealers initially signed up to sell the new product line.

By far the most serious criticism comes from industry analysts who claim that the big RVs still represent the fastest-growing segment of the market. Countering Hanson's demographic conclusions, these analysts point out that the baby-boom consumers were also the individuals who earlier purchased the big muscle cars of the 1960s and 1970s (e.g., Pontiac GTO, Olds 4-4-2, Plymouth Roadrunner). Assuming readily available fuel supplies, it is projected that these people would rather purchase an RV with sufficient power and comfort. This large RV market has been neglected by Winnebago for years. Lacking new large models or innovative features, the company has slipped from first place in a market that it had continually dominated.

Undaunted, Hanson is moving ahead on other plans to rejuvenate the company. In addition to the new vans, he has also set up a new ventures group that is spinning off fresh ideas. These include producing open-air trams for amusement park transportation systems, as well as building vehicles designed to transport wheelchair passengers. In accordance with the recreational mission of the firm, Hanson is licensing Winnebago's name (for a hefty fee) to a wide array of products including outdoor clothing, sleeping bags, and other camping gear. The company will also introduce a new 35-foot RV in 1983. Do you think Hanson is listening to his critics?

Adapted from H. S. Byrne, "Recreation Vehicles Start Selling Better, Sparked by Falling Rates, Gasoline Prices," *Wall Street Journal* (April 14, 1983): 29; and "Winnebago Industries: Gambling on Two Hybrids to Win Back Lost Territory," *Business Week* (November 15, 1982): 147.

Questions for Discussion

1. What is your evaluation of Hanson's turnaround strategy?
2. The success of Winnebago's two new van products will depend on the accuracy of the environmental analysis. Do you agree with Hanson or the industry analysts? Why?

3. How will the new strategy be implemented? Do you think it will work?
4. In one paragraph, write out a mission statement for Winnebago today that would be acceptable to Mr. Hanson. Would your personal mission statement be any different from Mr. Hanson's? In what way?

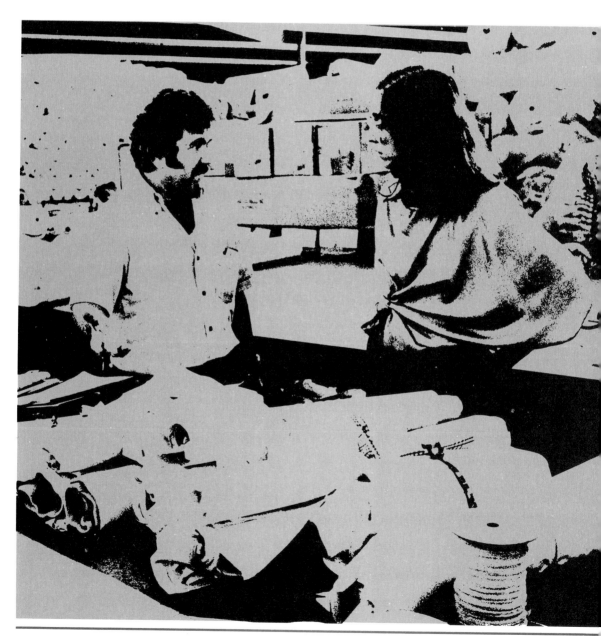

Planning in Action

Chapter Outline

Key Points

1. The cycle of planning involves different times, people, levels of management, topics, and responsibilities.
2. The dimensions of planning involve type of plan, time frame, elements, repetitiveness, and focus.
3. MBO is a process that enables individual managers to get involved in the planning process.
4. Contingency planning concerns anticipating the occurrence of possible events and the changes in the plan that might be required.
5. Scenarios, nominal group technique, and computer simulation models are some of the many planning aids available to managers.

Gulf Oil Corporation

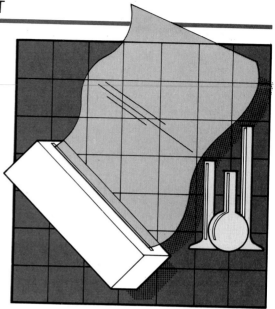

In 1978, Gulf Oil Corporation received what might be called a nasty surprise from a competitor. Halfway toward its five-year goal of gaining and holding the number two position in the market for low-density polyethylene film (used in household food wrappings, sandwich and garbage bags), Gulf was jolted by Union Carbide's announcement that it had developed a new process to make low-density polyethylene at a cost 20 percent less than Gulf's conventional method.

In seeking to attain the number two position in the low-density polyethylene film market, the chemicals division went about its planning: looking at its industry potential for growth, its competitors, its market position, and any inherent risks, as well as the funds needed to reach its goals. But Gulf's problems show that any plan is only as good as the assumptions and savvy underlying it. Gulf had forecast a projected growth in demand of 10 percent or more in each of the plan's five years. To meet such a demand, Gulf added into its plan the cost of a new plant to be built in 1979. In addition, a major assumption of the plan was that since technological breakthroughs in the manufacture of polyethylene were highly unlikely, research and development spending could be kept to a minimum. Not only did the Union Carbide announcement throw a rock into these assumptions, but market growth turned out to be only 8 percent annually, calling the new plant into question.

The conception of Gulf's initial strategy for its chemicals business, the dovetailing of this into the overall organizational plan, and now the problems in those plans are typical of what organizations throughout the U.S. are facing these days. Questions of how to design plans and how to meet—or better still, anticipate—

threats from competitors and a host of other outside factors have become of prime concern.

Divisional plans and corporate plans are two very different animals. A business plan usually covers a plan for a single product or group of related products, while a corporate plan seeks to unify all the product and service lines of an organization and point them toward an overall goal. Today most of the action is at the divisional level, where sophisticated tools and techniques permit analysis of such things as market growth, pricing, and the impact of governmental regulation and also permit the establishment of a plan that can sidestep threats from competitors, economic cycles, and social, political, and consumer changes.

But today corporate planning is still very fuzzy and ill-defined. The people who have risen to power now are simply continuing what was for them a successful strategy— stability and minimum risk. The new style of planning, which requires line managers to be creative, flexible, and entrepreneurial, could end up breeding a whole new type of manager.

Adapted from "The New Planning," *Business Week* (December 18, 1978): 62-68.

6

In the last chapter on strategic planning, we focused our discussion on planning efforts aimed at major directional changes in the organization. While this corporate, or total organizational view of planning is important, the effects of planning are felt throughout the entire firm.

Much of what goes on in the organization feels the results of planning. Planning can involve the chief executive as well as department managers; it can concern broad strategies or unit policies and procedures; functions affected include marketing, manufacturing, personnel, R&D, finance, and so on; and the time frame can involve day-to-day activities or those five years down the road. As the introductory case illustrates, planning (particularly contingency planning) also can involve abrupt *revisions* due to unforeseen changes.

In this chapter, our objective is to discuss some of the finer points of planning activities in organizations. In the first of three parts, we will focus on how strategic plans work their way through the organization. This includes discussions of the planning cycle, the basic elements of planning, and the use of management by objectives (MBO) in support of planning directives. Part two will concern how plans are changed in response to changing conditions. We have called this contingency planning. Finally, we will close the chapter with a discussion of some of the most popular planning aids.

 ## The Planning Cycle

From the time broad corporate goals and strategies are formulated to the time final department budgets are approved and the plan is put into action, many people are involved in the planning process. As shown in exhibit 6-1, the degree of involvement and the subjects discussed involve what we will call the planning cycle.

Consider the case of Kellogg Company, the largest producer of breakfast cereals in the U.S. Facing changing consumer tastes and a projected slow growth of traditional cereals (e.g., Corn Flakes), company executives decided to increase their product line by adding health-oriented cereals that are low in sugar and sodium.[1] How would this new strategy cycle through the organization?

According to exhibit 6-1, *Cycle 1* involves top- and middle-level managers who develop the overall plan.[2] This could include establishing product-line goals (e.g., 4 percent market share with $200 million in sales within two years after introduction); concentrated efforts by the health cereal product manager (i.e., middle-level manager) to set priorities, timetables, and revised strategies, and approval of the program by top management.

In *Cycle 2*, all major levels of management are involved. We see the formal strategic plan reviewed, approved, and given to each of the functional managers (e.g., sales, production, finance) for study and recommendations. This latter step concerns, for example, what production will need to do in producing this new product, and the costs, quantity, and equipment involved. Other functional managers would be given responsibility for their part of the product.

Exhibit 6-1
Organizational Planning Cycles

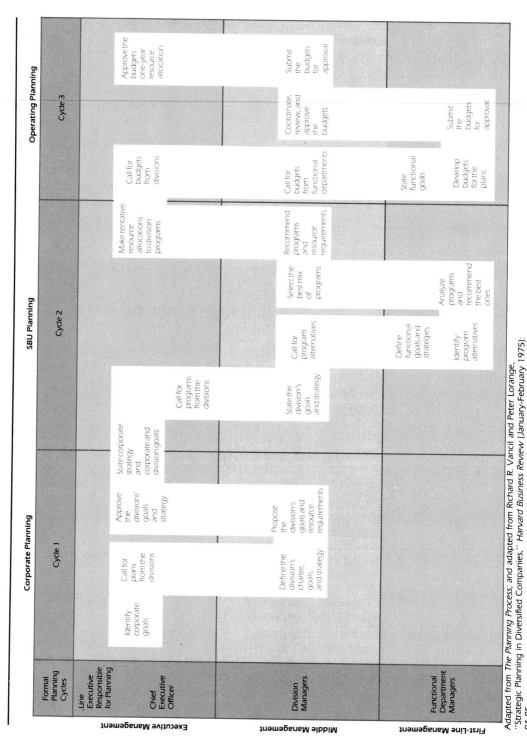

Adapted from *The Planning Process*; and adapted from Richard R. Vancil and Peter Lorange, "Strategic Planning in Diversified Companies," *Harvard Business Review* (January-February 1975): 84-85.

Finally, in *Cycle 3*, the focus is on the financial aspects of the plan. Budget development at all levels and from all divisions is the issue; budgets are planned, coordinated, submitted, reviewed, and approved.

The planning cycle involves many people, levels, functions, approaches, topics, and time frames. This is what we call the *dimensions* of planning, which is the subject of the next section.

Dimensions of Planning

With our discussion of the planning cycle, we have given an overview of the various details associated with planning in organizations. As shown in exhibit 6-2, we refer to these details as the dimensions of planning. Five dimensions are most frequently discussed—type, time frame, elements, repetitiveness, and focus.

Exhibit 6-2
Organizational
Planning
Dimensions

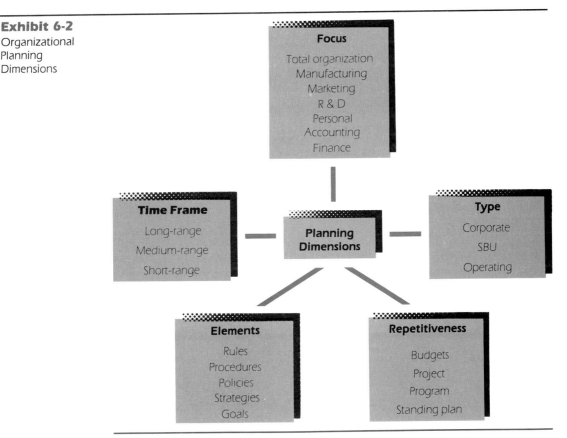

Suggested from G.A. Steiner, *Top Management Planning* (New York: Macmillan, 1969), p. 12.

Types of Plans

Categorizing plans by type may mean different things to different people. It could mean the level of management involved, from chief executive to middle-level manager to first-line manager. It can also be interpreted as the particular unit affected, from the total organization down to the department level. Finally, it could involve the differences between developing the plan (formulation) and putting it into effect (implementation).[3]

We prefer a method of categorizing that includes all of the above. That is, our method involves concern for the level, affected units, and place in the planning process. As shown in exhibit 6-2, the first type of plan, with which we should be quite familiar, is *corporate strategic planning*. Here we are concerned with plans that affect the entire organization, are usually developed by top managers, and often (but not always), are long-term in nature.

The most important aspect of this type is that it is original, energizing, and decisional. It is original because it is the starting point of the formal planning process for the total organization. It is energizing because it stimulates and motivates employees to work toward achieving the organization's goals. Finally, it is decisional because it sets the foundation for all plans, policies, and procedures to follow.

The second type of plan is the *strategic business unit (SBU) plan*. Here, as we discussed in chapter 5, attention is focused on the unit that has primary responsibility for the particular product, product line, or service. In the earlier example, Kellogg may establish three main SBUs: cereals (including the new health cereals), frozen foods, and dairy products. Taking the lead from the corporate strategic plan, the focus of this type of plan is on the product affected and how it fits into the total organization.

Finally, the third type of plan is called an *operating plan*, or sometimes, a tactical plan. Here, as shown in exhibit 6-3, attention switches to the ''nitty-gritty''—promotional programs, labor needs, cash flows, product development, inventories, distribution systems, and the like. In most cases, this type of plan involves the lower levels of management and is oriented toward day-to-day or month-to-month concerns. The key aspect of operating plans is that, more than any other type of plan, they involve coordination and control of critical internal flows of resources.

Time Frame

A second important planning dimension concerns the time frame, or length of the planning horizon. Three planning horizons are usually identified—long-range, medium- or intermediate-range, and short-range plans.

Long-range plans are those that deal with the decisions about the broad competitive and technological aspects of the organization, as well as the allocation of resources over an extended period of time. Inherent in a long-range plan is its congruence with stated goals and strategies, its particular degree of involvement with various organizational units and functions, and a provision for periodic review and revisions.

Medium or *intermediate* plans generally have a planning horizon of between two and five years. These plans are usually more detailed than long-range plans in their involvement of organizational functions (i.e., marketing, production, R&D).

Exhibit 6-3
SBU and Operating Plans

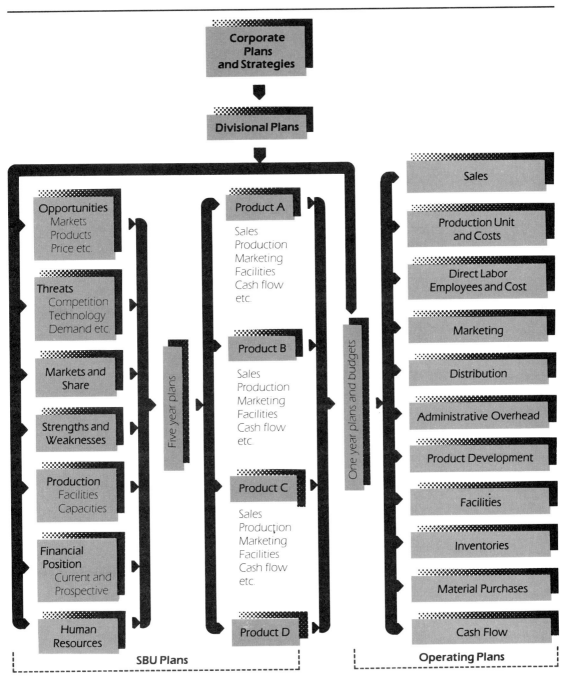

Adapted from G.A. Steiner, J.B. Miner, and E.R. Gray, *Management Policy and Strategy*, 2nd ed., (New York: Macmillan, 1982), p. 426.

Short-range plans, like medium-range plans, are an extension of long-range plans. The planning horizon usually extends to about a year and includes more specific plans with respect to plant locations, work methods, inventory plans, employee training, and budgeting requirements.

The time frame of long-range plans varies by industry. Typically, most people consider plans incorporating five, ten, or fifteen years long-range plans. However, as shown in exhibit 6-4, this can vary by industry. For example, retail firms may plan ahead only one to two years in clothing goods, but five to eight years concerning store construction. A natural resource company, such as Weyerhaeuser, may plan ahead for twenty or more years when considering the planting and harvesting of trees.

Planning Elements

A number of different elements are involved in an organization's planning effort, some of which we have already discussed. The major difference between the elements is the scope of the activities involved. These are shown in exhibit 6-2.

Goals and strategies, as we have discussed, concern desired end results and particular choices of action. As such, they have the broadest scope of any planning element.

Policies, which are narrower in scope, are standing guidelines for decision making. Policies not only flow from goals and strategies, they also set up boundaries around which decisions are made. In doing so, policies direct the behavior and actions of employees so that they are consistent with stated goals. Examples of policies are shown in exhibit 6-5.

Procedures are even narrower guides to decision making. Unlike policies, which many times involve the entire organization, procedures tend to be applied to departmental or interdepartmental activities. Examples include how customer orders are to be handled, how people are hired, how suppliers are paid, how price changes by competitors are monitored, and so on.

Exhibit 6-4
Time Span Covered by Long-Range Plans

| | | | | | Time | | | | |
| Industry | 3-5 Years | | 6-10 Years | | Over 10 Years | | Other | | Total |
	No.	%	No.	%	No.	%	No.	%	
Food	22	84	3	11	0	0	1	4	26
Chemicals	40	87	5	10	0	0	1	2	46
Oil	10	58	5	29	1	6	1	6	17
Steel	7	63	2	18	0	0	2	18	11
Machinery	26	92	1	3	0	0	1	3	28
Electronics	34	91	1	10	0	0	2	5	37
Retail sales	25	89	3	10	0	0	0	0	28
Total	164	84	20	10	1	0	8	6	193

Source: L. W. Rue, "The How and Who of Long-range Planning," *Business Horizons* (December 1973): 29.

Exhibit 6-5
Example of
Organizational
Policies

Product Policies
1. Determining factory layout.
2. Maintaining movement of materials and work in process.
3. Production control and scheduling.
4. Machine utilization and inventory control.

Marketing Policies
1. Product—nature of product line, sizes, and quality of product or service.
2. Price—methods of pricing, trade, and quantity discounts.
3. Promotion—advertising, personal sales effort, and sales promotion.
4. Place—channels of distribution, types of outlets, and transportation methods.

Financial Policies
1. Established fixed and variable expense relationships.
2. Determining the degrees of risks involved and cost of capital in capitalizing potential earnings.
3. Utilizing financial ratios and control techniques in analyzing sources of funds.
4. Determining the methods used in valuing inventories in depreciating fixed assets.

Personnel Policies
1. Developing job descriptions.
2. Recruiting and hiring employees.
3. Use of testing programs in establishing applicant capabilities.
4. Implementing training programs.
5. Developing fair compensation and fringe benefit programs.

Purchasing Policies
1. Deciding if established suppliers will be used exclusively, or if orders will be placed with any available vendor.
2. Determining how much should be bought on each order.
3. Determining the minimum inventory size of each item in computing the reorder point.
4. Making use of purchase discounts.

Rules are the narrowest element, since they deal with specific activities or behaviors. In general, rules usually guide the activities of individual employees who take care of specific assignments on their jobs. A requirement for safety glasses in a plant, employment hours, and deadlines for submission of reports are examples. As the most explicit planning element, rules do not serve as general suggestions for decision making, but act as substitutes for them.

Repetitiveness

Plans can also be categorized by how often they are used, or the degree of repetitiveness. Two distinctions are usually made—standing plans and single-use plans.[4] *Standing plans* are those developed by the organization to direct activities that will occur frequently over time. These include certain policies, methods, and standard operating procedures. Examples include methods for computing employee overtime, the procedure for taking an x-ray in a hospital, and the policies for handling an overdrawn checking account.

Single-use plans deal with ill-structured, novel, or non-repetitive problems that are designed to fit a specific situation and may become obsolete in time. Three types of single-use plans can be found in organizations. First, *programs* are broad activities that include many different functions and interactions. Examples include implementing a new motivation program based on profit sharing, or a store expansion program by a retail organization.

Second, *projects* are single-use plans that are much narrower and complex than programs. Examples are a project to review and revise de-icing procedures on aircraft to improve wintertime safety or a project to redesign packages for over-the-counter drugs. The outcome of a project may become a policy of the organization.

Finally, the third single-use plan is the *budget*. A budget is a plan for allocating certain financial resources to organizational activities and units. We will cover the topic of budgets in greater detail in chapter 15.

Focus

The final planning element concerns the particular function, unit, division, or department affected by the plan. This can mean marketing, personnel, accounting, production, R&D, finance, information services, or the total organization.

Exhibit 6-6 illustrates the interrelationships between the different planning dimensions. Note that while all managers are involved in some facet of planning, there are important differences between management levels and what these managers do.

 # Management by Objectives

Putting any type of plan, especially a strategic plan, together is a major project for most organizations. Getting individual managers working together to follow the plan and achieve stated goals is another issue itself. One of the most popular and frequently used approaches to effectively integrate individual managers and employees into a plan—one that is used in at least half of the country's business organizations—is *management by objectives* (MBO). In its most basic form, MBO is defined as:

> A process whereby the superior and subordinate managers of an organization jointly identify common goals, define each individual's major areas of responsibilities in terms of the results expected of them, and use these measures as guides for operating the unit and assessing the contribution of each of its members.[5]

Exhibit 6-6
Organizational Planning Dimensions: A Summary

Organizational Level	Type	Time	Focus	Elements	Repetitiveness
Executive Management	Corporate planning	Long-range planning	Total organization	Corporate: Strategies Policies	Corporate: Standing plans Programs Projects Budgets
Middle-level Management	SBU planning	Long-range planning Medium-range planning	Divisional or business unit	Divisional: Strategies Policies Procedures	Divisional: Standing plans Programs Projects Budgets
First-line Management	Operating planning	Short-range planning	Unit, function, or department	Unit: Policies Procedures Rules	Unit: Standing plans Programs Projects Budgets

In essence, MBO is an applied managerial technique that not only stresses the importance of mutual understanding between a superior and a subordinate, but is concerned with initiating and stimulating better performance through a "proactive" rather than a "reactive" style of managing.

The idea of giving employees a specific amount of work to be accomplished—a task, a quota, a performance standard, a deadline, or a goal—is not new to the management profession. The task concept and performance standards were well-founded over seventy years ago with Taylor's scientific management (see chapter 2). As we discussed, Taylor used the system to increase the productivity of first-line workers. It was not until about twenty years ago that the idea of goal setting reappeared under a new name, management by objectives. This time, however, the technique was designed for managers.

The Foundations and Process of MBO

MBO has evolved in many organizations because it addresses certain important factors inherent in a person's job:

- Employees can perform better when it is clear to them not only what is expected of them, but how their individual efforts contribute to the organization's overall performance.

- Employees usually want to have some say about the particular results that are expected of them.

- While performing, employees have a need to know how well they are doing.

- Employees want to be rewarded (e.g., with money, recognition, opportunities for growth, and a sense of achievement) in line with their levels of performance.

These foundational elements have been translated into operational terms. As shown in exhibit 6-7, an operational MBO process usually involves at least eight steps:

Step 1—*Diagnosis* This first step concerns the preliminary activities that managers do to analyze the important employee needs, jobs, technology, and issues in the organization.

Step 2—*Planning* Involved in this MBO step are issues related to the overall goals and strategies of the organization, receiving management commitment to the MBO process, and training and development in learning how to use the technique.

Step 3—*Defining the Employee's Job* Possibly one of the most difficult steps, the employee is required to describe his or her particular job, its content, duties, requirements, and responsibilities. This step is important because before individual goals can be set, one must know what work is being done.

Step 4—*Goal Setting* The employee initiates the superior-subordinate interaction by developing a set of goals for the upcoming period, usually one year. The type of goal (maintenance, project, and development—see chapter 1), setting priorities, target dates, and methods of measurement are all important.

Step 5—*Superior Review* The employee's superior reviews the initial goals, offers suggestions for improvement, and so on.

Exhibit 6-7
The MBO Process

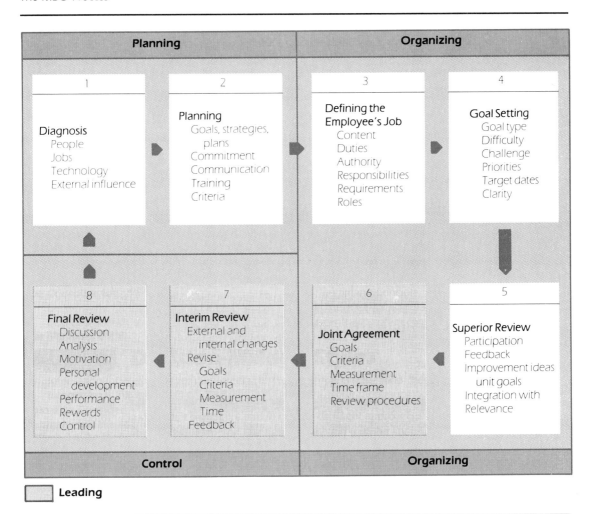

Planning		Organizing	
1	**2**	**3**	**4**
Diagnosis People Jobs Technology External influence	Planning Goals, strategies, plans Commitment Communication Training Criteria	Defining the Employee's Job Content Duties Authority Responsibilities Requirements Roles	Goal Setting Goal type Difficulty Challenge Priorities Target dates Clarity
8	**7**	**6**	**5**
Final Review Discussion Analysis Motivation Personal development Performance Rewards Control	Interim Review External and internal changes Revise Goals Criteria Measurement Time Feedback	Joint Agreement Goals Criteria Measurement Time frame Review procedures	Superior Review Participation Feedback Improvement ideas unit goals Integration with Relevance
Control		**Organizing**	

Leading

Step 6—*Joint Agreement* Steps 4 and 5 are repeated until both the employee and the manager agree on the established set of goals for the period.

Step 7—*Interim Review* During the period of evaluation, the employee and manager get together to review the progress toward goal accomplishment. These meetings can be scheduled for once, twice, or more during the year and focus not only on what progress has been made, they also allow for adjustment should new information or changing environmental events become important.

Step 8—*Final Review* At the end of the goal-setting period, the employee and manager formally get together to review the results. Emphasis is placed on analysis, discussion, feedback, and input to the next MBO cycle. At the end of this step, the cycle is repeated for the next period.

As noted in exhibit 6-7, the MBO process is closely related to the major functions of management. That is, the *planning* function deals with steps 1 and 2; *organizing* concerns steps 3 through 6; *leading* relates to steps 6 through 8; and *control* concerns steps 7 and 8. Managerial change relates to the recycling of the process.

Since MBO has this direct relationship to managerial functions, organizations sometimes use it for different purposes. Some organizations use MBO to clarify the employee's job (planning and organizing); others use it to motivate employees (leading); while still other organizations apply MBO as a control mechanism to check performance and to adapt to new conditions (control and change).

Nowhere is this difference in application more pronounced than in how organizations use the results of the MBO process (step 8). Some organizations tie the results directly into the merit review process (see chapter 16). In this way, the employee sees a direct monetary impact of MBO on his or her salary. Other organizations use MBO to improve planning performance. Finally, still other organizations use MBO to identify managers for development and future advancement. There is no best application of MBO. The organization generally identifies its own needs and then adapts the MBO process to them.[6]

Exhibits 6-8 and 6-9 show how MBO can be used for a production supervisor's job. Exhibit 6-8 represents the result of the objective setting process (step 6), while exhibit 6-9 is the final outcome at the end of the process period (step 8). In exhibit 6-9, note that the type of goal varies by maintenance ("90 percent of all orders delivered on time"), project or improvement ("increase minority employee percentage by 19 percent"), and personal development ("complete preventive engineering correspondence course with at least an 85 percent average"), and that some of the goals have been prioritized (*A* equaling the highest priority, *B* being the next-highest priority), or assigned target dates, depending on the goal.

MBO Applications

Because of its popularity, MBO has been the subject of many organizational applications and studies. Some of the most notable studies have been conducted at General Electric, Wells Fargo, Purex, Weyerhaeuser, and Black and Decker. These studies have revealed the following:[7]

- Setting clear and specific goals has a greater positive effect on performance improvement than does the "do the best you can" approach.

- Employee goals that are perceived to be difficult but achievable lead to better performance than do easy goals, as long as the goals are accepted by the individual.

- Superior-subordinate participative goal-setting has been shown to improve performance better than superior-assigned goal-setting.

- Using frequent performance feedback in the MBO process results in higher performance by individuals than not using feedback.

Exhibit 6-8
Goal-Setting (MBO) Plan for a Production Supervisor

RESPONSIBILITIES (Major headings of job responsibilities.)	PERFORMANCE FACTORS AND/OR RESULTS TO BE ACHIEVED (A more specific statement of the employee's key responsibilities and/or goals employee can reasonably be expected to achieve in the coming period. Indicate how results will be measured. When specific quantitative indicators are not possible, state what conditions will exist when a job is well performed.)	PRIORITY AND/OR TARGET
Production	93% of all job lots delivered on time.	A
	90% of all orders delivered on time.	A
	Improve utilization of key equipment from 86% to 91%.	9/1/19—
	Production rate will meet monthly efficiency plan.	A
Quality	Finished product will meet standards within ± .5 of specification. No justifiable customer complaints attributable to my department.	A
Maintenance	Scheduled downtime will be utilized for preventive maintenance. No downtime will result from inadequate spare parts availability.	B
Employee Relations	Grievances processed and disposed within specified contract period.	B
Safety	No disabling injuries in my department.	B
Affirmative Action	Increase minority employee percentage to 19%.	6/30/19—
Personal Development	Complete preventive maintenance engineering course with at least 85% average.	10/31/19—
INTERIM REVIEW: CHANGES IN THE PLAN		
Quality	Finished product standards changed to ± .07 of specifications (by product engineering).	A

- There is growing evidence that unless successful goal achievement is reinforced, the performance levels of individuals will begin to decline.

These and other studies, however, also have pointed out a number of important criticisms in the use of MBO. The most prominent complaints include:

- The program was used as a whip by management to get employees to do what it wanted them to do, not what employees felt was best.

- The program significantly increased paperwork in the organization.

- The program not only failed to reach the lower managerial levels, staff positions were frequently excluded as well, creating a problem of ''haves and have nots.''

- There was an overemphasis on achieving quantitative results. This ignores some of the more important aspects of a manager's job that can only be assessed through qualitative or subjective means.

- Rewards for good performance did not equal either the level of subsequent performance or the efforts put in by employees in the MBO program.

Exhibit 6-9
Superior's Evaluation of Production Supervisor's Goal Achievement

---

(SUPERIOR'S EVALUATION)
LEVEL OF ACTUAL ACHIEVEMENT

Job lot deliveries averaged 92.6%. Orders delivered, averaged 91.1%.

His study of key equipment utilization in cooperation with our I.E. staff caused production planning change which has improved his utilization rate to 87.8% (the best we've ever done).

Monthly efficiency plan standards were within ± 1% of average expected.

Product engineering changes these specs. during the year. He ran consistently at ± .06%.

He received two (2) customer complaints during the year compared to his predecessor's average of 7/year.

He developed a "preventive maintenance program schedule" which permitted maximum use of downtime. We're using it in other control.

Spare parts availability did not cause any downtime within his control.

He had a real problem with one overtime grievance which is now in arbitration (due to advice of corporate labor relations).

His department had two disabling injuries, which I consider were within his control.

Minority employees now average 23%. He is our best supervisor from an affirmative action standpoint.

He completed preventative maintenance engineering course on July 1 with an 89% average.

ADDITIONAL SIGNIFICANT ACCOMPLISHMENTS

Served as "United Way" chairman for our plant and brought in our best pledge record to date.

CONTINUING RESPONSIBILITIES indicate additional responsibilities whenever they have had a significant positive or negative effect on the overall results achieved.
As "energy control coordinator" for his department, he achieved a 1% reduction from last year.

RELATIONSHIP WITH OTHERS— (JOB RELATED) Give significant positive or negative influence this employee has had on the results achieved by other employees.
He and the safety director are "polarized." I feel it is affecting his safety judgment and his record.

OVERALL RATING

Review actual level of achievement against overall performance plans. Consider performance in key results areas: that is actual performance against important priorities, dates, amounts and other factors listed above. Check the definition which best describes the employee's overall performance.

☐ Results achieved were unsatisfactory — performance did not meet expectations and must improve.

☐ Results achieved were adequate — performance met expectations in most key areas.

☐ Results achieved were satisfactory — performance exceeded expectations in a few key results areas.

☒ Results achieved were above average — performance exceeded expectations in many key results areas.

☐ Results achieved were outstanding — performance exceeded expectations in most key results areas.

Keys to Success with MBO

MBO has been used by managers for more than two decades. What have these managers learned? Although not exhaustive, the following list can be look upon at least as a start to determining some keys to success with MBO.

- *Top management support,* commitment, and involvement is mandatory. Without it, MBO will probably slowly decline in usage and effectiveness.

▪ MBO should be *integrated* into the manager's normal, everyday activities. Managers must accept it as part of the total management system, not just something they pull out of their desks once a year.

▪ MBO should emphasize goals that when achieved can benefit the organization and the manager. In other words, *personal development goals* must be included in an MBO program.

▪ Recognition of *differences* in units, departments, and functions in an organization is essential. Forcing a standardized program on units that involve different processes, methods, and constraints may meet with resistance and possible failure. Slight modifications to an MBO program at the unit level can prove to be quite valuable.

▪ Overemphasis on *quantitative* goals (e.g., dollars, time) can undermine success. Because managerial jobs are difficult to evaluate and measure, *qualitative* goals can be equally useful.

▪ *An MBO system need not generate too much paperwork.* An effective program can be conducted without the overuse of forms, memos, reports, and the like. Remember, the key aspect of MBO is the interaction between the superior and the subordinate, an interaction that need not be spelled out on paper every time.

▪ Great emphasis should be placed on *evaluation*.

▪ *Overnight results* should not be expected. Because of MBO's complex nature and time frame, past experience has shown that concrete results probably will not be seen until eighteen to twenty-four months into the program. In other words, don't abandon the program after only one year.

The work on MBO evaluation and application is really just beginning, despite over twenty years of study. There will undoubtedly be more work on the process of MBO, the impact of MBO on minority employees, the training requirements of MBO, and so on. The work to date has shown that MBO can result in improved performance, but in doing so it requires careful diagnosis, training, implementation, and reinforcement. These results clearly indicate that although MBO appears to be quite simple on paper, it is a complex process and difficult program to make work at any level in any organization.

 ## Contingency Planning

To this point in our discussion of planning, we have taken what may be considered a "single-future" or "straight-line" approach—goals are set, and specific strategies, plans, policies, procedures, rules and budgets are developed to meet these goals. This straight-line approach is based on a series of expected events and certain assumptions regarding the internal and external environment. Such plans, however, do not make provisions for unexpected events or situations that could significantly alter the accuracy of the total planning process.

Taking unexpected events into account in the planning process is the focus of one of the fastest-growing planning techniques—contingency planning. Basically, *contin-*

gency planning is the preparation, *in advance,* of a course of action to meet a situation that is not expected, but that, if it occurs, will have a significant impact on the organization.[8] Similarly, it has been defined as a plan that can be put into effect when an unforeseen event actually occurs. For example, a divisional manager may develop an intermediate-range plan for the sale of a product line that is based on projection of the growth in the nation's economy. What happens to the manager's original plan when the economy begins taking a dip toward a recession not anticipated by the manager? Needless to say, not only has the original plan been significantly affected, a totally new plan may be needed.

Contingency planning has a number of benefits. First, it helps avoid, or cushion, the effects of *surprise* in the planning process. For an organization, the occurrence of unexpected events can cause what we can term *crisis management*—the scrambling for answers and guidelines and the sometimes ineffective decisions that can result. Contingency planning usually permits more rational decisions, because they are made in advance in a less critical fashion.

Second, involvement in contingency planning can sharpen managers' *skills*. It forces managers to anticipate problems and opportunities and prepare for them with different courses of action. Third, it requires managers to gain a better *understanding* of their environments. They are therefore not wedded to a particular plan, and they are able to get a "second look" at the environment. Finally, the result is an organizational planning product that emphasizes *speed* and *flexibility*—speed in foreseeing an event, and flexibility in reacting to it.

There are two main sources of contingencies: those that are within the planning process, and those that are outside the planning process.

Sources of contingencies *within* the planning process are similar to those we discussed at length in chapters 3 and 4. These may include, for example: (1) changes in raw material sources or costs; (2) new product introductions by competitors; (3) mergers of firms that may upset the competitive balance; (4) labor problems; (5) stiffening of governmental regulations; and (6) increased influence of foreign governments. These factors are termed sources within the planning process because they are generally known, at least as far as their range of effects and probability of occurrence.

Sources of contingencies *outside* the planning process concern those events that may be considered unexpected or a surprise to the organization. Examples include: (1) natural disasters; (2) a takeover by another organization; (3) a major internal fraud uncovered in an audit; (4) product recalls; (5) a major legal suit brought by a governmental agency or competition; and (6) a death of high-level manager.

Contingencies outside the planning process can sometimes be built into a contingency plan. For example, an organization may limit or refrain from doing business in an area subject either to severe weather disruptions or political upheavals. In addition, many organizations have insured the lives of executives or provided for a sudden leadership vacuum through management training and succession programs.

Contingency planning applies to the entire organizational planning process, including type of plan (corporate, divisional, and unit), planning horizon (long-range, intermediate-range, and short-range), or particular focus (marketing, manufacturing, personnel, and so on). Unexpected events can occur anytime and anywhere.

The contingency planning process generally consists of three distinct steps: (1) identifying the contingent event; (2) establishing the point at which action should be taken (the action point); and (3) determining the nature of the response. The process is shown in exhibit 6-10. To help our understanding of the process, the Gulf Oil example in *The Practice of Management* section will be developed further.

CROCK

CROCK by Rechin and Parker © 1980 Field Enterprises, Inc., Courtesy Field Newspaper Syndicate.

Exhibit 6-10
Example of a Contingency Planning Process

Planning Steps	Actions	Description		
STEP 1: Identify the Contingent Events				
What if . . . ?	List events that may occur in the future that are important.	Competitor develops new process.	Decline (20%) in market growth.	Substitute product
What is impact of event?	Evaluate impact of contingent event on corporate goals.	"B"—moderately severe	"C"—slightly severe	"A"—very severe
How probable is event?	Establish the likelihood of contingent event occurrence.	"I"—highly likely	"II"—somewhat likely	"III"—unlikely
STEP 2: Establish Action Points				
How known that event is about to happen?	List indicators and set action points that signal the impending occurrence of event.	Various media sources	Economic data	Various media sources
Who will alert us?	Assign responsibility for tracking indicators and issuing warnings.	Division manager	Market research manager	Marketing manager
STEP 3: Develop Strategies and Plans				
What will we do when it occurs?	Determine the strategy that will neutralize (or capitalize) on the effects of the contingent event.	1. Develop new process; 2. Cut prices; 3. Get out of market.	1. Delay plant construction; 2. Maintain status quo.	1. Compete with new product; 2. Get out of market.
What effect will this have on the event?	Estimate the financial impact of the new strategies.	1. Will neutralize, if successful, in time; 2. Declining profit margin; 3. Significant reduction in revenue and profits.	1. Cost of construction plans; 2. Little impact.	1. Reduction in profit margin if price cutting occurs; 2. Significant reduction in revenue and profits.

Identifying Contingent Events   The process of identifying a contingent event is the most critical, but most difficult, part of the contingency planning process. The problem is not so much in being able to identify events, but in identifying *too many!* Most managers have found it helpful to limit the identification of those "key risks," as they are called, to no more than a half-dozen events that can have a significant impact on the goals of the organization.[9]

How are these key risks identified? There are a number of ways. The most popular is the formal planning process itself. These formal plans usually contain "assumptions'' about the environmental situation such as economic data, market conditions, competitive behavior, and socio-political trends. In a contingency framework, managers are forced to *challenge* the validity and accuracy of these assumptions. This process forces managers to possibly rethink their assumptions.

A second method is the use of an informal or formal environmental monitoring and warning system. Data are constantly received from various internal and external sources and compiled for evaluation. Sources include the media, meetings with customers, financial analysts' reports, and the ''grapevine.'' A final method is the ''nominal group'' technique, which we will discuss later in this chapter.

In our example, Gulf has set a goal of being the number two (behind Union Carbide) producer of low-density polyethylene, which is used to make household food wrappings and large garbage bags. A contingency analysis may identify three important key risks: (1) development of a more cost-efficient manufacturing process by a competitor; (2) a significant decline (e.g., 20 percent) in the market growth; and (3) introduction of a substitute product not made of polyethylene.

Two other steps occur within this first phase. First, the identified key risks are evaluated on their severity to the organization should they occur. The usual procedure is to assign subjective characters or letters to represent the degree of severity. For example, ''A''—very severe, ''B''—moderately severe, and ''C''—slightly severe.

The final step is to estimate the likelihood of the occurrence of the key risk. This is done either by actual probabilities or through a subjective evaluation system (e.g., I—highly likely, II—somewhat likely, and III—unlikely).

Establishing Action Points   An action point is an event, or series of events, that signals the manager that one of the identified key risks is about to happen. Three steps or activities are crucial to this stage:

- *Gather information and track the contingent event.* This can be the function of an environmental monitoring system. For example, in the Gulf Oil situation, if market growth is expected to be around 10 percent, then economic data should be gathered frequently on the actual situation. For the other key risks, constant monitoring of various sources should give the manager some idea as to what is occurring.

- *Set the action point.* This is the point, quantitatively or qualitatively measured, that tells the manager when the contingency plan should be thrown into effect. For Gulf, if market growth is only 8 percent per year instead of the planned 10 percent, the action point would signal the manager that the original goals and plans are in doubt.

- *Assign responsibility for initiating the action point.* Someone in the organization, possibly the manager in charge, should be given the responsibility to collect the data as well as to signal when the contingency plan should be used.

In most organizations, the action point probably has already been established. That is, the process just described is nothing more than what a good *control* system would do. Since most control systems incorporate monthly and quarterly reports, the necessary data may already be available. The responsibility, however, for signaling the action point must still be determined.

Develop New Strategies and Plans   Once the action point has been initiated, the process of determining the response—selecting new strategies and activities— involves the same sort of process that developed the original plan. The main difference is that the new goals take on a two-level orientation. The first goal is to somehow neutralize the effects of the unexpected event as much as possible—in other words, the first actions are directed at reducing costs quickly. With this done, the second goal is to try to regain as much of the lost performance as possible. Both development of the basic strategies and a contingency plan require that a variety of alternatives must be weighed and evaluated in order to find the most favorable outcome.

In our ongoing example, if a major competitor develops and puts into operation a new, more cost-efficient manufacturing process for polyethylene, the response by Gulf could be twofold. First, since the new process may enable the competitor to sell the product more cheaply, Gulf may decide to cut prices in order to protect its share of the market. By this action the company hopefully could temporarily neutralize the impact of the new process. Second, in order to regain some of the lost position, the company must decide whether it can internally develop a similar process or attempt to license the process from another organization. Of course, a possible strategy could be to get out of the polyethylene business if a new manufacturing process cannot be acquired internally or externally, or if the price-cutting actions result in an unprofitable product.

 # Aids in Planning

As we have suggested throughout this book, the management of organizations has become a much more dynamic and complex activity over time. It has, therefore, become more important—and more difficult—for managers to make plans that are more effective and accurate. To help managers improve the quality of their planning, a variety of tools and techniques, some from the management science school, have been developed. This section will present a brief overview of three techniques that have been applied to the planning function: (1) scenarios; (2) nominal group technique; and (3) simulation models. These by no means include all the planning techniques in use by organizations today. However, they do represent the most popular and frequently used methods.

Scenarios

In a formalistic sense, a scenario is a *hypothetical* sequence of events constructed to focus attention on causal processes and decision points.[10] In more practical terms, a scenario is a written description of a set of events *apt* to occur in the future that bears on organizational effectiveness. A scenario, then, is nothing more than a story describing a "what if" situation.

Similar to contingency planning, to which they are compared, scenarios have come into prominence only because of managers' dissatisfaction with the usefulness of "single future" plans. Managers recognized quickly that single-future plans are not very valuable when there is a high probability of the occurrence of unexpected events. Scenarios are intended to raise awareness and prevent surprises. Alternate scenarios help broaden the outlook of managers to the external forces that shape the future of the organization and sensitize them to their vulnerabilities and to opportunities that lie within other possible futures.[11]

Developing Scenarios Three scenarios are considered the most practical to work with: (1) the "most likely" or most probable, on which the regular plan is developed; (2) a pessimistic or "worst case"; and (3) an optimistic or "best case" scenario. The "most likely" case usually carries a 50 to 70 percent probability; the worst and best cases each account for a 20 percent probability or less. While it might be perfectly valid to prepare more than three scenarios, it is doubtful that many managers would bother to prepare, read, or base their actions on so many cases.

The process of preparing a scenario can consist of the following steps:[12]

- Identify and make explicit the organization's basic goals and strategies.
- Determine how far into the future you wish to plan.
- Develop a good understanding of the points of leverage and vulnerability.
- Determine factors that you think will definitely occur *and* may occur within the planning horizon.
- Make a list of key variables that will have make-or-break consequences for your organization.
- Assign reasonable values to each key variable.
- Build three scenarios (most likely, worst case, and best case) from which the organization may operate.
- Develop a strategy for each scenario that will most likely result in achieving the organization's goals.
- Check the feasibility of each strategy in each scenario.
- Select—or develop—an optimum response strategy and present it to management.

In most cases, the process of developing scenarios follows the same steps of a regular planning exercise. The main difference is that at least three situations are evaluated, not just one.

Subjects and Sources of Scenarios The scenario writer faces a number of areas of managerial concern. The easiest to develop, and the most immediate, are those scenarios that relate to the organization's performance. Many organizations ask for scenarios based on upturns or downturns in sales, inventories, or products. Other possible subjects for scenarios include economic (GNP, inflation, and interest rates), sociopolitical issues (energy problems), legislative and regulatory behavior (FTC, OSHA, and the like), climatology (for agriculturally based industries such as tobacco and fruits), labor, and foreign activities.

A variety of individuals and groups can be responsible for preparing scenarios. Some external sources, such as universities, institutes, and consultants, are primarily used when the organization lacks expertise on the issue. Internally, ad hoc committees, task forces, and formal planning groups prepare scenarios. Past experience has shown that internal groups that are interdisciplinary or interdepartmental produce the best scenarios because of the diversity in resources and points of view.

Nominal Group Technique

The nominal group technique is a limited but extremely useful technique that has been used in conjunction with contingency planning and scenario development. It is particularly useful for planning tasks or elements that require a high degree of innovation, idea generation, and creativity.[13] Examples include product development, future missions of the organization, and the development, of new manufacturing and information processes.

Process   The technique is usually applied to a group of knowledgeable people with different backgrounds and experiences whose pooled skills and judgments are needed to identify desirable goals and strategies. The typical steps followed in a nominal group exercise are as follows:

- The manager brings together a group of about six to twelve individuals and outlines the problems to be discussed (e.g., what product lines should the organization be involved in within the next ten years).

- Each member *separately,* without communicating with any other member, attempts to generate a number of ideas in writing.

- At the end of a short period (e.g., fifteen to thirty minutes), each member verbally presents one idea to the assembled group. Each idea is recorded on a blackboard or a large sheet of paper, and discussion is limited only to clarifications of the presented idea.

- The cycle is repeated until all developed ideas are presented and recorded. Each idea is then openly discussed as to its merits and realism.

After sufficient discussion, the manager asks each member to evaluate—usually by ranking in order—the presented ideas by secret ballot. The group decision is the pooled or summed outcome of the members' evaluations. The manager can then accept or reject the results.

Evaluation of the Nominal Group Technique   A number of organizations, including those in the industrial, service, and government sectors, have successfully used the nominal group technique for many years. Most of its successes have been with issues or problems that are exploratory in nature, or where fresh ideas are needed.

The main benefit of the technique is that it minimizes some of the inhibiting effects of group interaction, at least in the early discussions. In particular, the following benefits have been reported: (1) in the absence of personal criticism—since only the idea, not the person, is discussed—there is a greater sharing of ideas; (2) there is a greater concentration on the task as opposed to side issues; and (3) nominal groupings prohibit the dominance of the group by strong individual personalities since persuasion is not permitted, only open discussions.

Two concluding factors should be noted. First, on the positive side, individuals who participate in the exercise can develop a sense of ''ownership'' of the finalized idea. This can be translated into a high level of commitment should some of these ideas reach the formal planning stage. Second, on the negative side, since individual members put in a significant amount of time and effort into the exercise, the manager is put on the spot if he or she decides not to accept some of the group's ideas. In the future, the manager in charge may find that these members do not want to participate again.

Simulation Planning Models

One of the fastest-growing planning tools is computer simulation modeling, by which planners construct sophisticated models of an organization showing characteristics that are desired based in reality. With the aid of the computer, managers can test certain hypotheses on a wide range of decisions at a much lower cost and with greater speed than ever before. From a definitional point of view, computer simulation in planning is a quantitative modeling technique developed to test alternative courses of action based on historical facts and managerial assumptions.[14]

Many different forms of planning models exist in organizations. Some models attempt to simulate a particular function, such as manufacturing, marketing, or finance. Others simulate the interaction and interrelationships between functions. Still others, called corporate planning models, are capable of simulating almost the entire operation of an organization. The overall objective of these models is to assist in the development of long-, medium-, and short-range plans. A well-designed model is capable, at least in theory, of projecting the results (e.g., financial, sales, and manufacturing costs) of particular strategies over a number of years.

Process   In preparing a simulation planning model, a number of steps are required. Among the most important are the following:

First, as shown in exhibit 6-11, a simulation model depicts a *logical* sequence of activities and functions. Of crucial importance are the interactions and interrelationships between the components, or submodels, of the larger model. For example, the marketing and manufacturing submodels must show the important relationships between these two functions. The marketing submodel must specifically describe how marketing demands affect production capabilities; production capacities and requirements (e.g., maintenance, downtime) must be shown to affect the total number of products available for sale.

Second, the formulation of the model and the important interrelationships are based on the *assumptions* of managers. These aspects are usually translated into some form of mathematical equation that can be manipulated by the computer. The assumptions are based on historical data, managerial opinions, and certain forecasts of events, such

Exhibit 6-11
A Corporate Planning Model

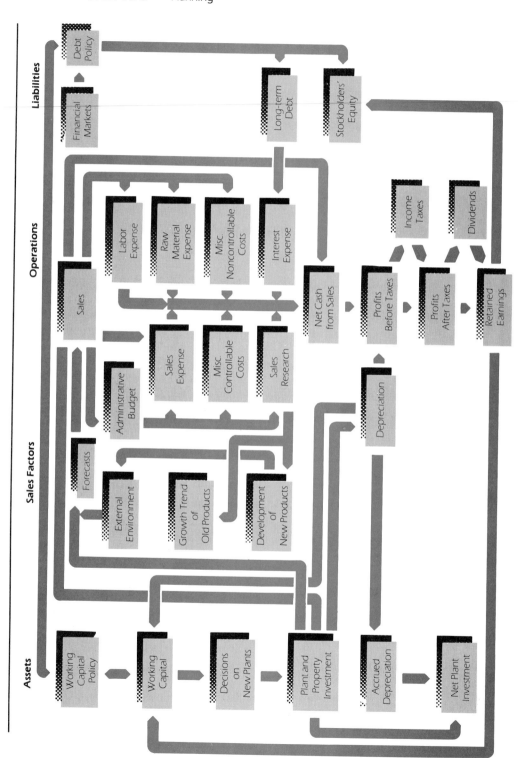

Adapted from James J. Morgan, Robert M. Lawless, and Eugene C. Yehle, "The Dow Chemical Corporate Financial Planning Model," in Albert N. Schrieber, ed., Corporate Simulation Models (Providence, R.I.: Institute of Management Science, 1970): 379.

as revenue growth, personnel and equipment costs, availability of raw materials, and so forth.

Finally, the model is tested on the computer to verify the validity of the assumptions and the input data. In other words, can the model predict today's results with today's data? Once this has been satisfactorily shown, the model is made more forward-looking by changing some of the input data and analyzing the results in an orderly fashion. Examples include changes in sales growth, impact of inflation and interest rates, manufacturing cost changes and price.

Many organizations, such as Ralston Purina, Digital Equipment, and R. J. Reynolds Industries, work with their models almost on a continual basis. For example, at Public Service Electric & Gas Co., the total corporate planning model is run on the average of once a day to test the impact on the New Jersey utilities costs, equipment use, and the financial effect of such events as an unexpectedly warm winter week on fuel purchases.[15]

Evaluation of Simulation Planning Models   With continuing advances in computer technology, simulation models in planning activities will become one of the dominant techniques in our future. It not only can be used in long- and short-range planning studies, but special studies solving the ever-present ''what if'' problems can be accomplished with a high degree of accuracy.

Now let's look at the problems. As should be readily apparent, the performance of such models depends to a great extent on how it was constructed and on what assumptions the calculations were based. If the model is not a true representation of reality, the output will be equally unrealistic. Second, problems can arise if managers do not have a clear idea of the kind of information they want to get out of the computer. A common problem is to attempt to simulate too many variables, resulting in an unmanageable model. Finally, a simulation model has no perspective of some of the important qualitative aspects of organizational functioning. In other words, while it can help to find answers to certain questions, it cannot tell managers which questions to ask and what are the most important answers to get.

 ## POINTS TO CONSIDER
An Emphasis on Managerial Skills

1. **The success of planning efforts depends as much on operating plans as it does on strategic plans.**
    The details of putting together and implementing an operating plan are important, because the process gets most of the managers in the organization into the actual planning. Good strategic plans will fail unless they are translated into operating terms.

2. **The concept of time and planning are interrelated.**
    Time is a double-edged sword to managers involved in planning. First, it concerns the length of the planning cycle, usually one year. Second, it concerns the length of the planning horizon (i.e., how long the plan will be in effect).

3. **MBO should not be considered a panacea for managers.**

   If used properly, MBO can improve performance and enhance the planning process, but it should not be considered a solution to all of the manager's problems.

4. **Contingency plans should be kept secret.**

   Normal plans are kept from competitors for obvious reasons. So too should contingency plans be kept secret from employees, especially if plant closings and project cancellations are part of the plan.

5. **Contingency plans should not be limited to crises.**

   Too often, contingency plans are couched in terms of negative impact on the organization. Experience has shown that there are many unexpected positive opportunities that need quick reaction from management. These, too, can be part of a contingency plan.

6. **The value of planning aids depends on what goes into them.**

   Planning aids are just that—aids. It is important for managers to insure that the assumptions and data behind the planning aids are valid and reliable. Poor assumptions and data will yield poor results.

SUMMARY FOR THE MANAGER

1. Planning usually involves three cycles: *cycle 1*—setting the direction; *cycle 2*—establishing the duties and responsibilities of key people; and *cycle 3*—allocating resources.

2. The dimensions of planning involve types of plans (corporate, strategic business unit, and operating), and time frame (long-term, intermediate, and short-term).

3. Additional planning dimensions concern elements (goals, strategies, policies, procedures, and rules), focus, and the degree of repetitiveness.

4. While most levels of management are involved in some form of planning, they differ in the particular planning element used.

5. MBO is a process which, when used in the planning process, can enhance the involvement of managers.

6. Contingency planning provides a way for managers to adjust their plans when unforeseen events occur.

7. Scenarios, nominal group technique, and simulations are some of the most popular planning aids.

REVIEW AND DISCUSSION QUESTIONS

1. What managerial skills are important in the planning process?
2. What is the difference between a strategic business unit plan and an operating plan?
3. Is long-range planning only done by top management?
4. Give an example of a standing plan and a single-use plan.
5. Would you consider MBO a policy or a procedure?

6. Why has contingency planning become so important and popular to a growing group of managers?
7. How can MBO increase the effectiveness of planning efforts?
8. Who should be responsible for putting together a contingency plan?
9. How often should a plan be reviewed by management?
10. What are some of the advantages and disadvantages of computer simulations in planning?

NOTES

1. "Kellogg Looks Beyond Breakfast," *Business Week* (December 6, 1982): 66-69.
2. R. R. Vancil and P. Lorange, "Strategic Planning in Diversified Companies," *Harvard Business Review* (January–February 1975): 80-94.
3. W. Kiechel III, "Corporate Strategies Under Fire," *Fortune* (December 27, 1982): 34-39.
4. F. Kast and J. E. Rosenzweig, *Organization and Management* (New York: McGraw-Hill, 1974), p. 444.
5. G. S. Ordiorne, *Management by Objectives* (New York: Pittman, 1965), p. 8.
6. J. M. Ivancevich, J. T. McMahon, J. W. Streidl, and A. D. Szilagyi, "Goal Setting: The Tenneco Approach to Personal Development and Management Effectiveness," *Organizational Dynamics* (Winter 1978): 58-80.
7. See J. N. Kondrasuk, "Studies in MBO Effectiveness," *Academy of Management Review* (July 1981): 419-30; and G. P. Latham and E. A. Locke, "Goal Setting: A Motivational Technique That Works," *Organizational Dynamics* (Autumn 1979): 68-80.
8. R. O'Connor, *Planning Under Uncertainty* (New York: Conference Board, 1978), p. 13.
9. Ibid, p. 17.
10. H. Kahn and A. Weiner, *The Year 2000* (New York: Macmillan, 1967), p. 6.
11. O'Connor, *Planning Under Uncertainty*, p. 5.
12. R. E. Linneman and J. D. Kennell, "Shirt Sleeve Approach to Long-Range Plans," *Harvard Business Review* (March-April 1977): 141-50.
13. A. Delbecq, A. Van de Ven, and A. Gustafson, *Group Techniques for Program Planning: A Guide to Nominal Group and Delphi Processes* (Glenview, Ill.: Scott, Foresman, 1975).
14. See A. N. Schrieber, ed., *Corporate Simulation Models* (Providence, R. I.: Institute of Management Science, 1970); and J. S. Hammond III, "Do's and Don'ts of Computer Models for Planning," *Harvard Business Review* (March-April 1974): 110-23.
15. "The New Planning," *Business Week* (December 18, 1978): 66.

A CASE FOR ANALYSIS

Planning in Action
The Hoover Company

Many a consumer products company would covet Hoover Co.'s widely recognized brand name for vacuum cleaners, its 100,000-outlet marketing network, and its rock-solid balance sheet. Indeed, such assets attracted a suitor unwanted by management—Fuqua Industries, Inc., the Atlanta-based conglomerate. In 1979, Fuqua offered $22 a share, or double the stock's then-current price, in a bid to acquire the 42 percent of the company's shares held by Hoover family members as a base for a future tender for the remaining shares.

But if Hoover's assets are enticing, its performance decidedly is not. Despite a 29 percent increase in sales over the past five years to $692 million, Hoover's 1978 earnings of $24.6 million fell short of the peak 1973 level. By the accounts of insiders and outsiders, it appears that Fuqua has set its sights on putting the resources of a weakly managed company to better use by installing more aggressive managers.

Even some of Hoover's executives privately conceded that the company's conservative, slow-moving management has failed to capitalize further on the familiar red and white Hoover trademark, both in domestic markets, and, more importantly, in markets overseas, where Hoover chalked up 70 percent of its sales in 1978. "I don't think they've been aggressive at all in utilizing their resources," says William M. Kreckmann, an investment officer at Philadelphia's Provident National Bank, which has held a large block of Hoover shares.

Management's cautious bent all but doomed the company's only major move to diversify. In the mid-1960s, Hoover introduced small appliances, such as toasters and blenders, but the new products fell victim to brutal competition. The company now seems reluctant to venture beyond its traditional floor-care products in the U.S. Eyeing sluggish demand for household vacuum cleaners, Hoover acquired Chemko Industries Inc., a $2.4 million per year maker of industrial carpet-cleaning equipment in May 1979.

Perhaps the boldest move in recent years has been the company's desperate effort to stave off Fuqua. In mid-May 1979, Herbert W. Hoover, Jr. (no relation to the former President), grandson of the company's founder and former chairman, announced that he planned to accept Fuqua's offer for his 1.1 million shares, or 8.2 percent of the outstanding stock. But Chairman Merle R. Rawson did not favor any linkup with Fuqua, a $1.6 billion per year concern with interests ranging from movie theaters to lawn mowers. "Fuqua Industries has been built over buying and selling companies," he says.

The Hoover board voted to exercise its right of first refusal on any sale of Herbert Hoover's shares, a byproduct of the settlement of a lawsuit launched by the former chairman following his ouster fifteen years ago. The company began looking for other merger partners, and it filed lawsuits claiming that Fuqua's moves violated federal securities laws and state anti-takeover statutes. In turn, Hoover family members owning half a million shares have sued to keep the company from buying the former chairman's stock, fearing the purchase might discourage Fuqua.

While Hoover has failed to diversify into faster growing markets, it has at least attempted to bolster its position in vacuum cleaners in recent years. Earlier in the decade, plagued by intense competition from the number two maker, Eureka Co., and by a design flaw in one of its own models, Hoover lost several points of its roughly 30 percent domestic market share. But the company managed to regain the ground it lost with the introduction in 1978 of a more powerful line of cleaners, dubbed Concept One. Still, few observers believe the new models will stimulate much new growth in a mature market that has remained stagnant at just over 9 million units a year for three years. In 1969, Hoover stepped up its efforts to move into more glamorous consumer product lines by acquiring a manufacturer of small appliances, but its offerings were not competitive in price, and Hoover was either unable or unwilling to roll out the continuing stream of new gadgets that success in the small appliance field requires. The company sold off the operation in 1977.

Hoover is also taking a drubbing in Britain, its chief overseas market and one that supports a broader line of Hoover appliances. The company claims half the market for vacuum cleaners in Britain, but it has been hard hit by European over-capacity in the appliance business, and imports of Italian laundry equipment have cut its 40 percent share of Britain's market for clothes washers to 35 percent. Earnings of Hoover Ltd., in which Hoover Co. has a 55 percent interest, slid from $23.8 million in 1975 to $5.8 million in 1978.

The company is responding by scaling back new product and plant expansion plans and by cutting its British work force. However, some of its British managers are reportedly upset that the popular Hoover brand is not reaching its full potential because of the limits corporate headquarters has put on planning and new product development. Such caution leads many observers to speculate that the new management that might result from an unfriendly tender by Fuqua is just what Hoover needs.

Adapted from "Hoover: How Stodgy Management Made it a Takeover Target," *Business Week* (June 18, 1979): 149.

Questions for Discussion

1. Discuss Hoover's strategies and policies since 1969.
2. Can you identify the existence of corporate plans and operating plans in this case?
3. Discuss Hoover's reaction to the takeover attempt in terms of contingency planning.
4. Discuss the comment that Hoover is weakly managed. Is it justified?

EXPERIENTIAL EXERCISE
Organizational Planning:
The Simpson Sporting Goods Company

Purpose
To study the steps in the organizational planning process.

Required Understanding
The student should be familiar with the elements of organizational planning.

How to Set Up the Exercise
Set up groups of four to eight persons for the thirty- to forty-five-minute exercise. The groups should be separated from each other and asked to converse only with members of their own group. Before joining their groups, each member is asked to complete the exercise alone and then join the group to reach a consensus.

The Situation
The Simpson Sporting Goods Company is a medium-sized recreational product manufacturer with headquarters and the main manufacturing plant located in Kansas City, Missouri. Founded in 1948 by Mr. John Simpson, Sr., the company specializes in the manufacture and sales of sporting goods for use in tennis (rackets), baseball and softball (bats and gloves), and skiing (water and snow skis). The products are sold directly to retail stores across the country through a twenty-five-person sales force. The company has attained an average growth in sales and net income of 14 percent over the last eight years; sales revenues at the end of 1982 were $8.7 million.

The current chairman of the board, Mr. John Simpson, Jr., has concluded that present and future economic and leisure time trends offer the company a unique and positive opportunity to expand its product line and significantly grow in sales and profitability. While the present product lines have proven to be quite successful, he believes that they are too narrow for the rapidly expanding recreational field.

To formalize his objective of future growth, Mr. Simpson made two important announcements during a meeting of the company's top managers. First, he set the following company goals he wishes the company to achieve within the next five years:

The company shall show a growth rate in sales and net income of a minimum of 20 percent annually.

The company shall introduce at least three new product lines in areas in which they currently do not manufacture or market.

Second, in order to manage the growth process better, he formed a new department of corporate planning, staffed by a director, four planners, and two clerical workers.

Instructions for the Exercise

In one of your first duties as Director of Corporate Planning, you have asked your planning staff to identify and develop a set of agenda items to be covered at the initial meeting of the planning unit. After a review of the individual lists, you have identified a set of items for discussion. These are shown in exhibit 6-12. A closer examination of the combined lists indicates, however, that the identified topics represent different stages of the planning process, thus necessitating a scheme for setting priorities. In response, you have developed the following classification or system for setting priorities:

Exhibit 6-12
Topics for the Simpson Planning Group Meeting

Planning Topics	Individual Priority	Group Priority
1. Analysis for internal and external environmental contingency factors.		
2. Develop five-year economic forecast.		
3. Development of the total company manpower resource base to achieve the stated goals.		
4. Identifying market opportunities for the company's existing product being manufactured.		
5. Procedures for reviewing established and implemented plans.		
6. Development of capital budgets and profit and loss statements for the next five years.		
7. Establishing a timetable for the implementation and evaluation of the plans.		
8. Analysis of the external environment influencing the demand for sporting goods.		
9. Analysis of the company's present resource base.		
10. Identification of the required level of physical facilities needed to achieve the stated goals.		

I. Those topics that deal with the direction in which the company should head in order to achieve the stated goals. These topics concern the broad, corporate issues and the criteria for judging the quality of the final plan.

II. Those topics that come after consideration of the topics labeled ''I.'' These topics should concern the more operational aspects of a plan.

III. Those topics that are related to the implementation of a plan, which should be considered after those topics labeled ''I'' and ''II.''

1. *Individually,* each member should classify the topics in exhibit 6-12 as I, II, or III.

2. As a *group,* the same topics should be classified using the same scheme.

3. The group results should be displayed, and each group should justify its scheme.

Managerial Decision Making

Chapter Outline

Key Points

1. Decision making is a managerial activity that affects and involves all managerial functions.
2. Decision making is a process that involves a sequence of rational steps.
3. Decisions vary by type and conditions.
4. The managers's position in the organization, culture, and certain organizational factors can act as constraints to decision making.
5. The manager's particular style can result in significant variations in how decisions are made.
6. Creativity and innovation can be looked at through a decision-making framework.
7. The management science school has helped solve many complex managerial problems.

Sears, Roebuck & Company

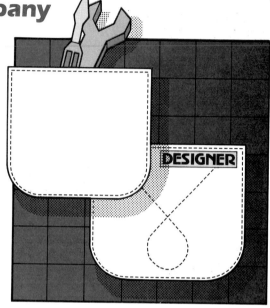

Sears, Roebuck & Company has always been associated with superlatives—biggest, best, and sharpest. According to *Business Week* and *Fortune*, it has been the envy of its competitors. Sears was second to none in its ability to ferret out innovative products and to get suppliers to provide them at the lowest cost. Its nearly 900 stores were located in convenient shopping centers, it had one of the world's largest catalog operations, and its employees were highly motivated, due in part to liberal stock option and retirement programs.

But early in the 1980s, the situation had become less than rosy. Profits dropped significantly in Sears' retail operations, to the point that only its insurance and real estate operations were bright spots. Behind the problems were a series of scattershot decisions aimed at countering the inroads made by the big discount firms like K-Mart, Target, Toys "R" Us, and the growing number of successful local department stores. Some of these decisions:

- Sears began stocking expensive, high fashion merchandise in many of its stores. Not only did the affluent members of the community show little interest in clothing or jewelry sporting the Sears label, but the traditional and solid blue-collar customers were turned off by the new and higher prices.
- Sears tried to woo the specialty store customers by stocking such products as an extensive line of sporting goods. Customers still saw no reason to buy these products at Sears rather than go to a better-known specialty store.
- K-Mart customers became the next target, when Sears embarked on a wide-ranging price-cutting war. Sales shot up 16 percent, but management soon discovered that the price cuts had destroyed profits.
- Sears' suppliers were next on the decision list. Management ordered a get-tough policy with suppliers by informing them that Sears would no longer inventory slow-selling products. Suppliers responded by finding new customers and expanding their product lines. When they sold to Sears, it was higher.

A ponderous management structure was really at the root of most of these ill-conceived decisions. Layer upon layer of management created a situation in which local department store managers had little autonomy. Decisions made in Chicago headquarters frequently were not appropriate for stores in Fresno, California, or Atlanta, Georgia.

By 1981, Sears' management belatedly recognized the problems created by their earlier decisions. Many of these decisions have been reversed, but management knows that things will not change overnight.

Adapted from "How Sears Became a High-Cost Operator," *Business Week* (February 16, 1981): 52-57; and A. M. Morrison, "Sears' Overdue Retailing Revival," *Fortune* (April 4, 1983): 133-37.

7 Decision making is an integral part of every manager's job. In fact, many people prefer to call managers "decision makers." Decisions involve everything from something as minor as where to hold a meeting to a major resource allocation decision as discussed in our Sears introductory case.

The common theme running through these and other examples is that decision making involves some *action* or, in our terminology, making a choice of particular actions. Going from here, we will define *decision making* as a process involving information, choice of alternative actions, implementation, and evaluation that is directed to the achievement of certain stated goals.[1] The strategic planning process discussed in chapter 5 is a form of decision making.

Our discussion of decision making breaks down into four parts. First, we will focus on the process of decision making, types of decisions, and the factors influencing decision making. Second, we will investigate the relationship between the decision-making process and the manager's style of decision making. Third, we will look at creativity and innovation through a decision-making framework. Finally, we will introduce certain decision-making aids that the management science school has brought to light.

The Process of Decision Making

Decision making is a process that involves the following steps: (1) recognition and identification of the problem; (2) development and evaluation of alternatives; (3) choice among the alternatives; (4) implementation; and (5) evaluation of the results. Exhibit 7-1 shows this process. We see, first of all, that decision making is a logical *sequence* of activities. That is, before alternatives are evaluated, the problem must be defined, and so on. Second, decision making is an *iterative* activity. As shown by the feedback loop, decision making is a recurring activity, and managers can learn from past decisions.

Recognition and Identification of the Problem

This first step, that of recognizing and identifying the problem, is the *energizing* factor in the decision process. The questions are important to this step—what is defined as a problem, and what are the sources for identifying problems?

Defining a Problem Managers usually encounter problems from two sources. First, organizational goals, while not considered problems, are certainly energizing factors for decision making. Achieving such goals as "improving return on invested capital to 15 percent by 1985" or "reducing service cost by 25 percent this year" is the purpose of the decision-making process.

The second source of decision-making problems is related to the first—that is, there is a *gap* between the desired level of goal achievement and the actual level. This may be as simple as an operator in a power-generating plant recognizing that the flow

Exhibit 7-1
Decision-Making
Process

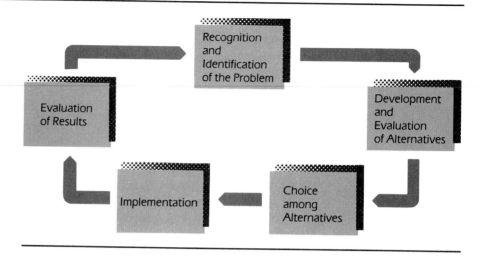

of coal into the equipment is below standard, or as significant as the ''action point'' in contingency planning. In essence, signaling an action point (i.e., that a contingency has occurred) is a decision in itself.

Sources of Identifying Problems   The process of identifying problems, sometimes called ''problem finding,'' relates to the particular information source available to the manager. These sources include:[2]

- *Internal sources.* To determine whether performance has increased, decreased, or remained the same, managers can use comparative, or historical, data. Information from organizational plans indicating that results do not meet planned goals is another internal source.

- *External sources.* Customers, suppliers, actions by competitors and governmental agencies, either from written or verbal sources, act to initiate the decision process.

There are times when the identification and recognition of a problem is clear cut, such as the case of the decision process involving goal achievement. There are other cases in which there is a lack of information to identify a problem, but the manager has a hunch that something has or will go wrong. These situations should not be passed off as folly—many hunches are founded on sound managerial experience.

Development and Evaluation of Alternatives

Once the problem (or problems) has been identified, the search for solutions can begin. This step is broken down into two separate factors—developing alternative solutions, and evaluating each alternative.

Developing Alternative Solutions   At this point, managers are concerned with gathering different ideas, thoughts, and resources to try to solve the problem. For example, Uniroyal faces the problems of high labor costs and inefficient equipment in its Akron, Ohio tire plant. Among the possible alternatives for solving these problems are: (1) remodel the plant; (2) close the Akron plant and build a new plant in a more favorable area; or (3) do nothing.

Evaluation of Alternatives   Each alternative, first of all, is considered for its *realism* and *feasibility*. This "weeding out" process eliminates those alternatives that are not practical or are too costly. For example, Uniroyal may eliminate the plant-remodeling alternative because it still would be faced with high labor costs.

Following the feasibility analysis, managers must ask specific questions about the degree to which the problem can be solved by adopting a particular alternative. The focus is one of *criteria*. As discussed in chapter 2, many different criteria can be used to evaluate an alternative, such as costs, potential profit contribution, maintaining a competitive position, and so on. For example, consider the decision on equipment for a new manufacturing plant. On one hand, the manufacturing manager may propose the purchase of a new packaging machine that has the latest technology and is the most cost efficient. It, however, will not be delivered for six months. The marketing manager, on the other hand, suggests that the company instead purchase another packaging system, one that is less cost efficient but can be delivered and installed within eight weeks. According to the marketing manager, this alternative would enable the organization to get the product into the market for sale earlier than any competitor, providing a significant competitive advantage. This illustrates the issue of criteria (in this case, multiple criteria—costs savings versus time) in selecting alternatives.

Choice Among Alternatives

The final choice among a variety of alternatives depends on how well the alternatives serve the goals of the organization. Choice is an act of *judgment*. The basis of judgment is how close the outcomes or consequences of the alternatives come to meeting the desired goals, or which alternative offers the most favorable combination of results. Some judgments made by managers are reasonably objective; others, however, are more subjective and are influenced by personal value systems.

Choice is influenced by the *quality of the information* used in evaluating alternatives. As we discussed in the last chapter, managers must be aware of this information quality/effective choice relationship. The choice of a particular course of action can also be altered if *new information* is received (which happens in contingency planning), or if managers higher in the organization do not approve the decision. From experience, managers make their most effective presentations of a decision to higher level executives when they thoroughly explain the problem, review the several actions that might be taken, offer a definite proposal, and explain what results are expected and why it is the best action.

Implementation

Implementing a decision involves a number of important steps. Consider the decision by an office equipment manufacturer to open a new sales office in a previously untapped territory. Initially the decision must be *communicated* to all involved employees. This is usually done through written communications and verbally to those who are most directly affected. Second, resources must be *organized* and *allocated* to the new office. This means appointing a sales manager and sales representatives, acquiring office space, and hiring the staff. Finally, *feedback* mechanisms are developed in order to check on the progress of the new office's sales performance. These topics will be covered in greater detail in Part Three.

Evaluation of Results

Evaluating the results of decisions can be a time for cheer, a time for deep introspection, or a time to pick up the pieces. For every successful decision, such as the introduction of felt-tip pens or low-calorie beers, there is a less-successful one, such as the Edsel. In analyzing decision results, at least three questions should be asked by the manager.

First, to what degree have the goals been *achieved?* This is the most important to the organization. For example, Miller Brewing's goal of obtaining the largest market share in low-calorie beer was achieved with its ''Lite'' product.

Second, how *committed* are employees and customers or clients to the decision in the long run? This is crucial, for many times a decision can be successful in the short run, but a failure as time goes by. For example, a high level of commitment and participation is part of instituting a new employee performance evaluation system. But after the initial euphoria has worn off, some of the deficiencies of the new system become apparent, and, commitment and enthusiasm decline.

Finally, what has been *learned* from implementing the decision—in other words, could we have done better making another decision? This is similar to second guessing a result that was successful but may have been better had some changes been made earlier. For example, in the case of McDonald's, some people have looked beyond the company's tremendous successes in fast food marketing and suggested that McDonald's has missed out on even higher profits by not diversifying sooner into foods such as pizza and other specialty sandwiches. Fact is, McDonald's *is* diversifying (Chicken McNuggets, McRib sandwiches), and the results so far show that only the breakfast foods are consistently reaping high profit. The benefit of this type of analysis is that the organization has learned from experience what has worked, and what may have worked better, so that the next time a similar decision is to be made, a different approach may be taken.

Organizational Framework for Decision Making

Managers make decisions within a framework and under conditions usually dictated by the organization. In essence, the process of decision making can vary significantly depending on the situation that the manager faces. For our purposes, this framework is determined by the types of decisions, conditions of decision making, and the focus of the decision.

Types of Decisions

Each of us has been in situations in which we have made decisions that were well defined and straightforward. We have also encountered other situations in which the decisions were quite ill-defined and not readily adaptable to a straightforward approach. In managerial terms, the former are defined as programmed decisions, while the latter are called nonprogrammed decisions.[3]

Programmed decisions are well-structured problems that are generally routine and repetitive. Such decisions can be made using a systematic procedure, rule, or habit. For example, the decision to hire a new employee, the manner in which a patient is admitted into a hospital, and the way a product is checked for quality can be called programmed decisions because they are quite similar each time they occur.

Nonprogrammed decisions are those that are loosely structured, unique, and for which standard routines cannot be developed. For example, negotiating a merger, introducing a new product line, or selecting a new organization president are not well suited to structured rules or policies because they happen so infrequently.

Managers are faced with many nonprogrammed decisions in their work, and the ability or *skill* to make good nonprogrammed decisions can determine how effective a manager really is. Managers must rely heavily on their problem-solving ability, judgment, and common sense when they are faced with nonprogrammed decisions. Many organizations have developed training programs to help their managers make nonprogrammed decisions in a logical manner.

Conditions of Decision Making

Managers make decisions so that certain goals can be achieved. Sometimes a particular decision assures the achievement of these goals. Unfortunately, most managerial decisions are made when the future is not so predictable. The difference between these decisions is the *amount of information* that managers have at their disposal and the *degree of confidence* managers have in the usefulness of that information in predicting the future. The information input into decision making determines the following conditions—certainty, risk, and uncertainty.[4]

Certainty   When managers have enough information to make decisions so they know the exact results in advance, they are making decisions under *certainty*. For example, a worker in a chemical plant may be responsible for monitoring the reaction between certain materials. The worker may watch a dial that measures the reaction temperature and notice that the temperature is too low. Since a continued low temperature results in an inferior product, the worker turns certain valves that raise the reaction temperature. This decision (in essence, a programmed decision) is made under conditions of certainty, because the worker knows that raising the temperature produces an acceptable product.

Risk   Under conditions of *risk* the manager faces a situation in which the results are not totally known, but will probably fall within a certain range of outcomes. With the use of the word "probably," we are introducing the concept of probability to managerial decision making. *Probability* is defined as the percentage of times a specific outcome will result over a large number of occurrences.

For example, consider the marketing manager of a firm that manufactures machine tools who decides to raise prices on a particular product line by 5 percent. The decision to raise prices is based on two assumptions: (1) the added revenue is needed to cover rising manufacturing costs; and (2) the price rise will hold because competitors will probably follow suit with their own price rises. From past experience the manager knows that competitors have matched price rises in 80 percent of recorded situations. However, there is a 10 percent chance that some competitors will not raise prices, and another 10 percent chance that other competitors will raise prices, but less than 5 percent. In other words, the marketing manager is operating under conditions of risk.

Uncertainty   When managers have difficulty assigning probabilities to outcomes, either because there is a lack of information or an absence of knowledge concerning what outcomes can be expected, we say that the manager is operating under conditions of *uncertainty*.[5] In other words, there are too many variables, many unknown facts, or both, and therefore the manager cannot predict the outcome with any degree of confidence.

This situation is faced frequently by managers when new, innovative products or services are introduced. For example, such products as Chrysler's K car, microwave ovens, and videotape recorders and personal computers for home use were first introduced with much uncertainty.

Focus of the Decision

In the last chapter, we pointed out that there are different types of plans tying into the three main managerial levels. In much the same manner, the focus of decisions is different at varying management levels. We shall identify these as strategic, administrative, and operating decisions.[6]

Strategic decisions are usually oriented toward establishing organizational goals, selecting strategies, and solving problems that concern the relationship between the organization and its environment. They are fundamentally executive or top-management oriented.

Administrative decisions are directed toward developing divisional plans, structuring work flows, distribution channels, developing material sources, personnel training, acquisition of facilities, and the like. They are primarily middle-management oriented.

Operating decisions maximize the performance of current operations. For example, setting production schedules, determining inventory levels, and deciding on the relative expenditures for the organization's functional areas are in this category.

The components of decision type, conditions, and management level can be integrated. That is, at the lower management levels (i.e., first-line managers), one can expect to be confronted with mostly operating decisions that lend themselves to programming and that contain a great deal of certainty. At the highest management level, however, decisions are more strategic in nature, are mostly nonprogrammed, and contain a high degree of uncertainty (see exhibit 7-2).

	Type	Conditions	Focus	Examples
Exhibit 7-2 Decision Types, Conditions, and Focus	Programmed	Certainty to Risk	Operating and Administrative	Hiring clerical personnel Quality control Hospital admissions
	Nonprogrammed	Risk to Uncertainty	Administrative and Strategic	Negotiating a merger Introducing a new product Testing a new drug

Factors Influencing Decision Making

We cannot assume that decision making is a straightforward, checklist approach that varies little over time. Decision making does vary, because managers and the situations they face change. Both organizational factors and culture appear to have a significant influence on managerial decision making.

Organizational Factors

Possibly nothing can facilitate or constrain decision making more than organizational factors. Typically, the manager has very little control over these factors and must learn to adjust to them. In essence, organizational factors establish the *boundaries* for managerial decision making. The manager's *level* or *position* in the organization influences the degree of freedom the manager has in making a decision. Some managers have flexibility and discretion in making a decision, while others must closely follow standard rules and procedures. This concerns the topic of organizational structure, which will be discussed in chapters 8 and 9.

Another organizational factor is the relative *importance* or *significance* of the decision to the organization. Decisions are not the same in terms of the impact they will have. For example, a decision to promote a manager is less important than one to close down a series of inefficient plants or offices.

The significance and importance of the decision is related to the amount of resources that are involved or can be affected. Promoting one person or laying off 400 people obviously represent different levels of significance. The impact on the *financial stability* of the organization should also be considered. A decision to introduce a new product line that could affect the total survival of an organization is certainly more important than how the office space is designed. Finally, *time* is an important factor in and of itself. Time relates not only to how long it takes to make a decision, but to what is the long-term impact of the decision.

The third organizational factor concerns the different *groups* that influence the manager. The influencing groups can include advisory committees, informal groups, and labor unions. Many times groups act as constraining factors in managerial decision making. For example, with labor contracts, the manager is limited in ability to motivate, discipline, or assign work to subordinates. Contractual wage increases remove the powerful influence of merit increases, discipline in many cases is not permitted, and managers may have to assign specific workers to jobs not on the basis of skill, but seniority. In chapter 14, we will discuss the influences of groups in more detail.

Culture

In earlier chapters, we discussed the importance of culture in the activities of organizations and managers. Nowhere is cultural influence more pronounced than in decision making. Consider the difference between Western and Japanese managers.

For Westerners, the organizational decision-making process stresses individual responsibility and accountability. The Japanese, however, take a different approach by emphasizing *collective* or *consultative* decision making. This is primarily due to the fact that employees, managers and nonmanagers alike, spend more time in corporate activities than do their Western counterparts. They have tenure, are almost never fired, and job switching is quite rare.

Termed *hara gei* (where hara means ''guts'' and gei is translated as ''art''), this collective decision making occurs in Japanese industrial and commercial organizations when an important strategic decision must be made that can affect many people both inside and outside the organization. The process is usually initiated by a series of memos and reports discussing the elements of the decision and the possible consequences. These memos and reports are then passed up and down the ranks in the organization and initialed by all recipients.

Whenever an individual wishes to express reservations about the decision, he will put his initials sideways on the circulating document. To express severe reservations, he may even sign it upside down. This prepares his colleagues for a future memo that outlines his dissent, possibly discussing important aspects that might have been overlooked.

To the Japanese, there are a number of advantages in the use of a collective form of decision making:

■ *The thoroughness of the process insures that fewer aspects will be overlooked.* It is believed that satisfactory decisions are made when they agree with the overall goals of the organization, are based on adequate information about the present and future, include all relevant factors, have been considered in the light of their long-term consequences, and so forth. The Japanese believe that when more people are involved in the decision process, each element in the process will be covered more thoroughly.

■ *Broad participation creates a sense of commitment by employees.* It has long been believed that people work harder to implement decisions when they understand and approve them. Several Western management techniques are also based on the principle of explaining goals and methods to those who are charged with implementation. For the Japanese, it is even more motivating to have employees participate in the process leading to the decision. The opportunity to study background memos and reports used to reach a decision is more informative than an ex post facto explanation or justification.

■ *The decision can be bolder and more radical in a collective decision system.* In Japan, the consultative decision process between workers and management has resulted in unanimous agreement on harsh but necessary courses of action. For example, the entire bicycle industry was abandoned and the workers were retrained for positions in new industries with greater potential, such as motorcycles, automobiles, and trucks. Through participation in decision making, it is easier for the workers to trade off short-term problems and disruptions against their long-term benefits.

While there are obvious benefits in the adoption of a collective system of managerial decision making, there are certain factors that make it difficult to integrate into other systems. First, the collective system does not work well when decisions must be made quickly. Second, when secrecy is important, the collective system fails outright. A degree of participation can be used quite effectively in certain types of decisions, but on an overall basis the collective system seems to be culturally bound.

Recent research has shown that certain changes are occurring in the Japanese system of decision making.[7] One study has shown that there is a growing tendency for the Japanese to adopt a more Western style; they are moving away from the consultative process.

 # Decision-Making Styles

Since decision making is influenced by a number of situational factors, one would expect that managers would exhibit different approaches or styles. One way of studying the differences in managerial decision-making styles is to examine the steps in the decision-making process. As we will discuss, these different styles reach across the individual decision-making steps as well as work within them.

Problem Identification

Although it is widely assumed that managers are concerned with the solutions to work-related problems, there is some evidence that some managers (and nonmanagers) *actively* go out of their way to *find* problems. In the same manner, we are all aware of some people who thrive in situations of high uncertainty, while others can be effective only in situations of calm certainty. This phenomenon relates to what has been called a manager's *problem-sensing style*.

Research in this area has shown that there are at least three types or styles that managers exhibit in problem-sensing situations.[8]

■ *Problem avoider.* A problem avoider is a person who expects order and predictability (i.e., certainty), and is motivated to maintain these conditions. Such people tend to block out or eliminate problems in advance either by ignoring information or by attempting to curb uncertainty with detailed planning efforts.

- *Problem solver.* This style applies to a manager who expects and strives to maintain a mix of certainty and uncertainty. Problem solvers do not tend to ignore problems, but attempt to handle them as they arise.

- *Problem seeker.* A problem seeker is one who actively seeks out and thrives on uncertainty and the novelty that it provides. Managers who adopt this style usually go after problems to satisfy their needs for the challenge of uncertainty. They would be expected to be active in contingency planning efforts.

As we discussed in chapter 3, and will point out further in this chapter, an organization's environment plays an important role in determining where these styles are most effective. That is, an environment of relative stability may be conducive to a problem-solver style, whereas a complex and dynamic environment in which problems abound would fit a problem-seeker style of decision making.

Developing and Evaluating Alternatives

The process of developing and evaluating alternatives for decision making is based on *information*. Managers differ in their styles of gathering, interpreting, and evaluating information. Two distinct approaches can be identified—information processing and information integration.

Information Processing   If we view decision making as a process through which managers organize the information they receive from the environment, we must try to imagine how these individuals think. How a manager thinks through the process of developing and evaluating alternatives depends very much on certain consistent modes of thought. These thought patterns develop through training and experience in much the same way as managerial skills develop.

As shown in exhibit 7-3, a manager's decision-making style in developing and evaluating alternatives can vary along two information processing dimensions—information gathering and information evaluation.[9]

Exhibit 7-3
Information Processing
Decision Styles

Information Evaluation

Information Gathering		Systematic	Intuitive
	Preceptive	Manufacturing manager Statistician	Marketing manager Psychologist
	Receptive	Accountant Physician	Architect Research chemist

Adapted from J.L. McKenney and P.G.W. Keen, "How Managers' Minds Work," *Harvard Business Review* (May–June 1979): 83.

Information gathering relates to the way managers organize the various sources of information they receive daily. In a sense, it involves a framework or standard by which some information is rejected while other information is summarized and categorized. Two specific managerial styles can be identified:

- *Preceptive style.* A manager who adopts a preceptive style is one who emphasizes the process of "filtering" data or information. All incoming information is compared against some internal standards—information that matches the standard is retained, and information that does not meet the standard is eliminated. Consider a manufacturing manager who attends a meeting where the divisional vice president outlines the division's plans for the next five years. The manufacturing manager with a preceptive style would listen attentively to the vice president's comments concerning production aspects, but may filter out comments that are of little concern to his or her job, such as changes in the organization of the market research department.

- *Receptive style.* The manager with a receptive style of information processing is attentive to *all* sources of information. Instead of trying to categorize information through filtering, he or she looks at all the information for some meaning or new knowledge. Consider a doctor specializing in internal medicine. In order to gain some understanding of a patient's condition, a doctor with a receptive style would examine *all* test results in total in order to pinpoint any possible source of illness.

Information evaluation is sometimes referred to as the process of problem solving. The different styles of information evaluation relate to the particular sequence of analysis a manager uses. Two distinct styles can be described:

- *Systematic style.* This style refers to managers who approach problems by structuring them in terms of some accepted method that if followed will lead to a solution. An accountant auditing the books of an organization would use a systematic style of information evaluation.

- *Intuitive style.* In contrast to the systematic style, a manager with an intuitive style would avoid being bound by a particular approach to a problem. An intuitive manager prefers to see the meaning of information from a trial-and-error framework and is much more willing to jump from one method to another. Consider the reaction of United Airlines in their attempt to regain lost business after their lengthy strike in 1979. In the past, airlines that come off a long period of inactivity would attempt to win back customers in a slow "business as usual" manner. Since competition in the air-travel business had significantly increased due to deregulation, the United's management felt that a more dramatic and quick reaction was needed. This intuitive response, the half-fare coupon to passengers, not only regained lost business quickly, it sent reverberations throughout the airline industry.

Exhibit 7-3 also shows that the two information processing dimensions can be combined to describe particular managerial jobs. For example, statisticians use a preceptive and systematic style of information gathering and evaluation. They normally tend to filter out superfluous information and go about their decision making systematically. On the other hand, an architect is more receptive to a variety of information sources and depends on a certain intuition to solve design problems.

The Manager's Job

John Finn of Carborundum

Mergers and acquisitions have become a way of life in American industry. Frequently, the financial considerations of a merger or acquisition far overshadow other organizational activities, such as decision making. If management is not cognizant of newly created problems, the financial benefits of an acquisition will go down the tubes.

Carborundum Company, maker of abrasives such as grinding wheels and sandpaper, was acquired in 1977 by Kennecott Corporation, a mining company. In 1981, both Kennecott and Carborundum were acquired by the energy giant Standard Oil Company of Ohio (Sohio).

According to John Finn, executive vice president of Sohio Chemicals & Industrial Products, the time between 1977 and 1981 was crucial for Carborundum. During this time, Kennecott's management decided to use the earnings from the abrasives business to invest in other areas of the corporation. Product development slipped, as did most manufacturing plants. Most significant was the fact that many of Carborundum's key managers left the company.

Kennecott's managers, who lacked the experience to oversee the abrasives business, were unable to fill the vacuum. Even the way decisions were made and executed differed at the two companies. Because of the huge projects involving mining, Kennecott's managers were accustomed to long analysis of a few major investment decisions. In contrast, an action-oriented management at Carborundum exerted tight control but gave managers great leeway, so they could make decisions quickly. Even modest decisions took up an inordinate amount of time, as Carborundum managers struggled to explain their business to their Kennecott bosses. The result was that Carborundum's market share dropped by one-third, on-time deliveries fell to about 60 percent from 90 percent, and profits went into the red.

Finn, a Carborundum veteran, is now in charge of the troubled company. He is part of an aggressive new management team running Carborundum. Their first order of business—to get decision making back to basics.

Adapted from "How Kennecott Has Mismanaged Carborundum," *Business Week* (May 23, 1983): 127-130.

Information Integration In what ways does the manager *combine* or *integrate* information from various sources in developing and evaluating alternatives? Consider the case of a manager making a decision to promote one employee from five candidates to a supervisory position. Suppose that the manager has four pieces of information on each candidate: tenure in the organization; individual performance data over the past two years; previous supervisory experience; and test scores measuring supervisory capability. In evaluating the five candidates (i.e., alternatives), how does the manager combine or integrate the information? Exhibit 7-4 suggests that three approaches can be used.[10]

First, the manager could treat the information in a *compensatory* manner for each candidate. This approach is based on the assumption that a low score on one criterion can be *offset* or *compensated* by a high score on another criterion. One employee, for

Exhibit 7-4
Information Integration Decision Styles

Style	Description	Supervisory Selection Example
Compensatory	High value on one criterion can offset low value on another criterion.	High test score on capability test offsets lack of supervisory experience.
Conjunctive	Minimally acceptable levels must be achieved on all criteria.	Must minimally have: (1) five years employment with the organization; (2) two years supervisory experience with any organization; (3) top 20 percent in performance; and (4) top 25 percent on scores of supervisory capability test.
Disjunctive	High value on any one of the criteria is acceptance.	Four years supervisory experience with the organization is sufficient to make decisions.

example, may have almost no previous supervisory experience, but scores high on the supervisory capability test. Because the high test score can offset the lack of experience, this candidate will be evaluated at the same level as a candidate who has an average amount of supervisory experience and who achieves an average score on the capability test.

A second approach, termed the *conjunctive* or multiple hurdles approach, can also be used by the evaluating manager. In this case, the manager establishes *minimally* acceptable levels that must be attained on *each* criterion. If candidates fall below the cuttoff level on any one criterion, they can no longer be considered for promotion to supervisor. The manager, for example, may set the following minimum cutoff points: (1) five years with the organization; (2) two years of supervisory experience; (3) past performance that would place the candidate in the top 20 percent of fellow employees; and (4) test scores that place the candidate in the upper 25 percent of those who take the test. Note that in contrast to the compensatory model, under a conjunctive approach high scores on one criterion cannot offset a score below the minimum cutoff on some other criterion.

Finally, the manager might adopt an evaluation approach that is *disjunctive* in nature. Under this approach, the manager simply scans the information about a candidate looking only for some *outstanding characteristic*. If found, the candidate is promoted on the basis of this characteristic alone, and other pieces of information are ignored. In this case, the manager might determine that one of the candidates has had over four years experience as a supervisor in another organization and that this information alone warrants promoting the individual.[11]

Alternative Choice

When the problem or goals have been stated and the major alternatives have been identified and evaluated, the manager is faced with making the actual decision. The different decision-making styles that managers have been known to use now can take two approaches—classical decision approach and behavioral decision approach.

Classical Decision Approach   To illustrate the classical approach to decision making, consider the problem facing the administrator of a private hospital that specializes in rehabilitation care for patients with spinal cord injuries and nerve and muscle system disorders. Because of the relatively small size of the hospital (only 80 beds) and the growing patient load, a planning decision concerning the physical facilities must be made soon. The three strategies open to the administrator are: (1) maintain the present size; (2) remodel the existing facilities to increase the number of beds to 110; or (3) add a new patient ward to increase the number of beds from 80 to 150. The administrator wants to begin planning revisions to the hospital, if any are justified, as soon as possible. From a decision-making point of view, which alternative should be chosen? Two different approaches can be used—probabilistic, and nonprobabilistic.[12]

The *probabilistic* approach, known as a "decision tree," deals directly with the probabilities associated with various environmental events. The development of the decision tree for this example involves the following steps. (The complete analysis is shown in exhibit 7-5.)

▪ *Identify the possible strategies.* The three strategies that have been chosen for analysis include no change, remodeling, and ward expansion.

▪ *Identify the possible events that can affect the strategies.* Crucial to the analysis is the variation in patient load that could possibly occur. Three possible patient loads are identified—no change, 20 percent *decrease,* and a 20 percent *increase.*

▪ *Estimate the probability of occurrence of each event.* On the basis of past experience and a recognition of current trends, the administrator estimates that there is a 50 percent probability that patient load will increase, a 30 percent probability that there will be no change in patient load, and a 20 percent probability that the patient load will decrease.

▪ *Calculate the expected payoff of each event and strategy.* The expected yearly payoff is calculated by multiplying the expected profit by the estimated probability of occurrence. Expected profits are the result of subtracting operating costs from expected revenue. For example, for decision tree branch 2 (maintain present size with no change in patient load), the expected payoff is ($2.2 million – $2.0 million × 0.3) $60,000. Similarly, for decision tree branch 6 (remodel with an increase in patient load), the expected payoff is ($2.7 million – $2.3 million × 0.5) $200,000.

▪ *Choose the strategy that results in the highest expected payoff.* As shown in exhibit 7-5, the strategy to maintain the present size results in a $300,000 expected payoff, $230,000 for the remodeling strategy, and $330,000 for the ward expansion strategy. Therefore, the decision tree analysis indicates that the administrator should expand the hospital because it results in the highest expected profits, the original goal.

Nonprobabilistic rules ignore the probabilities of the occurrence of various outcomes. In other words, decision makers act as if they had perfect information. Three different styles can evolve from this approach.

Maximax Rule   Some managers act *optimistically* about the occurrence of the events influencing a decision. By following this style, the manager will select the

Exhibit 7-5
Decision Tree Analysis for Hospital Expansion

Strategy	Patient Load	Revenue (Millions)	Expense (Millions)	Profits (Millions)	Probability	Expected Payoff	
Expand —	Increase	9 [$3.0	− 2.4	= $0.6]	× 0.5 =	$300,000	
	No Change	8 [$2.5	− 2.4	= $0.1]	× 0.3 =	$ 30,000	$330,000
	Decrease	7 [$2.0	− 2.0	= $0.0]	× 0.2 =	$ 0	
Remodel	Increase	6 [$2.7	− 2.3	= $0.4]	× 0.5 =	$200,000	
	No Change	5 [$2.4	− 2.3	= $0.1]	× 0.3 =	$ 30,000	$230,000
	Decrease	4 [$2.0	− 2.0	= $0.0]	× 0.2 =	$ 0	
No Change	Increase	3 [$2.4	− 2.0	= $0.4]	× 0.5 =	$200,000	
	No change	2 [$2.2	− 2.0	= $0.2]	× 0.3 =	$ 60,000	$300,000
	Decrease	1 [$2.0	− 1.8	= $0.2]	× 0.2 =	$ 40,000	

strategy under which it is possible to receive the most favorable or highest payoff. This is called a style that maximizes the maximum possible payoff, or *maximax*. As shown in table A of exhibit 7-6, the maximum payoff occurs when the hospital expands and patient load increases ($600,000). Using this style, the manager will decide to expand the hospital.

Maximin Rule   A *pessimistic* manager may make a decision believing that only the worst possible situation will occur. This is called the style that maximizes the minimum payoff, or *maximin*. Table A of exhibit 7-6 suggests that if the administrator adheres to a maximin rule, the choice will be to remodel or expand under a decrease in patient load condition because it maximizes the minimum payoff ($0).

Minimax Rule   If a manager chooses a particular strategy but the most favorable environmental event does not occur, a certain degree of *regret* develops. A decision-making style that takes regret into account is called minimizing the maximum regret, or *minimax*. For our purposes, we will define *regret* as the payoff for each strategy under every environmental event subtracted from the most favorable payoff that is possible with the occurrence of the particular event. The minimax analysis is shown in table B of exhibit 7-6. For example, if the hospital administrator decides to expand the hospital and patient load increases, the regret is $0 ($600,000 − $600,000). On the other hand, if the decision is to remodel and patient load increases, the regret would be $200,000 ($600,000 − $400,000). Taking all strategies into consideration, the manager adopting a minimax style would choose to do nothing because such a decision would be a "minimum of maximum regret" of $200,000.

The reader should note carefully that the various decision styles can yield vastly different results. Using maximax and maximin expected payoff rules, the manager would decide to expand; a maximin rule would dictate remodeling as one of the decisions; and the minimax rule would result in a no-change decision.

Exhibit 7-6
Classical Decision
Style to
Alternative Choice

Table A—Maximax and Maximin Rules

Strategy	Patient Load Increase	No Change	Patient Load Decrease
Open new ward	$600,000	$100,000	$0[2]
Remodel	$400,000	$100,000	$0[2]
No change	$400,000	$200,000	$200,000

1 = Maximax rule choice   2 = Maximin rule choice

Table B—Minimax Rule

Strategy	Patient Load Increase	No Change	Patient Load Decrease	Raw Total
Open new ward	$0	$100,000	$200,000	$300,000
Remodel	$200,000	$100,000	$200,000	$500,000
No change	$200,000	$0	$0	$200,000[1]

1 = Minimax rule choice

Behavioral Decision Approach   In contrast to the classical approach, the behavioral approach to decision making suggests that many managers often make decisions without knowing all the possible alternatives and consequences. In other words, there is a *limit* to how rational the decision can be. Under these circumstances, many researchers have implied that managers make decisions within what has been called *bounded rationality*.[13]

If we accept the bounded rationality approach, we must consider two things. First, there is the quality of the information available to the manager—in other words, the state of certainty, risk, or uncertainty. Under conditions of uncertainty, managers many times have incomplete or highly speculative information on which to base a decision. This may mean that not all alternatives have been considered, or there are far too many complex variables and relationships for one person to handle effectively. Without placing some "boundaries" on this information, few decisions could ever be made.

Second, managers differ in their psychological approach to decision making. Some are problem avoiders, others are problem finders; one may adopt a systematic-preceptive approach, while another may prefer an intuitive-receptive approach; some may identify with a compensatory format, while others may focus on a conjunctive model. There is no one best way; therefore, managers choose the approach that they feel is the most effective under the circumstances.

Under conditions of bounded rationality, managers make the most *logical* decisions they can, limited by the quality of the information and by their ability to use the information. Rather than make the "maximum" or "optimum" decision as suggested by the classical approach, managers more realistically make a decision that will *adequately* serve their purposes. We call this making a *satisficing* decision. (The word is coined from "satisfy" and "suffice.")

BROOMHILDA

HARRY S. TROLL, HOW DID YOU JUDGE MEN WHEN YOU WERE IN OFFICE?

I'D BRING 'EM ALL INTO MY OFFICE AND KNOCK THEIR HEADS TOGETHER...

THE ONES THAT **DIDN'T** MAKE A HOLLOW, RINGING SOUND HAD SOMETHING IN 'EM...

THOSE WERE THE ONES YOU HAD TO WATCH OUT FOR!

Reprinted by permission: Tribune Company Syndicate, Inc.

As an example of satisficing behavior, consider the process of buying an automobile. Under the classical decision approach, to buy a car one would search out all models at all dealers within an area and bargain with the sales rep until the best or "optimum" price or decision has been reached. But if the buyer were to use a *satisficing* approach, he or she would make a number of initial assumptions. For example, perhaps the decision would be limited to small, four-cylinder, two-door models that are manufactured by U.S. auto companies. Second, if the person lives in a large urban area, contacts may be limited to dealers in a particular part of the city. In bargaining, the person may have established a range of desired prices. Whenever a price is quoted that is within this range, the person may consider it because it minimally satisfies (or satisfices) the criteria set.

Managers who act in a satisficing mode do not give up trying to make the best possible decisions. Rather, they recognize that at some point it becomes too expensive, difficult, and complex, (or simply too much of a "hassle") to try to acquire or analyze additional information.

Implementation

Managerial decision making is not a solitary process, whether it concerns actual choice or implementation. At times, it is appropriate for a manager to make and implement the decision alone. Other times, however, putting the decision into effect requires the involvement and participation—and hopefully the commitment—of others.[14] In 1974, Vroom and his associates developed and tested a model that focused on the degree of *participation* between a manager and subordinates when making and implementing decisions.[15]

The model begins by making a distinction between two major types of decision problems—individual and group. Individual problems are those whose solutions affect only one of the manager's subordinates. Problems that affect several of the subordinates are defined as group problems. A number of decision-making styles that lead to solutions have emerged from research on Vroom's model. These are presented in exhibit 7-7.

The letters A, C, G, and D represent decision processes that increasingly involve subordinate participation. "A" processes are very autocratic, not involving the sub-

Exhibit 7-7

Decision-Making Implementation Styles

For Individual Problems	For Group Problems
AI You solve the problem or make the decision yourself, using information available to you at that time.	**AI** You solve the problem or make the decision yourself, using information available to you at that time.
AII You obtain any necessary information from the subordinate, then decide on the solution to the problem yourself. You may or may not tell the subordinate what the problem is in getting the information from him. The role played by your subordinate in making the decision is clearly one of providing specific information that you request, rather than generating or evaluating alternative solutions.	**AII** You obtain any necessary information from subordinates, then decide on the solution to the problem yourself. You may or may not tell subordinates what the problem is in getting the information from them. The role played by your subordinates in making the decision is clearly one of providing specific information that you request, rather than generating or evaluating solutions.
CI You share the problem with the relevant subordinate, getting ideas and suggestions. Then *you* make the decision. This decision may or may not reflect your subordinate's influence.	**CI** You share the problem with the relevant subordinates individually, getting their ideas and suggestions without bringing them together as a group. Then *you* make the decision. This decision may or may not reflect your subordinates' influence.
GI You share the problem with one of your subordinates and together you analyze the problem and arrive at a mutually satisfactory solution in an atmosphere of free and open exchange of information and ideas. You both contribute to the resolution of the problem with the relative contribution of each being dependent on knowledge rather than formal authority.	**CII** You share the problem with your subordinates in a group meeting. In this meeting, you obtain their ideas and suggestions. Then, *you* make the decision, which may or may not reflect your subordinates' influence.
DI You delegate the problem to one of your subordinates, providing him with any relevant information that you possess, but giving him responsibility for solving the problem by himself. Any solution that the person reaches will receive your support.	**GII** You share the problem with your subordinates as a group. Together, you generate and evaluate alternatives and attempt to reach agreement (consensus) on a solution. Your role is much like that of chairman, coordinating the discussion, keeping it focused on the problem, and making sure that the critical issues are discussed. You do not try to influence the group to adopt ''your'' solution and are willing to accept and implement any solution that has the support of the entire group.

ordinate at all; The roman numerals denote variants of the same process. ''C'' processes are consultative; they involve the group in the actual decision. ''D'' processes constitute delegation of the entire decision to individual subordinates or groups of subordinates. The exhibit, then, shows five decision strategies each for individual and group problems that are commonly used by managers in actual situations.

The investigators also asked under what conditions will each of these alternative decision processes result in a good solution? They identified three basic criteria for evaluating the success of a decision: (1) the quality or rationality of the decision; (2) the acceptance or commitment on the part of the subordinates to execute decisions effectively; and (3) the amount of time required to make the decision.

These three criteria have been combined into a series of questions confronting the manager about the decision situation. Once these questions are answered, the model indicates the best decision process to use under the given circumstances. Vroom and his associates arranged these questions in sequential fashion and designed a decision tree (reproduced in exhibit 7-8).

The first step in using the model is to state and examine the problem. Questions A through H, arrayed in sequential fashion across the top of the decision tree, are a series of questions representing the criteria for effective decisions. They can be answered with a "yes" or "no" response. The decision maker works through the tree in sequential fashion until he or she finds an acceptable decision process. For example, according to the tree, if decision process 1 is reached after analysis, AI is the best decision strategy for both group and individual problems. If the result is 2, GII is the best for group problems, and DI is the best for individual problems. You are urged to examine the decision tree and use it to work through several hypothetical problems.

The Vroom model was an important improvement over classical decision theory with rather immediate implications for decision making. The study identified major, commonly used decision strategies and established criteria for evaluating the success of the strategies under a variety of conditions. In addition, the Vroom approach is an applied model for selecting decision strategies. It can improve the quality of decisions, the acceptance of the decisions by subordinates, and it can minimize the time consumed in decision making.

Evaluation of Results

Once the decision has been made and implemented, the manager becomes concerned with the performance the decision has generated—the evaluation stage. As we have suggested earlier in this chapter, the evaluation of decisions involves looking at criteria, the long-run commitment to the decision by employees and customers, what has been learned, and finally, how future decisions benefit from the organization's experience with this particular decision.

Similar to the other decision-making stages, managers can use different decision-making styles in evaluation. One way of describing decision styles is to return to our discussion of the dimensions of the external environment in chapter 3. We stated that at least two dimensions, shown in exhibit 7-9, can describe an organization's environment—degree of change and degree of complexity. The four-quadrant grid provides a framework upon which to place decision-making styles at the evaluation stage.[16]

Computational   In this first quadrant, decision-making evaluation is seen as being relatively mechanical and technical. This is attributed to the external environment,

Exhibit 7-8
Decision Process Flow Chart for Both Individual and Group Problems

A. Is there a quality requirement such that one solution is likely to be more rational than another?
B. Do I have sufficient information to make a high quality decision?
C. Is the problem structured?
D. Is acceptance of the decision by subordinates critical to effective implementation?
E. If I were to make the decision by myself, is it reasonably certain that it would be accepted by my subordinates?
F. Do subordinates share the organizational goals to be attained in solving this problem?
G. Is conflict among subordinates likely in preferred solutions? (This question is irrelevant to individual problems.)
H. Do subordinates have sufficient information to make a high quality decision?

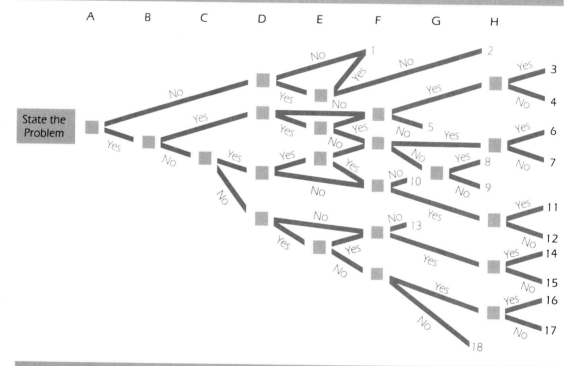

The recommended strategy for each problem type (1-18) for group (G) and individual (I) are as follows

	Group	Individual		Group	Individual		Group	Individual
1	AI	AI	7	GII	GI	13	CII	CI
2	GII	DI	8	CII	CI	14	CII	DI
3	AI	AI	9	CI	CI	15	CII	CI
4	AI	AI	10	AII	AII	16	GII	DI
5	AI	AI	11	AII	DI	17	GII	GI
6	GII	DI	12	AII	AII	18	CII	CI

Exhibit 7-9
Decision-Making Evaluation Styles

Degree of Change

		Stable	Dynamic

Degree of Complexity	**Simple**	**Computational**
		Type: Programmed
		Condition: Certainty
		Criteria: Efficiency
		              Costs
		              Consistency
			Compromise
			Type: Nonprogrammed
			Condition: Risk to uncertainty
			Criteria: Reaction
			              Flexibility
			              Stability

	Complex	**Judgmental**
		Type: Programmed
		Condition: Certainty to risk
		Criteria: Efficiency
		              Quantity/quality
		              Variety
			Adaptive
			Type: Nonprogrammed
			Condition: Uncertainty
			Criteria: Reaction time
			              Innovation
			              Growth

which is both simple and stable, resulting in a low degree of environmental uncertainty. Decisions are made on problems for which there are well-established procedures that can be followed in a programmed format. Due to the environment, decisions are made with a high degree of certainty, and there is an emphasis on efficiency, cost control, and consistency.

As an illustration, consider a manager of loan processing in a small, rural savings and loan. Decision making is fairly routine and follows a definite sequence of steps. The evaluation of the decision is based on established interest rates and payback periods—in other words, it is computational.

Judgmental   A judgmental decision evaluation style can be used when the environment is stable, but more complex when compared to the first quadrant. Decisions are still somewhat programmed, but due to the increased complexity of the environment, a degree of risk becomes more apparent. Efficiency is still a primary criterion for evaluation, but additional emphasis is also placed on quantity and quality as well as the variety of responses.

Consider the manager of the pension fund for a large industrial corporation. When they deal with the collection and distribution of funds to employees and retirees, the manager's decisions are somewhat programmed. However, in investing collected funds into market securities (stocks and bonds), a degree of risk is interjected. In an evaluation, the manager must be concerned with the quality and variety of the investments and the efficiency with which the total funds are handled.

Compromise   When the external environment becomes dynamic (but remains simple), a compromise decision evaluation style is dictated. Compromise is a situation of "give and take" between interacting parties, where, for example, the achievement of one performance criterion can come only at the expense of another. Decisions are generally nonprogrammed, and an increasing degree of uncertainty is present. Evaluation is made with such criteria as flexibility, stability, and reaction time.

An example can be the management negotiating team of a newspaper publishing company in discussions to write a new labor-management contract. The management team recognizes that, in order to reach an agreement with the labor team, a degree of compromise and bargaining over certain points will be necessary. For example, in order to agree on productivity levels, a concession on cost-of-living advances or working hours may have to be made. This compromise style enables the management team to obtain a certain degree of stability in a dynamic environment.

Adaptive   In an external environment characterized by dynamic change and complex relationships, the manager is faced with many nonprogrammed decisions that are inherently high in uncertainty. Given this environment, an adaptive decision style for evaluation is usually adopted, stressing reaction time, innovation, and growth.

Consider the situation facing market development managers at Walt Disney Productions. With the decrease in the company's primary market age group (five- to thirteen-year olds) and growing competition from other theme parks, the company's environment has shifted to one of complexity and dynamism. This increase in uncertainty and nonprogrammable decisions contributes to a need for decisions that stress innovation, growth, and reaction time. For example, in early 1983, Disney opened a large theme park similar to Walt Disney World in Japan. To attract older audiences, the development managers planned and built EPCOT (Experimental Prototype Community of Tomorrow) Center in Florida, which opened in late 1982. They are also considering building a ski resort in California and producing more PG-rated films. Each of these decisions were evaluated on the basis of their reaction time to environmental events, innovativeness, and contribution to the organization's growth.

The key point is that no one style or combination of styles is ideal. Each one works best in the right environment where there are differences in the types of decisions, conditions of uncertainty, and evaluation criteria.

Creativity, Innovation, and Decision Making

In a world dominated by turbulence and change, management cannot stand still and expect to survive in the long run. Faced with increasing competition, scarcity of all types of resources, opportunities and threats from domestic and international sources, and ever-increasing labor and raw material costs, most organizations would welcome anything that can lead to more efficient and effective operations. While traditional decision making can apply, what may be needed are decisions that incorporate creativity and innovation.

Examples of the impact of creativity and innovation in organizations abound. Xerox saw the novel promise of Chester Carlson's copying machine—IBM initially rejected it; Edward Land recognized the market for instant photography, enabling Polaroid, through protective patents, to exclude competition, especially giant Kodak, from the market for years; RCA was able to envision the innovative opportunity in radio—the Victor Talking Machine Company did not; Henry Ford saw the promise of the automobile—yet it was General Motors that recognized the need to segment the market by price and performance components. The following sections discuss the key characteristics of creativity and innovation.

Creativity and Innovation

In studying the dynamics of change in organizations, many people conclude that creativity and innovation are related but distinct factors. For our purposes, we will define *creativity* as the process of generating a new idea, while *innovation* involves the translation of the idea into a new product or service.[17]

This distinction has significant implications to managers. Creativity abounds all around us, whether we are working in an organization or not. We can all point to people we interact with each day who are virtual idea-generation machines. True innovation in organizations is much rarer because it involves taking an idea and finding a *useful* application for it. The effective manager not only recognizes the difference between these two factors but understands that an organization needs both creative *and* innovative employees to achieve its goals. An organization full of creative people may never get a product or service to the marketplace, while a heavily innovative orientation simply could not exist without someone to generate ideas.

The creative and innovative process is shown in exhibit 7-10, which points up two major features. First, creativity and innovation are sequentially related to each other. Second, the innovation step may require far more time and organizational resources than the creative stage. Let's examine the components of creativity and innovation.

The Creative Process   Creativity, contrary to the belief of some people, is not simply the sudden feeling of "Eureka, I've found it." It is, in fact, a process that involves a number of distinct steps.[18]

- *Identification.* The individual selects or identifies a problem to concentrate on. Usually the issue arises because of some difficulty the person is having doing his or her normal work. This can happen in all jobs.

- *Preparation or immersion.* After selecting a problem, the individual immerses himself or herself in collecting information and data, looking back into the past, or just "getting dirty" in the issue. Illustrations include the extensive preparation George C. Scott put in for his movie role as General Patton; in baseball, Lou Brock and Rod Carew studied films of various pitchers to develop their basestealing and hitting skills; anthropologists Richard and Mary Leakey worked the Olduvai site for years before they made some of their initial discoveries.[19]

- *Incubation.* A little-understood but extremely important part of the creative process is the time the individual relaxes or stands back and mulls over (consciously and/or

Exhibit 7-10
The Creativity
and Innovation Process

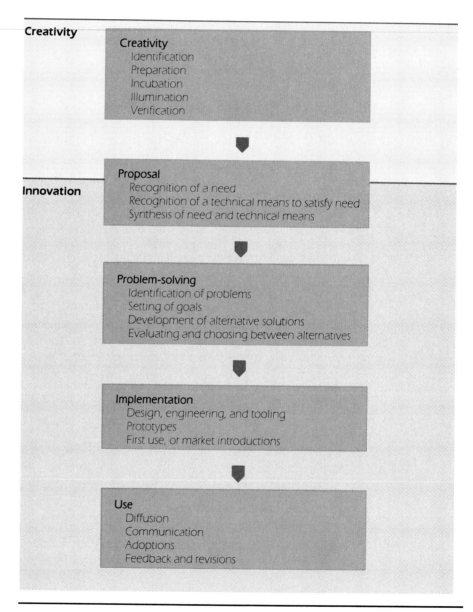

Creativity

Creativity
Identification
Preparation
Incubation
Illumination
Verification

Innovation

Proposal
Recognition of a need
Recognition of a technical means to satisfy need
Synthesis of need and technical means

Problem-solving
Identification of problems
Setting of goals
Development of alternative solutions
Evaluating and choosing between alternatives

Implementation
Design, engineering, and tooling
Prototypes
First use, or market introductions

Use
Diffusion
Communication
Adoptions
Feedback and revisions

Adapted from James M. Utterback, "The Process of Technological Innovation within the Firm,"
Academy of Management Journal (March 1971): 83.

subconsciously) the collected information. What may look like daydreaming or idle time is actually time used to arrange, integrate, and make sense of the information.

- *Insight or illumination.* Insight or illumination occurs when the individual first becomes aware of the value of a new idea or association. It is the breakthrough, the solving of the problem that has been sought. Insight can appear in many forms, such as Newton's inspiration (a gradual awareness growing out of research or hard work), or by accident (as in the discovery of the vulcanization process in rubber manufacturing).

- *Verification.* Verification is the process the individual uses to prove, through logic or experiment, that the idea is valuable and can be implemented. In its most basic form, verification is the cutting, polishing, and knocking off the rough edges of an idea. It may come from continued individual work on an idea, or in seeking the opinions of other people.

The Innovation Process   Exhibit 7-10 suggests that the process of innovation involves three separate steps. These steps are the proposal, problem-solving, and implementation stages.[20]

Proposal   The proposal stage is probably the most important of the entire creativity-innovation process because it involves the "go/no-go" decision the organization must make of whether the idea can be applied. It involves the recognition of a *need,* the recognition of the *technical* means to satisfy the need, and the *synthesis* of the need and technology for the further development of the idea. In essence, this stage asks: (a) Who is interested in our idea? (b) Can the idea be translated into a product or service? and (c) Can the product or service be efficiently and effectively produced and successfully marketed?

The studies over the past two decades on this part of the innovation process have yielded some interesting findings. First, most of the information leading to innovations in many industries comes from *outside* any given firm. This has been found in such diverse industries as textiles, machine tools, steel, railroads, housing supplies, and computer equipment. For example, of Du Pont's twenty-five major product and process innovations over the last fifty years, nearly 60 percent had their origins in external sources. Du Pont, in essence, was more a developer than an innovator.[21]

Second, the size of the firm has little effect on its relative ability to originate innovations. For example, of the seven major innovations in the aluminum industry, only one was initiated by a primary producer, such as Alcoa. There is, in fact, some evidence that in certain mature industries such as textiles and machine tools, innovations are more likely to come from smaller new firms than older and larger organizations.

Problem Solving   Once the idea has received the support of the organization, the innovation process is concerned with setting product or service goals, resolving the many problems, and evaluating design priorities and policies. This stage not only relates to the process of decision making, but, as we will soon show, it relates as well to the different roles people perform (see chapters 1 and 14) and the strength of the internal and external communication systems (see chapter 11).

Implementation   This stage emphasizes the manufacturing, engineering, tooling, and plant start-up required to bring the prototype product or service to its first use or market introduction. While implementation generally involves greater commitment and expenditures by the firm than the other innovation stages, the technical uncertainties are usually less than those of the earlier stages. Implementation also concerns projections of economic or market success, testing, acceptance, and an increased emphasis on internal and external communication.

The Manager's Job
Paul Breedlove of Texas Instruments

When Paul Breedlove proposed the idea of a handheld calculator that could "talk" in 1976, it evoked a round of laughter from his colleagues at Texas Instruments. Even though management felt the idea was "too wild," they still gave the project $25,000 from a special kitty used to finance long-shot projects. That seed money for innovation led to a multimillion-dollar-a-year business for TI.

The money came from the company's IDEA program for Identify, Develop, Expose, and Action. About 40 IDEA representatives throughout the company can award funds, without special executive approval, for projects by lower level managers, such as Mr. Breedlove, who don't have the influence to get developmental funds through regular R&D channels.

Without the IDEA program, TI would not have developed Speak & Spell, the result of Mr. Breedlove's concept. The product, introduced in 1978, is a learning aid for children that uses a microcomputer to announce a word. The company since has developed other variations, including Speak & Math and Speak & Read. The result of Mr. Breedlove's effort was more than creating one new product—it was creating a new business.

Adapted from L. Ingrassia, "How Four Companies Spawn New Products by Encouraging Risks," *The Wall Street Journal* (September 18, 1980).

Aids for Creativity and Innovation

Organizations can use other means to facilitate creative and innovative activities. First, as discussed in the last chapter, special units or task forces can be established (i.e., venture groups) to investigate an idea or problem. Second, two group processes can be utilized—brainstorming and synectics.[22]

Brainstorming in groups involves six to twelve persons who get together to search for solutions to a problem. It was used many years ago in its initial application to help solve advertising problems for a commercial food-products company. Since then it has received wide application. The main idea is to have group members produce as many solutions to an issue or problem as they can without permitting judgments or criticisms to inhibit the free flow of ideas. Due to the freewheeling environment, brainstorming groups can come up with a wide range of usable ideas. As with any group, the composition is of great importance—that is, most people in the group should be experts or people who are familiar with the issue at hand.

Synectics, developed by the Arthur D. Little Inc. consulting firm, is not as well known or widely used as brainstorming. A synectics team is defined by two major characteristics. First, the group members are chosen only after thorough testing and screening. This selection process results in a tailor-made team composed of individuals best equipped intellectually and psychologically to deal with problems unique to their organization. Second, only the group leader knows the exact nature of the problem. The group members are given a very broad description of the issue and then allowed to talk out loud about a variety of issues related to the broad issue. For example, management at Kellogg's may be interested in developing new breakfast cereals for children. In the synectic team, the group leader suggests that the initial discussion center on the issue of "breakfast." After a number of give-and-take sessions, the group leader might focus the discussion on other breakfast cereals that it might be possible to produce and market. In reality, Kellogg's used this process not only to develop new cereals for children that were lower in presweetened qualities (i.e., sugar content), but a whole new line of cereals for health-conscious young adults.

These are some of the many mechanisms that organizations can use to facilitate the creative and innovative process. The key factor is that the organization takes an active role in providing the means and resources to further these important activities.

Aids in Managerial Decision Making

In our discussion of the management science school in chapter 2, we pointed out how the development and use of mathematical models and the computer have revolutionized many parts of the manager's job. In a sense, the discussions of forecasting and planning aids have introduced the reader to some of the most important management science techniques and tools.

Classifying Management Science Models

Management science models for decision making can be classified in at least three ways.[23] This is shown in exhibit 7-11.

First, models can be classified as either *descriptive* or *normative* in *purpose*. Similar to the discussion in chapter 2, descriptive models describe things *as they are.* They are used to define a situation more clearly, identify possible areas of change, and study the impact and consequences of various decision strategies. They cannot, however, identify the best choice among all possible alternatives. A normative model, on the other hand, is used to identify the best available alternative on the basis of some decision criteria—in other words, things *as they should be.* They are sometimes referred to as *optimizing* models since their purpose is to identify the optimal solution under a given set of conditions.

Exhibit 7-11
Classification of Management Science Models in Decision Making

Use of Models	Purpose		Types of Variables	
	Descriptive (As Things Are)	Normative (As Things Should Be)	Deterministic (Certainty)	Probabilistic (Uncertainty)
Inventory				
EOQ		X	X	
Inventory control models		X		X
Resource Allocation				
Linear programming		X	X	
Assignment		X	X	
Transportation		X	X	
Scheduling and Sequencing				
Queuing	X			X
Simulation	X			X
PERT		X	X	
Prediction				
Break even		X	X	
Regression		X	X	
Decision tree		X		X
Expected payoff		X		X
Monte Carlo simulation	X			X

Adapted from H. L. Lyon, J. M. Ivancevich, and J. H. Donnelly, *Management Science in Organizations* (Glenview, Ill.: Scott, Foresman, 1976), p. 26.

Second, management science models can be *deterministic* or *probabilistic*. A variable that is deterministic is one that contains no element of chance—conditions of *certainty* in our framework. For example, the accounting model of assets equals liabilities plus capital ($A = L + C$) is deterministic because the variables are all known quantities, and the exact solution is stated by the given relationship.

When variables in a decision situation have an element of chance or *uncertainty* in them, the models for their analysis are termed *probabilistic*. Our decision tree example in the last section is a probabilistic model.

The third way of classifying management science models in decision making is by their *use*. As shown in exhibit 7-11, there are at least four major areas of use.

Inventory Control   Most organizations cannot exist without some form of inventory, either of raw materials or finished products. Inventories, however, create a dilemma for managers. On one hand, inventories must be kept on hand to insure the smooth flow of materials to production facilities and final product to the customer. On the other hand, maintaining inventories is costly, not only in terms of idle goods but also in the physical space necessary to hold them. The management science school has developed a number of decision-making techniques that have helped managers balance product availability with cost considerations.

Resource Allocation   A common problem for all types of managers is how to allocate the organization's resources effectively—people, space, finances, and equipment—to specific situations. The two biggest problems are *where* to allocate resources for their maximum potential and *how* to allocate resources when there are not enough available. Managers have used assignment, transportation, and linear programming methods to help solve their resource allocation problems.

Scheduling and Sequencing   When a manager must design facilities to meet a demand for services, or in decide in what order the parts of a job or project are to be performed, he or she is concerned with scheduling and sequencing. Queuing models and network models have been used in solving these problems.

Prediction   Managers' jobs would be made significantly easier if they knew in advance the exact impact and result of their decisions. Under conditions of certainty, managers can approach this. However, as we have pointed out throughout this book, managers are increasingly coming face to face with high degrees of uncertainty in their work. Management science tools have been developed to help the manager make predictions about the occurrence of future events or outcomes of their decisions. Regression analysis (chapter 3), decision trees, and simulation are some of the most popular techniques.

Issues Concerning Decision-Making Aids

The examples we have given to illustrate different decision-making aids are simple and straightforward. In most managerial situations, the problems are usually more complicated, requiring the use of more sophisticated techniques or more complex versions of the described methods.

The use of these more sophisticated methods has not received the high level of managerial support one would expect. The more important reasons for this situation are noted below.

Limited Time   The process of developing a complex model, gathering data, and testing the model can be extremely time consuming. The model may prove to be quite accurate and valid, but this is little help when a decision must be made quickly.

Inaccessibility of Information   Some data necessary to test decision models may be difficult to obtain or may be totally unavailable. This can add time and frustration to the decision-making process.

Resistance to Change   The use of decision aids may be a relatively new development in many organizations. This can be a problem if managers have developed their own particular ways of making decisions, causing them to be unreceptive to new ways of doing things. The fact that mathematical techniques seem so complex and mysterious to many managers makes it more difficult for them to accept these techniques.

Oversimplification   The problems addressed by decision aids are quite adaptable to mathematical formulations. The problems frequently confronting managers, however, are not so easily quantifiable. These include motivation problems, politics, and power struggles. The models can develop so-called optimum decisions but prove to be useless because they have been oversimplified by leaving out some important variables.

POINTS TO CONSIDER
An Emphasis on Managerial Skills

1. **Be as much problem oriented as solutions oriented.**
    Business schools have been frequently criticized for producing problem solvers, not problem finders. Whether this is true or not is for others to discuss. The point here is to stress the need for managers to develop diagnostic skills.

2. **Always check the accuracy of the information.**
    Decision making is founded on the use of information. If that information is bad, the decision will be as well.

3. **Decisions need not always be hastily made.**
    There are obvious situations where a quick decision needs to be made. In other situations, it may be wise to wait a short time and let additional information collect or just sit on the initial decision. Waiting may pay-off in the long run.

4. **Common sense plays an important role in decision making.**
    Too often managers get pushed into a rut of trying to maximize, optimize, or minimize a solution. As a result, they apply quantitative models to situations where only common sense may be needed. There is nothing wrong with the use of common sense, in its proper place.

5. **Encourage new ideas.**
    As the Texas Instruments example in the chapter illustrated, even the wildest of ideas can turn out to be successful. Try to avoid a hasty "it won't work"—instead, give new ideas a fair hearing.

6. **Learn how to tolerate failures.**
    For every successful innovation, there are fifty failures. However, each failure is a learning experience, and they add up over time, possibly leading to that one success.

SUMMARY FOR THE MANAGER

1. Decision making is one of the most important activities in which managers engage daily. There are some, in fact, who prefer the term *decision maker* to manager. Decision making pervades the entire management process, from planning to control. A manager's success as a decision maker, however, is made up of a combination of scientific analysis, experience, and common sense.

2. In making most decisions, managers follow a number of rational steps including problem identification, evaluation of alternatives, choice, implementation, and evaluation of results. Many of the problems managers face in making decisions result from not following these steps in a sequential order. Managers take short cuts either because of time constraints or their own personal characteristics (procrastination). Whatever the reasons, the effectiveness of a decision depends on how well the individual process steps are followed.

3. Decisions vary by the type and the conditions of the problem. Many decisions faced by lower level managers are programmed decisions. The routineness and repetitiveness of these decisions make them amenable to set policies and procedures. Higher level managers many times

face unprogrammed decisions, which are unique and for which there is a scarcity of information. The amount of information also establishes the conditions of certainty, risk, and uncertainty.

4. Managers should be aware that certain internal and external factors in their job can act as constraining factors in decision making. Such factors as the manager's position in the organization and cultural influences may set boundaries around what type of decisions they can make or how effective they can be.

5. While the decision-making process is sequential, significant variations can develop in how each step is followed. Most of the variations can be attributed to the manager's particular style. For example, managers can be problem avoiders, problem solvers, or problem finders in the problem identification stage; preceptive-receptive or systematic-intuitive in the way they process information in the evaluation of alternatives stage; optimizers or satisficers when it concerns decision choice; or participative-nonparticipative in how they implement decisions. These different styles create significant variations between managers who may be making the same decisions.

6. Two of the most important factors in facilitating the creative and innovative process in organizations are improving information flow and creating a climate for innovation. A lack of information flow coupled with a coercive team environment deters the development of new ideas, new products, and new services.

7. A key factor for managers to understand is that creativity and innovation are functions more of the immediate environment than of the size of the organization or industry. The organization can provide the basis for creativity and innovation; however, one-on-one relationships are the real heart of this process.

8. A number of aids to decision making are available to managers. These aids, which originate primarily from the management science school, have had a significant impact on the effectiveness of a manager's decision. The manager should be aware, however, that these decision aids are not the final answer to making good decisions. Important issues such as resistance to change, time and cost constraints, and oversimplification may severely limit how many decision techniques can be applied.

REVIEW AND DISCUSSION QUESTIONS

1. Can you distinguish between problem finding and problem solving?
2. What is the difference between *optimize* and *satisfice?*
3. Discuss the difference between normative and descriptive models.
4. Identify some jobs that: (a) involve mostly programmed decisions; and (b) involve many unprogrammed decisions.
5. What important criteria should managers use to evaluate the effectiveness of their decision making?
6. How are diagnostic skills for managers and decision making related?
7. What is the relationship between decision making and planning?
8. How are creativity and innovation different?
9. What is meant when someone says, ''That was an innovative decision''?
10. Why is it said that many new ideas for products fail because they have not successfully passed through the innovation proposal stage?

NOTES

1. See I. L. Janis and L. Mann, *Decision Making* (New York: The Free Press, 1977); and R. Hogarth, *Judgement and Choice* (New York: John Wiley, 1980).
2. W. F. Pounds, "The Process of Problem Finding," *Industrial Management Review* (Fall 1969): 1-19; and C. A. O'Reilly, "Variations in Decision Makers' Use of Information Sources: The Impact of Quality and Accessibility of Information,"*Academy of Management Journal* (December 1982): 756-71.
3. H. A. Simon, *The Shape of Automation* (New York: Harper & Row, 1965), p. 61.
4. See F. H. Knight, *Risk, Uncertainty, and Profit* (New York: Harper & Row, 1920); and S. A. Archer, "The Structure of Management Decision Theory," *Academy of Management Journal* (December 1964): 269-84.
5. C. A. Holloway, *Decision Making Under Uncertainty* (Englewood Cliffs, N.J.: Prentice-Hall, 1979).
6. H. I. Ansoff, *Corporate Strategy* (New York: McGraw-Hill, 1965).
7. See W. M. Fox, "Japanese Management: Tradition Under Strain," *Business Horizons* (August 1977): 76-85; F. Kaufman, "Decision Making-Eastern and Western Style," *Business Horizons* (December 1970): 81-86; and R. T. Pascale, "Communication and Decision Making Across Cultures: Japanese and American Comparisons," *Administrative Science Quarterly* (March 1978): 91-110.
8. See M. J. Driver, "Individual Decision Making and Creativity," in *Organizational Behavior,* ed. Steven Kerr (Columbus, Ohio: Grid, 1979): 76; and S. Kiesler and L. Sproull, "Managerial Response to Changing Environments: Perspectives on Problem Sensing from Social Cognition," *Administrative Science Quarterly* (December 1982): 548-70.
9. See J. L. McKenney and P. G. W. Keen, "How Managers' Minds Work," *Harvard Business Review* (May-June 1974): 79-90; and G. R. Ungson, D. N. Braunstein, and P. D. Hall, "Managerial Information Processing: A Research Review," *Administrative Science Quarterly* (March 1981): 116-34.
10. M. J. Wallace, Jr. and D. P. Schwab, "A Cross-Validated Comparison of Five Models Used to Predict Graduate Admissions Committee Decisions," *Journal of Applied Psychology* (October 1976): 559-63.
11. R. M. Dawes and B. Corrigon, "Linear Models of Decision Making," *Psychological Bulletin* (1974): 95-106.
12. See R. D. Luce and H. Raiffa, *Games and Decisions* (New York: Wiley, 1957); and R. Schlaiffer, *Probability and Statistics for Business Decisions* (New York: McGraw-Hill, 1959), pp. 445-46.
13. J. G. March and H. A. Simon, *Organizations* (New York: Wiley, 1958).
14. J. M. Ivancevich, "An Analysis of Participation in Decision Making Among Project Engineers," *Academy of Management Journal* (June 1979): 253-69.
15. See V. H. Vroom and A. Jago, "Decision Making as a Social Process: Normative and Descriptive Models of Leader Behavior," *Decision Sciences* (1974); and R. H. G. Field, "A Test of the Vroom-Yetton Normative Model of Leadership," *Journal of Applied Psychology* (October 1982): 523-32.
16. See H. Leblebici and G. R. Salancik, "Effects of Environmental Uncertainty on Information and Decision Processes in Banks," *Administrative Science Quarterly* (December 1981): 578-96.
17. L. B. Mohr, "Determinants of Innovation in Organizations," *American Political Science Review* (1969): 112.
18. See N. Howard, "Business Probes the Creative Spark," *Dun's Review* (January 1980); and G. F. Kneller, *The Art and Science of Creativity* (New York: Holt, Rinehart, and Winston, 1965).
19. H. J. Reitz, *Behavior in Organizations* (Homewood, Ill.: Irwin 1977), pp. 235-42.
20. J. M. Utterback, "Innovation in Industry and the Diffusion," *Science* (February 15, 1974): 620-26.

21. J. M. Utterback, "The Process of Innovation," *Naecon Record* (1970): 19-26.

22. I. Summers and D. E. White, "Creativity Techniques: Toward Improvement of the Decision Process," *Academy of Management Journal* (April 1976): 99-107.

23. See H. L. Lyon, J. M. Ivancevich, and J. H. Donnelly, *Management Science in Organizations* (Glenview, Ill.: Scott, Foresman, 1976); and J. W. Ulvila and R. Brown, "Decision Analysis Comes of Age," *Harvard Business Review* (September-October 1982): 130-41.

A CASE FOR ANALYSIS

Decision Making
Roy Ash of Addressograph-Multigraph

In 1977, Roy Ash staked his managerial reputation and a substantial part of his personal fortune on an effort to turn around the troubled company that Wall Street analysts privately dubbed "Addressogrief-Multigrief." As both the chief executive and the largest individual stockholder, he jumped into what he called "a classic case of corporate decision making." The full recovery of Addressograph-Multigraph, he said at the time, was to take four or five years.

Ash seemed determined to recapture the luster he had in the 1960s as president of glamorous Litton Industries and one of the brightest stars on the U.S. business scene. In Washington, he created the idea of an Office of Management and Budget, a considerable accomplishment that was obscured in the general ruin of the Nixon administration. Ash was eager to prove that the managerial success of the glory days at Litton was not a fluke.

Rescuing a creaky maker of mechanical office equipment was a very different kind of challenge from founding and running a high-technology conglomerate, but Ash believed that the right executive decisions can shape up any organization. "At a sufficiently high level of abstraction," he said, "all businesses are the same."

Ash's plans for testing that theory were summed up in the notes he continually penciled on yellow legal pads. One of the most revealing of these notes says: "Develop a much greater attachment of everybody to the bottom line—more agony and ecstasy." As he saw it, the really important change in a company is a process of psychological transformation.

In trying to do that, Ash employed a decision technique he called "immersion management." To reach the core of problems, he probed deeply into operations through relentless questioning, which one executive called "excruciating." Ash battered down bureaucratic practices in the belief that they tend to become an end in themselves. He forbade long memos, which managers submit, he says, "to have the record show the right thing for a defense later." And to make managers fully aware of the impact of their decisions, he demanded a penetrating financial analysis of everything the company did or considered doing.

Ash found plenty that seemed to need changing. A-M, in his words, was "slow in pace, conservative in attitude, and living in the past." Its once dominant line of "clanking machinery" for offset printing and addressing was being overwhelmed by quiet, more efficient electronic products of rivals that include Xerox, IBM, and Eastman Kodak. The previous management had floundered about, never coming up with a clear plan for the company's future.

Ash began his corporate revolution very quietly. The new chairman showed up in Cleveland without a single personal aide to become, he half-jokingly says, "the lion in the den, all alone." He told everyone to continue whatever they were doing and promised, "I'll catch up to you." This helped reassure A-M's management, which was still reeling from past reorganizations and personnel changes that had proved disastrous. "Lots of us," said one vice president, "were anxious about how we might fit into his plans."

Instead of immediately starting to revamp the company, Ash spent his first several months visiting its widely scattered operations and politely asking a lot of searching questions. That alone was a dramatic and generally welcomed change. His predecessors had always summoned subordinates to the headquarters building, which had long lived up to its official name, the Tower. But Ash's aim was substantive as well as symbolic. He wanted to get a handle on all the operations and assess the key people who ran them.

As he learned about the company, Ash kept jotting down what he saw as the issues that had to be resolved. Those notes, still being revised, became what he called "my brick pile" for redesigning A-M. They included some 200 items, ranging from problem products to organizational difficulties. Summing up his overall goal in his own form of mental shorthand, he wrote: "Rethink, redesign, rebuild, and re-earn." In the same spirit, he said that he wanted to make the company's executives "requestion everything."

Rather than announcing his ideas, Ash demonstrated them. He left his office door open, placed his own intercom calls to arrange meetings, and always questioned people in person, not in writing. By casually asking office secretaries to suggest ways to "debureaucratize" the company, he received some clues about which executives were heavily engaged in paper shuffling. Then he removed some of the company's copying machines "to stop breeding paperwork." Spotting a well-written complaint from an important customer in Minneapolis, Ash quickly flew off to visit him. As he now explains, "I wanted the word to get around our organization that I'm aware of what's going on."

Soon others began emulating him, even before they grasped his broader objectives. Above all, Ash wanted to "raise the excitement content" of A-M. And he wanted to make its managers personally accountable. "There's nothing like fear of failure," he said, "to motivate all of us."

Ash stirred both excitement and fear by his early discovery that no one in the corporation knew precisely which products were profitable. "I assumed that it was an innocent question," he recalled, "but the data didn't exist." Older hands at A-M had analyzed the profitability of broad product lines that included many different items, but Ash demanded that they break it down further—including the amount of salesman's time devoted to each product. Said one surviving manager, "Roy opened a lot of closets that we hadn't gotten into yet."

Finally, fifteen weeks after taking over, Ash gathered five of his key executives in St. Petersburg, Florida, and revealed his ideas for giving the company "a sense of direction." Working from his collection of notes, Ash told them, "I don't have nearly as many answers as you, but I am beginning to know some of the questions." He spent the working weekend reviewing and refining his list of problems, then assigned them to various subordinates with deadlines for action. Accustomed to Ash's style by then, the five had their own pads and pencils ready. In essence, Ash's plan was to extend the life of the company's mature products as long as possible while gradually acquiring new electronic office equipment to replace them. A-M steadily continued to sell offset duplicators and expected that its more than two hundred thousand operating machines will chug along for years—consuming supplies and requiring service. "This company," Ash said, "has a big flywheel that gives us the time and the cash throw-off to do other things." What is more, the corporation's ample hoard of cash, he said, "allows us to deal with this task deliberately, rather than frantically."

But within two weeks of the strategy session in Florida, Ash started shedding what he calls "millstone products"—either unprofitable or unpromising. "One of the things that I learned in Washington," Ash stated, "is that a new guy doesn't have a proprietary interest in earlier decisions—or in impending mistakes."

As he began swinging the ax, a sense of alarm swept through the company, but Ash's management style eased the psychic pain. He guided the managers he had inherited into solving their own problems. "Rather than just pronouncing the outcome from on high," he explained, "you lead others through joint analysis to the same conclusion."

Ash concentrated on "structuring the problems"—posing the hard questions, which forced others to provide the answers that determined the fate of dubious products. Cancelling the model 9000 lithographic copier, which had been introduced with great fanfare, came as a major blow to sales managers, says Robert Hagy, the senior vice president for marketing. "But when all the facts and figures were in," he adds, "it was the obvious thing to do."

Despite Ash's emphasis on cool, objective decision making, he was highly sensitive to the need for diplomacy with his board and stockholders. By initiating radical changes slowly and methodically, he won over even the wariest directors. As one says, "Roy had a reputation from Litton of being fast on the draw, but his prudent way of dealing with A-M's problems impressed everyone." For example, when Ash and Mellor decided to drop vice president Edwin Bruning, whose family owns nearly 3 percent of the corporation, Ash first went to Chicago to break the news gently to the family patriarch, Herbert Bruning.

Even though Ash made important and key decisions, they may have been too late—the company floundered. Asked to resign by the board of directors in 1981, Ash used his severance pay to invest in a gold-mining operation in Nevada. The new company (Newmont Mining) made the biggest U.S. gold strike of the century.

Adapted from W. Guzzardi, "The Huge Find in Roy Ash's Backyard," *Fortune* (December 27, 1982): 48-65; and L. Kraar, "Roy Ash is Having Fun at Addressogrief-Multigrief," *Fortune* (February 27, 1978): 46-52.

Questions for Discussion

1. Discuss Roy Ash's style of decision making in terms of the five process steps.
2. What interpersonal, informational, and decisional roles did Ash perform?

3. Were any elements of Ash's approach to decision making factors in his termination and the subsequent bankruptcy of the company?

EXPERIENTIAL EXERCISE
The Templeton Manufacturing Company

Purpose

1. To study the elements of a manager's decision-making style.

2. To consider the important criteria that are used to make a decision.

Required Understanding

The reader should have a basic understanding of the process of managerial decision making and the various elements that constitute a decision-making style.

How to Set Up the Exercise

Set up groups of four to eight students for the thirty to forty-five minute exercise. The groups should be separated from each other and the students asked to converse only with the members of their own group.

Background Information

The Templeton Manufacturing Company is a medium-size company that specializes in the manufacture and assembly of mobile communications equipment. The company is located in Indianapolis, Indiana, and is not unionized.

A significant decrease in international sales of the company's main product line has forced management of Templeton to consider laying off one, two, or possibly three of the poorest performers on the transmitter assembly line. The layoff may be only temporary, but the company wants to be as fair as possible in its decision choice. The layoff decision will be made by the immediate line supervisor, with approvals from the personnel manager and the plant manager.

The eight employees on the transmitter line that is to be cut back to at most five workers are as follows:

- *Julie Budde:* White; age twenty-four; single; high-school graduate; three years with the company.

- *Tom Bare:* White, age forty-three; divorced; four children to support; high-school graduate; six years with the company.

- *Rich Gomez:* Hispanic; age twenty-nine; married; two children; junior-college graduate; six years with the company.

- *Dick Jackson:* Black; age thirty-eight; married; three children; high-school graduate; ten years with the company.

- *Jack Lustig:* White, age thirty-one; single; high-school graduate; five years with the company.

- *Tina Pastore:* White; age twenty-eight; married; no children; junior-college graduate; three years with the company.

- *Sam Morrison:* White; age fifty-five; widower; three grown children; high-school graduate; three years with the company.

- *Ken Carlson:* White; age forty-nine; married; two children; high-school graduate; seventeen years with the company.

The company has evaluated these transmitter line employees on a number of factors, including productivity data and supervisory evaluations. The performance information to be used in making the layoff decision is shown in exhibit 7-12. The information represents the average performance for each of the employees over the past twelve months.

Instructions for the Exercise

1. Each group member, alone, is to *rank* the eight employees from 1 (the first to be laid off) to 8 (the last to be laid off).

2. The group should then be convened and the same ranking decision should be made as a group. When this has been accomplished, the ranking for all groups should be displayed and a spokesperson for each group should explain how the rankings were reached.

Exhibit 7-12

Templeton Manufacturing Company Employee Performance Data

Employee	Productivity			Supervisory Evaluation			
	Average Weekly[1] Output	% of Defective Units[2]	% Absent[3]	Depend-ability[4]	Ability to Take Directions[4]	Coopera-tiveness[4]	Advancement Potential[5]
Julie Budde	21.2	9.8	9.2	Poor	Fair	Fair	Low
Tom Bare	20.9	5.3	6.2	Good	Good	Good	Moderate
Rich Gomez	20.9	3.8	6.0	Good	Fair	Good	Moderate
Dick Jackson	22.8	5.7	7.8	Fair	Fair	Fair	Moderate
Jack Lustig	19.2	5.2	4.9	Excellent	Excellent	Good	High
Tina Pastore	18.7	1.9	1.1	Excellent	Good	Excellent	High
Sam Morrison	23.7	7.4	3.5	Good	Good	Good	Moderate
Ken Carlson	21.3	5.1	13.0	Fair	Good	Good	Low

1. Higher score indicates more quantity performance.
2. Lower score indicates fewer defective units.
3. Lower score indicates less absenteeism.
4. Ratings are poor, fair, good, excellent.
5. Evaluation range is low, moderate, high.

PART THREE

INTERVIEW

Clyde R. Keller

Vice President of Human Resources
Norwest Corporation
Minneapolis, Minnesota

Q: What elements are considered in Norwest's human resource planning system?

A: Our starting point is the Corporate Human Resource Mission Statement, which ties into the strategic plan for the corporation. The plan is divided into the functions and activities necessary to make the mission statement happen. Activities of our planning system include career pathing, succession planning, manpower development, organizational development, training, and management systems.

Q: To what extent are line managers involved in developing the corporate human resource plan?

A: Norwest is in a transition period—moving from a fixed-line organization to a flexible matrix design for the future. The matrix design has line managers (regional presidents) as well as business managers, along with the corporate hierarchy having input to the development of the Norwest Human Resources plan.

Q: What factors does Norwest's management consider in developing the organization's structure?

A: The main consideration for the current matrix structure was flexibility, quick decision-making, and problem-solving. Norwest's process of changing a traditional organizational structure to a matrix structure involves the arrangement of nine regions and four businesses joined by vice chairmen to whom both report.

Q: What essential responsibilities do the company's officers have?

A: The business managers decide what product or service is to be created/offered. The regional presidents decide how the product/service will be delivered. The business managers design and develop—the regional presidents implement and refine.

Establishing Order, Function, and Design: Organizing

Q: Can you explain how you identify problems within the current structure?

A: Indicators for problems include duplication of efforts and lack of communication between regions, business managers, and support staff. If subtle power struggles to determine who runs the organizations become evident, we know we need solutions.

Q: What is the relationship between Norwest's overall corporate strategy and its human resources planning?

A: The human resource planning activities support the overall corporate strategy. Input from the nine regional presidents and the four business managers is the primary planning method. Human Resources is included in the strategic planning process and can guide and/or respond to the company's human resource needs as required.

Q: What emphasis do you place on effective communication between managers in your organization?

A: Communication is the most important of all management skills. It affects all management functions and all other skills. We think there must be continuous communication between and through all levels of the company.

Q: How much formal training in communications do you recommend for your managers?

A: We have formal and informal communications. A management council composed of the chairman, vice chairmen, regional presidents, and business managers meets regularly. Our management system (performance, planning, evaluation, and development) requires communication training, which is expressed informally with meetings, committees, publications, and, more formally, with training and development programs, as well as a roll-up system of reporting and sharing of data. We do social survey research regularly. Norwest has a serious commitment to creating effective interpersonal, managerial, and organizational communications. We build communication training into all levels and types of training (management, sales, technical, and other). There is never too much communication training.

Q: What important skills should future managers develop to become effective in the human resources area?

A: The major requirement for success in human resources in present and future organizations is flexibility. Managers must acquire the ability to handle, change, and develop their knowledge, skills, and abilities to respond to interpersonal as well as managerial and organizational needs or requirements.

The technical human resource skills will not be enough in the future. Human resource managers must understand and approach their functions much like line managers do. Human resources is any organization's most important resource. And the manager of the human resource function must be one of the organization's best.

8

Dimensions of Organizations

Chapter Outline

Key Points

1. There are three key dimensions of organizations: grouping, influence, and coordination.
2. The grouping dimension, which concerns the process of grouping jobs and departments, involves the concepts of job specialization, departmentalization, and line-staff relationships.
3. Establishing authority within the newly formed units is the function of the influence dimension. Three sources of authority are identified: legitimate, acceptance theory, and the unity of command principle.
4. The chain of command, span of control, and the centralization/decentralization issues relate to how authority is implemented in organizations.
5. One of the most important authority implementation issues concerns the degree of decentralization the organization adopts. This decision depends on such factors as culture, cost and risk of decisions, managerial philosophies, locus of expertise, and the availability of capable managers.
6. Coordination requirements in organizations are determined by the level of interdependence and the differences in time and goal orientation between interacting units.
7. Rules and procedures, hierarchial referral, planning, liaison persons, task forces, teams and integrating departments are identified as some of the mechanisms available to the manager to ensure coordinated effort.
8. An organization adapts to increased international activity by forming an international division or by developing an integrated structure. The success of decentralization attempts is highly dependent on cultural practices.

Allied Corporation

The process of taking absolute control of a firm's direction while giving managers the illusion that they have more freedom than ever before is perhaps many an executive's wildest dream. But in the short time that Edward L. Hennessy, Jr. has managed Allied Corporation (formerly Allied Chemical Company) as chief executive, he has demonstrated that it can be done. Many of the changes instituted by Hennessy have dealt with reorganization.

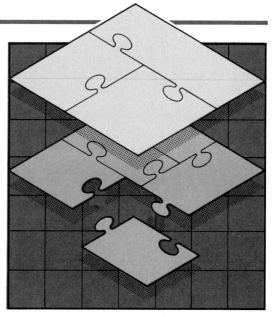

One of the first things Hennessy did after assuming command was to restructure the organization, reducing the nine previous divisions to three operating companies—Fibers and Plastics, Chemicals, and Union Texas Petroleum. He has since added Eltra Corporation to form the nucleus of a new electrical division, and subsequently he created a fifth division to specialize in laboratory equipment, centered on his acquisition of Fisher Scientific Company.

Further reorganization concerned a radical change in the firm's hierarchy. Hennessy's predecessor surrounded himself with a large corporate staff that frequently overruled divisional managers' authority to handle purchasing, engineering, and basic marketing functions. Hennessy's belief in strong centralized control didn't include large numbers of staff personnel. He trimmed the staff by over 700 people, for a savings of $30 million.

As part of Hennessy's control orientation, managers are required to set specific, measurable goals that they must meet. He admits to being a "return on assets" nut, and he expects his managers to be as bottom-line oriented as he is. Managers are given sufficient authority and responsibility to reach these goals. For example, the manager of an oil-drilling project previously had a spending ceiling of $1 million. Beyond that, he had to get several corporate approvals. Currently, his maximum is $6 million, which enables him to make quicker decisions. The other side of the coin, however, is that he can no longer blame the corporate staff for missed opportunities or less than satisfactory results.

Hennessy has made it clear that bonuses are directly tied to outstanding performance, with no excuses permitted. "I'm very demanding. I'm also results oriented, and I reward accordingly." True to his word, one recent year Hennessy divided up $1.5 million in bonuses to his top managers.

In a few years, Hennessy has taken Allied from three core businesses into five, and is moving toward achieving a corporate goal to "have more businesses in young, growing industries to balance our mature businesses." The main problem is Hennessy's predilection for buying companies, not all of which have paid off. Some experts not only question some of these acquisitions, they also wonder how Hennessy can maintain centralized control over a dispersed empire.

Adapted from "The Hennessy Style May Be What Allied Needs," *Business Week* (January 11, 1982): 126-29.

8

We now move into a four-chapter sequence about how organizations are ordered and designed—the organizing function. We will devote the first two chapters to the important subject of designing an effective structure for an organization. Once we see how a structure is developed, we will discuss the process of acquiring and training a work force to staff an organization. We will complete our presentation with an analysis of the communication process that occurs within the organization's structure.

The Allied Corporation *Practice of Management* section is a good illustration of the many elements that make up an organization. In it, we are introduced to the dimensions of structure, line-staff relationships, authority, and responsibility. A look at these basic organizational dimensions will answer the following questions:

- What should be the content of employee jobs and how should these jobs be grouped together? The answer to this question of *grouping* involves the concepts of job specialization, departmentalization, and line-staff positions.

- How can patterns of *influence* be established within the groupings or units? Issues of authority, scalar chain of command, span of control, and centralization and decentralization relate to this question.

- What mechanisms are needed to insure the proper *coordination* between the different organizational units? To answer this question, we must analyze the determinants and mechanisms for coordination.

A discussion of each of these questions forms the major sections of this chapter. In the next chapter, we will investigate a fourth question: What is the effect of the external environment, the organization's strategies, and its technology on its structure?

The Organizing Function

In the previous four chapters, our focus was on establishing the *framework for performance* in the manager's job. Setting goals, developing plans, and making decisions to achieve these stated goals, however, requires the *coordinated* effort of all individuals and groups within the organization. In other words, the previous chapters emphasized the *formulation* part of the manager's job; the next chapters deal with the process of *implementing* these formulated goals, strategies, and plans.

We will define the *organizing function* as the process of achieving a coordinated effort through the design of a structure of tasks, authority, people, and communication. This definition draws attention to at least three points:

- The meaning of the word *design* implies a rational and conscious *process* on the part of managers to develop the most effective interactions and interrelationships within the organization.

- The *result* of the design effort is a structure or framework within the organization.

- This structure includes grouping similar jobs, establishing authority relationships across and among different jobs, placing the most capable people in these jobs, and developing the most effective means of communication between those who define jobs and jobholders.

Exhibit 8-1
Dimensions Defining Organizational Structure

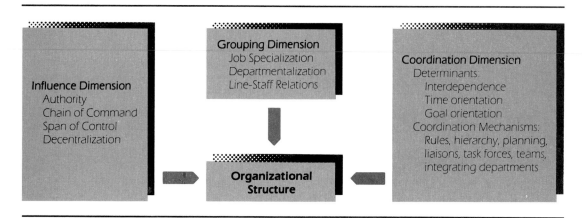

An effectively structured organization, then, develops the framework for the organization to achieve its goals. It permits employees to know what their responsibilities are so that they can concentrate on the tasks at hand. Structure enhances the process of coordinating the activities of managers and subordinates so time and effort are put to the best use.

This chapter focuses on the following structural dimensions: the grouping dimension—aggregating or clustering jobs and units; the influence dimension—establishing authority, command, and control; and the coordination dimension—developing coordination mechanisms.[1] These relationships are outlined in exhibit 8-1.

The Grouping Dimension

One of the first and probably most important dimensions of an organization's structure is that of defining the content of jobs and then grouping these jobs into units. Formally, this is a *grouping* function called the division of labor. We will discuss three aspects of the division of labor: (1) defining individual jobs, or job specialization; (2) the horizontal division of labor, or departmentalization; and (3) line-staff relationships.

Job Specialization

In order to accomplish the required work, managers generally divide it into specialized tasks to be filled by employees. For example, the personnel department may have a training specialist, a wage and salary specialist, a college recruiting specialist, and a labor relations and contract negotiation specialist. On a different scale, a building contractor may employ carpenters, plumbers, electricians, and bricklayers. This specialization of tasks provides an identity for the job and those performing it. This indicator is often called the *job definition* because it establishes what the workers are to do, how they are to do it, and what the organization will give in return for the effort (e.g., wages).

The concepts of job scope and depth may be used to describe the extent or degree of job specialization.[2] *Job scope* refers to the number of movements a job involves. Sometimes called *job variety,* scope relates to the different things a worker does within a certain cycle of work. *Job depth,* on the other hand, concerns the relative freedom the worker has in planning, organizing, and controlling the assigned duties. This relates to such factors as the degree of autonomy, responsibility, and the extent of decision-making freedom.

For example, consider two jobs within a manufacturing organization such as the Fisher Body Division of General Motors. A stamping press operator's job can be considered to be quite narrow in scope and depth. The task is to operate the press that stamps out car doors from a flat piece of sheet steel. Variety is limited in this job to positioning a sheet of steel from the conveyor belt in the press, starting the stamping by pressing a button, and moving the stamped piece onto the conveyor belt to the finishing operation. The cycle for this job is relatively short, something less than one minute per unit. The operator's responsibilities are also limited by well spelled out safety and operating rules and procedures.

On the other hand, consider the job of plant manager of this GM facility. This manager's job is quite broad in scope and depth. There is considerable variety in what this manager does, involving responsibility for overall effectiveness of the production, maintenance, personnel, and accounting functions. From our view of the manager's job, the plant manager's position involves many aspects of planning, organizing, leading, controlling, and change. The manager operates relatively autonomously because that job contains a high degree of freedom in decision making.

The degree of job specialization is highly dependent on the particular school of management thought adopted, as discussed in chapter 2. For example, a manager who believes in the principles of the classical school (scientific management) would define an employee's job with the objective of improving efficiency. In defining the stamping press operator's job, the manager would break it down into its fundamental movements and then attempt to make these movements as efficient as possible. One could expect that the result would be a job quite narrow in scope and depth.

The manager who adopts an approach similar to that of the behavioral school, however, is concerned with the problems associated with overspecializing jobs, such as boredom, fatigue, and monotony. These problems can lead to adverse effects such as increased absenteeism, turnover, and poor workmanship. As we will discuss in chapter 12, the manager making job specialization decisions must be concerned not only with criteria for economic efficiency but with psychological criteria as well.[3]

Horizontal Division of Labor: Departmentalization

Once the manager has decided on how *individual* jobs are defined, the next step is to determine how to group these jobs into different units or departments. When this grouping is done horizontally in an organization, it is called *departmentalization.*

The basis for making departmentalization decisions is one of *focus,* either internal or external. An internal focus is called departmentalization by function; an external focus involves an orientation toward product, geographical dispersion, customer type, time, type of equipment, and so forth.

Internal Focus—Functional Departmentalization   The functional approach is by far the most widely adopted form of departmentalization. Exhibit 8-2 shows an example of a functional arrangement in a manufacturing firm. (When an organization's structure is shown in schematic form, it is sometimes referred to as an organization *chart*). It is termed an *internal* focus because it is designed on the basis of the operations or functions performed by employees. In exhibit 8-2, the functional arrangement is by manufacturing, marketing, research and development, finance, and personnel. This approach also applies to many other organizations. For example, a medical school can be arranged by such specialties as surgery, pediatrics, psychiatry, or internal medicine.

The functional form has two advantages. First, it can be highly cost efficient because the individual specialties are grouped together, which eliminates costly duplication of effort. Second, it makes management easier because managers have to be experts in only a narrow range of skills.

There are also two major disadvantages of the functional structure. First, as the organization becomes large and more complex, this arrangement can prove to be quite cumbersome. For example, a functional arrangement in a hospital may have a single department of nursing. However, within the department there may be included such specialties as trauma nurses (i.e., emergency rooms), heart attack specialists, cancer ward specialists, pediatric emergency nurses, nurses specializing in paraplegic/quadriplegic patients, and so forth. Second, the functional arrangement does not readily adapt to change. Obtaining quick decisions or actions on specific problems may require more time because such decisions have to be made by higher level managers. In exhibit 8-2, if a problem of product quality arises with a customer, the marketing vice president must involve the manufacturing vice president and the president to solve it. This takes valuable time from executives who might be better invested in such activities as environmental analyses and planning.

External Focus—Product Departmentalization   In a product arrangement, departments are grouped together on the basis of product or family of products and services marketed to customers. Exhibit 8-2 shows an example. This type of arrangement is particularly applicable to those organizations that market a wide variety of products and services and require production technologies and/or marketing methods that differ markedly between products. For example, two of the main product lines for General Electric are consumer products (e.g., televisions) and electrical turbines. General Foods could be another example, since it produces and markets both breakfast cereals and dog food. There are too many *dissimilarities* between these product lines for them to be grouped together in a functional design.

The major advantages and disadvantages of the product arrangement are just the opposite of the functional form. That is, because it specifically is developed along external lines, the product form can be quite adaptable to change. It provides the mechanisms for the organization to react quickly to, for example, competitive

Exhibit 8-2
Functional and Product Departmentalization

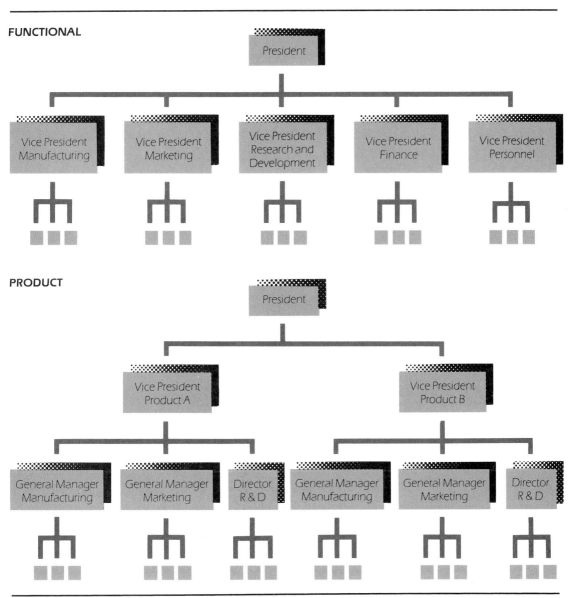

changes or new customer needs. The main disadvantage is that there may be situations in which there is a duplication of effort or functions (see exhibit 8-2). This can be costly to the organization in terms of equipment and personnel. For example, in a product arrangement there may be two or more research and development labs, while in a functional arrangement there would be only one laboratory. This situation relates to the concept of "economies of scale."[4]

A variation of the product form is the *project* arrangement. This form groups jobs into departments by the particular project that is being performed. This is a popular arrangement used by large construction companies such as Brown and Root, Fluor, and Bechtel. That is, project A may be an oil refinery in the Middle East, project B may be a large bridge in the state of Washington, and so forth. The other characteristics are similar to the product arrangement.

External Focus—Geographic Departmentalization   As shown in exhibit 8-3, a geographic arrangement groups units on the basis of location. The exhibit is a partial illustration of the geographic departmentalization used by Federated Department Stores and its regional merchandising operations. The rationale is that if the markets are widely dispersed in different regions, response time to consumer needs will improve if the particular units in each region are grouped together.

Two additional factors or principles concerning departmentalization should be pointed out. First, in most cases, the particular arrangement does not remain intact as one goes up or down managerial or organizational levels. This represents the principle of *alternation*. For example, as depicted in the product form of exhibit 8-2, the first organizational level after the president is arranged along a product departmentalization. The next level, however, is a functional arrangement, and so on. In another organization, the first level may be formed with a functional arrangement, and the next level would usually be a product departmentalization. The important point for managers to recognize about this situation is that departmentalization by different arrangements can and does occur at each level in the organization.

Second, exhibit 8-4, the organization chart for the Mead Corporation, illustrates the concept of *mixed* departmentalization. There are times when an organization does not want to become a fully functional- or product-structured firm. For instance, top management may feel that a product arrangement will work effectively with groupings of manufacturing and marketing. However, they also may believe that keeping planning, personnel, finance, research and development, and legal counsel in a functional form would be best. In the Mead Corporation example, we see where international, corporate staff, and corporate development are grouped functionally.

Using our cost and adaptive criteria, we see a dual effect of mixed departmentalization. That is, for purposes of quick reaction time, manufacturing and marketing are structured product-wise, while for control purposes, finance and personnel retain a functional arrangement.

Line-Staff Relationships

As an organization increases in size and complexity, it may become necessary to introduce personnel with specialized knowledge and skills. When these specialists are

Exhibit 8-3
Geographical Departmentalization: Federated Department Stores

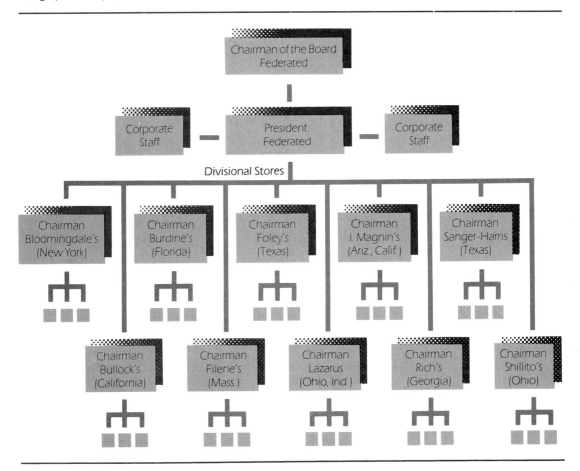

departmentalized in a separate structure, what is created are line and staff relationships.[5] Line groupings, represented by manufacturing and marketing, are those units directly involved in producing and selling the product or service. Staff groupings, characterized by personnel and finance, are those units that perform in support of the line functions but are generally not involved in direct production or selling. We will look at two aspects of staff relationships—type and role.

There are at least two *types* of staff positions. The first, the executive staff, assists other managers and executives in their work. Characterized by such titles as "assistant to the vice president" or "staff assistant," individuals who hold these jobs generally advise, counsel, or take on special projects for the executive. The functional staff generally consists of an entire unit or department of specialists. Examples include purchasing and personnel.

Staff personnel assume many *roles* in organizations. They can perform market research (planning), acquire employees and procure equipment and raw materials

Exhibit 8-4
Mixed Departmentalization: The Mead Corporation

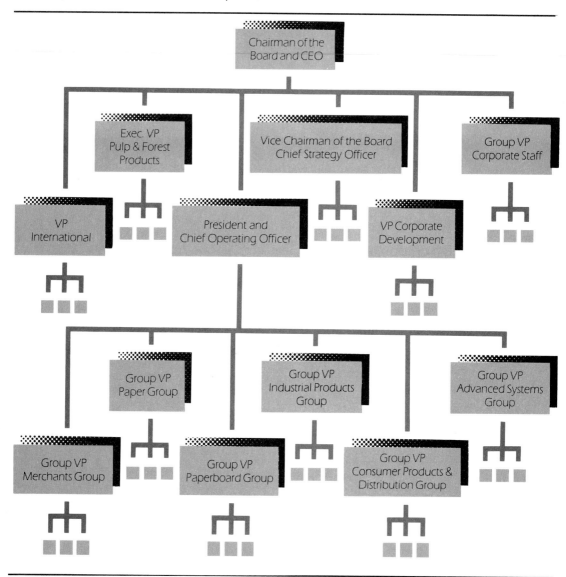

(organizing), prepare manuals and specifications (leading), or assist in quality control and financial analysis (controlling). In each case, the role nearly always has an advisory nature. Staff personnel run into problems due to the limits of their specialized training, the social distance imposed by structural differences, and the need to rely on voluntary cooperation rather than formal authority. These problems will come to the surface when we discuss authority and coordination activities.

The Influence Dimension

Once methods of departmentalization have been chosen and jobs have been grouped or clustered, mechanisms are needed to influence the behavior of employees within the departments. This influence dimension is referred to as *authority*. Before we discuss the sources of authority in organizations, the difference between authority, power, and responsibility should be pointed out.

For our purposes, *authority* is defined as the right to command and allocate resources.[6] Lines of authority link and integrate the various organizational departments in order to achieve stated goals. *Power,* often confused with authority, is the ability to influence another person with the control of resources.[7] Power is thus related to the concept of dependence. Person A has power and can influence person B when A controls certain resources that are needed by B. For example, the manufacturing department of an organization has power over the packaging and shipping department because without manufactured products, no packaging and shipping can occur. In a sense, authority is a subset of power, since a manager controls certain resources (e.g., job assignments, wage increases, and so forth) that are desired by subordinates.

Finally, *responsibility* is accountability for the achievement of goals, the efficient use of resources, and the adherence to organizational plans, procedures, and rules. Once a manager accepts responsibility, it becomes an obligation to perform the assigned work.

Sources of Authority

At least three sources of authority can be identified in most organizations. These include legitimate authority, the acceptance theory of authority, and the unity of command.

Legitimate Authority   Authority can be viewed as one individual's right to influence other members of the organization. This is termed the *legitimate* source of authority.[8] An organization gives its managers the right to influence others. A vice president has authority over subordinate managers, and each of these managers has the right to influence subordinate employees.

Acceptance Theory of Authority   One of the foundations of the authority concept was stated in 1938 by Barnard in *The Functions of the Executive*.[9] He stated that a person can and will accept a form of communication as authoritative only when four conditions exist: (1) the person can and does understand the communication; (2) at the time of the decision, the person believes it is not inconsistent with the purpose of the organization; (3) the person believes that the acceptance of the communication is compatible with personal interests; and (4) the person is able both mentally and physically to comply with it. These four conditions have been called the "acceptance theory of authority" because the right to command depends upon whether or not the subordinates obey. The manager can use punishment (or the threat of punishment) to assure acceptance. However, the subordinate may decide to endure the punishment or quit the organization rather than accept an effort at influence through authority.

Unity of Command   The principle of unity of command originates from the classical school of management and concerns the relationship between managers and their subordinates.[10] Stated simply, the unity of command suggests that an employee should have *one and only one* immediate supervisor or manager. This principle is founded on two beliefs. First, it further legitimizes the manager's authority by clarifying lines of authority. Second, it helps eliminate the problem of conflicting orders. Under this conflict, the employee is put into an uncomfortable position—obeying one order will leave the other manager dissatisfied. When there are clear lines of authority, these problems are removed, and the employee may concentrate on the task at hand.

Implementation of Authority

Because authority is a key element in management, there are a number of ways it is implemented in organizations. Three specific implementation concepts will be discussed: (1) scalar chain of command; (2) span of control; and (3) the centralization-decentralization issue.

Scalar Chain of Command   The scalar chain of command states that authority in the organization flows, one level at a time, through a series of managers ranging from the highest to the lowest managerial ranks.[11] Each link is a single manager, and the meshing of individual links forms a unified chain. A manufacturing firm's chain of command was shown earlier in exhibit 1-3.

The chain of command concept is founded on the unity of command principle. The latter is related to the interaction between superior and subordinates, and the chain of command takes this further by detailing how the principle works its way through the entire organization. The more clearly the lines of authority and responsibility flow from top management to every subordinate, the more likely there will be effective decision making and proper communication.

Span of Control   The span of control is measured by the number of subordinates that report directly to a single supervisor or manager.[12]

Various mechanisms of determining the optimum number of subordinates that should report to a single manager have been discussed. One of the first versions of the span of control argument was presented by Sir Ian Hamilton during World War I.[13] He stated that a system with no more than six subordinates reporting to a superior would enable the superior to get his job done effectively. Surprisingly, this number has held up for many years, even though the origins of Hamilton's number are unclear. In today's organizations, however, a manager's span of control can vary with many factors. Steadfastly adhering to a particular number may prove to be a much less effective strategy than a careful analysis of situational factors.

A. V. Graicunas later developed a mathematical representation of the span of control concept.[14] He pointed out that in selecting a workable span of control, managers should consider at least three points: (1) the direct one-to-one relationships with the people they directly supervise; (2) the relationships the manager has with groups of two or more subordinates; and (3) cross-relationships between and among the individual subordinates.

From an analysis of these three possible relationships, Graicunas developed this formula to give the number of superior-subordinate relationships that may require managerial attention:

$$C = n(2^n/2 + n - 1)$$

where C designates the total potential contacts, and n is the number of subordinates reporting directly to the manager. According to the equation, the number of relationships increases geometrically as the number of subordinates increases arithmetically. For example, two subordinates require a total of 6 relationships; five subordinates require 100 relationships; and ten subordinates require 5,210 relationships.

Even without the use of this formulation, it was clear that managers' span of control directly relates to the level of obtained effectiveness. It has been stated, "Harassed supervisors and frustrated subordinates often mean that the supervisor has too broad a span of control." Conversely, harassed subordinates and frustrated supervisors often are indicators of too narrow a span of control.[15]

Given this situation, what are the elements the manager should consider in selecting a span of control? There are at least three components:

Types of Control Spans   Two types can be identified: executive and operative. *Executive* span of control includes middle and top management positions in the organization. Since these positions deal primarily with matters of planning and policy, a narrow span of control on the order of three to nine is usually adopted. *Operative* span of control is within the realm of first-line managers and some middle-level managers. The primary activities performed by these managers can many times be fairly routine, which requires less direct contact and interaction. In this case, the span of control can increase to as many as thirty. In essence, this argument suggests that span of control can and does vary by level in the organization—smaller for executives and larger for lower level managers.

Situational Factors   Many internal situational factors can affect the decision on managerial span of control. There are at least six factors for the manager to analyze: (a) The manager's ability to supervise large numbers of people; (b) the relative similarity or dissimilarity of the work being performed; (c) the frequency and quality of employee interactions needed for effectiveness; (d) the incidence of new problems to be faced; (e) the need for supervision—the extent that rules, procedures, and other guidelines can direct the work of employees; (f) the physical dispersion of employees.[16]

Tall Versus Flat Structures   The selection of a span of control can have a significant effect on the "shape" of the organization, commonly termed *tall vs. flat structures*. At issue is the number of managerial or supervisory levels involved. A flat structure is one with few managerial levels, while a structure with many managerial levels is termed tall.[17] Generally speaking, a tall structure requires more personnel due to the increased number of managerial people involved.

The proponents of both flat and tall structures point out certain advantages and disadvantages for each. The flat structure is said to be more cost efficient and, by providing more variety of work, may result in high employee job satisfaction. On the negative side, it is not very adaptable to change and the large span of control may result in coordination problems. The tall structure can adopt to change better and there is better coordination, plus the narrow span of control facilitates the development of skills. The disadvantages include increased costs due to the added managerial levels, as well as problems of employee dissatisfaction associated with performing routine, more specialized jobs.

The many research studies that have been conducted over the years to study these factors, however, have been inconclusive, indicating that we cannot select the best span of control on the basis of a formula or set of rules. There are just too many variables involved in any organization. For example, in the next chapter, we will suggest that the nature of an organization's work (what we will call *technology*) is an important factor. In a manufacturing firm, the routine and repetitive nature of the work may be appropriate for a tall structure. On the other hand, the innovative and creative work in a research and development laboratory may be handled by a rather flat structure.

Centralization/Decentralization   The words *centralization/decentralization* have been discussed for many years, usually creating confusion. For our purposes, we will present these concepts as the degree to which the *power to make decisions* is transferred to lower level managers. When all the power for decision-making is in the hands of a single, high-level executive, it is called a *centralized* structure. When the power to make decisions is dispersed among lower-level managers, it is called a *decentralized* structure.

Centralization/decentralization are not two separate concepts but opposite ends of a single continuum of *delegation*. At the decentralized end of the continuum, the phrase "You make the decision" would be representative; the phrase "I will make the decision" implies a centralization. In the middle of the continuum, the statement "Study this problem, but don't make a decision until you've checked with me first" would be appropriate.

There are two types of decentralization that can be identified in most organizations—vertical and horizontal. *Vertical decentralization* concerns the dispersal of power *down* the chain of command. This is the case of a higher-level manager delegating the power to a subordinate manager to make a decision. In some cases, this may also be called vertical division of labor.

Horizontal decentralization relates to line and staff relationships. When, as in the case of vertical decentralization, the authority and power to make a decision remains within a particular function, this is called *line* authority. When decision authority flows to managers outside the line structure to analysts, support specialists, and other experts, such a delegation is called decentralization to *staff* authority. Staff authority is auxiliary and sometimes temporary. For example, many organizations have created the positions of assistant to the president, assistant to the senior vice president, and so forth. In some cases, the line manager will instruct the "assistant to" positionholder to attend a meeting and make inputs or decisions as if the line manager were present.

The use of centralization or decentralization has its value to the degree that it assists the organization in achieving its stated goals. The decision whether or not to decentralize is a complex process that involves a number of considerations. These include:[18]

External Environmental Factors   The impact of such environmental factors as governmental legislation; unions; federal, state, and local tax policies; and variations in the economic trends in different countries in which the organization operates are important influences on the decision whether to decentralize or not. As the environmental problems faced by an organization become more complex and dispersed, we would expect that some form of decentralization would be used. For example, many large multi-division/multi-product corporations face the prospect of negotiating labor contracts with ten, twenty, or more different labor unions. Rather than conduct the negotiation on a centralized basis with a headquarters unit, these organizations usually choose to delegate such decisions to the divisional level. This is also the way many organizations have decided to handle international operations. Rather than make decisions in the U.S., sometimes many thousands of miles away from the foreign operations, these organizations permit many of the day-to-day and long-term decisions to be made by the managers on site.

Growth of the Organization   In managing a complex organization, it is nearly impossible to make all decisions in one location or in one head. This is especially true for organizations in the midst of significant growth phases. Because situations, problems, and opportunities are developing at a rapid pace, top management may have to delegate the decisions on these issues to lower levels in the organization. Unless this decentralization occurs, the organization may bypass a significant opportunity or be faced with a problem that has mushroomed from inattention. In some cases, organizations build decentralization into their strategic plans to ensure proper attention.

Cost and Risk   Many managers are reluctant to delegate authority on a decision when the consequences may have a significant impact on the organization now or in the future. When the risks and costs are high, the tendency to centralize is strong. In the framework we developed in the last chapter, we can expect strategic decisions to be centralized, while administrative and operating decisions normally would be decentralized.

Management Philosophies   Some managers and organizations pride themselves on a policy, sometimes historical in nature, of making all the important decisions. Others point to a past practice of successful delegation to subordinate managers. This is nothing more than the adherence to a habit formed from past activities. As we all know, it is sometimes difficult to break a habit, whether it be smoking or centralizing decisions.

In the decade since SCM Corporation acquired it, the company's Cleveland-based Glidden-Durkee division evolved into a big conglomerate in its own right. Its centralized approach to management, however, was getting in the way of successful operations. A capital expenditure proposed by a Glidden-Durkee plant manager, for example, would take seven months to wend its way through operating managers, be analyzed by the Glidden-Durkee financial staff, and then go to New York, where the SCM staff would do it all over again. The same lead time existed in budgeting and planning.

To solve this problem, Paul H. Elicker, president and chief executive officer of SCM, decided to restructure Glidden-Durkee. His main move was to split Glidden-Durkee into four separate units: coatings and resins, with headquarters in Cleveland; food, also in Cleveland; chemical-metallurgical, based in Baltimore; and organic chemicals, with headquarters in Jacksonville, Florida. Decentralizing this way allowed for greater concentration of operations, and the promise of better performance.

In effect, Elicker recognized that the businesses that Glidden-Durkee was in were different and required specialists to run them. He noted that it was hard to mix a high-growth business, such as foods and chemicals, with low-growth operations, such as coatings and resins. Managing them requires a different approach. Coatings and resins growth will come primarily from expanding marketing and R&D efforts, and success in chemicals will come as a result of the skill with which capital investments are made.

So far, the restructuring has gone smoothly—no small feat considering the types of managerial jobs that were involved. One key reason for the smooth transition was that there was no loss of pay to any manager. Another factor is that a manager's chances of heading a division are greatly enhanced, since there are more divisions to go around. In addition, bonuses are now awarded based on the performance of the smaller divisions, where managers can have a more direct effect.

Adapted from "Streamlining the Management at SCM," *Business Week* (February 21, 1977).

Locus of Expertise   There are many instances when managers just do not have the necessary knowledge and understanding to make a decision. This *expertise* may reside at some lower level in the organization. For example, in selling consumer products in Europe, it may be a more effective policy to permit the European marketing manager to make decisions rather than make them from the home office.

Abilities of Lower-Level Managers   One of the basic assumptions of a policy of decentralization is that capable managers at lower levels are available to make effective decisions. However, too often there is a shortage of skilled and trained managers, forcing top management to centralize most decisions. This situation is somewhat circular in nature. That is, if decision-making authority is not decentralized because of lack of capable and skilled managers, how will these managers become skilled and capable unless they make important decisions? Also, if the organization is reluctant to decentralize some decisions, it will have a difficult time retaining young and ambitious managers who want to get more involved in the decision-making process. When good people leave the organization, it makes the decision to decentralize that much harder. It is apparent that some form of decentralization should occur if the organization wishes to train and hang onto future managers. In fact, many organizations use decentralization as a means of identifying future managers—those who perform successfully are moved quickly up the promotion ladder, and those who perform less successfully move much slower, if at all.[19]

Managers should be aware of certain factors that can alter the way decentralization is implemented in organizations. First, the decision to decentralize need not be permanent. Decentralization can occur over a period of time and then change when the situation changes. For example, in the 1970s Levi Strauss & Company created 17 marketing units, each with its own sales force, to cover its new segments in men's, women's, and children's wearing apparel. Sales growth in some areas failed to justify the large overhead and a few of the new marketing units found their stiffest competition coming from other Levi's groups. By the early 1980s, the 17 marketing units were replaced with six regional marketing units that handled all product lines.[20]

Second, various levels of decentralization can occur within the same organization. A multiplant chemical company may decentralize its manufacturing division at the plant level, but keep finance and accounting centralized at the corporate level.

Finally, managers must recognize that subordinates may be reluctant to accept decentralization attempts by managers. This is especially true in organizations where decentralization has not been widely practiced. In these cases, managers must try to remove the barriers to decentralization attempts. He or she can do this by establishing goals, providing incentives, training subordinates in making decisions, and giving direction and guidance.

The decision to decentralize decision-making authority is obviously not as straightforward as you may have first thought, nor is it universally accepted in organizations. General Electric, Sears, E.I. Du Pont, and General Motors have been successful with decentralized decision making. On the other hand, General Dynamics and International Harvester have had equal success with a more centralized approach. Managers must closely diagnose their own situations before deciding on the degree of centralization. Blind obedience to any single approach may lead to less than satisfactory levels of effectiveness.

 **The Coordination Dimension**

In our discussion of the grouping dimension of an organizational structure, we focused on the most effective means of grouping jobs and units. The influence dimension deals with establishing authority and command within units or departments. Finally, in our discussion of the coordination dimension, we will focus on developing mechanisms to *integrate* separate units and departments in order to achieve organizational goals. Without some form of coordination, individuals and larger units would go about their divided work activities and lose sight of their important roles *within* an organization.

Determinants of Coordination Needs

There are many examples of the need for coordination in all types of organizations. Consider the emergency room in a hospital. In order to treat an automobile accident patient, the attending physician needs the assistance of members of the nursing staff, pathology lab personnel for blood analyses, X-ray technicians, and possibly other specialized physicians. In the same manner, the production control manager at a large chemical plant needs the help of manufacturing and sales personnel in order to schedule production rates and product grades that can satisfy both consumer demands for product and the needs of the manufacturing manager for steady and efficient production. Coordination is both an important and complex managerial task.

Before discussing the mechanisms for coordination, it is necessary to identify the basic determinants and origins of coordination needs. For our purposes, three determinants will be discussed: (1) interdependence; (2) time orientation; and (3) goal orientation of interacting units.

Interdependence   Interdependence between two or more departments is the degree to which the interactions between departments must be coordinated to attain a desired level of performance. Three types of interdependence are most frequently discussed: (1) pooled; (2) sequential; and (3) reciprocal.[21]

Pooled interdependence describes the relationship of departments that are relatively *independent* of each other but that provide a discrete contribution to the larger organization. The Chevrolet assembly plant in Oklahoma is independent of the Cadillac assembly plant in Michigan on most manufacturing or coordination matters. They are, however, interdependent in a pooled fashion because each contributes to the overall performance of General Motors.

Sequential interdependence exists when an output of one group becomes an input to another group. For example, sequential interdependence exists between the departments of manufacturing and shipping in an organization. The outputs of the manufacturing department—finished products—are the major inputs for the shipping department.

Reciprocal interdependence exists when certain outputs of each department become inputs to these same departments. In other words, the departments are highly dependent on one another and thus require a significant degree of coordination. For example, consider the departments of operations and maintenance of a domestic airline company. These two departments are reciprocally interdependent because, on one hand, the outputs of the operations department—an aircraft needing repair—serve as an input to the maintenance department. On the other hand, the output of the maintenance department—a fully repaired aircraft—is an input to the operations department.

For successful performance, it is important for managers to understand that as one progresses from pooled to reciprocal, the three types of interdependence require greater interaction and hence greater coordination efforts. That is, when advancing from pooled to sequential and finally to reciprocal interdependence, everyone involved must be aware that the activities of one department depend on the actions of other departments. Effective performance is a direct result of how this interdependence is successfully coordinated. A summary of this concept is shown in exhibit 8-5.

Exhibit 8-5
Summary of Interdependence Types

Type	Degree of Dependence	Description	Example
Reciprocal	High	Certain outputs of each group become inputs for other groups, or to each other. 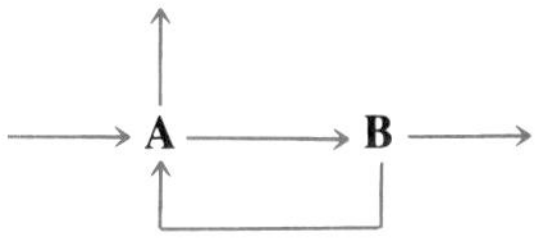 ⟶ A ⟶ B ⟶	The interaction between operations and maintenance in a domestic airline company.
Sequential	Moderate	Outputs of one group become inputs of other groups.  ⟶ A ⟶ B ⟶	Automobile assembly line activities.
Pooled	Low	Groups or units are relatively independent of each other, but contribute to the overall goals of the organization. 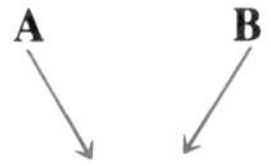 A B	Separate manufacturing plants of a single organization that only infrequently interact.

Time Orientation   Managers who spend several years in a particular type of job tend to become accustomed to organizing their work in a predictable fashion that helps them perform that job effectively. Many factors within the manager's job contribute to this situation, one of which is the *time orientation*.[22] We can define *time orientation* as the length of time required to obtain information or results relating to the performance of a task. Manufacturing managers, for example, usually are concerned with problems that can be solved within a short time. A production rate problem or an equipment malfunction requires the manager to seek a solution as quickly as possible. On the other hand, a research chemist may require months, or even years, to develop a new product or process.

The coordination issue posed by time orientation is important for units or departments that must get together to solve problems or perform joint activities. For example, a serious problem has arisen in the quality of an important product of a plastics manufacturer. Because the problem is unlike anything the company has previously encountered, the divisional vice president appoints a task force made up of representatives from manufacturing, marketing, production control, and research. Because of individual time orientations, the manufacturing representative may move for a "let's find a quick solution" approach while the research representative may opt for a more lengthy "let's investigate all the alternatives" route. Given these divergent approaches, it may be difficult for the task force to reach a satisfactory solution.

Goal Orientation   *Goal orientation* focuses on the particular set of goals that are of major concern to the manager.[23] To be effective, managers must focus clearly on goals that are related to their own work. For example, manufacturing managers concern themselves with raw material costs, processing and inventory costs, production volume, and the quality of the product. Marketing managers orient their goals toward sales volume and revenue, market share, and customer satisfaction. Research scientists often concentrate on goals involving the development of scientific knowledge and translating this knowledge into potential market applications.

These examples point to three different goal orientations: (1) *techno-economic,* dealing with cost control and the implementation of manufacturing techniques (e.g., manufacturing and accounting departments); (2) *market* goals, concerning the response of the market to the organization's goods and services (e.g., marketing department); and (3) *science* goals, concerning contributions to scientific knowledge (e.g., research and engineering departments).

The different goal orientations provide a basis for establishing criteria for evaluating the performance of a particular unit or department. We would expect that the main criteria of performance for manufacturing would be quantity, quality, and cost considerations (i.e., techno-economic), sales volume and market share for the marketing department (i.e., market goal), and the number of new products, new processes, and other contributions to scientific knowledge for research and engineering (i.e., science goal).

Two additional factors should be pointed out. First, as in the case of time orientation, the greater the difference in goal orientation, the greater the difficulty in achieving coordination between units or departments. Different department orientations may force managers to act in dissimilar ways and when managers representing these units are asked to integrate their activities, they try to maintain their particular perspectives about work and how it should be done. A high degree of coordinated effort by management is required to fully integrate the activities of widely different units.

Second, as shown in exhibit 8-6, time and goal orientations are closely related to each other. That is, we would expect that manufacturing managers have a relatively short time orientation along with a techno-economic goal emphasis. On the other hand, the director of a research laboratory should have a much longer time orientation and goals that are more scientific in nature.

Coordination Mechanisms

A number of different methods or mechanisms are available to managers to achieve good coordination. A total of seven methods will be discussed: rules and procedures, hierarchy, planning, liaison roles, task forces, teams, and integrating departments.

Two points should be noted about these coordination methods. First, advancing from the use of rules to integrating departments involves an increased level of difficulty and commitment of resources by the organization to achieve coordination. That is, the use of rules and procedures is the easiest coordination method, particularly appropriate for those situations that require low coordination. However, when organizations use integrating departments, coordination needs are great and they are willing to commit significant organizational resources to achieve coordination.

Exhibit 8-6
Differences in Time and Goal Orientation

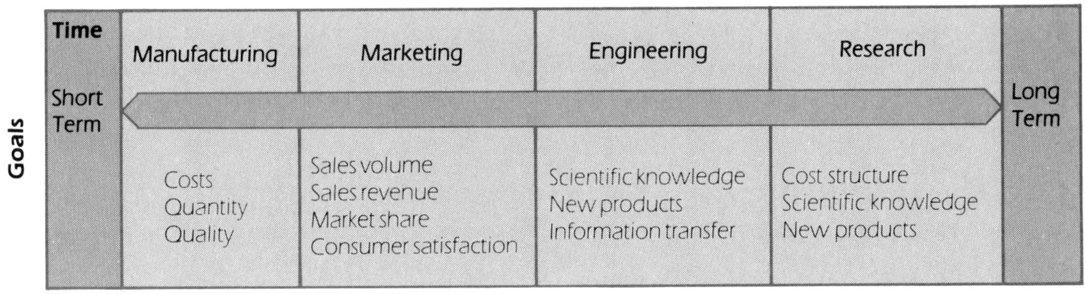

Time	Manufacturing	Marketing	Engineering	Research	
Short Term	←				→ Long Term
Goals	Costs Quantity Quality	Sales volume Sales revenue Market share Consumer satisfaction	Scientific knowledge New products Information transfer	Cost structure Scientific knowledge New products	

Second, in moving from the use of rules and hierarchy to teams and integrating departments, a coordination method previously used will probably still be used along with other methods. That is, even though the organization may depend on task forces as the main coordination method, it is highly probable that it will still use rules, hierarchy, and planning.

Rules and Procedures   The most basic or simplistic method for managing coordination is to specify in advance, through rules and procedures, the required activities and behavior of group members.[24] Interacting employees learn that when certain situations arise, they should follow a particular set of actions. For example, the packaging and shipping department knows that when the manufacturing department changes its process from producing the medium-grade product to the higher-grade product at 10:00 a.m. each day, it must use a different packaging container and labeling method. Little, if any, interaction between the two groups is necessary, because the procedures have spelled out in advance the required actions.

The principal benefit of rules and procedures is that they eliminate the need for extensive interaction and information flow between groups or units. Rules and procedures also provide a means of stability. Employees may come and go, but the procedures remain for future interactions.[25] Rules and procedures, however, are limited methods for managing coordination. They are most applicable when interacting activities can be anticipated and when the responses or required behaviors can be developed.

Hierarchy   When rules and procedures are inadequate for effective coordination, the hierarchy, or common supervisor, becomes the primary managerial strategy. For example, when there are departmental problems between manufacturing and shipping, such as inadequate inventory to load a boxcar, the problem is brought to the attention of the manufacturing general manager by the supervisors of the two units.

The basic assumption for using hierarchy in coordination is that higher level managers have the power and authority to make these decisions. However, as in the case of rules and procedures, this method has its limitations. Whenever interdependence and/or time and goal orientation differences become a problem, the manager's time may be totally taken up resolving these exceptions or problems of coordination. The manager has less time to devote to more pressing issues, such as planning the construction of a new plant. Additional difficulties are encountered when problems between two separate units, such as shipping and sales, arise. The common supervisor may be the divisional vice president, who becomes the sole arbitrator of day-to-day problems—an ineffective way of using an executive's skills and time.

Planning   As coordination problems between interacting departments develop beyond the control of rules, procedures, or hierarchy, organizations increasingly turn to planning activities. Planning involves setting targets and schedules that can lead to task accomplishment.[26]

For example, consider the construction of a new manufacturing plant. Various interdependent and interacting groups are involved in erecting the frame of the building, installing the electrical and utility lines, installing the manufacturing equipment, and connecting all raw material and finished-product processing lines. Rather than having constant interaction between these groups, plans have been made so each group or unit can perform its task over a specific period of time. Each division has a set of goals or targets for required hours of construction, delivery of construction materials, and completion dates.

Liaison or Internal Boundary-Spanning Roles   When the number of interactions and volume of information between two or more units or groups grows, a specialized role to handle these requirements may be established. Such a role has been variously termed a *liaison,* or more formally, an internal boundary spanner.[27]

In the example shown in exhibit 8-7, a liaison role could be set up between the applied research and market research functions. Individuals who operate in this role provide *lateral* communications and facilitate interaction between the two functions in a number of areas. One important area is coordination of efforts to determine the potential of a new product developed by the applied research unit. When the liaison is performing effectively, decisions about the new product are often made. Either the product may progress more quickly, or research scientists may be forced to revise their work in light of a negative evaluation from the market research unit.

There are a number of negative consequences to a liaison role strategy. First, performing in liaison roles may have negative effects for the individuals who hold these positions. A number of research studies have found people in boundary-spanning roles to experience lower job satisfaction and higher stress.[28]

Basically, employees in boundary-spanning roles must face conflicting performance expectations from the different groups with which they interact. A person dealing only with performance expectations from one group would face less conflicting and ambiguous expectations. Second, the effectiveness of interdepartmental relations is limited by the ability of the liaison person to handle the complexities and information flow between the groups. In addition, as these aspects increase, more and more individuals begin functioning in liaison roles, which removes them from per-

QUEENIE   By Phil Interlandi

"Why complain now? You should have asked what 'Special assistant to the President' meant before you took the job."

Exhibit 8-7
Liaison Role

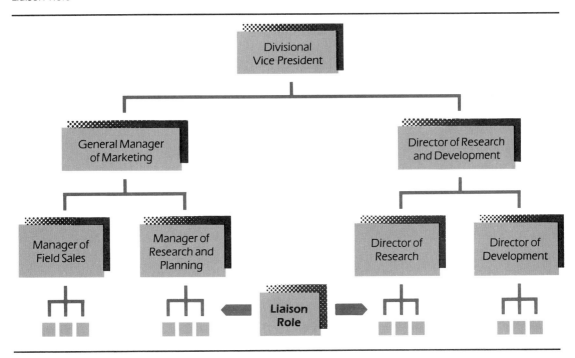

forming their primary functions. When this situation arises, organizations look for other methods to manage coordination.

Task Forces   When the complexities of interaction increase, such as when there are more than two or three interacting departments, the coordinating or decision-making capacity of the liaison role becomes overloaded. One mechanism to overcome these problems is to establish a temporary task force (see exhibit 8-8) consisting of one or more representatives from each of the interacting units. Task forces exist only as long as the problem of interacting remains. When a solution is reached, each member returns to normal duties.[29]

Teams   Similar to task forces, teams are collections of individual members used to manage coordination activities when there are more than two or three interacting units. What distinguishes the team concept is that the problem to be solved usually is long term in nature, requiring a relatively permanent formal assignment of the team. In addition, team members have two responsibilities—one to their primary functional unit, the second to the team. When the team has accomplished its task, each member returns full-time to his or her functional assignment.

Exhibit 8-8
Product Development Task Force

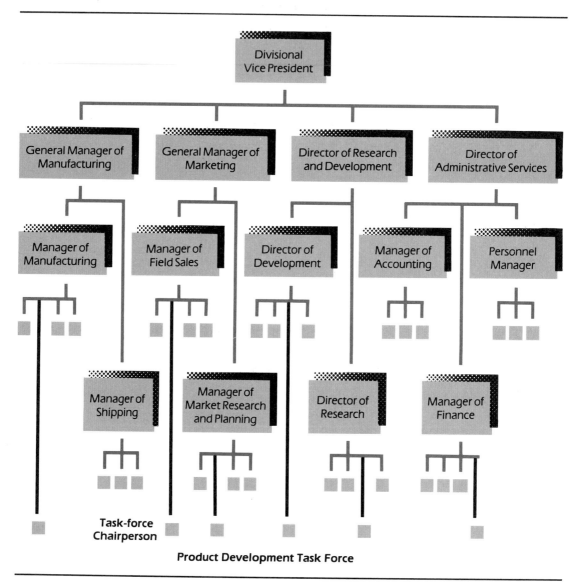

Product Development Task Force

Integrating Departments   As the complexities of interdependence and time and goal orientations increase, the magnitude of coordination requirements may grow beyond the capacity of plans, task forces, or teams. In response to this situation, organizations may seek more permanent, formal, and authority-based mechanisms that represent the general manager's perspective. Such mechanisms are known as integrating departments.

In its basic form, an integrating department is a single person who carries a title such as product manager, project manager, brand manager, or group manager. This manager rarely supervises any of the actual work required in departmental interactions. He or she is, however, generally held responsible for the effective coordination of activities. The integrator's decision-making authority is acquired through a direct reporting relationship to a higher management position; by increasing his or her staff with specialists from marketing, finance, and production; by giving the manager a major influence in the development and allocation of resources; or by allowing the manager to control a large budget. For example, with budgetary responsibility, the manager of the integrating department would have the authority to approve budget allocations in the engineering department in the process of product development.

Summary   A summary of the various mechanisms or strategies for managing coordination is shown in exhibit 8-9. This table indicates that as the complexities associated with coordination requirements increase, the organization may respond in two ways. It may: (1) increase the number of employees involved in managing coordination; and (2) move from informal to more formal managerial involvement. Whether

Exhibit 8-9 Coordination Strategies	**Strategy**	**Description**
	1. Rules and procedures	The required activities and behaviors between interacting groups are spelled out in advance. Employees learn that when certain situations arise, a particular set of behaviors should be used. Rules are a limited strategy; they cannot specify all behaviors in advance.
	2. Hierarchy	When rules and procedures prove inadequate as a coordination strategy, the emphasis switches to the use of the hierarchy, or common superior. This is a limited strategy in that the higher level manager's time may be totally devoted to resolving intergroup plans.
	3. Planning	Goals and targets are set for group interaction. The effectiveness of the strategy is limited by the complexities of interaction and how precisely future interaction patterns can be detailed in advance.
	4. Liaison roles	A specialized, generally informational role is created to transmit vital information and coordinate activities. Certain dysfunctions, such as job stress, may affect the behavior of the liaison person.
	5. Task forces	Selected members of interacting groups are brought together to form a task force. Task forces generally coordinate intergroup activities for a specific period of time, and thus are temporary. They are also limited to an advisory role, leaving the final decision making to higher level managers.
	6. Teams	Similar to task forces, teams are more permanent and may be given certain decision-making authority.
	7. Integrating departments	These provide the most formal strategies for managing intergroup performance. The department manager generally reports to the highest management level and may be given great decision-making authority, consisting of a large staff and budgetary responsibility.

the organization achieves a high level of performance depends not only on the choice of a management strategy but also on commitment to the improvement of coordination relations. Choosing such mechanisms as teams and integrating departments may require a significant departure from the organization's management philosophy.

Organizational Dimensions in the International Realm

As an organization develops international operations, its structure must adapt to accommodate these foreign activities. The structure that emerges depends on many factors, including the scope, location, and type of international facilities; the goals and strategies of the organization; the impact of foreign operations on total organizational performance; and the degree of international management experience and competence. The relationship between strategy and structure is discussed in the next chapter.

An organization that begins operating in more than one national market normally encounters problems that require changes in its internal structure. The international organization must learn how to cope with geographically dispersed operations, personnel from many different cultures, diverse political and social environments, and a high rate of change in the economy. Many managers have found that an organizational structure designed for purely domestic purposes is ineffective for international operations. To illustrate the dimensions of organizations in international activities, we will briefly point out differences in the grouping and influence dimensions.

International Grouping: Evolution of Structure

The evolution of the grouping dimension, particularly departmentalization, can be viewed as a series of stages, with each stage modifying or adapting the structure of the previous stage. The rate of passing through the stages varies from organization to organization—some proceed cautiously one step at a time, while others move through quickly. At least three stages have been identified—exporting, international division, and integrated structure.[30]

In order to enter international markets, many organizations *export* products. Organizationally, this can be done by assigning export responsibility to an independent trading company, by forming an internal export department, or by establishing sales, service, and warehousing facilities abroad. In this first stage, the structure of the organization remains essentially unchanged.

The second stage of evolution involves the establishment of an *international division* within the organization's structure. Exhibit 8-10 is a simplified structure for Bendix; similar arrangements can be found in IBM, General Motors, and Coca-Cola. An international division, which is usually headed by a vice president who reports directly to the president, normally results from four conditions: (1) the level of commitment to international operations has reached an absolute size and importance to justify a separate unit; (2) the complexity of international operations requires the centralization of activities; (3) the organization has recognized the need for a group of specialists who are skilled in handling the special requirements of international activities; and (4) there is a need to improve the organization's ability to identify and evaluate external opportunities and threats by scanning the global horizon rather than simply responding to situations as they develop.[31]

During the 1960s and well into the 1970s, the international division was the most common structure in large U.S. organizations with foreign interests. However, in many organizations, the structure became quite cumbersome and problem ridden. For instance, the international division normally does not have its own product development, engineering, research and development, and other staff units. The domestic divisions controlling these important activities were frequently reluctant to give priority to overseas needs because their performance was usually measured solely by their domestic operations. More importantly, top management recognized that, to function effectively, the control over strategic planning and policy decisions must

Exhibit 8-10
International Structure for Bendix

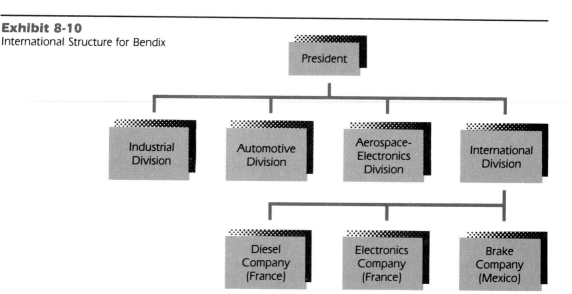

Source: Daniels/Ogram/Radebaugh, *International Business*, © 1979, 2nd ed., Addison-Wesley
Publishing Company, Inc., Chapter 18, pp. 403, 404, figure 18.2, "Placement of International
Activities Within the Organizational Structure." Reprinted with permission.

shift from the decentralized international division to the headquarters unit, where a
worldwide perspective could be used.

The third stage of structural evolution in the international realm is termed the
integrated structure. Besides the need for a global strategic approach, managers
became aware of the probable gains of coordinating functions and motivating personnel to perform in accordance with the organization's international interests.

As shown in exhibit 8-11, at least three forms of grouping can be found in organizations adopting this structural approach—functional, geographic, and product.
The functional structure (exhibit 8-11A) has the advantage of tight control over operations and uses only a relatively small group of executives to maintain line control
over operations. On the other hand, the important functions of sales and manufacturing are separated, creating coordination problems. The geographic structure (exhibit
8-11B) is appropriate for organizations with a narrow range of products whose end-
use markets, technological base, and production methods tend to be similar. The
major oil companies also prefer this structural form. The geographic structure permits
the handling of market-to-market variations quite easily due to its decentralized
approach. However, it requires a large number of internationally experienced managers to staff the regional operations and can prove to be quite inefficient when
product lines become diverse.

Finally, the product international structure (exhibit 8-11C) is best when an organization's product line is widely dispersed, when products go into a variety of end-use
markets, and when a high technological capability is required. Problems arise with

Exhibit 8-11
Integrated Structures in International Operations

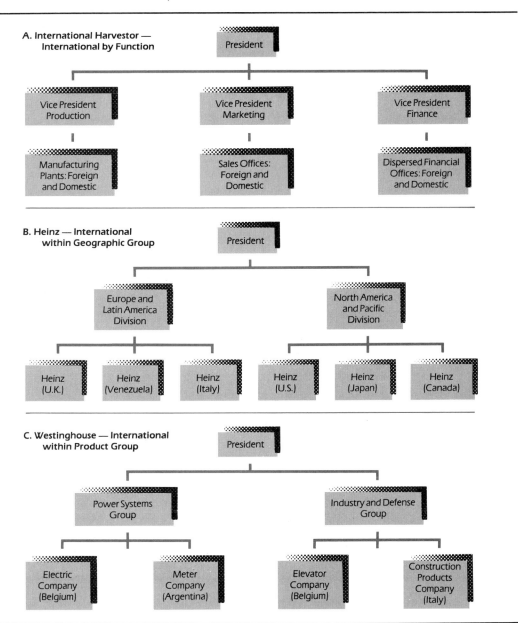

A. International Harvestor —
International by Function

President

Vice President Production

Vice President Marketing

Vice President Finance

Manufacturing Plants: Foreign and Domestic

Sales Offices: Foreign and Domestic

Dispersed Financial Offices: Foreign and Domestic

B. Heinz — International
within Geographic Group

President

Europe and Latin America Division

North America and Pacific Division

Heinz (U.K.)

Heinz (Venezuela)

Heinz (Italy)

Heinz (U.S.)

Heinz (Japan)

Heinz (Canada)

C. Westinghouse — International
within Product Group

President

Power Systems Group

Industry and Defense Group

Electric Company (Belgium)

Meter Company (Argentina)

Elevator Company (Belgium)

Construction Products Company (Italy)

Adapted from S.H. Robock, K. Simmonds, and J. Zwick, *International Business and Multinational Enterprises* (Homewood, Ill.: Irwin, 1977), p. 436, © 1977 by Richard D. Irwin; and from Daniels/Ogram/Radebaugh, *International Business*, © 1979, 2nd ed., Addison-Wesley Publishing Company, Inc., Chapter 18, pp. 403, 404, figure 18.2, "Placement of International Activities Within the Organizational Structure." Reprinted with permission.

this structure when managers are too narrowly trained in product responsibilities and when coordination is needed between the product divisions.

Some interesting variations happen when foreign organizations also attempt to go international. For example, many Japanese firms export through large trading companies that have grown to be quite powerful in international trade. In addition, some European organizations, because of their fast growth and diverse product lines, have bypassed the international division approach and have gone directly to the integrated structure from exporting.[32]

International Influence: Decentralization

As the international nature of management gains importance, so does concern over the applicability of managerial concepts and the integration of these concepts with the dominant culture of the country. This is especially important for the centralization/decentralization issue.

Consider, for example, the differences among the U.S., Sweden, and Great Britain.[33] In the U.S., many decisions on decentralization are determined for the most part by the six factors previously discussed. In other words, it is a concept that is dictated by the needs of the particular situation. To the Swedes, decentralization of decision making, or participation, implies a classless cooperation between workers and management. Decentralized decision making is a fundamental belief of the Swedish culture, an assumed concept. On the other hand, the British look at decentralization as another arena for a class struggle. Their system is based on the adversary roles of bargaining for power, not in the cooperative roles of decentralization in decision making. Britain's "them versus us" philosophy is as strong between levels in the organization as it is in education (elitist or democratic) or housing (public or private). In other words, decentralization occurs as a result of one group gaining power over another, rather than the problem at hand.

In summarizing a study of European managers, *Business Week* states:

> Clearly, the problems facing the various managers—as well as their solutions—vary sharply from country to country and from industry to industry. There is no such thing as a purely European management style. . . . The deeply entrenched egalitarianism of the Scandinavian cultures has made it easier for companies such as Volvo to introduce less formal, more delegatory styles of management. By contrast, formal management relationships are still the rule in Switzerland and the Netherlands . . . French and Italian managers are far more comfortable operating in a rigid hierarchy, while Scandinavian and German managers prefer a looser organization structure.[34]

Though countries differ significantly in their views on the degree of decentralization, these cultures are beginning to experience a growing demand from lower level managers and workers alike for more involvement in decisions.[35] This is an important trend that managers need to recognize and monitor.

POINTS TO CONSIDER
An Emphasis on Managerial Skills

1. **An organizational structure is more than an organization chart.**
   An organization chart, as shown in many of the chapter's exhibits, is a diagram that shows only select organizational dimensions such as departmentalization, span of control, and chain of command. Other important dimensions such as authority patterns, centralization, and coordination needs are not so clearly shown. As a manager, be careful not to accept an organization chart for more than what it is.

2. **Organizational dimensions offer suggestions, not accepted laws or facts.**
   The discussions on the grouping, influence, and coordination dimensions do not offer the "one best way" to organize. Rather, consider them guidelines for action.

3. **An organization's structure should be adaptable to change.**
   A successful structure is one that captures the key organizational dimensions but also can change with changing conditions. For example, situations may arise that make decentralization less effective than centralization, or a wide span of control may not prove as good as a much narrower span.

4. **Organizing requires a high level of conceptual skill.**
   Developing a "total picture" of the organization is a necessity for effective organizing. This involves recognizing which units to put together, how much decision making authority can be moved to lower management levels, and who needs coordination and how.

5. **Organizing foreign operations may require a different approach.**
   Many managers have learned the hard way that certain organizing concepts do not work well in foreign countries. Cultural differences, legal considerations, readiness to accept decision-making authority, and the like can vary from country to country and managers must consider them when designing structures for foreign organizations.

SUMMARY FOR THE MANAGER

1. Analyzing the external and internal environments, establishing goals, and developing extensive organizational plans will only work when the manager gives a great deal of attention to the organizing function. In other words, goals and plans do not implement themselves—a formal framework that permits the organization to use its resources effectively and efficiently is needed. We call this framework the organization's structure.

2. Three basic dimensions make up the organization's structure—grouping, influence, and coordination. The important thing for managers to realize about organizational dimensions is that they represent a sequential process. That is, the first concern is clustering or grouping jobs (grouping), followed by establishing authority and responsibility patterns within the newly formed units (influence), and finally integrating the various units into a single effort to achieve the organization's stated goals (coordination).

3. The grouping component consists of three aspects—job specialization, departmentalization, and line-staff relations. Job specialization, which involves grouping various jobs into units, can either contribute significantly to effectiveness or be a big problem area. The key factor is the

degree of specialization employed and the way workers react to this specialization. The manager must recognize that, on one hand, specialization provides the necessary mechanism for the development of skills and job expertise, and, on the other hand, too much of it may create jobs that are routine and boring, resulting in adverse employee reactions.

4. Departmentalization, the second grouping factor, involves putting departments into such arrangements as functional, product, geographical, or mixed designs. The selection of one of these designs is based on a number of criteria; two of the most important are costs and adaptiveness. Which of these two criteria apply determines the choice of the particular design. Functional is best for control of costs; the product form is much more adaptive to changing conditions.

5. The influence component consists of assigning or recognizing authority, power, and responsibility relationships within a newly formed structure. The main concept, authority, has its origins in the legitimacy placed on the job by the organization, the degree of acceptance by subordinates, and the important unity of command factor. Authority is implemented in organizations with the use of the chain of command, span of control, and the principles of centralization/decentralization.

6. The centralization/decentralization decision is one of the most important a manager can make because it involves giving important authority to certain subordinate managers to make decisions formerly made only by higher level managers. The external environment, the size of the organization, the costs and risks, basic managerial philosophies, the locus of expertise, and the availability of competent managers all factor into making a decentralization decision.

7. With the growing importance of international management, managers should be aware that various cultures around the world will adapt quite differently to decentralization attempts. That is, in some countries, such as Sweden, decentralization is a way of life, while in Great Britain attempts at decentralization may meet great resistance.

8. Coordinating the units and departments of an organization is an extremely important but massive and costly managerial activity. The need for coordination is founded on three factors—the degree of interdependence, the difference in time orientation, and the difference in goal orientation between interacting units. As the degree of interdependence and the differences in time and goal orientation become more severe, the need for coordination also increases.

9. Depending on how much coordination is needed, a number of mechanisms are available to managers. From the most basic mechanism, rules and procedures, to the most complex, integrating departments, these mechanisms vary in terms of the degree of managerial commitment required and the amount of organizational resources that must be used.

 REVIEW AND DISCUSSION QUESTIONS

1. What is the purpose of the organizing function?
2. How are goals, planning, and organizing related?
3. What are the sequential steps in developing an organizational structure?
4. What is the difference between organizational structure and an organizational chart?
5. What are some of the problems a manager should look for if an organization's structure is not working effectively?
6. What is the difference between authority and responsibility?
7. What are the positive and negative aspects of performing in a liaison position?

8. What is the relationship between span of control and coordination?
9. Discuss the relationship between decentralization and the development of managerial skills.
10. Discuss the differences between functional and product departmentalization.

NOTES

1. See R. S. Blackburn, "Dimensions of Structure: A Review and Reappraisal," *Academy of Management Review* (January 1982): 59-66; and D. R. Dalton, W. D. Todor, M. J. Spendolini, G. J. Fielding, and L. W. Porter, "Organizational Structure and Performance: A Critical Review," *Academy of Management Review* (January 1980): 49-64.
2. J. L. Pierce and R. B. Dunham, "Task Design: A Literature Review," *Academy of Management Review* (October 1976): 83-97.
3. See D. McGregor, *The Human Side of Enterprise* (New York: McGraw-Hill 1960); A. Turner and P. Lawrence, *Industrial Jobs and the Worker* (Boston: Harvard University Press, 1965); and *Work in America: Report of a Special Task Force to the Secretary of H.E.W.* (Cambridge, Mass.: MIT Press, 1973).
4. R. T. Gill, *Economics*, 3rd ed. (Santa Monica, Calif.: Goodyear, 1978), pp. 111-18.
5. See G. G. Fisch, "Line-Staff is Obsolete," *Harvard Business Review* (September-October 1961): 67-79; and L. A. Allen, "The Line-Staff Relationship," *Management Record* (September 1955): 346-49; and R. C. Sampson, *The Staff Role in Management* (New York: Harper & Row, 1965), pp. 42-44.
6. H. A. Simon, *Administrative Behavior* (New York: Macmillan, 1961), pp. 133-34.
7. D. C. McClelland, *Power* (New York: Wiley, 1975).
8. J. R. P. French and B. Raven, "The Bases of Social Power," in *Studies in Social Power*, Dorwin Cartwright, ed. (Ann Arbor, Mich.: University of Michigan, 1959), pp. 150-67.
9. C. I. Barnard, *The Functions of the Executive* (Boston: Harvard University Press, 1938), pp. 165-66.
10. H. Stieglitz, "Optimizing the Span of Control," *Management Record* (September 1962): 25-29; and D. Van Fleet and A. G. Bedeian, "A History of the Span of Management," *Academy of Management Review* (July 1977): 356-72.
11. L. F. Urwick, *The Elements of Administration* (New York: Harper & Brothers, 1943), p. 46.
12. H. Fayol, *General and Industrial Management*, trans. J. A. Conbrough (Geneva: International Management Institute, 1929), p. 36.
13. Sir I. Hamilton, *The Soul and Body of an Army* (London: Arnold and Co., 1921), p. 229.
14. A. V. Graicunas, "Relationships in Organization," in *Papers on the Science of Administration*, ed. Gulick and Urwick, pp. 183-87.
15. Stieglitz, "Optimizing the Span of Control," p. 28.
16. E. J. Walton, "The Comparison of Measures of Organization Structure," *Academy of Management Review* (January 1981): 155-60.
17. R. Carzo, Jr., and J. N. Yanouzas, "Effects of Flat and Tall Organization Structure," *Administrative Science Quarterly* (June 1969): 178-91.
18. See E. Dale, *Organization* (New York: American Management Association, 1967).
19. W. D. Wooldredge, "Fast Track Programs for MBA's: Do They Really Work?" *Management Review* (April 1979): 8-12.
20. "It's Back to Basics for Levi's," *Business Week*, (March 8, 1982): 77.
21. J. D. Thompson, *Organizations in Action* (New York: McGraw-Hill, 1967), pp. 54-55.
22. P. R. Lawrence and J. W. Lorsch, *Organization and Environment* (Homewood, Ill.: Irwin, 1967), pp. 34-39.
23. Ibid., p. 40.
24. J. G. March and H. A. Simon, *Organizations* (New York: Wiley, 1958), p. 44.
25. M. Weber, "The Theory of Social and Economic Organization," trans. A. M. Henderson and T. Parsons (New York: Oxford University Press, 1947).

26. J. W. Galbraith, *Designing Complex Organizations* (Reading, Mass.: Addison-Wesley, 1973), p. 12.
27. R. L. Kahn et al., *Organizational Stress: Studies in Role Conflict and Ambiguity* (New York: Wiley, 1964), p. 101.
28. R. T. Keller and W. E. Holland, "Boundary Spanning Activity and Research and Development Management," *IEEE Transactions on Engineering Management* (November 1975): 130-33.
29. Galbraith, *Designing Complex Organizations,* p. 80.
30. S. H. Robock, K. Simmonds, and J. Zwick, *International Business and Multinational Enterprises* (Homewood, Ill.: Irwin, 1977), p. 428.
31. H. Schollhammer, "Organizational Structures of Multinational Corporations," *Academy of Management Journal* (September 1971): 345-65.
32. Robock, Simmonds, and Zwick, *International Business,* p. 426.
33. N. Foy and H. Gadon, "Worker Participation: Contrasts in Three Countries," *Harvard Business Review* (May-June 1976): 71-83.
34. "Europe's New Managers," *Business Week,* (May 24, 1982): 116-22.
35. L. Donaldson, "Divisionalization and Diversification: A Longitudinal Study," *Academy of Management Journal* (December 1982): 909-14.

A CASE FOR ANALYSIS

Organizational Dimensions
Cutting Staff Expenses

More and more U.S. managers are recognizing that excessive overhead costs, particularly in top-heavy staff units, are one of the main reasons American companies are losing their competitive edge to foreign producers. For example, salaried staff costs at Ford Motor's North American automotive operations have reached $4 billion a year—a figure most people admit is probably twice that of rival Japanese automakers. One reason is that Ford works with twelve layers of management, compared to just seven for competitor Toyota. At issue are the skewed ratios of costs to revenues that have built huge, lumbering organizations.

Not surprisingly, consultants and professors are quick to offer guidelines to remedy this situation. Most suggestions involve some realigning the corporate structure, including: (a) decentralizing decision-making down to operating units; (b) increasing every manager's span of control by eliminating excess units and divisions; and (c) significantly reducing the number of staff personnel. How the last suggestion is implemented is open to debate. Two approaches seem to dominate—the ax and the surgeon's knife.

The ax approach appears to be the simplest and most popular. Adopting it means eliminating a flat percentage of employees, such as 10 percent. This can be done by laying off personnel, instituting large-scale early retirement programs similar to those of Exxon and Sears, or simply eliminating layers of management.

The surgeon's knife approach takes the individual, not the department, as the unit of study. What recently occurred at Acme-Cleveland, the large machine toolmaker is an example. When B. Charles Ames took over as chief executive in 1981, he found that while earnings had dropped nearly 50 percent from the previous year, the corporate staff overhead remained constant. In solving this problem he avoided cutting a flat percentage—instead, he tried to understand the needs of the organization.

Although he came to Acme-Cleveland from Reliance Electric's executive ranks, many of the rules and policies he applied came from his fourteen years as a management consultant. He believes, for example, that there should be no more than one salaried worker for every three hourly workers, that computer costs should never exceed 1 percent of sales, and that overall corporate expenses should never total more than 1.5 percent of sales. At Acme, he found its worker/manager ratio was closer to 1-to-1, its centralized computer facilities cost about 3 percent of revenues, and its total overhead represented 5.7 percent of sales.

Ames forced each corporate department and division head to pinpoint where costs could be cut and then let each of them decide who to retain and who to fire. What happened was that corporate personnel was reduced by 900 people (most in mid-management positions), the large centralized computer was eliminated and replaced by smaller divisional units (savings: $8 million), marketing was moved to the divisional level by eliminating the corporate department, corporate advertising expenses were reduced, and two corporate aircraft were sold. Rather than an across-the-board cut, some departments were eliminated or reduced by as much as 20 percent in personnel, while others actually gained employees. College recruiting was also reduced to a minimum effort.

Opponents of staff reductions scoff at both approaches for three main reasons. First, eliminating massive numbers of staff personnel could do permanent psychological damage to the organization—morale will go down and stay down. Second, without a good performance evaluation system, giving divisional managers the authority to fire at will can result in nothing more than lay-offs based on personalities and friendships—the "it's who you know, not how good you are" syndrome. Finally, these critics point out that when better times return, the type of person who will be hired is the same type who was let go. A smooth-running organization, claim these critics, needs a professional group of staff specialists. The frequent hiring and firing of staff personnel may improve short-term profitability, but it can severely mortgage the future of the organization.

Adapted from A. Patton, "Industry's Misguided Shift to Staff Jobs," *Business Week* (April 5, 1982); and "A New Target: Reducing Staff and Levels," *Business Week* (December 21, 1981): 84-85.

Questions for Discussion

1. What organizational dimensions are involved in this case?
2. Why do you think many managers turn to staff reductions when the economy goes into a downswing or when profitability problems occur?
3. What are the advantages and disadvantages of the ax and surgeon's knife approaches to staff reduction?
4. Evaluate the points made by opponents to staff reductions.

CHAPTER

9

Organizational Design

Chapter Outline

Key Points

1. The organizational design process can be studied on the basis of three approaches: classical, behavioral, and contingency.
2. The classical approach, most closely aligned with the bureaucratic model, offers the "one best way" to organize. It has been successful, however, only in specific environments.
3. The behavioral approach stresses participation, decentralization, and communication.
4. The contingency approach is based on the interaction of the environment, strategy, and technology, which determines the most effective structure.
5. Studies of organizational environments have shown that mechanistic or functional structures are best applied in stable environments, while product-type structures work best in dynamic environments.
6. Historical analysis of organizations has shown that organizations not only follow a similar strategic development process, but that structure follows strategy.
7. Technology is both a determinant and a constraining factor in choice of organizational structure.

Oki Electric Industry Company

Japanese managers are often amused when Americans ask about their keys to success. Many people are surprised to know that for years, the Japanese have implemented management concepts they learned from attending U.S. business schools and reading the works of American experts such as Peter Drucker. Now, they are adopting another U.S.-bred concept that is reshaping their organizational structures—the business unit.

Business units are self-contained organizations formed in reaction to complex environments. Three criteria characterize them: a set of clearly defined external competitors, managers with full responsibility for formulating and implementing plans, and profitability that can be measured in real income.

At Oki Electric Industry Company, the move to business units was almost the last-ditch effort to save the firm. Known for years as a company that generated nearly all its profits from selling telecommunications equipment to Japanese government agencies, it ran into hard times during the 1970s when the government turned to other manufacturers for such products. Unable to compete in the private sector, its sales and profits dropped sharply.

In 1978, Oki turned to Masao Miyake, former managing director of Nippon Telephone & Telegraph and Oki's largest customer, for help. As soon as he assumed the presidency, Miyake reorganized the firm along the business concept used by General Electric. He set up fifteen units, all oriented toward high technology and, hopefully, high profits, for computer terminals, integrated circuits, computer printers, and more. Within two years, Oki made a significant turnaround.

How the business unit concept works can be seen by looking at the computer printer market. Prior to reorganization, products were developed almost solely according to requests from government agencies. Company engineers would be assigned to customer teams, not knowing that other teams could be working on similar products for different agencies. The result—duplication of effort on a large scale.

After the reorganization, Oki assigned engineers in each business unit to product planning teams. The new teams were expected to seek out new markets for new products rather than simply meeting customers' known needs. Previously, a customer team would focus its attention only on its customer and not the total potential printer market. The new concept has provided welcomed economies of scale, better responsiveness to market changes, increased international sales, and a "matrix dot" printer that produces near perfect letters at high speeds.

Miyake is watching the business center concept closely. He is particularly aware of what Toshiba Corporation faced when it earlier adopted the business unit concept. Toshiba carved out too many small units, making each one meaningless from a marketing and planning viewpoint.

Adapted from "A U.S. Concept Revives Oki," *Business Week* (March 1, 1982): 112-13.

9 In the previous chapter, we began our discussion of the organizing function by identifying three major structural dimensions of organizations—grouping, influence, and coordination. The focus was on how to group jobs and units, how to establish authority within the units, and what mechanisms can ensure proper coordination between units.

In this chapter, we will direct our attention to the process of developing a structure for the organization—a subject called *organizational design*. The important issues are the impact of the external environment, strategies, and internal technologies of grouping, influence, and coordination. The impact of one of these factors—the external environment—is seen in our *Practice of Management* section. In the international realm, we see how a changing environment and a new strategy (sales to the private sector) require a company to closely examine the appropriateness of its structure.

The chapter is divided into two main sections. First, we will review a number of studies that represent the three major organizational design approaches—classical, behavioral, and contingency theories. Second, we will attempt to integrate the three approaches into a framework for designing today's organizations.

Classical Approach to Organizational Design

A number of theoretical perspectives have emerged over the years that can be categorized as belonging to the classical approach. Among these, for example, is the work of Taylor and his scientific management.[1] However, the most dominant classical organizational design approach is the one we hear the most about but probably understand the least—*bureaucracy*.

Characteristics of an Ideal Bureaucracy

The bureaucratic approach to organizational design was conceptualized by German sociologist Max Weber in the early part of this century.[2] Like Taylor, Weber believed that the key to an organization's survival was through mechanisms that increased the *efficiency* of its activities. The Weberian model can be considered a rigid approach, since it was proposed to be superior to any other structure. In other words, Weber promotes the "one best way" to structure all types of organizations.

The Weberian model is based on a number of important characteristics. Among these are:[3]

Division of Labor   All tasks necessary to accomplish organizational goals must be divided into highly specialized jobs. A worker needs to master the trade, and expertise can be more readily achieved by concentrating on a limited number of tasks. This is an example of the important *grouping* dimension of organizational structure. Weber proposed highly specialized jobs, and with high specialization the worker can easily master the necessary activities and skills, becoming an expert in one area.

Rules and Procedures   Each task is performed according to a "consistent system of abstract rules." This practice allows the manager to eliminate the uncertainty of individual differences in job performance. As discussed under the classification of the *coordination* dimension, the use of rules and procedures helps provide some of the order needed to achieve the organization's goals. Rules and procedures in a bureaucracy have sometimes been called "red tape," the seeming effect of excessive use of forms, policies, systems, and so on.

Authority   Offices or positions must be organized into a hierarchial structure which clearly defines the scope of authority of managers over subordinates. This system, termed the *influence* dimension, gives the organization mechanisms to establish and hold some form of order.

Impersonality   Superiors must assume an impersonal attitude in dealing with each other and with subordinates. This psychological and social distance enables the superior to make decisions without being influenced by prejudices and preferences. The thrust of this belief is that everyone in the organization, managers and nonmanagers alike, would be subject to the same rules and that all employees would be evaluated on the basis of expertise and performance, not personality or emotion.

Careers   Employment in a bureaucracy must be based on qualifications. In addition, promotion must be decided on performance (i.e., merit). Because of this careful and firm system of employment and promotion, it is assumed that employment will involve a lifelong career for workers, and their loyalty. In other words, job security, incremental salaries, and retirement benefits are guaranteed as long as the employee is qualified and performs at acceptable levels. In government, this has evolved into the civil service system.

These characteristics of an "ideal" bureaucracy established a major organizational movement that still appeals to many people. Managers find the idea that effectiveness as an organization can be achieved by an emphasis on efficiency, stability, and control a very attractive concept.

Issues with the Bureaucratic Model

Weber assumed that strict adherence to these characteristics was the "one best way" to organize to achieve organizational goals. The benefits of implementing a structure that emphasized efficiency, stability, and control offered many organizations an opportunity to become more effective. As history has shown, the bureaucratic model became the most widely adopted and successful form of structuring an organization that had yet been devised. Few alternatives, however, existed at that time.

As one may have suspected, some of the "ideal" characteristics of bureaucracy have undergone a transition over time and are now considered drawbacks. Exhibit 9-1 shows a number of these negative effects which have emerged.[4] Some of the drawbacks are:

Excessive Red Tape   The use of formal rules and procedures was adopted to help remove the uncertainty of coordinating a variety of activities in an organization. In a bureaucracy, rules produce two negative effects. First, their use is only a limited strategy for achieving coordination. Other strategies may be required, but bureaucracy's approach is to *add* more rules to try to cover all contingencies, resulting in the frequently heard cry of "too much red tape." Second, once established, it is very

Exhibit 9-1
Characteristics,
Benefits, and Problems
of Bureaucracy

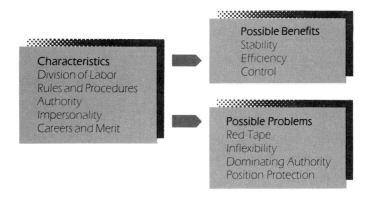

difficult in a bureaucracy to eliminate ineffectual rules or procedures. This results in more confusion, frustration, and reduced motivation.

Inflexibility A careful examination of Weber's works reveals an absence of the word "environment." As we have stressed throughout this book, to be effective, managers and organizations must be flexible and adaptable to the changing environment. Experiences with bureaucratic structures in organizations continue to show that the "one best way" is not really best when faced with a rapidly changing external and internal environment.

Dominance of Authority The authority factor is one of the most powerful characteristics of the bureaucratic model. It is so strong and dominant that many managers are reluctant to give up some of their authority—for example, by decentralization—when the situation warrants. The end result is less effective decision making. Another form of the dominance of authority in a bureaucracy is managers' attempts to acquire as much authority, power, and status as possible. This "empire building" takes the form of adding unneeded subordinates, acquiring excessive space (e.g., office space), having to be in on every decision, and so forth. This is a way managers seek to promote their own power, not try to achieve the organization's goals.

Position Protection The bureaucratic characteristic that stresses lifelong careers and evaluations based on merit is idealistic and rarely found in actual practice. In some bureaucracies, advancement in jobs and salary is more due to seniority and position than to actual skill and performance. The idea of having the most competent people in the positions is not fully realized. Loyalty is obtained, but it is usually toward the protection of one's job and rank, not to the effectiveness of the organization.

Many of these negative effects have led to some classic "bureaucratic blunders." For example:

A governor of a southern state a few years ago nominated to a state job a man who had been dead for two years.

THE WIZARD OF ID

by Brant parker and Johnny hart

By permission of Johnny Hart and Field Enterprises, Inc.

One large drug company spends over $20 million a year filling out 27,000 government forms, thus adding nearly $1 to the price of each prescription.

The Food and Drug Administration took eleven years to decide how many peanuts should be required in peanut butter.

Former Secretary of HEW (now split into two cabinet positions, Health and Human Resources and Education) Joseph Califano issued a 402-word job description for a chef to staff HEW's executive dining room and never once mentioned cooking skills.

Due to the foresight of the Board of Education of financially strapped New York City, at the current rate of consumption the city's schools have enough rubber softballs in warehouses to last students 23 years, enough magnets on hand for 32 years, and wooden beads sufficient to outfit kindergartens until the year 2626.[5]

Ideally, bureaucracy offered a number of features that were very valuable to organizations in their formative stages. Many changes, however, have been made to the bureaucratic model that have significantly altered the purposes designed by Weber. Bureaucracy is not yet dead nor unsuitable for use as an organizational design. As we will discuss later, the bureaucratic model works well in situations where the emphasis on stable, routine tasks matches a stable external environment.

Behavioral Approach to Organizational Design

Dissatisfaction with the classical design approaches led to the development of the behavioral approach to organizational design (see chapter 2). The Hawthorne research and the more recent findings by researchers such as Rensis Likert have offered significant modifications to the classical approach. These modifications are more scientifically based rather than derived from the personal experiences of the classicists. The work of Likert and Warren G. Bennis highlights the behavioral approach.

Likert's System 4

Likert's research led him to propose that effective organizations differ markedly from ineffective organizations along a number of important structural lines.[6] It is Likert's position that an effective organization encourages managers to focus on building effective work groups with challenging performance goals. In contrast, less effective organizations encourage managers to:

- Introduce a high degree of job specialization.

- Hire people with the skills and aptitudes to perform specialized job tasks.

- Train these employees to do their jobs in the best and most efficient manner.

- Closely supervise the performance of these job specialists.

- Where feasible, use incentives in the form of individual or group piece rates.[7]

These five points are associated with the core features of the bureaucratic design. By examining organizations with such tendencies, Likert concluded that a more behaviorally or people-oriented design that encourages groups to work together is more effective. He describes this more effective, people-oriented organization in terms of eight dimensions and calls it a System 4 organization. The classical design is designated as System 1. Likert believes that System 1 organizations are ineffective because they cannot respond or cope with changes in their environments. Environmental changes naturally create pressures for change, and to react to them the organizational design needs to be more flexible. The System 4 and System 1 dimensions described by Likert are compared in exhibit 9-2.

The System 4 organization contains the features required to cope with changing environments, according to Likert. Communication flows freely, and this process is required to reach decisions, exercise control, and lend emphasis. Likert, like Weber, assumes that there is a "one best way" organizational design. In Weber's case, it was the bureaucracy; in Likert's, it is System 4.

Bennis: A Behavioral Prescription

Bennis, like some of the classical organizational theorists, has forecast the demise of bureaucracy.[8] He assumes that bureaucracy largely will wither and die in organizations because managers will be unable to manage the tension, frustration, and conflict between individual and organizational goals. Bureaucracy also will fade because of the scientific and technological revolution in industrialized nations. The revolutionary changes require adaptability to the environment, and bureaucracies have experienced difficulty doing this.

Based on experience, but no empirical foundation, Bennis outlines organizational life into the 1990s.

- The environment will show rapid technological change with a large degree of instability or turbulence.

- Because of their better education, people in jobs will want more involvement, participation, and autonomy in their work.

Exhibit 9-2
Classical Design and System 4 Organization

Classical Design Organization	System 4 Organization
1. *Leadership process* includes no perceived confidence and trust. Subordinates do not feel free to discuss job problems with their superiors, who in turn do not solicit their ideas and opinions.	1. *Leadership process* includes perceived confidence and trust between superiors and subordinates in all matters. Subordinates feel free to discuss job problems with their superiors, who in turn solicit their ideas and opinions.
2. *Motivational process* taps only physical, security, and economic motives through the use of fear and sanctions. Unfavorable attitudes toward the organization prevail among employees.	2. *Motivational process* taps a full range of motives through participatory methods. Attitudes are favorable toward the organization and its goals.
3. *Communication process* is such that information flows downward and tends to be distorted, inaccurate, and viewed with suspicion by subordinates.	3. *Communication process* is such that information flows freely throughout the organization—upward, downward, and laterally. The information is accurate and undistorted.
4. *Interaction process* is closed and restricted; subordinates have little effect on departmental goals, methods, and activities.	4. *Interaction process* is open and extensive; both superiors and subordinates are able to affect departmental goals, methods, and activities.
5. *Decision process* occurs only at the top of the organization; it is relatively centralized.	5. *Decision process* occurs at all levels through group processes; it is relatively decentralized.
6. *Goal-setting process*, located at the top of the organization, discourages group participation.	6. *Goal-setting process* encourages group participation in setting high, realistic objectives.
7. *Control process* is centralized and emphasizes fixing of blame for mistakes.	7. *Control process* is dispersed throughout the organization and emphasizes self-control and problem solving.
8. *Performance goals* are low and passively sought by managers who make no commitment to developing the human resources of the organization.	8. *Performance goals* are high and actively sought by superiors, who recognize the necessity for making a full commitment to developing, through training, the human resources of the organization.

Source: Adapted from Rensis Likert, *The Human Organization* (New York: McGraw-Hill Book Co., 1967), pp. 197-211.

▪ The tasks of organizations will be more technical, complicated, and non-programmed. There will be a need to group specialists together by project design.

▪ Organizational structures will be more temporary and adaptive. These adaptive organizational structures will gradually replace classic bureaucracy.

As we have shown, the classical design approach sought to solve the problems of efficiency by emphasizing vertical, or top down, functional structure by relying on the hierarchical power of managers. Likert and Bennis, on the other hand, elevate the individual and groups to a prominent status in design decisions. Both approaches, classical and behavioral, are "one best way" recommendations that are simplistic because they are either/or choices. Organizational design decisions are anything but simple today. Consequently, we consider contingency design strategies.

Contingency Approach to Organizational Design

The experiences of managers functioning in complex organizations have led to their seriously questioning the universal "one best way" proposals of the classical and behavioral approaches to organizational design. In most cases, they are rather simplistic in that they exclude many of the important variables that affect a manager's decision to structure the organization. In response, what has emerged in management literature and practice is the *contingency* approach. It seems more reasonable to discuss approaches because no one model has been adopted as the final answer to design problems.

Definition and Importance of the Contingency Approach

Using the theories and research of classical and behavioral scholars enables one to offer a broad definition of the *contingency approach* to organizational design:

> A contingency approach attempts to understand the interrelationships within and among organizational units as well as between the organization and its environment. It emphasizes the complex nature of organizations and attempts to interpret and understand how they operate under varying conditions and in specific situations. The approach strives to aid managers by suggesting organizational design strategies which have the highest probability of succeeding in a specific situation. The success criteria revolve around the accomplishment of organizational goals.[9]

The contingency approach to organizational design appeals to practicing managers for a number of reasons. First, it *supports no one particular design;* rather it encourages searching through the many important variables and making a design decision for the organization that is appropriate for a given period of time and in the existing environment.

Second, the contingency approach, although empirically based, incorporates personal opinions about an organizations's particular situation. It encourages using different models, systems, scientific management, classical organization theory, bureaucracy and/or System 4, if they properly fit the situation. This openness and willingness to use what fits best is realistic, especially if one considers the dynamic nature of organizations and their environments.

Finally, the contingency approach clearly points out that various departments of a single organization may require different organizational designs to accomplish goals. Thus, the same organization may have multiple designs as opposed to a strictly bureaucratic or System 4 structure. The exact designs of separate departments are based on the situational mix of variables affecting how they progress toward their goals.

Exhibit 9-3
Contingency Factors
in Organizational
Design

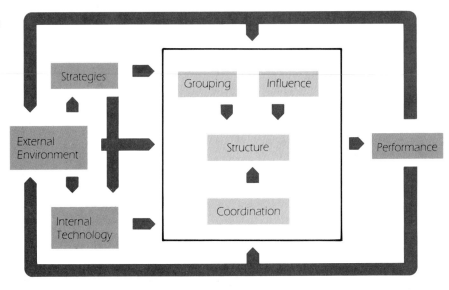

Contingency Factors in Organizational Design

As shown in exhibit 9-3, we have identified three major contingency factors that can influence the structure of an organization. Note that the central figure in the exhibit is a reproduction of exhibit 8-1. In other words, contingency factors affect the grouping, influence, and coordination dimensions of an organization's structure.

The major contingency factors include the organization's external environment, strategies, and the internal technology used by the organization. In the following sections we will discuss the impact of these factors on organizational design.

 # External Environment and Structure

One of the most important influences on the development of an organizational structure is the external environment. As shown in exhibit 9-3, not only does the external environment directly affect structural dimensions, there is an indirect impact through the environment's influence on the organization's strategies and technology.

The relationship between environment and structure has been the subject of a growing body of literature. Among the most quoted and important are the studies of Burns and Stalker and Lawrence and Lorsch. These studies are briefly discussed here.

Burns and Stalker: Mechanistic and Organic Structures

Burns and Stalker examined approximately twenty industrial organizations in the United Kingdom.[10] They were interested in determining how the pattern of managerial activities in planning, organizing, and controlling was related to the external environment. Gathering their data by performing field interviews, it was their intent to analyze the responses and reach some useful conclusions about how the environment and organization interact.

Early in the course of their work, Burns and Stalker discovered that management processes were different in various industries and environments. They reached the conclusion that each firm in their study sample could be viewed as an information-processing network.

The Burns and Stalker study treated the predictability of environmental demands facing organizations. They rated environments on a five-interval scale, from "stable" to "least predictable." Each of the five environments was then discussed with regard to the different management processes.

They studied a rayon manufacturer, an engineering company, and an electronics firm. The rayon company operated in the most stable or predictable environment. Because of this stability, the organization was run on the basis of clearly defined roles, specialized tasks, limited information flowing downward, concentration of decision-making authority at the upper managerial levels, and a distinct scalar chain of command.

The engineering company operated in a rapidly changing commercial environment. The environmental fluctuations required frequent organizational design changes. Thus, the structure was more flexible or fluid. Tasks were not as clearly defined as in the rayon firm, and lines of authority and responsibility were not emphasized.

The organization operating in the least predictable environment was a newly created electronics development organization. Job tasks were not well defined; the specific task assignments were made on an individual basis between superiors, peers, and subordinates. This type of interactive and dynamic task decision making was the result of the organization's rapidly changing situation. The structural dimensions of this firm were matched with the unpredictability of the environment.

From their analysis of the studied companies, Burns and Stalker identified two management systems: mechanistic and organic. The characteristics of mechanistic and organic organizations are presented in exhibit 9-4. A number of important points need emphasis. First, structure in the organic organization is based on expertise in handling current problems. This type of organization has a less rigid hierarchy but also a structure that is used to avoid confusion and chaos. Second, in the organic organization the individual's loyalty develops around work unit membership. The group has a special value in satisfying needs of employees. Finally, organic systems are associated with unstable environmental conditions. This type of system is more flexible and able to cope with and adjust to changes in technology and the market. Rigidity of structure in the mechanistic organization hinders its ability to adapt to change. Thus, its use is most appropriate to a more stable environment.

Lawrence and Lorsch: Differentiation and Integration

If an organization's environment is complex and varied, specialized subunits may be necessary to deal with the parts of the environment. Lawrence and Lorsch conducted field studies to determine what kind of organizational design was best able to cope with various economic and market environments.[11]

Exhibit 9-4
Differences Between Mechanistic and Organic Structure

Factor	Mechanistic	Organic
External Environment	Stable and changing	Dynamic and unstable
Goals	Short range, efficiency oriented	Long range, development oriented
Decision Making	Programmed	Nonprogrammed
Structural Dimensions	Formal structure	Flexible structure
	Emphasis on rules	Fewer rules
	Centralized	Decentralized
	Low job scope	High job scope
Locus of Authority	In a select group of executive managers (position power)	At whatever level skill or competence exists (skill power)
Communications	Directions and orders	Advice, counsel, and information
	Vertical	Vertical and lateral
Loyalty	To the organizational system	To the project or group
Performance Criteria	Objective measures	Objective and subjective measures
	Focus on results	Focus on activities and results
	Short time span between actions and results	Longer time open between actions and results

To sharpen their analytical procedures and theoretical propositions, they studied six firms in the plastics industry. After this phase of study, they examined one *highly effective* and one *less effective* organization each in the plastics, food, and container industries. The study focused on these three industries because they were assumed to be operating in environments that showed varying amounts of uncertainty (see exhibit 4-4). To assess environmental certainty, they asked executives in the organizations about clarity of market information, the rapidity of technological change in the industry, and the length of time normally required to determine product success in the marketplace.

In their research, Lawrence and Lorsch wanted to analyze the relationship between the environmental uncertainty facing an organization and its internal organizational design. They concentrated on three main subsystems—marketing, economic-technical, and scientific—and hypothesized that the structural arrangement of each subsystem or department would vary with the predictability of its own environment. They proposed that the greater the degree of environmental certainty, the more formalized or rigid (bureaucratic) the structure would be.

These contingency researchers also were concerned with what they called the *differentiation* and *integration* within the system. They assumed that by separating or grouping job tasks into departments, a need for coordination would develop. The unit members would become specialists in dealing with their tasks and would assume particular work styles. Thus, *differentiation* is defined as the state of segmentation of the organization's subsystems, each of which contains members who form attitudes and behaviors and tend to become specialized experts (see time and goal orientation in chapter 8).

A potential consequence of differentiation is the problem of bringing these individuals together to accomplish organizational goals. Because the members of each subsystem develop different attitudes, interests, and goals, they often find it difficult to reach agreement. These built-in organizational conflicts illustrate the importance of integration. Lawrence and Lorsch define *integration* as the quality of the state of collaboration that exists among departments, which is required to achieve unity of effort (i.e., coordination mechanisms).

Results of the researchers' questionnaire and interviews revealed that subsystems within each organization tended to develop a structure that was related to the certainty of their own environments. For example, a production subsystem tended to be faced with a relatively stable or certain environment. They had the most formal and structured design of the subsystems studied. On the other hand, research subsystems operated in a less predictable environment and had the least formal or rigid structure. Marketing operated in what Lawrence and Lorsch refer to as a moderately predictable environment and had a less formal structure when compared to production and research. Exhibit 9-5 illustrates the structural factors for high performing firms in these industries.

The Lawrence and Lorsch findings point out that successful firms in different industries achieve a high level of integration. The amount of managerial time and effort required to achieve successful integration seems to depend on two factors—diversity and interdependence. The more diverse the tasks of the firm's main units, the more differentiated those units will be in an effective organization. However, by

Exhibit 9-5
Dimensions of High-Performing Organizations in Three Industries

	Containers	**Food**	**Plastics**
External Environment	Low uncertainty	Moderate uncertainty	High uncertainty
Key Interdependencies	Marketing-production	Marketing-research; research-production	Marketing-research; research-production; marketing-production
Degree of Differentiation	Low	Moderate	High
Key Unit to Goal Achievement	Production	Marketing	Integrating department
Major Problem	Scheduling; control	Consumer preferences	Innovation; change
How Conflict is Resolved	Confrontation	Confrontation	Confrontation
Type of Structure	Functional (mechanistic)	Functional/product (mechanistic/organic)	Product (organic)
Main Integrating Mechanisms	Rules; hierarchy	Plans, liaison person; task forces	Task forces; teams; integrating department

creating and encouraging different viewpoints, differentiation generates conflict. Thus, the greater the state of differentiation, the larger the potential conflict, and the more time and effort it takes the manager to resolve these conflicts to benefit the firm. Furthermore, the more interdependent the tasks of the major subsystems, the more information processing is required for effective integration.

In our framework of investigating the determinants of organizational structure, one of the most important findings of Lawrence and Lorsch is the relationship between an organization's structure and its environment. As shown in exhibit 9-5, stable environments are best suited for a *functional* structure (mechanistic), with its emphasis on rules, procedures, and authority. On the other hand, the more dynamic the environment, the more a *product-type structure* (organic) is suited, for a focus on authority, decentralization, and coordination mechanisms.

Strategy and Structure

Why do some growth-oriented, multi-industry organizations such as Texas Instruments and General Electric have internal organizational structures that are significantly different from such stable, single product or industry organizations as Alcoa? This question has been the subject of the writings of many management scholars for a number of years.

In the early 1960s, Alfred D. Chandler was the first to give a concise answer to this question in his book *Strategy and Structure*.[12] Chandler studied over seventy of America's largest firms—Du Pont, General Motors, Sears, and Standard Oil, for example—and formed several principles about the relationship between an organization's strategy and its structure. First, he proposed that structure *follows* the growth strategy of the organization. Second, he concluded that organizations do not change their structures until they are provoked or forced to by a state of inefficiency.[13]

Structure Follows Strategy

Chandler's best-known contribution was his statement that an organization's structure follows its growth strategy. In other words, as an organization changes its growth strategy—in order to use its resources most effectively in the face of changing external environmental conditions—the new strategy creates its own internal structural problems. These internal problems, such as ineffective departmentalization, lack of proper authority over projects, or an absence of coordination, can be solved only by changing the structure of the organization. If a structural rearrangement does not occur, then the strategy will be less than effective.

Chandler's historical studies identified four different growth strategies that were followed in his example firms. In stage I, *Volume Expansion,* many organizations began as single offices or plants. In most cases, only one function was performed, such as manufacturing, sales, wholesaling, or warehousing.

Stage II, *Geographic Expansion,* multiple field offices or plants were created in the same function or industry, but in different locations. Coordination, standardization,

Since its founding, TRW Inc. has evolved a split personality in its product mix and geography. Units in the Eastern U.S. specialize in mature businesses—bearings, fasteners, and automotive parts. The Western U.S. units, however, are distinctly high technology—electronics, space, and defense weaponry. As Chairman Ruben F. Mettler knows, managing such diversity is a large task in itself. Add to this the rapidity of technological change and increased world competition and you have an almost overwhelming job. Mettler responded to this environment by emphasizing integration in the total organization—trying to get his managers to work as a team.

Insisting on teamwork and gaining compliance from managers in a firm that is highly decentralized (i.e., differentiated), however, are two different matters. Managers who are accustomed to great independence are usually reluctant to give up part of their autonomy to work as a team. They also worry that on one hand, they may be asked to risk time, talent, and money on cooperative ventures, while on the other hand, they are evaluated on the bottom-line performance of their units.

Mettler approached integration in three ways. First, he reorganized the business into sectors, larger groupings of products. One such sector was formed by merging the electronics and defense units into a single function. Second, he set up a number of formal committees across units and sectors to encourage cross-fertilization of ideas on everything from productivity to technology. Finally, he revised the reward and evaluation system to include not only bottom-line results in the short-term, but also long-term issues related to the performance of the total company. At the heart was the company's strategic plan.

Adapted from "TRW Leads a Revolution in Managing Technology," *Business Week* (November 15, 1982): 124-30.

and specialization problems arose almost immediately. To counter these problems, the *functional* department was established. Geographic expansion problems were faced early in the development of the railroads. Later, these same problems were faced by the financial industry with the development of branch banking and by the retail industry with the geographic expansion of department stores.

Stage III, *Vertical Integration*, involved the organization staying within the same industry but expanding its functions. Retail stores initially specialized in clothing but expanded to sell appliances, furniture, yard products, and so on. The new structural problems that developed included issues of interdependence and the coordination of product flow. The resulting structural arrangement we now know as a *functional* structure (see exhibit 8-2).

Stage IV, *Product Diversification*, involved the process of organizations moving into new industries with new products and services in order to employ existing resources as the primary markets began to decline. Structural problems with this new strategy concerned the appraisal and evaluation of new products, decisions on allocation of resources, and issues of departmentalization and coordination. The new structural arrangement created a division of labor that was based on time horizon and product/service class—or the *product structure* (see exhibit 8-2).

General Motors, Du Pont, Sears, and Standard Oil were some of the first multi-divisional firms that Chandler studied. In each case, the firms followed the four-stage pattern from volume expansion to product diversification by altering their structures from the simple unit structure to the more complex product structure.

Not all organizations in Chandler's study went completely through the four-stage pattern. For example, metal-processing firms in the copper and aluminum industries did not move into the product diversification stage (stage IV). Instead, they grew only in one industry, supplied the same customers, and employed strategies that were consistent with the stage, vertical integration. In other words, in each case structure followed strategy—General Motors adopted a product diversification strategy and implemented a product-type structure, while Alcoa was successful by staying within a vertical integration strategy and using a functional structure. Those firms that remained in and grew within a single industry retained the centralized functional structure; those that diversified adopted the multi-divisional, product structure. The strategy-structure linkage held true.

Initiating Change

Chandler's historical studies pointed to a second important finding. He found that the process of changing strategy and structure was usually a painful one, especially during the early stages.[14] He found that the individual who started the organization—the *entrepreneur*—became entrenched and protective of the organization. As a result, entrepreneurs were resistant to change. On the other hand, the next generation of managers—the *professional organizers/managers*—had acquired different knowledge and skills that were more adaptable to the latter growth stages (i.e., vertical integration and product diversification).

The entrepreneur wanted a "business as usual" approach; the professional organizer/manager, skilled in analysis and diagnosis, saw the necessity for change in order to survive and grow. It was only when economic inefficiency and mounting internal problems surfaced that the entrepreneur gave up control and the new structure was developed and implemented. Thus, basic differences between the entrepreneur and the professional organizer/manager created a delay in the formulation of new strategies, and the implementation of a new organizational structure occurred only after a forced and sometimes painful situation. Historical analyses of such entrepreneurs as Henry Ford I and Andrew Carnegie generally support Chandler's position.

Current Views on Strategy and Structure: International Development

Vertical integration, product development, and market development were some of the strategies presented in chapter 5. In the last chapter, we discussed the evolution of structure in the international realm. By integrating this material, we can develop a framework like the one shown in exhibit 9-6. The exhibit illustrates the most popular

Exhibit 9-6
Current View
of Structure Follows
Strategy

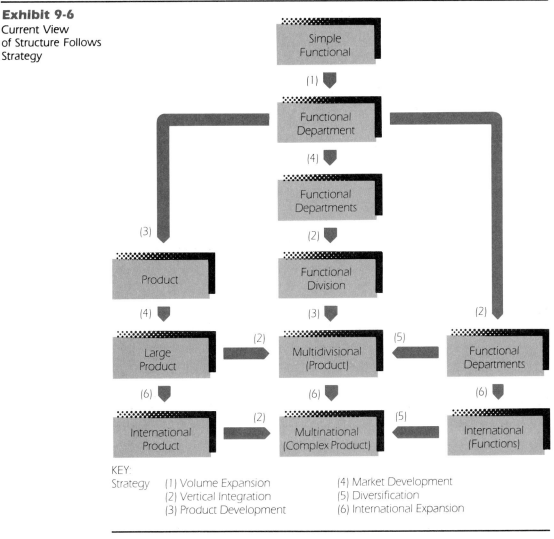

KEY:
Strategy   (1) Volume Expansion   (4) Market Development
           (2) Vertical Integration   (5) Diversification
           (3) Product Development   (6) International Expansion

Adapted from J. R. Galbraith and D. A. Nathanson, *Strategy Implementation: The Role of Structure and Process* (St. Paul, Minn.: West, 1978), p. 115.

structural approaches organizations use during their growth phases. It is not an all-inclusive view, since the retreat strategy is not shown. (When a retreat strategy is adopted, the organization usually reverts back to a former structure.)

One of the most important aspects of exhibit 9-6 is that international development can result in a functional or product structure. This confirms the last chapter's statement that organizations with a narrow product line prefer to maintain a functional structure when they go international, while a wide range of products may necessitate an international product structure.

Technology and Structure

Few concepts in the study of organizations are so important, yet so ill-defined or misunderstood, as organizational technology. In recent studies, the concept of technology has been seen in terms of the extent of task interdependence (see chapter 8), degree of equipment automation, uniformity or complexity of materials used, and the degree of routineness of the task.[15]

There seems, however, to be some convergence of certain important points on the technology concept. First, most experts agree that technology concerns either the mechanical or intellectual processes by which an organization transforms raw materials into final goods or services. In other words, technology refers to a *transformation* process by which mechanical and intellectual efforts are used to change inputs into products.

Second, the diversity of opinions on a definition may relate to the level of analysis on which technology is viewed. Some individuals may study technology as an organizationwide concept, such as an assembly line process in auto manufacturing. Others may view technology at the individual level, relating to the concepts of job depth and scope (see chapter 8).

Finally, there seems to be some agreement that technology is influenced by the environment *and* in turn influences the structure of the organization (see exhibit 9-3). As one example of the former, consider pocket calculators in the office machine industry. Only a few years ago business calculators were bulky, slow, expensive, and generally a business as opposed to a personal possession. With the development of microcomputer circuitry, coupled with a growing consumer demand (technological and economic environment in chapter 3), office machine companies were forced to develop new manufacturing technologies to produce the new, inexpensive pocket calculators. An example of technology influencing structure is the steel industry. The process for manufacturing steel is well defined, standardized, and expensive (i.e., capital intensive). Since steel technology is fairly rigid, the structure of the organization must provide effective control and maintenance functions. In other words, structure adapts to technology.

Types of Technology

To study the relationship between technology, structure, and performance, we need a scheme for categorizing or classifying different technologies. One of the best-known approaches to technology classification was presented by Thompson.[16] This classification scheme, based on how units are organized for task accomplishment, involves three types of technologies: (1) mediating; (2) long-linked; and (3) intensive. Exhibit 9-7 gives a summary of these technology types.

A *mediating technology* links otherwise independent units of an organization (pooled interdependence in chapter 8) through the use of standard operating procedures. A simple example would be a commercial bank, characterized by low interdependency between the different functions (e.g., savings, investments, loans). Rules, procedures, and other control mechanisms maintain effectiveness. Such a technology is moderately adaptable to changing demands.

Long-linked technology stresses sequential interdependency between different units. Characterized by an automobile assembly line, this type of technology attains effectiveness through planning and supervisor control, coupled with a moderate emphasis on communication. The rigid sequential nature of interdependence (along with the usual high cost of equipment and materials), renders this type of technology not very flexible or adaptable to changing demands.

Finally, an *intensive technology* draws upon a variety of techniques to transform an object from one state to another. The key point is that the choice of techniques is influenced by feedback from the object itself; that is, how the object responds to the application of the different techniques. A hospital is one of the best examples. The object being transformed is the patient and the patient's health; the techniques are the various specialties of the hospital (e.g., surgery, pediatrics, X-ray, nursing, physical therapy). How the patient responds to one of the specialties (e.g., knee surgery) determines how other specialties (e.g., physical therapy) are applied. As shown in exhibit 9-7, this type of technology is characterized by a great deal of interdependence between units, coupled with a need for good cooperation and high levels of flexibility and communications.

A number of studies have investigated the technology-structure relationships. One of the most important and most cited is the work of Woodward.

Exhibit 9-7
Technology Types

Technology Type	Illustration	Characteristics			
		Interdependence	Basis of Coordination	Flexibility	Communication Demands
Mediating	Bank 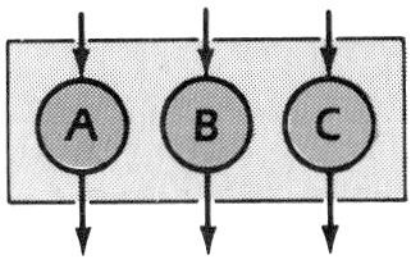 (A) (B) (C)	Low (pooled)	Rules, standard procedures, and supervisory control	Medium	Low
Long-Linked	Auto Assembly Line 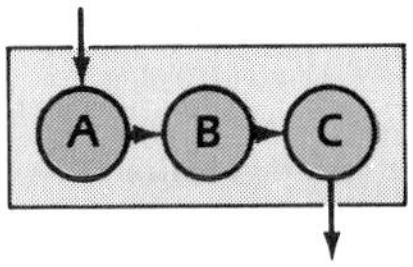 (A)-(B)-(C)	Medium (sequential)	Planning and supervisory control	Low	Medium
Intensive	Hospital 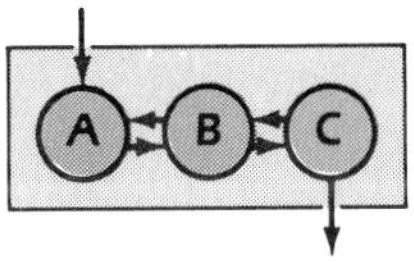 (A)-(B)-(C)	High (reciprocal)	Cooperation and mutual adjustment	High	High

Woodward: Technology

The studies of Joan Woodward and her associates involved a sample of 100 firms in South Essex, England, that employed at least 100 people. Through reviewing company records, interviews, and observation, they developed a profile of specific dimensions for each organization in the sample.[17]

Analysis of the profiles resulted in a number of disconcerting discoveries. First, the researchers found that the data did not relate, as they had hypothesized, to the size of the organization or to its general industry affiliation. For example, job specialization did not seem to be more intense in larger companies than in smaller ones. Second, the twenty organizations that were classified as effective had few organizational properties in common. This was also true among the twenty least effective organizations. These two findings implied that the classical design principles (bureaucracy) were not significantly related to organizational effectiveness. Approximately one-half of the successful organizations made use of an organic management system, which, of course, is contrary to the prescriptions of Weber.

In trying to interpret their data, the Woodward team found they could do better classifying firms on the basis of technology. The Woodward system of classification seems to interpret technology as "who does what with whom, when, where, and how often."[18] The three categories of technology were:

- Unit and small batch (custom clothing, furniture, and electronics).

- Large batch and mass production (automobiles, industrial equipment manufacturers).

- Long-run process production (oil refinery and chemical plant).

This three-category system and the subgroups comprising it provided Woodward's team with a rough scale of *predictability of results* and the *degree of control* over the production process. In unit and small-batch manufacturing, each unit of production is made to order for a customer, and operations performed on each unit are nonrepetitive. Mass-produced products, such as automobiles, are usually more or less standardized, and the production steps are predictable. Within our framework, the unit and small-batch group could be considered an *intensive* technology, large batch and mass production a *long-linked* technology, and process production a *mediating* technology.

Exhibit 9-8 summarizes the results of classifying organizations on the basis of technology among effective firms in the sample. The number of managerial levels varied among the three technological categories, with process production firms having the longest chain of command. Similarly, the chief executive's span of control varied with technology, with managers in process manufacturing having the widest span. The first-level supervisors' span of control also varied with type of technology, but in this case the relationship was curvilinear. Unit, small-batch, and process first-level supervisors tended to have smaller spans of control; those in mass production had the highest. Furthermore, the more advanced technologies utilized proportionately more administrative and staff personnel.

Woodward's research team also found that there were differences in operational procedures in the different technology categories. At what she calls the "top and bottom of the technical scale" (i.e., unit and process firms), there was a tendency for

Exhibit 9-8
Summary of Woodward's Research Findings for Effective Organizations

	Technologies		
Levels of Organization and Characteristics	**Unit and Small-Batch Production**	**Large-Batch and Mass Production**	**Process Production**
Lower levels	Informally organized	Organized by formal structural arrangements	Organized by task and technological specifications; wide spans of control
Upper levels	Informally organized; no clear distinction between line and staff	Organized hierarchically with clear line and staff distinction	Informally organized; no line-staff distinction
Overall characteristics	Few levels; broad span of control; no clear hierarchy; low ratio of administrators to operating employees	Clear job specialization; clear chain of command	Many hierarchical levels
Keys to success	Sense and adapt to market changes	Efficient production of a standardized product	Product development and new scientific knowledge
Focus	External	Internal	External
Most effective structure	Organic (product)	Mechanistic (functional)	Organic (product or project)

fewer rules, controls, definitions of job tasks, and more flexibility in interpersonal relations and delegation of authority compared to the middle-range mass-production firms. In addition, organizations in the technological category that deviated from this general pattern were most often less effective. The most effective mass-production firms were those that emphasized job specialization, tight controls, rigid chain-of-command adherence, and that in general followed classical design principles. A mass-production firm that was more flexible or organic tended to be less effective. On the other hand, organic and flexible process production firms were more effective than more rigid and bureaucratically inclined process firms.

Woodward aptly summarized the thrust of her contingency-oriented research by using the Burns and Stalker concepts: "Successful firms inside the large-batch production range tended to have mechanistic management systems. On the other hand, successful firms outside the range tended to have organic systems."[19]

What are the implications for managers from the research of Woodward? Let's examine the basic organizational functions and the keys to success (see exhibit 9-8). The unit and small-batch organization, such as a manufacturer of furniture, functions by taking customer specifications, developing the product, and manufacturing it. The keys to success depend on the organization's ability to sense and adapt to environmental change through the product development function. Since the focus is *external*, a product or organic structure seems more appropriate.

On the other hand, the mass-production technology depends on producing a standardized product or service—automobiles, food, appliances—for an existing market. The keys to success concern the degree to which the product can be produced efficiently and economically through routine methods. The focus is *internal*, which supports scientific management, bureaucracy, and the adoption of a functional or mechanistic structure.

Finally, organizations that use a process technology also depend on product development as the focal point. The key to success is the ability to discover a new product, or a new use for a product—such as a new chemical compound, a new fabric for use in radial tires, or a new additive in detergents—through scientific research and development. New production facilities or the use of existing facilities also work into the scheme. Since the focus is *external*—adapting to changing scientific knowledge—a product or organic structure is most appropriate.

Current Technology/Structure Views

Since the publication of Woodward's study, a number of other research efforts have been conducted to verify, refute, or further develop her findings. Besides noting that organizational size (i.e., number of employees) can influence structure, one of the most important findings was that an organization can consist of a variety of technologies, and hence, a variety of structural forms.[20] For example, a production department using a long-linked technology may effectively operate with a function structure, while the marketing department or research and development function may successfully adopt a product structure. This confirms the fact that, more and more, organizations are using a ''mixed'' structure (see exhibit 8-4).

A Contemporary Organizational Design Framework

If there is a dominant and unifying concept that characterizes a contemporary outlook, it would be the focus on the impact of the *external environment*. As we have shown, the environment not only directly influences an organization's design alternatives, it also has an indirect influence through the choice and implementation of the organization's strategies.

Technology, as well, is an indirect environmental influence on organizational design. In essence, technology acts more as a *constraint* to an organization. Operating a bank usually requires the adoption of a mediating technology; manufacturing automobiles almost automatically assumes a long-linked or assembly-line technology. The degree to which the technology matches the requirements of the environment will be reflected in the effectiveness of the organization's structure. That is, a long-linked technology is usually heavily capital intensive (i.e., requires large amounts of expensive equipment and processing mechanisms), and thus is not very adaptable to change. If an organization with a long-linked technology, such as a radio manufacturer, is placed in a relatively stable environment, the technology and environment are closely matched.

On the other hand, if the long-linked technology is confronted with a dynamic and complex environment, such as manufacturing business calculators, the need for adaptation to the environment cannot be satisfied with the stable technology. In this situation, the organization is faced with a need for an "organic" structure, but an internal technology that is primarily effective with a "mechanistic" structure. This organization must, therefore, depend on such complex and costly coordinative mechanisms as task forces and integrating departments to ensure some level of acceptable performance.

Exhibit 9-9 expands our discussion of a contemporary organizational design framework. It is based on exhibit 4-4, which identified two major dimensions of the external environment: *degree of change* (stable/dynamic) and *degree of complexity* (simple/complex). The four quadrants establish the elements that link organizational structure to effectiveness.

In *quadrant I*, the external environment for an organization is characterized by a relative lack of rapid change (stable) and a minimum number of interactions with external entities (simple). An example could be a city government or a paper products company, which usually adopt a stable strategy and use a mass-production form of technology. The design characteristics that lead to high performance are detailed job specialization, centralization of authority, narrow span of control, and low coordination needs. The recommended structure would be a mechanistic or *functional* design. Since the environment is not rapidly changing, the keys to success for this type of organization reside in the control of *costs*, the strength of a functional structure. You probably recognized that under these conditions, a bureaucratic form of organization would work well. In other words, bureaucracy can be considered as an element of the contingency approach, being most effective in this particular environment.

In *quadrant II*, the external environment remains fairly stable, but the degree of complexity increases because the number of external interactions (e.g., customers, suppliers, and competitors) has grown. Manufacturers of home appliances—washing machines, dryers, and refrigerators—are an example of organizations that sell a variety of products across different markets, all of which exhibit a fairly stable demand. Strategies usually involve improved or expanded competencies and market development (see chapter 5), and the dominant technology is one of mass production. Internally, there is a moderate degree of job specialization and centralization, wide spans of control, and moderate coordination needs. A *functional* structure, using task forces, or a *product* structure would be a recommended design form.

A dynamically changing but simple environment characterizes organizations in *quadrant III*. Specialty producers, such as clothing manufacturers, are an example. Such organizations generally deal in only a few products that are made to order (or fashion) in a rapidly changing environment. A strategy of product development coupled with a unit/batch or continuous technology is usually found. The key design

Exhibit 9-9
Contemporary Organizational Design

Environment			Design Characteristics					
Degree of Change	Degree of Complexity	Example Strategies	Example Dominant Technology	Job Specialization	Decentralization	Span of Control	Coordination Needs	Structure
Stable	I Simple	Maintain existing competence; stability; vertical integration	Mass production or long-linked; high capital investment; programmed decisions	High	Low	Narrow	*Low* Use of rules, procedures, and hierarchy	Mechanistic or functional structure (exhibit 8-2)
	II Complex	Expand competences; market development; vertical integration	Mass production or long-linked; high capital investment	Moderate	Low to Moderate	Wide	*Moderate* Use of rules, hierarchy planning, and task forces	Functional or product structure (exhibit 8-2)
Dynamic	III Simple	Expand and improve competences; product development or diversification	Continuous/process or unit/batch; mediating technology	High	High	Narrow	*High* Use of rules through integrating department	Organic or product structure (exhibit 8-2)
	IV Complex	Adapt to rapid change; seek new competences; product development; market development; merger	Unit/batch; continuous/process; mediating or reciprocal	Low	High	Wide	*High* Use of rules through integrating departments	Product or matrix structure (exhibits 8-2 and 9-10)

characteristics are high job specialization and decentralization, narrow spans of control, and high coordination needs. In this case, a *product* (or organic) structure would probably be most effective.

Finally, in *quadrant IV,* organizations are faced with a highly complex and rapidly changing environment. Energy companies, engineering firms, electronics manufacturers, and some multinational firms fall within this quadrant. Organizational strategies usually emphasize adaptation to change, diversification, and mergers coupled with a unit/batch or process technology. Job specialization is low, a wide span of control exists, and decentralization and coordination needs are high. Many organizations prefer a complex product structure, but the matrix structure is also gaining popularity.

The Matrix Design

The term *matrix* has been used to describe organizations that include a number of projects, programs, or task forces.[21] Decentralization was and still is a typical response to growth in organizational size, markets, and competition. Decentralization is feasible because it is possible to break the organization up into fairly autonomous units. However, rapid changes in technology, the environment, and preferences of the work force have posed problems for decentralized organizational design. These changes have made it necessary for organizations to have large numbers of specialists to handle research and development, market research, and human resources development. Thus, the matrix or program management approach has been appealing as a solution to problems of the decentralization of decision-making authority.

Exhibit 9-10
Matrix Structure for an Engineering and Construction Organization

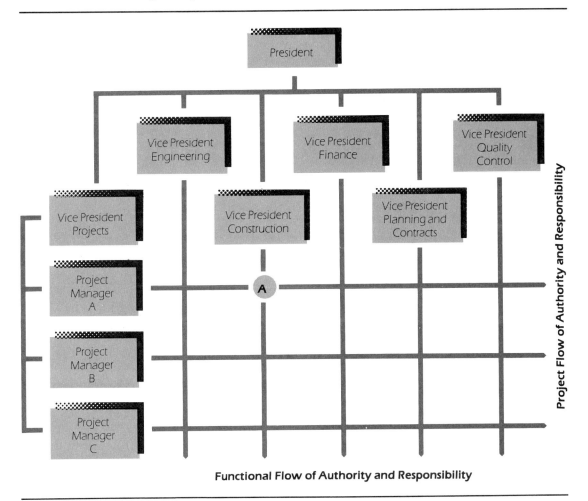

Functional Flow of Authority and Responsibility

The easiest way to describe a matrix design is as a product structure *superimposed* on a functional structure. For example, exhibit 9-10 depicts the structure of an engineering firm that specializes in the construction of large projects, such as bridges, oil refineries, and dams. The vertical components of the matrix structure reflect the typical functional departments of manufacturing, marketing, contracts, and so on. Since each project requires a different orientation with different needs, the product structure is placed on the functional structure—the horizontal components of exhibit 9-10. The result is that the *control* advantages of a functional structure and the *adaptive* advantages of a product structure are contained in one design.

To function effectively, a matrix design must incorporate certain important factors. First, the *classical scalar chain of command* principle (i.e., each subordinate has only one supervisor) is thrown out. In our example, a construction engineer reports to both the functional construction vice president and the project manager (point *A* on exhibit 9-10). Second, the key managers in this design must agree on a balance or *sharing of power* over resources. Decisions over financial, physical, and human resources must be made *jointly* and with a knowledge that power will be shifting between the two units over time. Third, since conflict inevitably will occur, there must be free use of *confrontation* as a resolution mechanism. Conflict over financial resources, for example, will create severe problems unless confronted and solved early.

A properly designed and functioning matrix structure can benefit the organization in a number of ways. With it come greater information processing, better responsiveness to the environment, and human resource economies of scale. On the other hand, the experiences of user firms have revealed a number of negative features that all managers must consider.[22]

Definition of Roles   Knowing what to do, how to do it, and when to do it is a recurring problem with matrix designs. For example, the functional manager must learn how to share resources with the project manager and work with a loss of status; the project manager must learn to manage people differences and varying authority and power situations; and the two-boss manager (noted as ''A'' in exhibit 9-10) must learn how to take direction from two superiors and how to control anxiety and stress.

Power Struggles   Balance of power is an important theoretical concept in matrix designs. Given human nature, power struggles between functional and project managers will occur. In these situations, top management must quickly step in to resolve the problem.

Groupitis   Frequently, managers operating in a matrix design get so engrossed in their cooperative work that they almost always turn to group activity or group decision making to reach accord. Managers must remind themselves that not all decisions require the input of others.

Collapse During Economic Decline   Matrix designs seem to blossom during periods of rapid growth, but they stagnate or are discarded during poor economic times. In bad times, when simplicity and low overhead is desired, a complex matrix design is frequently abandoned. Experience has shown that once a matrix is removed, it is extremely difficult to reinstall.

Despite its relative youth, matrix designs can be found in many large companies, such as IBM, General Electric, and Honeywell. It is not, however, the final answer to

In the mid-1970s, Tony Cascino, vice chairman of International Minerals and Chemicals Corporation (IM&C), faced a crisis that threatened to break down the company's problem-solving and decision-making processes. The company, a major producer of fertilizers, animal products, energy, and such chemicals as phosphates, potash, and nitrogen, was operating with an organizational structure that did not fit with its growing and dynamic environment.

The company's structure had evolved from a simple functional design to one that was a complex array of project management and decentralization. Cascino recognized, however, that internal complexities and external environmental turbulence can increase to such a degree that a more effective structure has to be devised. To IM&C and Cascino, the answer was a matrix structure.

After six years with matrix management. Cascino learned a number of important lessons from which other managers may benefit. Some of the most important include:

—In the early stages of implementation, the structure should not only be put in place in manageable degrees, but minimal concern should be given to rules, titles, and authority. Experience is the best guide to establishing procedures.

—Success rests more on the behavior of people than on structure—the internal operations, therefore, must stress cooperation, not power plays.

—Avoid the condition of "two bosses"—the preference was to refer to the "peer group," which minimized authority challenges.

—Keep top management informed, but don't let them get too involved in day-to-day activities; whenever this occurred, otherwise good working sessions deteriorated into a series of unproductive meetings and presentations.

—The compensation package for managers must be structured to accommodate both vertical (functional) and horizontal (product) obligations.

—Top management must, in spirit, philosophy, and practice, promote and support the matrix approach.

Matrix structure has helped IM&C improve operations, productivity, profitability, and overall working relationships. Its major contribution has been in the development of managers—experience with the matrix approach has improved managerial skills and performance.

Adapted from A. E. Cascino, "How One Company Adapted Matrix Management in a Crisis," *Management Review* (November 1979): 57-61.

the issue of organizational design, nor is it applicable to all situations. Texas Instruments, for example, has discarded its matrix in favor of a structure that depends more on temporary task forces and teams for integrative work.

Before the matrix design is even remotely considered as effective as bureaucracy or System 4 in various settings, it must be studied more thoroughly. It is different and offers many appealing elements, but determining where and when to use it is a key managerial decision requiring the use of important conceptual and diagnostic skills.

POINTS TO CONSIDER
An Emphasis on Managerial Skills

1. **Designing an organization's structure is a complex and involved process.**
    Do not underestimate the time, effort, and commitment of resources required to restructure an organization. Reorganizing is not simply redrawing an organizational chart, rather it means considering the grouping, influence, and coordination dimensions.

2. **Most organizations consist of many different technologies, not just one.**
    While technology may be a simple concept, do not be misled. In reality, organizations are made up of many technologies. If the technology structure argument is valid, you can better understand why certain parts of an organization are functionally structured, while others are structured in a product/project form.

3. **An organization's structure influences and is influenced by many factors.**
    Managers must recognize that an organization's structure, while providing needed order and design, is not an isolated concept. It is important to understand that structure is determined in part by the environment, by organizational strategies and technologies—*and* that structure can influence the way people act and behave.

4. **The matrix design is not the final answer to organizational design problems.**
    Matrix designs are a new alternative, but still just one of many different structures that managers must consider. The essence of this argument is that a manager should choose a structure that best fits the particular situation.

SUMMARY FOR THE MANAGER

1. Organizational design is the managerial process that concerns the development of a structure for the organization. In essence, it focuses on the investigation, analysis, and decisions that establish the grouping, influence, and coordination dimensions of organizations. The process is organizational design; the result is the organization's structure. Three approaches to organizational design are more frequently discussed—classical, behavioral, and contingency.

2. The classical approach to organizational design usually relates to a discussion of the bureaucratic model as developed by Weber. In its ideal state, the bureaucratic approach offers the manager—with emphasis on rules, authority, impersonality, and lifelong career development—a means to stress stability and control. In many situations, however, bureaucracy has come under severe criticism because its problems—red tape, inflexibility, dominance of authority, and the protection of position. It is important for the manager to recognize that the bureaucratic approach is quite effective for organizations operating in a relatively stable and unchanging environment where there is strong need for control. However it is not the "one best way" to structure all organizations as its founder and supporters claim.

3. The behavioral approach to organizational design, like the classical approach, proposed the "one best way" to organize. The emphasis, particularly Likert's, was on the behavioral and humanistic issues of people working in an organization. Likert's approach emphasized participation, decentralization, and frequent communications as the means to overcome the problems associated with bureaucracy. It, too, found success in some organizations, but not all.

4. The contingency approach has been suggested by many as the most appropriate way of organizing. It presents no single answer but is more a diagnostic approach that stresses the interaction of the external environment, the organization's strategies, and the internal technology as factors determining structure.

5. The work of Burns and Stalker and Lawrence and Lorsch drew attention to the importance of the environment in the organizational design process. For managers, the lesson to be learned is that as the environment becomes more dynamic and complex, the structures of the organization should become more decentralized and flexible. In our framework, a dynamic and complex environment is most appropriate for the product type of structure.

6. Chandler's major contribution is the finding that "structure follows strategy;" in other words, structure is determined, in part, by the strategies the organization chooses.

7. Technology is viewed as another contingency factor in organizational design. It works, however, more as a constraining factor than a pure determinant. That is, the technology of a bank, hospital, or assembly plant, for example, is a given item, as it is in any company that chooses to produce a particular good or service. The question for organizational design specialists is how flexible is this technology to the needs imposed on the organization by the environment? A heavily capital and equipment intensive organization may not have the flexibility of an organization that is more labor intensive, especially in a dynamic environment. To counteract this enviromental constraint, many organizations have made use of temporary task forces or permanent project managers to ensure flexibility.

8. The matrix design, which is simply a product structure superimposed on a functional structure, is fast becoming the most popular form of organizational structure. It is certainly not the final answer, particularly with the many problems that have arisen for organizations that have adopted this design. It is appropriate for organizations that operate in dynamic and complex environments but that need both the cost control *and* flexibility of the functional and product structures.

 REVIEW AND DISCUSSION QUESTIONS

1. What is the difference between organizational design and organizational structure?
2. What are the major proposals or elements of the bureaucratic model? Why has the model failed to be the "one best way" to organize?
3. How do bureaucracy and Likert's System 4 differ?
4. Why does the contingency approach to organizational design not subscribe to a "one best way" system?
5. How are the external environment, strategy, and structure related?
6. Does Chandler's analysis pertain only to large organizations?
8. Why is the concept of technology important to the study of organizational design?
9. What are some of the advantages and disadvantages associated with the matrix structure?
10. How are managerial skills and organizational design related?

NOTES

1. F. W. Taylor, *Principles of Scientific Management* (New York: Harper & Brothers, 1911).
2. M. Weber, *The Theory of Social and Economic Organization*, trans. A. M. Henderson and T. Parsons (New York: Oxford University Press, 1947), p. 330.

3.   C. Perrow, *Complex Organizations,* 2nd. ed. (Glenview, Ill.: Scott, Foresman, 1979), pp. 4-6.

4.   See B. Reimann, "On the Dimensions of Bureaucratic Structure: An Empirical Reappraisal," *Administrative Science Quarterly* (1973): 462-76; and T. Parsons, *Structure and Progress in Modern Societies* (New York: Free Press, 1960).

5.   R. Levy, "Tales From the Bureaucratic Woods," *Dun's Review* (March 1978): 94-96.

6.   R. Likert, *New Patterns of Management* (New York: McGraw-Hill, 1961).

7.   R. Likert, *The Human Organization* (New York: McGraw-Hill, 1967), p. 6.

8.   W. G. Bennis, *Changing Organizations* (New York: McGraw-Hill, 1966).

9.   F. S. Kast and J. E. Rosenzweig, *Contingency Views of Organization and Management* (Chicago: Science Research Associates, 1973), p. 313.

10. T. Burns and G. M. Stalker, *The Management of Innovation* (London: Tavistock, 1961).

11. P. R. Lawrence and J. W. Lorsch, *Organizations and Environment* (Homewood, Ill.: Irwin, 1969).

12. A. D. Chandler, *Strategy and Structure* (Cambridge, Mass.: MIT Press, 1962).

13. J. R. Galbraith and D. A. Nathanson, *Strategy Implementation: The Role of Structure and Process* (St. Paul, Minn.: West, 1978), pp. 12-16.

14. Ibid.

15. J. D. Ford and J. W. Slocum, "Size, Technology, Environment and the Structure of Organizations," *Academy of Management Review* (October 1977): 561-75.

16. J. D. Thompson, *Organizations in Action* (New York: McGraw-Hill, 1967), pp. 15-18.

17. J. Woodward, *Industrial Organization: Theory and Practice* (London: Oxford University Press, 1965).

18. E. D. Chapple and L. R. Sayles, *The Measures of Management* (New York: Macmillan, 1961); and C. Perrow, "A Framework for the Comparative Analysis of Organizations," *American Sociological Review* (1967): 194-208.

19. Woodward, *Industrial Organization,* p. 71.

20. See J. Child and R. Mansfield, "Technology, Size and Organization Structure," *Sociology* (1972): 369-93; D. J. Hickson, D. S. Pugh, and D. C. Pheysey, "Operations Technology and Organization Structure: An Empirical Re-Appraisal," *Administrative Science Quarterly* (1969): 378-97; C. Perrow, *Organizational Analysis: A Sociological View* (Belmont, Calif.: Wadsworth, 1970); and A.H. Van De Ven and A. L. Delbecq, "A Task Contingent Model of Work Unit Structure," *Administrative Science Quarterly* (1974): 183-97.

21. S. M. Davis and P. R. Lawrence, *Matrix* (Reading, Mass.: Addison-Wesley, 1977).

22. Ibid, chapter 6.

A CASE FOR ANALYSIS

Matrix Organization
Bausch & Lomb

To most people, Bausch & Lomb, the New York-based firm, is known for its contact lens products. A wide array of eyecare products generate the majority of revenues and profits for the firm. In 1981, the instruments unit (i.e., microscopes) received increased attention from top management because of the fierce price competition and arrested growth of contact

lens products. The instruments group, facing such high-technology heavyweights as Hewlett-Packard and Perkin-Elmer, would be asked to carry a bigger load for Bausch & Lomb.

To start the turnaround, James D. Edwards was hired as president of the instruments group in May 1981. Edwards brought with him years of experience as an executive with IBM and Xerox. Many felt that if he was successful, Edwards would be a prime candidate for promotion to the unfilled position of corporate chief operating officer.

Edwards' first turnaround action was a radical overnight reorganization of the instruments group. He divided manufacturing responsibilities among three newly formed divisions—microscopy and image analysis, spectroscopy, and graphics and control—and created a fourth division to manage all sales, service, and marketing. To replace the shattered lines of authority, Edwards introduced a matrix design similar to one he was part of at IBM.

In operation, the spectroscopy manufacturing manager, for example, might retain responsibility for the unit's profits while giving up control over the sales force. Sales authority would go to the new marketing division. The seven product managers, each with complete responsibility for one product, would act as coordinators between the separate manufacturing and marketing divisions.

On paper, Edwards' new organizational design was appealing. It could possibly integrate Bausch & Lomb's formerly autonomous businesses into a more manageable whole for the first time. Costly redundancies and manufacturing duplications

could be eliminated along with a hoped-for improvement in competitive reaction time.

On paper is one thing, but reality is another. Unaccustomed to operating in a dual authority arena, Bausch & Lomb instruments division managers immediately resisted the change. Issues, problems, and conflicts went unresolved. Sales representatives who had sold only simple microscopes wondered how to sell complex, computer-driven chemical analysis devices. Division managers complained that without authority over the sales force, they could not control their businesses. Edwards developed brochures and videotapes that explained the changes to managers, but many remained confused and dissatisfied. To add to these problems, the budget for the marketing division was "out of control" and the 1982 recession was having an effect on sales, particularly to customers in the steel, machine tools, and construction industries.

With sales dropping, Edwards began a massive cost-cutting campaign that reduced the 500-member sales force by some 10 percent, significantly trimmed R&D expenditures, and delayed the introduction of many new products. Finally, in October 1982, Bausch & Lomb simultaneously announced a 32 percent drop in net income for the third quarter and Edwards' resignation.

Adapted from S. P. Sherman, "Bausch & Lomb's Lost Opportunity," *Fortune* (January 24, 1983): 104-105.

Questions for Discussion

1. On a piece of paper, draw the new organization chart for the instruments group.
2. What were the reasons behind this unsuccessful reorganization? What would you have done differently in implementing the new matrix design?
3. Would another form of organization work for the instruments group? Discuss the possibilities.

Human Resources in Organizations

Chapter Outline

Key Points

1. Human resource management has increased in importance in many organizations recently, due to a wide variety of changing internal and external environmental events.
2. The human resource process consists of human resource planning, recruitment, selection, orientation, training and development, performance evaluation, rewards, and separations.
3. Human resource planning involves the analysis of current and future trends as they relate to the organization's resource base.
4. Recruitment concerns the process of securing people and insuring that they remain with the organization.
5. Selection involves identifying the most capable people to fill a position. For managerial selection, the concept of assessment centers has grown in importance.
6. Orientation relates to the process of induction and socialization.
7. Training and development activities are used to develop managers and increase management skills.
8. Current issues in human resource management include issues for women in management, staffing international operations, and the effects of automation.

Procter & Gamble

Consider the following statement: "We don't believe in mothering our managers. We grow our own managers by giving them responsibility very quickly, which sometimes means putting them in jobs they aren't quite ready for." If you think an organization adopting such a philosophy is asking for trouble, think again—it is the basic management development philosophy of Procter & Gamble, a company with an uninterrupted profit growth that is impressive by any industry's standards.

P&G starts the process by finding the right people through an extremely intensive selection process, continues with on-the-job training, and ties it neatly together with a substantial compensation system. The details of the compensation system are a guarded secret, but it is known to consist of competitive salaries, bonuses, and a significant profit-sharing program. A manager's profit share is invested in P&G stock, which is a powerful incentive to work hard—that is, the better the company performs, the better the manager will do.

The essence of the P&G system is to put new managers through their paces—a process that draws talent out early. At P&G new managers go to work, not to school. Except for a limited amount of training for those in technical areas, formal classroom training is not the P&G way. Instead, managers get something to do.

That "something" is responsibility for a piece of business and, if the manager does well, quick promotions into other jobs. Some of these jobs may require skills and abilities that the manager may not be fully equipped to handle. Yet the risks are much less than one might imagine. For one thing, the new manager, who is labeled a "development person," is backed up by a superior who is always close by (i.e., a mentor). By strictly limiting the number of people reporting to any one individual, the bond between superior and subordinate managers can grow tight. In addition, there is P&G's policy to promote from within, and managers are expected to train their successors. From day one, managers get the message that the best way to advance is for the people under them to be so good that they push the manager out of a job.

Just as important, the P&G system of management development gives managers a built-in loyalty and sense of respect for company traditions. Confidence is built because managers prove able to handle jobs that may have originally been over their heads.

If consistency is the keyword of P&G's management development, it pays off in corporate stability. While its executive ranks are not totally immune to raiding by other companies, turnover is surprisingly low. Many managers spend their entire careers at P&G. One advantage of this outcome is that employees know if there is a change in the management the basic conduct of the business will be the same.

Adapted from R. Rowan, "The Tricky Task of Picking an Heir Apparent," *Fortune* (May 2, 1983): 56-64; and "P&G: We Grow Our Own Managers," *Dun's Review* (December 1975): 48-51.

10 To this point in our discussion of management and the manager's job, we have: analyzed the organization's environments; stressed the importance of goals; seen how planning can provide valuable direction to the firm; discussed how decision making can pervade all managerial activities; and, through the organizational design process, gained an appreciation for how the structure of an organization establishes a framework for order. The next step is to place people in the established jobs and within the structure so they can perform the organization's work.

As *The Practice of Management* section on Procter & Gamble shows, one of the most important resources of an organization is its people. Employees supply the talent, skills, and creativity and exert the effort and leadership that contribute to the organization's level of performance. Managers in all types of organizations are taking a greater interest in the management of human resources and are supporting many innovative and practical changes in longstanding human resource activities.[1] This interest is prompted by such factors as increased governmental interventions (e.g., equal employment opportunity and affirmative action), rising labor costs, changing human needs, and questions about the supply of competent and skilled managers and employees.[2]

The topic of human resources in organizations will be presented in three main parts. First, we will discuss the human resource process—sometimes called the staffing function.[3] Second, five important elements of the human resource process—human resource planning, recruitment, selection, orientation, and training and development—will be singled out for discussion. Finally, three contemporary issues in human resources management—women in management, staffing in the international realm, and the effects of automation—will be highlighted.

The Human Resource Process

The human resource process, like many other organizational activities, is a dynamic system. Changes in the external environment (e.g., competitive pressures, consumer needs, technological advances, and demographic characteristics), organizational goals and strategies, and other internal factors add up to a need for a flexible human resource system. In our discussion, the human resource process consists of two major components—the premises of the process, and the actual steps in the process.

Premises of the Human Resource Process

The premises of the human resource process involve those factors that come *before* the development of the human resource plan. This is shown in exhibit 10-1. For instance, as presented in chapter 4, *organizational goals* describe the state of affairs or desired results the organization attempts to achieve. From a human resource point of view, this involves not only developing knowledge of the numbers, skills, competencies, and weaknesses of the current work force but also defining the changes needed in a future work force in order to achieve the stated goals.

Exhibit 10-1
Premises of the
Human Resource
Process

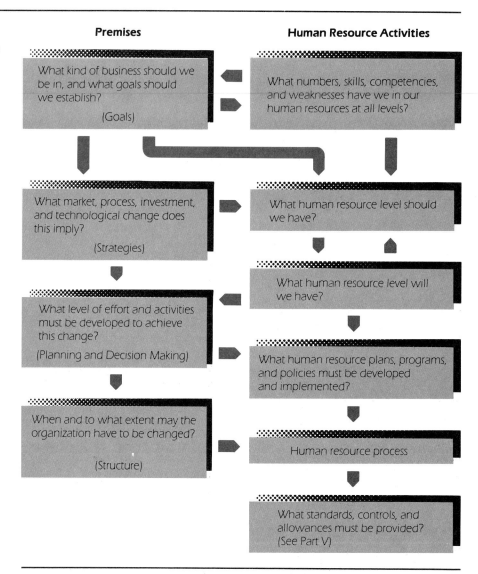

Premises

Human Resource Activities

What kind of business should we be in, and what goals should we establish?
(Goals)

What numbers, skills, competencies, and weaknesses have we in our human resources at all levels?

What market, process, investment, and technological change does this imply?
(Strategies)

What human resource level should we have?

What human resource level will we have?

What level of effort and activities must be developed to achieve this change?
(Planning and Decision Making)

What human resource plans, programs, and policies must be developed and implemented?

When and to what extent may the organization have to be changed?
(Structure)

Human resource process

What standards, controls, and allowances must be provided?
(See Part V)

As we have seen in chapters 5, 6, and 7, the process of translating goals and strategies into specific activities concerns *planning* and *decision making*. Organizational plans that contain subplans for the development of an effective work force must be developed. Finally, establishing the framework within which performance will occur—the grouping, influence, and coordination components of the organization's *structure*—evolves from the stated goals, strategies, and plans. From a human resource view, this means developing a comprehensive staffing plan.

Elements of the Process

The human resource process can be viewed as consisting of a series of steps that all managers perform continuously. The steps, shown in exhibit 10-2, include:

Human Resource Planning Meeting current and future human resource needs begins with a plan. The manager analyzes the organization's goals and strategies and the needed skills, abilities, positions, and competencies coupled with a knowledge of trends in employment laws and in personnel availability.

Recruitment Once human resource needs have been identified, an effort is made to locate acceptable candidates. This may involve placing newspaper and professional journal ads, college recruiting, recommendations from employees, placement firms, and so forth.

Exhibit 10-2
The Human
Resource Process

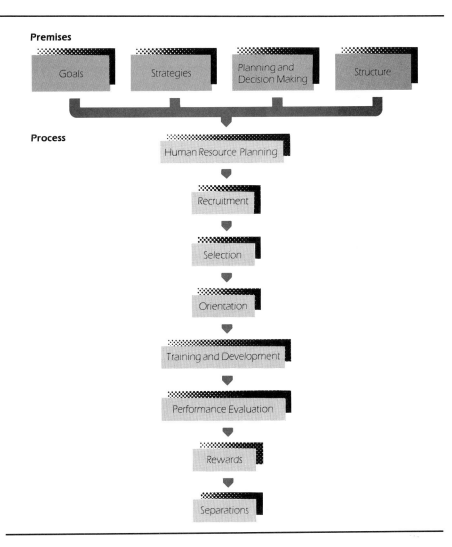

Selection   The selection process evaluates various candidates and selects those who match the organization's requirements. Methods of evaluation include application forms, interviewing, testings, reference checks, and assessment centers.

Orientation   This important step integrates the newly hired employee into the organization. Included are formal activities, such as acquainting the individual with the organization's rules, benefits, and policies, along with informal activities of "socializing" them into the work group.

Training and Development   Activities directed toward improving the employee's capability to contribute to the organization's performance fall under training and development. Training involves improving employee skills; development concerns preparing the employee for additional responsibility or advancement.

Performance Evaluation   This step is the process of evaluating the employee's performance in relationship to standards or goals. Features of this step are the *feedback* to the employee, and the *direction* needed to continue or improve performance.

Reward System   To maintain an effective work force, the organization must be able to reward good performance or punish poor performance. This is the function of the reward system. Included within this step are aspects related to compensation, promotion, career development, transfers, demotions.

Separations   Because the human resource process in an organization is dynamic, there will be a constant inflow and outflow of people. Voluntary turnover, retirements, layoffs, and discharges all concern managers.

This chapter discusses the steps in the process through training and development. The last three steps—performance evaluation, reward system, and separations—will be the focus of chapter 16.

Human Resource Planning

A few years ago, a large farm equipment manufacturer was in the process of building a plant in one of the southern states. Financial planning had been conducted and the actual construction of the plant had begun. One element was missing—no one had given much thought to the issue of staffing the new plant. When the issue finally did come up, the new manager indicated that when the plant was finished, then they would start worrying about hiring employees.

To the human resource planner, such a statement is not only a frequent occurrence, it is sure to bring on premature gray hair! Fortunately, most managers have come to realize that the process of acquiring and allocating human resources cannot be turned on and off like a lightbulb. It takes time, effort, and a commitment by management—lack of attention to the process results in many problems, such as higher costs and lower performance.

The human resource planning function involves at least four different factors, including: (1) the organization's goals and strategies; (2) the recognition of important labor force trends; (3) the current human resource audit and replacement analysis; and (4) the legal environment.

Organizational Goals and Strategies

The organization's stated goals and strategies identify what the future human resource needs are for the organization. In other words, how many people will be needed (an increase or decrease) to staff the organization in the near and distant future, and what skills and abilities will they require?

For example, vertical integration, market development, product development, and diversification (see chapter 5) strategies may require the organization to increase its number of employees, as well as necessitate the development of new skills. Consider the situation faced by AT&T.[4] Long protected as a monopoly, the huge telecommunications conglomerate is now faced with increased competition in sales and services from other companies. Since these products and services do not fall under the monopolistic umbrella, AT&T altered its strategies in an attempt to meet the new competition. Their main effort has been aggressive marketing, with an emphasis on *selling*. AT&T has found, however, that it has needed to go further—and American Bell was formed in 1983 to cover new, high-tech products and services.

A strategy of stability will probably mean that an organization will attempt to reach a status quo, being concerned with replacements for terminated workers. A retreat strategy, on the other hand, may require some major work force reductions.

Labor Force Trends

In human resource planning, managers must be aware of certain trends in the distribution of the labor force. For example, consider the data shown in exhibit 10-3, which represents the actual and projected numbers in the national labor force by sex and age. The exhibit's data make at least two important points.[5] First, the decrease in the 20-24-year-old group represents the well-known decline in birth rate that the U.S. has been experiencing. To management, this may signal a potential shortage of managerial talent during the latter part of this century. The knowledge of this situation may force organizations to rethink some of their expansion plans, or to revise their selection and training processes in order to provide for early identification and development of future managers.

Second, the increases in the 35-54-year-old groups represent the "baby boom" population. By the end of this century, organizations will be faced with a large group of people who will be entering retirement. Thus, an effort may be needed to revise and reemphasize the organization's retirement programs. Coupled with the first point, many organizations will be faced with the problem of retiring a large group of experienced managers, but having an insufficient number of younger managers to replace these retired executives. The time to plan for this situation is now, not in 1990.

The process of forecasting human resource needs has evolved into a major management activity in all types of organizations. The available forecasting techniques are much the same as those we discussed in chapter 3 for environmental forecasting. The most frequently used techniques include judgmental (Delphi, trend extrapolation), quantitative (linear programming), and computer simulations. As human resource problems continue to grow in importance and complexity, the use of sophisticated forecasting techniques will increase commensurately.

Exhibit 10-3
Labor Force Data (Actual and Projected) by Age and Sex

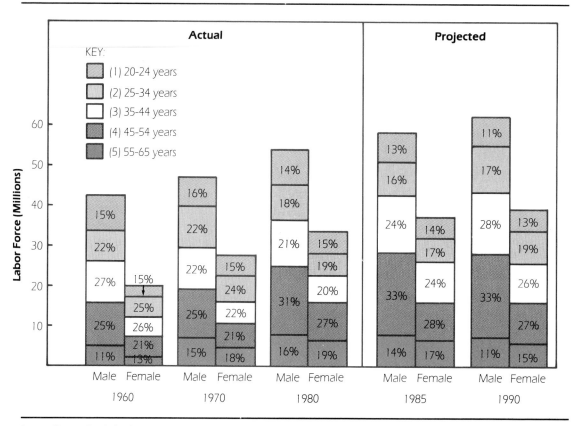

Source: *Current Population Reports,* Series P-35, no. 493; and W. Guzzardi, Jr., "Demography's Good News for the Eighties," *Fortune* (November 5, 1979):96; and J. Cook, "The Moulting of America," *Forbes* (November 22, 1982): 161-67.

Human Resource Assessment

At the same time, or shortly after the analysis of human resource trends, the emphasis switches to an examination of the organization's present personnel. This is called the human resource assessment or audit. The objective of the assessment is to evaluate current strengths and weaknesses of personnel and to match this evaluation against future requirements. Most organizations emphasize finding the needed skills and potential in *current* employees because, for reasons of cost and morale, it may be better to develop and promote from within than to recruit and hire from the outside.

Two examples can be used to clarify the human resource assessment process. First, consider the data presented in exhibit 10-4, which depicts the distribution by age, turnover rates, and replacement ratios (i.e., the ratio of employees at one age bracket who are waiting to fill each opening that occurs at the next-oldest age bracket) for

Exhibit 10-4
Resource Audit: Age, Turnover, and Replacement

Ages	Age distribution				Turnover rates			Replacement ratios		
	A	B	C	TOTAL	A	B	C	A	B	C
60-64	7	6	7	20	4%	3%	3%	0	0	0
55-59	14	10	22	46	0	4	2	6	7	2
50-54	22	21	20	63	0	3	5	30	20	34
45-49	73	22	30	125	0	1	6	25	21	16
40-44	47	15	18	80	12	3	2	50	13	17
35-39	38	7	8	53	4	2	4	13	5	8
30-34	45	14	12	71	3	2	5	16	14	7
25-29	44	15	20	79	0	2	3	22	8	6
20-24	20	4	10	34	2	3	2	4	5	3
	310	114	147	571	3	8	6	31	18	22
					(Divisional Averages)			(Divisional		Averages)

Adapted from W. E. Bright, "How One Company Manages Its Human Resources,"
Harvard Business Review (January-February 1976): 85.

managers in three divisions of a hypothetical company.[6] Such an analysis, known as a *resource audit*, reveals any problems associated with age distribution. Turnover rates can be too high, indicating excessive replacement costs, or too low, indicating insufficient weeding out. In addition, high replacement ratios indicate that some blocking of lower level personnel is occurring; low ratios indicate that a shortage of capable managerial replacements exists.

If you were a manager in division A, you might be concerned with this analysis from exhibit 10-4:

- Of your 310 managers, there are 73 who are in the 45-49-year age bracket, which is not only disproportionate with the other age groups, it is the worst of the three divisions. Questions about the morale of the lower age group may develop. It is possible that some of these younger managers may move to other firms where there is more advancement potential. Or, these same managers may lose some of their effectiveness while waiting for slow-coming promotions.

- The turnover rates for your division are the lowest of all the divisions and are one-half that of the organization as a whole. This is good from the point of reducing turnover costs, but it may also be a signal that you may not be weeding out poor performers or younger managers may be getting blocked from promotions (note the turnover rate for the 40-44-year-old group).

- The analysis of replacement ratios supports the previous results. Your division has the highest replacement ratios, indicating that many more younger employees are waiting for promotion and advancement than in the other divisions.

In summary, while on the surface your division may appear to be in good shape, a serious problem may be on the horizon concerning younger employees and their career development. You can consider a number of solutions, including more frequent

Since R. S. Reynolds founded Reynolds Metals Company in 1928, the firm has always been run by a member of the family. After Mr. Reynolds stepped down from day-to-day management, he turned the company over to his four sons who pursued the aluminum business with great intensity.

Now, however, the family tradition is about to fade. Two of the Reynolds brothers died in 1980, while David P. Reynolds, the chairman, is 66 years old, and J. Louis Reynolds, who manages the international operations, is 71. In addition, most of the company's other top managers are 60 years of age or older.

Analysts predict that most of the growth in aluminum usage will come from transportation, building material, and construction, with automobiles holding the brightest prospects. Recognizing this, along with the tough competition from Alcoa and Canada's Alcan Aluminium Ltd., David P. Reynolds hired William O. Bourke, 54, a former vice president at Ford Motor Company to head up most of the company's operating divisions. His strategy is to use his extensive automobile manufacturing knowledge to convince automakers to use more aluminum in cars. As Mr. Bourke says, "I know a bit about automakers' problems with aluminum and what they are looking for. . . . I can talk their lingo." The movement to bring in new management expertise continued with the hiring of Rodney Hanneman from General Electric. Hanneman's knowledge will be put to a test early, as he was given responsibility for energy-related projects.

If Bourke performs well, he will probably succeed David Reynolds as chairman. A Reynolds family member may lead the company in the future—two younger Reynolds executives are currently in with the organization. Owning 14 percent of the company, the Reynolds family will continue to have an influence on who is the chief executive.

Adapted from A. Nag, "Reynolds Metals Family Hires Outsiders as Firm Plans Expansion into New Areas," *The Wall Street Journal* (December 1, 1981).

promotions, use of special assignments, and so on. The most important factor, however, is that you have *diagnosed* the problem before it becomes critical. This, as we have stressed throughout this book, is an extremely important managerial skill.

A second form of human resource assessment is the *management replacement analysis*. As shown in exhibit 10-5, the replacement analysis for division A consists of three steps: (1) developing the organization chart; (2) evaluating the current performance of the existing managers; and (3) evaluating the promotion potential of the managers. The results are twofold. First, you get an evaluation of each department, which provides higher level management with an assessment of human resource strengths and weaknesses. Second, the analysis provides the first step in the development of a *managerial succession plan*, identifying the managers who are likely candidates for future promotion.

In a simple way, the analyses provided in exhibits 10-4 and 10-5 are very valuable to the manager. Not only have certain problems been uncovered, but the future needs and potential of the managerial staff have also been identified. These data, plus an analysis of labor force trends, provide the foundation of the human resource plan.

Exhibit 10-5
Management Replacement Analysis

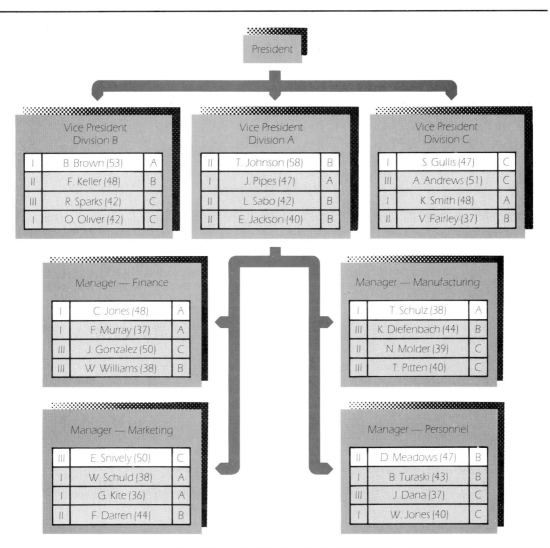

The Legal Environment of Human Resources

One of the most important developments in the human resource planning process has been the evolution and growth of the legal environment. Based primarily on civil rights legislation, the legal environment has had a significant impact on human resource activities for all types of organizations.

Exhibit 10-6 shows a number of the most important laws affecting the human resource process. By far the most dominant are those legislative acts that prohibit

Exhibit 10-6
Major Federal Laws Related to Human Resources

Federal Law	Description
1. U.S. Constitution: 1st, 5th, and 14th Amendments	Prohibits deprivation of employment rights without due process of law—federal, state, and local governments.
2. Civil Rights Act of 1866 and 1870	Prohibits race discrimination in hiring, placement, and continuation of employment for private employers, unions, and employment agencies.
3. Title VI, 1964 Civil Rights Act	Prohibits discrimination based on race, color, or national origin—employers receiving federal financial assistance.
4. Title VII, 1964 Civil Rights Act	Prohibits discrimination based on race, color, religion, sex, or national origin—private employers; federal, state, and local governments; unions; employment agencies.
5. Executive Orders 11246 and 11375 (1965)	Prohibits discrimination based on race, color, religion, sex, or national origin (affirmative action)—federal contractors and subcontractors.
6. Title I, 1968 Civil Rights Act	Prohibits interference with a person's exercise of rights with respect to race, religion, color, or national origin.
7. National Labor Relations Act	Prohibits unfair representation by unions that discriminate on the basis of race, color, religion, sex, or national origin.
8. Equal Pay Act of 1963	Prohibits sex differences in pay for equal work—private employers.
9. Age Discrimination in Employment Act of 1967 and 1975	Prohibits age discrimination against those between the ages of 40 and 65 years—all employers.
10. Rehabilitation Act of 1973	Prohibits discrimination based on physical or mental handicap (affirmative action).
11. Vietnam Era Veterans Readjustment Act of 1974	Prohibits discrimination against disabled veterans and Vietnam era veterans (affirmative action).
12. Occupational Safety and Health Act (OSHA—1970)	Established mandatory safety and health standards in organizations.
13. Revised Guidelines on Employee Selection (1976)	Established specific rules on employment selection practices.
14. Mandatory Retirement Act	Employee cannot be forced to retire before age 70.
15. Privacy Act of 1974	Employees have legal right to examine letters of reference concerning them unless they waive the right.

discrimination in the workplace on the basis of age, race, and sex. These laws are the foundation for affirmative action programs, which require organizations to have a positive plan to reduce and/or eliminate internal imbalances or inequities among affected groups. Failure to do so can result in fines, loss of government contracts, or other actions.

AT&T, for example, agreed to pay over $15 million in back wages to women and other minority groups whose pay was "arbitrarily" low because of discriminatory practices. In addition, AT&T's affirmative action plan required that the number of women and blacks in lower-level management positions be increased by over 80 percent and 40 percent, respectively. The plan also called for a 150 percent increase in the number of men in clerical positions and a nearly 120 percent increase in the number of women in craft and skilled jobs. The result is that women now climb telephone poles to repair circuits and men answer requests for long distance assistance.

The effect of affirmative action policies has been significant on organizations. Recent research has shown that the existence of such policies, supported by top management, has greatly helped counteract racial and sex biases in selection and promotion decisions.[7]

Due to the significance and complexity of human resource legislative acts, managers at all levels must become aware of the fairness of their employment policies and behavior. Support and commitment to the laws must come from all managers, from the chief executive to the lowest levels.

Recruitment

Recruiting concerns the set of activities that an organization uses to attract job candidates who have the abilities and skills needed to assist the organization in the achievement of its goals. For our purposes, recruitment will be concerned with the dual problem of *securing* people the organization needs and *insuring* that these people remain.[8]

Recruiting to Secure People

In recruiting future employees, most organizations divide their process into at least two categories. First, for lower level positions, the organization employs a process we will call *general* recruiting. This continual process is directed at filling positions that frequently open up in most organizations. Examples include clerical personnel, janitorial staff, and other nonskilled or semiskilled workers. Second, to fill particular positions, an organization may opt for a *specific* recruiting orientation. This is most appropriate for positions in management, professional employees such as engineers and nurses, and certain skilled workers such as specialized equipment operators.

College recruiting can fall into either category. For example, most of the tire and rubber companies and financial institutions hire a number of college graduates for their management training programs. In this general classification, the new recruits enter the training program for a period of up to two years, after which they join a particular department where there is a match between the needs of the unit and the skills of the individual. Some recruiting of MBA graduates can be specific in nature, particularly if the graduate is being hired for an identified position, such as financial analyst or cost accountant.

Two issues are important in this recruiting category—job analysis and recruitment sources.

Job Analysis   Before the organization can recruit personnel, it must know what type of position is open. This is the purpose of job analysis. *Job analysis* consists of a statement that is: (1) a description identifying the title, duties, and responsibilities for that position; and (2) an acknowledgment of the desired background, experience, and personal characteristics an individual must have in order to perform effectively in the position. For example, a description of an open position for an auditing manager in an accounting firm may state: ''Position requires a BS or MS in accounting, CPA, minimum five years experience, some as a supervisor; motivated with well-established interpersonal and analytical skills.''

Recruitment Sources   Organizations can use two broad sources of recruitment. First, there are *internal* sources within the organization. These may include job posting systems, friends of present employees, or the replacement analysis. Many organizations have found it beneficial to recruit or promote existing employees to open positions. Promoting within has at least two advantages: (1) it significantly reduces the sometimes excessive recruiting and placement costs; and (2) it improves morale and loyalty among employees because they believe their good performance can be rewarded with a promotion.

External sources are also frequently used by organizations. These include walk-ins, agencies or placement/search firms, newspaper and journal ads, school and college recruiting, unions, military services, and professional associations. External sources offer mixed advantages and disadvantages to the organization. On the positive side, the vast variety of sources almost ensures that the organization is able to find an adequate number of candidates. On the negative side, sources such as college recruiting can be quite costly. Most organizations must interview twenty to thirty candidates before one is hired. Newspaper and journal ads can also be expensive, as is using a placement firm for more specialized or high-level managerial positions.

The growing body of research that has investigated the relationship between recruiting source and rates of turnover have yielded surprisingly consistent results.[9] These studies indicate that internal sources, particularly employee referrals, were consistently good in hiring people who remained in the organization for a significant length of time. Employment agencies, on the other hand, were poor sources of long-term employees.

Realistic Recruiting

Recruiting philosophies and policies in many organizations are too often based on the objective of filling the immediate job opening, as opposed to the more long-term objective of finding a person who will both be productive and stay in the job. The first is called the *flypaper* approach to recruiting—if the organization is able to attract people, they will get stuck and stay.[10] The latter approach is the *realistic* method, which emphasizes telling the prospective employee what to expect in the job to avoid establishing unrealistic expectations that may lead to later dissatisfaction.

The realistic recruiting approach stresses, through a variety of mechanisms, what the prospective employee will actually find on the job. This can be done with the use of interviews, booklets, films, and other forms of communication.

A number of studies have been conducted to investigate the effects of the realistic recruiting approach.[11] Some of the people studied were telephone operators, insurance sales representatives, and assembly-line workers in an electronics plant. In each study, the results were nearly the same: (1) newly hired employees given realistic job previews had greater job survival rates than those hired by traditional methods; (2) higher levels of job satisfaction were reported by realistic job preview employees; and (3) contrary to the belief of many people, the use of realistic job previews did not reduce the flow of highly capable applicants.

In summary, the traditional approach to recruiting (i.e., flypaper approach) may result in the short-term benefit of hiring capable people, but can create long-term problems with respect to dissatisfaction and turnover. The realistic approach, on the other hand, has resulted in lower turnover rates with no decrease in the number of people applying for jobs.

 # Selection

The basis of the selection process is *matching*. On one hand, the organization decides whether the candidate's qualifications match the needs of the job; on the other hand, the candidate decides whether or not the job in the organization matches personal goals and needs.

Ideally, both the organization and the candidate enter the selection process on an equal basis. In reality, however, many factors, particularly the nature of the external environment, create a state of inequality. For example, if the labor market is "tight"—known as a buyer's market, because there are more candidates than jobs—the organization can usually choose from a number of qualified people. If the labor market is "open"—known as a seller's market, because there are more jobs than qualified candidates—the candidate may be able to choose from a number of job opportunities. In the early 1980s, the labor market for elementary school teachers was quite tight, while an open market was apparent for secretaries and certain accountants. For engineers, the labor market has varied from tight to open frequently over the past fifteen years.

The Selection Process

Exhibit 10-7 presents an example of the selection process for an organization. While there are many variations in the degree of formality that organizations adopt, the detailed steps usually are followed.

Step 1   First, the organization establishes the *criteria* for selection. As in the job analysis procedure, the criteria usually consist of information related to formal education, experience, physical characteristics, and other specific skills.

Step 2   This step includes the *initial screening interview* and the completion of an application form. The objectives of this step are to: (1) get basic information; (2) determine the level of interest of the candidates; and (3) determine if the selection process should continue.

Exhibit 10-7
The Selection
Process

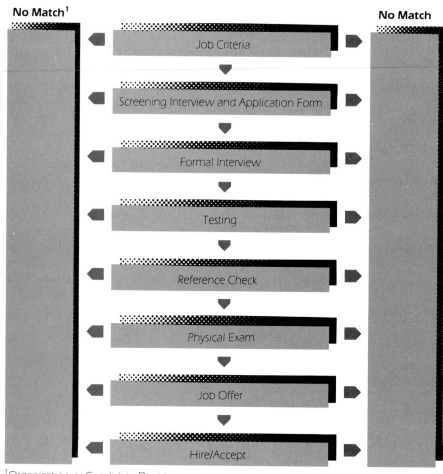

¹Organization or Candidate Decision

Step 3   The *formal interview* is part of almost all selection procedures and probably one of the most important steps. It is important for two major reasons. First, it provides a great variety and volume of information about the candidate (for the organization) and the organization (for the candidate). Second, the candidate generally meets face to face with many organizational members, which is valuable for determining whether individual and organization fit or match each other.

There are three general types of interviews that are most frequently used—structured, semistructured, and unstructured. In the *structured* interview, the interviewer prepares a list of questions in advance and does not deviate from the list. If the responses are to be made in a forced-choice manner (i.e., yes or no), a great deal of objective information can be gathered, because the structured interview eliminates idle chatter. The *semi-structured* interview consists of a limited set of questions asked of the candidate. This procedure allows needed data to be collected, while the extra time permits the interviewer or interviewee to delve deeper on a number of points. Finally, the *unstructured* interview uses little preparation other than a set of example topics. The overriding advantage of this type of interview is that it allows a great deal of freedom to the interviewer to adapt to the situation and cover areas of interest to the candidate.

While the organization wishes to gain as much information as possible from the candidate, there are limitations that have been imposed as a result of antidiscrimination laws. Many questions that may appear harmless can function as discriminatory in selection decisions. The important criterion is that unless a question relates directly to the job, or to specific needs, such as future insurance needs, it normally cannot be asked.

Step 4   *Employment testing* involves a number of different procedures, each attempting to estimate the candidate's ability to perform effectively on the job. Two general categories of tests are usually employed by organizations. First, in *performance tests* or simulations, candidates actually perform the work or a portion of it. Examples are typing tests for secretaries, speed and accuracy tests for computer keypunch operators, and a standardized driving exam for forklift drivers. The second category concerns *pencil-and-paper tests* designed to measure the general intelligence and aptitude levels of the candidate. *Psychological tests* that are oriented toward measuring certain personality and temperament traits are also in this second category.

In the use of employment tests, the manager needs to be concerned with three characteristics. First, does the test relate to *actual performance* on the job? If not, it may possibly lead to a charge of discrimination. Second, is the test *valid?* That is, does the test measure a component of performance, or something else? For example, a speed and accuracy test for computer keypunch operators is quite valid for measuring

Cooper, if I had wanted someone who squealed every time I told him to come in on Sunday, I would have hired Porky Pig!

© Valen Associates

or predicting future performance, but a psychological test supposedly measuring "achievement motive" may not only *not* be measuring this factor, but the factor itself may not be an important determinant of future performance. Finally, is the test *reliable?* The key to reliability is whether the test gives approximately the same score each time it is taken over a short period of time, assuming that nothing affective has occurred between tests.

Step 5   Background and *reference checks* are one of the most valuable, but equally controversial, aspects of the employment selection process. Usually the candidate is asked to provide letters of reference or the names of people who are knowledgeable about his or her background. If the reference person is sufficiently knowledgeable and is truthful, then valuable information is obtained. However, many times this does not occur. Either the references do not know the person well enough or they hide the truth for a variety of reasons. For this reason, reference checks have been criticized for their lack of reliability.

Another problem closely related to reference checks was created by the Privacy Act of 1974. Under this law, persons have a legal right to examine letters of reference concerning them *unless* they waive the right to do so. Because of this, many people are reluctant to provide negative information for fear of being sued by the candidate. Besides attempting to have candidates waive their right to view the letters, many organizations have tried two techniques to obtain the valuable information from references. First, they may decide to telephone the reference and ask for a verbal recommendation. This helps somewhat to eliminate the problem of having the data down on paper. Second, the organization may contact people *other* than those identified by the candidate. This provides wider coverage to the needed information.

Step 6   Some organizations require future employees to take a *physical examination.* The reasons are threefold: (1) to eliminate insurance claims for injuries or illnesses contracted outside the workplace or before the individual was hired; (2) to prevent the hiring of people with communicable diseases; and (3) to verify that the candidate can actually do the required work. The most important point is probably the third—organizations must carefully state and prove that certain specific physical requirements are needed for acceptable on-the-job performance. For many years, certain handicapped persons were excluded from jobs because of non-performance-related physical requirements. In the same manner, women were not permitted to apply for jobs in city fire departments for reasons based on standards for physical stamina that have since been revised. With time—and the influence of anti-discrimination laws—discriminatory practices are slowly being eliminated.

Step 7   The job offer generally concludes the first cycle of the selection process. A person who has successfully passed through the key steps in the process is offered employment. As we pointed out in the recruiting discussion, many offers can be turned down before someone accepts. This means that the selection process is a *continual activity* that is time consuming, costly, but necessary.

The American flag and the McDonald's flag fly high over the expressway running through the backyard of Hamburger University in a suburban Chicago town. Inside, McDonald's franchisers and company managers learn skills to reinforce what the golden arches have come to symbolize: predictability in atmosphere and taste, or, as McDonald's founder Ray Kroc puts it, ". . the gospel of Quality, Service, Cleanliness, and Value."

A high school dropout, Mr. Kroc is committed to employee training, especially if it is trade oriented. Two thousand students each year "graduate" from the school (Hamburger U.). One lucky student in each course receives a golden chef's hat for making the largest contribution to class discussion. . . . Another walks away with a ceramic abstract model of a hamburger for highest academic honors.

Mr. Kroc points out that the American Council of Education recommends college credit of up to six semester hours for Hamburger U. courses for those who are pursuing a diploma at a two- or four-year college. At Hamburger U., there are 18 courses, from one-day seminars to week-long sessions covering such topics as market evaluation, management skills, and area supervision.

McDonald's success has been largely based on fast food and friendly service. Management training goes a long way to support the continuation of this success.

Source: S. S. Anderson, "Hamburger U. Offers a Break," *The New York Times* (August 30, 1981): 27-28.

development are necessary for the spirit, survival, and performance of an organization—it must develop those who will manage the organization in the years to come.

The training and development function in an organization involves a multi-faceted purpose and definition. *Training* is an activity that is primarily directed at improving an employee's current job performance. It generally involves the acquisition of technical skills, and some human skills, by nonmanagerial and managerial personnel. Learning to operate a computer terminal, how to write a business report, or the right way to conduct a performance evaluation are examples.

Development, on the other hand, involves two equally important components.[20] First, there is *management development,* which is concerned with the question, "What kind of managers and professionals will the organization need tomorrow in order to achieve its goals in a changing environment?" Management development is oriented to issues of the age and skills of the managerial staff and what is needed in the future. It is also concerned with the structure of the organization and the types of managers that are required to operate within it. The focus of management development is *outside* or *external*—it is heavily oriented toward responding to strategic questions.

The focus of *manager development* is internal—on the manager. The objective is to improve the skills and advancement potential of individuals so they may better contribute to the organization and to society in the future.

This chapter focuses on management development and training activities. In chapter 20, we will provide a more detailed discussion of the process of manager development.

Training and Development Process

Exhibit 10-9 is an example of the training and development process that occurs in many organizations. There are a number of important steps in this process:

- The first step is to conduct a "training and development needs analysis." As shown in exhibit 10-9, a needs analysis has a threefold focus: *organizational analysis* (analyzing the needs of the total organization now and in the future); *operational analysis* (analyzing the needs of a specific group of jobs); and *individual analysis* (analyzing the needs of the specific employee).[21]

- Once the needs have been identified, the specific goals and criteria for training and development activities must be set. This includes establishing both the short-term and long-term objectives of the programs, as well as the criteria on which the programs will be evaluated.

- Training and development methods are selected that emphasize both on-the-job and off-the-job programs.

- Program evaluation provides an important assessment of the training and development process. Evaluation occurs during three stages: (a) during training and development; (b) at the end of the training and development experience; and (c) after a length of time on the job.

Because of its particular importance to organizations, the topic of training and development sources and techniques will be discussed separately.

Training and Development Sources

A number of sources of training and development programs are available to the organization.[22] Programs conducted *within* the organization (internal) usually involve on-the-job or off-the-job activities. On-the-job activities are programs designed for the individual to learn during work. Examples include apprenticeship programs and internships. Off-the-job activities are more oriented to separate classroom-type instructions by the training and development staff.

Training and development programs can also be conducted *outside* the organization (external). Such activities generally involve sending the individual to an association-sponsored program, such as the American Management Associations; or through one of the many university-sponsored programs. These external activities usually cover topics in more depth or completely new topics that the organizational staff are unable to cover.

A continuing debate in many organizations is the comparative value and effectiveness of internal and external programs. Internally sponsored training and development programs are generally less expensive and require less of the individual's time than external programs. On the other hand, external programs typically present concepts

Exhibit 10-9
The Training and Development Process

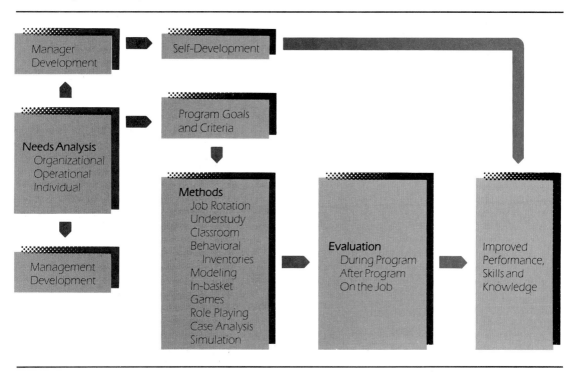

and topics from experts in a field, which can be quite a plus. In addition, a frequently overlooked factor is that an individual may learn new skills and approaches more effectively when he or she is removed from the day-to-day activities and demands of the job. This allows a greater concentration on the concepts being presented. There is also the positive feature of meeting and interacting with managers from other organizations. The interchange of ideas and approaches to problems among program participants is itself a very valuable learning experience.

There is no pat answer to which is best, internal or external programs. Managers should diagnose the particular needs of the organization and the individual before choosing between the different techniques. Cost and learning value must be carefully weighed.

Training and Development Techniques

With the growing importance of training and development, the number of techniques that have been used has grown commensurately. The various techniques range from basic classroom instruction to complex simulation gaming and experiential learning. To simplify our presentation, we will discuss them as they relate to the specific managerial skills that they are intended to influence. Exhibit 10-10 summarizes.

Exhibit 10-10
Training and Development and Managerial Skills

Skills	Criteria	Job Rotation	Under-study	Class-room	Behav. Inven.	Model.	In-Basket	Games	Role Playing	Cases
Technical	Improved Performance	X				X		X		
	Skills Development	X	X			X	X	X		
	Knowledge	X	X	X	X	X				
Human	Improved Performance	X				X		X	X	
	Skills Development	X	X	X	X	X		X	X	
	Knowledge	X	X	X	X	X		X		
Conceptual	Improved Performance	X						X		X
	Skills Development	X	X	X	X	X	X	X		X
	Knowledge	X	X	X	X	X	X		X	X
Diagnostic	Improved Performance	X	X			X	X			X
	Skills Development	X	X			X	X	X		X
	Knowledge	X	X	X		X	X		X	X

Adapted from T. J. Von Der Embse, "Choosing a Management Development Model," *Personnel Journal* (October 1978).

Technical Skills   Three techniques are most frequently used to help an employee gain technical skills. These include: job rotation; understudy or mentoring relationships; and classroom instruction.

Job Rotation   With job rotation, the individual employee works on a series of jobs in the organization or in a specific unit. The primary benefits of job rotation are that it provides for learning of a wide variety of tasks, the individual is made aware of the critical interdependencies and the need for cooperation, and it enables the individual to develop a better view of the entire unit or organization.

Understudy or Apprenticeship   Like job rotation, this technique is highly oriented to on-the-job activities. The understudy is asked to observe, follow, and emulate an experienced worker for a period of time until he or she has mastered the particular technical skills. In such skilled trades as carpentry, electrical installation, and others, the approach is known as an *apprenticeship*. At the managerial level, the *mentoring* relationship discussed in chapter 1 could be considered an understudy approach.

Classroom Instruction   Similar to that of formal instruction in educational institutions, many organizations use lectures and seminars to conduct training activities.

Human Skills Since managers recognize the importance of human skills, they are quite often included in most training and development programs. Yet their complexity makes them equally difficult to present. Many techniques, including role playing, have been created for purposes of developing human skills. Among the most used are behavioral inventories and behavioral modeling.

Behavioral Inventories A number of pencil-and-paper instruments provide an evaluation or description of certain behaviors exhibited by the manager. Examples include descriptions of the manager's leadership style, communications patterns, and orientation toward working in groups.

Behavior Modeling Behavior modeling is a technique that uses a combination of role playing and videotape feedback to present a new concept or skill.[23] For example, to introduce a new approach to college interviewing, the participants review a series of films or videotapes that depict acceptable and unacceptable interviewing techniques. For realism, employees in the organization are used as the actors in the role-playing episodes. The participants are then asked to do the role playing using the new interviewing techniques, after which the tapes are evaluated and repeated.

Conceptual and Diagnostic Skills The development of conceptual and diagnostic skills is more difficult to accomplish through training and development programs. As we implied in chapter 1, these skills are primarily developed through time and experience. Certain techniques, however, can facilitate the recognition and development of these two important skills.

In-basket exercise, simulation gaming, and leaderless group discussions, as used in assessment centers, have been used in the development of conceptual and diagnostic skills. One of the most popular techniques is the comprehensive *case analysis*. Either through internal programs or more frequently through externally sponsored management development programs (or graduate school courses), the participant is forced to: (1) identify the main problems and their causes; (2) develop a set of alternative actions to resolve the problems; and (3) choose the most appropriate solution. The group discussions that result not only force the participant to justify a position, they may help promote tolerance of others' viewpoints in solving complex organizational problems, which itself is a valuable human skill.

Successful Management Development Programs

Organizations such as Xerox, Citibank, General Motors, AT&T, Kaiser Aluminum, IBM, Caterpillar, and Raytheon have been known for their successes in developing effective managers. It may be helpful to note the similarities and differences in the way these programs are conducted. A recent analysis of some of the best-managed companies in the United States revealed some interesting findings regarding management development practices.[24] The study revealed that there is no universal approach followed by these companies. AT&T, for example, depends heavily on the assessment center approach to identify managers with potential and then involves them in a long series of formal training activities along with frequent job rotations. IBM emphasizes formal training programs that can last from one to four weeks. Lower-level managers participate primarily in in-house programs, and higher-level executives may be sent to university programs or other external associations. Raytheon almost totally depends on in-house training programs.

Second, without exception, the companies studied believe that the vast majority of actual management development occurs *on the job,* when managers handle progressively more responsible assignments and problems under fire. On-the-job experience, coaching by superiors (mentoring), and job rotation were identified as the most important development means.

Third, formal training in management skills required at different organizational levels helps prepare for and enhance on-the-job development. Specific job assignments allow managers to use their new skills after they develop them.

Fourth, the content of formal management training varies by organizational level. At the supervisory level, the emphasis is on handling organizational policies and procedures, communication, personnel practices, and motivation of subordinates. At the middle-management level, performance evaluation, effective leadership styles, group dynamics, time management, and counseling of subordinates are stressed. Finally, at the executive level, the focus is on effective decision making, dealing with the external environment, and the development of strategies and policies.

Fifth, the larger the organization, the greater the probability that it will have its own training operations physically separated from its headquarters. Thus, internal programs are preferred over external programs. This allows the organization to tailor the training programs more closely to on-the-job development activities.

Finally, it was unanimously believed that managers have a primary responsibility to develop their subordinates. Their ability to develop capable people is a significant element in their own development and advancement.

Current Issues in Human Resource Management

The human resource process, not unlike the other facets of the managerial functions, faces many complex and difficult issues today. We have selected three of these issues for a brief discussion—women in management, international staffing, and automation.

Women in Management

During the past two decades, women have made significant inroads into this nation's work force. Today, four out of ten workers in the U.S. are women. Among the professions, they account for about 12 percent of doctors, up from 6 percent in 1950, and close to 15 percent of the nation's lawyers, up from only 4 percent in 1950. Even more dramatic has been the increase in the managerial ranks, where nearly 15 percent hold management jobs, more than double the rate of twenty years ago.[25]

The management field is reflecting the major changes of society as a whole. But studies have given a number of specific reasons for the increase of women in managerial positions.[26] First, there has been significant *governmental pressure* in enforcing equal opportunity for women through various legislative acts, including Title VII of the Civil Rights Act and the Equal Pay Act of 1963.

Second, there are the clear cut and dramatic shifts in *social trends* in this and other countries. Women are more highly educated than ever before—nearly one-half of business school graduates today are women.

The rising cost of living has influenced the entry of married women into the managerial labor market to supplement the inflation-crushed family income. Often it is the woman's salary that provides the family with the larger home, car, and vacations that would be impossible on one income. And it frankly can be a matter of survival as well.

There is women's increased awareness of their need for self-satisfaction and fulfillment in their careers. Women are no longer satisfied with clerical jobs when higher positions are available. So, no matter what management's view has been concerning the ''woman's place,'' the fact is that women are working and must be considered a valuable resource and part of the same work force as men—one that needs to be effectively managed, motivated, utilized, and rewarded.

Many organizations are finally concerned over their *public image* as it relates to 51 percent of the population—women. Product-based organizations now seriously consider the implications on their market activities of their internal discrimination. Because women are the prime buyers of this nation's goods and services, they are taking a hard look at the policies of the companies that produce the products. For example, a recent General Mills training program consisting of sixty-five people, sixty-four of them white males, was the target of a formal charge filed by the National Organization for Women (NOW) and the Urban League. Not only was the publicity damaging, but both groups threatened to launch a nationwide boycott against the company's Betty Crocker products, Wheaties, Cheerios, and Gold Medal flour.[27]

Finally is the issue of *human resource availability*. Many managers are coming to the recognition that industry's biggest problem in the coming years will be a shortage of capable people at all levels of management. Organizations can no longer ignore one-half the population when they are looking for creative executive talent. It has long been obvious that organizations are not utilizing the capabilities of women, having kept them in jobs in which their aptitudes, skills, intelligence, and education are not fully appreciated. From a resource point of view, the female work force constitutes an important reservoir of talent that all organizations need to remain competitive and successful.[28]

Human Resources in the International Realm

One of the most significant changes in management during the last twenty years has been the development of the multinational corporation, the natural result of the evolution and growth of organizations in taking advantage of prevailing market opportunities and demands. The importance of an international awareness is vividly illustrated by the fact that companies such as Gillette and Ford Motor derive a large percentage of their sales and profits from overseas operations.

Stages of Human Resource Development   In the industrial organization viewpoint, the international human resource development and usage process generally goes through four stages.[29]

Stage One—Transfer   This first stage involves the transfer of an executive or executives from the home country to fill key positions in a foreign operation. In many cases, the vast majority of the jobs are held by U.S. personnel, and only a minimum of jobs are held by foreign nationals. Such decisions are normally not made out of prejudice toward foreign employees but a concern that there is a lack of needed expertise to handle the work.

Stage Two—Mixed Resources   In this second stage, sometimes due to pressures from the foreign government (or because foreign nationals have been suitably trained for the work), most foreign operations jobs are held by local personnel, and the top management team is still from the home country of the firm. The organization wishes to be a good neighbor to the country by employing some of its citizens, but it is reluctant to relinquish total control of operations.

Stage Three—Unitary Resources   At this stage in the evolution process, the entire operation is staffed by foreign nationals, including the top management positions. Such a situation may be forced on the organization, as in Japan and Zambia where it is expected that the top management positions are to be filled by executives from that country. In other situations, the organization's operations may have matured to the point at which foreign nationals have the experience to handle jobs at all levels effectively.

Stage Four—Interchange   In this final stage, there is the recognition that a manager's skill and competence rather than his or her passport should be the basis of advancement, privileges, and rewards. In other words, there is not only the opportunity for U.S. managers to obtain international assignments, but foreign managers within the organization can hold assignments at the home office. There are few organizations that have fully passed through this stage, but in time many will, because the forces behind this movement are quite strong. The main force is the search for excellence and performance—choose the manager best for the job without consideration of nationality.

One of the most successful international staffing efforts was conducted by American Standard, Inc., a large New-York-based manufacturer of plumbing supplies, transportation equipment, and mining machinery. In order to instill a more global orientation, the company began tapping foreign managers to run its key U.S. operations, along with sending U.S. nationals overseas. Nearly one-third of all vice-presidential positions at corporate headquarters have been filled by foreign-born personnel.[30]

Besides differences in managerial style, American Standard's biggest problem was getting qualified foreign managers to come to the U.S. The company found out that many foreign managers resisted the potentially career-boosting move because their cultural roots were deep in their countries. American Standard overcame this problem with the use of a careful selection program. Interestingly, they found that the most successful moves were by foreign managers who were educated in U.S. universities.

Issues in International Human Resource Development   The development of the human resource function on an international basis has been one of the most troublesome problems faced by many organizations. The reluctance on the part of many organizations to go from stage one to stage two and/or stage three in the development process has been a major stumbling block to effectiveness. The salient problem, however, has been the insistence on the part of organizations to impose U.S. management methods and techniques on foreign operations without certain modifications that are important to the particular culture. As we discussed in earlier chapters, for example, assigning authority and responsibility to a manager, so accepted in our culture, is not so readily accepted in others. Similar problems related to differences in cultural norms regarding employee terminations or the acceptance of high levels of foreign national absenteeism have also been difficult for managers to adjust to in the short run.

In addition to these points, there are other important issues that organizations face in performing in the international sphere. A recent survey of executives of U.S.-based multinational corporations identified the major problem in their foreign operations as the lack of qualified personnel in the particular country.[31] In order to have as many foreign nationals in their operations as possible, many organizations are investing millions of dollars in developing extensive training programs to teach people the skills and knowledge needed for high performance.

Finally, there are the problems associated with transferring a U.S.-based manager to a foreign operation. Beyond learning the language, a person simply must adapt to the customs of another country. This is a particular problem for managers who wish to take their spouses and families with them on a job assignment in the Middle East, where the role of women is quite different from what it is in the U.S. Other family adjustment problems can occur concerning education for the children or simple housing needs. To counter some of these problems, many organizations ask managers *and* their families to participate in orientation and training programs before the transfer so that their "socialization" goes smoothly.

Recognizing the importance of U.S. managers in overseas assignments, Congress recently changed the Tax Code to make such positions more attractive. Effective January 1983, an expatriate manager does not have to pay U.S. income tax up to $75,000 per year. This exception will not only rise to $95,000 by 1986, but housing allowances, once heavily taxed, will become largely tax exempt. As some experts have stated, this tax code change will allow top management to fill a job with the best qualified person without being overly constrained by governmental policies.[32]

Automation and Human Resources

By the year 2000, automation will be one of the important factors influencing the management of human resources. Largely the outgrowth of computer technology, it is predicted that by the end of the century nearly one-half of all U.S. workers will be affected by some form of automation on the job. This change is already visible today in word processors, office computers, and robot welders.[33]

Managers are looking to automation to help reduce costs, improve product quality, and possibly make workers' jobs more interesting. Overall, it is hoped that automation will increase the ability of U.S. industries to compete more effectively with foreign imports.

Even though experts in the field do not expect the rapid substitution of automated machinery for human labor to increase unemployment, there are a number of issues managers should consider from a human resource point of view.[34] First, automation may require painful adjustments for workers and organizations alike. For example, automating some processes—whether assembly line or an office secretarial pool—will require job and skills upgrading for many workers. Training is already a costly operation in most organizations, and in the future, this cost is expected to increase.

Second, the push to automate has so far focused primarily on jobs that are dirty, dangerous, and boring. Yet some automation may also displace workers or require them to take jobs in which the primary responsibility is to babysit equipment. In other words, automation can lead to a dead-end job.

Third, automation can create health problems. Long hours at a video-display terminal can cause eye, neck, and back fatigue. Many postal workers suffer from something called *carpal tunnel syndrome* when they work on letter-sorting machines.[35] This is a nerve disorder of the hand and wrist that leads to loss of feeling and may require surgery. Workers may feel increased job pressure from working on automated equipment. Word processing is a classic case. Since managers and supervisors have recognized the value of word processing in improving the quality and quantity of information transfer, they have tended to push harder for improved productivity with the new equipment. Some workers, as those at Blue Cross of Texas, have resisted attempts to significantly increase productivity without a commensurate increase in pay.

There is no question that the issue of automation and human resources will be a challenge to management in the future. Training costs, job upgrading, worker motivation, health problems, and the increased interest shown by unions on the effects of automation will have to be confronted by managers in their quest for improved performance in the office and the plant.

POINTS TO CONSIDER
An Emphasis on Managerial Skills

1. **Managing human resources is every manager's job.**
   Some people may think that managing human resources is the job of the personnel department. Actually, it is a process that cannot be completely delegated to someone else with the expectation of continued success.

2. **Managing human resources in the 1980s and beyond will be a challenging task.**
   The entire human resource process—from hiring to firing—involves many new problems and issues. Governmental intervention, changing worker needs, demographic pattern changes, women rising in management, automation, and many more issues will increase the complexity of managerial decision making.

3. **Managerial skills and roles are closely related to the human resource process.**
   Selection, orientation, and training and development are three key steps in the human resource process that act as sources of managerial skills and roles. Where managers are placed, how they learn what is to be done, and what additional training they receive all impact their current and future performance.

4. **Developing capable future managers should be an important performance criterion for today's managers.**
   We often look at the performance of a manager from a short-term perspective (e.g., making decisions on time, maintaining or exceeding production capacity). The long-term performance, survival, and growth of any organization, however, is related to the degree to which it can continue to provide a steady stream of skilled and competent managers. Managers who are able to handle the changing and dynamic role of management. Thus, it is important for every manager to pay particular attention to identifying and developing the managers of the future.

SUMMARY FOR THE MANAGER

1. The acquisition, training, and allocation of human resources in organizations is one of the most important functions of management. No longer can management assume the existence of an unlimited employee pool that can be easily trained to accomplish the organization's goals. Issues of equal employment opportunity, the need for improved productivity, and the development of the managers of the future all highlight the need for a revised view of the human resource function. The effectiveness of this function is the job of every manager, not just the personnel department.

2. The human resource process—consisting of resource planning, recruitment, placement, selection, orientation, training and development, performance evaluation, reward system, and terminations—begins with an analysis and knowledge of its premises. These premises involve much of the material covered up to now in this book—goals, strategies, decision making, and organizational design. These components serve as the starting point for the human resource process.

3. Human resource planning involves the analysis of at least the following points: what does the organization want to do (i.e., goals and strategies); what are the significant labor forces and legal trends that can impinge on this organization; and, what is our present state of evaluation with respect to our human resources? By responding to these issues, managers can have a good start in identifying the organization's human resource needs now and in the future. Of particular concern for managers at this stage is the growing body of laws regulating the human resource process.

4. Recruiting involves the twofold process of securing people and making sure they stay in the organization. Beyond the growing variety of recruiting sources, the issue of realistic recruiting is particularly important to the manager. Unless a true picture of the organization is given, the possibility of increased turnover may develop.

5. Selection is a process that concerns establishing criteria for the job, interviews, testing, reference checks, and the like. The selection of managers requires a special emphasis by the organization because of the key role that managers play in the survival of the organization. Particular emphasis is placed on the individual's potential, past performance, and the evaluation of

extensive interviews. Management assessment centers have been given increased attention during the past few years.

6. Orienting the new employee to the organization must go beyond the simple induction activities. The process of socialization—learning the ropes—undergoing a significant revision in many of today's organizations. The effectiveness of the unlearning and relearning phases of socialization can have a tremendous impact on the employee's subsequent performance.

7. The training and development stage of the human resource process is one of the most important. It is at this stage that the key managerial skills and roles are learned. Organizations use a wide variety of methods and techniques to train and develop their managers and nonmanagerial employees; by far the most used and successful relate to job rotation and on-the-job training. The important function of mentoring also can be used to give the manager new skills.

8. Many human resource issues face today's manager. Among them are the growing importance of women in management, staffing the international operation, and automation. These and others will continue to make the human resource aspect of the manager's job much more complex.

 # REVIEW AND DISCUSSION QUESTIONS

1. Why is the concern over human resources the responsibility of every manager?
2. What are the premises of the human resource process?
3. Distinguish between a resource audit and management replacement analysis.
4. Why do many organizations resist the use of realistic recruiting?
5. What are some of the positive and negative features of managerial assessment centers?
6. Why are interviews so important in management selection?
7. What is meant by the term *organizational socialization?*
8. What is the difference between manager development and management development?
9. Can conceptual and diagnostic skills be acquired in training and development programs?
10. What are the forces behind women in management today?

NOTES

1. See M. A. Devanna, C. Fombrun, and N. Tichy, "Human Resources Management: A Strategic Perspective," *Organizational Dynamics* (Winter 1981): 51-67.
2. A. D. Szilagyi, "Keeping Employee Turnover Under Control," *Personnel* (November-December 1979): 14-28.
3. H. Koontz and C. O'Donnell, *Management*, 6th ed. (New York: McGraw-Hill, 1976), p. 449.
4. B. Uttal, "Selling Is No Longer Mickey Mouse at AT&T," *Fortune* (July 17, 1978): 98-104.
5. W. Guzzardi, Jr., "Demography's Good News for the Eighties," *Fortune* (November 5, 1979): 92-106.
6. W. E. Bright, "How One Company Manages Its Human Resources," *Harvard Business Review* (January-February 1976): 81-93.
7. B. Rosen and M. F. Mericle, "Influence of Strong Versus Weak Fair Employment Policies and Applicant's Sex on Selection Decisions and Salary Recommendations in a Management Simulation," *Journal of Applied Psychology* (August 1979): 435-39.

8. B. Schneider, *Staffing Organizations* (Santa Monica, Calif.: Goodyear, 1976), p. 99.

9. P. J. Decker and E. T. Cornelius, "A Note on Recruiting Sources and Job Survival Rates," *Journal of Applied Psychology* (August 1979): 463-64.

10. Schneider, *Staffing Organizations*, pp. 99-100.

11. J. P. Wanous, "Tell It Like It Is at Realistic Job Previews," *Personnel* (July-August 1975).

12. R. B. Finkle, "Managerial Assessment Centers," in *Handbook of Industrial and Organizational Psychology*, ed. M. D. Dunnette (Chicago: Rand McNally, 1976), pp. 861-88.

13. C. L. Jaffe and F. D. Frank, *Interviews Conducted At Assessment Centers* (Dubuque, Iowa: Kendall/Hunt, 1976), p. 93.

14. J. M. Bender, "What Is Typical of Assessment Centers?" *Personnel* (July-August 1973): 51.

15. W. C. Byham, "Assessment Centers for Spotting Future Managers," *Harvard Business Review* (July-August 1970): 158.

16. See P. R. Sackett and G. F. Dreher, "Constructs and Assessment Center Dimensions: Some Troubling Empirical Findings," *Journal of Applied Psychology* (August 1982): 401-10; and P. R. Sackett and M. A. Wilson, "Factors Affecting the Consensus Judgment Process in Managerial Assessment Centers," *Journal of Applied Psychology* (February 1982): 10-17.

17. L. W. Porter, E. E. Lawler, III, and J. R. Hackman, *Behavior in Organizations* (New York: McGraw-Hill, 1975), pp. 173-76.

18. D. C. Feldman, "A Practical Program for Employee Socialization," *Organizational Dynamics* (Autumn 1976): 64-80.

19. J. Van Maamen, "People Processing: Strategies of Organizational Socialization," *Organizational Dynamics* (Summer 1978): 19-36.

20. P. F. Drucker, *Management: Tasks, Responsibilities, and Practices* (New York: Harper & Row, 1974), p. 425.

21. M. L. Moore and P. Dutton, "Training Needs Analysis: Review and Critique," *Academy of Management Review* (July 1978): 532-45.

22. H. Levinson, "Executive Development: What You Need to Know," *Training and Development Journal* (September 1981): 84-95.

23. See A. I. Kraut, "Behavior Modeling Symposium," *Personnel Psychology* (1976): 325-69; and "Imitating Models: A New Management Tool," *Business Week* (May 8, 1978): 119.

24. L. Digman, "How Well Managed Organizations Develop Their Executives," *Organizational Dynamics* (Autumn 1978): 71.

25. A. L. Malabre, Jr., "Women at Work: As Their Ranks Swell, Women Holding Jobs Reshape U.S. Society," *Wall Street Journal* (August 28, 1978): 1.

26. M. B. Boyle, "Equal Opportunity for Women Is Smart Business," *Harvard Business Review* (May-June 1973): 85-95.

27. Ibid., p. 87.

28. K. Anundsen, "Keys to Developing Managerial Women," *Management Review* (February 1979): 55-58.

29. H. V. Perlmutter and D. A. Heenan, "How Multinational Should Your Top Managers Be?" *Harvard Business Review* (November-December 1974): 121-32.

30. "American Standard's Executive Melting Pot," *Business Week* (July 2, 1979): 92-93.

31. U. E. Weichmann and L. G. Pringle, "Problems that Plague Multinational Marketers," *Harvard Business Review* (July-August 1979): 120.

32. S. Grover, "Employees Start Looking Again at Jobs Abroad," *The Wall Street Journal* (October 28, 1982): 1.

33. *Business Week*, "The Speed-Up in Automation" (August 3, 1981): 62.

34. L. Edison, "Slaves to Industry," *Across the Board* (July-August 1981): 24-28.

35. J. S. Lublin, "Unions and Firms Focus on Hand Disorders That Can Be Caused by Repetitive Tasks," *The Wall Street Journal* (January 18, 1983): 1.

Human Resource Management

Delta Airlines and Hewlett-Packard

Delta Airlines of Atlanta is one of the very few airline firms to go through deregulation with few problems and a good record of strong financial performance. Delta's last strike was in 1942, and the last attempt by a union to organize employees was in 1955—it failed. As a union executive stated, Delta has ". . . a relationship with their employees that is most difficult to break into."

Delta is a people company—it advertises and lives by "the Delta Family Feeling" philosophy. This includes promoting from within, paying better than most airlines, hiring people carefully, going to great lengths to avoid laying workers off, and generally caring for their workers. For example, flight attendants are culled from thousands of applications, interviewed twice, and then sent to a company psychologist to determine their sense of cooperativeness and sense of teamwork. Also, during recessionary times, it is likely that one can find pilots selling tickets and mechanics cleaning the inside of aircraft.

Success in the management of human resources includes a number of activities. For example, there is a true "open door" policy for all employees. Ex-president William Beebe explains, "My rug has to be cleaned once a month. Mechanics, pilots, flight attendants—they all come in to see me. If they really want to tell us something—we'll give them the time . . . The chairman, president, vice-president—none of us has a single administrative assistant to screen people out." Of course, what makes this policy work is that something happens when the open door is used.

Success also involves Delta's policy of interchangeability of management parts. The chairman insists, for example, that all senior vice presidents be trained to step into any job in the company (excluding, of course, piloting an aircraft). All managers are supposed to know one another's areas well enough to step in when the need arises. At Christmastime, it is a tradition for top management to pitch in and help baggage handlers.

At Hewlett-Packard, the concern for human resources started early. In the 1940s, Bill Hewlett and Dave Packard decided not to be "a hire and fire company." Given the fact that during this time the electronics industry was almost totally supported by the government, such a position was courageous. Even during economic down times, the policy is followed. Rather than lay people off during the 1970 recession, everyone, including Hewlett and Packard took a 20 percent cut in pay and work hours. As a result, HP survived the recession without having to resort to layoffs.

HP's strong orientation toward the effective utilization of its human resources is reflected in the firm's corporate objectives. The very first sentence reads, "The achievements of an organization are the result of the combined efforts of each individual. . . ." A few sentences later, HP reinforces its commitment to innovative people—a cornerstone in the organization's success. "First, there should be highly capable, innovative people throughout the organization. . . . Second, the organization should have objectives and leadership which generate enthusiasm at all levels. People in important management positions should not only be enthusiastic themselves, they should be selected for their ability to engender enthusiasm among their associates."

A case in point is HP's "open lab stock" policy. The lab stock area is where the electrical and mechanical equipment components are kept. The policy means that not only do the engineers have free access to this equipment, but they are encouraged to take it home for their personal use. The idea is that whether or not what the engineers are doing is directly related to the project they are working on, by fooling around with the equipment at home or at work, they will learn how it works—thus, reinforcing the company's commitment to innovation. Legend has it that Bill Hewlett visited a plant over a weekend and found the lab stock area locked. He went to the maintenance department, grabbed a bolt cutter, and proceeded to cut the padlock off the lab stock door. Monday morning, workers found the following note on the door: "Don't ever lock this door again. Thanks, Bill."

Adapted from T. J. Peters and R. H. Waterman, Jr., *In Search of Excellence* (New York: Harper & Row, 1982), pp. 242-46, and pp. 253-55.

Questions for Discussion

1. In less than ten words, describe Delta Airlines' human resources policy. Also describe Hewlett-Packard's. How are they similar and different?
2. Would these policies work in most organizations? Why or why not?
3. If a new top management team would take over either company and attempt to radically change the policies, what do you think would happen?
4. Would you want to work for either Delta Airlines or Hewlett-Packard? Why?

11

Communication

Chapter Outline

Key Points

1. Communication is the most time-consuming of all the managerial activities. Managers communicate to influence others, to express feelings, for information exchange, and to control.
2. Interpersonal communication generally involves the interaction between two people; it can be either one-way or two-way in nature.
3. Three main types of communication are found in organizations—verbal, written, and nonverbal.
4. A manager's interpersonal communication style concerns the degree of emphasis he or she gives to the dimensions of exposure (giving information) and feedback (receiving information).
5. Perceptual errors, language, filtering, and information overload are among the many barriers to effective interpersonal communication.
6. Organizational communication occurs within networks that vary according to speed, accuracy, centrality, and member satisfaction.
7. Organizational communication flows both vertically and laterally.
8. In the international realm, important differences exist among verbal, written, and nonverbal communication.
9. Communication relates closely to the manager's informational roles of monitor, disseminator, and spokesperson.

Communication

Learning How to Talk to the Public

In today's complex and dynamic environment, an organization's success in the public's eye depends heavily on its ability to respond quickly and effectively to public concerns and opinion. Unfortunately, managers are not good communicators, particularly when it involves communicating to elements external to the organization. Robert J. Wood, a communication consultant, relates the following incident to illustrate this point:

The chief executive of a major company called me last winter and said, "I've spent 32 years of my life working to get this job, and now my staff wants me to learn show biz!" He had been invited to appear on the program of a well-known tv reporter, and his colleagues felt their boss needed professional advice before tangling on national television with a man famous for putting his guests on the spot. To decline to appear on the program, in view of certain delicate developments within his company that had recently been made public, would have been unwise.

The executive was reluctant and resentful of this supposed criticism of his managerial skills. But reluctance vanished when we played back the videotape of the simulated interview with which we started his session. Our staff members spent a week studying his company, familiarizing themselves with public statements of every officer, and poring over congressional records in which the company had been involved. One of the group took the role of the host and threw the book at our guest, firing one difficult question after another. When the videotape was played back there was a long moment of silence. Then he said, "Let's get to work. I need help."

It began with each member analyzing his performance. First time around they criticized it for content. He had contradicted a previously published statement of one of his senior officers. He had hedged on two other questions. It would have been better to say, "I don't know that answer, but I'll be glad to send it to you." In answering another question he had taken almost three minutes to get to the heart of the matter. Start with your major point. Say, "Our company believes in doing such and such because . . . ." Then tell them why.

Next they criticized his style. He looked more at the camera than at the interviewer. He fingered the knot of his tie too often. He didn't use the interviewer's name in answering the questions. He should have said, "I'm glad you asked that question, Pete. It gives me a chance to tell you about . . . ."

I don't remember how many simulated interviews took place during the two-day cram session, but the progress was visible, vertical, and exciting to watch. He began to criticize himself: The tv screen is a great teacher.

This manager spent two days that he later described as among "the hardest working days of my life." But on the day of the interview, he acquitted himself well. He had the facts at his fingertips, made his points clearly, quickly, and concisely. He was confident and looked at ease.

Adapted from R. J. Wood, "Communication: Top Executive Priority," *Management Review* (May 1979): 49-51.

11 One of the most important activities in organizations is communication. Yet, it also can be the domain of confusion and ambiguity. Consider the following statements:[1]

■ Dagwood, you're being impacted by job discontinuance, and you're getting assigned to the mobility pool for decruitment. (Meaning: you're fired!)

■ Jayne, an impromptu meeting of department heads will be held at 4 o'clock—it's nothing to worry about if you can't come. (Meaning: better attend because management may be reorganizing your unit.)

■ We're a people-oriented company. (Meaning: salaries are low, but we give out turkeys at Christmas.)

These examples, along with *The Practice of Management* introductory section, reveal the many uses and abuses of communication in organizations.

In this last chapter of part III—the organizing function—the focus will be on the various mechanisms people use to communicate within the organization's structure. After a discussion of the importance of communication to the organization, we will highlight two major types of communication: interpersonal, dealing with information exchange between two or more people, and organizational, concerning the network of information exchange between people and groups of people inside and outside the organization. This will be followed by an analysis of communication in the international realm, particularly the difficulties of communicating across different cultures. In chapter 17, we will reintroduce the subject of communication with the discussion of management information systems (MIS).

The Purposes of Communication

In one way or another, managers spend the vast majority of their time communicating, whether presenting a long-range strategic plan or directing a subordinate to do a particular task. If communication is hampered, the entire organization suffers; when it is accurate, thorough, and timely, the organization can move effectively toward achieving its goals.

There are at least four major purposes served by communication that make it central to management.[2] The first major purpose is to *influence* the performance of organizational members—to motivate, direct, instruct, and evaluate. Second, communication networks are made up of people, and much of what people communicate has emotional content. Communication, formal and informal, is the primary way people express and clarify their *feelings*. Third, communication is a vital activity that serves as an *information input* or *exchange* to many of the managerial functions. As we have already seen, information is important in setting goals, planning, and decision making. Finally, communication and organizational structure are closely related. Organization charts, for example, represent *formal channels* of communication in organizations.

 # Interpersonal Communication

Over the years, many studies have examined how managers spend their time (see chapter 1). Concerning communication, these studies have generally found that managers: (1) spend between 50 and 80 percent of their time at work communicating with other individuals; and (2) not only prefer face-to-face communications, but spend most of their time in this type of communication.[3]

This form of communication is referred to as *interpersonal* communication because it concerns the one-on-one exchange of information between two organizational members. In our discussion of interpersonal communications, four topics are of importance: (1) the process of interpersonal communication; (2) types of communication; (3) interpersonal communication styles; and (4) barriers to effective communication.

Interpersonal Communication Process

In its most basic form, interpersonal communication involves a sender, a message, and a receiver.[4] However, as the model shown in exhibit 11-1 illustrates, we need to be more specific about these terms.

First, the *sender* is the source, or initiator of the communication. In initiating interpersonal communication, there are two important factors about the sender that must be considered—sender intent and sender expression. Concerning *intent,* the sender is a person with ideas, intentions, information, and a purpose for communicating. In other words, the sender has something with a meaning to communicate to another person. Consider again the socialization example in the last chapter, where the sales representative incorrectly contacted the plant manager of the facility that produced the defective goods. The sales rep's supervisor, the sales manager, wishes to communicate (intention) to the rep that such behavior is not acceptable and that future instances like this should come through the sales manager (meaning).

The *expression* of the intent by the sender, sometimes termed *encoding,* involves translating the sender's intent or ideas into a systematic set of symbols or gestures. The symbols, gestures, or words chosen must enable the receiver to understand what is being communicated.

Second, the sender's intent and expression are communicated by means of a message sent through a channel. The *message* is the physical form into which the sender encodes or expresses the information, and it may take the form of speech, written words, or gestures. In the example of the sales rep, the sales manager may choose to use a verbal message, such as a simple conversation on a face-to-face basis. Physical gestures are also frequently used. For example, most children learn at an early age the meaning of "yes" and "no" from a parent nodding or shaking his or her head. A baseball umpire raising one hand may indicate a strike or that the runner is out trying to steal; in football a referee raising both hands indicates a touchdown.

The *channel* is the carrier of the message and is many times inseparable from the message. In organizations, the channel or medium of information exchange can mean

Exhibit 11-1
An Interpersonal Communication Model

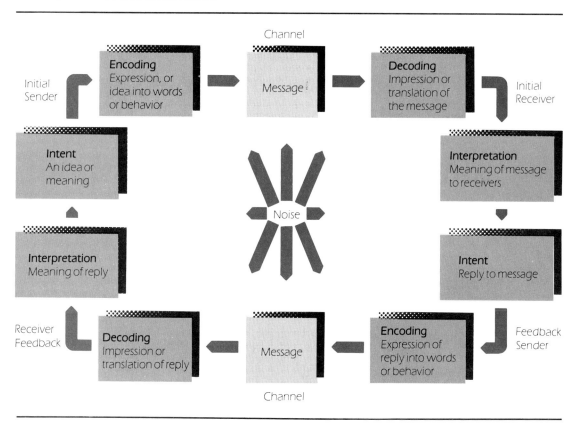

face-to-face communication, telephone calls, meetings, written memos, computer outputs, or other written reports.

Third, the receiver of the sender's message must sense and interpret the meaning of the communication. This involves two factors. First, there is the translation or *impression* of the message, or what is heard or sensed by the receiver. Second, the *interpretation* or *decoding* factor is the process of translating the message into meaning for the receiver. Receivers interpret the message in light of their own past experiences and their personal frames of reference. The important aspect is that for effective communication, the meaning of the message sent by the sender must be interpreted in the same manner by the receiver.

For example, the sales manager in our illustration could tell the sales rep—and mean it—that direct contact with manufacturing personnel is not acceptable. The sales rep, on the other hand, could interpret the message in one of at least three ways: (1) don't repeat that behavior; (2) you can repeat that behavior only in serious situ-

Lamar Muse founded his firm, Muse Air, in 1981 to serve the lucrative air travel market between Houston and Dallas. Mr. Muse knew that his new firm would have to challenge already established and successful Southwest Airlines for a piece of the action. Having worked for Southwest for a number of years, Muse was no stranger to the ins and outs of this competitive business.

Besides offering larger aircraft than Southwest, complimentary cocktails, and a total non-smoking cabin, Muse sought to give the firm a distinct image. He accomplished this with the use of a large logo placed on each aircraft. Painted in script black on an all-white airplane, the logo was not easily missed by the public.

Being distinctive was one thing, but if the logo contained a hidden message, Muse wanted to know about it. So he hired a handwriting expert to do an analysis of the logo. The results:

- The backstroke of the letter *M* indicates that this person examines past experiences and goes a short distance into the past and then sweeps forward with strength.

- The large *A* is an indication of pride.

- The dot over the *i* close to the stem is a sign of good memory and close attention to detail.

- The overall writing style indicates a tendency against doing things impulsively.

Needless to say, Muse thought this was appropriate communication to the traveling public.

Adapted from *The Wall Street Journal*, "Expert Signs Off on Muse Air Logo" (August 4, 1981): 29.

ations; or (3) you have been told the rules, now go about your business and contact the plant manager when you feel it is necessary.

Communication Noise and Feedback As exhibit 11-1 also shows, two other aspects are important to the interpersonal communication process. First, in the framework of interpersonal communication, *noise* is any factor that disturbs or distorts the message. The sender may write a confusing memo, the sender may speak too softly or indirectly to the receiver, the receiver may not be paying attention, or there are other sounds or sensations in the environment. One example is the manager who attempts to conduct a conversation while simultaneously taking telephone calls.

Second, there is the *feedback* from the receiver to the sender, this time with the roles reversed. Because the receiver now becomes the sender, feedback goes through the same steps as the original communication with the same encoding and decoding problems. Feedback can take the form of verbal expression, a simple nod of the head, or questions directed at clarifying the original communication.

In organizations, three types of feedback are usually found—informational, corrective, and reinforcing.[5] *Informational* feedback is not evaluative; that is, it does not stress whether something is right or wrong. It is merely information one person gives another that may be of value to the work of the first. Examples include giving a credit manager information on the account of a specific customer, a staff specialist giving sales revenue and market share information to a sales manager, or laboratory results concerning a patient sent by a lab technologist to a physician.

The second type of feedback is called *corrective* feedback. This type of feedback is evaluative and instructional, because it deals with the need of the receiver to correct something in the sender's message. Examples include an engineer correcting an assumption about a project design specification, or an accounting manager resolving a problem with an accounting report that contains an improper procedure.

John Wooden, who led his UCLA basketball teams to ten national championships in twelve years, was the master of corrective feedback. Observations of his behavior in practice sessions showed that 75 percent of his contacts with players were instructional.[6] He used instructions simultaneously to point out a mistake *and* indicate the correct way of performing. An interesting part of Wooden's behavior that may be of value to managers is that corrective feedback is always centered on the task, not on the personality of the player as an individual.

The third type of feedback is termed *reinforcing* feedback. That is, when a particular message has been sent clearly and/or correctly, the receiver makes a positive acknowledgment. For example, a personnel manager may say to a staff member, "well done," with respect to a recently submitted comprehensive human resource audit for the organization. We will discuss the reinforcement approach in more detail in the next chapter on motivation.

One-Way and Two-Way Communication   The existence or absence of feedback gives rise to the concepts of one-way and two-way communication. In *one-way* communication, such as statements of organizational rules and policies, the sender communicates without expecting or asking for feedback from the receiver. *Two-way* communication occurs when the receiver is permitted to or actually does provide information in return. A manager giving a project to a subordinate and receiving clarifying questions in return is an example.

Over the years, a number of research studies have investigated the various features of one-way and two-way communication.[7] In general, the results have shown:

- One-way communication takes less time than does two-way.
- Two-way communication is more accurate, since both parties may refine their messages.
- While receivers feel more secure about their interpretation of communication in the two-way manner, senders sometimes feel threatened when the receiver questions the sender's lack of clarity or mistakes.

▪ One-way communication, although less accurate, appears to be more orderly than two-way communication in certain situations.

What implications are there for managers from this research? The answer deals with the criteria of time and accuracy. If communications must be made fast, and accuracy is not a problem or is easy to achieve, then one-way communication is preferred. Consider a divisional manager presenting changes in the organization's compensation plan to a large group of employees in an auditorium. Because of time considerations, executives cannot speak to each employee individually; therefore, a large meeting is appropriate. It also is much more organized, which is important in getting the point across.

When the accuracy of the communication is important, then two-way communication is required. Such cases as evaluating an employee's performance and assigning a complex task are examples. The feedback from the receiver provides the sender with a better understanding of how the receiver interpreted the message.

Types of Communication

As shown in exhibit 11-2, a number of methods are available to the manager for sending messages in an organization. These are verbal, written, and nonverbal types. The choice of the particular communication type depends on a number of factors, which are discussed below.

Verbal Communication   By far the most prevalent form of communication in organizations is simply a verbal exchange of information. Usually taking the

Exhibit 11-2
Types of Communication

Type	Description
Verbal	
Personal	Face to face or telephone conversation
Group	Face to face in a meeting
Impersonal	Public address system, closed circuit or video-tape television
Written	
Personal	Letters, memos, reports
Organizational (impersonal)	Newsletters, posters, announcements, policies, rules, computer outputs, and other organizational publications
Nonverbal	
Body language	Hand signals, body and eye movements, facial expressions, pitch and tone of voice
Physical or symbolic	Signs, horns, sirens, "beeping" paging devices, office size, desk, carpet, number of secretaries, number of windows, badges, clothing, and so on.

form of face-to-face conversations or telephone calls, verbal communication can be both accurate and timely. On the other hand, unless one of the participants tapes the conversation, there is no record of the exchange, which leaves open questions of clarity and the chance that certain aspects of the communication may be forgotten.

In recognition of the importance of verbal communication, two major innovations have been coming to the forefront. First, the use of telecommunication equipment, such as picturephones and videotape, has grown immensely. One of the most intriguing forms of interpersonal communication is known as *télématique* or *compunications*.[8] This is the merging of telephone, computers, and television into a single system that allows for transmission of data *and* interaction between persons through cables, microwaves, or satellites. Thus, the total communication message can be packaged and organized into a much faster and accurate channel.

Second, increased attention is being given to the physical layouts of the workplace, particularly office design. Managers are coming to realize that verbal communication among organizational members is facilitated when the ability to interact with other members is improved. For example, consider the designs of two hypothetical offices shown in exhibit 11-3: the first represents the ''typical'' office design with floor-to-ceiling walls and solid doors; the second is the newer ''open plan'' design using partitions and no doors. We see that the two offices are similar when it comes to physical density (i.e., the straight line distance between members), but quite different in social density (i.e., the walking distance needed for members to interact physically). Recent studies have shown that the open plan design improves communication and performance between organizational members when there is a need for frequent verbal (face-to-face) communication.[9]

Written Communication   Written communication within organizations can take many forms, including memos, reports, procedures manuals, and other organizational publications. They are preferred by managers who wish a record of their interactions, or for such items as technical reports, which would be impossible to communicate verbally. Written communication also forces the sender to use clear and concise thinking to present the message.

On the negative side, since written communication (such as memos) is essentially one-way, there is no opportunity for the receiver to question or comment on the message, at least not initially. A second problem, one we alluded to in our discussion of bureaucracy, is that overreliance on written communication may create a state of ''red tape'' confusion. Having a record of everything may put a severe burden even on the most effective organization. Finally, having a record of an interaction may backfire on the participants. One such case discussed in the last chapter is the letter of reference.

Organizations differ in their emphasis on written communications. Some managers prefer verbal communications and shy away from a written memo as if it were a plague (see National Can case at the end of this chapter); other managers prefer to put everything in writing. For example, a part of Procter & Gamble's management development program is the emphasis given to written reports:

Exhibit 11-3
Physical Density
and Social Density
in Offices

1. Offices can be similar in physical space and worker locations . . .

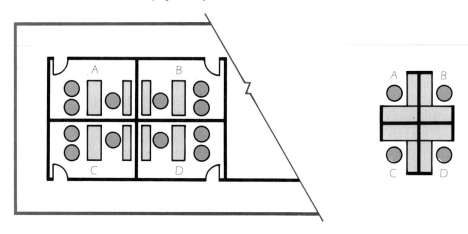

2. But different in social density relationships.

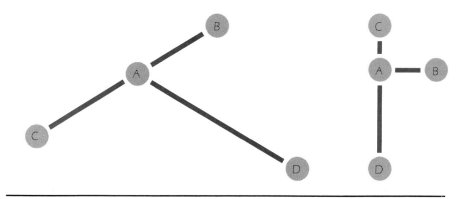

Source: A.D. Szilagyi, W.E. Holland, and C. Oliver, "Keys to Success with Open Plan Offices," *Management Review* (August 1979): 26-41.

The manager . . . first has to learn how to write the P&G memo, a one-page report considered essential to analytical thinking. The idea, of course, is that if a manager can put his thoughts down on paper in a concise and orderly fashion, they are, in fact, rational and orderly thoughts. Conversely, if his recommendations or analysis contain illogical elements, they are immediately apparent. Memos by the typical trainee . . . are scrutinized with the same kind of care that a writer's story is blue-penciled by an editor.

Why all the fuss? At P&G, memos are not only central to the communication system, they are a basic decision-making tool. P&G's conservative management approach rests on written analyses that must go through a series of endorsements up the line. . . . As one top company executive says, "We don't go in for any of this 'Let's get together and rap' nonsense. A brief written presentation that winnows out fact from opinion is the basis for decision-making around here."[10]

To be most effective, most managers use a combination of verbal and written communication to exchange information. After a conversation, one may hear the phrase, "Fine—why don't you confirm our agreement in a memo." In this way, the positive features of one-way and two-way communication can be obtained.

Possibly the most significant advance in written communication has been the introduction of *xerography,* or photocopying equipment. Because of this technological advance, various forms of written communication (memos, reports, and other documents) can be distributed more widely, hopefully to communicate a better understanding and knowledge. Another advance having an impact on management is the *facsimile* system. With this system, written documents can be sent electronically by telephone lines or satellites much faster than by postal systems.

Nonverbal Communication   When we transmit a message without the use of the spoken or written word, we are using nonverbal communication.[11] Such communication can take two forms—physical and body. *Physical* or symbolic nonverbal communication involves the various symbols with which we come in contact each day. Examples include traffic lights, stop signs, no-smoking signs, and sirens. Sometimes organizations use nonverbal communication to imply status of an individual. The size of an office, its location, the thickness of the office's carpet, or a private elevator all factor into status.

The second form of nonverbal communication involves expressions by a person's *body.* Voice tones, facial expressions, eye movements, and other gestures, either consciously or unconsciously frequently give away what a manager is thinking. People can show their tension by crossing their arms or legs and clenching their fists. A person can show boredom by yawning or slouching down in a seat.

Interpersonal Communication Styles

As we have all experienced, people differ in their style of communicating with others. Consider the following example dealing with the communication styles of two U.S. presidents:

> Soon after President Eisenhower took office, I asked one company's vice president of governmental affairs to comment on the different communication styles of President Eisenhower and President Truman. She told me that President Eisenhower depended almost completely on all news going through regular channels, with each key man giving him a briefing on what was happening. As a result, he had to see very few people.
>
> President Truman, on the other hand, saw practically everyone. People came and went constantly, until it was almost like having Andrew Jackson back in the White House. To the casual observer, President Truman was the most disorganized person in the world. But through his methods, he was able to personally determine the things that were important. He really *knew* what was going on.[12]

Exhibit 11-4
The Johari Window

Feedback

	Known to self	Unknown to self
Known to Others	I Arena	II Blindspot
Unknown to Others	III Hidden	IV Unknown

(Exposure — vertical axis label on left)

Source: J. Hall, "Communication Revisited," *California Management Review* (Spring 1973): 30-48.

In the organizational world, some managers find comfort in following formal communication channels; others prefer an open-door policy. Both may be successful in their own particular situations.

In an attempt to assess a manager's interpersonal communication style, a pencil-and-paper instrument known as the "Johari Window" has received widespread use in many organizational training programs.[13] The instrument, named after the first names of the developers (Drs. Joseph Luft and Harry Ingram), attempts to measure a person's tendency to facilitate or hinder the flow of interpersonal communication.

The model, shown in exhibit 11-4, consists of two dimensions—exposure and feedback. *Exposure* involves the open and candid expression of one's feelings, knowledge, and information in a conscious attempt to communicate with others. The greater the exposure—the more one communicates—the more information others have. The second dimension, *feedback*, entails the active requests by the manager for information held by others. The more information provided, the greater the feedback, and the more the manager knows. The combination of exposure and feedback is an example of the two-way communication process. The manager sends information to others (exposure) and receives it from others (feedback).

Various combinations of exposure and feedback can create, as shown in exhibit 11-4, four different regions or cells of interpersonal communication—arena, blindspot, hidden, and unknown. The *arena* represents the amount of information known by both the manager and others. The larger the arena, the more effective the communication process between two or more persons. The second cell, the *blindspot*, concerns information that is known to others, but not known to the manager. It represents the information others are withholding from the manager, or information not perceived or heard by the manager for reasons such as excessive noise in communications channels.

The *hidden* cell, like the blindspot, can contribute to decreased communication effectiveness because it concerns the amount of information that is known by the manager but not communicated to others. In some cases, managers use it as a protective strategy, out of fear or desire for power, or because the managers feel others know that they know. Finally, the *unknown* relates to information that neither the managers or others know. In a sense, it represents unconscious or repressed feelings, hidden skills, and creative tendencies.

Because managers vary in their use of exposure and feedback, different interpersonal communication styles result. As shown in exhibit 11-5, at least four different styles can develop. *Type A* style reflects a minimal use of both exposure and feedback. A manager adopting this impersonal approach would tend to withdraw from interactions, substituting a preference for rules and procedures that limit interpersonal communication. To others, this manager would seem to be aloof, rigid, and uncommu-

Exhibit 11-5
Interpersonal
Communication
Styles

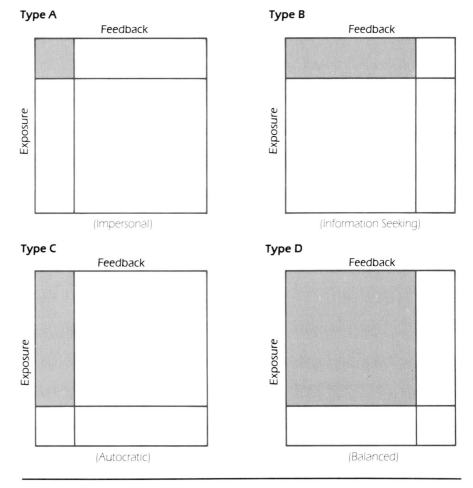

Source: J. Hall, "Communication Revisited," *California Management Review* (Spring 1973): 30-48

nicative. *Type B,* on the other hand, is a style characterized by an aversion to exposure, but a desire for feedback. The typical manager using this interpersonal style would continually seek information from others, but would provide little in return. An aversion to the use of exposure can be interpreted as a sign of basic mistrust of others, which can lead to feelings of anxiety and hostility on the part of subordinates. With time, the manager using this style would be treated as a superficial person. As a result, effectiveness may suffer.

The *type C* style reflects an overuse of exposure with a neglect of feedback. Managers adopting this style may feel very confident of the value of their own opinions and a mistrust of the opinions of others. Such managers are sometimes referred to as autocratic because they prefer to tell people what to do, but wish to hear nothing in return that might be critical of their decisions. Since the manager using this style has little use for the contributions of others, people begin to develop feelings of hostility, insecurity, and resentment toward the manager.

The final interpersonal style, *type D,* reflects a balanced use of both exposure and feedback. Openness and a sensitivity to others' needs to participate in interpersonal communication are the major features of this style. The arena is the dominant cell of the model, and effectiveness is the expected result.

If one believes that improved communication through exposure and feedback results in higher levels of performance, then the Johari Window has a value to managers. Before managers decide to adopt the model's framework, however, they must answer three major questions. First, what happens when a type D manager interacts frequently with other employees who are not the same type? Will the type D manager become the frustrated participant? Second, how are managerial interpersonal communication styles acquired and developed? One might speculate that similar to a manager's style of decision making, one's interpersonal communication style also is acquired through a complex process of culture, work experience, and personality traits over time. Finally, is a manager's style of communicating rigid, or can it change and be flexible with the situation? This leaves open the potential positive influence of training and development programs to assist managers in their communication processes.

Barriers to Effective Interpersonal Communication

In the well-known movie *Cool Hand Luke,* the chain gang boss stands over a beaten prisoner (played by Paul Newman) and shouts, ''What we have here is a failure to communicate.'' While most managers would not be expected to find themselves in such a physical predicament, it is highly likely that in many of their interactions with others, they would find themselves feeling on one side or the other!

Communication problems happen frequently in organizations and can have many complex sources. To illustrate this phenomenon, four major types of barriers to effective interpersonal communication have been chosen for discussion. These include perceptual errors, filtering, language, and information overload.

Perceptual Errors   Perception involves the process of the stimulation of a person's senses. We see, hear, touch, and taste aspects of the world around us that not only cause us to interpret what we have sensed but serve as significant learning situations.

Perception, and more specifically perceptual errors, play an important part in contributing to communication problems. Two perceptual errors are most prominent—stereotyping, and halo effect.[14] In *stereotyping,* managers seek to *simplify* their perceptual process by categorizing people into specific classes where there is a similarity of traits and characteristics. For example, a male manager may receive a memo from a woman manager describing a potential safety hazard in one of the organization's facilities. Because this manager stereotypes women as being "nonanalytical," he may disregard the memo's legitimacy. Similarly, a manager of an engineering design group may ignore a recommendation by a young engineer on improving a design procedure because the manager has stereotyped young staff members as "lacking experience."

The second perceptual error, *halo effect,* concerns the biasing of an evaluation, either to the negative or the positive, because of a single trait or incident. For example, a college recruiter for an organization may be on campus interviewing prospective employees. A particular candidate may have an excellent academic record, but may come to the interview wearing jogging shoes. This single appearance trait may cause the interviewer to rate the candidate quite low. Similarly, if a manager believes very strongly in the value of eye contact and a firm handshake, he or she may be unduly impressed by a person who might have little else to offer.

Eliminating perceptual errors from the interpersonal communication process may be a difficult proposition, because many of the errors have developed over time and may be culturally influenced. Some stereotypes, particularly those that are discriminatory, are clearly illegal, as in the case of refusing to hire a person on the basis of race. Halo effects, especially those related to the interviewing process, can be corrected through training programs. Even some stereotype errors can be changed through proper training. Others, however, may be changed only with the passage of time, or with the replacement of the individual.

Filtering Filtering happens in communications when the sender purposely modifies the message to highlight the strong or weak points. For example, a manager may report to an executive committee that the "present high turnover rate of employees in the department is only a passing situation that will correct itself with time." The manager has filtered out some important facts that point to significant internal problems that are at least contributing to the turnover problem.

The manager can correct filtering problems only by helping promote an environment in which subordinates feel free to pass on all information without fear of coercion or punishment. We will discuss this point further in chapter 12.

Language Language factors have at least a twofold impact on communication barriers in interpersonal communications. First, from the study of semantics, we know that: (1) words mean different things to different people; (2) words vary in degree of abstraction; and (3) the use of particular words reflects not only the personality of the individual but also the culture of the society. On the first point, consider a manager's statement to a subordinate that, "It's important that we have your part of the report

Frank and Ernest

finished by the fifteenth of the month. Try to get it in on time, if you can.'' To the subordinate, these two sentences do not make sense. The first stresses the importance of the completion of the report; the second takes a weaker stand. How would you react to such a communication? In communicating one must consider the clarity of the message and how the receiver will react.

Concerning the second point, look at the plight of a plumber who wants to know whether to use hydrochloric acid to clean stopped-up drains. A reply such as, ''The efficacy of hydrochloric acid is indisputable, but chlorine residue is incompatible with metallic permanence,'' certainly does not tell the plumber much. A better reply would have been, ''Don't use hydrochloric acid—it eats the heck out of the pipes.''[15] For the manager, keeping communication straightforward and simple is a worthwhile rule to follow.

Information Overload   One of the major problems all managers face is the fact that they are frequently deluged with all types of incoming communications. Phone calls, memos, written reports, computer outputs, or people just dropping in to the office create a state of information overload, the efficient handling of which can be beyond even the best manager. Many people attribute this situation at least partially to the computer, photocopying machines, and the growth of telecommunication.[16]

Many successful managers alleviate this problem by setting priorities. They divide the communications into different categories on the basis of when and what action must be taken. Another method to help reduce information overload is to delegate some of the communication to subordinates to handle. This assumes that subordinates are capable and skilled to do this. A third strategy is to insist that all communication be direct and without excessive frills. This is why most business reports emphasize the use of a beginning abstract section, a short but direct narrative section, and an extensive, but optional appendix section. Remember a key managerial credo—a manager's time is most valuable—success will come when this time is used most efficiently.

Organizational Communication

Communication between individuals is of obvious importance; the flow of data and information through the various channels and networks within an organization is of equal importance. In our discussion of organizational communication, we will focus on general communication networks, vertical and horizontal (lateral) communication, and communication from the organization to elements of the environment.

Communication Networks

An organization can develop a variety of networks to channel communication. Some networks can be very rigid. For example, a number of years ago telephone operators were prohibited from talking with anyone other than their supervisors while on duty. On the other hand, some networks can be much more loosely designed so that communications between people is encouraged. A director of an R&D lab may encourage the organization's scientists to frequently interact in the hope that the pooling of knowledge may help solve a complex research problem.

Communication networks have been the subject of many research studies. The emphasis has been on comparing the advantages and disadvantages of various networks in handling the communication process in organizations. Using five people in a two-way communication pattern, four of the most popular networks, termed the chain, wheel, circle, and all-channel are shown in exhibit 11-6.[17] To apply these to the organization, we can see the chain as the typical chain of command, from executive management to the lowest management levels; the wheel is closely aligned with the communication from a single manager to four subordinates; the circle can be viewed as the communication that flows between members of a task force; and the all-channel is similar to the informal communication network in organizations (i.e., grapevine).

As exhibit 11-6 indicates, the four networks offer managers different advantages and disadvantages. The chain is a moderately decentralized network with moderate communication speed, predictability of leadership, and a high degree of accuracy. For participants in this network, however, the satisfaction level is moderate because of its formalistic nature and the low degree of participation. For simple communication tasks, the centralized wheel network is both accurate and fast, and leadership predictability is very high, but satisfaction is low for the participants for essentially the same reason as with the chain. On the other hand, for more complex tasks, the speed of communication is reduced along with the level of accuracy. The reason is that with more complex tasks, the central person in the network may become overloaded with communication and feedback, which may have an adverse effect on accomplishing the task.

The circle is slow with a low degree of accuracy and leadership predictability. The participants, however, report high degrees of satisfaction because of their involvement in the communication process. In a task force, where the need for speed is not crucial, accuracy can be improved with constant interactions of members. The high

Exhibit 11-6
Organizational Communication in Networks

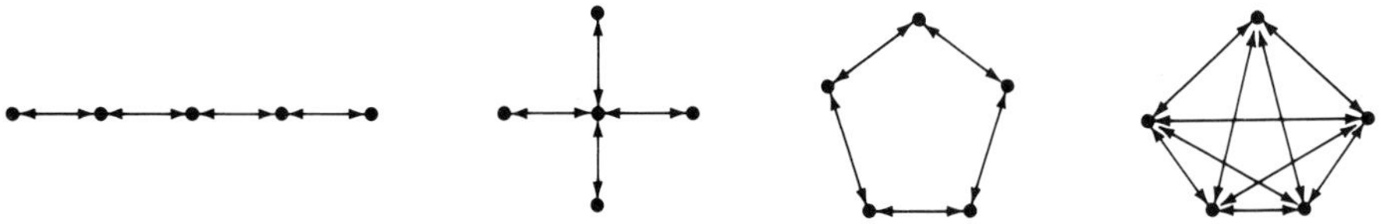

Evaluation Criteria	Type of Network			
	Chain	**Wheel or Star**	**Circle**	**All-Channel**
Centrality	Moderate	High	Low	Very low
Speed	Moderate	1. Fast (simple tasks) 2. Slow (complex tasks)	Slow	Fast
Accuracy	High	1. High (simple tasks) 2. Low (complex tasks)	Low	Moderate
Predictability of leadership	Moderate	Very high	Low	Very low
Average group satisfaction	Moderate	Low	High	Very high
Example	Chain of command	Supervisor to four subordinates	Task force	Informal communication (grapevine)

satisfaction level of participants will help keep the members' attention directed on the task at hand.

Finally, the all-channel network is very decentralized. The speed of communication is fast; accuracy is moderate, with a very low level of leadership predictability. For the same reasons as the circle, the satisfaction level of participants is very high.

What implications are there for managers from this information? Clearly, if the task being performed is simple and employee morale is not an issue, then a centralized network is preferred, particularly a wheel arrangement. If the task is complex, a decentralized network, either a chain or a circle, is recommended. If speed and accuracy in accomplishing a complex task are important, then clearly the chain is best.

Vertical Communication

Vertical communication is information that flows through the chain of command of an organization. In general, two categories of vertical communication are used—downward and upward communication.[18]

Downward Communication   This system involves the transmission of information from higher levels of management to lower levels in the organization. The goal-setting and planning processes are examples of downward communication. Another example of downward communication is the process of informing employees of changes in their benefit program. With the rapid change and complexity of today's organizations, it is important that close ties between the organization and its employees be maintained. Downward communication must be current, effective, and personal.

As shown in exhibit 11-7, the identified types of downward communication vary in terms of how effectively they communicate the message to the employee. It appears that those mechanisms that are both personal and direct (small group meetings, company publications, and supervisory meetings) are the most effective. Those mechanisms that are both indirect and impersonal (bulletin boards and posters) are the least effective.

Because most of the information that is transmitted to employees is through such impersonal and indirect means as employee manuals, there is now greater concern over whether or not the information presented this way can be understood. Many organizations are making such impersonal mechanisms, when used, more readable for the employee. To improve this form of communication, many other organizations are trying to use more of the small group meeting where the communication is direct and mechanisms for two-way communication are available.

Upward Communication   In downward communication, often the positive benefits of two-way communication are lost. Upward communication is that form of communication that originates at the lower levels in the organization and flows to the higher levels.[19] An effective upward communication system not only can help management evaluate the performance of the downward communication system, but it enables management to find out about some of the problems that the employees are facing.

Exhibit 11-7	**Downward Communications**	**Upward Communications**
Effectiveness Ranking of Downward and Upward Communication Types	1. Small group meeting 2. Direct organizational publications 3. Supervisory meetings 4. Mass meetings 5. Letters to employees' homes 6. Bulletin boards 7. Pay envelope inserts 8. Public address system 9. Posters 10. Annual reports, manuals, media advertising	1. Informal discussions 2. Meetings with supervisors 3. Attitude surveys 4. Grievance procedures 5. Counseling 6. Exit interviews 7. Union representatives 8. Formal meetings 9. Suggestion boxes 10. Employee newsletters

Adapted from "Upward and Downward Communication Channels," *Small Business Report* (October 1979): 12-14; and *Employee Communications, Bureau of National Affairs & Personnel Policies Forum Survey No. 110* (July 1975): 5-9.

In general, four major types of information are involved with upward communication: the level of performance and achievement of employees; identification of any unresolved problems and issues faced by employees; ideas and suggestions for improvement in the organization; and how employees generally feel about their jobs, fellow employees, and the organization. All this information is valuable to management because it provides a needed evaluation of how the organization is viewed by its important human resources.

Exhibit 11-7 also shows some of the many types of upward communication that exist in most organizations, along with a ranking of their relative effectiveness as evaluated by a sample of organizations. In much the same manner as downward communication, the most effective means are those that have direct and personal characteristics (informal discussions and meetings with supervisors). The least effective are those that are both indirect and impersonal.

Issues with Vertical Communication   Vertical communication is the most formal and probably the most important type of communication found in organizations. But it can present the most problems for a manager. First, because downward and upward communication must flow through different layers of management, they are highly subject to distortion, condensing, modification, or blockage. As we pointed out in our discussion of barriers to interpersonal communication, perceptual errors, filtering, language, and/or information overload can happen at any management level. The key concept to remember is that the more people there are in a network, the greater the chance that problems in vertical communication will occur.

Second, since vertical communication involves differing levels of management, one must also consider the effects of status and power. Research has shown that the more dissimilar the people are who must communicate, the less vertical communication is aided. For example, a general manager communicating to a vice president usually does so quite formally. Because of this situation, the general manager's true feelings and attitudes may be hidden.

Finally, vertical communication networks are enhanced when there is a high level of trust and respect among the participants. Without such factors, subordinates usually will not communicate information that may be interpreted as weaknesses in their ability, skills, or performance. Likewise, subordinates are likely to screen out problems and complaints when they perceive a possibility that the higher-level manager will use this information to punish them in some way.

Lateral Communication

Vertical communication systems in organizations generally follow the chain of command. As we pointed out in chapters 8 and 9, in today's increasingly large and complex organizations, communication *across* the chains of command is quite important to organizational performance. This type of communication is referred to as *lateral* communication.[20]

The need for lateral communication is primarily due to problems with the organization's structure. First, there is the issue of *time*. Frequently, information must be

Most managers recognize the value of good communication and look for ways of strengthening it within their organizations. One of the more popular methods is the executive conference. Commonly referred to as "gripe sessions," most take the form of an executive meeting with a small group of employees to listen to their comments about improving work.

Consider Patrick Foley, president of Hyatt Hotels Corporation. About twice a month, Foley ventures to one of the hotels to conduct an employee communication session. In a typical session, which usually lasts from two to three hours, Foley knows it will take about half the time for employees to warm up to talking to a high-level executive. The real substantive comments won't emerge until much later in the session. For example, at a recent session some initial concerns focused on the style of uniforms, whether or not to remove Mexican food from the Coffee Shop menu, and the like. As the meeting progressed, however, more important issues such as low morale, poor career progression, and non-cooperative workers were discussed.

Employee gripe sessions are not without some disadvantages. Supervisors, for example, don't like the idea of their employees talking directly to an executive, fearing that it will turn into a witch hunt; each session is costly in terms of lost work hours; non-participating employees wonder why they were not selected to attend a session; the credibility of these sessions decreases if the executive takes no corrective action on some of the major issues; and, often, insufficient time is given to discussing the *good* things about working for the organization.

Foley understands these problems, but as he states, "It's as good a communication tool as we've found. . . . I think it really makes them feel part of the company."

Adapted from L. Rout, "Hyatt Hotels' Gripe Sessions Help Chief Maintain Communications with Workers," *The Wall Street Journal* (November 11, 1981): 23.

transmitted across organizational functions because a decision must be made, such as a sales rep handling a customer complaint on product quality, who must get the problem to the production unit manager (see exhibit 11-8). Under normal circumstances, this information would be transmitted along the chain of command of the marketing function, across to the manufacturing function, and then down the manufacturing chain of command to the responsible manager (this is also an example of a chain network as shown in exhibit 11-6). When time is critical, as in solving a serious customer problem, this form of communication can be less than satisfactory.

The second need for lateral communication, closely aligned with the first, concerns the need for *coordination* between different units in an organization. In a hospital, for example, before the nursing staff can administer medication to a patient, the lab results must be communicated to the right people. In a university, there must be close coordination between the registrar's office and the director of facilities during the

Exhibit 11-8
Vertical and Lateral Communication Example (Customer Quality Complaint)

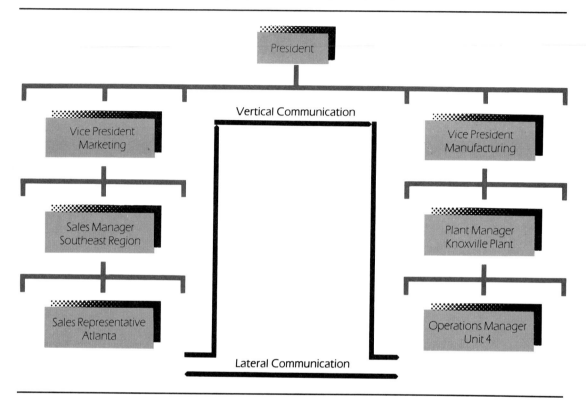

registration process, particularly in making sure that there is adequate classroom space.

Because of the need for lateral communication, many organizations have adopted a number of facilitating mechanisms. The most frequently used mechanism, especially when time is important, is *direct contact* and communication across functional boundaries. In the hospital example, lab personnel may be given the go ahead to phone in the results of tests to the physician or nursing staff. As discussed in chapter 8, another frequently used mechanism for channeling lateral communication between different units is the *liaison role*. For example, a project coordinator at NASA during the space program was responsible for making sure that there was impeccable communication between private contractors and the particular NASA unit. Finally, some organizations facilitate the flow of lateral communication between a number of units with the formation of *task forces*. Instead of fighting the problem of communicating information vertically and across many functional divisions, representatives from the involved units form a task force.

These examples are certainly not all-inclusive of the mechanisms organizations can use to facilitate lateral communication. The key point for managers to recognize, however, is that the structure of the organization, with all its formalistic components, may actually impede important communication. The need for lateral communication is not a failure of management, only the legitimate concern that most organizational structures cannot effectively adapt to the growth, complexity, and dynamism of today's organizations without looking at new ways to communicate within themselves.

External Communication

To this point in the discussion of organization communication, our focus has been on the *internal* communication process. The way the organization communicates with elements of its external environment is growing in importance as well.

A number of serious situations have compelled organizations to pay more attention to how they communicate with the public. Consider, for example, the reaction by the public to the 100 to 200 percent increases in profits by the oil companies in 1978 and 1979. Regardless of the validity or justification of these profits by the oil companies, it is hard for the general public to accept them when they personally are fighting high inflation. Or consider the significantly higher rates by auto and health insurance companies, increases in utility rates by gas, electric, and telephone companies, or rapidly increasing health care expenses.

From a communication viewpoint, organizations are beginning to adopt a number of new strategies for a link with the general public. A mechanism frequently used by organizations, the *speakers' bureau,* is a volunteer group of employees who devote a portion of their time to discussing various important issues with community organizations. For example, a plant manager of a manufacturing facility may speak to a local civic club on the topic of the plant's plans to reduce air and water pollution, hire the hard-core unemployed, or possibly expand the plant.

In addition, many organizations are reemphasizing the power of the press in communicating to the public. This usually involves more frequent *news releases* on organizational activities, interviews with managers and employees, and so on. The strategy, however, runs the risk of the copy being misquoted or misunderstood by the media representative, which may end up doing more harm than good.

More frequently, various *professional associations* of which individuals and organizations are members present an organization's views. For example, the National Association of Manufacturers, the American Medical Association, and the Off-Shore Technology Association serve as communicators to the general public.

Finally, one of the main mechanisms for transmitting information to the public is the growing number of business councils. The most prominent are the Conference Board and the Business Roundtable. The latter is a group of nearly 200 chief executives who analyze issues, take positions, and argue them at the White House, on Capitol Hill, with regulatory agencies, or state or local bodies.[21] Their strategy is relatively simple—they suggest that organizations begin presenting their responses to the issues brought up by consumer and environmental groups in a more forceful and positive manner.

As the external environment becomes more dynamic and turbulent, organizations increasingly will be faced with having to state their cases to the public on a variety of issues. Managers can no longer take an "avoidance" view, hoping that the problem will blow away with the next breeze. The issues of our times need open and straightforward information and communication if they are to be solved.

Communication in the International Realm

Communication across cultures and in different languages has presented many perplexing and sometimes embarrassing problems for organizations.[22] For example, consider the following illustrations:

- Coca-Cola's management was disturbed over the decline in sales of their soft drink in some Asian markets. The reason was that consumers were confused over the company's advertising claims—the "Coke Adds Life" theme had been translated as "Coke Brings You Back From the Dead."

- Colgate Palmolive had to change the name of their toothpaste in French-speaking countries—the name "Cue" is a pornographic word in French.

- Exxon's "Put a Tiger in Your Tank" ad was offensive to people in Thailand.

- In Germany, General Motors' "Body by Fisher" translates to "Corpse by Fisher."

- In some South American countries, the name "matador" has criminal implications. For American Motors, this presented problems because one of its car lines had this name.

- In marketing a new tire cord in Germany, Goodyear demonstrated its strength by showing how the cord could break a steel chain. The German government intervened and stopped the advertising claim—it seems that it is illegal to imply another product is inferior in Germany.

Before managers can use communication to the fullest, they must really understand international differences. Among the most important differences are consideration of language, especially in verbal and written communication, nonverbal communication, issues of etiquette, and formal versus informal communication.

Language difficulties can have a significant impact on verbal and written communications between managers and organizations. These differences surface not only in translations, but also in the actual meaning of words and phrases. For example: (1) in Spanish, the word *empleados* refers to white-collar workers and *obreros* relates to laborers—and these important class differences must be recognized by the manager; [23] (2) in Japan, the word for yes—*hai*—does not indicate agreement, only that the other person has understood what has been said; and (3) the terms *corn, maize,* and *graduate studies* in the United Kingdom translate into *wheat, corn,* and *undergraduate studies* in American English.

What can the manager do to lessen language problems? He or she can take at least three approaches. First, the manager can attempt to learn the local language. With concentrated effort, a person can acquire a casual speaking knowledge of another language within six to twelve months. A casual knowledge may not be enough given the complexities of many languages. Second, many organizations prefer to employ a good interpreter when there is a lack of well-versed or bilingual managers. Finally, English is rapidly becoming the international language of business, thus overcoming outright some of the language barriers. Among non-U.S. organizations, such firms as Siemans and Hoechst (German), Phillips (Dutch), Hoffman-LaRoche (Swiss), and Volvo (Swedish) have adopted English as their official tongue.[24]

Still, a working knowledge of the language spoken where one is operating usually helps a person adapt to the foreign country as well as gain acceptance there. However, unless fully fluent in the language of the country, managers should not attempt serious negotiations in it or expect the foreigners to do so in English. Good translators are essential in these circumstances. Perhaps more important than a manager's ability to use a language is an awareness of the importance of language in the decision-making process. The capacity and structure of a language to a significant degree determines the nature of a person's thought and emotion and hence of behavior. In other words, for a manager to understand how foreign managers think and make decisions, they must have established clear communication channels.[25]

Managers should also be aware of nonverbal communication differences. For example, color conjures up meanings to us based on experience within our own cultures. Black in most Western countries historically has been associated with death, yet in parts of the Far East and in Latin America, white and purple mean the same thing, respectively. In some countries, particularly in Latin and South America, people doing business prefer to stand quite close to each other while they are communicating. Not knowing this approach, the U.S. manager continues to back up. In the end, both parties may have developed an unexplained distrust of each other. In addition, clues concerning a person's relative position may be particularly difficult to grasp. A U.S. manager may underestimate the importance of a foreign counterpart because he or she has no large private office with a wooden desk and plush carpeting. Similarly, the foreigner may feel the same because the U. S. manager opens garage doors or mixes drinks without benefit of a servant.

Even etiquette can influence communication between managers in the international realm. For example, if a U.S. manager in the Far East fails to bring small but thoughtful gifts to the Far Eastern counterpart, that official may not only consider it rude, but may also feel that the U.S. manager places little interest or emphasis on the meeting. At the same time, if shuttled back to a lonely hotel and not invited into private homes, the U.S. manager may develop the same wrong opinion of the Far Eastern associate, not realizing that such invitations are not customary.

Taken together, many organizations have found that for the best results, communication in the international realm should be conducted on a formal basis. This means the frequent use of an interpreter and much reliance on written reports, both between headquarters and a foreign operation and between two organizations.

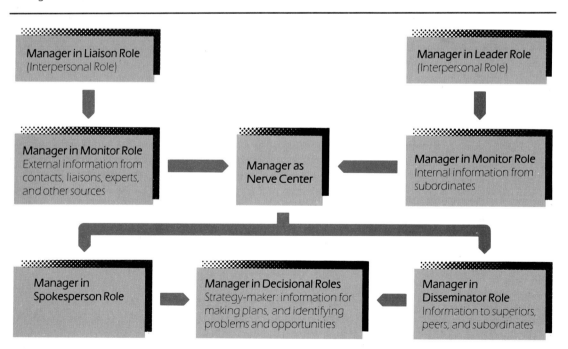

POINTS TO CONSIDER
An Emphasis on Managerial Skills

1. **Develop your own information system.**
    This includes not only being aware of all sources of information that concern one's job, but building important *liaison* contacts (see exhibit 11-9) with key people internal and external to the organization. A brief conversation with a sales respresentative or a customer may provide as much information as a year-long market-research study.

2. **Train subordinates to be equally aware of important information.**
    A manager's subordinates are an important part of the information system. Properly trained, they can make valuable contributions to the understanding of the manager's situation.

3. **Develop good listening and reading habits.**
    Important information can be lost unless the manager operates with a clear set of senses. This includes learning how to listen carefully when another person is trying to communicate. Also, since much of the communication received by a manager is in written form, good reading habits are of great value. Three types of reading are most important: (1) inspectional reading, or skimming to identify key points; (2) analytical reading, or in-depth analysis of the important

Exhibit 11-9
Managerial Roles in Communication

| Manager in Liaison Role (Interpersonal Role) | | Manager in Leader Role (Interpersonal Role) |

| Manager in Monitor Role External information from contacts, liaisons, experts, and other sources | Manager as Nerve Center | Manager in Monitor Role Internal information from subordinates |

| Manager in Spokesperson Role | Manager in Decisional Roles Strategy-maker: information for making plans, and identifying problems and opportunities | Manager in Disseminator Role Information to superiors, peers, and subordinates |

Adapted from H. Mintzberg, *The Nature of Managerial Work* (New York: Harper & Row, 1973), p. 72.

points; and (3) comparative reading, which is the process of examining a number of messages simultaneously in order to determine or detect trends, relationships, and so on.[26]

4. **Whether factual or value oriented, make sure your information is accurate.**
    When a supposedly important piece of information comes to the attention of a manager, there is a tendency to communicate it upward and/or downward before giving much thought to its validity. Before communicating any information, take time to check it out with other sources. There are few things more damaging to a manager than to be known as one who "cries wolf" too often.

5. **Choose communication methods and channels carefully.**
    Try to disseminate information when there is less interference or fewer barriers to communication. This means learning the *timing* of communication (usually when you have the receiver's attention) and the most appropriate method and channel to fit the situation.

6. **Follow up your communication.**
    This can be done by asking questions, calling to check in after first using written communication, encouraging the receiver to express reactions, or using informal contacts. The key factor is to ensure that every important communication allows enough feedback for the best possible understanding.

7. **Make sure the information communicated to the environment is accurate.**
    For much the same reasons as apply to the disseminator role, the accuracy of the information you communicate determines the respect the public has for your position.

8. **Share information with liaison sources.**
    A manager's personal information system is not a one-way system; it entails two-way communication. To make sure you keep receiving information from other sources, it is wise to keep sending them information they consider to be valuable. In this manner, the liaison network is strengthened.

9. **Become recognized as an expert source of information.**
    A manager's ability to be influential in a spokesperson role depends largely on whether or not the receivers consider the manager to be an expert. This means that the manager must demonstrate current, up-to-the-minute knowledge of the organization and its environment. Just as "crying wolf" too often will hurt one's performance in a monitor role, not having done your homework in a spokesperson role will be detrimental to your overall performance.

 SUMMARY FOR THE MANAGER

1. Of all the activities and functions that are performed by a manager, none takes up more time than communication. Communication in organizations helps managers influence others, express feelings, exchange information, and use control. The way managers communicate has a significant effect on their overall levels of performance.

2. The interpersonal communication process involves a sender, a message sent through a channel, and a receiver. The process can be one-way or two-way in nature. While one-way takes less time, it is less accurate than two-way communication. An important part of two-way communication is the feedback the sender gets. Whether informational, corrective, or reinforcing, feedback is extremely important given the growing complexity and dynamism of today's organizations.

3. Three main types of communication are found in most organizations—verbal, written, and nonverbal. It is important for managers to recognize that in trying to communicate a message, using more than one form of communication is a wise strategy. Examples include following up a conversation with a phone call or asking for comments on a memo or report during a face-to-face interaction.

4. One of the most popular ways of presenting a manager's interpersonal communication style is the Johari Window. The major dimensions of the model, exposure and feedback, relate to how the manager provides *and* receives information from others. The key point is that one should not stress one dimension over another—effectiveness is a function of the maximum use of both exposure and feedback.

5. Interpersonal communication is not without problems or barriers. Four of the main barriers are perceptual errors, language, filtering, and information overload. Overcoming these errors involves a combination of training, experience, guidance, and practice.

6. Organizational communication—that form of communication that may involve more than two people—is conducted through communication networks. The four networks that were discussed—chain, wheel, circle, and all-channel—differ in many characteristics, including centrality, speed, accuracy, and member satisfaction. For highest performance, the manager should carefully analyze the situation and choose the network that will work best. In formal superior-subordinate interactions, the chain and wheel are appropriate; for committees or task forces, the choice should be the circle or all-channel.

7. Communication in organizations flows both vertically and laterally. The most effective vertical communication methods (upward and downward) are those methods that are both direct and personal. Lateral communication needs generally develop because of the need for speed and the deficiencies in the structure of the organization. Direct contact, liaisons, and task forces are used to speed communication throughout various units.

8. Communication in the international realm presents a number of problems to the manager. Among these are the problems of language (should the manager learn the local language or use a skilled interpreter), nonverbal communication, and etiquette. Because of these concerns, formal communication is stressed heavily.

9. Communication relates directly to the manager's roles. Information is gathered from performance in the liaison role (external information) and the leader role (interpersonal role). It is processed through the monitor, disseminator, and spokesperson roles, and then put to use through the decisional roles. Effectiveness in these managerial roles involves developing one's own information system, learning how to read effectively, making sure the information is accurate, following up on communication, and being recognized as an expert in the material that is communicated.

REVIEW AND DISCUSSION QUESTIONS

1. Why are organizational structure and communication closely related?
2. What are some examples of noise in the communication process?
3. Why is filtering a significant barrier to interpersonal communication?
4. Why are vertical communication methods emphasizing a direct and personal approach rated the most effective?
5. Give an example of the three main forms of feedback. Why is feedback important to the communication process?
6. What key characteristics should a manager consider when choosing a communication network?
7. Identify some of the reasons that many managers and organizations are increasing their emphasis on external communication to the general public.
8. How can the organizational grapevine be used effectively by a manager?
9. Identify some of the reasons for the need for lateral communication.
10. Discuss the importance of the manager's monitor role in organizational communication.

NOTES

1. M. Bralove, "Taking the Boss at His Word May Turn Out to Be a Big Mistake at a Lot of Companies," *The Wall Street Journal* (June 4, 1982): 23.
2. See R. K. Allen, *Organizational Management Through Communication* (New York: Harper & Row, 1977); D. S. Ellis, *Management and Administrative Communication* (New York: Macmillan, 1979); and R. Huseman, J. Lahiff, and J. Hatfield, *Business Communication: Strategies and Skills* (Hinsdale, Ill.: Dryden Press, 1981).
3. H. Mintzberg, *The Nature of Managerial Work* (New York: Prentice-Hall, 1980).
4. See W. V. Haney, *Communication and Organizational Behavior* (Homewood, Ill.: Irwin, 1973); and J. J. Wofford, E. A. Gerlof, and R. C. Cummins, *Organizational Communication* (New York: McGraw-Hill, 1977).
5. See R. Kreitner, "People Are Systems, Too: Filling the Feedback Vacuum," *Business Horizons* (November 1977): 54-58; and D. A. Nadler, *Feedback and Organizational Development* (Reading, Mass.: Addison-Wesley, 1977).
6. R. G. Tharp and R. Gallimore, "Basketball's John Wooden: What Coach Can Teach a Teacher," *Psychology Today* (January 1976): 74-78.
7. See D. M. Herold and M. M. Greller, "Feedback: The Definition of the Constrict," *Academy of Management Journal* (March 1977): 142-47; and H. J. Leavitt and R. A. H. Mueller, "Some Effects of Feedback on Communications," *Human Relations* (November 1951): 401-10.
8. D. Bell, "Communications Technology—For Better or for Worse," *Harvard Business Review* (May-June 1979): 20-42.
9. A. D. Szilagyi and W. E. Holland, "Social Density: Relationships with Functional Interaction and Perceptions of Job Characteristics, Role Stress, and Work Satisfaction," *Journal of Applied Psychology* (February 1980): 28-33.

10. "P&G: We Grow Our Own Managers," *Dun's Review* (December 1975): 48.

11. L. R. Cohen, "Nonverbal (Mis)Communication Between Managerial Men and Women," *Business Horizons* (January-February 1983): 13-17.

12. H. O. Golightly, "The What, What Not, and How of Internal Communication," *Business Horizons* (December 1973): 49.

13. J. Hall, "Communication Revisited," *California Management Review* (Spring 1973): 30-48.

14. S. S. Zalkind and T. W. Costello, "Perception: Some Recent Research and Implications for Administration," *Administrative Science Quarterly* (September 1962): 218-35.

15. See S. Chase, *Power of Words* (New York: Harcourt Brace, 1953); and M. McCaskey, "The Hidden Messages Managers Send," *Harvard Business Review* (November-December 1979): 135-48.

16. C. A. O'Reilly, "Individuals and Information Overload in Organizations," *Academy of Management Journal* (December 1980): 684-96.

17. See H. J. Leavitt, "Some Effects of Certain Communication Patterns on Group Performance," *Journal of Abnormal and Social Psychology* (January 1951): 38-50; and M. E. Shaw, "Communication Networks," in *Advances in Experimental Social Psychology*, ed. Leonard Berkowitz (New York: Academic Press, 1964): 111-47.

18. See B. Harriman, "Up and Down the Communication Ladder," *Harvard Business Review* (September-October 1974): 143-51; and J. B. McMaster, "Getting the Word to the Top," *Management Review* (February 1979): 62-65.

19. W. H. Read, "Upward Communication in Industrial Hierarchies," *Human Relations* (February 1962): 3-15.

20. R. L. Simpson, "Vertical and Horizontal Communication in Formal Organizations," *Administrative Science Quarterly* (September 1959): 188-96.

21. W. Guzzardi Jr., "Business is Learning How to Win in Washington," *Fortune* (March 27, 1978): 52-58.

22. D. A. Ricks, M.Y.C. Fu, and J. S. Arpas, *International Business Blunders* (Columbus, Ohio: Grid, 1974).

23. J. D. Daniels, E. W. Ogram Jr., and L. H. Radebaugh, *International Business* (Reading, Mass.: Addison-Wesley, 1979), p. 78.

24. Ibid., p. 512.

25. R. D. Robinson, *International Business Management* (Hinsdale, Ill.: Dryden, 1973), p. 267.

26. M. Adler and C. Van Doren, *How to Read a Book* (New York: Simon & Schuster, 1972).

A CASE FOR ANALYSIS

Communication
National Can Corporation

Before Frank W. Considine arrived at National Can, the firm had succeeded largely on the strength of its skillful, old-fashioned salesmanship. The company was adept at patiently cultivating close relationships with customers and in providing extra help and service. National still has important customers who have remained faithful because of special efforts made on their behalf decades ago.

Even as National grew into a billion-dollar company, Considine deliberately preserved a lean and informal style of management. One of National's most valuable assets today is a small-company spirit rare among corporations of its size. Sales have doubled since 1973 (excluding the food and pet-food divisions), but with Considine keeping iron control over executive staffing, the number of salaried employees has remained virtually unchanged.

This strategy, however, leads to a lean, if not austere, corporate life. The company's four-year-old headquarters building, which stands alone out near Chicago's O'Hare Airport, is a plain tower of the sort that generally houses a swarm of small-time sales offices and one-person law firms. Most of National's vice presidents work out of spare, white-painted cubicles; senior vice presidents get offices that are not much larger, though most are at least corner rooms. There are no company planes—Considine purposely located near the airport to take advantage of what he calls "our corporate jet fleet, the largest in the world: American, United, TWA. . . ." Everybody, including Considine, flies coach unless the flight is long or a customer is going too.

Informality is crucial to National's operating style. Because of the lean managerial staff, no one ever has trouble knowing whom to call when a problem arises. The only expensive-looking things in those executive offices are multibuttoned phone consoles, backed up with a system of WATS and tie lines, through which practically any National executive can reach practically any other. Written memos play a small part in National's communication flow.

Considine's own operating style sets the tone. He is very much a hands-on manager, with a relish bordering on obsession for involving himself in operations. He has a keen eye for detail and a memory for names, faces, numbers and minutiae that endlessly amazes his executives. Considine takes the phone in hand dozens of times a week to call down the executive line. One day recently, for example, the president of Jos. Schlitz Brewing Co. asked Considine for help on a problem involving printing on cans. Considine wanted to waste no time in putting the right person to work; he called directly to a plant where he knew he could find a suitable technician.

It could be argued, of course, that a chief executive should not spend a great deal of his time on such matters. But attention to details is an essential part of Considine's management style and a reflection of his philosophy. Good managers, Considine thinks, must be highly involved with their work and with their fellow managers. For a leader, he believes that involvement consists of asking the right detailed question at the right time. The results of doing that lie not just in getting the question answered, but in setting a pattern of managerial involvement.

Considine's style of close involvement works both ways. His executives feel free to call him directly, without going through channels, if they have problems too pressing to wait for someone above them who may not be available. They are free to call anyone else, up or down the chain of command, without observing hierarchical priorities. At National, customers get their problems attended to quickly, and manufacturing lines do not sit idle awaiting the appropriate executive's decision on a production problem. The freedom of communication in all directions undoubtedly contributes to National's prowess as an efficient maker and marketer of cans.

Considine has taken original and unconventional measures to improve the flow of communications. Typical of his whole approach to management is a major structural reorganization he sponsored a number of years ago. He had hired a new head of operations, a shrewd and down-to-earth veteran of twenty-three years in plant management at Continental Can. Considine had observed that engineers and plant operations supervisors, although linked by a common corporate interest, were not good at communicating with each other. It was almost as if they spoke different languages.

With Considine's backing, managers got together to work out a program for integrating the two staffs, with the goal of achieving smoother and more efficient plant operations. It took two years to bring the project off, but since 1974, National's engineering department has reported to manufacturing. The integration works at all levels, from senior management to factory floor. Executives can visit a plant and talk about either engineering or manufacturing.

A notable aspect of Considine's character as a manager is an unusual degree of concern for the people who work under him. He believes that a corporation doesn't have to hurt people to be successful. He is perpetually interested in the well-being of his employees' families. Not many billion-dollar corporations have ever held anything quite like the open-house fiestas, complete with refreshments and circuses, that took place at two National Can plants. Considine's purpose was to make it possible for spouses and children to see firsthand the workplaces that were such an important part of employees' lives. The open-house program was a smashing success, and Considine plans more such events for the future.

Considine's hands-on, highly personal operating style has clearly served National well to date, but there are questions about how well it will continue to do so. National's officers and directors are unanimous in saying that Considine is overly involved, given the size of the company today. Moreover, there is no chief operating officer to share the burdens.

Even if National seems not to have suffered from Considine's overinvolvement, he himself has: a little over a year ago, he was hospitalized for three weeks after a mild heart attack. Since then he has taken his directors' advice to bring in help.

Pulling back is not likely to be easy for Considine. Past experience has convinced him that someone needs to be on the lookout for problems. For instance, he recently caught a major underbilling that just slipped by everyone else. Spotting even a major underbilling, however, is not part of the chief executive's job in a large corporation.

Adapted from C. G. Burck, "How Frank Considine Runs a Billion-Dollar Company," *Fortune* (July 3, 1978): 74-77.

Questions for Discussion

1. Describe and evaluate Frank Considine's communication style and its effects on the company and other employees.
2. How would you describe the company's communication networks?
3. Using exhibit 11-9, what managerial roles does Mr. Considine perform?
4. Can Mr. Considine continue to use his communication style? Can others?
5. What is the relationship between communication and organizational structure in this case?

EXPERIENTIAL EXERCISE
The Fog Index

Purpose

The purpose of this exercise is for you to become familiar with problems of bloated writing style in managerial communication.

Preparation

Each student should read and become familiar with the *Fog Index*, developed by the Gunning-Meuller Clear Writing Institute. The Fog Index works as follows:

1.   Find the average number of words per sentence in a sample of writing. Treat clearly independent clauses as separate sentences. Example: "In school we read; we learned; we improved." This counts as three sentences.

2.   Calculate the percentage of words having three or more syllables. Don't count capitalized words, compound words like *pawnbroker,* or verbs that reach three syllables by the addition of *-es* or *-ed.*

3.   Add the average sentence length to the percentage of big words and multiply by 0.40. The resulting number is the years of schooling needed to understand what you've written.

Instructions

Each student should read the following passage and compute the Fog Index:

As President, I am delighted and gratified to be able to report and animadverize on Dewey, Cheatum, and Howe's performance last year, pontificate on exteriorities, prognosticate with regard to subsequent performance potentialities, and epexegesize our conglomerations. Unfortunately, energetic disassemblies at three of our nuclear generating modalities, the dynamic negative development of constituency components extramundane to the organization, and rapid oxidation of our competitive position have effectuated a neglible fungible situation for this year. Indeed, as the end of the fiscal year approaches, restoration of our previous position is deemed impossible and it appears that we will have to finalize the termination of the corporation.

After calculating the passage's Fog Index, each student should rewrite it, aiming for an index reduction of at least 3 points.

PART FOUR

INTERVIEW

John K. Robinson

Vice President/General Manager
Catalysts and Technology
Sohio Chemical Company
Cleveland, Ohio

Q: Do you personally follow any particular theory of motivation, or do you adapt to situational conditions?

A: I have spent a lot of effort to become aware of current theories in motivation. I also try to stay up-to-date with new thinking in this field. A sound theoretical background is most important . . . *but* flexible, knowledgeable responses to individual situations are critical.

In many ways the first managerial jobs are the toughest. A bright, highly ambitious young person, early in his or her career, often is handed responsibility for a group of folks who would just as soon be fishing. Adapting to this situation and rising to this leadership challenge takes all the flexibility one can muster.

Q: In your view, what factors motivate today's young managers?

A: I think today's young managers, as a group, are less single-minded than many of the old duffers who are currently in senior management positions. These younger managers, therefore, require that the demands and rewards of their jobs be accommodated to their overall *package* of ambitions. In my own case, I observe that not only do the younger generation of managers, again as a group, exhibit broader interests

today, I believe that today's top executives were more narrowly focused when they were younger.

Which attitude is fundamentally superior is an interesting philosophical question. I am convinced that excellence in a field will continue to demand sacrifice. Those among today's young managers who concentrate their efforts will find themselves with a much better chance to climb to the top.

Q: Do you believe a manager's style of leadership is rigid or flexible?

A: It seems as though I am going to keep contrasting the way things are with the way they "oughta" be. I really think most people have one style and stick with it come hell or high water. The key word here is *most*.

This conviction has led me to accept the theory that one should *compensate* for, rather than try to *correct*, any perceived weaknesses. For example, if you inherit an organization that in general has been flying by the seat of its pants and doing quite well until recently—but now needs a more analytical approach—for heaven's sake, add an analyst to your staff. Don't try to teach the guys who have been doing well *some other way* how to be analytical.

The same feeling about the rigidity of style leads me to conclude that you should be very cautious in rewarding a manager who has just turned around your most mature, most unprofitable business by giving her the chance to head up your most attractive new business opportunity. Most likely, the different style required to do those two jobs will mean it won't work.

Now let's talk about the chosen few. In the cases I have had the opportunity to observe, it seems to me that those people, the really successful top managers who endure the test of time, are *flexible* managers. Probabilities limit you too much if you can only win one kind of game. Having said this, I run out of any detailed advice. Maintaining a flexible style of management is a tough goal.

Directing Performance: Leading

Q: How important was your formal education in making you an effective leader?

A: My formal education has been both technical (PhD in Chemistry) and managerial (MBA). Unquestionably, the MBA is an asset for me in answering the demands of my present job.

Regarding the value of a technical background in the area of business one manages, I believe it can be very helpful for the young manager; but I also believe it's a crutch one should learn to do without as soon as possible. As your responsibility in an organization increases, you simply have to decide whether you are going to be a technical expert or a manager. As a manager of the commercial activities of a very complex business, you can't try to set yourself up as a technical expert as well. Later in a career a really good technical background can retard the development of a manager by providing a too easy—and too limiting—security blanket.

The key to getting out of this rut is learning how to judge the quality of technical information as a manager; that is, without the luxury of having equal or superior technical knowledge. At some point every aspiring manager faces this issue. Frankly, if I ever learn a solid answer to this dilemma, I'll write my own text on the subject.

Q: When assuming their first managerial position, many young managers are surprised at the large amount of time that is spent in various group activities (e.g., committees, task forces, etc.). From your experience, how can the future manager prepare himself or herself for this situation?

A: In a complex organization, satisfactory implementation of any important decision requires concurrence of several different functions. Sometimes one group can reach a decision and make an *attempt* to get going in a particular direction. But the bigger the decision, the more the need for commitment and support from the organization as a whole if the undertaking is to be successful.

To recognize this is to understand the need for broad concurrence. And for this purpose, task forces, or similar groups with different names, are often used. In today's environment the ability to persuade and negotiate is most important.

From my experience, many good *younger* managers really excel in this regard when they have the chance. Maybe this is because more established managers have their own way too often and too easily within their own organizations. The opportunity to participate on such a work group or task force is a forum to display one's talents and therefore should be viewed as a real opportunity for the new manager. It's also an excellent chance to embarrass yourself in front of some important people if you don't do your homework.

Q: What important skills should future managers develop to become effective managers?

A: Learn to *listen* and *understand* the position of the other interested parties—and to *persuade* them through persistent negotiation. This is just as important in one's own organization as it is when two separate companies are dealing with one another.

A lot of the thrill of anticipating a serious leadership role comes from the idea that, all of a sudden, one will be able to introduce sweeping changes at one's whim or edict. Given the diversity of power in large organizations, the brilliance of individual insight has to be supplemented by the accommodation and persuasion of other sources of power.

And don't be misled by positions on conventional organization charts. The names of some mighty important sources of power will be found lower down on the page than your own. If you need their contribution, treat them with the appropriate regard.

Motivation

Key Points

1. The process of motivation has been examined through two major approaches: content theories (arousal factors) and process theories (arousal and direction factors).
2. Maslow's need hierarchy, a content theory, concerns motivation from the desire to satisfy needs.
3. Herzberg's two-factor theory, also a content theory, focuses on the nature of the job as the key motivator.
4. Expectancy theory is a process approach concerned with how individuals choose motivated behaviors that lead to valued rewards.
5. The second process theory, reinforcement theory, emphasizes learning motivated behaviors from the rewards received for performance.
6. Job design is an applied managerial approach to motivation that stresses the use of intrinsic rewards.
7. Behavior modification, founded on reinforcement theory, emphasizes the use of extrinsic rewards to motivate subordinates.
8. Through assigning work, identifying subordinate needs, guiding work, and evaluating and rewarding performance, the manager is a key factor in the motivation process.

Motivation: Differing Views

On the Datapoint Corporation assembly line in San Antonio, where desktop office calculators take shape, employees appear to have special individual ways of making time pass. At 9 a.m., the assembly line has been moving for only an hour, but already the day is dragging. In position five on line four, Annette Fulbright catches the next circuit board crawling down the line. At the current pace, one board passes her work station every minute and a half. Forty down, 280 to go today.

Over in quality control, Ismeal Hernandez puts his soldering gun back in his holster, fidgets with his left shirt sleeve and steals a quick glance at his watch. Thirty more minutes before a coffee break, two and a half hours to lunch, and seven hours until quitting time. Two aisles over to the right, Della Pena checks the dates on a calendar hanging near her work station. She smiles—tomorrow is payday.

Since few workers want to make a career out of working on the line, Datapoint has some turnover headaches. Management reports that workers on the line stay for an average of 18 months, meaning that a line must be adjusted occasionally to accommodate new, frequently slower workers. As a supervisor stated, "They take their money and go."

It is a rare person who finds life on an assembly line exciting or rewarding. Yet, the line does offer a certain peace of mind that comes from knowing you'll be doing the same thing tomorrow that you did today. Some people actually seek out this type of work where there is a minimum of hassle and a steady paycheck—no decisions, no tough responsibilities.

Across the country at another electronics plant, a different story unfolds. George Stewart, engineering technician, works in a plant that is clean, pleasant, and quiet enough to permit Stewart to work on a challenging job, but also

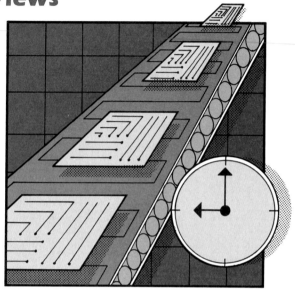

affords time to talk with other workers. Stewart, whose job is to assemble the company's complicated electrical-signal analyzer, takes a craftsman's pride in his work. He has even come up with a couple of tools and methods to make the assembly task easier and more efficient. "They like it when you come up with new ideas. When they have this policy, you think more and work harder."

Stewart is also pleased with the company's other policies, such as profit sharing, which he says makes you feel more a part of the company. Recently, the plant initiated a flexible schedule that allows employees to come to work any time between 6:30 and 8:30 a.m. and leave between 3:15 and 5:15 p.m. Stewart is usually at his work station by 6:30. "These hours give you a lot of freedom in the afternoon," he points out. When he goes home, Stewart does chores around the apartment building that he and his wife manage, or spends time with his three sons.

Adapted from R. Thurow, "Assembling Computers Means That Happiness Doesn't Come Til 4:30," *The Wall Street Journal,* (June 1, 1981).

12 With the topic of motivation, we begin a three-chapter sequence on the important managerial function of leading. We will start with an overview of the basic process of motivation, analyze the manager's activities as a leader, and examine how to understand and lead individuals in groups.

As *The Practice of Management* introductory section reveals, even workers who have similar jobs can exhibit different levels of motivation. Many factors contribute to this situation, including the person, the job, and the organization. There are no universals to motivating employees. Hopefully, this chapter will provide a basic framework for a better understanding of this important behavior.

Three major sections make up the chapter. First, the study of motivation itself and a basic model will be discussed. Second, we will briefly cover some of the main approaches to motivation in organizations. Finally, we will look at two important managerial motivation strategies—job design and behavior modification.

The Study of Motivation

Managers in all types of organizations are continually faced with the fact that vast differences exist in the performances of individual employees. Some employees always perform at high levels, need little or no direction, and appear to enjoy what they are doing. Other employees perform only at marginal levels, require constant attention and direction, and are often absent. The reasons for these differences in performance are varied and complex, involving the nature of the job, the behavior of the manager, and the characteristics of the employee. But at the core of each of these aspects is *motivation*.

Consider this statement from a recent General Electric publication:

When it comes to being highly productive on the job, to feeling a sense of success and achievement, to being a real contributor, what do you really believe about yourself and others? Does money count first—the desire to draw a bigger paycheck? Is it the competitive instinct—the urge to win over others? Is fear the principal factor or does motivation come from the promise of reward? Is it just ego—the desire for recognition, approval and status? Or is it the sheer enjoyment of being part of a busy, cooperative, professional team?

These are questions to which behavioral scientists have been addressing themselves for years. Yet, oddly enough, few of their findings and theories have been effectively applied by managers who have learned their managing skills from bosses or from managerial courses that have stressed techniques, rather than a fundamental understanding of the manager's role in the human resource area.[1]

It appears that motivation has not only a complex meaning, it is applied in a variety of ways in organizations. This chapter will look at the reasons for this variety.

Definition of Motivation

From years of research, behavioral scientists have developed slightly different viewpoints of motivation, emphasizing different components. In general, the views have led to these conclusions:

- The analysis of motivation should concentrate on factors that *arouse* or *energize* a person's activities. These include needs, motives, and drives.

- Motivation is *process* oriented and concerns behavioral choice, direction, goals, and the rewards received for performing.[2]

From these conclusions, we can build a basic model of motivation that incorporates the concepts of needs, direction, and rewards. The model, shown in exhibit 12-1, presents motivation as a multistep process. First, the arousal of a *need* creates a state of tension (or disequilibrium) within the individual that he or she will try to reduce through behavior. Second, the individual will *search for and choose* particular behaviors or strategies to satisfy these needs. Third, *goal-directed behavior,* or actual performance occurs. An important individual characteristic, *ability,* intervenes between the choice of behavior and actual behavior. This is because individuals may not have the necessary background (skills, experience, or knowledge) to satisfy a need. Fourth, an *evaluation* of the individual's performance is conducted by the individual or by others. The individual usually evaluates his or her own performance directed at satisfying a need such as developing a sense of pride in one's work. On the other hand, another person, such as a supervisor, generally evaluates performance directed toward satisfying a financial need, for example. Fifth, *rewards or punishment* is given, depending on the level of performance. Finally, the individual *assesses* the degree to which the chosen behavior has satisfied the original need. If this motivation cycle has satisfied the need, a state of equilibrium or *satisfaction* exists. If the need remains unsatisfied, the motivation cycle is repeated, with the possibility that the individual will make a different choice of behavior.

Consider, for example, a civil engineer newly assigned to the design and construction of a large bridge. Because the engineer has been with the company for a number

Exhibit 12-1
A Basic
Motivation Model

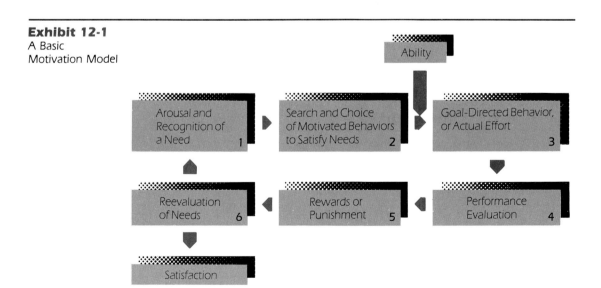

of years, he or she recognizes a desire or need to be promoted to the position of project engineer (arousal of a need). A number of ways to satisfy this need are available, including continued excellent performance, obtaining an advanced degree, asking for the promotion outright, or moving to another company (search for behaviors). The engineer decides, after a discussion with higher-level management, to excel on this project as the strategy to satisfy the need (choice of behavior). Recognizing he or she has the necessary ability to excel in performance, the engineer works hard toward the successful completion of the project (ability and goal-directed behavior). After the project has been completed, the engineer's performance is evaluated by higher management (performance evaluation), resulting in a promotion to project manager (reward). Because the original need for promotion has been satisfied, our engineer is in a state of equilibrium (satisfaction) with respect to this particular need. Other needs may arise, such as a need for recognition, that will start the motivation cycle all over again.

Approaches to Motivation

Managerial approaches to motivation have existed for many decades. In previous chapters, the work of Taylor in scientific management and McGregor's theory X and theory Y represent contrasting views of how to motivate employees. These early approaches, however, lacked the specificity and concrete suggestions today's managers require. Now we need more comprehensive approaches.

We will present four contemporary approaches to motivation. These approaches will be classified into two broad categories that correspond to our definition of motivation. Two approaches—Maslow's need hierarchy and Herzberg's two-factor theory—are classified as *content* approaches, since they concern those factors that energize or arouse motivated behavior. The approaches that deal with the direction of motivated behavior—Vroom's expectancy theory and Skinner's reinforcement theory—are *process* approaches.

Content Theories

Content theories of motivation focus on the question of what arouses, energizes, or starts behavior. First we have to assume that needs drive people to behave in a particular manner. A need is considered to be an internal quality of the person. Hunger (the need for food), a steady job (the need for security), or career advancement (the need for promotion) are seen as needs that arouse people to choose specific acts or patterns of behavior. Two of the most popular content theories are Abraham H. Maslow's need hierarchy theory and Frederick Herzberg's two-factor theory.

Maslow's Need Hierarchy Theory

Maslow's need hierarchy suggests that people in organizations are motivated to perform by a desire to satisfy a set of internal needs (Step 1 in exhibit 12-1). Maslow's framework has three basic assumptions.[3]

■ People are beings who want and whose wants (needs) influence their behavior. Only *unsatisfied* needs can influence behavior; satisfied needs are not motivators.

■ A person's needs are arranged in an order of importance (hierarchy), from the most basic (food and shelter) to the complex (ego and achievement).

■ A person advances to the next level of the hierarchy (or from basic toward complex needs) only when the lower need is at least *minimally* satisfied. That is, the individual will be concerned with satisfying a need for safe working conditions before being motivated by a need for achievement from the accomplishment of a task.

From these assumptions, Maslow proposed five classifications of needs that represent the order of importance to the individual. These needs are (1) physiological; (2) safety and security; (3) social; (4) ego, status, and esteem; and (5) self-actualization. Exhibit 12-2 is a general representation of the need hierarchy.

Physiological needs—food, shelter, and relief from and avoidance of pain—are the primary or basic level needs of people. In the workplace, such needs concern base salary and working conditions.

When the primary, or physiological, needs have been minimally satisfied, the next higher level of needs, *safety and security needs*, assume importance as motivators.

Exhibit 12-2
Maslow's Need Hierarchy

General Factors	Need Levels		Organizational Specific Factors
1. Growth 2. Achievement 3. Advancement	Self-actualization	Complex ↑	1. Challenging job 2. Creativity 3. Advancement in organization 4. Achievement in work
1. Recognition 2. Status 3. Self-esteem 4. Self-respect	Ego, Status, and Esteem	Ascending Order ↑	1. Job title 2. Merit pay increase 3. Peer/supervisory recognition 4. Work itself 5. Responsibility
1. Companionship 2. Affection 3. Friendship	Social		1. Quality of supervision 2. Compatible work group 3. Professional friendships
1. Safety 2. Security 3. Competence 4. Stability	Safety and Security		1. Safe working conditions 2. Fringe benefits 3. General salary increases 4. Job security
1. Air 2. Food 3. Shelter 4. Sex	Physiological	Basic	1. Heat and air conditioning 2. Base salary 3. Cafeteria 4. Working conditions

These are needs such as freedom from threat, protection against danger and accidents, and security of the job. In organizations, individuals view these needs in terms of safe working conditions, salary increases to meet inflation, job security, and an acceptable level of fringe benefits to provide for health, protection, and retirement.

Social needs become dominant when safety and security needs have been minimally satisfied. These needs concern such aspects as friendship, affiliation, and satisfying interactions with other people. In the workplace, these needs relate to the desire to interact frequently with other workers, good supervision, and peer acceptance.

The next level in the hierarchy, *ego, status, and esteem needs,* focuses on the need for self-respect from others for one's accomplishments, and a need to develop a feeling of self-confidence and prestige. Successful completion of a particular project, recognition by others of the person's skills, and the acquisition of organizational titles (e.g., manager, senior analyst, and director of nursing) are examples of these needs.

The highest need level in Maslow's framework, *self-actualization,* concerns the need to maximize the use of one's skills, abilities, and potential. People with dominant self-actualization needs could be characterized as individuals who seek work assignments that challenge their skills, permit them to learn and to use creative or innovative talents, and provide for advancement and personal growth.

To illustrate Maslow's approach, consider a newly graduated accounting student from a well-respected university in Indiana who takes a job as staff accountant for a large accounting firm in California (see exhibit 12-3). The initial interview trip plus the follow-up visit to locate housing remove his concerns about base salary and housing (physiological needs in exhibit 12-3a). Because the new accountant is married and has a small child, he seeks out information about medical coverage, job stability, the tuition reimbursement program, and so on (safety and security needs in exhibit 12-3b). The information he collects, coupled with a long discussion with his supervisor about job security, satisfies his concerns over these factors. The frequent interactions the accountant has with his supervisor, fellow workers, and clients prove to be most satisfying (social needs in exhibit 12-3c).

As time passes, the accountant concentrates more and more effort toward doing his job as effectively as he can. Within three years, he receives a promotion to the position of senior staff accountant (ego, status, and esteem needs in exhibit 12-3d). Subsequent years find the accountant in the newly created position of director of administrative services, the external consulting arm of the accounting firm. His outside activities include participating in civic, school board, and charitable affairs, plus a revitalized interest in building furniture in his garage workshop (self-actualization needs in exhibit 12-3e).

This example illustrates Maslow's basic concepts. That is, needs are: (1) motivational; (2) ordered in an importance, or basic-to-complex hierarchy; and (3) ascending the hierarchy, based on the satisfaction of lower-level needs.

The Need Hierarchy in International Operations   Since managers are becoming increasingly involved in international operations, it is important to know what motivates workers in other countries. While our understanding of this is just emerging, what we know to date suggests that important differences exist.[4] For example, the

Exhibit 12-3
Maslow's Need Hierarchy: Career of an Accounting Graduate

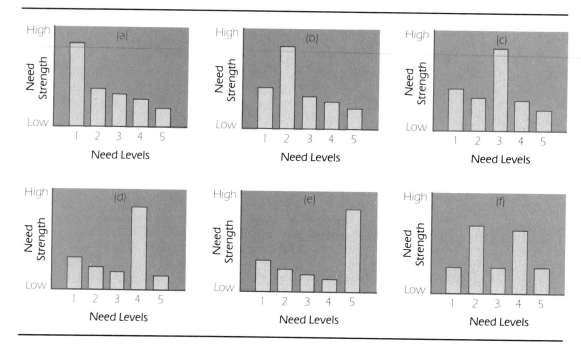

analysis of needs for technical personnel in ten countries indicates that some employees are motivated by higher-order needs (e.g., in U.S. and United Kingdom), others
are motivated by a combination of higher- and lower-order needs (e.g., Japan), while
still others have dominant, highly motivational lower-order needs (e.g., Chile).

Issues and Implications of the Need Hierarchy Theory   Since its development,
the need hierarchy has stimulated a great number of research studies of organizations.
Among the most interesting findings is the recognition that ego and self-actualization
needs become more important as one climbs the management career ladder from
first-line supervisor to higher-level executive.[5]

Even with these and other supportive findings, managers must be aware of the
serious limitations of this theory. First, there is some question as to whether five need
levels for individuals are found in all organizations. Some research has shown that the
number of need levels can range from two to as many as seven.[6]

Second, managers must acknowledge that needs are not static, but are quite dynamic—in other words, one can go down the hierarchy as fast as up. For example,
managers in troubled organizations such as Lockheed or Penn Central can go from
being motivated by ego needs to security needs quite quickly after the announcement
of impending manpower cutbacks.

Third, as shown in exhibit 12-3f, more than one need level can be operative at any
one time, which is counter to the theory. Such a need profile was representative of

your author shortly after graduating with a bachelor's degree in engineering. The high ego needs represent a desire to do well and the seeking of recognition for high performance. However, the equally high safety and security needs relate to the fact that your author had a young and growing family, plus his job involved production engineering in a chemical plant that manufactured highly toxic products. Such a need profile is inconsistent with the theory, but in fact, is found frequently.

Finally, the theory states that a satisfied need is not a motivator. Although in a general sense this may be true, it is also true that individual needs are never fully or permanently satisfied as a result of a single act or behavior. Human needs must be continually fulfilled if the person is to perform effectively. If a number of needs are operating at one time—as is probably the case with most people—this would seem to contradict the idea of need satisfaction occurring in a fixed hierarchical order.[7]

Herzberg's Two-Factor Theory

A second popular content theory of motivation was proposed by Herzberg. The theory, called the two-factor theory or the motivator-hygiene theory, has been widely applied by managers.[8] Herzberg accepted Maslow's concept of the importance of needs, but went further by suggesting that not all needs are motivational. Herzberg's research led to the following conclusions:

First, there are *extrinsic* job conditions whose *absence* or inadequacy causes dissatisfaction among employees. However, if these conditions *are* adequate, it does not necessarily mean the employees are motivated. These extrinsic-contextual factors are

---

The Manager's Job

Motivation in a Business With a "For Sale" Sign

Mergers, acquisitions, and divestitures have become commonplace in many industries today. When it is known that a business or unit is up for sale, managing and motivating in such a situation can be an onerous task. Many employees quickly find new jobs rather than live with the uncertainties of another owner's plans. Those employees who stay spend as much time worrying as they do trying to do their jobs. Even such routine cost-savings moves, as eliminating jobs through attrition, are often viewed as the beginning of the end of all jobs. Clearly, employee motives have changed. For example:

▪ In 1980, RCA sold its Banquet Foods division to Con Agra Inc.. Prior to the sale, managers and salespersons spent more time counteracting rumors that the firm was going out of business than they did developing new customers, according to one former employee. "The company stood still. We didn't lose market share, but we certainly didn't gain any. . . . All we did was spend time putting out fires."

▪ Similarly, eight divisions of GAF Corporation were scheduled for sale. As one division executive admits, he spends at least one third of his time on matters related to the sale. "It's the time I used to spend on planning the business' future." As time passed with no serious buyers, other problems emerged— morale dropped and more and more people left the firm.

Adapted from "Running a Business with a 'For Sale' Sign," *Business Week* (March 23, 1981): 104.

the dissatisfiers, or *hygiene* factors. They include: job security; salary; working conditions; status; company policies; quality of technical supervision; quality of interpersonal relations among peers, supervisors, and subordinates; and fringe benefits.

Second, *intrinsic* job factors exist whose *presence* helps to build levels of motivation that can result in good job performance. However, if these conditions are *not* present, it does not cause dissatisfaction. These conditions are intrinsic-content factors of the job and are called motivators, or *satisfiers*. These include: achievement; recognition; challenging work; responsibility; advancement; and personal growth, learning, and development.

As shown in exhibit 12-4, Herzberg has reduced Maslow's five need levels to two distinct levels. The hygiene factors, or dissatisfiers, are similar to Maslow's lower-level needs (physiological, security, and social). They are essentially *preventative* factors that reduce dissatisfaction. In other words, hygiene factors, if absent in the job, lead to high levels of dissatisfaction; if present, they create "zero dissatisfaction" or neutrality. By themselves, hygiene factors do not motivate individuals to better performance.

The motivators, or satisfiers, correspond to Maslow's higher-level needs. These are the factors that motivate people to perform. According to Herzberg, the presence in a job of factors such as job challenge is motivational; when they are absent, the level of satisfaction is reduced to the zero point. Absence of these factors is, however, not dissatisfying.

Exhibit 12-4
Herzberg's
Motivator-
Hygiene Theory

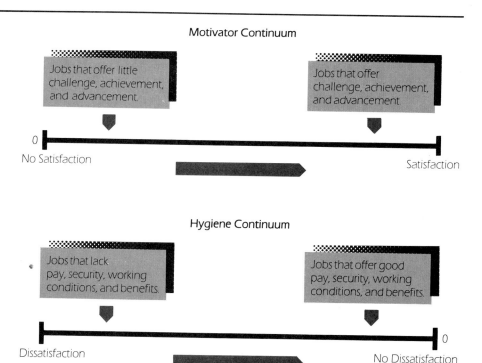

Issues and Implications of the Two-Factor Theory   The implications of Herzberg's theory are significant. For example, consider assembly-line workers in the auto industry. For many years, these firms have experienced severe worker motivational problems, lower productivity, high turnover, absenteeism, grievances, and so on. In response, the industry—usually with the blessing of the unions—has instituted costly fringe-benefit programs, significant wage increases, and elaborate security and seniority programs. Yet, many of these problems remain.

According to Herzberg's framework, the problems remain because these firms try to motivate through hygiene factors, which he claims are nonmotivational. To remedy the situation, according to Herzberg, management should direct its attention to the motivators—for example, changing jobs to remove the routineness, boredom, and lack of challenge.

Managers in many organizations have accepted the two-factor theory.[9] But it has also been criticized by behavioral scientists on a number of points, including research methodology (short, written essays) and the research sample (engineers and accountants in Pittsburgh).

More importantly, the theory stresses the importance of *satisfaction,* rather than motivation. As shown in exhibit 12-1, satisfaction is more an *outcome* of actual motivated behavior. Finally, the two-factor theory fails to account for differences in individuals. Herzberg basically assumes that all employees will react similarly to motivational factors. Just looking closely at the people around us, however, can reveal that some will indeed be motivated by a challenging job, achievement, and advancement, while others will be highly motivated by money, security, and status symbols. In other words, trying to motivate employees through the content of the job is bound to result in only partial success.

Although the list of major criticisms is significant, the value of the theory should not be underestimated. As in the case of the need hierarchy approach, Herzberg's theory has common-sense appeal to some managers. The serious management student, however, should be cautious of approaches that have a subjective appeal and which scientific study has seriously questioned.

Process Theories

The content theories, while identifying the key factors that arouse or energize motivated behavior, provide little understanding of why people *choose* a particular behavior to satisfy specific needs. Choice is the focus of two *process* theories—expectancy theory and reinforcement theory.

Expectancy Theory

In its basic form, expectancy theory concerns choosing behavior that can lead to desired rewards. Specifically, the theory states that individuals evaluate various strategies of behavior (e.g., working hard every day versus working hard three days out of five) and then choose that behavior they believe leads to those work-related outcomes or rewards that they value (e.g., pay increase, promotion, or recognition). If a worker believes that working hard every day will lead to a desired pay increase, expectancy theory predicts that this is the motivated behavior he or she will choose.

Building on the work of other behavioral scientists, Victor H. Vroom presented expectancy theory in its most complete formulation.[10] As shown in exhibit 12-5, the theory involves three main variables—expectancy, instrumentality, and valence—that are derived from the relationship between effort, performance, and outcomes or rewards.

Expectancy is the perceived relationship between effort and performance. Similar to a probability, expectancy can range from 0 to +1.0. For example, if a financial analyst is given a project that he or she knows can be completed on time, the value for that expectancy would approach certainty, or +1.0. On the other hand, if completing the project on time (i.e., performance) would be difficult or near impossible, the value for this expectancy would approach zero.

Instrumentality is the perceived relationship between performance and outcomes or rewards and can vary in value from −1.0 to +1.0. For example, if high performance in an organization is always rewarded, then instrumentality would have a value approaching +1.0; if high performance usually yields no rewards, the value for instrumentality would be zero; finally, in the unlikely state that performing at a high level would result in a reprimand, instrumentality would have a negative value.

Exhibit 12-5

Expectancy
Theory of
Motivation

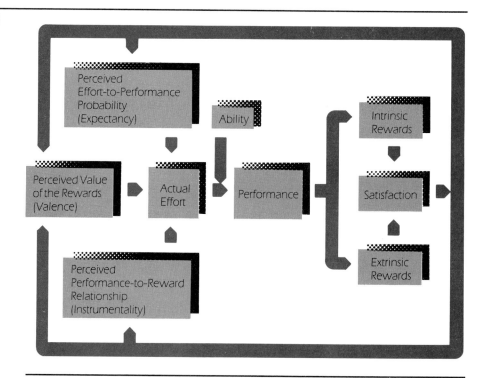

Valence is the strength of an employee's preference for a particular outcome or reward, which can be either intrinsic or extrinsic. Valence can either be given a positive or negative value by the person. In a work situation, we would expect outcomes or rewards such as pay increases, promotion, and recognition by superiors to have positive valences; outcomes such as reprimands, job pressures, stress, and interpersonal conflicts may have negative valences. Theoretically, an outcome or reward has a valence because it is related to the *needs* of the individual; therefore, this variable provides a link to the content theories.

Consider, for example, a laboratory technician who must analyze the results of an experiment for a research chemist. The technician has a dilemma: on Friday afternoon, only an hour before normal quitting time, she has yet to complete the analysis. The technician knows that it will probably take at least two hours to finish.

At least two options are available to the technician. First, she could work to complete the analysis (i.e., performance). It would take a concentrated effort, possibly involving some extra time, but she knows that it can be done (i.e., expectancy). The technician also knows that her effort would not go unnoticed by the supervising chemist (i.e., instrumentality), since some form of valued praise or recognition would be given for the extra effort (i.e., valence). On the other hand, the technician could stop what she is doing at quitting time (i.e., performance). This behavior, which is easy (i.e., expectancy), would also not go unnoticed (i.e., instrumentality); however, this time the result would be an undesired reprimand (i.e., valence). The choice of behavior by the technician would probably be to work hard to complete the analysis, since this form of motivated behavior would lead to a valued reward (i.e., recognition).

The expectancy model in exhibit 12-5 identifies three additional factors.[11] First, as in the original motivation model (see exhibit 12-1), the relationship between actual effort and actual performance is moderated by the employee's ability. Unless the employee has necessary ability, no amount of effort will yield acceptable performance. Second, rewards for performance can be either or both intrinsic and extrinsic. In the case of the laboratory technician, an extrinsic reward could be recognition from the supervising chemist, while an intrinsic reward could be the feeling of accomplishment and pride of successfully completing an important task. Finally, the level of rewards leads to a state of satisfaction with work, which also acts as feedback into the main expectancy theory variables.

Issues and Implications of Expectancy Theory Expectancy theory, which stresses that people are motivated to choose behaviors that result in valued rewards, has a number of implications for practicing managers. Among the most important points are:

Clearly define good performance levels. Before subordinates can be motivated to high performance, they need to know what is defined as good performance. Managers must identify what they want, when they want it, how it is to be done, and what rewards are available.

Make sure the employee can reach good performance levels. Unless the organization has provided adequate training and resources and the individual exhibits the necessary skills and abilities, motivation levels may be low.

Determine what rewards are valued by the employee. If motivated behavior is directed toward obtaining rewards, the manager needs to know what rewards are valued by the employee. It is important to recognize that when it comes to rewards, people are different. Some employees value praise and recognition highly, while others see their motivated behavior as leading to a good pay increase or advancement.

Expectancy theory is not without significant criticisms.[12] The major issue is complexity; not only is it too difficult to fully research, but do people actually consider expectancies, instrumentalities, and valences every time they are motivated? Overall, however, the theory is a valuable addition to the study of employee motivation, if for no other reason than that it emphasizes that motivation involves *both* arousal and behavioral choice.

Reinforcement Theory

The second process theory of motivation, reinforcement theory, emphasizes the application of rewards by the manager. Sometimes referred to as operant conditioning, reinforcement theory has its foundations in the work of B. F. Skinner.[13] Stated simply, reinforcement theory suggests that behavior (or motivation) is a function of its consequences (or rewards). In other words, if people are rewarded for performing at a high level, they should again perform at a high or higher level because they know they will be rewarded.

The reinforcement process is illustrated in exhibit 12-6. This process introduces formally a factor in motivation that is extremely important for all managers to consider. That is, much of a person's motivated behavior is *learned* behavior. Through experience, managers learn to be good managers or poor managers; in a similar manner, subordinates learn over time what is considered acceptable performance and what is not. This is the concept of learning.

The crucial element in this reinforcement process is the consequences or rewards for performance, because it is through the administration of rewards that the person learns acceptable or motivated behavior. Consider again the laboratory technician in the expectancy theory discussion. By choosing to work hard to complete the analysis (motivated behavior), the technician receives a valued reward. If a similar situation arose in the future, the technician would probably repeat that behavior because the reward would still be valued and desired. From a reinforcement point of view, the

Exhibit 12-6
The Reinforcement
Process

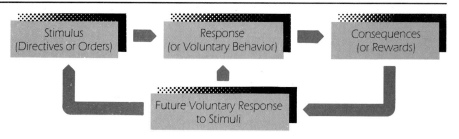

technician's improvement in performance would be a learned behavior that was the result of the proper use of the consequences of performance, or rewards.

Four fundamental principles are the foundation for reinforcement theory in motivation. These principles concern focus, types of reinforcement, schedules of reinforcement, and the nature of the reward.

Focus   The focus of reinforcement theory is *objective, measurable* behavior (e.g., number of units produced, percentage of quality rejects, or adherence to budget and time schedules), as opposed to inner-person states (e.g., needs), which are difficult to measure. This is one of the main distinguishing characteristics of reinforcement theory in comparison to the need hierarchy, two-factor, and expectancy theories. The latter approaches directly or indirectly involve the concept of human needs, while reinforcement theory does not, emphasizing instead those behavioral components that can be easily observed and measured.

Types of Reinforcement   In reinforcement theory, four major types of reinforcement can be used to motivate or modify a person's behavior in an organization— positive reinforcement, punishment, avoidance, and extinction (see exhibit 12-7).

Exhibit 12-7
Types of Reinforcement

Reinforcement Type	Stimulus	Response	Consequence or Reward
Positive Application increases the likelihood that a desired behavior will be repeated.	Promotion will result from continued excellent performance ⟶	Continued excellent performance ⟶	Promotion
Punishment Application decreases the likelihood that an undesired behavior will be repeated.	Tardiness will not be tolerated ⟶	Tardiness ⟶	Reprimand
Avoidance Likelihood of desired behavior is increased by knowledge of consequence.	Reprimands will result from tardy behavior ⟶	Punctuality ⟶	No reprimand
Extinction Removal of positive reinforcement to eliminate a now undesired behavior.	1) Prizes awarded for attracting new savings account customers ⟶	High effort directed toward attracting new customers ⟶	Prizes
	2) Prizes for attracting new savings account customers halted. ⟶	Reduction of effort to attract new customers ⟶	No prizes

Positive reinforcement is used to *increase* the likelihood that a behavior desired by the organization will be repeated by the employee. *Punishment* is the use of negative consequences to *decrease* the likelihood that an undesired behavior by the individual will be repeated. Managers use *avoidance,* like positive reinforcement, to strengthen the recurrence of a desired behavior. The employee avoids punishment by performing in the correct manner. The distinction between positive reinforcement and avoidance should be kept clear. With positive reinforcement, the employee performs to *gain* certain rewards; with avoidance, the employee performs in a manner to *avoid* undesired consequences. *Extinction* is used like punishment to reduce or eliminate undesired behavior. In its simplest form, extinction involves the withholding of positive reinforcement for a previously acceptable behavior. With continued nonreinforcement, the behavior will disappear.

The objective of each of the four reinforcement types is to modify the individual's motivated behavior to lead to goal achievement. Reinforcement will either increase the strength of desired behavior or decrease the strength of undesired behavior, depending on the goals of the organization.

Schedules of Reinforcement   The degree of effectiveness of any reinforcement type is a function of time; the closer the reinforcement to the behavior, the greater the impact. Two broad classifications of reinforcement schedules have been identified and studied—continuous and intermittent. *Continuous* reinforcement is when each behavior is reinforced every time it is exhibited. Workers who assemble pocket calculators know that their behavior is correct when each unit passes a quality control check. A reprimand given after each tardiness is another example.

When a manager recognizes that it would be impossible to reinforce each and every behavior, an *intermittent* schedule can be followed. With intermittent reinforcement, two distinctions are made. First, reinforcers can be given after a certain amount of time (an *interval* schedule) or after a certain number of acceptable behaviors (a *ratio* schedule). Second, reinforcers can be given in an unchanging format (a *fixed* schedule) or a constantly changing format (a *variable* schedule). As shown in exhibit 12-8, combination of these generates four reinforcement schedules: fixed interval (weekly paycheck), fixed ratio (sales commission), variable interval (promotion), and variable ratio (recognition).

A number of research studies have shown that the variable ratio schedule of reinforcement is the most powerful in sustaining motivated behavior in employees.[14] The reason is that reinforcement is tied to the behavior of the individual and is timed closer to that particular behavior. This finding has significant implications for managers. Typically, organizations depend highly on such rewards as money and advancement to motivate employees; yet, the schedules associated with these rewards are not as effective as other schedules (see exhibit 12-8).

Nature of the Reward   The nature of the reward, in terms of size and value to the person, can have a great effect on subsequent behavior. Again managers must remember that individuals differ in their preferences for particular rewards. One subordinate may respond effectively to frequent praise and recognition. On the other hand, a subordinate desiring a promotion may not respond well to "pats on the back."

Exhibit 12-8
Intermittent Reinforcement Theory

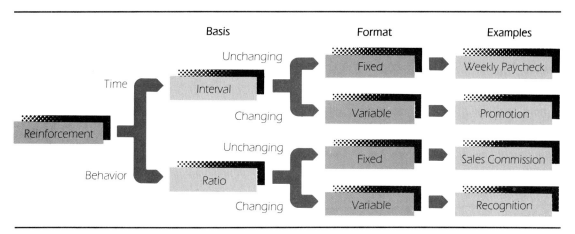

Issues and Implications of Reinforcement Theory   Reinforcement theory has a number of implications for managers.[15] The manager should:

Tell subordinates what they can do to get reinforcement. By setting performance goals or standards, the manager lets employees know what performance will lead to rewards. In this way, people can plan their work and behaviors.

Administer rewards as close to the occurrence of the behavior as possible. To ensure continued high motivated behavior, the appropriate reward must not only be clearly associated with the level of performance, but it must be given within a short time after performance.

Understand that failure to reward or punish can be reinforcing. Managers can influence motivation not only by what they do, but by what they don't do. Failing to recognize a deserving employee may cause the person to perform less effectively the next time. And, failing to punish poor performance may cause that performance to recur.[16]

Use punishment wisely. Two points are key. First, use punishment as soon as possible after the poor performance for quick correction. Second, don't punish in public. A public reprimand often humiliates the subordinate in front of his or her peers, causing embarrassment or possibly increased resentment toward the manager. The effect on others (an avoidance reinforcement) of a private reprimand will still be present. Either the person will tell others, or the "grapevine" will pass on the information. Most people know what is going on when a person is called into the supervisor's office, without actually being there to see and hear.

Although reinforcement theory has many positive implications for managers, some nagging problems persist. First, critics point out that the theory may oversimplify behavior. In particular, it does not take into account important individual characteristics such as needs. Second, others claim that it is not really reinforcement that occurs, but manipulation and control. This, critics say, has tones of inhumanity. Third, with its heavy emphasis on extrinsic rewards, the theory may ignore the fact that some employees can be motivated by the job itself.

Finally, there is the issue of what rewards are available to the manager to administer. While an organization's reward system may contain pay, advancement, praise, and recognition, not all these rewards are available to every manager. For example, promotions may not be within the domain of the immediate supervisor. Often recognition can only go so far.

Managerial Approaches to Motivation

In the first sections of this chapter, we focused on theoretical presentations of the content and process theories. In this section, we show how some managers have applied these theories to motivate employees. We will look at two specific approaches—job design and behavior modification.

Job Design—Domestic and International Approaches

It has only been within the last few decades that the job as a motivational influence has gained the attention of management practitioners and scholars. Previously, most job design programs were guided by the principles of scientific management. As discussed in chapter 2, adopting a scientific management perspective meant that jobs were designed to be as efficient as possible (i.e., narrowly defined, routine, with short work cycles), and monetary incentives were used to motivate workers.

This managerial attitude began to change in the 1950s as more and more workers began to voice displeasure with jobs that were boring and routine. As this feeling among workers grew more intense, organizations began to see increases in turnover, absenteeism, grievances, work slowdowns, and so on. This forced management to reevaluate its thinking about what motivates workers and, in particular, what role the job plays in this process.

Early Approaches   Two of the earliest managerial approaches, or reactions to this worker dissatisfaction, were job rotation and job enlargement.[17] *Job rotation,* very simply, involved moving workers between a series of jobs within a particular unit. For example, a worker on an auto assembly line assigned to the interior of the car would work one week installing seats, followed by two weeks assembling dashboard components, and so on. Unfortunately, this approach did not solve worker motivational problems, since it became clear that all that was done was subject the worker to a series of boring tasks, not just one. (But, as we saw in chapter 10, job rotation has also assumed a role as an effective training method.)

Job enlargement was the first approach that involved a change in the job. The enlargement entailed giving the worker more to do by increasing the work cycle (i.e., providing more job variety).

Applications of job enlargement have met with more success in organizations than have applications of job rotation. Many organizations, including IBM, Ford, and Maytag, adopted job enlargement programs to help solve worker problems. For example, at Maytag the job of assembling the washing machine pump was a focal point of one study.[18] Prior to enlargement, the task involved six operators assembling the pump on an assembly line. After enlargement, the work previously done on the assembly line, or conveyor belt, was done at four one-person benches.

Some job enlargement programs have shown improvements in worker morale, production costs, and product quality. A number of problems have also arisen. Some workers did not have the necessary skills and abilities to handle an enlarged job; because workers were asked to do more, they wanted more pay; and finally, since fewer workers were required to accomplish the tasks, layoffs resulted, creating tension between workers and management. Adjusting wage levels and keeping the size of the work force steady not only took away some of the strong features of the approach, but it became clear that job enlargement was not the only way to motivate workers through changes in the job. This led managers to consider the approach known as job enrichment.

Job Enrichment   Job enrichment as a managerial tool was founded on Herzberg's two-factor theory of motivation.[19] As noted earlier, the theory stresses the concepts, or motivators, of challenge, achievement, autonomy, and responsibility. Applying job enrichment to organizations involves two important factors—giving employees more variety in their work, and giving them more authority and responsibility. In other words, job enlargement is part of a job enrichment strategy.

To illustrate this job-related approach to motivation, consider a technologist in a hospital pathology laboratory. Prior to enrichment, this person's job involved analyzing blood samples according to standard procedures and reporting the results on the patient's record.

How could the technologist's job be enriched? The following changes, involving Herzberg's motivators, could be considered:

- *Responsibility.* Increase the level of responsibility by making the individual responsible not only for daily productivity, but also for quality control over his work and the scheduled maintenance on the blood analysis equipment.

- *Decision making.* Increase the technologist's authority and autonomy through setting productivity standards per shift, controlling the pace of the work, and removing some supervisory controls.

- *Feedback.* Provide direct feedback to the technologist by making productivity data available to him. In some cases, permit him to collect and maintain such data.

- *Personal growth and development.* The technologist may offer suggestions about improvements that can be made to the analysis system. In addition, the manager could structure training programs or career paths beyond the present job that are dependent on the level of performance.

- *Achievement.* By increasing such aspects as responsibility, autonomy, and feedback, the technologist can develop a sense of accomplishing something worthwhile.

Since its introduction, job enrichment has found its way into a variety of organizations, such as utilities (AT&T), insurance (Traveler's), investments (Merrill Lynch), financial (Chemical Bank), airlines (American Airlines), and manufacturing (Texas Instruments, Polaroid, and Bosch).[20] Applications can be found in all parts of the globe.

At Texas Instruments, a group of employees who had been assembling radar equipment according to specifications drawn up by the engineering department was asked to develop its own methods, manufacturing processes, and production goals.[21] After job enrichment, not only had the total time for assembling a unit been reduced from 136 hours to 36 hours, it was determined that the number of supervisors could be reduced, since the workers exercised a high degree of self-control.

At Bosch, a large German electronics manufacturer, two units reported successes with job enrichment.[22] The automobile radio assembly unit of sixty employees was redesigned so each worker does the entire assembly job, resulting in greater flexibility, elimination of rigid time frames, and improved worker morale. In the autospeaker unit, the employees were broken down into five three-person groups, with each group building the entire unit. Each worker was required over time to learn all the individual tasks, providing an excellent training and learning opportunity.

Whether job enrichment is consistently successful is unresolved.[23] Some applications have been successful; others, however, have resulted in high implementation costs, and resistance from workers—particularly older people—has caused the program to be terminated. This points out the need for the development of diagnostic skills before the enrichment program begins, and the need for conceptual skills in evaluating how well the program is being implemented.

Job Redesign—Need Satisfaction and Job Characteristics   The successes and problems managers have experienced with job rotation, enlargement, and enrichment identify at least two important points that must be considered in any job design program. First, not all people will react favorably to a job that has been changed. Many workers at all organizational levels are quite happy and satisfied working on routine and repetitive jobs. This may be because certain workers seek out routine jobs because they want only the satisfaction of lower-level needs (e.g., pay, employee benefits, job security) from their jobs. They may seek fulfillment of higher-order needs outside of work. Others simply are not happy with a great deal of responsibility. An attempt to "enrich" jobs for these workers would probably be met with resistance and possible failure.

Second, a closer analysis and diagnosis of particular jobs is needed. A job should be looked at from the basis of strengths and weaknesses for employee motivation. In other words, a job may not need to be enriched with increased responsibility, decision making, feedback, and so on, if some of these components are already at acceptable levels. Changing all of these components at the same time (the shotgun approach), when only one or two need enriching, is both unnecessary and costly. What is needed are better ways of analyzing jobs in order to identify what can and should be changed.

An approach that incorporates both of these points was developed by J. Richard Hackman and his associates.[24] Shown in exhibit 12-9, this approach to job redesign emphasizes four specific points. These are translated into managerial questions:

What are the desired outcomes of work? The identified outcomes—motivation, performance, satisfaction, turnover, and absenteeism—focus on aspects that relate

Exhibit 12-9
A Job Redesign
Model

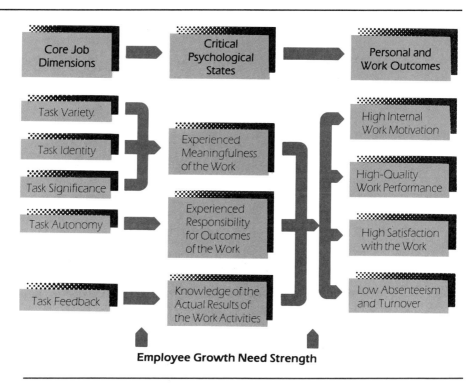

Employee Growth Need Strength

Source: J.R. Hackman and G.R. Oldham, "Development of the Job Diagnostic Survey," *Journal of Applied Psychology* (1975): 159-70. Copyright 1975 by the American Psychological Association. Reprinted by permission.

not only to the improved effectiveness of the organization, but the satisfaction of individual needs. In other words, the organization *and* the worker should benefit from job redesign.

What psychological states are important to job redesign? Three key psychological states are identified: the experienced meaningfulness of the work, the experienced responsibility for work outcomes, and the knowledge of the results from the work. A manager needs to carefully analyze specific jobs for these key states to see which are missing and, more importantly, which can be changed within the constraints of the work.

What important job characteristics are involved? Five important characteristics of the job are noted.[25] These are: (a) *task variety*—the degree to which a job requires employees to perform a wide range of operations in their work; (b) *task identity*—the extent to which employees do an entire or whole piece of work and can clearly identify with the results of their efforts; (c) *task significance*—the degree to which employees feel that they are contributing something worthwhile to the organization; (d) *task autonomy*—the extent to which employees are involved in scheduling their work, selecting their equipment, and deciding the procedures to be followed; and (e) *task feedback*—the degree to which employees receive information as they are working that tells them how well they are performing.

For effective job redesign, the manager must link the psychological states with the core job characteristics. That is, if a job is found to lack ''experienced responsibility,'' the Hackman approach suggests that increased emphasis on task autonomy would be effective. Thus, the ''shotgun approach'' can be decreased.

What is the level of employee growth need strength? Possibly the most important component of the approach, this factor really asks how ready employees are for a change in jobs. This relates to the concept of growth need strength, which is similar to a combination of Maslow's ego and self-actualization needs. In essence, it is sug-

"I FIND THIS WORK TRULY FULFILLING IN MANY
WAYS — THERE'S THE EXERCISE, THE SENSE OF
ACCOMPLISHMENT, AND, MOST IMPORTANT THE OPPORTUNITY
TO MAKE LOTS OF NOISE."

© 1975 Sidney Harris

gested that workers with high growth needs will react more favorably to efforts to redesign a job than employees with low growth needs.

Once the manager has identified the right people for job redesign and diagnosed the task, there are a number of factors that can be altered to change the job characteristics. For example, if there is a need to improve the "meaningfulness" of the job, the manager can combine tasks (enlargement), assign natural units of work methods, and permit self-paced control. Improved "responsibility" can result from the creation of autonomous work groups and greater worker participation in decision making. Finally, increasing the "knowledge of actual results" can occur through making production data available to the worker, holding frequent meetings between superiors and subordinates (see chapter 11), or setting up self-evaluation programs.

Since this approach is relatively new, there have been few direct tests of its validity or applicability. However, a number of organizations have made indirect applications. Among the most interesting are found in General Motors and in Volvo of Sweden.

At GM's assembly plant in Tarrytown, New York, job-related problems among workers had reached a critical stage in the late 1960s and early 1970s.[26] Operating costs were high, frustration, fear, and mistrust of management reigned, absenteeism and turnover were rampant, and over 2,000 labor grievances remained unresolved.

To help solve some of these problems, both management and labor began a program designed to give workers greater participation in deciding the makeup of their tasks. The program began with a request by management to have workers comment on a revised layout for two departments. Surprising management, the workers came up with ideas that made the transition and revised operations more efficient. Since then, the program has expanded to include more than 3,500 workers. Workers have a greater say in the design of jobs; in addition, more data on their performance are being fed back to employees, and there is greater emphasis on communication between superiors and subordinates. During the eight years since the program's inception, the plant has gone from one of the worst performers to one of the best, quality has improved, and turnover, absenteeism, and grievances have declined.

Some words of caution should be mentioned about the Tarrytown project. First, the situation prior to the job redesign was so bad that something had to be done. Thus, both management and labor were more accepting of change. Second, the program did not result in overnight improvement. In fact, many years passed before positive results were found. Finally, the program did not supersede the goal of economic performance. During the time of the program's development and introduction, there were significant layoffs due to an economic decline, plus the speed of the assembly line was increased from fifty-six to sixty cars per hour. It was a credit to the people involved that under such trying times, the program even continued to exist.

In Sweden, Volvo faced many of the problems of the GM Tarrytown plant—turnover exceeded 50 percent per year and absenteeism approached 20 percent.[27] One important difference between the two organizations was that Volvo was also facing a significant cultural problem. Only four out of ten students graduating from high school in Sweden indicated a willingness to take rank-and-file jobs. This resulted not only in increased difficulty in filling factory jobs, but also increased dependence on foreign workers (58 percent of the work force was foreign).

Among the many projects begun by Volvo to counter this problem was the assembly plant at Kalmar.[28] The plant contained many job redesign features including compartmentalized workshops with large windows, employees who worked in teams and could vary the work pace or change teams as they wished, instant productivity data provided by a computerized display screen, and individual autos mounted on trolleys that rolled 90 degrees on the side and permitted work to be done in a less fatiguing manner.

While this job redesign program has proven successful for Volvo, there are a few cautionary notes. First, from a survival and societal view, the company had to do something. The country's present and future work force was highly educated, possibly indicating that routine and mundane jobs were no longer attractive (i.e., a high growth need). Second, as discussed in earlier chapters, worker participation is accepted in Sweden. Thus, worker involvement in job redesign efforts did not meet much resistance. Finally, the plant layout, with holding stations, trolleys, and flexible schedules, was easily adapted to a product that was essentially high cost and low volume. If the Kalmar plant design were adopted in the U.S. with present costs and production rates, it would cost from 10 to 30 percent more to build.

These examples of job design indicate that the redesign of jobs can contribute significantly to the motivation of workers. An important fact is that job redesign is not for every organization. It works when there is a definite need, when the key factors have been diagnosed, and when it has been properly planned and implemented.

Behavior Modification

Earlier in this chapter, we discussed reinforcement theory as a process motivation approach that depends heavily on the use of extrinsic rewards. One of the formats for reinforcement theory in organizations has been termed *behavior modification*.[29]

In the use of behavior modification by managers with subordinates, positive reinforcement is stressed heavily. Research findings suggest that positive reinforcers are more effective than punitive reinforcers (i.e., punishment) in achieving *lasting* changes in behavior. Contrary to the belief of many managers, all that punishment does is buy the manager a little time (you have told the subordinate what not to do) but you still need to strengthen behavior; that is, what should be done.

Behavior modification also emphasizes that rewards should be administered as close in time to the actual behavior of the employee as possible. This is probably one of the reasons why pay is considered a hygiene factor by Herzberg: the employee receives pay long after the occurrence of the desired behavior. Behavioral scientists recommend the use of such reinforcers as praise, recognition, compliments, and other verbal approaches. They are easier to apply and can be administered soon after the desired behaviors. Monetary reinforcers in the form of incentive pay or bonuses, if available, can also be used as positive reinforcers.

Exhibit 12-10 shows the sequences involved in a typical behavior modification program in an organization. Consider a manager of the receiving and marking department in the warehouse operations of a large retail chain. The manager supervises a group of fifteen workers responsible for unloading, inspecting, pricing, and distributing women's fashions to the organization's five branch stores. How can behavior

Exhibit 12-10
Behavior
Modification
Program

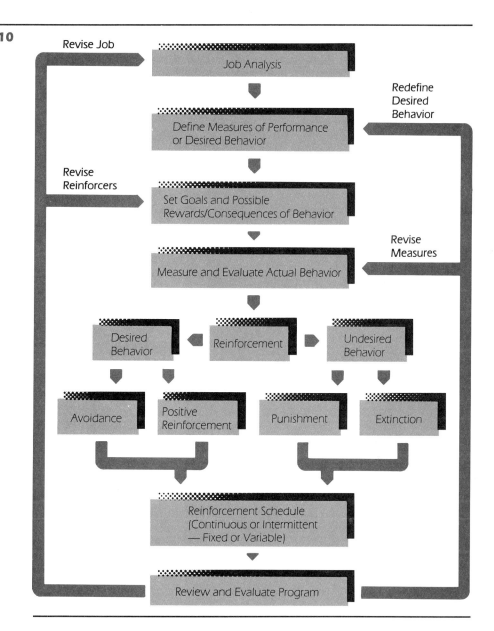

modification help this manager motivate her subordinates to higher productivity?
Let's follow the steps in exhibit 12-10:

▪   *Job analysis* is the process of defining the requirements of the job, the areas of
responsibility and authority, and so on. Since everyone in our example performs the
same task (unload, inspect, price, and distribute), this step can be accomplished easily
and quickly.

- *Defining performance measures* is defining the criteria for job performance. This may be difficult for organizations that use subjective, or qualitative factors to measure performance (e.g., cooperativeness and ability to get along with others, as opposed to number of units produced), or those that have no formal performance evaluation system at all. In the warehouse example, three criteria may be chosen: number of units handled per day, percentage rejects from branch stores (i.e., clothing that is defective or missing price tags), and monthly absenteeism.

- *Setting goals* is the important step of stating what is (or is not) desired behavior of the subordinates. For example, goals for the warehouse employees could be: (a) 500 units processed per day; (b) store rejects held at monthly levels of 4 percent; and (c) no absences per month. *Identifying rewards/consequences of behavior* entails telling employees what they will receive for their performance. Examples include praise and recognition (awards for high performance or just a simple ''thank you''), a major input into the yearly performance review, a year-end bonus, or an extra day off.

- In *measurement of actual behavior,* the manager or the employee keeps a record of daily and monthly performance data. This can be done through observation or actual record keeping. Having the employee keep a performance record has the added effect of a self-feedback mechanism.

- The *reinforcement* stage involves the administration of a reinforcer dependent upon the employee's behavior. For desired behavior, praise and recognition could be given daily, while more lengthy good performance could result in more formal recognition and possibly monetary rewards. Undesired behavior would result in some form of punishment (reprimand initially, possibly followed by termination).

- *Reinforcement schedules* concern the timing of the reinforcer. Continuous reinforcement can be used for undesired behavior (after each occurrence), while a fixed or variable schedule may be used with positive reinforcement.

- Finally, the program is continually *reviewed and evaluated*. If the program is successful, little or no change may be needed. On the other hand, a review of the program may require a change in any of the individual components. For example, the warehouse manager may want to revise the output goal to reflect the differences in processing coats as opposed to blouses or scarves, which take longer to process.

The important aspect for managers to recognize about a behavior modification program is that it is a *continuous* program, not a one-shot deal. For maximum effectiveness, the program must be revised and strengthened as needed.

Since the initial applications, the list of organizations using behavior modification has grown steadily with positive and interesting results.[30] For example, Emery Air Freight has been using a positive reinforcement program for over ten years to improve productivity and the quality of service.

While the program resulted in a cost savings of over $2 million per year, Emery's management noticed a major flaw in their program—praise was overused as a reward, dulling its effect as a reinforcer through sheer repetition, even to the risk of making praise an irritant to employees.

To counter this, Emery managers were trained and encouraged to expand their reinforcers beyond praise. The reinforcers now include a public letter or a letter home, being given a more enjoyable task, invitations to business luncheons, delegating responsibility and decision making, and special time off for good performance. In a similar manner, Connecticut General Life Insurance Company uses positive reinforcement in the form of an attendance bonus system for its clerical personnel. Employees receive one extra day off for each ten weeks of perfect attendance. As a result, chronic absenteeism and lateness have been dramatically reduced.

Additional successes have been reported in other companies. For example, Weyerhaeuser uses a cash bonus (over and above regular salary) for tree planters who exceed production goals. The sanitation department of Detroit used a positive reinforcement system with its refuse collectors. The plan provided for sharing the savings from productivity improvement with workers. General Electric used a behavior modification program—positive reinforcement and feedback—in training employees. The initial program centered on teaching male supervisors how to interact and communicate with minority and female employees, and teaching minority and female employees how to become successful by improving their self-images. Using a format similar to behavior modeling (see chapter 10), the program stressed the use of role playing and videotape feedback.

It is apparent that the use of behavior modification will continue to expand, probably taking various forms in different organizations. The same criticisms as noted for reinforcement theory in general apply to behavior modification, so managers should accept it with caution.[31] Overall, however, it should be clear to managers that tying rewards to performance is a powerful approach to motivating employees.

POINTS TO CONSIDER
An Emphasis on Managerial Skills

1. **There is no universal theory or approach to motivation.**
   While each of the motivation theories we discussed has a certain degree of intuitive appeal to managers, none can be accepted as the one best way. Since different elements are involved—needs, jobs, expectancies, and rewards—the manager would be wise to diagnose the situation and apply the motivation approach that fits best.

2. **The job is a foundational element for motivation.**
   Managers must recognize that what the employee does—his or her job—is at or near the core of the motivation process. Thus, how jobs are designed and how workers move through different jobs in their careers are important concerns.

3. **Rewards are powerful motivators.**
   People in organizations generally are motivated to perform in relation to what they get in return—in other words, ''what they get for what they do.'' A manager also must learn to use a blend of extrinsic and intrinsic rewards. Just as a challenging job may eventually prove dissatisfying without proper monetary benefits, a highly paid job that is boring may lead to motivation problems.

4. **Managerial skills and roles and motivation are closely related.**
   Human skills directly affect a manager's ability to motivate subordinates. From a perspective of roles, the manager motivates through the leader role. It is through this position of authority that the manager directs and rewards employee performance.

SUMMARY FOR THE MANAGER

1. Motivation is a complex process that involves unsatisfied needs, direction of behavior, actual effort, evaluation of performance, and the resulting rewards. While no single motivation theory has yet been developed that encompasses all components of the motivation process, it is helpful to classify the various motivation theories by focus (content approach or process approach).

2. Maslow's need hierarchy was one of the first scientifically based approaches to the study of motivation in organizations. It is a content theory that considers unsatisfied needs to be arousal or behavior-energizing factors. People are motivated to satisfy these needs. The five levels of needs—physiological, safety, social, ego, and self-actualization—indicate to the manager how mature an individual's motivation process is at that time. While it is not a complete motivation theory, it strongly suggests that managers be aware of employee needs because they usually *start* the motivation process.

3. Another content theory, Herzberg's two-factor theory, suggests that needs can be classified as hygiene factors or motivators. Aspects such as pay, fringe benefits, and working conditions do not motivate employees; only those factors that relate to the job—challenge, responsibility, and advancement—act as motivators. A manager accepting this approach would try to improve motivation by making changes in the employee's job. However, this theory has a number of significant shortcomings, which make its total acceptance a tenuous proposition.

4. Expectancy theory, classified as a process theory, stresses the importance of both arousal factors *and* analyzation of the direction of motivated behavior. According to the theory, employees are motivated to adopt behavior that will lead to valued rewards. By clarifying and strengthening effort-to-performance and performance-to-reward relationships, the manager can significantly affect a worker's behavior.

5. Reinforcement theory emphasizes that motivation is a *learned* behavior. If a valued reward is given for following a managerial directive, then the employee will probably repeat that motivated behavior the next time a similar directive is given. Positive reinforcement coupled with a variable schedule of reinforcement has been found to influence motivation most. Punishment, when used properly, can eliminate undesired behavior; however, the employee must be told what to do right, not just what was done incorrectly.

6. One of the main applied-motivation techniques is job design. Job design focuses on altering the employee's job so that it is challenging and intrinsically rewarding. A variety of approaches, including job rotation, enlargement, enrichment, and job redesign, have developed. For best results, the manager must recognize that not all employees will react favorably to a more challenging job. In addition, the success of these programs depends a great deal on how well the manager has diagnosed what changes are needed, what the potential side effects are, and what level of management commitment has been given to the program.

7. Behavior modification, which is based on reinforcement theory and heavily stresses the use of extrinsic rewards, is another popular applied-motivation technique. In a number of organizations, behavior modification has improved employee motivation. Managers, however, must recognize the importance of measurable behavior, the proper use of rewards, the value the subordinate places on the reward, and what rewards the manager can offer.

8. While motivating employees is an important human skill, conceptual skills and diagnostic skills are also important. In much the same manner, motivation heavily involves the leader role, but

the informational and decisional roles also play important parts. Overall, the manager is the key element in motivating subordinates. The manager assigns the work, recognizes the needs of subordinates, guides the work, evaluates it, and rewards it—all part of the motivation process.

 REVIEW AND DISCUSSION QUESTIONS

1. Compare the need hierarchy and expectancy theory approaches to motivation. What are their similarities and differences?
2. How can a manager influence an employee's perceptions of expectancy (effort-to-performance) and instrumentality (performance-to-reward)?
3. Discuss the advantages and disadvantages of reinforcement theory in organizations.
4. How would you present expectancy theory to a group of managers?
5. Why is Herzberg's two-factor theory so popular among managers, even though the many criticisms are significant?
6. Why has job rotation been considered only a short-term job design strategy to counter worker morale problems?
7. Why is feedback an important element in any job design program?
8. Discuss the impact of cultural differences on job design programs.
9. Why do some workers resist having their jobs made more challenging?
10. What is the difference between intrinsic rewards and extrinsic rewards?

NOTES

1. "Managing Motivation," *General Electric Monogram* (November-December 1975): 2-5.
2. See M.R. Jones, ed. *Nebraska Symposium on Motivation* (Lincoln: University of Nebraska, 1955); J.B. Miner and N.R. Smith, "Decline and Stabilization of Managerial Motivation Over a 20-Year Period," *Journal of Applied Psychology* (June 1982): 297-305; and T.R. Mitchell, "Motivation: New Directions for Theory, Research and Practice," *Academy of Management Review* (January 1982): 80-88.
3. A. H. Maslow, *Motivation and Personality* (New York: Harper & Row, 1954).
4. See J. M. Ivancevich, "Perceived Need Satisfactions of Domestic versus Overseas Management," *Journal of Applied Psychology* (August 1969): 274-78; and D. Serota and J. M. Greenwood, "Understand Your Overseas Work Force," *Harvard Business Review* (January-February 1971): 53-60.
5. L. W. Porter, *Organizational Patterns of Managerial Job Attitudes* (New York: American Foundation for Management Research, 1964).
6. E. E. Lawler III and J. L. Suttle, "A Causal Correlational Test of the Need Hierarchy Concept," *Organizational Behavior and Human Performance* (April 1972): 265-87.
7. D. T. Hall and K. E. Nougaim, "An Examination of Maslow's Need Hierarchy Concept," *Organizational Behavior and Human Performance* (February 1968): 12-35.
8. F. Herzberg, B. Mausner, and B. Snyderman, *The Motivation to Work*, 2d ed. (New York: Wiley, 1959).
9. R. J. House and L. Wigdor, "Herzberg's Dual-Factor Theory of Job Satisfaction and Motivation: A Review of the Empirical Evidence and a Criticism," *Personnel Psychology* (Winter 1967): 369-80.
10. V. H. Vroom, *Work and Motivation* (New York: Wiley, 1964).

11.   See R. J. House, H. J. Shapero, and M. A. Wahba, "Expectancy Theory as a Predictor of Work Behavior and Attitudes: A Re-examination of the Empirical Evidence," *Decision Sciences* (July 1974): 481-506; T. Janz, "Manipulating Subjective Expectancy Through Feedback: A Laboratory Study of the Expectancy-Performance Relationship," *Journal of Applied Psychology* (August 1982): 480-85; and L.R. Walker and K.W. Thomas, "Beyond Expectancy Theory: An Integrative Motivational Model from Health Care," *Academy of Management Review* (April 1982): 187-94.

12.   See F. Schmidt, "Implication of a Measurement Problem for Expectancy Theory Research," *Organizational Behavior and Human Performance* (April 1973): 243-51; and J. M. Feldman, H. J. Reitz, and R. J. Hilterman, "Alternatives to Optimization in Expectancy Theory," *Journal of Applied Psychology* (December 1976): 712-20.

13.   See B. F. Skinner, *Contingencies of Reinforcement* (New York: Appleton-Century-Crofts, 1969); and R. M. Tarpy, *Basic Principles of Learning* (Glenview, Ill.: Scott, Foresman, 1974).

14.   F. Luthans and R. Kreitner, *Organizational Behavior Modifications* (Glenview, Ill.: Scott, Foresman, 1975).

15.   W. C. Hamner, "Reinforcement Theory and Contingency Management in Organizational Settings," in *Organizational Behavior and Management: A Contingency Approach*, H. L. Tosi and W. C. Hamner, eds. (Chicago, Ill.: St. Clair, 1974), pp. 86-112.

16.   See J. L. Komaki, R.L. Collins, and P. Penn, "The Role of Performance Antecedents and Consequences in Work Motivation," Journal of Applied Psychology (June 1982): 334-40; and R.M. McFatter, "Purposes of Punishment: Effects of Utilities of Criminal Sanctions on Perceived Appropriateness," *Journal of Applied Psychology* (June 1982): 255-67.

17.   See R. W. Griffin, *Task Design: An Integrative Approach* (Glenview, Ill.: Scott, Foresman, 1982).

18.   M. D. Kilbridge, "Reduced Costs through Job Enlargement: A Case, *The Journal of Business* (October 1960): 357-62.

19.   F. Herzberg, "The Wise Old Turk," *Harvard Business Review* (September-October 1974): 70-80.

20.   R. Ford, "Job Enrichment Lessons for AT&T," *Harvard Business Review* (January-February 1973): 96-106.

21.   M. S. Myers, *Every Employee a Manager* (New York: McGraw-Hill, 1970).

22.   Ohio Human Relations Commissions, *World of Work Report I* (May 1976).

23.   See J. R. Hackman, "Is Job Enrichment Just a Fad?" *Harvard Business Review* (September-October 1975): 129-39; and M. Fein, "Job Enrichment: A Re-evaluation," *Sloan Management Review* (Winter 1974): 69-88.

24.   J. R. Hackman, G. Oldham, R. Janson, and K. Purdy, "A New Strategy for Job Enrichment," *California Management Review* (Summer 1975): 57-71.

25.   H. P. Sims, A. D. Szilagyi, and R. T. Keller, "The Measurement of Job Characteristics," *Academy of Management Journal* (June 1976): 195-212.

26.   R. H. Guest, "Quality of Work Life—Learning from Tarrytown," *Harvard Business Review* (July-August 1979): 76-87.

27.   See W. F. Dowling, "Job Design on the Assembly Line: Farewell to the Blue-Collar Blues?" *Organizational Dynamics* (Spring 1973): 51-67; and P. Gyllenhammar, *People at Work* (Reading, Mass.: Addison-Wesley, 1977).

28.   J. M. Roach, "Why Volvo Abolished the Assembly-Line," *Management Review* (September 1977): 50.

29.   W. C. Hamner and E. P. Hamner, "Behavior Modification on the Bottom Line," *Organizational Dynamics* (Spring 1976): 2-21.

30.   Ibid., p. 4.

31.   E. A. Locke, "The Myths of Behavior Mod in Organizations," *Academy of Management Review* (October 1977): 543-53.

Motivation

General Foods

In 1968, General Foods was considering the construction of a plant in Topeka, Kansas, to manufacture pet foods. Because of continuing problems at their existing plants—product waste, sabotage, frequent shutdowns, and low morale—the management of General Foods wanted to try a set of innovative motivational techniques at this new plant. The basic design of the new plant was oriented around the principles of skills development, challenging jobs, and teamwork.

Autonomous work groups. The work force of seventy employees was divided into teams of seven to fourteen employees. Three types of teams were created: processing, packaging, and shipping. These teams were self-managed by the workers; they were involved in making work assignments, screening and selecting new members, and the added responsibility of the decision making for large segments of the plant's operations.

Challenging jobs. The basic design of each job was developed to eliminate the boring and routine aspects as much as possible. Each job—whether on the manufacturing line or in the warehouse—was designed to include a high degree of variety, autonomy, planning, liaison work with other teams, and responsibility for diagnosing and correcting mechanical or process problems.

Job mobility and rewards for learning. Because each set of jobs was designed to be equally challenging, it was possible to have a single job classification for all operators. Employees could receive pay increases by developing new skills and mastering different jobs. Team members were, in essence, paid for learning more and more of the plant's operations.

Information availability. Unlike most manufacturing plants, the operators at this new plant were provided the necessary economic, quantity, and quality information normally reserved for managers.

Self-government. Rather than working with a set of predetermined rules and procedures, such policies were developed as the need arose. This resulted in fewer unnecessary rules to guide the work. Only critical guidelines or rules were developed, and generally these were based on the collective experience of the team.

Status symbols. The typical physical and social status symbols of assigned parking spaces, wide variations in the decor of offices and rooms, and separate entrance and eating facilities were eliminated. There existed an open parking lot, a single entrance for both office and plant workers, and a common decor throughout the entire plant.

Learning and evaluation. The most basic feature of the plant was the commitment to evaluate continually both the plant's productivity and the state of employee morale. Before any change was made in the plant, an evaluation of the impact on both productivity and worker morale was made.

As in any major redesign program, management at the new plant was faced with a number of implementation problems. First, tension among employees developed concerning pay rates. There were four basic pay rates in the plant: (1) starting rate; (2) single rate (mastery of one job); (3) team rate (mastery of all jobs within the team); and (4) plant rate (mastery of all operator jobs within the plant). Because the decision on pay rates was primarily the responsibility of the team leader, certain questions about the judgment of job mastery and whether workers had an equal opportunity to learn jobs developed.

Second, because the management philosophy at this particular plant was quite different from that at the other plants, difficulties arose whenever employees of the new plant interacted with other General Foods personnel. Problems of resistance and a lack of acceptance and support developed.

Finally, the expectations of a small minority of workers did not coincide with the new teamwork concept of the plant. Certain employees resisted the movement toward greater responsibility. Again, individual differences among employees were shown to be important to the job redesign movement.

Was the new plant successful with its innovative work arrangement? A review after eighteen months of operation suggested positive results. For example, fixed overhead costs were 33 percent lower than in older plants, quality rejects were reduced by 92 percent, and the safety record was one of the best in the company. Focusing on the human resource side, morale was high, absenteeism was 9 percent below the industry norm, and turnover was far below normal.

The plant was widely heralded as a model for the future, and General Foods claims that it still is. In fact, GF has applied a similar system at a second dog food plant in Topeka and at a coffee plant in New Jersey. And it says it may eventually do the same at two plants in Mexico and among white-collar workers at its White Plains headquarters.

But management analysts and former employees tell a different story. And General Foods, which once encouraged publicity about the Topeka plant, now refuses to let reporters inside. Critics say that after the initial euphoria, the system, faced with indifference and outright hostility from some GF managers, has been eroding steadily.

"The system went to heck. It didn't work," says one former manager. Adds another ex-employee: "It was a mixed bag. Economically it was a success, but it became a power struggle. It was too threatening to too many people." He predicts that the plant will eventually switch to a traditional factory system. In fact, he says, the transition has already begun.

The problem has been not so much that the workers could not manage their own affairs as that some management and staff personnel saw their own positions threatened because the workers performed almost too well. One former employee says the system—built around a team concept—came squarely up against the company's bureaucracy. Lawyers, fearing reaction from the National Labor Relations Board, opposed the idea of allowing team members to vote on pay raises. Personnel managers objected because team members made hiring decisions. Engineers resented workers doing engineering work.

Consequently, critics say, there has been a stiffening of the Topeka system: more job classifications, less participation, more supervision. GF has added seven management positions to the plant, including controller, plant engineering manager, and manufacturing services manager. GF says these were necessary because of a plant expansion. When GF geared up a plant adjacent to the first one to produce Cycle, a canned dog food, it introduced the Topeka process but deferred several elements of the system.

Suggested from R. E. Walton, "How to Counter Alienation in the Plant," *Harvard Business Review* (November-December 1972); and *Business Week*, "Stonewalling Plant Democracy" (March 26, 1977): 78-82.

Questions for Discussion

1. What basic motivational principles were involved in the General Foods Topeka plant?
2. Initially, why did the job redesign program work effectively?
3. What were some of the reasons for the slow decline in the commitment by managers to the program?
4. What can other managers learn from the Topeka experience?

EXPERIENTIAL EXERCISE
Motivation Factors

Purpose

1. To examine the application of motivation approaches to organizations.

2. To understand the relationship between motivation and differences in individuals.

Required Understanding
The student should have a basic understanding of the different approaches to motivation.

Instructions for the Exercise
Exhibit 12-11 presents a list of ten job-related factors that can be found in most organizations. Examine these ten factors and *rank-order* from 1 (most influential to motivation) to 10 (least influential to motivation). (No ties, please.) Three rank-orders are required:

1. *Self-rating:* A rank-order of the factors as evaluated by yourself.

2. *Non-supervisory, assembly-line worker:* Rank-order the ten factors as you believe a nonsupervisory employee working on an assembly line would do.

3. *Middle-level manager:* Rank-order the ten factors as you believe a middle-level manager would do. *Note:* The instructor may wish to specify a particular industry or organization.

When completed, the rankings will be compared with a set of comparative data that has been made available to the instructor. The differences in the rankings, if any, should be discussed, particularly between the different jobs.

Exhibit 12-11
Motivation Factors

	Rankings		
Factor Description	**Self**	**Nonsupervisor/ Assembly Line**	**Middle-Level Manager**
1. **Recognition:** Receiving recognition from peers, supervisors, and/or subordinates for good work performances.	_____	_____	_____
2. **Pay:** A wage that not only covers normal living expenses but provides additional funds for certain luxury items.	_____	_____	_____
3. **Sense of Achievement:** The feelings associated with successful completion of a job, finding solutions to different problems, or seeing the results of one's work.	_____	_____	_____
4. **Supervision:** Working for a supervisor who is both competent in doing his or her job and looks out for the welfare of his or her subordinates.	_____	_____	_____
5. **Advancement:** The opportunity for advancement or promotion based on ability.	_____	_____	_____
6. **Job Itself:** Having a job that is interesting, challenging, and provides for substantial variety and autonomy.	_____	_____	_____
7. **Job Security:** Feeling good about job security within the company.	_____	_____	_____
8. **Working Conditions:** Safe and attractive conditions for doing work.	_____	_____	_____
9. **Fringe Benefits:** A substantial fringe benefit package covering such aspects as health insurance.	_____	_____	_____
10. **Personal Development:** The opportunity to develop and refine new skills and abilities.	_____	_____	_____

CHAPTER

13

Leadership

Chapter Outline

Key Points

1. Leadership in organizations is a process in which influence is founded on the strength of the leader's power base.
2. Trait theories of leadership attempt to identify certain managerial characteristics that can be used to distinguish successful from unsuccessful leaders.
3. Behavioral theories of leadership concern the leader's style or behavioral patterns. An attempt is made to identify the best style of leadership.
4. Fiedler's contingency model, the first situational approach to leadership, relates certain situational factors to the leader's style in order to develop the most effective match.
5. The path-goal theory, based on expectancy theory, is a situational approach that seeks to improve employee motivation through the use of different leader behaviors.
6. A manager's needs and preferred leadership style are influenced by cultural factors.
7. Leaders influence superiors and peers as well as subordinates.
8. Leadership is a learned skill that can be acquired through a variety of mechanisms, including experience, observation, and training programs.

American Can Company

When William S. Woodside assumed the chair of American Can Company in 1980, the company was faced with many serious problems. First and foremost, previous year profits had dropped by 33 percent. Then many of American's major customers began making their own containers. Finally, there were red ink problems at Pickwick International and Sam Goody, Inc., key units within the company that competed in the recording industry. Woodside's task was to put a disorganized and demoralized house back in order.

In less than a year, Woodside established himself as a leader who would move quickly and, if need be, ruthlessly. For example, he put American's billion dollar paper-related businesses on the auction block claiming that canmaking and paper production were too expensive and capital intensive for the financial health of the firm. When two key senior vice presidents objected strenuously to the proposed sale, Woodside responded swiftly by naming them president and executive vice president of the paper division. Meaning: the two executives would go with the division when it was sold.

Woodside's leadership was felt in other parts of the company. He restructured the company by changing what had been a breakdown along market lines to one organized around basic materials. As *Business Week* reports, previously one executive was responsible for containers and packaging, another handled consumer products and distribution, and a third was in charge of resource recovery. But now paper packaging, Dixie Cups, and ligin chemicals—once treated as totally different areas—are lumped together under a manager of fiber businesses.

Decentralization was also part of Woodside's restructuring plan. Corporate staff support services—personnel, research, purchasing, and the like—were pushed down to the business-unit level. The idea was to give managers in the new organization direct support from important staff departments that were under their control.

Not surprisingly, Woodside's leadership style has been described by American Can managers in such terms as hard-nosed, aggressive, tough, and no-nonsense. To some, this style has not been easy to digest, prompting claims of low morale. Whatever the state of internal attitudes, Woodside is turning his company around. A key question, however, is left unanswered: can Woodside develop a sound management team and groom a successor to continue the company's success after he retires?

Adapted from *Business Week*, "Where Different Styles Have Led Two Canmakers," (July 27, 1981): 80-81.

13

Both practicing managers and management scholars consider leadership one of the most important factors influencing organizational performance. Our *Practice of Management* section on American Can's William Woodside is a good example. For the manager, leadership involves directing employees to work toward the accomplishment of organizational goals. From a human resource point of view, a leader's actions also have a significant effect on the behavior, attitudes, and performance of employees.[1]

We will discuss the concept of leadership in organizations in three major parts. First, we will establish the foundations of leadership, with a definition of the concept and a discussion of the basic elements that make it up. Second, we will look at the major approaches to leadership—trait, behavioral, and situational. Finally, we will highlight a number of contemporary issues in leadership.

The Definition of Leadership

When asked to give a one- or two-word definition of leadership, it is likely that people would use words such as *direction, example, powerful, motivator, control, authority, reinforcer,* and *delegator*. Leadership probably involves each of these concepts. The one word, however, that seems to encompass the major focus of leadership is *influence*. With this word, we will define leadership as follows:

> Leadership is a process involving two or more people in which one attempts to influence the other's behavior toward the accomplishment of some goal or goals.

There are at least three important implications of this definition. First, leadership is a *process*. That is, it is an ongoing activity in an organization. Second, leadership involves *other people,* usually in the form of subordinates. By their willingness to be influenced by the leaders, subordinates formalize the leader's authority and make the leadership process possible. Finally, the outcome of leadership is some form of *goal accomplishment*. This suggests that the leader's attempts at influence are directional, aimed at some level of achievement.

Manager and/or Leader?

Management and leadership are not synonymous. A person can be a leader without being a manager. This is common in sports—Pete Rose (baseball), Joe Montana (football), and Wayne Gretsky (hockey) have been leaders of their teams without being the managers. That is, they did not plan, organize, or control the activities of the team, nor did they have this responsibility. Through their superior performance and example, however, they often influenced the behavior of other team members.

On the other hand, a person can be a manager without also being the leader. People are managers by virtue of the authority in their positions as given by the organization (see chapter 8). They have the *right* to influence because of their positions, but they may not choose to exercise this right, or subordinates may choose to be influenced by other individuals or factors. For example, a head nurse in a hospital is technically the manager over a group of floor nurses. Yet frequently the floor nurses' behavior at work is influenced by doctors' directives or their own knowledge of what a patient needs.

Informal Leaders

A second way to approach the manager versus leader issue is to discuss *informal* leaders. Consider a group of clerical personnel who are responsible for maintaining customer charge accounts for a large retail store. Who is the group's leader? A typical response might be, "Well, my direct supervisor is Emily, but Julie is really the leader of my group. Emily gives directions and orders and generally tells us what to do. She is the 'organization's person,' and we go to her with problems concerning rules, procedures, and policies. Julie, on the other hand, has the same clerical job as we do, but has worked here longer than any of us. She 'knows the ropes.' Julie helps us with our work by showing us the best way to do the job. Everyone feels good that Julie is around—she helps us build confidence in our work and is a real morale booster."

This example draws attention to two important sources of influence and leadership. Emily is the *formal* supervisor, and as such, exercises formal influence. Leadership, however, can be *informal,* and Julie exerts it. This type of leader is called the informal, emergent, or peer leader.

While not prescribed by the organization, informal leaders can significantly influence the behavior of others. Informal influence originates not from the position held by the individual, but from some special quality, ability, or skill that the group seems to want. In Julie's case, this influence is based on her work experience and willingness to help her co-workers.

In some situations, only a formal leader will exist. In our clerical example, if Emily, having the necessary skills, provided the support her subordinates needed as well as performed her formal role, an informal leader probably would not have emerged. Julie held her informal leadership role because Emily's behavior was not satisfying the work-related needs of the workers.

Informal leaders can play a very valuable role in organizations if their behavior and influence are congruent with the goals of the organization. Influencing others to work more efficiently and effectively is acting in support of the organization's purposes. But if Julie supported lengthy lunches and frequent "gab" sessions around the coffee pot, or refused to work overtime, she would be acting incongruent with the organization's purpose.

Foundations of Leadership

Two factors lay the foundation for our discussion of leadership in organizations. These are an analysis of the concept of power and identification of the process of leadership.

Power in the Leadership Position

As noted in chapter 8, the concepts of influence and power are closely related. In particular, power has been defined as the "capacity to influence another through the control over needed resources." It is important for the manager to understand that power to influence can originate from a variety of sources. In the example of clerical personnel, Emily's power came from her positional authority, while Julie's originated from certain skills and abilities. In other words, power in organizations includes positional and personal attributes.

One of the most widely used descriptions of organizational power was proposed by John R. P. French and Bertran Raven.[2] They stated that there are six different forms of power a leader may possess:

- *Legitimate power* is given the manager by the organization because of the manager's position in the hierarchy. The organization usually sanctions this form of power by titles such as manager, director, or supervisor.

- *Reward power* is based on the ability of the manager to control and administer rewards to others (money, promotions, praise) for compliance with the leader's orders or requests.

- *Coercive power* is based on the manager's ability to use punishment on others (reprimands, termination) for noncompliance with orders.

- *Expert power* is derived from some special ability, skills, or knowledge exhibited by the individual.

- *Referent power* can be shown in at least two forms in an organization. First, it can be based on a certain attractiveness or appeal of one person to another. A person may be admired because of certain characteristics that inspire or attract followers. For example, President John Kennedy and General George Patton were said to have had charisma, and they had followers both inside and outside their realms of authority. Referent power may also be based on a person's connection or relationship with another powerful individual. For example, the title "assistant to . . ." has been given to people who work closely with others with substantial power (see chapter 8). Although the assistant to the vice president may not have legitimate, reward, or coercive power, other individuals may perceive that this person is acting with the consent of the vice president, resulting in the assistant's power to influence. Before he became secretary of state, Henry Kissinger was President Nixon's national security advisor. That being a staff position, Kissinger had little organizationally based power. When he spoke in meetings, however, people assumed that he spoke for the president.

- *Information power* involves opportunity managers have to gain access to and transmit information about particular issues or activities concerning an organization's internal and external environments. This information power may or may not relate to the person's position or level in the organization. Certainly top-level executives have acquired information about the firm that others do not have. On the other hand, at a lower level, secretaries seem to be able to accumulate and use information as no one else can—giving them more power than their position technically allows.

Remember that legitimate, reward, coercive, and informational power are given by the organization and are based on the control of important organizational resources.

Expert and, to some extent, referent power are based on the characteristics of the individual and may or may not be given by the organization.

Many times, managers find they lack certain organizationally based power components. For example, managers may have legitimate power because of their positions, but decisions on pay raises or reprimands may be limited by organizational rules or procedures (e.g., union contracts). Thus, some of the manager's ability to influence others has been taken away. When faced with this situation, many managers compensate by strengthening an individually based power component. They accomplish this usually by becoming ''expert'' in their particular areas of responsibility. The stronger the manager's power base, the greater the chance that attempts at influence will be successful.

A Basic Leadership Model

Knowing the foundations, we can now present a basic model of the leadership process. As shown in exhibit 13-1, the model consists of three major parts.

▪ Power is the *basis* of the leadership process.

▪ A series of four process factors, or *leader behaviors,* are the main elements of influence. The first stage, *assignment,* is leader behaviors that start the influence, or goal-achievement, activities. Included are planning, directing, instructing, and so on. The second stage, *implementation,* is the leader's activities that guide, monitor, delegate, and support subordinates in their work. The *evaluation* stage is the leader activities that evaluate and control the work. Finally, in *rewards,* the fourth stage, the leader rewards, revises, and feeds back information regarding the degree to which the workers' performance has achieved the stated goals. Consider the manager of quality control in a farm equipment manufacturing plant who wants to put into operation a new quality control technique. At the beginning, the manager shows his or her subordinates how to use the new technique (assignment stage). As the subordinates begin using the technique, the manager makes sure that it is being done properly (implementation stage). As time passes, the manager evaluates how the technique has worked, how the technicians have adapted to it, and so on (evaluation stage). Finally, when sufficient data have been collected, the manager may revise some procedures associated with the technique, feeds this information back to the subordinates, and rewards them for their performance (reward stage).

▪ The third major part of the model is the *outcomes* of the leadership process. Outcomes can include increased productivity, increased satisfaction, or decreased turnover and absenteeism.

Approaches to the Study of Leadership

Having the basic leadership model, we can examine the various approaches to leadership. Three broad approaches have evolved over the last forty years—trait theories, behavioral theories, and situational theories.

Exhibit 13-1
A Basic Leadership Model

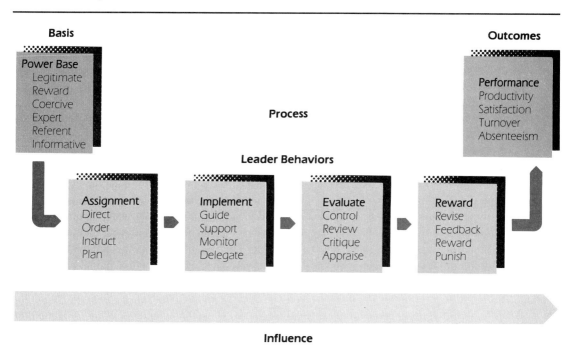

The early *trait theories* studied leadership by attempting to answer the question, "In terms of managerial characteristics, who are the most effective leaders?" Following the early trait theories came *behavioral theories,* in which researchers and practicing managers switched their emphasis from the characteristics of the leader to a concern for the style of leadership exhibited by the leader. The key question asked was, "Is one leadership style more effective than another?" In terms of the basic leadership model, the focus was actually on the leadership process itself. In other words, attention shifted from a concern of "who the leader is" to "what the leader does."

Finally, contemporary management scholars developed *situational theories.* These approaches expanded on our basic leadership model by seeing leadership as a complex process that involves the leader, subordinates, and the nature of the situation. These management scholars were directed by the belief that "effective leadership is a function of the characteristics of the leader, the style of leadership, the characteristics of the subordinates, and the situation surrounding the leadership environment." We will begin our discussion of the various approaches to the study of leadership with a brief analysis of the trait theories.

 # The Search for Leadership Traits

One of the first scientific efforts to study and understand leadership was directed at identifying the important characteristics of leaders. This research, which began in earnest after World War II, attempted systematically to analyze something that many of us have observed: there is some quality in military heroes, movie heroes and heroines, successful politicians, executives, and some everyday people that makes them seem naturally more intelligent, braver, more decisive, more articulate, or more loyal than anyone else.

A fascinating discussion of this special quality was presented by Tom Wolfe in *The Right Stuff*, which describes the behind-the-scenes selection and training of the first American astronauts.

> Herein the world was divided into those who had it and those who did not. This quality, this *it*, was never named, however, nor was it talked about in any way. As to just what this ineffable quality was . . . well, it obviously involved bravery. . . . The idea here seemed to be that a man should have the ability to go up in a hurtling piece of machinery and put his hide on the line and then have the moxie, the reflexes, the experience, the coolness, to pull it back in the last yawning moment—and then to go up again the next day, and the next, and every next day, even if the series should prove infinite. . . . The idea was to prove at every foot of the way that you were one of the elected and anointed ones who had *the right stuff* and could move higher and higher and even—ultimately, God willing, one day—that you might be able to join that special few at the very top, that elite who had the capacity to bring tears to men's eyes, the very Brotherhood of the Right Stuff itself.[3]

People recognized this "right stuff" in those American heroes, the first astronauts, but found it difficult to define.

Research on Leader Traits

The trait approach to leadership began with the question: Can a set of finite traits be found that can distinguish effective from ineffective leaders, such that the results can be used to select new leaders? This new approach to managerial selection was supposed to be the major contribution of the trait theories.

Exhibit 13-2 presents a list of example traits that have been investigated. The results of the many research studies indicated that there was a *tendency* for leaders (emergent and effective leaders) to be taller, more intelligent, self-confident, extroverted, and more effective in their communication.[4] In a study of Fortune 500 executives, it was found that a high percentage (but not a majority) of them came from a middle-class background, held Protestant or Episcopalian religious beliefs, identified with Republican or independent political stands, and had fathers who were professional or business executives.[5]

Edwin E. Ghiselli performed one of the most famous studies of managerial effectiveness.[6] He examined thirteen personality and motivational traits of managers to determine how these traits related to managerial success.

Exhibit 13-2 Examples of Studied Leader Traits	Physical Characteristics	Social Background	Intelligence
	1. Age	1. Education	1. Ability
	2. Weight	2. Mobility	2. Judgment
	3. Height	3. Social status	3. Decisiveness
	4. Appearance	4. Family background	4. Fluency of speech
	Personality	Task-Related Characteristics	Social Characteristics
	1. Independence	1. Achievement need	1. Administrative ability
	2. Self-confidence	2. Initiative	2. Attractiveness
	3. Dominance	3. Persistence	3. Cooperativeness
	4. Aggression	4. Responsibility need	4. Interpersonal skills

Supervisory ability—the capacity to direct the work of others and to organize and integrate their activities and behavior toward goal accomplishment—was the most distinguishing trait of managerial success.

Next in importance is a cluster of five traits: the need for (occupational) achievement, intelligence, the need for self-actualization, self-assurance, and decisiveness. This suggests two things: (a) successful leaders have the need to achieve, have the drive to act independently, and are self-assured in their work; and (b) leadership ability is strongly associated with good judgment and proven communication skills.

The results suggest that intelligence is an accurate predictor of managerial success within a certain range. At the extremes of this range—very high or very low intelligence—the chance of successful performance decreases. Ghiselli's findings imply that the leader's intelligence should not be too different from that of the subordinates. In other words, the leader who is too smart or not smart enough may lose the respect of subordinates and the ability to influence their behavior.

A number of traits were identified as contributing little to managerial success. The low level of importance given to the need for power and wealth points to a theory Y orientation of these managers, rather than a theory X philosophy.

McCall and Lombardo have reported a more current investigation of leadership traits.[7] In their research, they studied why certain managers *failed* to live up to their potential for success. Their results identified the following traits or factors that can lead to failure: a leadership style that is abrasive, intimidating, cold, aloof, arrogant, and generally insensitive to others; betrayal of colleague trust; being overly ambitious—playing politics; not being able to delegate, build a team, staff effectively, think strategically, and adapt to a boss with a different style; and overdependence on an advocate or mentor.

Ghiselli's and McCall and Lombardo's research, however, used small sample sizes, and the traits are not totally independent of each other. Nevertheless, these studies have contributed to our understanding of the elements of managerial performance from a trait point of view.

Issues and Implications of Trait Theories

Even with these sometimes interesting results, it has been generally thought that trait research has not provided an accurate analysis of the leadership process. First, the list of leader traits studied was not finite in number, but approached many hundreds. Thus, applying the findings to managerial selection in organizations was tenuous. Second, there were inconsistent findings across organizations. That is, the discriminating traits that were found in one organization frequently did not occur in others. Third, one can easily acknowledge that some, if not many, of these identifying traits are *learned* when a person is in a leadership role. A manager realizes, for example, that to improve performance, he or she needs to become more assertive, more decisive, and stronger in the ability to communicate. During this process, self-confidence may also increase.

Finally, there was the belated understanding that effective leadership depends not so much on *who* the leader is but on what the leader does and how well the leader adapts to the varying requirements of different situations. This led researchers to an examination of the behavior, or styles, of the leader.

 # The Behavioral Approach

Dissatisfaction with the trait approach motivated management scholars to refocus their attention on the study of actual behaviors. This approach has been termed the behavioral or leadership-style approach. Unlike trait theories, the behavioral approach emphasized what leaders do, not who they are in terms of individual characteristics. Similar to trait theories, however, the behavioral approach sought the "one best" style of leadership that would be effective in all situations.

Research on the Behavioral Approach

A number of definitions of leadership styles have been developed from the various behavioral theories of leadership. As we will see, although many terms were assigned to the different leadership styles, two dimensions were stressed in each theory—task orientation and employee orientation. *Task orientation* is the emphasis the leader places on getting the job done by assigning and organizing the work, making decisions, or monitoring and evaluating performance. *Employee orientation* is the openness, friendliness, and concern the leader shows subordinates.

In exhibit 13-3, the two orientations have been presented in a two-dimensional framework. This framework reflects the notion that a leader's behavioral style can vary along each of the dimensions, resulting in a great array of possibilities. For example, point A represents a manager whose style is moderate on task orientation, but low on employee orientation. Similarly, manager B shows a high degree of task orientation and a moderate degree of employee orientation, while manager C is depicted as low on task orientation but high on employee orientation.

Two research groups were most noted for work on leadership styles, Ohio State University and the University of Michigan. At Ohio State, the two leader dimensions

Exhibit 13-3
Dimensions of
Leadership Style

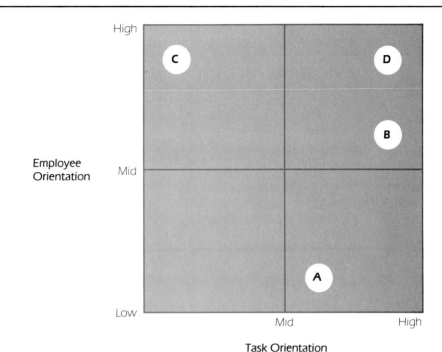

were called *initiating structure* (task orientation) and *consideration* (employee orientation).[8] Much of the early work was conducted with the belief that the most effective leadership style was high both on initiating structure and consideration (manager *D* in exhibit 13-3). It was assumed that leaders with this style supervised groups who were high performers and had equally high levels of job satisfaction. However, in numerous studies in such organizations as a petroleum refinery, a business machine manufacturer, an aircraft manufacturer, and military groups, no single leadership style emerged as the most effective. In certain organizations, a high initiating structure and high consideration style was found to be most effective; in others, a low initiating structure and high consideration style was best; while in still others, a high initiating structure and low consideration style was associated with high subordinate performance.[9]

In the University of Michigan studies, the dimensions of task orientation and employee orientation were called *job-centered* and *employee-centered* styles. In a major study that characterized much of their work, Michigan researchers compared the effectiveness of two units in a large corporation. The prevailing leadership style in one unit was highly job-centered, while a highly employee-centered style was dominant in the second unit. The study found that production increased in both units; however, the attitudinal and behavioral relationships among the study participants were quite different. In the unit with leaders having high employee-centered styles,

The Manager's Job

Charles J. Pilliod of Goodyear Tire & Rubber

In the early 1970s, Goodyear Tire & Rubber was having problems, according to *The Wall Street Journal*. Among other things: it was slow to introduce radial tires; it ignored opportunities to sell tires in Europe; and it watched France's Michelin win the lucrative Sears, Roebuck & Company contract for private label tires. The board of directors wanted a leader who would shake the company up as its new president.

What it got was a hip-shooting, autocratic executive named Charles J. Pilliod, formerly head of Goodyear's European operations. An Akron native and a college drop-out, Pilliod never lacked self-confidence. Until recently, he piloted the company plane on business trips, and in 1976, he personally drew the tread sketches that led to the first successful all-season radial tire, the Goodyear Tiempo.

Pilliod's demanding, autocratic style didn't win him any popularity contests at Goodyear. Some claim he was an egomaniac, others said he was more a megalomaniac. Former managers remember Pilliod's penchant for yelling at his employees, "What do you think that pointy little head of yours is for anyway?," when he found slow decision making. That style, however, may well have kept Goodyear from becoming an industrial dinosaur. Instead, it stands as a rare example of an old-line smokestack company that has pulled ahead of its domestic rivals and is successfully meeting growing foreign competition.

"Chuck dragged Goodyear kicking, screaming, biting, and scratching into the radial tire age. . . . He saved this company's apples," says a retired Goodyear executive. Firestone's president agrees, "Chuck Pilliod put Goodyear in a very good position. Maybe that's too nice a thing to say about my competitor, but it's the truth."

In 1983, Charles Pilliod stepped down as Goodyear's chief executive officer. His style of leadership appears to have worked; Goodyear is not only the number one tire maker in the world, it has also overcome Michelin's early lead in radials and blunted that company's move to increase tire manufacturing in the U.S.

Adapted from R. Winter and P. Ingrassia, "Chief's Style and Ideas Help to Keep Goodyear No. 1 in the Radial Age," *The Wall Street Journal* (January 18, 1983).

satisfaction increased, while turnover and absenteeism decreased; the high job-centered style unit reported decreased satisfaction and higher turnover and absenteeism.[10]

The main conclusion reached from these studies was that the effectiveness of a leadership style should not be evaluated solely by productivity measures. Other measures of organizational performance, such as employee job satisfaction, turnover, and absenteeism, should be considered carefully (see chapter 2). In the University of Michigan framework, the results would support a conclusion that employee-centered leader behavior would be the most effective.

The Managerial Grid®

The work of Robert R. Blake and Jane S. Mouton has also been identified with studies that adopted the task-orientation/employee-orientation approach to leadership styles.[11] Using *concern for production* and *concern for people*, Blake and Mouton created the "managerial grid." Shown in exhibit 13-4, the grid focuses on five main leadership styles:

- *The 9, 1 style*, termed task or authoritarian management, stresses a high concern for production and efficiency but a low concern for employees.
- *The 1, 9 style* is the country-club management style, where there is a high concern for employees but a low concern for production.
- *The 1, 1 style* is termed impoverished or laissez-faire management because of low concern on both style dimensions.
- *The 5, 5 style* is called middle-of-the-road management due to the intermediate emphasis placed on concerns for production and employees.
- *The 9, 9 style*, termed team or democratic management, expresses a high concern for both production and employees.

The managerial grid is related to both the Ohio State and Michigan studies. Similar to the Ohio State work, the 9, 9 style (called high initiating structure and high consideration in the Ohio State framework) was suggested as the most effective leadership style. Like the work at the University of Michigan, Blake and Mouton propose that the outcomes of the leader's influence attempts should include increases in both productivity and satisfaction.

Subsequent research on the grid resulted in only moderate support for the superiority of the 9, 9 style. As we will see later in this chapter, other management scholars and practicing managers believe the 9, 9 style tends to oversimplify the complexities of the leadership process. The growing belief was that situational factors surrounding the leadership environment would have to be considered much more thoroughly before a better understanding of leadership could emerge.

Issues and Implications of the Behavioral Approach

A number of important managerial implications can be derived from an analysis of the behavioral approach to leadership:

Leadership style is a multidimensional concept. At least two different leadership styles have been identified and studied, task orientation and employee orientation. The important implication is that varying one's style along each dimension seems to make a wide variety of leader behaviors available to the manager.

A manager's leadership style is flexible. Contrary to what was initially believed, there is no one best style of leadership that consistently leads to high levels of performance. There are too many complex relationships in leadership to make this pos-

Exhibit 13-4
The New
Managerial Grid®

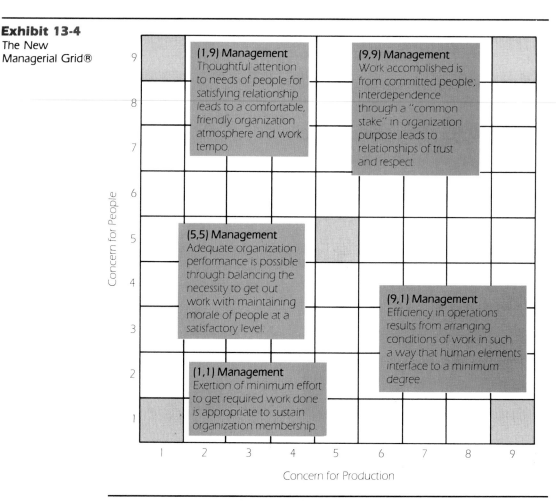

(1,9) Management
Thoughtful attention to needs of people for satisfying relationship leads to a comfortable, friendly organization atmosphere and work tempo.

(9,9) Management
Work accomplished is from committed people; interdependence through a "common stake" in organization purpose leads to relationships of trust and respect.

(5,5) Management
Adequate organization performance is possible through balancing the necessity to get out work with maintaining morale of people at a satisfactory level.

(9,1) Management
Efficiency in operations results from arranging conditions of work in such a way that human elements interface to a minimum degree.

(1,1) Management
Exertion of minimum effort to get required work done is appropriate to sustain organization membership.

Concern for People

Concern for Production

Source: The Managerial Grid figure from *The New Managerial Grid*, by Robert R. Blake and Jane Srygley Mouton. Houston: Gulf Publishing Company, Copyright © 1978, page 11. Reproduced by permission.

sible. One of the many situational factors—one that we discussed earlier in this chapter—is the power base of the leader. As shown in exhibit 13-5, the stronger the leader's power base (legitimate, reward, and coercive), the greater his or her ability to use a task-oriented style.[12] Conversely, the weaker the leader's power base, the more the leader will depend on an employee-oriented style.

Leadership style is a learned managerial skill. The ability of a leader to use task-oriented and employee-oriented styles is probably acquired through experience. Managers not only recognize what works for them in various situations, they usually take note of what leader behaviors work for other managers.

Exhibit 13-5
Power Base and Leadership Styles

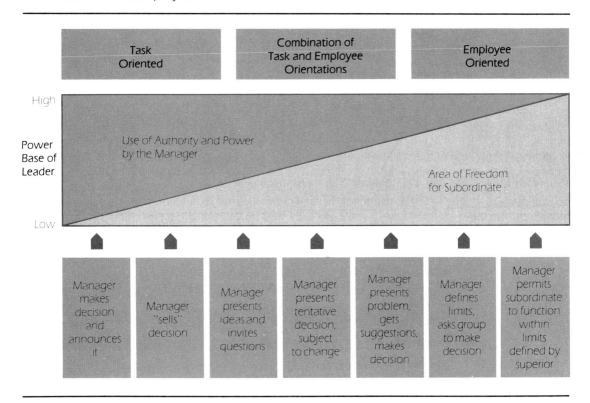

Adapted from Robert Tennenbaum and Warren H. Schmidt, "How to Choose a Leadership Style,"
Harvard Business Review (May-June 1973): 162-80.

The various theories that helped build the behavioral approach to leadership have made a large contribution to the study of leadership. While the main proposition that there was one best leadership style was not supported by research, the recognition that other factors must be considered was very important.

 ## Situational Approaches

The limitations of the trait and behavioral approaches to leadership led researchers to refine and refocus their efforts on the study. The result was an increased emphasis on the important situational factors that affect the leader's attempts at influence. There was the significant recognition that effectiveness in leadership is highly dependent on being able to diagnose and adapt to the dynamics of the particular situation.

This emphasis on diagnosis requires the leader to examine at least four factors. As shown in exhibit 13-6 (a revision of exhibit 13-1), these are managerial characteristics, subordinate characteristics, task characteristics, and organizational characteristics.

The *managerial characteristics* factor recognizes that what the manager brings to the leadership situation is very important. In essence, consideration of managerial characteristics is an application of the trait theories. The leader's personality, needs, past experience and reinforcement, and expectations are important characteristics to consider. A manager with high safety and security needs may use a different leadership style than a manager with high self-actualization needs, even though they may hold similar positions within the organization.

Subordinate characteristics is an important situational concept that was missing from the trait and behavioral approaches. This factor is what subordinates bring to the situation in terms of personality, needs, past experience and reinforcement, and expectations. Consider, for example, the supervisor in the x-ray unit in an outpatient clinic. One of the technicians under the supervisor always exhibits a high level of self-confidence, while another's behavior suggests low self-confidence. Situational approaches to leadership would suggest that the supervisor use different leader behaviors with the two technicians.

Exhibit 13-6
Situational Factors Affecting Leadership

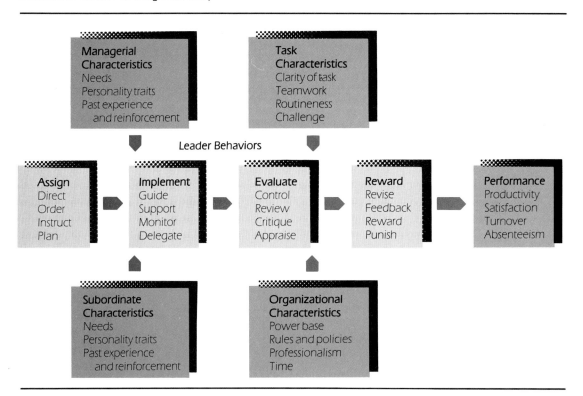

Task characteristics, or the nature of the subordinate's job requirements, will also affect the way the leader behaves. For example, the use of a high task-oriented style of leadership would be more appropriate in jobs that require exact and detailed instructions (assembling a pocket calculator), than in jobs that require more freedom (research chemist). Similarly, one would expect that a high employee-oriented style would work better in situations that require a high degree of teamwork (e.g., physical therapy) than in situations where there is a high degree of independence (sales representative).

Organizational characteristics are aspects within the organization that may alter or constrain the leader's influence. Examples include the leader's power base, the degree to which the organization operates on strict rules and procedures, and the level of professionalism of the employees. Many union contracts, for example, limit the supervisor's ability to reward, punish, or instruct workers. In a similar manner, professional employees such as accountants, nurses, and engineers may require less direction than workers on an assembly line.

This list of situational factors, although not exhaustive, should point out that leadership is indeed a complex process. Two theories—Fiedler's contingency model and the path-goal theory—illustrate how situational factors have been incorporated into the study of leadership.

Fiedler's Contingency Model

Fred E. Fiedler was one of the first to develop a situational approach to leadership.[13] In the contingency model (known also as the contingency theory), he proposed that a leader's effectiveness depends on the interaction between the leader's behavior and certain situational factors.

Contingency Theory Components

Five major components make up Fiedler's model: (1) leadership style assessment; (2) task structure; (3) leader/member relations; (4) the leader's position power; and (5) effectiveness. The first identifies the *motivational* aspect of the leader, while the remaining factors relate to the *situational favorableness* for the leader.

Leadership Style Assessment   The main variable used in the contingency model to assess leadership style is called the least preferred coworker (LPC). With the use of a questionnaire, the leader is asked to describe the person with whom he or she has worked least effectively on a recent task. The model suggests that a low LPC score— an unfavorable evaluation of the least preferred co-worker—indicates that the leader is ready to reject those with whom he or she has difficulty working. Therefore, the lower the LPC score, the greater the tendency for the leader to be *task oriented.* On the other hand, a high LPC score—a favorable evaluation of the least preferred co-worker—indicates a willingness to perceive even the worst co-worker as having some positive characteristics. Thus, the higher the LPC score, the greater the tendency for the leader to use an *employee-oriented* style.

CROCK

CROCK by Rechin and Parker © 1982 Field Enterprises, Inc., Courtesy Field Newspaper Syndicate.

Task Structure   This first situational factor concerns the nature of the subordinate's task. It measures the degree the task is routine (structured) or complex (unstructured). For example, an accounting clerk in a retail store may work on a fairly structured task, while the manager of planning for a health maintenance organization probably works on an unstructured task.

Leader/Member Relations   As the second situational factor, this variable measures the relationship between the leader and subordinates. It is the degree of confidence, trust, and respect subordinates have in the leader. It is evaluated along a continuum of good to poor, and the main idea is that the better the relationship between leader and subordinate, the easier it will be for the leader to exercise influence. When the relationship is poor, the leader may have to resort to special behaviors or favors to get good performance.

Leader Position Power   The final situational factor concerns the extent of the leader's power base. As discussed earlier in this chapter, this variable refers to the degree that the leader possesses, through legitimate, reward, and coercive power, the ability to influence the behavior of the subordinate. According to Fiedler, position power can vary from strong (vice president of manufacturing) to weak (committee chairperson).

Effectiveness   The major outcome variable in the contingency theory is effectiveness. In other words, the focus of this situational approach is on task or goal accomplishment, as opposed to job satisfaction.

Contingency Theory Framework

The various components of the contingency theory have been combined into a situational framework, which exhibit 13-7 shows. The combination of the three situational factors—task structure, leader/member relations, and leader position power—leads to an examination of an eight-cell framework that varies along a continuum of *situational favorableness*.

As the model indicates, the recommended leadership style also varies with the certainty of the situation. A task-oriented leadership style will be more effective than

Exhibit 13-7
Fiedler's Contingency Model

Cell		1	2	3	4	5	6	7	8
Situational Factors	**Leader/Member Relations**	Good	Good	Good	Good	Poor	Poor	Poor	Poor
	Task Structure	Structured	Structured	Unstructured	Unstructured	Structured	Structured	Unstructured	Unstructured
	Leader Position Power	Strong	Weak	Strong	Weak	Strong	Weak	Strong	Weak
Situational Favorableness		Favorable			Moderately Favorable			Unfavorable	
Situational Certainty		Very Certain Situation			Moderately Certain Situation			Very Uncertain Situation	
Recommended Leadership style		Task	Task	Task	Employee	Employee	Employee	Task	Task

Adapted from Fred E. Fiedler, *A Theory of Leadership Effectiveness* (New York: McGraw-Hill, 1967), p. 37.

an employee-oriented style under extreme conditions—that is, where the situation is either highly certain or highly uncertain. For example, a task-oriented style would be recommended for a manager of a large restaurant (cell 1). The tasks are highly structured for the waiters, waitresses, chefs, and support staff. Moreover, if the owner backs the manager's decisions (or if the manager is the owner), the position power is strong. Finally, if the manager gains the respect and trust of the subordinates through fair treatment and is able to gain significant pay increases, the leader-member relations may be good. Under these conditions, a task-oriented style is preferred to an employee-oriented style in order to achieve high performance.

An employee-oriented style is more appropriate for moderate levels of certainty and situational favorableness. For example, in many research laboratories, the tasks of the scientists are quite unstructured and the leader may have weak position power, but leader-member relations are good (cell 4). Since research scientists prefer to follow their own creative tendencies as opposed to being told what to do by the research director, an employee-oriented style would be recommended.

Issues and Implications with the Contingency Model

Possibly the most important implication for managers of the contingency model is the relationship between the leader and the situation. On one hand, the manager's leadership style is not only considered to be unidimensional, but because it is part of the leader's characteristics, it is a rigid behavioral quality. This has led supporters of Fiedler's model to suggest that leader effectiveness is a function of fitting the manager to the job. In other words, since the leader's style is rigid, for the highest level of effectiveness one must first diagnose the situation and then select the manager whose style fits the favorableness of that situation. Thus, task-oriented leaders would find themselves placed in situations represented by cells 1, 2, 3, 7, and 8 in exhibit 13-7, while employee-oriented leaders would be selected to manage in situations represented in cells 4, 5, and 6.

Since its introduction, Fiedler's model has been the subject of a growing body of research.[14] As one would expect, a number of significant criticisms have developed.[15] These include questions of whether managerial style is indeed unidimensional and rigid, what the LPC scale really measures, and about the interaction between leadership style and the situation. For example, it is highly probable that an employee-oriented style can change leader-member relations from poor to good. If this happens—as in cell 5—the situation can change to one represented by cell 1. Cell 1, however, requires a task-oriented style. Managers with the employee-oriented style would, thus, have worked themselves out of their jobs! According to the model, they must be moved to other situations where their style would be more appropriate.

Even with these and other major concerns, Fiedler's contingency model has proven to be a significant addition to the study of leadership in organizations. With its emphasis on diagnosing the situation, the model has emphasized the importance of considering other factors that can affect the leader's attempt to influence the behavior of subordinates.

The Manager's Job

Robert C. Hazard
and
Gerald W. Petitt
of Quality Inns

Contemporary management thought suggests that a manager's skills and leadership style should be linked to the life-cycle stage of the product line he or she is managing. It is claimed, for example, that an entrepreneur who brings a product from, say, a 2 percent share of market to 20 percent in a few years is the wrong person to manage the line once it has become mature. At that point, someone whose style emphasizes cutting costs and increasing productivity, rather than risk taking and innovating, has to move in. The entrepreneur could then be placed in charge of another fledging product line.

Consider the case of Robert C. Hazard and Gerald W. Petitt. Between 1974 and 1980, the two men brought the Best Western chain from 800 hotels to over 2,500. They expanded into 18 countries and set up one of the most sophisticated computerized reservations systems around. But during 1980, the hotel owners' board of directors were ready to put the brakes on growth, while Hazard and Petitt continued to push full steam ahead. The problem was that neither Hazard nor Petitt possessed the political skills or leadership qualities to work with a confrontation board or in a non-growth situation.

Quality Inns, by contrast, emerged from several years of losses into financial stability in 1977. A recent merger further enhanced the company's cash position. When Quality Inns' president resigned in 1980, the company immediately went after Hazard. The board was different, and more importantly, as *Business Week* reports, the whole company saw itself as being in the early stages of its life cycle. Thus, the same entrepreneurial spirit that made the Hazard-Petitt team so unpopular at Best Western is making these men and their leadership styles welcome by the people of Quality Inns.

Adapted from "Matching Managers to a Company's Life-Cycle," *Business Week* (February 23, 1981): 62.

A Path-Goal Theory

A second situational approach to leadership was recently developed from the work of Martin G. Evans and Robert J. House.[16] Named the path-goal theory, the model attempts to study leadership effectiveness in a variety of situations. In brief, the model suggests that leaders are effective by means of their impact on employee motivation. It is termed path-goal because it focuses on how the leader influences the perceptions of work goals or rewards of subordinates and also focuses on the paths, or behaviors, that lead to the successful accomplishment of work goals.

Path-Goal Components

As shown in exhibit 13-8, the expectancy theory motivational approach is the foundation for the path-goal theory. From our discussion in chapter 12, recall that the expectancy theory suggests that employees will be motivated to perform on the job when: (1) they believe they can accomplish a specific task (expectancy); (2) rewards are given that relate to the person's level of performance (instrumentality); and (3) the rewards are of value to the person (valence). Path-goal theory states that certain situational factors can adversely affect the employee's perceptions of expectancy, instrumentality, or valence. When this happens, motivation is reduced. If the leader can help remove, or clarify, these perceptions, then motivation will improve, along with increased effectiveness.

Beyond expectancy, instrumentality, and valence, there are three main components of the path-goal approach to leadership—situational factors, leader behaviors, and outcomes.

Exhibit 13-8
Path-Goal Theory of Leadership

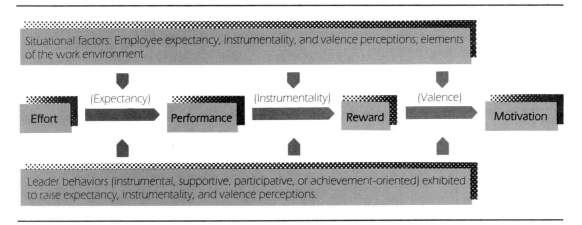

Situational Factors   Two situational factors are considered important in path-goal theory, subordinate characteristics and elements of the work environment. The key *subordinate characteristics* include ability, self-confidence, and needs. In the theory's framework, ability is the degree to which the person believes he or she can do the work (expectancy), self-confidence concerns the degree to which the employee believes that he or she has control over what happens to himself or herself (instrumentality), and needs are the internal desires of the individual (valence).

The *elements of the work environment* involve such factors as the employee's task, relationships with co-workers, and the nature of the reward system. For example, an employee working on a structured task (nurse's aide) may have clearer expectancy perceptions than one performing an unstructured task (physicist). In the same manner, co-workers who interfere with the employee's activities—through constant goofing-off and frequent interruptions—can lower expectancy and instrumentality perceptions. Finally, a complete, performance-based reward system can result in higher instrumentality and valence perceptions.

Leader Behaviors   One of the major contributions of path-goal theory has been the identification of a more complete set of leader behaviors. In particular, four, not two, leadership styles have been most frequently studied through path-goal theory—instrumental, supportive, participative, and achievement-oriented.

Instrumental behavior is the planning, task assignment, monitoring, and control aspects of the leader's behavior. It is similar to the traditional dimension of task orientation in that the leader's style emphasizes letting subordinates know what is expected of them. An instrumental leadership style can be used to increase an employee's effort-to-performance perception (expectancy) that had been low due to ability problems or because of an ambiguous or unstructured task.

Supportive behavior includes giving consideration to the needs of subordinates, displaying concern for their well-being, and creating a friendly and pleasant work environment. For instance, employees with high social needs (valence) may relate more positively to a supportive leadership style. Or, in a boring-type task such as janitorial services, the leader can make the path from performance-to-rewards (instrumentality) easier to travel by being supportive of subordinates.

Participative behavior, like supportive behavior, can be considered within the larger classification of employee-oriented leadership style. It is characterized by the sharing of information, emphasis on working with subordinates, and use of their ideas in making managerial decisions. A subordinate who shows ability to do the work and/or is highly self-confident (high expectancy) will probably react more favorably to a leader's participative style rather than an instrumental style.

Achievement-oriented behavior is setting challenging goals, expecting subordinates to perform at the highest levels, and continually seeking improvement in performance. The leader wants good performance—a task-oriented type of leader behavior—but at the same time displays confidence in the ability of the subordinates to do a good job. An achievement-oriented style would work well with employees who have high ego needs (valence). On the other hand, this style can help clarify an employee's low performance-to-reward perception (instrumentality), by working with him or her to seek high goal accomplishment.

Outcomes   Unlike Fiedler's model, the path-goal approach stresses the concern for outcomes that benefit the organization (productivity) and the employee (job satisfaction). Because of this emphasis on multi-outcome measures, the path-goal approach is a much more complete—and, maybe, more realistic—situational theory of leadership than the contingency model. Exhibit 13-9 presents a set of typical situations.

Issues and Implications of the Path-Goal Theory

Even though the path-goal theory of leadership is of recent vintage, it has made a number of contributions to both the study and practice of management.[17] The more important implications for the manager include:

A manager's leadership style may include more than two dimensions. The results of the behavioral approach suggested that a manager's leadership style was multidimensional, involving the dimensions of task orientation and employee orientation. Path-goal theory, however, promotes the position that leadership style is even *more* complex. The important factor for managers to consider is that their style of leadership is neither unidimensional and rigid as proposed by Fiedler, nor as simple as being task- and/or employee-oriented.

Effective leadership is a function of proper situational diagnosis. By far the most important implication of path-goal theory is that before leaders use a particular style of leadership, they must diagnose the situation. Since improved effectiveness comes from increasing the motivation of subordinates, the manager should first analyze the factors that enhance or constrain the level of motivation of the subordinate. The manager can then choose the necessary behavior.

Exhibit 13-9
Examples of Path-Goal Theory of Leadership

Situation	Important Expectancy-Theory Perceptions	Recommended Leadership Style for High Performance
1. Employee with low ability to perform	Low expectancy	Instrumental style
2. Highly capable employee	High expectancy	Supportive style
3. Employee exhibiting low self-confidence	Low instrumentality	Instrumental and supportive styles
4. Employee exhibiting high self-confidence	High instrumentality	Participative style
5. Employee working on an unstructured task	Low expectancy and instrumentality	Instrumental and supportive style
6. Employee working on a structured task	High expectancy and instrumentality	Achievement-oriented and supportive style
7. Employee with a low achievement need	Low valence	Achievement-oriented and participative style

The leader is not the only source of influence on the subordinate. The classical or traditional view of leadership has suggested ways in which the leader can influence the subordinate toward goal accomplishment.[18] Path-goal theory also supports this notion, but adds that other sources of influence exist in the work environment. For example, individuals who exhibit high levels of self-confidence and/or have the necessary ability to do the job effectively, may not need much guidance from the leader. In essence, they are self-motivated to perform at high levels. Similarly, highly skilled or trained employees depend more on their education and experience to influence their work than on the behavior of the leader. In these and similar examples, path-goal theory would suggest the use of supportive and/or participative behavior by the leader.

Managers should act with caution in adopting the path-goal approach. For one, due to the relatively recent introduction of the theory, there is a lack of supporting research.[19] In addition, because path-goal theory uses expectancy theory as a basis, the criticisms of expectancy theory, discussed in chapter 12, still apply. Yet, overall, managers would do well to consider path-goal theory, if for no other reason than it has identified key leadership styles and suggested when and how these behaviors should be used.

Contemporary Issues in Leadership

The study of leadership in organizations has made significant strides during the last twenty years. Much of this progress is the result of both management scholars and practicing managers recognizing and emphasizing the important factors that can lead to improved effectiveness.

As in the case of many scientific fields, the various theoretical approaches can be applied to a number of contemporary issues. These applications include leadership in the international realm, relationships with superiors and peers, and learning how to be a leader.

Leadership in the International Realm

As illustrated throughout this book, management is *international,* and cultural differences are important concerns in leadership situations. Culture influences people and their needs, wants, aspirations, and behavior whether they are managers or not.

A recent study of the cross-cultural aspect of management, involving over 3,000 managers in 12 countries, reported some interesting findings on the motivating needs of managers and their leadership style preferences.[20]

■ Even with the supposed vast differences in cultures, there is a remarkable consistency across the different countries concerning many of the needs.

■ What are the dominant motivating needs of these managers? Clearly the higher-level needs—particularly self-actualization and independence—are most salient. This supports Ghiselli's findings discussed earlier in this chapter.

■ What needs are of less importance to the managers? Again, there is some consistency which suggests that the lower-level needs related to money, security, and affection (social) are of less importance.

■ The need for leadership, which may be considered as an ego, status, esteem need in Maslow's framework, was moderately important to the sampled managers. It appears that achieving a leadership position is not an end in itself, but a means whereby the more important self-actualization and independence needs get satisfied.

While these findings represent only a small sample, they do suggest some important differences and similarities about leadership in the international realm.

And what are the leadership styles preferred by managers in different countries? A common stereotype is that German managers use more task orientation than their U. S. counterparts.[21] In fact, the opposite is true. German managers are not only less task-oriented than U.S. managers, they also exhibit greater employee orientation.

The reasons for this focus on the German concept of collective responsibility. Under German law, nonmanagement personnel have equal representation on two management boards, the board of directors and the board of managers. Because of this, German managers are more concerned with the views of their workers and are more sympathetic to workers' efforts to assert their rights. Having this representation and being better informed about the organization may be a reason why strikes and walkouts are not as common as in the U.S.

Also, German managers, because of their attitudes toward authority, are able to issue an order and assume it will be carried out without close monitoring. In the U. S., we tend to place more emphasis on individual capabilities and independence; consequently, U. S. managers are more inclined to be task-oriented—to monitor the behavior of subordinates and use monetary incentives (or punishment) more frequently.

Japanese managers report a leadership style profile that is similar to German managers', but for different reasons. In Japan, there is a greater emphasis on achieving harmony, cooperation, and teamwork than in most countries. Because of this, managing in Japan is rarely accomplished with the use of high task orientation. Instead, consultation, with emphasis on getting the opinions of most workers, is stressed to the point that even low-level supervisors get involved in the planning and policy formulation processes. Getting everyone involved before actions are taken results in less conflict and resistance to change. Such a process, however, is time consuming and may result in decision delay.

Another important factor is the state of economic development. In developed countries, because individual initiative is such a dominant assumption, managers need not heavily use task orientation. This may explain why managers in such developing countries as India and Latin America place a strong emphasis on continued use of task orientation. They may feel that subordinates have less ability and little to offer other than muscle. Initiative, therefore, comes from the task orientation of the leader.

This discussion is not suggesting that any one leadership style is better than any other. What is important is what works within a particular culture. Successful managers in the U.S., Germany, and Japan are those individuals who have correctly diagnosed and adapted to their situations.

Relationships with Superiors and Peers

Throughout this chapter, the emphasis has been on how managers can influence the behavior of subordinates toward better performance. While this is certainly one of the manager's major roles, the manager's relationships with superiors and peers are equally important. The key question is how can managers influence the behavior of people they do not supervise?

The answer is complex and can involve many different approaches. For our purposes, we will focus on influence from personal and positional sources. *Personal* sources of influence concern relationships with superiors and peers, or, more simply, how the manager may satisfy important needs of others so that improved interpersonal relations result.

Drawing on motivational theories, managers should consider at least four need-satisfying behaviors. First, the manager can get work done or help a superior or peer solve a difficult problem. This not only establishes the manager as a dependable person, it satisfies certain *physiological/safety needs* of the other person. Second, the manager can get to know the superior or peer, in both formal and informal activities, and *social needs* are satisfied. Third, the manager can treat the other person with respect, which can help the person satisfy the *esteem need*. Finally, by observing and interacting with superiors and peers, the manager can learn effective behaviors. This activity will help satisfy the other person's *self-actualization needs*.

A manager can also influence the behaviors of superiors and peers because of the importance of his or her *position* in the organization. This positional influence can originate from at least three sources—controlling uncertainty, substitutability, and centrality.[22]

No one likes to be taken by surprise, including managers. Surprise (i.e., *uncertainties*) can create disruptions, confusion, and lower performance. If a manager can control the effects of uncertain events so that they do not affect others, he or she can have a significant level of influence. The maintenance manager can prevent costly plant shutdowns through an effective preventative maintenance system; the market research or planning manager can successfully detect and monitor environmental events; the manager of personnel or the legal department can shield line managers from constant governmental intervention.

Another source of positional influence is the lack of *substitutability*—that is, the manager controls activities or resources that no one else in the organization can. In such situations, the manager can have a tremendous effect on the performance of other units. For example, purchasing managers control the purchase of raw materials and equipment for a manufacturing plant, and the director of the x-ray unit in a hospital has control over this much-needed diagnostic activity. The x-ray unit director can affect the activities of physicians, nurses, and even the accounting department.

The final source of positional influence concerns the degree to which the manager's activities are interlinked into the organization. This *centrality* relates to how important the manager is in producing the products and services of the organization. The more central the activity, the greater the level of influence. For example, a hospital cannot operate for long without nurses, nor can a manufacturer of pocket calculators function without computer chips.

Consider the case of Tandem Computers, a Silicon Valley computer company.[23] Known for its relaxed approach—the company has a swimming pool and tennis courts on its grounds and sponsors a beer party each Friday—the company also has adopted an approach to management and leadership that may be interesting to other firms. Among other things, its philosophy states:

- All people are good.
- People, workers, management, and company are all the same thing.
- Every person in the company must understand the essence of the business.
- Every employee must benefit from the company's success.
- You must create an environment where all of the above can happen.

Whether this philosophy will be a major contributor to the company's success remains to be seen. Right now, employees are enjoying the benefits of explosive growth.

Learning to Be a Leader

Throughout this chapter, we have suggested that leadership is primarily a learned quality. Given this situation, how can the aspiring manager learn to become a more effective leader? The experience of many managers suggests four points to study:

Learn from experience, practice, and observation. If leadership is primarily a learned quality, then it benefits the manager to participate in as many learning experiences as possible. Examples include mentoring (see chapter 1), practice, and observation of the behavior of other leaders. Through these and other learning experiences, the manager can develop knowledge in the important interpersonal, informational, and decisional roles effective leaders perform.[24]

Learn from continuing education and training and development programs. In-house or outside programs, coupled with job rotation (see chapter 10), provide an opportunity to develop many of the technical, human, conceptual, and diagnostic skills required of a leader.

Learn from subordinates. For too long, management scholars assumed that the influence process in leadership was one-way—from the leader to the subordinate. In reality, the influence process is two-way; subordinates can significantly influence the behavior of the leader.[25] There are at least two ways the manager can learn from subordinates. First, make note of what behaviors are effective, not only in different situations, but with different subordinates. The situational approaches have stressed this point strongly. Second, continually viewing employees from a theory X framework ignores the fact that many times subordinates are equally, if not more, skilled in the work being performed than the manager. If given the opportunity, employees can teach the manager better ways of performing the department's work, which may lead to greater effectiveness.

Know yourself. Many times, behavior as a manager is influenced by personal characteristics. For example, in the last chapter, we emphasized the importance of needs as energizing factors in motivation. This framework would be just as valuable a mechanism for self-analysis as it is for understanding the behavior of subordinates. A manager with high social needs—one who is seeking respect and friendship from others—may use a different leadership style than a manager with high ego needs—one who strives for recognition and status. We will cover this point further in chapter 20.

The key emphasis is for the manager always to be aware of learning experiences. With today's complex environments and organizations, managers cannot afford to stand pat in their approach to leadership.

 ## POINTS TO CONSIDER
An Emphasis on Managerial Skills

1. **The manager must understand the strengths and limitations of his or her power base.**
   The ability to influence others is strongly founded on the strength of the leader's power base. A leader who functions with all six power factors—legitimate, reward, coercive, expert, referent, and informational—is in the best position to influence subordinates, but such a situation is often more ideal than real. Most leaders find themselves in managerial situations in which they must attempt to influence others with a limited power base. In these cases, try to strengthen what you have and acquire power from other sources.[26]

2. **A manager's style of leadership is not infinitely flexible.**
   We have stressed, through situational theories, that a manager should try to adapt his or her behavior to the conditions of the situation. This, however, does not suggest that successful managers can adapt to *every* situation that confronts them. The fact is that most managers have leadership styles that can be adaptable to many situations, but not all. Requiring primarily human skills, leadership is at least partially shaped at an early age. Training and experience can help managers expand their sets of behaviors. In other words, it is probably as incorrect to believe in a "one best way" as it is to think that a manager can be "all things to all people."

3. **Leader behavior includes both style and reward components.**
   Literature in both the academic and practitioner fields has stressed the importance of leadership styles in the influence process. Leadership style, as we have seen it, does not totally define the managerial situation. Exhibiting task- and employee-oriented styles in a balance is appropriate for getting the work done. Equally important is what subordinates get for what they do—the rewards for work.[27] Rewarding subordinates is just as important as telling them what to do and being friendly and approachable.

4. **Leadership is a team-oriented activity.**
   The manager/subordinate/peer/superior unit establishes the most basic organizational team for goal accomplishment. As such, it is important for the manager to maintain good relations with each group.[28] Emphasize influence, coalitions, communication, and integrity rather than manipulation, politics, lack of trust, and information distortion and/or suppression.

5. **Effective leadership depends heavily on developing good diagnostic skills.**
   We know that leadership involves a complex interaction among personal, task, organizational, and environmental forces and conditions. Before a manager can approach a problem, he or she must be able to identify the key interacting variables. This calls for accurate and well-developed diagnostic skills.

6.   **The manager should look at each task, project, or position as a learning experience.**
The manager or future manager should view new activities and experiences for their long-term
learning impact, not so much from the perspective of the short-term problems that must be
faced. It is rare that a good manager would say he or she didn't learn something useful from
both challenging and boring assignments. The key is this: don't go into a new job with a
preconceived notion about what you will face and how you will react; keep an open mind and be
willing to adapt, because this is when you learn the most.

 # SUMMARY FOR THE MANAGER

1.   Leadership is the process of influencing others toward goal accomplishment. The most important aspect for managers is that leadership is an ongoing, everyday activity that involves power,
desired outcomes, and other people. A person can be a leader without being a manager, and
vice versa. To be both a manager and a leader, the person needs to be given the title by the
organization and must be able to influence subordinates through behavior.

2.   Influence in leadership is based on the concept of power. The power to influence can originate
from organizational sources (legitimate, reward, and coercive) or from the individual's particular characteristics (expert and referent). The greater the leader's power base, the greater the
capacity to influence others. Leaders who recognize that their organizationally based power is
not as strong as desired may attempt to compensate by acquiring power in other areas. In most
cases, leaders attempt to become expert in their fields to enhance their power bases.

3.   Trait theories, which were the first real scientific analyses of leadership, sought to determine if
there are any individual characteristics or traits that distinguish successful from less successful
leaders. If these select traits exist, then they could be used in future managerial selections. The
results suggested, albeit weakly, that successful leaders are more intelligent and decisive, report
higher achievement and self-actualization needs, and have good communication skills. These
results, however, were not consistent across different organizations, which decreased the
importance of trait theories in the study and practice of leadership.

4.   Behavioral theories came after the trait approach, and emphasized what the leader does in a
leadership situation—leadership style. While at first the one best leadership style was sought, it
became clear that no such style exists. For the manager, the behavioral approach made three
important contributions: (a) leadership style is multidimensional; (b) style is flexible; and (c)
styles of leadership are learned behaviors.

5.   Fiedler's contingency model, the first of the situational approaches to leadership, analyzed the
relationship between leadership style and three situational factors: task structure; leader-member relations; and position power of the leader. Task-oriented style was suggested as more
appropriate when the situation is either good or poor, while employee-oriented style is best
when the situation is only moderately good for the leader. Fiedler's suggestion that a manager's
leadership style is both unidimensional and rigid undermined the usefulness of the theory.

6.   The path-goal theory, based on the expectancy theory of motivation, provided a more complex
framework to study the interactions between the leader, the subordinate, and the situation.
Since one of the main functions of the leader is to motivate subordinates, path-goal theory
suggested that if the leader, through style, can remove some of the barriers to motivation,
enhanced performance will result.

7.   Culture is an important consideration in leadership. Across a number of countries, there are more similarities than differences in what motivates managers. In particular, higher-level needs (ego and self-actualization) are more important contributors to managerial motivation than the lower-level needs (social and safety/security).

8.   Relationships with superiors and peers require managers to attempt influence. Two approaches are most widely used: personal (interpersonal relationships with others that result in satisfying an important need of the other person), and positional (controlling uncertainty, substitutability, and the centrality or importance of the position).

9.   Effectiveness as a leader depends on the ability of the manager to learn new skills and roles from a variety of sources, including experience, practice, observation, training programs, subordinate activities, and self-knowledge. Since managers can learn from boring jobs as well as exciting ones, they must keep an open mind and be adaptable.

 # REVIEW AND DISCUSSION QUESTIONS

1.   Discuss the relationship between power and influence.
2.   Under what conditions can the behavior of an informal leader be dysfunctional to the organization?
3.   Why was trait theory unsuccessful in predicting leadership effectiveness?
4.   What is the relationship between the style dimensions of task and employee orientation and McGregor's theory X and theory Y?
5.   According to Fiedler, how can the organization engineer the job to fit the manager?
6.   Is a manager's leadership style flexible or rigid?
7.   How does mentoring relate to learning to be a leader?
8.   Besides the leader's behavior, what organizational factors can have a significant influence on the employee's performance?
9.   Why must one study the leader's reward behavior in any analysis of leadership?
10. Why is it important for the manager to develop good diagnostic skills in order to become an effective leader?

NOTES

1.   R. M. Stogdill and B. M. Bass, *Stodgill's Handbook of Leadership,* rev. ed. (New York: Free Press, 1981).
2.   See J. R. French and B. H. Raven, "The Bases of Social Power," in D. Cartwright, *Studies in Social Power* (Ann Arbor: University of Michigan Press, 1959); and B. H. Raven, "A Comparative Analysis of Power and Preference," in J. T. Tedeschi, ed., *Perspectives on Social Power,* (Chicago: Aldine, 1974).
3.   Tom Wolfe, *The Right Stuff* (New York: Farrer-Strauss-Giroux, 1979), p. 24.
4.   See R. M. Stogdill, "Personal Factors Associated with Leadership: A Survey of the Literature," *Journal of Applied Psychology* (January 1948): 35-71; and Stogdill, *Handbook of Leadership,* pp. 74-75.
5.   See C. G. Burck, "A Group Profile of the Fortune 500 Chief Executive," *Fortune* (May 1976): 172-77; and D. C. McClelland and R. E. Boyatzis, "Leadership Motive Pattern and Long-Term Success in Management," *Journal of Applied Psychology* (December 1982): 737-43.
6.   E. E. Ghiselli, *Explorations in Managerial Talent* (Glenview, Ill.: Scott, Foresman and Company, 1971).

7. M. W. McCall and M. M. Lombardo, "What Makes a Top Executive," *Psychology Today* (February 1983): 26-31.

8. E. A. Fleishman, "Twenty Years of Consideration and Structure," in *Current Developments in the Study of Leadership*, E. A. Fleishman and J. G. Hunt, eds. (Carbondale, Ill.: Southern Illinois University Press, 1973), pp. 1-37.

9. See R. J. House, A. C. Filley, and S. Kerr, "Relation of Leader Consideration and Initiating Structure to R and D Subordinates' Satisfaction," *Administrative Science Quarterly* (March 1971): 19-30; and A. K. Korman, "Consideration, Initiating Structure, and Organizational Criteria—A Review," *Personnel Psychology* (Winter 1976): 349-61.

10. R. Likert, *The Human Organization* (New York: McGraw-Hill, 1976).

11. R. R. Blake and J. S. Mouton, *The New Managerial Grid* (Houston: Gulf Publishing, 1978), p. 11.

12. R. Tannenbaum and W. H. Schmidt, "How to Choose a Leadership Pattern," *Harvard Business Review* (May-June 1973): 162-80.

13. F. Fiedler, *A Theory of Leadership Effectiveness* (New York: McGraw-Hill, 1967).

14. See G. Graen, J. B. Orris, and K. W. Alvares, "Contingency Model of Leadership Effectiveness: Some Experimental Results," *Journal of Applied Psychology* (June 1971): 196-201; and J. T. McMahon, "The Contingency Theory: Logic and Method Revisited," *Personnel Psychology* (December 1972): 697-710.

15. See J. Stinson and L. Tracy, "Some Disturbing Characteristics of the LPC Score," *Personnel Psychology* (1974): 477-85; and R. Vecchio, "An Empirical Examination of the Validity of Fiedler's Model," *Organizational Behavior and Human Performance* (June 1977): 180-206.

16. See R. J. House, "A Path-Goal Theory of Leader Effectiveness," *Administrative Science Quarterly* (1971): 321-32; and M. G. Evans, "The Effects of Supervisory Behavior on the Path-Goal Relationship," *Organizational Behavior and Human Performance* (May 1970): 277-98.

17. See R. J. House and T. R. Mitchell, "Path-Goal Theory of Leadership," *Journal of Contemporary Business* (Autumn 1974): 81-98; and A. D. Szilagyi and H. P. Sims, "An Exploration of the Path-Goal Theory of Leadership in a Health Care Environment," *Academy of Management Journal* (December 1974): 622-34.

18. S. Kerr, "Toward a Contingency Theory of Leadership Based Upon Consideration and Initiating Structure Literature," *Organizational Behavior and Human Performance* (1974): 62-82.

19. House and Mitchell, "Path-Goal Theory of Leadership."

20. B. M. Bass and P. C. Burger, *Assessment of Managers—An International Comparison* (New York: Free Press, 1979).

21. W. Grunwald and W. F. Bernthal, "Controversy in German Management: The Harzburg Experience," *Academy of Management Review* (April 1983): 233-41.

22. D. J. Hickson, D. S. Pugh, and D. C. Pheysey, "A Strategic Contingencies Theory of Intra-organizational Power," *Administrative Science Quarterly* (1971): 216-27.

23. M. Magnet, "Managing by Mystique at Tandem Computers," *Fortune* (June 28, 1982): 84-91.

24. See J. P. Kotter, *The General Managers* (New York: Free Press, 1982); and T. Levitt, "The Managerial Merry-Go-Round," *Harvard Business Review* (July-August 1974): 120-28.

25. See C. N. Greene, "The Reciprocal Nature of Influence Between Leader and Subordinate Performance," *Journal of Applied Psychology* (April 1975): 187-93; and A. Lowin and J. Craig, "The Influence of Level of Performance on Managerial Style," *Organizational Behavior and Human Performance* (1968): 440-58.

26. J. P. Kotter, "Power, Dependence, and Effective Management," *Harvard Business Review* (July-August 1979): 125-36.

27. P. M. Podsakoff, W. D. Todor, and R. Skov, "Effects of Leader Contingent and Noncontingent Reward and Punishment Behaviors on Subordinate Performance and Satisfaction," *Academy of Management Journal* (December 1982): 810-21.

28. N. C. Hill, *Increasing Managerial Effectiveness* (Reading, Mass.: Addison-Wesley, 1979), pp. 84-100.

Leadership
The Computer Software Department

Jill Prince is manager of software systems for a large international manufacturer of plastic products. Jill's department consists of eighteen computer programmers and systems analysts responsible for developing computer application systems (i.e., payroll, accounting, and financial systems) for the corporation's many divisions. All of Jill's subordinates are college degreed and classified as professional. Jill has undergraduate and graduate degrees in computer science and has been with the company for over six years.

It was almost 7 p.m. on a Friday evening in late December, nearly two hours past her usual time to go home. In her office, she sat staring out the window with a very concerned look, trying to piece together what had happened over the past two months. She kept trying to understand why the performance of her unit had dropped off so dramatically during this time.

Her first thoughts recalled a three-day management training seminar she attended, sponsored by the company, but led by a well-known behavioral consultant. The most vivid experience involved a session on leadership style where she completed a self-report questionnaire that was supposed to measure her style of leadership on two dimensions: task orientation and employee orientation. The results—she scored high on task orientation but very low on employee orientation—were a surprise to her. She had always thought of herself as very people oriented. She remembered that the seminar leader suggested that the most effective leadership style was one that was high on both task and employee orientation.

The timing of the leadership seminar was of particular importance to Jill due to the problems she was having with a number of people in her department. The busy year-end season was at hand, which meant a big push by the divisions to have new analyses programs on-line. Many of her problems centered on the performance of her subordinates. She felt that she could divide her people almost equally into two groups: those who consistently performed above standard, and those whose work was usually late and/or done poorly.

Two subordinates seemed to her to illustrate the behaviors of the two groups. First, there was Jack Domec, who had worked as a systems analyst for the past three years. Jack was dependable, quality conscious, and Jill could count on him to put out 110 percent effort. On the other hand, there was Art Roman, a computer programmer who had been working a little over two years. In Jill's opinion, Art spent too much time goofing off when work needed to be done, was overly concerned with socializing with fellow workers over coffee, and was usually the first one out the door at quitting time each day. Because Art's performance rarely reached standard, Jill warned him many times about his performance and the effect on his yearly evaluation and potential for advancement. These warnings usually had an effect on him for a few days, but his old habits returned.

The management training convinced Jill that what she needed to do to improve the performance of people like Art was to increase her employee-oriented behavior toward them—in other words, to conform to the ideal of being high on both leader style dimensions. As a result, she made a special effort to be more open and friendly to people like Art, to take more interest in their personal lives, and to try to be more sympathetic about the constant pressures for more work out of the department.

As Jill sat looking out the window, she was

both upset and puzzled. Her attempt at being more employee-oriented was a flop. Not only had Art's performance not changed, but many high-performing subordinates, including Jack, were showing dramatic drops in their quality and quantity of performance. The drop in performance couldn't have come at a worse time. Her direct supervisor and many of her divisional contacts were on her back to improve her unit's performance. She sat there wondering what to do next.

Questions for Discussion

1. Evaluate Jill's experience at the management training program.
2. Why was her attempt to be more employee-oriented a failure?
3. What change in Jill's behavior is needed to improve the performance of the unit?

Leadership

Texas Commerce Bancshares

Texas Commerce Bancshares, the multi-billion dollar bank-holding company of Houston, is a dynamic organization that has, like the Texas economy, boomed during the last ten years. *Fortune* says much of the bank's success can be traced to its dynamic chief executive, Ben F. Love, fifty-seven, who has turned Texas Commerce into one of the best performers among the country's banking organizations.

Fortune declares that success for Love means growth, which he has pursued with the zeal of a crusader. His employees keep in mind that one of his ambitions for the bank is growth in earnings per share each year of at least 15 percent. Love claims that every employee could state that objective. But Love also insists that growth cannot be achieved by foregoing Texas Commerce's traditionally conservative approach to lending. He wants it both ways—growth and caution—and remarkably, he has achieved it.

Ben Love is a complex, electric leader, says the magazine. Flowery in speech and courtly in manner, he can also pressure those around him—a tactic that some have found intimidating if not oppressive. He has a hard-edged, analytical bent, along with an uncanny memory, and can come up with names and numbers with astonishing accuracy. His background, however, is sales, not finance, and he spends much of his time selling his state, his bank, and himself.

Love was in a hurry the moment he walked through the door of the bank's lobby—prodding and cajoling his people to take to the streets and sell Texas Commerce. *Fortune* says a Texas Commerce vice president recalls that before long he was greeted on Monday mornings with clippings from the Sunday paper showing pictures of new construction projects—and notes from Love wondering why Texas Commerce wasn't involved.

A huge volume of clippings, memoranda, and letters flow from Love's second-floor office. In the *Fortune* article, the bank's officers joke that they always can tell when Love is in the bank, even if they haven't seen him; the stack of reading in their in-boxes becomes mountainous.

Ben Love assumes a number of different guises. Love is tall, lean, austere—and most of all intense. He can be charming and humorous when the occasion calls for it and can praise subordinates, often sending a note to thank them for good work. But with his withering gaze and rapid-fire, penetrating questions, Love can also "embarrass, humiliate, and bring to the knees" those with whom he is displeased or wishes to press on a particular point, states the magazine.

Keeping the pressure on seems to work, but some executives do not like the pressure-cooker atmosphere of Texas Commerce and have left. One top executive has nearly resigned at least once, only to reconsider his decision, and other officers are reported by *Fortune* to be on the brink of departing. Nevertheless, most of Love's senior management team has been able to adjust to his style. "You get used to the pressure," one of them says. "I'm not sure I could function without it." Most observers agree that Texas Commerce would probably not have come as far as it has, as fast as it has, without Ben Love at the helm.

Central to Love's operating philosophy is a belief in the value of setting narrowly defined objectives. At Texas Commerce, Love has established a set of rigid goals. *Fortune* says these goals include increasing earnings per share at a compound annual rate of 15 percent or better; earning a return on equity of between 15 and 18 percent; and achieving a return on assets of at least 9 percent.

Love's reaction to subpar results is

even-handed—no one is allowed to produce them. If after a down quarter, a division manager tries to say that the market was against him or that loans had slacked off unexpectedly, Love will listen and stare hard at the speaker, then ask: "What are our three corporate goals?" The goals are recited. "Then let's achieve them."

A legitimate question is raised concerning Ben Love's exacting approach to management.

It has driven some stars from the fold, stars who, under less rigorous conditions, might succeed Mr. Love. During the past few years, he has delegated more to those around him, but it is by no means clear who would take over if he were not there to run things. There are a couple of possible candidates, but as one former officer says, it just wouldn't be the same at Texas Commerce without Ben Love.

Suggested from Alexander Stuart, "Ben Love Conquers All In Houston," *Fortune* (November 19, 1979): 122-32.

Questions for Discussion

1. Describe Ben Love's power base. What are his most effective power sources?
2. How would you describe his style of leadership? Is it rigid or flexible, unidimensional or multidimensional?
3. Where did Love learn his particular leader behaviors? What were the most important skills that he learned?

4. Are leadership traits important to Love's success?
5. Do you think that Love can adapt to future conditions—lower growth and a need to develop replacement managers?

14

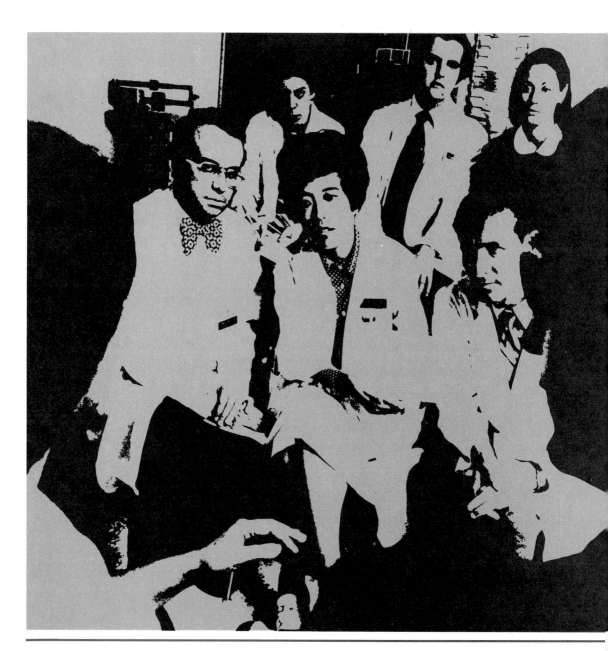

Managing Groups

Chapter Outline

Key Points

1. A variety of types of groups exist in organizations for a number of purposes. Since the manager spends a great deal of time in some form of group activity, he or she needs a good knowledge of group behavior.
2. Groups develop in stages; the early stages focus on learning to perform, while the later stages actually concern performance activities.
3. Group norms—behavioral and performance norms—not only can influence the level of performance, but members' nonadherence to norms can mean the group's rejection.
4. Status systems exist in all types of groups. It is the concept of status congruence, however, that is important to managers, because it strongly affects group performance.
5. Lack of clarity of one's responsibilities in a group (role ambiguity) and multiple demands on a member (role conflict) can adversely influence the level of group performance.
6. Group solidarity, or cohesiveness, is a significant determinant of group performance.
7. The uses of groups in organizations include typical superior-subordinate groups, committees, quality circles, venture groups, computer management groups, and the like.
8. With respect to the manager's job: group behavior relates to the leading function; effective group activities involve all the managerial skills, especially human and diagnostic skills; and leading, transmitting information, and making allocation (resource) decisions concern the concept of managerial roles.

Groups
How They Influence Our Behavior

We are all quite aware that groups can greatly influence our behavior. Consider, again, Tom Wolfe's book on America's first astronauts, *The Right Stuff*, and this incident.

When a pilot named Gus Grissom first went to Korea, the Air Force used to take the F-86 jocks out to the field before dawn, in buses, and the pilots who had not been shot at by a MiG in air-to-air combat had to stand up. At first Grissom couldn't believe it and then couldn't bear it—those b_____ sitting down were the only ones with the right stuff! The next morning, as they rumbled out there in the dark, he was sitting down. He had gone up north toward the Yalu on the first day and had it out with [the enemy] just so he could have a seat on the bus. Even at that level of combat, the main thing was not to be left behind.

To be accepted as part of a group, one has to obey the group's rules—what we will later discuss as group norms. Norms, however, can change over time. Studs Turkel, in his book *Working*, provides this example of a 1970s flight attendant.

They say you can spot a stewardess by the way she wears her make-up. At that time we all had short hair and everybody had it cut in stew school exactly alike. If there's two blonds that have their hair cut very short, wearing the same shade of make-up, and they get into similar uniforms, people say, "Oh, you look like sisters." Wonder why? (Laughs).
The majority of us were against it because they wouldn't let you say how you'd like

your hair cut, they wouldn't let you have your own personality, your make-up, your clothes. They'd tell you what length skirts to wear. At one time they told us we couldn't wear anything one inch above the knees. And no pants at that time. It's different now. Wigs used to be forbidden. Now it's the style. Now it's permissible for nice women to wear wigs, eyelashes, and false fingernails. Before it was the harder looking women that wore them. Women showing up in pants, it wasn't ladylike. Hot pants are in now. Most airlines now change style every year.

Source: T. Wolfe, *The Right Stuff* (New York: Farrar, Strauss, Giroux, 1979), p. 41; and S. Turkel, *Working* (New York: Random House, 1974), p. 44.

14 Many assume their first managerial positions expecting that much of their time will be devoted to independent thought, planning, individual decision making, organizing, and the like. For the vast majority, these expectations usually remain unfulfilled. The newly appointed manager is often amazed by the enormous amount of time and energy he or she devotes to managing groups, including participating in task forces and committees. In fact, some have estimated that as much as 50 percent of a manager's time goes to one form of group activity or another. In this chapter, we will examine how groups fit into the manager's job.

The chapter is divided into four main parts. First, we will discuss the basic elements, functions, and types of groups. This will be followed by a presentation of the key characteristics of groups in organizations. As *The Practice of Management* section shows, some of these characteristics can have a significant effect on individual behavior. In the third section, we will discuss the situation of Japanese-backed companies operating in the U.S. This Japanese boss/American workers situation provides some interesting insights into the interaction of culture and group behavior. Finally, we will look at the various uses of groups in organizations, such as committees, venture groups, and quality circles.

Groups in Organizations

Management scholars and practicing managers have provided numerous, varied, and sometimes overlapping definitions of a group.[1] This is because these individuals are studying different aspects that are related to the same phenomena—namely, groups and the management of groups. For our purposes, we offer this definition:

> A group is a collection of two or more individuals who are interdependent and interact with one another for the purpose of performing to achieve a common goal.

The main characteristics of this definition—goals, interaction, and performance—are critical to management effectiveness. These characteristics also distinguish a group from a collection of people attending a baseball game or waiting for a bus.

The Importance of Groups

The study of groups is important to the manager for a number of reasons. First, the group is a key element in the social order of our culture. Groups serve not only as the focal point of social life, but they provide an important source of direction to individuals for understanding social values and norms. Second, through participation in groups, individuals may satisfy important economic, status, safety, security, and friendship needs. Finally, the behavior and performance of groups provide a major mechanism for the achievement of organizational goals. Lack of group direction, a tense and stressful climate, continual conflict, and a lack of employee need satisfaction all can contribute to the performance or lack of performance of the group. This strong link to performance makes the study of groups valid to our understanding of management.

Types of Groups

There are at least two ways of classifying groups in organizations, by purpose and by orientation.[2] As shown in exhibit 14-1, classification by *purpose* involves three types of groups.

Functional or command groups are the most frequently occurring groups because they are specified by the structure of the organization—in other words, a combination of the chain of command and span of control identifies superior/subordinate relationships. Examples include the dean of a school of education with a group of administrators (i.e., department chairpersons), and the director of hospitals of a medical center with subordinate administrators at the various center hospitals.

Task or project groups relate to problem solving—employees are brought together to accomplish a specific task. For example, a divisional manager of a manufacturing

Exhibit 14-1
Types of Groups in Organizations

Group Type	Characteristics	Examples
Functional Groups	Member relationships specified by the structure of the organization. Involves superior-subordinate relationship. Involves accomplishment of ongoing tasks. Generally can be considered a formal group.	Head nurse supported by registered nurses, practical nurses, and nurses' aides. Manager of accounting supported by staff accountants, financial analysts, computer operators, and secretaries.
Task or Project Groups	Member relationships established for the accomplishment of a specific task. Short-term or long-term duration. Can involve superior-subordinate relationship. Generally can be considered a formal group.	Project-planning teams. Committees. Special task forces.
Interest and Friendship Groups	Member relationships formed because of some common characteristic such as age, political beliefs, or interests. Generally can be considered a formal or informal group. Goals can be congruent or incongruent to the organization's goals.	Trade unions also can be a functional group. Social groups. Recreation clubs.

Exhibit 14-2
The Linking Pin
Concept of
Groups

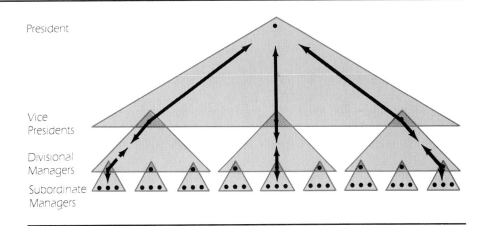

President

Vice
Presidents

Divisional
Managers

Subordinate
Managers

company may establish a task force to study the problem of why so many customers are receiving damaged products.

Interest and friendship groups develop in organizations to satisfy employee needs that are not satisfied by normal organizational means. Company baseball teams and weekend poker clubs are examples. One may even classify the beginnings of unions as this type of group because they form to present a united front to management.

Classifying groups by *orientation* makes the important distinctions between formal and informal groups. *Formal* groups exist in organizations to carry out the purposes and goals of the organization. Groups that are classified as functional and/or task and project groups when classified by purpose are usually considered formal when classified by orientation. Because of the influence of the structure of the organization, all employees belong to one or more formal organizational groups. As shown in exhibit 14-2, managers are the "linking pins" that integrate the various formal groups in the organization.

Informal groups generally are considered interest and friendship groups because employees are brought together for a common interest or because of their proximity of interaction.[3] Informal groups can either support *or* oppose the purposes of the organization. Recreational clubs, for example, strengthen the employees' ties with the organization. On the other hand, since there can be a strong bond among members of an informal group, they may object to or oppose the setting of high production goals by management. For example, workers on assembly lines often object to and work against management's goal of increasing the speed of the line.

Besides supporting the goals and policies of the organization, informal groups offer other benefits.[4] First, they can provide status and social satisfaction. In many large organizations, the individual might feel just like another "small cog in a big wheel." Within the confines of a small, informal group, however, the employee can enjoy recognition for good work or gain valued friendships. Second, informal groups can help the communication system. As discussed in chapter 11, the "grapevine," an informal group component, can improve the effectiveness of communication networks.

There are some disadvantages to informal groups as well. First, as noted previously, such groups can oppose the goals of the organization, or simply resist change. Most groups develop norms, or standards of behavior, that guide behavior. For example, a clerical group may develop an informal norm for dress that is more casual than the organization wants. The group may then resist the imposition of a formal dress code by the organization.

Another problem is communication systems that go awry because of the influence of informal groups. There is a fine line of distinction between a ''grapevine'' and a ''rumor mill,'' and the latter essentially transmits incorrect information. When employees are not well-informed, there is the tendency to spread false rumors that may prove damaging to employee morale. For example, when pay raises are awarded, unless the organization has an open-information pay system, informal groups tend to pass on data that inflate the actual amounts.

Management scholars have studied the various types of groups in organizations for a number of years. In the next section, we will focus on the key characteristics of groups and how these characteristics relate to performance.

Group Characteristics and Performance

Groups in organizations, whether formal or informal, develop characteristics or structural components that govern their members' behavior. Exhibit 14-3 shows these. At least five characteristics have been identified—group development stages, norms, status, roles, and cohesion.

Group Development Stages

The performance capacity of a group does not emerge with the group's formation, but develops over time.[5] Group members must get to know one another, they must resolve internal problems, and goals and procedures must be established before the group can devote its attention to accomplishing a task. This is the concept of group formation and development stages. While it is sometimes difficult to identify where a group is in its developmental sequence, it is important for the manager to help the group move quickly through these stages, particularly the early stages, because performance is highly dependent on what stage the group is in.

Group development usually consists of four stages—orientation, internal problem-solving, growth and productivity, and evaluation and control. Consider a city fire department that has decided to form a new arson investigation unit. The group will consist of six experienced firefighters, one will be director, and the others will be investigators. This group is a formal, task or command group that has been charged with investigating the origins of fires within the city.

Orientation concerns the various activities that occur when a group gets together for the first few times. In our fire department example, this stage means establishing the structure, rules, and procedures of the group, clarifying member relations and inter-

Exhibit 14-3
Groups in Organizations

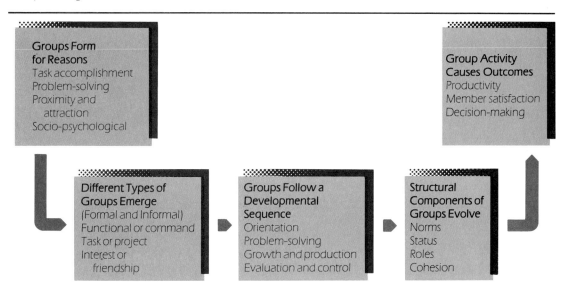

dependencies, and developing a plan of action. In other words, the emphasis is on who are members of the group, what this group is to do, and what it needs to do it.

Internal problem-solving relates to getting past problems that would bar goal accomplishment. Usually, the problems develop because something was not adequately covered in the orientation stage. In the arson unit, problems could arise over who takes over when the director is out of town, how arson reports should be presented, or personality conflicts.

Growth and productivity is one of the most important stages because at this time many of the group's internal problems have been solved and all member activities can be devoted to accomplishing the task at hand. Member relations in the arson unit at this stage are characterized by increased closeness, sharing of ideas and approaches, providing and receiving feedback, and exploring better ways of doing the job.

Evaluation and control concerns activities as the group approaches the conclusion of its task, or after the group has been in existence for a time. At this stage, the fire department unit would be involved in review of procedures, revising, reporting, and public communication programs.

An important aspect is that a group can revert to an earlier stage at any time. A new task, a new leader, or the addition or replacement of members can be the cause. A revision of the purpose of the fire department arson unit could cause it to revert to the orientation stage. Or a new member with a different background or expectations can force the group back into the internal problem-solving stage. Major league baseball has seen some changes with the emergence of highly paid free agents. The free agent, usually a high performer with another team, is added to a new team through a lengthy bidding process. A situation in need of internal problem-solving occurs when existing team members feel undervalued and become upset over the large salary the free agent is receiving.

Group Norms and Norm Conformity

Steve Hightower works as a buyer in the purchasing department of a large regional supermarket chain. Steve is responsible for the purchase of all breakfast food products (e.g., cereals). As such, a great number of food product sales representatives call on him each day. With Christmas less than a week away, Steve, who has been in the purchasing department less than a year, is called into his boss's office (the purchasing agent) for a discussion.

In a straightforward but nonpunitive manner, the purchasing agent informs Steve that he is doing two things wrong on his job he does not realize. First, he has accepted a number of Christmas gifts from some of the sales representatives who have called on him recently. Gifts that are offered during a presentation should be refused, he is told. Gifts received through the mail will be returned. Second, while going to lunch occasionally with an important supplier is fine, Steve is told he should suggest going to a nearby restaurant instead of frequently going across town to a fancier establishment. The reason is that eating at the closer restaurant will allow him to be back on the job sooner.

This illustration is an example of the function of *group norms* in organizations.[6] Norms are defined as *standards or rules of behavior* that are established by formal and/or informal group members to provide some *order* to individual and group activities. If individuals in a group were permitted to act, interact, or perform their functions as each saw fit, the result would be increased anxiety, stress, conflict, and chaos, along with decreased performance. Two important aspects of group norms are types of norms and norm conformity.

Types of Norms   There are basically two types of group norms in organizations. First are *behavioral* norms, which relate to specific behaviors of the person. For example, our buyer Steve Hightower did not adhere to the behavioral norm of refusing Christmas gifts from suppliers. Since this norm is also a formal rule of the organization, there is added impact.

The second type of group norm is the *performance* norm. Steve's long lunches prevented him from performing his assigned work. The key aspect of performance norms is their relation to the productivity of the group.

Managers need to understand that group norms can either support or oppose the purpose or goals of the organization. In Steve's situation, the established norms were congruent with the organization's purpose, since they emphasized both high productivity and ethical behavior. It thus is an important activity of the manager to understand the norms of the group and to evaluate their contribution to the organization. The manager can do little to stop the formation of norms—such qualities have existed in different societies for centuries. He or she can, however, try to alter certain nonproductive norms through direct orders or within a participative environment.

Norm Conformity   Group norms, whether congruent or incongruent with the goals of the organization, are a powerful influence on members' behaviors. In essence, to be considered a member of a group, one must adhere to the established norms. This *norm conformity* is important for managers to understand, because group members will attempt to enforce adherence to group norms on nonadhering members.[7]

For example, consider a group of workers responsible for the total assembly of a pocket transistor radio. Through lengthy interaction, group members have established an informal performance norm that they will assemble no more than eighteen units per hour. The group established this norm because it provided a level of productivity that was acceptable to management and did not push the group members to great fatigue.

A new worker is added to the group and immediately begins assembling at the rate of twenty-five units per hour. Since this behavior is contrary to the group performance norms, how will the group react? Generally, a three-phase reaction will be shown. First, select group members (usually the informal leader) will inform the new member of the norms of the group and suggest that they be followed. If the new employee ignores this comment, the reactions of the group become less friendly. They may speak directly and forcefully to him, telling him what he is doing wrong, or they will in isolated situations try to sabotage his work. Finally, if these approaches do not work, the group will ostracize the individual—no one will talk to him, eat at the same lunch table, help him fix a flat tire, and so on.

Such activities are not uncommon in many positions in organizations. It is the manager's job not only to recognize when such a situation is occurring, but to understand whether or not the group norm is actually beneficial to the organization.

Status Systems

Status is a social ranking within a group, and people have it because of their positions in the organization or important individual traits. Status can be a function of a person's title, wage or salary level, mobility, seniority, or expertise.

By far the most important factor is job title. A plant manager holds greater status than a supervisor. Likewise, the supervisor has greater status than a machine operator. Another important factor is seniority and/or expertise. The oldest nurse in a pediatric ward may enjoy higher status in her group because of age, tenure, or expertise.

Like norms, status systems have positive and negative aspects. The positive aspects are the clarification of relationships, authority, and responsibility. But an overemphasis on status can reduce both the frequency of interaction among members and their level of communication.

Status systems have a direct influence on group performance through the concept of *status congruence*, which is the agreement among group members on the level of status accorded to each member. When there is status congruence, the group can spend its time concentrating on task accomplishment. However, when there is disagreement on status levels (status incongruence), some group activity is diverted from task accomplishment and directed toward resolving the conflict.

As an illustration, consider a branch manager of a savings and loan association who attends a week-long training seminar out of state. The manager assumes, through the authority and status system, that the assistant branch manager will take over for him at the branch. However, the head teller believes that because he has been with the branch longer than the assistant branch manager (ten years compared to six months), he should take charge. Imagine the performance of the branch personnel with two people giving conflicting orders. The branch manager may have to return early to try to salvage the organization!

Groups and Member Roles

In chapter 1, we introduced the concept of roles when we discussed the main managerial roles—interpersonal, informational, and decisional. In essence, everyone in an organization, and in a group, has a role or roles that he or she must perform.

Managers need to understand two key characteristics of roles in groups—sources of roles, and the existence of multiple roles.[8] There are a number of *sources* in organizations that formulate an employee's role, whether the person is a manager or not. These include the considerations of the organization (e.g., job descriptions), the group (e.g., group norms), and the individual (e.g., expectations based on values and attitudes). A newly hired computer programmer in a bank develops an understanding of her role from job descriptions and communication with superiors (organizational sources), from observing and talking to colleagues (group norm sources), and from her own perceptions about the work, perceptions which have developed from educational training and her value system (individual sources).

The second key characteristic of roles is *multiple roles*—the fact that most people perform many roles during a typical day. For example, the owner of a small suburban hardware store may be the principal manager of the store, as well as the president of the local chamber of commerce and co-chairperson of the area United Appeal. Of course, there are important family roles that this person must also play. The more involved the person's work, the more complex the person's *role set*.

These two characteristics of roles give rise to two major role problems in organizations.[9] These role problems have a direct impact on the performance of the individual and hence, the group. First, when the person's role is unclear, a state of *role ambiguity* is created. If a manager is experiencing role ambiguity, he or she is unsure what to do, what is expected by the group and organization, and so on. For example, consider the dilemma many professionals—engineers, accountants, and medical personnel—face when they move into managerial positions. An engineer may be highly trained and experienced in the design of electrical circuitry for computers, but this may not have prepared him to perform well as manager of the Circuit Design Department. He may come to the recognition early that there is an important difference between being a technical/professional person and being a manager. Because of this lack of clarity, this engineer functions in a state of role ambiguity, and lower performance for both him and the group may result.

The second role problem is the situation in which there are multiple roles and/or role sources that conflict. This is *role conflict*. Consider the case of production supervisor in a plant manufacturing fertilizers. How would you react if, on any given day, the following happened to you? (1) The production manager wants you to increase production to 98 percent of rated capacity; (2) the maintenance supervisor wants you

In some organizations, groups—particularly the top management team—find that operating in an informal manner has many benefits over formal group activities. A case in point is Jordache Enterprises, which, *Business Week* points out, is a company like an Horatio Alger story. Joe, Ralph, and Avi Nakash, once penniless Israeli brothers, now each get about a million in salary. Fashion followers and cartoonists have had a field day with "the Jordache Look"—a slogan the company has made almost synonymous with tight, well-fitting jeans.

Business Week contends that, as an organization, Jordache is almost overripe for transition from the highly personal and often irreverent management style of the Nakash brothers to one that makes greater use of more conventional management and behavioral tools and controls. People worry that such a transition may not be made without killing the entrepreneurial spirit that made Jordache so successful.

Examples given by the magazine of the Jordache informal approach to people and groups are numerous:

- There are no formal meetings. Formality, and the stiffness it implies, runs counter to the brothers' style.

- The three brothers do most of their planning not in high-level executive conferences with other managers, but during their hour-long automobile commute from their Queens neighborhood. Major product-line decisions are as likely to be made while waiting for an elevator as around a table.

- Managers are hired, and operate, on the basis of trust and capability, not age, past experience, or other norms. Two of the top executives are under thirty years of age.

- Job-related duties for the brothers and other managers are divided on the basis of what they enjoy most, rather than by title or job description. Joe, officially chairman, is also the advertising and financial specialist. Ralph keeps his hand in production and merchandising. Avi is most involved in operations such as inventory control.

Adapted from "Jordache's New Executive Look," *Business Week*, (November 2, 1981): 121-22.

to shut the plant down for thirty-six hours to repair a poorly functioning piece of equipment; (3) the quality control manager informs you that during the past three days, quality rejects of batched product have increased 20 percent; and (4) a product manager calls and wants you to switch the plant's production to manufacture a special grade of product for a good customer as quick as you can. Where can you turn and what should you do first? Needless to say, if this situation was allowed to continue, the unit's performance and the supervisor's morale would suffer.

What can managers do if they recognize either of these role problems? For role ambiguity, the resolution may be as simple as asking for a clarification of one's role, or as complex as added managerial training. In the case of role conflict, a quick solution would be to appeal to a higher authority (see chapter 8). The production supervisor should immediately go to the direct manager (the production manager) and ask for guidance. In the case of matrix designs (see chapter 9), however, such conflict is built into the relationship because of the dual-authority system. Resolution, therefore, may not be that easy.

Role problems are common occurrences in many organizations. The important aspect for managers to consider is that high levels of either role ambiguity or role conflict will lead to performance and morale problems among group members. It is, therefore, important for the manager to recognize these problems, their causes, and the possible solutions.

Group Cohesiveness

Each one of us at one time or another has observed or been part of a group that possessed a degree of closeness or solidarity that made working with the group a pleasure. Termed *group cohesiveness,* this is a structural situation in which the factors acting on group members to remain and participate in the group are greater than those acting on members to leave it.[10]

Group cohesiveness presents at least two important implications for managers. First, cohesiveness is an important indicator of the degree of *influence* the group as a whole has on individual members—the greater the cohesiveness, the greater the group's influence on members. This is because highly cohesive groups generally have adopted strong behavioral and performance norms. Group members are not likely to violate the norms of the group to which they are strongly attached.

Second, highly cohesive groups are usually characterized by good feeling among members and an absence of tension, hostility, and major conflicts. For this reason, highly cohesive groups are potentially better performers than noncohesive groups.

If we assume that group cohesiveness is a positive factor that can lead to improved performance, managers need to understand what they can do to increase a group's cohesiveness. At least five different mechanisms or strategies are worth considering. As an example, let's examine the propulsion group in mission control for NASA's space shuttle program.

Group goal achievement. If the group agrees on the purpose and direction of its activities (i.e., to monitor, direct, and advise on the shuttle's propulsion systems), the group is bound together for better performance.

Frequency of interaction. When group members have the opportunity to interact frequently with each other, the probability for cohesion to develop will increase. For the shuttle group, the manager may want to schedule a number of meetings (formal and informal), and possibly, physically design the office layout so that offices are close together.[11]

Personal attractiveness and dependence. Cohesiveness is increased when members are attracted to one another, creating a state of mutual trust and support. This can be accomplished by adding members who get along well with others and have the expertise to perform at high levels. What the group stands for and what it does—its norms, friendships, communication networks—are bonds that attract the individual to the group.

Evaluation as a group. While it is important that individual performance be evaluated and rewarded (see chapter 12), cohesion can be increased by evaluating the group as a whole. NASA and other decentralized management structures in many organizations have used this technique to draw attention to the group as an important unit. It also is a mechanism that brings the group together to achieve a common purpose.

Group prestige and status. Cohesion can increase by according the group some prestige or status—in other words, aspects that make existing group members feel good that they are members and that cause other employees to want to become members. This can be done by openly recognizing the excellent performance of the group, frequently rewarding or promoting group members, stressing the important skills and abilities required for group membership, or allowing great independence of action among group members. During the Mercury, Gemini, and Apollo manned spacecraft programs, NASA began an extensive program of giving achievement awards to groups. Such awards create prestige, which further strengthens cohesiveness and supports continued outstanding performance.

Group Cohesiveness and Performance   Because group members highly value the membership in a cohesive group, we would expect that the individual would be more responsive to the demands and norms of the cohesive group. If this assumption is correct, two things should be apparent: (1) the major difference between high and low cohesive groups would be how closely members conform to group norms; and (2) group performance would be influenced not only by cohesion, but by the level or strength of group norms.

As shown in exhibit 14-4, research has supported the assumption that group performance is a function of both norms and cohesion—that is, the highest performance levels are found in groups that are highly cohesive and maintain high performance norms. As an example, consider two highly cohesive groups of machine operators.

Exhibit 14-4
Norms, Cohesion, and Group Performance

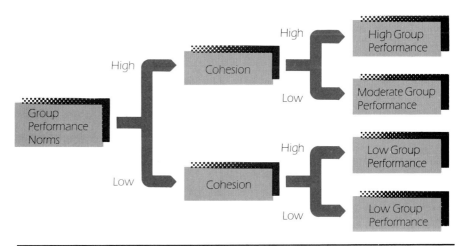

The first group has established a high and challenging performance norm of sixty units per day for each group member. Due to the high cohesion, we would expect that group members would work hard to conform to this norm. On the other hand, the second group has set a markedly lower performance norm (i.e., forty-five units per day for each member), which members also would adhere to, because of their level of cohesion.

Managers must understand, then, that cohesiveness by itself will not guarantee high performance. One must not only work to increase the group's cohesion, but he or she must also ensure that group norms are at a level that contributes to the overall good of the organization.

Decision-Making Groups

In many types of organizations, some groups have more than advisory capacity, they have actual decision-making authority. Examples include school boards, the Civil Aeronautics Board, executive committees in corporations, and so on. In these cases, the group analyzes the problem, looks at various alternative solutions, then makes the decision.

Benefits of Group Decision-Making

The major benefits of group decision-making can be expressed by this formula:[12]

$$\begin{array}{c}\text{Group}\\\text{Decision-Making}\\\text{Effectiveness}\end{array} = \begin{array}{c}\text{Sum of Independent}\\\text{Individual Effort}\end{array} + \begin{array}{c}\text{Assembly}\\\text{Effect}\end{array} - \begin{array}{c}\text{Process}\\\text{Losses}\end{array}$$

Sum of independent individual effort is a positive feature, reflecting that there is better information when more people are involved. In other words, two heads are better than one. *Assembly effect,* a second positive feature, is what some have called a "synergy" effect. In essence, the interaction of individuals with varied views can result in a decision that is better than a single individual's. *Process losses* is a negative feature that reflects two important aspects. First, groups take more time to make a decision than does an individual. Second, there are certain motivational effects. In essence, some group members may choose to be "hidden" in the group and not committed to the decision—a "let George do it" philosophy. And there is also the risk that some members would sublimate ideas so as not to go against the group.

Types of Decision-Making Groups

Three general types of decision-making groups can be found in organizations—the interacting group, and the nominal and Delphi groups. Exhibit 14-5 compares these three groups.

Interacting groups are the typical committees, where there is face-to-face interaction. Such decision-making groups are usually formed to solve a particular problem,

Exhibit 14-5

Comparison of Interacting, Nominal, and Delphi Groups

Dimension	Interacting Groups	Nominal Groups	Delphi Groups
Example	A product development task force	A group attempting to resolve intergroup conflict	A group attempting to forecast environmental events for the next ten years
Overall Methodology	Unstructured, face-face group meeting	Structured, face-face group meeting	Structured series of question-naires and feedback reports
	High flexibility	Low flexibility	Low flexibility
	High variability in the behavior of groups	Low variability in the behavior of groups	Low variability in respondent behavior
Relative Quantity of Ideas	Moderate	High	High
Search Behavior	Reactive, sometimes short-term focus	Proactive, long-term focus	Proactive, long-term but controlled focus
Conformity	High	Moderate	Low
Equality of Participation	High chance for mem-ber dominance	Member equality in search and choice activities	Respondent equality in pool-ing of independent opinions
Method of Problem Solving	Individual-centered	Problem-centered	Problem-centered
	Possible win/lose, smoothing, and with-drawal	Confrontation	Majority rule
Resources Utilized	Low administrative cost and time	Medium administrative cost, time, and preparation	High administrative cost and time
	High participant cost and time	High participant cost and time	Moderate participant cost and time
Time to Obtain Group Ideas	One to five hours	Three hours to two days	Three to five months

Adapted from A. Van de Ven and Andre Delbecq, "The Effectiveness of Nominal, Delphi, and Interacting Group Decision-Making Processes," *Academy of Management Journal* (1974): 605-21.

can be highly flexible in their approach, and can generate a moderate number of possible solutions. Consensus decisions are sought, but dominance and movement toward group norm conformity can be problems. Decisions can be made relatively quickly, but the combined amount of time members spend can add up.

Nominal groups are highly oriented toward idea generation and evaluation. They are more proactive in orientation (i.e., forward looking), decisions can be made in a moderate amount of time, and the effects of conformity and member dominance can be reduced through procedural means. Because of a structured nature, however, they show little flexibility.

Delphi groups can only be considered pseudo groups because members do not physically interact. As a result, idea generation and evaluation is high and the effects of group conformity are minimized. Such groups are highly inflexible; majority votes are sought, but they can be both time-consuming and costly.

As the exhibit indicates, each type of decision-making group has advantages and disadvantages. The manager should recognize these points when appointing these groups or participating in them.[13] Some rules may be helpful: (1) Use interacting groups in attempting to solve an immediate problem that needs fairly quick solution; (2) nominal groups are good for idea generation or for resolving intergroup problems such as conflict; and (3) use Delphi groups when idea generation is desired and when the experts are physically dispersed.

Problems with Decision-Making Groups

Despite the potential advantages of group over individual decision-making, some important disadvantages to group decision-making have been pointed out. Perhaps the most notable of these is the phenomenon of *groupthink* as discussed by Irving L. Janis.[14] In studying several major governmental fiascos involving high-level decisions (the Bay of Pigs incident of the Kennedy administration, the Johnson administration decision to escalate the Vietnam War, the failure to be prepared for the attack on Pearl Harbor, and the stalemate of the Korean War during the Truman era), Janis concluded that group processes actually prevented effective decision-making.

Groupthink usually occurs in highly cohesive groups where the need to conform to group norms pressures members toward consensus. Groupthink has some of the following symptoms:

- *Invulnerability*. Do group members develop an illusion of invulnerability that leads them to ignore obvious dangers or warnings? This may lead to becoming overly optimistic and possibly to taking unnecessary risks.

- *Rationale*. Closely related to a feeling of invulnerability, group members develop rationalizations to discount sources of information that contradict the group's thinking. Usually the source is discredited as unreliable.

- *Morality*. The closeness of the group may raise the group's moralistic level. In other words, the group members strongly believe that they are morally right in action.

- *Stereotypes*. If an external person doesn't go along with the group's views, he or she is discredited, or viewed as ignorant. "Who could not possibly understand our logic?" is the group's view.

- *Pressure*. If any member doubts the position of the group, he or she is branded as subverting the welfare of the group, or even banished.

- *Self-censorship*. Members who hold doubts about the group's views restrain themselves from expression. Janis cites several examples of individuals who regretted, after a group decision proved erroneous, not having spoken up and expressed doubts. This self-censorship is seen as a response to the pressure to conform to group norms.

- *Unanimity*. Self-censorship leads to the illusion of unanimity of opinion within the group. The false assumption is that anyone who remains silent is automatically in favor of the decision.

- *Mindguards.* Members affected by groupthink appoint themselves as "mindguards"—people who have the duty to protect the leader and other group members from adverse information about the group's position. Janis cites the instance of Attorney General Robert Kennedy warning Arthur Schlesinger not to share his doubts about the Bay of Pigs invasion with the President, because the President's mind was already made up.

If the manager recognizes some of these groupthink symptoms in his or her policymaking group, what can be done to reduce the adverse impact of this phenomenon? The following strategies would be helpful in reducing the groupthink problem.[15]

Appoint an individual to act as a critical evaluator and/or a devil's advocate. Since it is difficult for opposing views to be brought out in a groupthink situation, the chairperson should appoint (on a rotating basis) individual group members to act as critical evaluators during group discussions. This may force the group to slow down and rethink its options.

If the group is large enough, break it up into subgroups for discussions. In groups of ten or larger, it is easy for members to withhold information or opinions (i.e., self-censorship). Breaking up into smaller subgroups will usually create a better climate for discussion.

Seek out opinions from qualified people outside the group. To prevent an insulation of the group from the outside, it may be worthwhile to discuss the group's deliberations (confidentially) with trusted colleagues, or to invite external experts to the group's meetings. New information can be gathered in this way that may challenge the group's position. During the Iranian and Cuban crises of 1979, President Carter brought in outside experts, Henry Kissinger being one, to present their views on the situation.

Allot specific time for the group to discuss contingency plans. As we pointed out in chapter 6, situations arise that can make the best-laid plans obsolete. In order to alleviate the invulnerability, morality, and rationality groupthink symptoms, the chairperson should force the group to consider "what if" the decision is not accepted.

Hold second-chance meetings. When it becomes clear that the group has made a decision, many managers have found it good policy to hold "second-chance" meetings, at which time members are expected to express as vividly as they can all their residual doubts and to rethink the entire issue before making a definite choice. As stated by Alfred P. Sloan, former chairman of General Motors, "I take it we are all in complete agreement on the decision here. . . . Then I propose we postpone further discussion of this matter until our next meeting to give ourselves time to develop disagreement and perhaps gain some understanding of what the decision is all about."

Managing the effective decision-making group is not an easy task. There are many forces, both internal and external, that the manager must understand and adapt to. We return to the diagnostic skills that managers need to adjust to the situation.

# Japanese Boss, American Workers

In 1980, it was estimated that more than 1,200 Japanese-backed firms were operating in the United States.[16] These firms employed over 10,000 Japanese managers and more than 81,000 American workers. Since Japanese management customs, methods, and practices are sometimes quite different from American ones, the expatriate Japanese managers face the problems of adapting their managerial style to a new environment. Nowhere is this distinction more apparent than in the dealings between the Japanese manager and subordinate managers and workers in group-related activities, recent studies have shown.[17]

Overall Attitudes and Feelings

Two distinct attitudes were identified among the studied Japanese managers—those pertaining to themselves, and those pertaining to American workers. It was clear that Japanese managers were quite proud of their country's economic and technical accomplishments, their ancient and distinctive culture, and the uniqueness of their race. Having been considered for a high-level position in the U.S. was also viewed positively. Such a move was looked on as a good sign for promotion to a top executive position when the manager returned to Japan.

On the negative side, certain inferiority feelings were revealed. These included the negative connotation of Japan's rather late emergence into the modern world, as well as concern about their physical size. Many Japanese are shorter than the average American, which made them feel somewhat overpowered in the presence of their larger, more assertive American colleagues and workers.

The Japanese people typically emphasize the compatibility of a person with his or her environment. Each Japanese manager studied was concerned with successfully fulfilling his economic and cultural role as part of the larger web of family and social relations. In the workplace, the Japanese managers ponder the way American workers can compartmentalize their lives, being able to separate job, family, and friendships. Since this behavior is foreign to the Japanese, it has proved difficult to adapt to for some.

The American penchant for individualism has also been troublesome to certain Japanese managers working in the U.S. In Japan, a directive from a superior or an elder is accepted and implemented. Japanese managers have found it unnerving for their American workers to not only disagree with their bosses, but frequently, in "thinking for themselves," to take the initiative to try something new and different. In Japan, one generally waits for the wisdom of the elders or of the group as a whole before being innovative.

Relationships with Employees

These overall attitudes set the stage for individual and group activities. The more consultative, less authoritarian role of top management introduces levels of uncertainty and complexity in dealing with groups of American workers. The Japanese empha-

The Manager's Job

Japanese Boss, American Workers: Honda Motors

In planning the operations of its first American manufacturing facility, a motorcycle plant in Marysville, Ohio, Honda Motors faced a dilemma: should it impose Japanese management practices or adapt to the local culture? In Japan, companies operate with a highly industrious and homogeneous work force, which speaks the same language and is tied together with a unifying culture. Unions are cooperative, and companies maintain cordial relations with the Japanese government. In the U.S., workers tend to be more individualistic, unions serve more of an advisory purpose, and relations with the government can become strained at times.

Honda's approach: try the Japanese way first. Among the mechanisms used to manage the plant are:

- Extensive training of workers is stressed, and product quality is emphasized. Honda even sent a number of Marysville workers to Japan to learn their methods.

- Assurances of job security are given to employees but, unlike Japan, "lifetime" jobs are not offered. What is stressed is that product quality and job security are strongly linked; in other words, quality products equal customer purchases and a steady job.

- Before hiring a job applicant, Honda asks him or her to agree to be moved from job to job at management's discretion. This, according to Honda, will increase flexibility and reduce the chance for layoffs.

- As in Japan, status differences between management and labor are played down, emphasizing that each is part of a team. Everyone, management and labor, eats in the same company cafeteria, there are no assigned parking spaces, all employees are called associates, and instead of ties, executives wear the white Honda uniform.

Has the Honda experience worked? On the positive side, after some initial start-up problems, both the production rate for motorcycles and the product's quality have increased to near expectation levels. On the negative side, a number of problems have emerged. The Japanese consensus approach to decision making is slowly being accepted. However, its accompanying system, **nemawashi,** is not. Nemawashi means laying the groundwork and maneuvering behind the scenes (political behavior) to obtain one's objective. American workers feel this takes too much time and have attempted to short-circuit the process. As expected, language remains a problem to the extent that two full-time interpreters are employed at the plant.

Most seriously, during the attempt by the United Auto Workers to organize the plant, workers began wearing UAW insignia on their hats and uniforms. Management allegedly ordered them removed, prompting the filing of an unfair labor practice suit to the National Labor Relations Board. In the end, it appears that Honda's attempt to impose pure Japanese management practices has had to be adjusted to the culture of its workers in the U.S.

Adapted from M. Kanabayashi, "How a Japanese Firm is Faring on Its Dealings With Workers in U.S.," *The Wall Street Journal* (October 2, 1981).

size a management practice of decisions "from the bottom up" (the ringi system). The key point is the achievement of a consensus from the interaction and inputs of most people concerned. American workers, accustomed to the "top down" form of management, are either uncomfortable with this practice, or interpret the failure to give a direct order as a lack of self-confidence and management ability.

At first, Japanese managers attempted to use verbal nuances, facial expressions, body language, or other "hints" to convey their messages. When these were frequently ignored by American workers, some Japanese managers adopted a more blunt and directive form of managerial behavior to let workers know what was expected.

A key to Japanese group relationships is mutual trust, under which workers discuss and work out any disagreements, stressing the team nature of the job. Japanese managers reported that in working with American workers, it was the employment relationship that was important, where an adversarial relationship could develop. This may, in part, be due to the American desire for well-defined titles, positions, and lines of authority and responsibility. The Japanese, seeking cooperativeness and constant favorable group and individual relationships, came up against a strict and imbedded authority system in their American operations. Finding the two systems at odds, Panasonic went to the extreme of establishing two separate personnel offices in the U.S.—one office of Americans to oversee Americans, and another to look over the activities of Japanese managers.

One of the major problems faced by Japanese managers is the difficulty of convincing American managers and workers to think in long-range planning terms. Japanese stress activities directed toward the achievement of, for example, five-year plans. American employees, on the other hand, saw it important to achieve this year's target or goal.

At the heart of this problem is the organization's reward system. American managers have been typically rewarded on the basis of their yearly performance and accomplishments. They are keenly aware of numbers, figures, rapid growth, and the successes against competitors. Japanese, on the other hand, are in it "for the long haul," where performance over time is emphasized.

Will the clashing of cultures continue, or will some accommodation be made? This will probably vary from location to location but, as *The Manager's Job* insert indicates, some adaptation on the part of both parties is evolving. More importantly, the Japanese are learning a lesson that confronted U.S. managers in the 1960s and 1970s when many firms were expanding overseas. That is, one cannot expect to totally ship one's culture and management practices to another country without some form of change and adaptation.

 # Uses of Groups in Organizations

Organizations have found a number of ways to use groups. The most obvious and frequent is the superior/subordinate relationship, or the task group. Beyond this, a number of uses are worth discussing. These include committees, quality circles, venture groups, computer management groups, public policy groups, and the group manager.

Committees in Organizations

To many managers, committee membership is a symbol of status; to others, it is a plague. Whatever the view, being a member of at least one committee is necessary for most managers. Surveys of managers have reported that they are members of an average of three committees; about four hours per week are spent in committee meetings, with another four hours required for preparation before the meeting; and the number of committees a manager belongs to increases as one goes up the organizational hierarchy.[18]

In organizations, committees can serve one or more purposes. The most frequently identified purposes are:[19]

- To provide managers with an opportunity to exchange information and differing views on a variety of subjects
- To generate ideas or solutions to organizational problems
- To make recommendations to higher-level management
- To actually make decisions.

The specific purpose of a committee depends on a number of factors. For example, the more decentralized the organization, the greater the decision-making authority given a committee. Similarly, the greater the problems of coordination between different units, the higher the probability that a committee, or committees, will be formed.

As a special form of groups, committees share many of the key characteristics inherent in group behavior. As shown in Exhibit 14-6, committees can exhibit a number of important assets and liabilities.[20]

Types of Committees   Committees differ in purpose, membership, decision-making authority, and frequency of meetings. In general, four types of committees can be identified—task forces, permanent committees, boards, and commissions.

Task forces are formed to deal with a specific purpose or problem. They exist until the problem is solved, and then the members return to their normal duties. For example, in developing a new aircraft design, the Boeing Company, which is functionally

Exhibit 14-6 Assets and Liabilities of Committees	Assets	Liabilities
	Greater knowledge and information	Premature decisions
	More approaches to a problem	Excessive conformity to the group norms
	Increased acceptance of solution	Individual domination
	Better understanding and comprehension of the decision	Conflicting interests
	Improved communication and cooperation	Excessive idle chatter; time and manpower commitments

Adapted from Norman R. F. Maier, "Assets and Liabilities in Group Problem Solving," *Psychological Review* (July 1967), pp. 239-49. Copyright 1967 by the American Psychological Association. Adapted by permission of the publisher and author.

organized, establishes a number of task forces to help coordinate these large projects. The task forces deal with various parts of the new plane. When the particular plane has been completed, the members return to their original functions.

Permanent committees, sometimes called standing committees, remain in existence to deal with a continuing organizational issue. Examples include a curriculum development committee in a college of business or a new product review committee in a consumer products company. These committees can make recommendations to higher management, or they may have the authority to make decisions.

Boards are groups that have been given the charge of managing an organization. They can exist in either public or private organizations, and the members are appointed or elected. Examples include the board of directors for a corporation, a school board, or a hospital board. The key feature of boards is that they frequently have a great deal of decision-making authority. Corporate boards of directors establish stock dividend policies and capital funding programs and select high-level executives. School boards hire superintendents, raise revenue through taxes, and approve textbook selection procedures.

Commissions are similar to boards in that they can have broad decision-making authority. The main difference is that the members usually are appointed by officials to carry out administrative duties. Examples include government commissions such as the Federal Trade Commission and the Securities and Exchange Commission.

These four types of committees differ in a number of dimensions, such as temporary or permanent status, elected or appointed members, and advisory or decision-making authority. Another important dimension is to whom the committee is responsible. Task forces and permanent committees generally are internal groups that are responsible to a higher-level manager. Boards and commissions usually have an external focus and are responsible to the public. For example, a corporate board is responsible to stockholders, a school board to the community, and a commission to the general public.

Guidelines for the Effective Committee

In a corporate meeting room high up in the New York headquarters of International Telephone & Telegraph, a number of executives sit around a long, felt-covered table. There, from all over the world, they are reporting to Harold S. Geneen, ITT's combative, contentious chairman who sits at the center of the table.

"John," says Geneen, speaking to one of the executives, "what have you done about that problem?"

Leaning forward, John responds, "Well, I called the manager, but I couldn't get him to make a decision."

"Do you want me to call him?" is Geneen's response.

"Gosh, that's a good idea. Would you mind?"

"I'll be glad to," says Geneen. "But it will cost you your pay check."

"Never mind," says a flustered John. "I'll call him again myself."[21]

This illustration of a high-level management meeting is used not so much to suggest how a committee meeting should be run as to show the management style of one of today's most interesting executives, Harold Geneen. While we may or may not agree with his handling of this situation, Geneen obviously has gotten what he wants—executive action.

Committees play an important role in organizations, and it is crucial for managers to learn how to use committees effectively. In Exhibit 14-7, we make certain suggestions to the chairperson and committee participants. Of equal, or greater, importance are those activities that take place *before* the committee convenes. Noted below are important guidelines for the manager.[22]

The purpose of the committee should be clearly defined. The appointing body, usually higher-level management, should ensure that the committee members know the group's purpose. This means knowing the specific charge (the goals), the level of authority (how far the committee can go in gathering information), and the time frame (when the committee is to finish its business). Without a clearly stated purpose, the committee may spend endless hours going in circles.

Give the composition of the committee close consideration. Any group or committee can be doomed without the right people as members. Three guidelines: (a) keep the number of members at a manageable size, usually five to seven—large-sized committees are difficult to coordinate, plus there is the increased probability of cliques; (b) make sure you have some experts who are familiar with the issue; and (c) keep status differences at a minimum—this will facilitate information exchange and reduce chances of domination by a single person.

Develop a habit of working from an agenda. Knowing what is to be done at each meeting will help eliminate idle chatter and keep the group on track toward goal accomplishment.

Choose the meeting site carefully. To remove outside influences, some managers hold committee meetings at neutral sites, such as conference rooms away from the

Exhibit 14-7
Elements of a Successful Meeting

For the Chairperson		For the Committee Member
Handling Committee Members	**Handling Committee Business**	
Encourage the participation of all members	Become knowledgeable in the committee's subject	State your point clearly and logically
Don't compete with other members	Keep the group's energy level high	Carefully examine each potential solution
Go to senior people or higher status members last	Avoid premature decisions	Try for consensus decisions, not majority votes
Seek out members who are experts on the committee task	End all meetings with a wrap-up	Focus on the task, not on personality differences between members

major activities of the organization. Also, the room should be set up so that there is face-to-face interaction among members. Since sitting next to the committee chairperson can be a status position, the chairperson may want to rotate his or her seat.

Provide information on the committee's charge to the members before the meeting. This strategy will allow the members to become familiar with the problem and will help to get the committee off on the right foot.

With the growing complexity of today's organizations, coupled with the rapid rate of change of the external environment, it appears that organizations will continue to require the information pooling, expert evaluation, communication, and coordination that committee structure can provide. There are many disadvantages to the use of committees, but with proper procedures and leadership, these can be far outweighed by the advantages.

There's another meeting in five minutes, Ed. Did you hear me, Ed? Ed?

© Valen Associates

Quality Circles

Within the past thirty years, Japan's annual productivity growth has been four times greater than that of the U.S. and twice that of major European nations. If current U.S. productivity trends continue, by 1990 the output per hour of American workers will lag not only behind that of Japanese workers but also Canadian, West German, and French workers.

Deeply troubled by this slumping productivity, American companies in growing numbers are adopting a system that many management and behavioral scholars believe is the key to Japan's productivity gains: *quality circles*. In these, small groups of employees are trained to spot and solve production problems in their areas. In many companies, quality circles can be found both on the production line and in the office.[23]

The idea of a quality circle is quite simple. A plant committee, composed of management and labor representatives, decides which area of the firm could benefit from group discussion. Eight to ten workers are then asked to serve on a circle. The group meets once a week on company time with their immediate supervisor and with a person trained in personnel and industrial relations. This specialist trains the workers in problem solving, elementary data gathering, and statistics. The circle members then identify and attack a problem and present their ideas to management using such common business methods as histograms and scatter diagrams.

Curiously, the idea for quality circles came originally from U.S. management consultants. The Japanese picked up the idea after World War II as a means of improving the quality of their products. With more than eight million workers in Japan involved in the system, it is used today as a means of increasing both quantity and quality of production.

Quality circles can now be found in many U.S. companies. For example:

■ General Motors has about 100 quality circles in its assembly plants. At one Michigan plant, the circle decided it should do something about the large number of automobiles leaving the assembly line with flat tires. Their analysis eventually traced the problem to a defective tire stem. The part was replaced, saving the company about $225,000 yearly.

- An assembly line circle at the solar-turbine division of International Harvester found a way to simplify the production of a compression disc for a turbine. As a result, several production steps were eliminated, resulting in a huge annual savings.
- A quality circle at American Airlines' maintenance and engineering center in Tulsa came up with savings of $100,000 a year by simply replacing old hand grinders with new, more efficient tools.

In some cases, employees are profiting from participating in quality circles. At Northrop, for example, members of circles are paid about 10 percent of the money the firm saves every year from their suggestions.

Union reaction to quality circles has been mixed. The UAW is favorably disposed, provided the new system does not result in layoffs or increase work pace. Other unions, such as the International Brotherhood of Electrical Workers at General Electric, are demanding a union co-chairperson in each circle. In the end, the ability to guarantee job security appears to be one of the most important trade-offs that management can offer to induce worker cooperation in quality circles.

Venture Groups

In many of today's organizations, the dynamic needs of the market are frequently constrained by the complexity, size, and bureaucracy of the organization's structure and process. The organization's activities can act as a barrier to innovation and new ways of conducting a business.

One new approach that seems partially to eliminate some of these barriers is venture management or venture groups. A *venture group* is an entrepreneurial concept that enjoys remarkable freedom from typical corporate restraints in seeking out growth opportunities and in preparing to capitalize on them.[24] Venture groups are springing up in many corporations and also in a variety of smaller, highly dynamic organizations. They are raising new problems for management, but they are also raising new opportunities for small-group planning, radical new product development, new market or service penetration, and the profitable extension of organizational capabilities in both the near and distant future.

Dow, General Electric, Monsanto, Westinghouse, Celanese, and Union Carbide are using venture groups as an established method of planning entry into new businesses. At Minnesota Mining and Manufacturing, at least two dozen ventures have been in operation at one time, and 3M reports that six of its current divisions have grown out of its venture group concept. Du Pont is also committed to the venture method, where as many as thirty to fifty new development teams can be operating at one time. And at General Mills, the venture operating philosophy has been incorporated into company structure as a New Ventures Department.

There are at least four distinguishing characteristics of venture groups.[25] First, most venture groups focus on this single, unifying goal—to plan their organization's profitable entry into a new business or service area. Second, most, if not all venture groups are formed by taking skilled experts and managers from the various functional areas of the organization and putting them under a single head. The groups generally have few members, and the manager of the group reports only to a higher-level executive. This establishes the all-important autonomy of the group.

Third, venture groups offer a number of distinct advantages to the organization. These include the following:

- A venture group is *unidirectional*. It is chartered for a single purpose; it always knows what business it is in.

- A venture group is *multidisciplinary*. It contains representative skills from the marketing sciences, research and development, finance, and manufacturing. It thus has an external opportunity orientation and an internal cost orientation.

- A venture group is *eclectic*. It enjoys relative freedom in probing market and service needs that offer new opportunities. Its tendency to be innovative is unimpeded by traditional ways of doing business.

- A venture group is a good *management training ground*. Its freedom of activities plus clear-cut purpose and written plan offers a unique opportunity to develop new managerial talent.

- A venture group is *action oriented*. It is dedicated to change, which becomes expected of it. Standing ready to fill new needs, its justification for existence lies in doing something innovative.

The final important characteristic is the eventual disposition of the venture group. Most venture groups are temporary groups in that they are established for a specific purpose and a particular length of time. Once a venture group has completed its charge (e.g., to plan and introduce a new product into the market), at least three actions can be taken with the group. First, the members can go back to their original departments. Second, they can go on to become members of new venture groups. Or third, the group stays together and forms the nucleus of a new division responsible for the newly developed product or product line. This alternative is frequently preferred by organizations because the expertise in the venture group allows the new product to get off on the right foot. It also moves managers and employees into more challenging and responsible positions.

Venture groups are not without some significant criticisms. Some of the negative comments range from claims that venture groups tie up too many valuable people, to accusations that they create a ''prima donna'' environment or that many of the generated ideas have little or no commercial application.

By far the most severe criticism that has been directed at venture groups concerns organizational spinoffs. Frequently, and instead of developing a bright new idea for the mother organization, they decide to form their own company. This has been a particular problem for high technology companies, such as Texas Instruments, which has seen more than a half-dozen new companies form in the last ten years from the ideas of former TI employees.[26] While there are certain legal considerations that can be brought to bear, it is clear that the entrepreneurial drive—the belief that you can do something better by yourself in your own organization—is a powerful motive for many managers.

Computer Management Groups

Although they possess strong technical expertise, computer specialists who manage data-processing systems at many companies often lack the business background needed to determine how these systems can improve the organization's processes and output.[27] In recent years, nearly 100 companies have filled that void by taking computer management out of the hands of technicians and putting it into the hands of computer management teams. These groups usually consist of managers and executives from the organization's various departments and functional areas who appear to be as comfortable talking about profits and losses as they are about bits and bytes.

The major objective in forming these intergroup units is to try to improve the organization's use of computers in everything from strategic planning to production and inventory control. Instead of letting computer technology determine how the company should operate, the computer management teams see to it that the needs of the organization dictate how the computer is used.

Since the per capita white-collar investment in computers and information systems is expected to hit $20,000 by 1990 (a four-fold jump from 1980), the responsibility given to these computer groups is significant. In determining how to fit computers to the company's needs, the groups also oversee the purchasing of computer hardware and software, limiting purchases to what is really necessary.

Computer task forces also try to increase the efficiency of their existing facilities. This often requires them to arbitrate among the demands of competing division heads for computer time. At Inland Steel, the systems review group, which consists of seven executives of vice-presidential rank and higher, decides the computer priorities among corporate sales, finance, and manufacturing. Similarly, at Security Pacific National Bank in Los Angeles, the administrative planning group formally reviews plans for information systems and resources every ninety days. Finally, at Massachusetts Mutual Life Insurance Company, all divisions that use computer services are represented on a steering committee, which is responsible for computer usage, planning new systems, and even implementation.

Even when companies eventually hire a computer expert capable of making both systems-oriented and business-oriented decisions, the computer task force that had been filling that void seldom disbands. The coordination, directional, and efficiency benefits that have resulted from the performance of computer task forces appear to be too valuable for managers to easily give up.

Public Policy Groups

In our discussion on computer management groups, the focus of attention was primarily internal to the organization. Frequently, the benefits of cross-functional task forces can be applied to external issues as well.

Such is the thrust of the public policy group, an approach that has been initiated in more than 100 major companies.[28] Begun by such firms as General Motors, the policy groups help management deal more effectively with many outside pressures. Public policy groups have become highly influential, especially in guiding firms on complex and controversial issues.

The characteristics of existing policy groups vary greatly across different companies; there is no set of common issues that policy groups discuss. For example, General Electric's public policy group once tabulated no fewer than 120 issues of concern, ranging from the environment, product safety, equal opportunity employment, energy conservation, and data privacy, to community relations, political action, charitable contributions, and relations with stockholders and employees.

Second, the mix of members also differs from company to company, including board members, management, employees, and academicians. At General Motors, AT&T, and J. C. Penney, the groups are made up entirely of outside directors. At Mobil, Travelers Insurance, and Beatrice Foods, outsiders make up a majority of the members, with a minority of management personnel. Phillip Morris's group of nine includes five company managers. Having management represented ensures that the person responsible for implementing a decision also helped make the decision.

Mead's corporate responsibility committee, as it is called, also includes employees as participating members. The employees, usually union representatives, are chosen by an elaborate nomination and election system. They bring up issues that would not usually be discussed—questions of internal communications, resolution of conflicts, and privacy of records, for example.

A third characteristic of the public policy committee is its dual role. It has to look outward to see what the trends are in the country (among environmentalists, consumer activists, stockholders) and how they are likely to affect the organization. At the same time, the group must look inward to determine exactly how the company is responding, or can respond. Not surprisingly, such discussions can become lively, as in the case of GM's decision to continue doing business in South Africa. Group member Reverend Leon Sullivan spoke against the decision in group meetings and even took the floor at the firm's annual meeting to voice his opposition.

Lastly, public policy groups need information. They are able to call on many sources, both inside and outside the organization, to help their deliberations. Because of the importance of the membership and the issues at hand, the information is usually forthcoming—sometimes too much so!

Public policy groups in organizations have gained a great deal of influence within firms, and there are signs that further expansion can be expected.

The Group Manager

John Agal is forty-two years old, prosperous, and by most measures a success. John, his wife, and their three children live in a large home in a suburban community, where they enjoy many of the pleasures of the "good life." Even with this seemingly positive situation, John's wife has seen him become increasingly discontented, frustrated, and irritable. He complains about a lack of sense of accomplishment, a growing feeling of isolation from both his peers and subordinates, and nagging doubts about his self-worth.

John's problem traces back to over a year ago, when he received his most recent promotion at AMT Industries, a manufacturer and distributor of a variety of industrial machinery. For five years, he was the successful divisional manager of specialty molded machinery for AMT. This performance led to his advancement to group manager of industrial products, where he has four divisional managers reporting to him. Even though he has advanced up the hierarchy, he feels he is no longer in the middle of the action. On one hand, he sees the exciting activity below him at the divisional level, and above him at the executive level. On the other hand, he is frustrated because his management role is unclear, his decision-making latitude appears to be narrower, and his direct authority over the divisions is questionable. He finds himself in the role of thinker, planner, and director, yet confronted with the responsibilities of a doer.

This hypothetical situation is reality to many individuals who hold what has become a popular organizational position—*the group manager*.[29] As shown in exhibit 14-8, the group manager position is the result of the growth and complexities of many of today's organizations. In its most basic form, the group manager position is created in multiproduct or multiservice organizations when it is recognized that a single executive can no longer handle the growing span of control. In response to this situation, a new layer of management is established and a group of product or divisional managers reports to the new group manager. As group manager of industrial products, John Agal may have divisional managers reporting to him who are responsible for specialty machinery, numerical control equipment, food processing equipment, and industrial cleaning machinery.

Group managers usually identify three factors that can lead to feelings of frustration, stress, and lack of accomplishment. First, he or she is neither a super-divisional manager nor a higher-level executive, but one who is sandwiched between these two organizational levels. As in John's case, the group manager position rarely carries either the *operational* decision authority of a divisional manager or the *strategic*

Exhibit 14-8
The Group
Manager Position

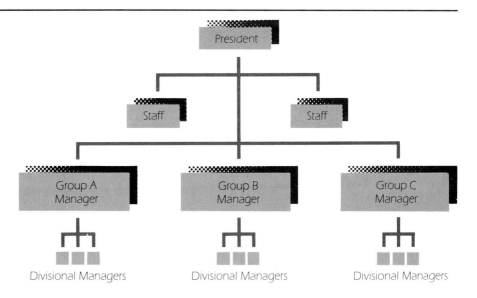

Divisional Managers   Divisional Managers   Divisional Managers

decision authority of an executive. Thus, the group manager is neither fish nor fowl. This problem, then, is one of *role definition*.

Second, the group manager's position often lacks the mechanisms or resources to contribute much to the performance of the divisions or to the overall direction of the organization. Group managers usually have few if any staff resources of their own and too little organizational staff support to help them participate effectively in either division or corporate affairs. The end result is a group manager who really has no true "group," but a collection of rather independent subordinate managers. The group manager becomes little more than an administrator, consolidator of numbers, information conduit, or liaison person (see Chapter 8).

Finally, there is the issue of motivation and rewards, where a paradox exists. On one hand, the group manager's income and bonus are directly tied to the collective performance of his or her divisions. But the group manager has little direct impact on the division's year-to-year performance. This reward paradox not only leads to concern over one's income, but questions of prestige and achievement arise when he or she attempts to identify particular contributions.

Given this all-too-frequent situation, one might argue that the group manager concept is a failure. Unfortunately, no alternative is available for diversified organizations that require a management layer between executive and numerous operating divisions. Somehow these sometimes-diverse organizational activities must be grouped into a manageable number of units. Enter the group manager.

Despite its faults and potential frustrations, the group manager concept will probably continue to be an integral part of the organizational world for some time to come. The group manager concept is also important in that it highlights the need for the person to develop a "general manager" as opposed to a "specialized manager" philosophy. We will cover this point in more depth in chapter 19.

 ## POINTS TO CONSIDER
An Emphasis on Managerial Skills

1. **Learn to live with group activities.**
   While many of us have had bad experiences working with groups, this should not cause us to shy away from future group activities. Since working with groups is almost inevitable in your jobs, knowing the advantages and disadvantages of group interactions is a valuable piece of knowledge.

2. **Informal groups can contribute much to the organization.**
   Many managers take the view that informal groups subvert or at least deter goal achievement in organizations. On the contrary, many informal groups can add a great deal. The key, however, is to ensure that the group's norms and purpose are congruent with those of the organization.

3. **Achieving high group performance involves many factors.**
   What does it take to get groups to perform at high levels? At minimum, factors such as successful movement to the latter stages of group development, organizationally congruent norms, clarity of roles, and a cohesive environment are important.

4.   **The task force chairperson holds a key organizational role.**
     To most people, it is clear that the leadership exhibited by the chairperson of a task force or committee is crucial to the group's successful performance. It is important to keep in mind that in the chairperson role, the manager represents not so much his or her functional area, but rather the total organization. This global, as opposed to narrow, viewpoint enables the group to study and discuss larger issues. Involved, then, is the development of key conceptual skills.

 # SUMMARY FOR THE MANAGER

1.   Groups in organizations serve many functions—from task accomplishment to socio-psychological satisfaction—and exist in a number of forms—functional groups, project groups, and interest groups. Since managers can spend a great deal of time in group activities, it is important to understand the key concepts that can lead to higher group performance.

2.   Groups develop in stages, involving orientation, internal problem-solving, growth and productivity, and evaluation and control. Groups can develop naturally through the stages or revert to an earlier stage due to the introduction of a new task, a new leader, or new members. The manager must recognize where his or her group is in its developmental sequence, because groups tend to perform better in the latter stages. If a group remains in its early stages of development, much of the members' time and energy is directed toward clarifying relationships, goals, and procedures, and resolving conflict.

3.   Norms, which have both behavioral and performance components, are one of the strongest factors in determining group performance. Norm conformity can be considered a ticket to group acceptance. Since norms will form in most groups that interact over a period of time, the manager needs to know what the norms are and at what level they operate. This is where some of the manager's diagnostic skills come into play.

4.   Status systems, much like norms, are an almost inevitable occurrence in organizational groups and committees. Job titles, seniority, and expertise can all lead to some form of status within the group. What is important is agreement among group members on individual status levels (i.e., status congruence). Without such agreement, confusion, conflict, and misdirected energies will develop.

5.   Roles represent what is expected of the individual in the group concerning his or her duties, authority, and responsibilities. Problems with roles—either role ambiguity or role conflict—can be barriers to high performance. Role ambiguity—the lack of clarity with respect to what one is supposed to do—can be countered through additional training and experience, or by directly asking for clarification from a higher authority. Role conflict—originating from multiple demands on one's time—can be alleviated by appealing to a higher authority or by ranking activities by priority.

6.   Cohesion is one of the most powerful determinants of group performance. The group solidarity associated with a cohesive environment creates a unity of purpose that is a positive influence on performance. The most important factor in increasing cohesiveness is seeing high performance as the result of the combined effect of both cohesion and norms. That is, higher-performing groups exhibit high cohesion *and* high group performance norms.

7.   In the form of a task force or a committee, groups can sometimes be given decision-making responsibility. The pooling of knowledge and the assembly effect are positive features, whereas time, premature decisions, and the possibility of groupthink are negative features.

8. With more and more Japanese firms operating in the U.S., the interaction between culture and group activities becomes important. This is especially critical in such issues as consensus decision making, authority systems, and long-range planning.

9. Groups have found wide application in many organizations. Examples include information exchange (committees), decision-making (computer management groups), planning and implementation (venture groups), and strengthening the management hierarchy (the group manager).

10. Groups influence many aspects of the manager's job. Groups are a focal element of the manager's leadership function, whether it is leading subordinates or chairing a committee. Following procedures and agendas, resolving conflict, identifying the group's contribution to the total organization, and pinpointing group problems all involve important managerial skills. In much the same manner, being the group leader, acting as a communication and information transmitter, and making resource allocation decisions concern managerial roles.

 # REVIEW AND DISCUSSION QUESTIONS

1. Describe the possible conditions that would cause a group in the control stage to revert to the internal problem-solving stage.
2. Can you identify particular jobs, occupations, or organizations in which group behavior is not important?
3. Discuss the development of trade unions in terms of type of group and stages of group development.
4. When a manager believes his or her group has set performance norms well below what they are capable of attaining, what can be done to raise these norms?
5. Under what conditions can status incongruence develop?
6. Can the manager control the composition of the group he or she manages?
7. Describe some sources of role ambiguity and role conflict.
8. Is cohesiveness a more important aspect of group performance for functional groups than for task or project groups?
9. How may the manager increase the frequency of group interaction to increase cohesiveness?
10. Would it be a sound managerial policy to break up a highly cohesive group that has low performance norms?

NOTES

1. See M. E. Shaw, *Group Dynamics: The Psychology of Small Group Behavior,* 2nd ed. (New York: McGraw-Hill, 1976).
2. See D. Cartwright and A. Zander, eds., *Group Dynamics: Research and Theory,* 3rd ed. (New York: Harper & Row, 1968).
3. R. Likert, *New Patterns in Management* (New York: McGraw-Hill, 1961).
4. K. Davis, *Human Behavior at Work,* 5th ed. (New York: McGraw-Hill, 1977), pp. 274-76.
5. W. Bennis and H. A. Shepard, "A Theory of Group Development," *Human Relations* (Summer 1963): 414-57.
6. See P. C. Andre de la Porte, "Group Norms: Key to Building a Winning Team," *Personnel* (September-October 1974): 60-67.

7. H. T. Reitan and M. E. Shaw, "Group Membership, Sex Compositions of the Group, and Conformity Behavior," *Journal of Social Psychology* (October 1969): 45-51.

8. R. Kahn, D. Wolfe, R. Quinn, and J. Snoek, *Organizational Stress: Studies in Role Conflict and Ambiguity* (New York: Wiley, 1964).

9. See J. L. Pearce, "Bringing Some Clarity to Role Ambiguity Research," *Academy of Management Review* (October 1981): 665-74; A. D. Szilagyi, "An Empirical Test of Causal Influences Between Role Perceptions, Job Satisfaction, Performance, and Organizational Level," *Personnel Psychology* (1977); and B. L. Toffler, "Occupational Role Development: The Changing Determinants of Outcomes for the Individual," *Administrative Science Quarterly* (September 1981): 396-418.

10. A. J. Lott and B. E. Lott, "Group Cohesiveness as Interpersonal Attraction: A Review of Relationships and Antecedent and Consequent Variables," *Psychological Bulletin* (October 1965): 259-309.

11. A. D. Szilagyi, W. E. Holland, and C. Oliver, "Keys to Success with Open Plan Offices," *Management Review* (August 1979): 26-28, 38-41.

12. See R. M. Hogarth, *Judgement and Choice* (New York: Wiley, 1980); and Shaw, *Group Dynamics,* p. 35.

13. See A. Van de Ven, A. Delbeq, and D. H. Gustafson, *Group Techniques for Program Planning* (Glenview, Ill.: Scott, Foresman, 1975).

14. I. L. Janis, "Groupthink," *Psychology Today* (November 1971).

15. I. L. Janis, *Victims of Groupthink* (New York: Houghton-Mifflin, 1972).

16. D. D. Buss, "Japanese-Owned Auto Plants in the U.S. Present a Tough Challenge for the UAW," *The Wall Street Journal* (March 23, 1983).

17. See S. Matsuno and W. A. Stoever, "Japanese Boss, American Employees," *The Wharton Magazine* (Fall 1982): 45-48; and T. Ozawa, "Japanese Chic," *Across the Board* (October 1982): 6-13.

18. G. M. Prince, "How to be a Better Meeting Chairman," *Harvard Business Review* (January-February 1969): 98-108.

19. See R. A. Golde, "Are Your Meetings Like This One?," *Harvard Business Review* (January-February 1972): 68-77; and A. Jay, "How to Run a Meeting," *Harvard Business Review* (March-April 1976): 43-57.

20. N. R. F. Maier, "Assets and Liabilities in Group Problem Solving," *Psychological Bulletin* (July 1967): 239-49.

21. "They Call it Geneen U.," *Forbes* (May 1, 1968).

22. See R. Tillman, Jr., "Committees On Trial," *Harvard Business Review* (May-June 1960); and "Committees: Their Role in Management Today," *Management Review* (October 1957): 4-10.

23. See "The Workers Know Best," *Time* (January 28, 1980): 65; "A Partnership to Build the New Workplace," *Business Week (June 30, 1980): 61-64; and K. A. Brooke, "QC Circles' Success Depends on Management Readiness to Support Workers' Involvement," Industrial Engineering* (January 1982): 76-82; and G. Munchus, "Employer-Employee Based Quality Circles in Japan: Human Resource Policy Implications for American Firms," *Academy of Management Review* (April 1983): 255-61.

24. See K. H. Vesper, *New Venture Strategies* (Englewood Cliffs, N.J.: Prentice-Hall, 1980).

25. M. Hanan, "Corporate Growth Through Venture Management," *Harvard Business Review* (January-February 1969): 43-61.

26. D. Clark, "Texas Instruments and Its Breakaway Off-Spring," *Texas Business* (September 1979): 36-41.

27. "Solving Computer Mismatch in Management," *Business Week* (April 2, 1979): 73-76.

28. J. Perham, "New Tool for Company Boards," *Dun's Review* (October 1980): 101-102.

29. J. H. Ransom, "The Group Executive's Job: Mission Impossible?" *Management Review* (March 1979): 9-14.

Managing Groups
The United Chemical Company

The United Chemical Company is a large producer and distributor of commodity chemicals with five chemical production plants in the United States. The main operations plant at Baytown, Texas, includes not only production equipment but also is the site of the company's research and engineering center.

The process design group consists of eight male engineers and the supervisor, Max Kane. The group has worked together steadily for a number of years, and good relationships had developed among all members. When the workload began to increase, Max hired a new design engineer, Sue Davis, a recent masters degree graduate from one of the foremost engineering schools in the country. Sue was assigned to a project whose goal was expansion of one of the existing plant facility's capacity. Three other design engineers were assigned to the project along with Sue: Jack Keller (age thirty-eight, fifteen years with the company); Sam Sims (age forty, ten years with the company); and Lance Madison (age thirty-two, eight years with the company).

As a new employee, Sue was very enthusiastic about the opportunity to work at United. She liked her work very much because it was challenging and it offered her a chance to apply much of the knowledge she had gained in her university studies. On the job, Sue kept fairly much to herself and her design work. Her relations with her fellow project members were friendly, but she did not go out of her way to have informal conversations during or after working hours.

Sue was a diligent employee who took her work quite seriously. On occasions when a difficult problem arose, she would stay after hours in order to come up with a solution. Because of her persistence, coupled with her more current education, Sue completed her portion of the various project stages usually a number of days before her colleagues. This was somewhat irritating to her because on these occasions she went to Max to ask for additional work to keep her busy until her fellow workers caught up to her. Initially, she had offered to help Jack, Sam, and Lance with their portion of the project, but each time she was turned down very tersely.

About five months after Sue had joined the design group, Jack asked to see Max about a problem the group was having. The conversation between Max and Jack was as follows:

- MAX: Jack, I understand you wanted to discuss a problem with me.
- JACK: Yes, Max. I didn't want to waste your time, but some of the other design engineers wanted me to discuss Sue with you. She is irritating everyone with her know-it-all, pompous attitude. She just is not the kind of person that we want to work with.
- MAX: I can't understand that, Jack. She's an excellent worker whose design work is always well done and usually flawless. She's doing everything the company wants her to do.
- JACK: The company never asked her to disturb the morale of the group or to tell us how to do our work. The animosity of the group can eventually result in lower quality work for the whole unit.
- MAX: I'll tell you what I'll do. Sue has a meeting with me next week to discuss her six-month performance. I'll keep your thoughts in mind, but I can't promise an improvement in what you and the others believe is a pompous attitude.
- JACK: Immediate improvement in her behavior is not the problem, it's her coaching others when she has no right to engage in publicly showing others what to

do. You'd think she was lecturing an advance class in design with all her high-power, useless equations and formulas. She'd better back off soon, or some of us will quit or transfer.

During the next week, Max thought carefully about his meeting with Jack. He knew that Jack was the informal leader of the design engineers and generally spoke for the other group members. On Thursday of the following week, Max called Sue into his office for her midyear review. Certain excerpts of the conversation were as follows:

- MAX: There is one other aspect I'd like to discuss with you about your performance. As I just related to you, your technical performance has been excellent; however, there are some questions about your relationships with the other workers.
- SUE: I don't understand—what questions are you talking about?
- MAX: Well, to be specific, certain members of the design group have complained about your apparent "know-it-all attitude" and the manner in which you try to tell them how to do their job. You're going to have to be patient with them and not publicly call them out about their performance. This is a good group of engineers, and their work over the years has been more than acceptable. I don't want any problems that will cause the group to produce less effectively.
- SUE: Let me make a few comments. First of all, I have never publicly criticized their

performance to them or to you. Initially, when I was finished ahead of them, I offered to help them with their work, but was bluntly told to mind my own business. I took the hint and concentrated only on my part of the work.
- MAX: Okay, I understand that.
- SUE: What you don't understand is that after five months of working in this group I have come to the conclusion that what is going on is a "rip-off" of the company. The other engineers are "goldbricking" and setting a work pace much less than they're capable of. They're more interested in the music from Sam's radio, the local football team, and the bar they're going to go to for TGIF. I'm sorry, but this is just not the way I was raised or trained. And finally, they've never looked on me as a qualified engineer, but as a woman who has broken their professional barrier.
- MAX: The assessment and motivation of the engineers is a managerial job. Your job is to do your work as well as you can without interfering with the work of others. As for the male-female comment, this company hired you because of your qualifications, not your sex. Your future at United is quite promising if you do the engineering and leave the management to me.

Sue left the meeting very depressed. She knew that she was performing well and that the other design engineers were not working up to their capacity. This knowledge frustrated her more and more as the weeks passed.

Questions for Discussion

1. Does Sue value her membership in the group? Explain.
2. What is Sue seeking from membership in the design group? What are the other members seeking from membership in the group?
3. How do you rate the way Max handled his meeting with Sue?

4. Discuss this situation in terms of the stages of group development.
5. Discuss this situation in terms of structural dimensions of groups.
6. What should Sue do next? What should Max do next?

EXPERIENTIAL EXERCISE
The Desert Survival Situation

Purpose

1. To examine the process of group decision-making.

2. To investigate and experience some of the benefits of group decision-making in comparison with individual decision-making.

Required Understanding

The student should have a basic understanding of the components of group structure and the elements of group decision-making.

How to Set Up the Exercise

Groups of between four to eight persons should be established for the 45–60-minute exercise. The groups should be physically separated and members asked to converse only with their own group members.

The Situation

It is approximately 10 a.m. in mid-August and you have just crash-landed in the Sonora Desert in the southwestern United States. The light twin-engine plane, containing the bodies of the pilot and co-pilot, has completely burned. Only the air frame remains. None of the rest of you have been injured.

The pilot was unable to notify anyone of your position before the crash. However, he had indicated before impact that you were 70 miles south-southwest from a mining camp which is the nearest known habitation, and that you were approximately 65 miles off the course that was filed in your VFR flight plan.

The immediate area is quite flat and except for occasional barrel and saguaro cacti, appears to be rather barren. The last weather report indicated the temperature would reach 110 degrees that day, which means that the temperature at ground level will be 130 degrees. You are dressed in light clothing—short-sleeved shirts or blouses, pants, and street shoes. Everyone has a handkerchief. Collectively, your pockets contain $2.83 in change, $85.00 in bills, a pack of cigarettes, and a ballpoint pen.

Instructions for the Exercise

Before the plane caught fire your group was able to salvage the fifteen items shown in exhibit 14-9. You may assume that the number of survivors is the same as the number on your team, you are the actual people in the situation, the team has agreed to stick together, and all items are in good condition. Your task is twofold:

1. *Individually,* rank order the fifteen items from 1, the most important, to 15, the least important. Do not discuss the situation until each member has finished. Take approximately ten minutes.

2. *As a group,* perform the same task of ranking the fifteen items. Once the group discussion has begun, do not change your individual rankings. You have forty-five minutes to perform this phase of the exercise.

All ranking should be placed on exhibit 14-9. An expert's evaluation of this situation will be provided by your instructor.

Exhibit 14-9
Ranking for the Desert Survival Exercise

Items	Step 1 Your Individual Ranking	Step 2 The Team's Ranking	Step 3 Survival Expert's Ranking	Step 4 Difference Between Step 1 & Step 3	Step 5 Difference Between Step 2 & Step 3
flashlight (4-battery size)					
jackknife					
sectional air map of the area					
plastic raincoat (large size)					
magnetic compass					
compress kit with gauze					
.45 caliber pistol (loaded)					
parachute (red and white)					
bottle of salt tablets (1000 tablets)					
1 quart of water per person					
a book entitled *Edible Animals of the Desert*					
a pair of sunglasses per person					
2 quarts of 180-proof Vodka					
1 topcoat per person					
a cosmetic mirror					
			TOTALS		
			(the lower the score the better)	Your Score Step 4	Team Score Step 5

Source: "The Desert Survival Situation," developed by Human Synergistics. Reprinted by permission.

INTERVIEW

Elizabeth H. Calderon

*Associate Hospital Director
Hermann Hospital
Houston, Texas
(Hermann Hospital is the
primary teaching hospital
for the University of
Texas Medical School at
Houston.)*

Q: What important elements make up your hospital's control system?

A: In a labor-intensive environment that must be staffed 24 hours daily, 365 days per year, the key controls focus on daily staffing requirements. The Hospital's daily census is calculated each midnight, and totals as well as breakdown by service (surgery, internal medicine, OB-GYN, pediatrics, psychiatry, critical care units, etc.) are graphed as are monthly and year-to-date patient days. These totals are reviewed by the Operations Council each morning at 8:00 o'clock.

Analysis of the daily census, along with the computerized nursing acuity system, which measures on an individual basis the level of required nursing care, enables the hospital to staff appropriately and cost effectively.

Q: How often are control variables monitored?

A: All staff positions are monitored bi-weekly through the Position Control Master printout that lists approved positions, open and filled, and no recruitment begins until the position-control coordinator approves.

Annual hospital goals and objectives are monitored monthly, and formal reports are filed quarterly and annually. Budget review is monthly, and department directors have ten days to explain 5% +/− variances to the appropriate administrator and chief operating officer. Other monthly controls include payroll distribution reports and accounts receivable/payable.

Continuous controls occur through productivity monitoring, the quality assurance program, and internal audit and purchasing reports. Except for goals and objectives, all reports are computerized.

Q: What type of performance appraisal system does your organization use for managerial and nonmanagerial employees?

A: A criterion-referenced evaluation form is used for both managerial and nonmanagerial employees. The system is based on seven points, and it provides specific questions for promotion-readiness, plans to assist employees in identified areas for needed improvement, and a section for narrative description of an employee's performance. Performance evaluation is conducted at the end of the 90-day probationary period, 90 days following a promotion, and annually. Appended narrative generally is used in addition to the standardized evaluation form for managerial personnel, especially at the department director and assistant director level.

The hospital administrator group measures department directors on their achievement of goals and objectives, turnover, and budget and personnel management. Outstanding directors are selected from

Evaluating Performance: Control

the group of approximately 60 and named as best directors of the fiscal year. Hospital administrators are provided with an oral performance review.

Q: Do you train your supervisors in methods of conducting performance appraisal interviews?

A: Supervisors are trained in performance appraisals both by the department director and through educational sessions offered by the hospital's Human Resources Department.

Q: How important is your management information system to your organization?

A: At Hermann Hospital, MIS is virtually totally computerized computation, dissemination, and monitoring of the hospital control systems.

Q: What key data are included?

A. Key data included in the MIS are census, disbursements, receivables, budget, payroll, position control, patient acuity, patient registration, patient-record location, billing, and patient diagnostic and procedural summarization.

Q: To what degree are middle- and lower-level managers involved in the budget process?

A: Responsibility for budget compilation and monitoring is at the department director level, following approval and consultation with the appropriate hospital administrator. Supervisor input varies based on the size of a department and the expertise of an individual supervisor. In most departments the final budget and its monthly monitoring is shared among the management staff, with individuals being encouraged to stay within budget guidelines through exposure to the budget performance.

Q: How is the budget monitored in your organization?

A: Accountability occurs through monitoring the revenue expense reports (RAS reports), the payroll distribution reports, and the position-control master list. A summarization reviewed by the appropriate area administrator each month and ultimately reviewed by the chief operations officer and budget director is an additional monitor.

Q: What important skills should future managers develop to become effective managers?

A: Future managers will have to be highly proficient in a variety of skills, with an increased emphasis on fiscal management. Specifically, future managers should know budgeting, accounting, statistics, and personnel management—including interviewing, training, counseling, and evaluating. A sure knowledge of labor relations is essential, along with a working knowledge of computer science.

Communication skills will increase in importance, and the ability to communicate orally and in writing possibly will mean the difference between the upwardly mobile manager and the one who remains static. The ability to develop goals and objectives in a well-articulated manner and to master forecasting and long-range planning will be key factors in success. Productivity monitoring is a major area—managers will need to know how to set standards and develop appropriate monitoring.

Working with other departments in a collegial manner for the good of the organization will set apart the successful manager in the organizations of the future.

CHAPTER

15

Elements of Control

Chapter Outline

Key Points

1. Control is a managerial function that assures that actual activities conform to planned activities. Three types of control are found in most organizations: input controls, process controls, and output controls.
2. Control indicates how effectively the other management functions—planning, organizing, and leading—are performing.
3. Operating and financial budgets are important parts of the manager's job.
4. Managers who are responsible for working within a budget should have some say in its development—this is the bottom-up approach.
5. Financial statements determine the state of the organization's financial resources during or at a particular time period.
6. Financial ratios are used to analyze the organization's current financial position and identify important trends.
7. External financial audits—usually performed by professional accounting firms—and internal audits are used to verify the organization's financial position and the validity of its financial statements.
8. A management audit includes an evaluation of the organization's goals, strategies, policies, and so on.
9. Financial statements, financial analyses, and audits vary greatly in the international realm.

Emerson Electric

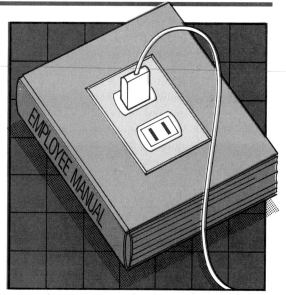

When a young management consultant named Charles F. Knight took over as chairman of St. Louis's Emerson Electric Company in the mid-70s, Wall Street had some doubts about the future of the company. The doubts soon faded as Knight took charge and quickened Emerson's growth pace.

Emerson's net profit of nearly 8 percent is well above the industry average of 4.6 percent, and its 18 percent return on capital compares with an estimated industry average of 12.5 percent. The company's success is attributed to the unique way it has engineered and managed that impressive record. Maintaining the flexibility usually associated with a small company, it has flourished through a meticulously orchestrated growth plan and a management control system that is considered one of the best in industry.

Emerson is decentralized by product lines into thirty-five divisions, each of which makes its own operating decisions and is run pretty much as an independent company. Knight keeps as much decision making as possible at the operating level because he feels that division managers are in the best position to respond quickly to the marketplace and determine what steps can be taken at the lowest cost in keeping with efficiency and product quality.

Knight has developed a sophisticated system of internal management controls that allows Emerson, which operates in markets where price competitiveness is often of top priority, to build sales by consistently underpricing the competition and yet maintain high quality and profit margins.

Planning and control start at the division level, where each manager must come up with detailed growth projections (one year and five year) for every product line—showing how much growth will come from acquisitions, internal sales, new product development, and overseas and government business. The priorities and strategies for attaining the next year's goals are refined in a corporate planning conference that top management holds with division managers. What emerges is a written plan of action and control systems for achieving the goals, product by product, with subordinate managers made responsible for dozens of lesser goals. That manual becomes the bible for every manager.

Emerson also motivates its managers through an incentive system that pays bonuses of up to 40 percent of salary for meeting goals. But most important, Knight believes, is the commitment of all managers to meet those goals. "There are a lot of companies that have systems to control profits," he says, "but what most of them lack is the dedication and commitment that goes down six and seven levels." Knight believes that the reason planning and cost control work better at Emerson is the flexibility, incentives, and discipline incorporated into their system.

Adapted from "Emerson Electric: The Unique Manager," *Dun's Review* (December 1977): 52-55.

15

With this chapter, we begin a four-chapter sequence dealing with the important managerial function of control. We will be concerned with those managerial activities designed to assure that both the actual operations and the final products or services of an organization conform to its stated goals and plans. As seen in our *Practice of Management* section on Emerson Electric, the link between planning and control is a key to managerial and organizational performance.

This chapter will be divided into three main parts. First, we will briefly outline the key elements of managerial control. We will follow this with a discussion of financial control, including budgets, financial analyses, and audits. The chapter will conclude with an overview of financial control in the international realm.

Elements of Control

The control function is one of the major guiding principles of the entire management process. All types of organizations use control. For example, Teledyne won't invest in a new project unless it can return 20 percent on assets; Polaroid not only wanted a debris-less film, but a camera that could fit into a coat pocket; Kellogg's will introduce a new cereal if it can capture at least 1 percent of the market; the Cleveland Clinic limits the number of research assistants according to available grant money.

Managers themselves have their own philosophy of control, which guides their behavior, and influences the behavior of those around them. For instance, consider the case of Harry Gray, the hard-driving chairman of United Technologies.

> Gray considers himself a prototype of the corporate generalist. He is as interested in financial management as he is in marketing, and he has introduced exceptionally tight-fisted financial controls on both operating expenses and capital investment. To generate more cash flow, he has reduced "days outstanding" on accounts by as much as 40 percent and has increased "turnover of inventories" significantly.
>
> Gray is also a very tough taskmaster. There has been a steady exodus of managers who have failed to meet his profit targets and controls. "Harry is a helluva driver who demands constant attention to detail," says a man who once worked for him. "Although he delegated responsibility, he wanted to be part of the process. He wanted to know what every one of his people was doing every minute of the day. Some people wouldn't go to the bathroom without calling Harry."[1]

Planning and control work hand-in-hand in organizations. For example, there are marked interrelationships among the concepts of direction, resources, problems, and performance.

Planning		Control
Provides a sense of direction and attention to goals	DIRECTION	Guides activities toward organizational ends
Allocates the resources of the organization	RESOURCES	Ensures the effective utilization of organizational resources
Anticipates problems	PROBLEMS	Corrects problems
Motivates employees to achieve organizational goals	EMPLOYEES	Rewards employees for goal achievement

More than anything else, these interrelationships emphasize that the elements of the management process must be integrated for acceptable performance.[2]

The Control Process

Control, like many managerial functions, is a process that involves a number of steps. As shown in exhibit 15-1, there are usually four:

Establish performance standards. Standards are reference points to which actual performance can be compared. In their most basic form, standards are the various goals and subgoals that have been set by the organization. Examples include load factors and seat-miles set by airline companies, as well as sales per square foot in department stores.

Measure performance. Measuring performance has at least two aspects. First, what *methods* will be used to measure the level of performance? As discussed in chapter 1, quantitative measures, qualitative measures, or a combination of both can be used. For example, a manager's performance can be measured according to the unit's profit contribution to the organization (quantitative measure) and the superior's evaluation of such subjective measures as the manager's initiative and ability to get along with others (qualitative measures). The second major consideration is *time*—when will the activity be measured? As pointed out in chapter 12, at least two time-frames can be used—continuous or intermittent. A continuous framework measures activities that occur on each unit, such as quality-control checks on tractors manufactured by John Deere. An intermittent framework measures activities at specified time intervals, such

Exhibit 15-1
Steps in a Control Process

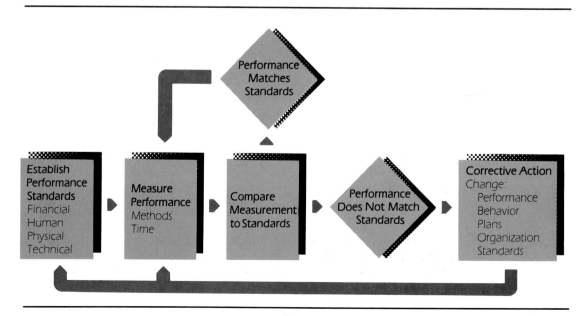

as a manager's yearly merit review or the bi-monthly evaluation of inventories by a business supply distributor. The important consideration for managers in choosing the time interval is that it should not be so short as to incur excessive control costs, nor so long such that performance problems are not detected.

Compare the performance to the standard. As shown in exhibit 15-1, this step involves a decision by the manager. If performance meets the standard, the control process returns to the measurement stage. If performance does not meet the standard, corrective action may be required.

Corrective action. Corrective action by the organization and/or the manager is required when the performance and performance standard do not match. This deviation between performance and standard can be favorable or unfavorable to the organization. A department store may establish a standard of $20 sales per square foot of store space for each store. If one store reports sales of $24 per square foot, the deviation is obviously favorable to the organization. In the long run, management may decide to revise the standard upward, or consider expanding the store. In contrast, consider a domestic airline in the monthly process of evaluating the performance of its individual routes. If a particular route is operating at only 45 percent of aircraft seat capacity (when 65 percent is the stated standard), the airline may contemplate such corrective measures as added promotion, fare decreases, or even discontinuation of the route. Corrective action can thus change the performance of the unit, or force a re-evaluation of the standard and its associated goals and plans.

As this brief discussion of the control process indicates, control is an important function that is performed by managers in all types of organizations. Control involves such aspects as financial performance, inventory cost control, sales force performance, absenteeism and turnover, employee productivity, safety, market share, and the like. It is, therefore, found throughout the organization.

Types of Control

Consider the position of director of area blood banks for a large metropolitan hospital district. As manager of the central source of blood units for the county health care institutions, the director is concerned with a number of control factors. Among the most important are acquiring sufficient supplies of blood from various donation programs, making sure that the units have been properly analyzed and stored, and keeping the departmental operating costs within budgetary limits. As shown in exhibit 15-2, this situation calls for three types of control—input controls, process controls, and output controls.[3]

Input controls. Sometimes called steering controls, input controls detect deviations from a standard or goal to permit correction *before* the major activity has begun. In the blood bank example, the director may compare present and planned inventories with planned surgery schedules and trends in emergency room usage. As noted in exhibit 15-2, other examples include analyzing job descriptions, selection and placement activities, raw material inspection, budget requirements, and training needs.

Process controls. This type of control acts as a *screening* process, so the main activity may not continue if the standard has not been met. In other words, it determines whether a unit in process is acceptable or unacceptable. Production and process

Exhibit 15-2
Types of Control

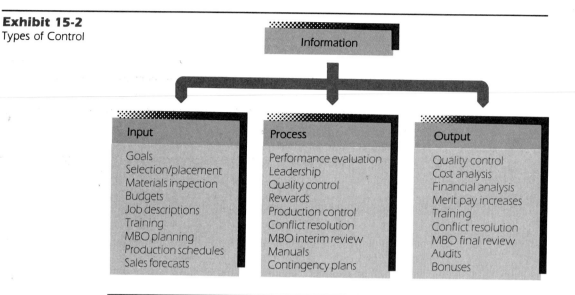

quality control activities are the most prevalent forms of process controls. For the blood bank, typing each unit and maintaining inventories are process controls.

Output controls. As the name suggests, this kind of control concerns those activities that analyze the final product or service. The monthly cost analysis by the blood bank director is an example.

The manager needs to consider at least three key aspects of control. First, each type has its own process—that is, its own standards, measurement activities, and possible corrective actions. Second, certain control activities occur across the three types of controls. For example, quality control deals with raw material inspection (input), ongoing examination of the operations (process), and analysis of the final product (output).

Finally, each of the control types and their inherent processes involve a rather detailed communication or information system. Standards must be communicated, the results need to be passed on to the involved parties, and information about corrective actions must be forwarded.

With this section serving as an introduction, we will focus on several specific control activities. Our first topic involves budgets, financial analyses, and audits—in other words, financial control.

 ## Financial Control: Budgets

Throughout this book we have noted the wide variations in the way managers emphasize and apply the tools and techniques of management functions. Some managers believe strongly in contingency planning, while others hardly plan at all; an executive may require strict adherence to a formal chain of command, while another executive may prefer a more informal approach; one manager may insist on the use of objective, quantifiable data in employee performance evaluation, while a second manager believes that subjective, qualitative performance data are sufficient, and so on. One area where there is a great deal of similarity is in emphasizing a knowledge of expenses, revenues, and profits over a period of time—the budget.

Budgets are formal statements of future expenditures, revenues, and expected profits developed to control the use of an organization's financial resources. Budgets form the last link in the management chain that began with goals and strategies. Thus, they are the most detailed management practice used to ensure that an organization's goals are achieved.

The Manager's Job

Herbert D. Kelleher of Southwest Airlines

In the eyes of its stockholders and the investment community, Southwest Airlines of Dallas is one of the world's most profitable commercial airlines. It has made those who have acquired its stock, including executives and employees, financially comfortable. Founded in 1970, the company originally served the Texas intra-state Dallas-Houston-San Antonio market with just four Boeing 737 jets. Today, its route system includes additional Texas cities along with Phoenix, San Diego, Las Vegas, Kansas City and Los Angeles, served with a fleet of nearly 40 jets.

To the traveling public, Southwest is a highly efficient, businesslike means of getting places at just about any time of the day or night. Flying Southwest is so ingrained with Texas commuters that they have apparently learned to endure the jammed airport terminals and boarding lounges, waiting lines, crowded planes and cramped seating—what critics call Texas' flying "cattle cars."

Why does Southwest perform so well, even during recessionary times? According to Herbert D. Kelleher, chairman and president, a key feature is its tight control in following the same formula it has had since the beginning—discount fares, high flight frequencies and on-time performance, productive and motivated employees, and squeezing every last minute of use out of its planes (Southwest's famous 10-minute turnaround). The aircraft maintenance unit strongly feels the company's efficiency and control orientation. Instead of pulling a plane off the line for lengthy scheduled repairs, Southwest works on its aircraft at night and in stages. The result is that Southwest has a perfect safety record and has been cited for exemplary maintenance practices by the FAA.

Concerning the infamous "cattle car" criticism, Kelleher smiles and leans forward in his unpretentious office at Dallas' Love Field and states, "We feel that, as one of the industry's lowest-cost operators, the greatest benefits we offer our passengers are low fares and the industry's best on-time record. We operate modern airplanes that cost $16 million and fly at 560 miles an hour. Most cattle haven't been exposed to that."

Adapted from W. G. Smith, "Will Success Spoil Southwest?," *Texas Business* (April 1983): 25-29.

Budgets are important to the manager for a number of reasons.[4] First, they aid in *planning* in that they force management to develop achievable goals and basic plans and policies associated with these goals. In other words, budgets set a standard of production (the budgeted amount of output). From an *organizing* point of view, budgets help clarify responsibilities among organizational members. This is particularly important in coordinating the activities of the organization. The interaction between managers and subordinates that occurs during budget development helps define and integrate performance-related activities. By specifying what resources are to be used, budgets help achieve goals through the successful implementation of the organization's strategies. This is an important part of the *leading* function. Finally, from a *control* view, budgets lead to the efficient use of resources, assist in preserving valuable resources, and establish a mechanism for periodic organizational analysis.

More than anything, budgets are important and universally read "money." Dollar figures are a common denominator among managers across a wide variety of organizational activities, including the purchase of raw materials and equipment in manufacturing, selling and advertising expenses in marketing, hiring and training of employees in personnel, and so on. Since profits are expressed in monetary terms, budgets are used by profit-oriented firms in estimating and guiding activities.

The Budgeting Process

Budgets can be prepared by at least two procedures—top-down or bottom-up.[5] In the top-down approach, a budget is almost totally developed by executive management and then imposed on lower management levels without much consultation. These budgets are usually prepared by the chief financial officer, such as the vice president of finance, or the controller. While lower-level managers can sometimes offer counter-proposals, their major duty is to implement the budget.

Most organizations, however, are beginning to follow a procedure in which the budgets are prepared by the managers who are responsible for their implementation. This bottom-up procedure offers a number of advantages, including: (1) lower-level managers have a more realistic view of their requirements, needs, and constraints; (2) there is less chance that important elements will be overlooked; and (3) managers who have had a voice in developing the budget are more motivated to work toward good performance.

Managers, however, should recognize some of the problems that could arise with the bottom-up approach.[6] First, increased political behavior may develop when a number of managers are competing for scarce resources; being overly friendly with superiors, talking down the skills and abilities of other managers, and attempting to discover the secret details of other managers' budgets through covert information systems are examples. Second, in order to ensure proper funding, many managers overstate their financial needs.

The budgeting process for a bottom-up approach includes the following key steps:

■ *Statement of goals* is communicating the organization's goals and strategies for the coming budget period. Included are many important forecasts of economic and competitive activity and a timetable for preparing and implementing the budget.

- *Budget preparation* is the responsibility of lower-level managers. Budgets allow for resource acquisition and utilization, and time requirements.

- *Review and approval* brings top management back into the budget process, usually in the form of a budget committee or department. Top managers review the individual budgets for their anticipated revenues, expenditures, and resource utilization, and integrate them into the organization's strategies and goals.

- Budget *evaluation and revision* occurs as the unit performs during the specified period. Unit managers are encouraged to meet the budget, and if a unit's performance is less than satisfactory, the manager is asked to take corrective action. This performance is then used as an input into the next budget period.

Budgets must be a flexible managerial instrument. Similar to forecasts—which budgets really are—there must be provisions for unforeseen events. For this reason, formal updating periods may be established at intervals.

Types of Budgets

An organization's overall budget is a composite of budgets for departments, divisions, and other organizational units. Three budget types frequently found in organizations are operating budgets, financial budgets, and variable versus fixed budgets.[7]

Operating Budgets   Operating budgets, as shown in exhibit 15-3, are those that allow for the raw materials, goods, or services the organizational unit expects to *consume* during the budget period. For a wood products company such as Boise Cascade, this includes the cost of the raw lumber, manufacturing expenses in converting the lumber into wood products, and the revenue generated from the products' sale. Operating budgets can be best analyzed from the basis of responsibility centers—expense centers, revenue centers, and profit centers.

Expense or cost centers are those units in which the budget relates to the efficiency of the operations. These budgets, sometimes called "engineered" budgets, are typically used in manufacturing units where material and labor costs are a concern, as well as estimated overhead costs. Exceeding the budget indicates that costs are higher than they should be and a certain level of inefficiency exists. Expense center budgets can be used in departments such as personnel, legal, and research and development, where measuring output is difficult. Termed "discretionary" cost budgets, the concern is not so much with efficiency as it is with controlling the number of tasks performed.

Revenue centers are concerned with outputs, as opposed to costs or expenses for inputs. An example would be sales budgets a regional sales office prepares for each product and salesperson. Revenue budgets are less precise than expense budgets, since managers lack control over the elements that determine their levels of effectiveness, such as products out of stock, rapid swings in the economy, or unforeseen decisions by competitors (e.g., a price cut).

Profit centers combine expense and revenue budgets into one statement. These budgets are usually found at the divisional level in an organization, where the manager is responsible for the best combination of costs and revenues. The goal is to maximize the bottom line—profits.

Exhibit 15-3
Types of Budgets in a Manufacturing Firm

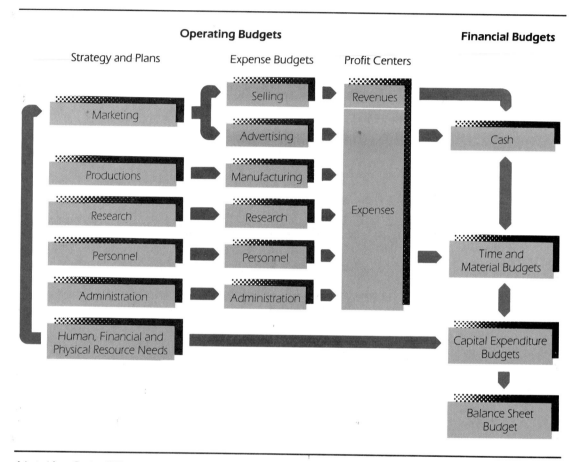

Adapted from Gordon Shillinglaw, *Managerial Cost Accounting*, 4th ed. (Homewood, Ill.: Irwin, 1977), p. 137.

Profit centers are one of the foundational elements of the planning and control system of BankAmerica Corporation, the largest financial institution in this nation. All operating authority is in the hands of unit managers at 150 profit centers around the world, while headquarters retains control of capital and major credit decisions.

Overall planning starts with BankAmerica's research policy council (i.e., top management), which early each year comes up with a list of economic assumptions likely to affect the bank over the coming five years. The list goes to the manager of each profit center, who must then turn the assumptions into a business plan. The plan—highly detailed for the next year, less so for the following years—charts such items as basic operating strategies, new services, and new market opportunities. Later in the year, the manager develops a detailed financial plan showing how the profit center will use the funds available to it. These two plans form the basic operating program for every profit center.

To measure financial performance of the profit centers, the bank relies on an elaborate control system, called the "building blocks," which features a method of pricing money transfers. Simply put, each profit center is credited for the funds it generates and is charged for the funds it uses. The result is one of the most efficient and lowest cost operations in the banking industry.[8]

Financial Budgets   Financial budgets deal with how the organization intends to spend money during a particular period. Cash budgets, capital expenditure budgets, time and material budgets, and balance sheet budgets are financial budgets.

Cash budgets are a projection of revenues and expenses for the budget period. They are designed to give the manager information about the amount of cash flowing through the organization and the pattern of cash disbursements and receipts. This information will tell the manager when excessive cash is available for short-term investments, or when a cash shortage may require some internal corrective actions.

Capital expenditure budgets describe the future investments of the organization in such physical resources as buildings, property, and equipment. Because they are very important to an organization's future, capital expenditure budgets are developed only after careful study. A major issue with capital expenditure budgeting is that money is being committed for several years in advance. Thus, this type of budget must be integrated with forecasts and long-range planning.

Capital expenditure budgets are made with a careful analysis of the external environment and the probability of certain events. For example, in 1975 Dow Chemical Company recognized during their long-range planning activities that funds for new plant construction would be needed in approximately two years. To most companies, this would have meant that they could wait at least a year before attempting to acquire capital money from investors in the form of stocks or bonds. Dow's management, through a detailed financial analysis, projected that interest rates on bonds would probably rise dramatically in the following years. With this information in mind, Dow sold over $200 million in bonds during 1975 at an interest rate of 8.5 percent. Even though the money was not needed immediately, this decision proved to be correct because when the money would have been needed, the interest rates had climbed more than 2 percent. Dow will save nearly $40 million over the thirty-year term of the bonds.[9]

Time and material budgets deal with the resources needed to produce a product or service. A time budget involves a forecast of labor costs, while a materials budget concerns the amount of material required to achieve an end result, such as producing a product or constructing a plant.

Finally, a *balance sheet budget* is a composite of all other financial budgets and shows the relationship between assets, liabilities, and equity at some future point in time. Usually called a pro forma balance sheet, it indicates the expected financial status of the organization at a future time if the various budgets are met.

Flexible Budgets   The previously discussed budgets are developed with the assumption of a single level of output. They are called *fixed budgets*. Included are the labor and material costs, plus the associated property taxes, depreciation, insurance, and administrative costs.

Situations arise, however, in which the level of output can vary significantly. In these cases, a *variable budget* is required. Costs for materials, labor and certain maintenance, energy, supplies, and selling based on output must be considered. Costs, such as advertising, are semi-variable and must be included in the variable budget.

The combination of variable, semi-variable, and fixed costs and revenues makes it almost impossible for the manager to prepare a simple graph or table of results. Computer simulations, however, are beginning to serve this purpose well.

Contemporary Budgeting Approaches

In recent years, many profit and not-for-profit organizations have adopted new approaches to budgeting. Among the most popular are the Planning-Programming-Budgeting System and Zero-Base Budgeting.

Planning-Programming-Budgeting System   During the Kennedy administration, a new approach to budgeting known as Planning-Programming-Budgeting System (PPBS) was introduced in the Defense Department. The system was designed to identify and eliminate costly program duplications within the Defense Department and integrate these programs into a more accurate overall budget.

The following steps are generally involved in a PPBS approach:[10]

- State and analyze the basic goals of a program or activity
- Analyze the output of the program in light of its stated goals
- Measure the total program costs for several years, not just one year
- Compare and choose the alternative that best achieves overall goals.

By analyzing each program on the basis of its impact on the total system, it was hoped the organization would use its resources more efficiently.

Unfortunately, PPBS never was fully implemented in the federal government, for two main reasons. First, many agencies and units resisted its use because they saw little benefit from it and because it was being forced upon them without consultation. Second, President Johnson's insistence that PPBS be put into use immediately resulted in different versions being developed, improper instructions and procedures, and generally poor efforts at communication and implementation.

Zero-Base Budgeting   In traditional budgeting exercises, managers start with the existing year's budget and then make adjustments for changing conditions. In other words, it is assumed that past expenditures are appropriate and should be continued. The manager's attention is directed, therefore, to justifying added expenditures for the coming year.

In zero-base budgeting, no such assumption is made. With each new budget preparation period, managers must justify every dollar expenditure as if they started from scratch, or a "zero base."[11] For example, a manager of marketing research who is developing a new budget must justify funds for any new market studies *and* those that are carried over from the previous period.

Zero-base budgeting, which is extensively used in such organizations as Xerox and Texas Instruments and was instituted in the federal government under President Carter, stresses three basic steps. First, activities are broken down into "decision packages" that include all the information needed to evaluate and compare the benefits, costs, and purpose of a program or activity. In the market research example, each project would be considered a decision package. Second, the individual decision packages are ranked according to their benefit to the organization during the budget period. Unit rankings are then given to higher-level management, who develop a rank order for the total organization. Finally, resources are allocated to the individual programs according to rank in the organization.

Zero-base budgeting offers advantages and disadvantages to managers. On one hand, it forces managers to scrutinize each program carefully, eliminating low-priority programs and possibly developing more effective activities. On the other hand, some managers are reluctant to give up pet projects, possibly forcing them to inflate their importance at the expense of better projects. Because it takes a total organizational viewpoint and stresses both the efficient and effective use of resources, a growing number of organizations are using zero-base budgeting.

Financial Controls: Financial Analyses

Budgets are primarily input controls—that is, they are established generally before any organizational activities have begun. During or after an operation, the manager's attention switches to other financial matters. These include financial statements, ratio analyses, and human resource accounting.

Financial Statements

Financial statements present an analysis of the use of organizational resources and the flow of goods, money, and services to, within, and from the organization.[12] The purpose of financial statements is fourfold:

- To determine the long-term and short-term financial condition of the organization
- To analyze the manner in which resources are being utilized
- To determine the liquidity of the organization
- To ascertain the profitability of the organization over a period of time.

Financial statements are usually prepared to indicate what financial events occurred since the presentation of the last statement, usually covering a twelve-month period. In our framework, we can consider the various types of financial statements a form of output controls.

It is beyond the scope of this book to cover in detail the different types of financial statements. A brief summary of the three main types—balance sheet, income statement, and cash flow statement—is provided. As an illustration, exhibits 15-4 and 15-5 present a company's balance sheet and income statements for 1979.

Exhibit 15-4
Consolidated
Balance Sheet

Year Ended 12/31/83

Assets

Current assets:

Cash, including time deposits	$ 520,296
Marketable securities at cost, which approximates market	548,553
Accounts and notes receivable	1,636,274
Inventories	719,109
Total current assets	3,424,232
Investments and advances	217,327
Long-term receivables	121,213

Property, plant, and equipment, at cost, less accumulated depreciation, depletion, and amortization

Owned	5,120,313
Leased under capital leases	227,907
	5,238,220
Prepaid and deferred charges	200,179
	$9,311,171

Liabilities and Stockholders' Equity

Current liabilities:

Notes payable	$ 79,225
Accounts payable	1,359,748
Accrued taxes, including income taxes	656,768
Other accrued liabilities	330,800
Long-term debt due within one year	49,250
Capital lease obligations due within one year	15,526
Total current liabilities	2,491,317
Long-term debt	1,367,392
Capital lease obligations	254,253
Minority interest in subsidiaries	284,797

Deferred credits and other liabilities:

Income taxes	716,597
Employee benefits	260,418
Other	153,286
	1,130,301

Stockholders' equity

Preferred Stock	502
Common Stock	566,469
Capital surplus	532,310
Retained earnings	2,715,296
	3,814,577
Less Common Stock in treasury	31,466
Total stockholders' equity	3,783,111
	$9,311,171

Exhibit 15-5		**Year Ended 12/31/83**
Statement of Consolidated Income and Retained Earnings	**Revenues:**	
	Sales and services (including excise taxes)	$12,851,369
	Interest and other income	231,515
		13,082,884
	Costs, Expenses, and Taxes:	
	Costs and operating expenses	7,835,780
	Selling, general, and administrative expenses	862,614
	Depreciation, depletion, and amortization	398,308
	Interest and debt expense	167,020
	Income and other taxes	2,952,853
	Minority interest in subsidiaries' net income	50,949
		12,267,524
	Net Income	815,360
	Retained Earnings:	
	Balance at beginning of year	2,083,131
		2,898,491
	Dividends paid:	
	Common Stock (1979—$1.70 per share)	182,870
	Preferred Stock ($2.00 per share)	325
		183,195
	Balance at end of year	$2,715,296
	Net Income Per Share of Common Stock	$7.58

Balance Sheet   In simple terms, a balance sheet indicates what the organization "owns and owes" at a particular point of time. What the organization owns are its assets, such as cash, land, inventories, and receivables. Its liabilities are what it owes: accounts payable, debts, and leases. A balance sheet also shows the organization's net worth, or that amount which represents stockholders' equity: common stock, preferred stock, and retained earnings (see exhibit 15-4).

Income Statement   As shown in exhibit 15-5, an income statement shows how much money an organization has made over a period of time. It starts with the firm's sales or revenues, then subtracts all costs, expenses, and taxes. The remaining amount—net income—can be distributed as stockholders' dividends or reinvested in the organization.

Cash Flow Statement   A cash flow statement, or sources and uses of funds statement, shows where cash or funds come from (sales, receivables, or sale of property) and where they are used (equipment purchases, reducing payables, or distributing dividends). Similar to the income statement, a cash flow statement concerns financial activities over time.

While financial statements are used primarily for internal control purposes, they may have significant external applications. For example, financial statements are used by bankers and other investment institutions in deciding whether or not to loan or invest money in the organization. In addition, it is wise for managers to study a firm's financial statements before they decide to work there.

Ratio Analysis

Most organizations perform ratio analysis to evaluate their financial condition. This activity basically involves taking figures from the financial statements and computing ratios or percentages for analysis. The evaluation of these results can involve at least two purposes: (1) comparison of the ratio over time within the organization, or (2) comparison of the ratio to similar organizations at one point in time or over a period of time.

The most commonly used ratios can be divided into a number of different categories. We have chosen four major categories for a brief discussion—liquidity, leverage, operating, and profitability ratios.[13] Exhibit 15-6 presents the method of calculating these ratios for the data presented in exhibits 15-4 and 15-5.

Liquidity ratios measure the organization's ability to meet its maturing financial obligations. In essence, an analysis of liquidity responds to the question, "Does the organization have sufficient cash and quickly convertible securities on hand to meet short-term obligations and still remain financially solvent?" The standard of acceptability is usually based on the organization's characteristics and the nature of its industry.

Leverage ratios compare the contributions of financing by owners to financing by creditors. Leverage refers to the influence of the fixed costs of the debt on profits or losses. Leverage ratios vary significantly by industry. For example, the debt-to-equity ratio for utility companies can run as high as 1.00, while for retail firms it can be as low as 0.20.

Operating ratios (activity ratios) indicate how effectively an organization is using its resources. By comparing sales or revenues to expenses used to generate them, the effectiveness of the operation can be established. As shown in exhibit 15-6, most operating ratios concern the relationship among sales and assets, inventory, and net working capital.

Profitability ratios measure the organization's success in achieving desired profit levels. In a profit-making firm, profitability ratios are used to measure the company's efficiency and effectiveness of operations. Exhibit 15-7 presents profitability ratios for a number of well-known organizations.

Human Resource Accounting

The basic idea behind human resource accounting is that employees have a quantifiable value to an organization which should be considered in managerial decision-making. Effective human resource management is important because employees are the resource that produces profits; the other resources, financial and physical, merely facilitate profit-making capabilities. Proponents of this concept point out that if we can dramatize the importance of human resources to the organization, greater attention will be given to the way they are managed.

A number of techniques have been formulated for evaluating human resources.[14] Four are most prominent—historical costs, replacement costs, economic value, and present value. With the *historical cost* method, the recruiting, training, and other acquisition costs for each employee are recorded, capitalized, and amortized over the

Exhibit 15-6
Financial Ratio Analysis

Ratio	Calculation	Measures	Example
Liquidity Ratios:			
1. Current ratio	Current assets / Current liabilities	Indicates the extent to which the claims of short-term creditors are covered by assets expected to be converted to cash.	$3,424,232 / $2,491,317 = 1.37
2. Quick ratio (or acid-test ratio)	Current assets —inventory / Current liabilities	A measure of the organization's ability to pay short-term obligations without the sale of its inventories.	$2,705,127 / $2,491,317 = 1.08
3. Inventory to net working capital	Inventory / Current assets —liabilities	A measure of the extent to which the organization's working capital is tied up in inventory.	$719,109 / $932,315 = 0.77
Leverage Ratios:			
1. Debt to assets ratio	Total debt / Total assets	Measures the extent to which borrowed funds have been used to finance operations.	$5,526,060 / $9,311,171 = 0.59
2. Debt to equity ratio	Total debt / Total stockholders' equity	Another measure of the funds provided by creditors versus the funds provided by owners.	$5,526,060 / $3,783,111 = 1.46
3. Long-term debt to equity ratio	Long-term debt / Total stockholders' equity	Measures the balance between debt and equity in the firm's overall capital structure.	$1,367,392 / $3,783,111 = 0.36
4. Times-interest-earned (or coverage ratios)	Profits before interest and taxes / Total interest charges	Measures the extent to which profits can decline such that the organization becomes unable to meet its interest expenses.	$3,986,182 / $ 271,369 = 18.33
Operating Ratios:			
1. Inventory turnover	Revenue / Inventory	Indicates the number of times inventory is replaced during the period.	$13,082,884 / $ 719,109 = 18.19
2. Net working capital turnover	Revenue / Net working capital	Measures the degree to which working capital is used effectively.	$13,082,884 / $ 932,315 = 14.03
3. Total asset turnover	Revenue / Total assets	Measures the relationship between sales and the assets needed to reach this level of sales.	$13,082,884 / $ 9,311,171 = 1.41
Profitability Ratios:			
1. Operating profit margin	Profits before taxes and before interest / Revenues	Measures the organization's profitability from current operations without regard to interest charges.	$ 3,986,182 / $13,082,884 = 0.30
2. Profit margin	Net income / Revenue	Measures profits per dollar of sales.	$ 815,360 / $13,082,884 = 0.06
3. Return on total assets	Net income / Total assets	A measure of the return on total investment in the enterprise.	$ 815,360 / $8,311,171 = 0.09
4. Return on net worth	Net income / Total stockholders' equity	Measures the rate of return on stockholders' investment in the organization.	$ 815,360 / $3,783,111 = 0.22
5. Earnings per share	Net income —preferred stock dividends / Number of shares of common stock outstanding	Shows the earnings available to the owners of common stock.	$ 815,035 / $6,177,965 = $7.58

Exhibit 15-7

Profitability Data for Select U.S. Firms

A. U.S. Industrial Companies (1979 & 1982)

Company	% Profit Margin		%Return on Net Worth		$Earnings Per Share	
	1979	1982	1979	1982	1979	1982
Anheuser-Busch	7.1%	6.3%	21.6%	18.8%	$4.34	$5.97
Boeing	6.2	3.2	27.4	10.4	7.88	3.02
Chrysler	(9.1)	1.7	—	51.6	—	1.84
Coca-Cola	8.5	8.2	21.9	18.4	3.80	3.95
Dupont	7.5	2.7	17.7	8.2	6.42	3.75
Exxon	5.4	4.3	19.0	14.7	9.74	4.82
General Electric	6.2	6.9	19.1	17.8	6.20	8.00
General Motors	4.9	1.6	15.1	5.3	10.04	3.08
Goodyear Tire	1.8	3.0	1.8	10.8	2.02	3.59
IBM	13.1	12.8	20.1	22.1	5.16	7.37
Kodak	12.4	10.7	18.6	15.4	6.20	7.12
Procter & Gamble	6.2	6.5	17.9	18.7	6.99	9.39
Texas Instruments	5.4	3.3	18.1	10.6	7.58	6.10
Time, Inc.	5.8	4.3	18.1	11.3	5.15	2.45
Uniroyal	(4.6)	1.3	—	4.8	—	0.78
U.S. Steel	(2.3)	(0.2)	—	—	—	—
Westinghouse	(0.1)	4.6	—	14.6	—	5.16
Whirlpool	4.8	6.1	16.5	15.9	3.06	3.83
Xerox	8.1	5.0	17.5	11.4	6.69	5.00

B. U.S. Retailing & Transportation Companies (1979 & 1982)

Company	% Profit Margin		%Return on Net Worth		$Earnings Per Share	
	1979	1982	1979	1982	1979	1982
American Airlines	2.7%	(0.1)%	11.1%	—	$2.63	—
Federated Stores	3.5	3.0	12.4	11.1	4.21	4.79
J.C. Penney	2.2	3.4	9.7	12.1	5.52	5.35
K Mart	2.8	1.6	16.4	10.1	2.54	2.06
Kroger	0.9	1.2	14.0	16.5	3.13	4.84
Pan Am	3.1	(0.1)	10.5	—	1.07	—
Sante Fe Industries	8.9	5.7	11.0	7.3	8.08	2.08
Sears, Roebuck	4.6	2.9	10.5	9.8	2.54	2.46
UAL	(1.9)	0.6	—	2.8	—	1.03
United Parcel Service	2.5	6.4	16.1	30.0	1.97	1.97
Yellow Freight	2.4	1.1	9.5	5.0	1.45	0.75

employee's expected tenure or another time period. When the employee leaves the organization, the unamortized balance of the investment is written off as a loss in the period of separation. The *replacement cost* method assumes that an employee should be valued according to the incurred expenses that would be needed to replace him or her. Costs include not only recruiting and training expenses, but also the costs of not having a capable replacement for a period of time. The *economic value* method usually uses salary as a measure of the individual's value to the firm. The assumption is that employees are compensated according to their worth to the organization. Finally, the *present value* method analyzes the stream of net future contributions of the employee to the organization. This method uses expected salary, probability of separation (i.e., turnover), and future productivity.

Human resource accounting is still in its infancy as a managerial tool, and as the description of the methods for calculation show, there are too many estimates and rough edges to overcome before the tool becomes widely used. Nevertheless, the concept draws much-needed attention to the fact that an organization's employees are important assets.

Financial Controls: Audits

To most people, *audit* means the process whereby one party attempts to determine if a second party has done something wrong. Governmental audits of the work of defense contractors such as Lockheed's C-5A aircraft, or of political campaign contributions during the Watergate investigation, have turned up surprising information. Even a letter from the IRS requesting an audit of your tax return is interpreted negatively.

While the discovery of misdeeds is a purpose of an audit, it is surely not its only purpose. An audit is basically an investigation of an organization's activities for purposes of analysis, verification, and correction. An audit may just as well be oriented to validating the honesty and fairness of an organization's financial statements—in fact, this is by far the main purpose of an audit.

Two basic types of audits are found in organizations. First, the external and internal audits deal with financial data. Second, the management audit evaluates various management practices and policies.

External audits are independent evaluations of the organization's financial statements, usually by public accounting firms. The task of the auditors is not to prepare the financial statements, but to verify that the organization has followed generally accepted accounting principles in valuing its assets and liabilities.

External audits have a number of advantages to organizations. First, because public accounting firms are independent organizations, there is a high degree of objectivity in their analyses. They are required by professional accounting standards to report the financial conditions and practices of the audited organization *as they exist*. Second, because the staffs of the accounting firms are highly skilled professionals, the audit can be useful in diagnosing problems involving the financial activities of the organization. Finally, because the external audit verifies that the financial statements were prepared and validated according to standard accounting principles, interested banks and investors are assured of the correct information.

In addition to external audits, many organizations use their own personnel to conduct ongoing *internal* audits. The purpose is the same—to ensure that the organization's financial statements accurately and honestly reflect the true financial condition of the organization.

The Manager's Job
Irvin Feld of Ringling Bros. and Barnum & Bailey

Throughout his life, Irvin Feld knew one thing for sure—he loved show business. At age 13, he hit the road with his brother Izzy to sell snake oil at carnivals. As an adult, he used profits from his drugstore chain to promote emerging talents such as Chuck Berry, the Platters, Bill Haley and the Comets, and Fats Domino.

In 1956, John Ringling North, head of an organization that was deep in debt, declared that Ringling Bros. and Barnum & Bailey had given its last performance under the big top—that is, until Irvin Feld heard about it. Within days, Feld bought the circus for $250,000 in cash and absorption of all the debts. Since then, Irvin and his son, Kenneth, have either owned or managed the world-famous circus. (The Felds sold the firm in 1971 to Mattel, Inc. for $50 million. Ten years later, the Felds bought the company back for $22 million!)

The Felds are committed to presenting quality performances to the public. They do this, in part, through careful managerial control. A typical day finds Kenneth Feld studying a sheet of paper from the performance director of the Blue Unit circus which presents information and data on last night's performance in Rosemont, Illinois. From the report, the younger Feld learns about certain mechanical failures, the slight injury to a trapeze artist, and the like. The sheet also tells Feld the timing of the show, attendance figures, gross and net dollars for each performance, the previous year's numbers from that town, and projections for the current year. Across the hall, Irvin reads a similar sheet from the Red Unit performance director, who is responsible for the second unit circus and the ice shows (e.g., Disney's World on Ice).

Irvin Feld's concern for quality and managerial control reaches all facets of the business. On the human side, he knows every employee, from rigger to lion tamer, by first name. He understands clearly that good workers put on good shows.

Even the pre-show operations are closely controlled. At 8 a.m. on the day of the first show, the seats are empty and the floor is bare. By 4 p.m., the miles of steel rigging is suspended, the heavy green mats have been put down, the sound system is set up, and workers are touching up the ring curbs with red, white, and blue paint. That night, the show goes on exactly as Feld approved it months ago.

"If I ever slipped up on what I was offering the public," says Irvin, "I'd bail out. It's really more than what the bottom line is. It's crazy, crazy, serious pride. . . . I would never compromise with quality." What is most important, says son Kenneth, is the show. "It has to function right. And it can't stop for any reason. It hasn't for 113 years."

Adapted from A. Solomon, "Lords of the Rings," INC (February 1983): 101-108.

On the plus side, because organizational employees make internal audits, their knowledge of inside operations allows them to go into more depth in their analysis. Also, such audits can occur throughout the year as opposed to once a year with external auditors. Thus, problems can be identified early. On the negative side, internal audits can not only be costly, but they may require hiring highly skilled professionals to develop the reports. A frequently occurring problem with internal audits is that some managers view them as a "police" action, rather than a constructive activity. Internal audit personnel need good interpersonal skills to help audited managers minimize their fears of repercussions if some error, even minor, is found.

A *management audit* involves an evaluation and assessment of the operations of the total organization.[15] Financial data can be analyzed, but this type of audit is not limited to that type of investigation. In particular, a management audit evaluates the organization's goals, strategies, plans, policies, resources (i.e., strengths and weaknesses), and future opportunities. The areas of investigation could include:

What market share should the organization strive for in each product line?

How effective are the key managers? How effective are the directors on the board?

Are the financial policies sound?

What is the state of the organization's research and development?

What environmental threats should the organization investigate?

Is the organization using the most effective structure?

What is the relationship between the organization and its stockholders?

How efficient are the organization's manufacturing operations?

Should the compensation system be revised?

How effective are the employment policies?

Management audits can be conducted by internal personnel, external consultants, or both. Public accounting firms are now commonly offering a management audit service to organizations. The rationale is that since the accounting firm knows about the strengths and weaknesses of the organization on the financial side, it could expand to include the entire operations of the organization.

Control in the International Environment

Controlling resources and operations in order to achieve organizational goals is just as important in the international environment as it is in the home country of the parent organization. The managerial control process in international operations, however, is complicated by a number of unique factors. The most important include consideration of distance, outside ownership interests, diversity, uncertainties, and host country

"What did you expect a financial wizard to look like?"

From the *Wall Street Journal*-Permission, Cartoon Features Syndicate.

goals.[16] In international control, both the cultural and geographic distance separating countries will increase the time, expense, and possibility of error. Not only may control systems not be fully understood by the organization's foreign managers, the time and expense of gaining verification may make the control systems worth less than their cost.

Many multinational organizations frequently have subsidiaries in which outside ownership interests are significant. Control becomes a problem when goals and strategies are not shared by the organization and the local partners. The diversity among countries in accounting procedures and economic, political, and cultural features complicates the task of setting standards, evaluating performance, and designing effective corrective actions. Uncertainties arise about the accuracy and completeness of economic and industry data across different countries. In addition, political and economic conditions can change rapidly from the basis on which global planning was established. Finally, in some countries—particularly the less developed ones—the organization's goals and methods of control may be on a collision course with host country goals.

To highlight the issues of control facing managers in the international environment, our discussion will be divided into two parts—international control elements and financial control in the international realm.

International Control Elements

As one would expect, there are many similarities and differences between domestic and international control activities. Three key control system elements are of special concern—evaluation measures, control reporting techniques, and possible corrective actions.

Evaluation Measures   The evaluation of performance of a unit in international operations is quite difficult, for the reasons we have mentioned. Consequently, many organizations have adopted systems of evaluation that depend on a number of different performance indicators. The measures most frequently used include market share, quality of distribution, new product development, productivity changes, product quality, profitability, output per worker, plant utilization rates, and prices relative to foreign competing firms. When the foreign operation is a joint venture or subsidiary (i.e., the organization may not have a 100 percent interest), each of the owners may want a different set of evaluation measures computed and analyzed. This can further complicate and confuse the control process.

One of the biggest problems of evaluation is comparability. As we will discuss in chapter 18, an organization may produce a similar product in two countries but use two different processes. For example, International Harvester may produce farm tractors in the U. S. with highly automated equipment, while producing the same product in South America with the use of more labor and fewer automated machines. A comparison of output per worker, labor costs, volume, maintenance expenses, and so on may prove to be of little value. In these situations, organizations usually separate the different operations for comparison purposes, or group operations by the similarity of the process. International Harvester may compare U. S. operations with those in Europe, while grouping South American and African facilities together for analysis.

Control Reporting Techniques   Timely reports from all operating units of an international organization are needed so management can allocate resources properly, make corrections in plans, and reward employees for their performance. Not surprisingly, several studies of reporting systems used in international organizations confirm that those used for foreign operations are essentially the same as those used domestically.[17] The reasons for this include the economy of carrying the same types of reports, the strong possibility that what is effective in the home country will prove the same overseas, and the fact that, where possible, comparability is enhanced.

The manager should recognize two important elements of international reporting systems—method and the type of information transmitted. Essentially, there are at least eight methods of sending control information—mail, telephone, cable, radio, telex, leased channel, alternate voice data, and travel. Because these methods vary considerably in cost, the choice in specific situations depends on message frequency, average length, destination, urgency, and ease of personal communication.[18] In terms of the type of control information sent, most is in the form of standardized reports, followed by finance, market, technical, and environmental information.

Enforcing Corrective Actions   Valid control standards and accurate reporting are of little use when the organization is limited in its ability to implement corrective actions. The important factors to consider include the degree of ownership of the foreign operation, the legal structure of the countries involved, and the national interest as perceived by political leaders.

In cases where the foreign operation is wholly owned, the use of corrective measures is simplified. This assumes that such corrective actions as worker layoffs, financial restructuring, or facility shutdowns are permissible under the country's legal system. However, what happens if a foreign operation is a joint venture, is substantially independent financially (that is, it generates its own operating funds), is managed by foreign nationals, or is not selling to or buying from the parent?

In these situations, the headquarters management can maintain control over a valued asset, such as patents, brand name, or raw materials. It can separate equity into voting and nonvoting stock, or as in the case of Westinghouse in Mexico, set up an operating committee in which its minority interest has a majority representation.[19]

Financial Control in the International Realm

One of the more complex problems the manager operating in the international realm has to face is financial control. Our focus will be on financial statements, financial analyses, and audits.

Financial Statements   The preparation of detailed and standardized financial statements is an accepted way of life for organizations operating in the U. S., but in overseas operations, a great variety of practices are followed. For example, the accounting profession in the U.S. has developed a set of "generally accepted accounting practices" (GAAP). Similar situations exist in Canada, the United Kingdom, and the Netherlands. In other countries, few standard practices exist, making the development and analysis of financial statements difficult.[20]

Another problem is currency. The problem is not so much translating other currencies into dollars, but that the exchange rate may vary widely and change rapidly. An exchange rate change can have a significant effect on a company. For example, when the dollar was devalued in 1971, many firms holding debt in stronger European currencies suffered large losses. Exxon alone suffered exchange losses of $70 million related to long-term debt it held in Europe.[21] To counter currency problems, many international organizations prepare two sets of financial statements—parent and consolidated. The parent books reflect the organization's operations in the headquarters country, while the consolidated books blend all operations into one set of financial statements.

Some standards have been set by the Financial Accounting Standard Board (FASB) with regard to financial disclosures. At minimum, the following information is now required to be disclosed for both domestic and foreign operations in the aggregate or by geographic area: revenue, sales to unaffiliated customers and between geographic areas, operating profit or loss of net income, and identifiable assets.

The Foreign Corrupt Practices Act of 1977 has had an effect on the way some organizations prepare their financial statements (see chapter 4). With the passing of the act, organizations can no longer "hide" bribes to foreign officials in their books. For example, prior to the act, the American Hospital Supply Corporation paid a 10 percent "commission" to certain officials to obtain a contract to sell hospital equipment to Saudi Arabia for the new King Faisal Specialist Hospital. The price of the equipment was increased to include the kickback, thus overstating revenues. The kickback was then recorded as a consulting fee, even though no such services were performed. This allowed the kickback to become a deductible expense and made the cash payment appear to be legitimate. Such activities are no longer permissible.[22]

Financial Analyses   If the organization can overcome some of the problems discussed above, the analysis of financial performance still remains complicated. For example, a comparison of financial ratios across different foreign operations may lead to incorrect conclusions. An operation in one country that is run with highly auto-mated equipment and few skilled workers is not equivalent to one which employs a large labor force and fewer automated machines. The assets and operating expenses are different; hence, the calculation of certain ratios will also be different.

Organizations have worked around this problem in two ways.[23] First, a comparison of ratios is permitted between similar countries, such as the United Kingdom and Germany. The most popular approach is to use budget performance as the main measure of financial effectiveness. Since the budget is stated in local currencies, bud-get performance (actual versus predicted) can be a significant performance criterion.

Audits   Many international businesses rely heavily upon the independent external auditor to verify the information in financial statements. Auditing standards, howev-er, vary considerably among different countries, as do qualifications for becoming an auditor.

For instance, in some countries all aspects of auditing are determined by the accounting profession itself, while in other countries the government determines who can perform the audit and the manner in which it is done. In many European countries, an audit merely states that financial statements adhere to the procedures of the *orga-nization*. At the other extreme, such as in the U. S. and the United Kingdom, there is greater reliance on GAAP from independent standards boards.[24]

As to the auditor, in West Germany, for example, it takes several years of study and practice and a difficult series of examinations before one is allowed to perform an audit. In Peru, on the other hand, a person need only graduate from a recognized university with an accounting major and receive an easy-to-get government license.

In response to the needs of organizations for consistency in auditing, many large U.S. independent accounting firms have established foreign offices or formed part-nerships with local accounting firms. In some cases, the foreign government will accept the more detailed audit of these U. S. firms; in other cases, these firms have to perform a second audit in conjunction with the audit approved by the government.

 ## POINTS TO CONSIDER
An Emphasis on Managerial Skills

1. **Control systems should be accurate, timely, and economical.**
   This is an all-encompassing suggestion that highlights some of the core concerns managers have with control systems. In essence, the effective control system measures the right things at the right times, without incurring excessive costs.

2. **Control systems can also anticipate problems.**
   Control systems can be quite valuable in evaluating "after-the-fact" activities (feedback con-trols), as well as providing a close look at the information for its predictive power (feedforward controls), much the same as leading economic indicators are used to anticipate changes in the economy. From the perspective of the manager's job, this involves key diagnostic skills.

3. **Involving lower-level managers in budget preparation is important.**
   Higher-level managers make a frequent error in imposing a budget on lower-level managers who have had little to say in its development. Participation of all managers in budget preparation not only provides more accurate information, it improves their commitment to the budget. Managers also develop an important human skill in this practice.

4. **Budgets should be flexible, not ends in themselves.**
   Budgets are not inflexible laws of organizational life. On the contrary, they help guide managerial activities and are adaptable to changing conditions, be they internal or external.

5. **Present control information clearly and concisely.**
   A frequent complaint by managers is that they do not have enough time to complete their duties—they are overloaded with information and ''just can't get to it.'' Don't present control data by dropping a two-inch thick computer output on a manager's desk. Summarize it and highlight the important points.

 ## SUMMARY FOR THE MANAGER

1. Control is a managerial function that assures actual organizational activities conform to planned activities. For managers, two aspects are important. First, control activities occur at all stages or steps in producing the organization's products or services—from input (raw material inspection), through the process (production control, contingency plans), to output controls (audits, cost analysis). Second, control is closely tied to the other managerial functions, especially planning. Good plans, in fact, have detailed control systems built into them.

2. Budgets are one of the most detailed and important parts of the manager's job. One of the keys to successful budget performance is permitting the participation of lower-level managers in its development. These managers not only have greater knowledge of the concerned operations, but since they will be responsible for its performance, they may be more motivated to work within its structure.

3. Budgets are not rigid, inflexible financial instruments. On the contrary, they must be flexible to the variable costs of the unit and to changes in the environment. It is also important for managers to recognize that short-term successful budget performance does not necessarily guarantee improved long-term performance. Cutting corners at the end of a budget period may allow managers to meet their current budget goals but have an adverse effect on the next period's performance.

4. Financial statements present the status of the organization's financial resources at a particular point in time. They are valuable to the person interested in investing in the organization, as well as to the individual contemplating employment with the firm.

5. Financial ratios are used to examine the current state of the organization and to analyze any important trends that have developed over years. The manager's diagnostic skills are particularly important in this analysis.

6. Financial audits verify the organization's financial statements. A trend in organizations is to form an internal auditing department to conduct ongoing audits. This permits the identification of problems much earlier than with the sole use of external auditors.

7. Management audits analyze the entire management process—from goals, strategies, and plans to control procedures. Whether performed by the professional accounting firm or a consulting

organization, management audits help pinpoint external opportunities and threats, as well as internal strengths and weaknesses.

8. Such factors as distance, outside ownership interests, diversity, uncertainties, and host-country goals must be taken into account when an organization develops and implements a control system for international operations. Additional problems include the development of evaluation standards, using the most effective control reporting techniques, and attempting to enforce corrective actions in foreign operations that are not wholly owned by the organization. The manager must also recognize that currency differences, exchange rates, and disclosure policies can affect the preparation of financial statements. Likewise, these differences make financial ratio analyses difficult.

REVIEW AND DISCUSSION QUESTIONS

1. Why is it suggested that planning and control are closely related?

2. Name key differences between input controls, process controls, and output controls.

3. How important are communication networks to the success of a control system?

4. What organizational units are usually associated with each of the budget responsibility centers?

5. Discuss the benefits and limitations of bottom-up budgeting.

6. What are the differences between cash, capital expenditure, and balance sheet budgets?

7. What are the main reasons PPBS has been unsuccessful in the federal government?

8. What role do financial ratios play in financial control systems?

9. What is the purpose of a management audit?

10. In reporting financial data on combined operations (foreign and domestic), what problems do multinational corporations face?

NOTES

1. "What Makes Harry Gray Run?" *Business Week* (December 10, 1979): 80.
2. R. J. Mockler, *The Management Control Process* (Englewood Cliffs, N.J.: Prentice-Hall, 1972).
3. W. Newman, *Constructive Control: Design and Use of Control Systems* (Englewood Cliffs, N.J.: Prentice-Hall, 1975).
4. R. N. Anthony and J. Dearden, *Management Control Systems,* 3rd ed. (Homewood, Ill.: Irwin, 1976), p. 453.
5. Ibid., p. 475.
6. H. L. Tosi, "The Human Effects of Budgeting Systems on Management," *MSU Business Topics* (Autumn 1974): 53-63.
7. G. Shillinglaw, *Managerial Cost Accounting,* 4th ed. (Homewood, Ill.: Irwin, 1977), p. 137.
8. R. F. Vancil, "What kind of Management Control Do You Need?" *Harvard Business Review* (March-April 1973): 75-86; and "Banking's Aggressive Conservative," *Dun's Review* (December 1976): 47-49.

9. "The Financial Chemistry at Dow," *Dun's Review* (December 1975): 50-57.

10. A. Schick, "A Death in the Bureaucracy: The Demise of Federal PPBS," *Public Administration Review* (March-April 1973): 146-56.

11. See L.M. Cheek, "Zero-Base Budgeting in Washington," *Business Horizons* (June 1978), p. 24; M. W. Dirsmith, S. J. Jablonsky, and A. D. Luzi, "Planning and Control in the U.S. Federal Government: A Critical Analysis of PPB, MBO, and ZBB," *Strategic Management Journal* (October-December 1980): 295-302; and J. C. Wetherbee and J. R. Montanari, "Zero-Base Budgeting in the Planning Process," *Strategic Management Journal* (January-March 1981): 1-14.

12. See J. D. Edwards and W. T. O'Keefe, "Financial Reporting in an Inflationary Environment," *Business Horizons* (July-August 1981): 21-29; and W. F. Frese and R. K. Mautz, "Financial Reporting-by Whom?," *Harvard Business Review* (March-April 1972): 6-21.

13. R. A. Bettis and W. K. Hall, "Diversification Strategy, Accounting Determined Risk, and Accounting Determined Rate of Return," *Academy of Management Journal* (June 1982): 254-64.

14. See R. B. Frantzreb, L. T. Landau, and D. P. Lundberge, "The Valuation of Human Resources," *Business Horizons* (June 1974): 73-80; and M. M. K. Fleming, "Behavioral Implications of Human Resource Accounting: A Survey of Potential Problems," *Human Resources Management* (Summer 1977): 24-29.

15. R. B. Buchele, "How to Evaluate a Firm," *California Management Review* (Fall 1962): 5-16.

16. J. D. Daniels, E. W. Orgram, and L. H. Radebaugh, *International Business: Environments and Operations*, 2nd ed. (Reading, Mass.: Addison-Wesley, 1979), p. 389.

17. See F. Hawkins, "Controlling Foreign Operations," *Financial Executive* (February 1965); and J. M. McInnes, "Financial Control Systems for Multinational Operations: An Empirical Investigation," *Journal of International Business Studies* (Fall 1971): 11-28.

18. R. D. Robinson, *International Business Management* (Hinsdale, Ill.: Dryden, 1973), p. 624.

19. Daniels, et al., *International Business*, p. 408.

20. W. P. Hauworth, "Problems in the Development of Worldwide Accounting Standards," *International Journal of Accounting* (Fall 1973): 24.

21. J. D. Daniels, E. W. Ogram, and L. H. Radebaugh, *International Business: Environments and Operations* (Reading, Mass.: Addison-Wesley, 1979), p. 446.

22. J. C. Taylor, "Preventing Improper Payments Through Internal Controls," *The Conference Board* (August 1976): 17-18.

23. S. M. Robbins and R. B. Stobaugh, "The Bent Measuring Stick for Foreign Subsidiaries," *Harvard Business Review* (September-October 1973): 85.

24. L. D. Tooman, "Starting the Internal Audit of Foreign Operations," *The Internal Auditor* (November 1975): 56-62.

Control
Returning to the U.S.A.

In 1983, Atari shifted home computer and video game production to Hong Kong and Taiwan, laying off 1,700 workers in California. Zenith closed a plant in Illinois that made electronics components and moved to Mexico.

Such situations have been the norm for U.S. manufacturers. But a surprising number of companies are shutting down foreign manufacturing operations and moving back to the U.S. Consider these cases:

- In the production of television sets, the average color tv was packed with nearly 750 electronic parts as late as 1979; by 1988, the number of parts should be reduced to close to 200. This fact, coupled with rising worker wages in foreign countries, enabled North American Philips, maker of Magnavox, Sylvania, and Philco, to move its Mexican operations to a new plant in Greenville, Tennessee. The company not only was able to hire skilled workers, especially key engineers, it saw product quality increase significantly (e.g., soldering defects were reduced from 80 per 10,000 joints to only 3 per 10,000).
- RCA (surveillance cameras) and Motorola (semiconductors) are moving their facilities from the Far East to the U.S. In each case, management found that savings from increased automation, transportation, and inventory costs, and the availability of skilled labor improved their competitive position by manufacturing back home.
- Increased productivity and quality control from computerized equipment enable Ford to manufacture automatic transmissions previously made abroad in a new Ohio plant.
- In 1977, Textron's Gorham division went to Japan to produce stainless steel flatware. By 1983, they were back at their Providence, Rhode Island, plant. Why? Gorham had to book orders from Japan six months in advance, which hurt marketing flexibility and caused inventory build-ups. Closeness to the market, coupled with modern machinery, has made the U.S. plant more competitive.

Adapted from J. A. Byrne, "Made (again) in the U.S.A.," *Forbes* (May 23, 1983): 35-36.

Questions for Discussion

1. What elements of control are represented in this case?
2. Which control variables are similar and unique to each illustration given?
3. Discuss the relationship between planning and control in this case.

A CASE FOR ANALYSIS

Control
The Singer Company

Late in 1975, the board of directors of Singer Company brought in Joseph Flavin to replace a chief executive who was seriously ill and had let the enterprise run out of control. The choice seemed inspired. Widely respected, Flavin had spent the first fourteen years of his career rising to controller of IBM World Trade Corporation and the last eight at Xerox, where he became an executive vice president. When he took the helm at Singer, he confidently predicted, "This company can be turned around." Within a month, he took a $411-million write-off.

The new CEO had the take-charge air of a man who could not falter. But when Singer stunned the business world with its second announcement of a $130-million write-off, the news raised serious questions about Flavin's stewardship. Unlike the earlier write-off, this one struck at the vitals of the enterprise that is synonymous with the corporate name. And Flavin admits that, for two years, he didn't know how bad the sewing-machine business was.

The day before the write-off, following a long session with Singer's board, Flavin took an overnight flight to Glasgow where he met with a delegation of Scottish trade unionists to deliver some very bad news: Singer would close down its ninety-three-year-old Clydebank plant by June of next year. The factory employs 3,000 workers, nearly a third of the total force at Singer's seven sewing-machine plants in Europe and North America.

Singer's top brass was woefully late to grasp what was happening. When Flavin was brought in, most outsiders—and, apparently, Singer insiders as well—were convinced that the business was basically sound. But in fact the U.S. market for sewing machines had peaked in 1972, and the European market had stopped growing in 1974, a year before Flavin came to Singer's rescue.

The trend line in the U.S. was dropping like an anchor when Flavin arrived in December of 1975, but Singer's executives blamed their own sales slowdown on the recession. Though the trouble was more fundamental, they had no way of knowing that. The company's market research was, at best, primitive. Singer had never gone in for polling its customers, as many appliance manufacturers do. And it suited the company fine that no trade association existed to collect market information; Singer executives assumed that the gathering of data could be valuable only to competitors.

In 1977, Flavin belatedly commissioned a study to get at why the market in the U.S. was in such a disturbing decline. Prepared by economist Norma Pace, it pointed out the obvious: women between the ages of sixteen and twenty-nine, Singer's great potential market, did not have a consuming interest in sewing or, for that matter, in possessing a sewing machine. "The downward trend is so strong," wrote Pace, "that it indicates only 18 percent of females in the sixteen to twenty-four ages will own machines in 1985, compared with an estimated 46 percent in 1970. The drop in the twenty-five to twenty-nine-year-olds is even more dramatic, with only 31 percent owning machines in 1985 in these age brackets, as compared with 79 percent in 1970."

On top of this, it was gently hinted that the working women of America (now 41 percent of the working population) had many alternative ways to fill their leisure time.

Though the decline in Europe began shortly after Pace delivered her analysis of the U.S. market, no one at Singer could accept the idea that European women were so quickly falling into step with their American counterparts. Said one Singer executive, "Whenever we had trouble, the motto was 'This too shall pass.' "

As 1978 unwound, Flavin finally woke up. The entire market for consumer sewing machines dropped dramatically on both continents, pulling Singer's unit sales down with it. For the first time in memory, Singer's U.S. operations lost money: $21 million. But the European operations stayed well in the black, so that the combined businesses eked out a $5-million operating profit on $701 million in sales. But it worsened. In the first half of 1979, the combined operations lost $6.8 million.

In announcing the write-off, Singer blamed most of its problems on a single devastating fact: the U.S. market for sewing machines has been cut in half since 1972. But the company's troubles really go back much further than that. The sewing business is international, and Singer has been attacked since the fifties in almost all markets. The Japanese came first, and they were followed by other Asian manufacturers. Though the company has shifted some of its production to low-cost locations such as Brazil, Mexico, and Taiwan, it has been unable to hold the more aggressive competitors at bay.

In many respects, the operations in Clydebank are symbolic of Singer's anguish. The nearly century-old plant is appallingly antiquated, with manufacturing operations on several floors and a casting process that would be out of date in Chungking. Productivity has been so low in recent years that even the unions have conceded that, in its present shape, the plant is incapable of competing with anyone, much less the producers on Taiwan. Over 90 percent of Clydebank's shipments go to Europe or North America, where they compete with lower-cost models. A competitor's machine comparable to one that costs Singer $123 to make at Clydebank can be turned out for $65 in Taiwan.

The closing of Clydebank is but the first of a series of efforts planned to treat Singer's numbing wounds. Flavin knows he has to batten down operations in Europe and North America to provide protection from the worst possible scenario, including a long and deep recession, a reduction in real purchasing power, and continued inroads by low-cost manufacturers.

For years Singer acted as if the sewing-products operation could run without a coherent business plan. Extraordinary latitude was given to the top managers. Small empires were created in this hands-off atmosphere, with scant communication among the emperors.

A very frank and downhearted Singer executive, looking back on the littered landscape, offers this summary: "What happened is not at all mysterious. We had no control systems. It's a classic case that will be studied for a long time to come."

The decision Flavin faced would test the mettle of any man. No one likes firing people, and Flavin is going to have to let thousands of workers go. "Most people need a lot of love," he said recently, "but here there is necessarily anger and hurt." Though his self-confidence appears to be intact, his own share of responsibility for Singer's predicament cannot have excaped him. He was late to diagnose the situation when he arrived, and now, assuming he survives as chief executive, he will have to live with it for some time to come.

Adapted from "Singer: Sewing Machines Finally Take a Backseat as it Expands into Aerospace," *Business Week* (June 13, 1983): 66-75; and Thomas O'Hanlon, "Behind the Snafu at Singer," Fortune (November 5, 1979): 76-79.

Questions for Discussion

1. Discuss the elements of the control system operating at Singer before the arrival of Flavin.
2. What type of control system does Singer need now and in the future?
3. Discuss the relationship between planning and control as it functions in the case.
4. What are the corrective actions that Flavin is taking to reverse Singer's problems?

CHAPTER

16

Behavioral Aspects of Control

Chapter Outline

Key Points

1. Performance evaluations in organizations vary by approach and method. The most popular methods include rankings, ratings, critical incidents, BARS, and MBO.
2. The appraisal interview is the heart of the evaluation process. Learning how to conduct this interview effectively is a crucial skill for managers.
3. Pay—which can involve base pay, pay increase methods, and supplemental pay—is one of the organization's most powerful reward system components.
4. Promotion programs in organizations are moving toward more openness. This includes an emphasis on job postings and improved communication with employees.
5. Employee benefits can be quite costly to an organization. Cafeteria plans and the use of executive perks are gaining in popularity.
6. A number of factors can cause conflict, including goal incompatibility, availability of resources, performance expectations, and organizational structure.
7. Avoidance, defusion, and confrontation are possible conflict resolution strategies. Confrontation is preferred because it attempts to get at the source of the conflict.
8. Employee terminations are originated by the organization or by the individual. Each have multiple sources, some of which are uncontrollable.

THE PRACTICE OF MANAGEMENT

Employee Evaluation

Faced with more dynamic and turbulent environments, changing demographic and labor force characteristics, and a widening variety of employee needs, many firms are attempting to overhaul or at least fine-tune their performance evaluation and reward systems. To motivate and retain good employees, companies are trying as never before to make distinctions between who should be rewarded and who should not. For example:

- The standard twelve-month review and merit increase is being replaced with other systems. At Citicorp, high performers may be reviewed and rewarded three, sometimes four, times per year. On the other side, less than satisfactory performers at Pullman-Kellogg may wait as long as eighteen months for a merit increase.
- Wider ranges of merit increases are becoming popular. At Digital Equipment, Westinghouse, and Xerox, the range from low performer to high performer can vary from nothing to 20 percent.
- One-time awards are also coming into fashion. At Security-Pacific and Pitney-Bowes, one-time awards averaging about 10 percent of the employee's annual salary are given for superior performance. While not a permanent raise, such awards can have a high motivation value. At Wang, one-time awards take the form of stock options.

Do most companies make a concerted effort to link performance and rewards for employees? In most cases, *Fortune* believes this to be true. There are, however, some interesting contradictions, especially for top executives. For example, in 1981, Thomas L. Phillips, chairman of Raytheon, earned $635,000. A good salary, but, for comparable firms, Phillips' pay puts him in the underclass.

In contrast, Rand V. Araskog, Chairman of International Telephone & Telegraph (ITT), earned $1,150,000 during the same period. This included $173,000 that ITT pays on a Manhattan cooperative apartment so that Araskog could live near the office, and over $50,000 for meetings he attended on company business (i.e., $1000 for board meetings and $750 for general management meetings).

How have each of these two similar, multi-industry firms performed under the direction of Phillips and Araskog? In the five-year period ending with 1981, consider this: average return on stockholder's equity (ITT 11 percent, 21 percent for Raytheon), annual growth rate in earnings-per-share (3.5 percent for ITT, 24 percent for Raytheon), and change in price of common stock (−12 percent for ITT, + 147 percent for Raytheon). Such comparisons have prompted *Fortune* to say that, in the compensation of chief executives, any similarity between rewards received and performance often seems coincidental.

Adapted from C. J. Loomis, "The Madness of Executive Compensation," *Fortune* (July 12, 1982): 42-52.

16 The managerial control function involves many activities. There are the clear-cut areas: finances (chapter 15), information (chapter 17), and production and operations (chapter 18). An equally important, but less well-defined, activity is the function of control as related to the organization's employees. As our *Practice of Management* section illustrates, two of the important behavioral elements of control concern performance evaluation and reward systems.

This second chapter on managerial control is divided into four main sections. First, we will highlight the importance of performance evaluation (or appraisal), emphasizing the purposes and methods of the evaluation process. Second, we will discuss various elements that make up an organization's reward system—pay, promotions, and employee benefits. In the third section, we will look at sources of conflict, along with ways that managers can control it. Finally, we will conclude the chapter with a discussion of a necessary, but controversial, control activity—employee terminations.

Performance Evaluation

One of the most important, yet perplexing, aspects of the manager's job is the appraisal and evaluation of employee performance. On one hand, management literature has touted its importance for years as a basic management function. It has been thought to contribute to employee development, identify employee potential, aid in human resource planning, determine employee compensation, and improve the performance of the employee and the organization.[1] On the other hand, managers involved in employee performance evaluation have voiced concerns about its objectivity, relevance, and validity. The complaint they most often voice is that the appraisal system simply does not work. In this section, we will point out both the benefits and problems associated with employee performance evaluation.

Performance evaluation can mean different things to different people. For example, consider the case of a major league baseball pitcher:

> You could always tell how you were doing by the way the pitching coach said good morning. If he said, "Well, now, good morning Jimsie boy," that meant that you'd won your last two or three games and were in the starting rotation. If he nodded his head to you and said, "Jimbo, how are you doin'?" you were still in the starting rotation, but your record probably wasn't much over .500. If he said, "Mornin'," that meant you were on your way down, that you'd probably lost four out of five and it was doubtful if you would be getting any more starts. If he simply looked at you and gave you a solemn nod, that meant you might get some mop up work, or you might not, but you definitely weren't starting anymore. . . . And if he looked past you, over your shoulder as if you didn't exist, it was all over and you might as well pack your bags because you could be traded or sent down to the minors at any moment.[2]

In most organizations, however, the process is more complicated.

For our purposes, employee performance evaluation or appraisal is the process of identifying, measuring, and developing human performance in organizations. An effective performance evaluation system must accurately measure current performance levels and contain mechanisms for reinforcing strengths, identifying weaknesses, and feeding the information back to the employees so they can improve future performance. In the most basic terms, performance evaluation answers these questions about an employee: "What is he doing?", "How well is he doing it?", and "What can be done either to maintain what he is doing well or improve on what he is doing less well?"

Our definition of performance evaluation has three major functions:

Observation and identification refers to the process of viewing or scrutinizing certain job behaviors. It concerns the process of choosing what behaviors to observe (e.g., the number of computer cards punched by a keypunch operator), as well as how often to observe them.

Measurement compares the information gained from observing employees' behaviors against a set of organizational goals or standards. The degree to which the observed behavior meets or exceeds the standards determines the level of performance it reflects (e.g., excellent or acceptable level of performance).

Development refers to performance improvement over time. A performance evaluation system must be able to point out deficiencies and strengths in people's behavior so they can be motivated to improve future performance.[3]

These broad-based functions of a performance evaluation system can be translated into specific purposes. The most important are:

- Feedback for employees about how the manager and organization view their overall performance

- Promotion, separation, and transfer decisions

- Criteria for allocating organizational rewards

- Criteria for evaluating the effectiveness of selection and placement decisions

- Ascertaining training and development needs, along with criteria for evaluating the success of training and development decisions.

Managers need to keep in mind that the performance evaluation process is at the focal point of the entire behavioral control system. That is, it not only evaluates the employee's behavior, but also initiates any corrective action.

The Performance Evaluation Process

Let's follow the typical performance evaluation process through the job of quality-control manager for a medium-sized manufacturer of home appliances. The manager's job consists of these responsibilities: develop, maintain, and revise quality-control standards for the firm's products; supervise a group of four quality-control technicians who perform tests; maintain quality-control costs within budgetary constraints; respond and act upon customer complaints; monitor the plant's air pollution emissions; and so on.

Exhibit 16-1 shows the steps in the manager's performance evaluation.[4] Note that this process and MBO are quite similar. There are two points to consider about these two processes. First, the similarity between them is why many organizations tie MBO and performance evaluation together, especially for wage and salary considerations. Since many of the same points are covered, they can sometimes be merged into a more comprehensive system. Second, performance evaluation covers more of a person's job than does MBO. MBO is usually concerned with "key results" areas—those aspects of a job that are deemed most important to the individual and to the organization. MBO generally covers somewhere between 50 and 75 percent of a person's job. Performance evaluation, on the other hand, deals with the total job. These are the steps in performance evaluation, shown in exhibit 16-1:

Step 1: Job analysis. As discussed in chapter 10, job analysis examines the elements that make up a job. For the quality-control manager, these elements include such responsibilities as cost control, quality testing, supervision, customer complaints, and so on.

Step 2: Identify performance criteria. This step concerns the question, "What are the important elements of performance?" The cost control responsibility for the quality control manager concerns the criteria of running the unit within the budget and the expenses incurred in developing a new test.

Step 3: Develop measuring instruments. Two aspects are related to this step: what is a valid representation of each criterion, and what is a reliable gauge of each measure? As discussed in chapter 1, most performance is measured using either quantitative or qualitative measures, or both. For example, the number of customer complaints is a quantitative measure, while the evaluation of the quality-control manager's supervisory performance is determined by the use of a subjective or qualitative measure.

Step 4: Establish performance standards. This step defines good performance. Responding to customer complaints within 30 days, the reduction of product reject rates by 15 percent, or developing a new air pollution emissions test by October 1 are examples for the quality-control manager.

Step 5: Performance appraisal and interview. This is one of the most important steps, because it concerns how the manager evaluates a subordinate's performance and how this evaluation is communicated. The content of the interview, its frequency and timing, and the quality of interaction between superior and subordinate are important.

Step 6: Intervention or corrective action. The level of performance will determine the nature of the activities in this step. If the performance of the subordinate is less than satisfactory, some form of corrective action or adjustment may be required. If the performance is satisfactory or exceeds standards, some form of positive reinforcement or plan for continued high performance would be discussed. We will present this step in greater detail with our coverage of reward systems.

We have selected two of the steps of the performance evaluation process for further discussion: developing measuring instruments (step 3), and the performance appraisal interview (step 5). These two steps have been chosen because of their centrality to the success of the evaluation and behavioral control system.

Exhibit 16-1
Steps in Performance Evaluations for a Quality-Control Manager

Job Analysis	Performance Criteria	Measuring Instruments	Performance Standards	Appraisal	Corrective Action
Develop, maintain and revise Q/C standards	Specifications and testing	Records	Prepare specs on products by April 1	Product specs developed on all products	None
Supervise Q/C technicians	Supervision (performance, absenteeism, etc.)	Rating scales	Maintain 90% inspection rate	92% inspection rate maintained	None
			Reduce absenteeism and turnover by 20%	Absenteeism and turnover increased by 10%	Formal analysis of causes
Work within a budget	Cost control	Budget and cost data	No excess costs during 19—	No excess costs	None
Respond to customer complaints	Quality rejects	Correspondence	Reduce complaints by 10% by year end—respond within 30 days	Complaints reduced by 3%	Discussions with manufacturing manager
Monitor air pollution	Environmental control standards	Records and data	Meet local, state and federal standards	Air pollution emission standards met only 45% of the time	Examine testing equipment
					Form air pollution task force

Selecting Measuring Approaches and Instruments

Assume you are the store manager in a branch of a large retail department store. You have a total of ten department managers reporting to you (men's, women's, and children's clothing, appliances, garden shop, and so on), along with a support staff (two assistant store managers, personnel, accounting, maintenance, security). To evaluate the performance of the department managers, you consider at least two issues—the approach and the method.

Performance Evaluation Approaches   The performance evaluation approach concerns the issue of *who* evaluates the performance of the department managers.[5] Let us assume you are evaluating the performance of the manager of children's clothing. There are at least five appraisal approaches you can use. The first, the *superior evaluating the subordinate,* is the most common in organizations. In other words, the subordinate department manager would be evaluated only by the store manager.

Second, a number of organizations have opted for a *group of supervisors evaluating a subordinate*. The idea is that a better appraisal can be had if more than one individual contributes to the evaluation. This approach is frequently found in a matrix structure. In our example, the department manager could be evaluated by the store manager and the two assistant store managers. A major problem is that this approach assumes that all the evaluators have knowledge of the manager's performance. This approach also can be time consuming and may dilute the subordinate's feelings of influence and accountability to the immediate superior.

A *group of peers evaluating a colleague* is the third approach. In the department store, a number of other department managers who understand the work of the children's clothing department would be asked separately for an evaluation. This approach is commonly used in the military and by scientists in research institutions. It is less common in other organizations because competition among peers for merit pay increases and/or promotions may bias their evaluations.

The fourth approach is *subordinates evaluating their superior*. Examples include student evaluations of a professor's teaching performance, or the sales staff appraising the performance of the department manager. While this is becoming a more frequently used evaluation approach, managers must make sure that subordinates are capable and trained in evaluation procedures.

Finally, in some cases organizations ask for a *self-evaluation*. Usually this approach is used as a supplement to the other approaches, rather than alone. Many managers believe that if self-evaluation is the only approach used, positive bias will become a problem (if you had a choice between giving yourself a C or an F in this course, which one would you choose?).

Because of the growing complexities of the managerial world today, many organizations use a *combination approach*. To evaluate the performance of the department manager, the store manager initially performs an appraisal. In addition, separate evaluations from the assistant store managers are provided, along with a number of one-on-one interviews with the manager's subordinates. Though this can become a time-consuming process, the cross-section of opinions may prove valuable, especially if the store manager is thinking of promoting the department manager.

Performance Evaluation Methods   There is a wide variety of methods for performance evaluation. The five most popular are global ranking, trait-based rating scales, critical incidents, behaviorally anchored rating scales (BARS), and effectiveness-based (objective) measures.[6]

Global ranking is a simple unidimensional rank order that involves a manager's *overall* estimate of performance of a group of subordinates without distinguishing between important job factors. With a ranking method, our store manager would take the ten department managers and rank order them from 1 (highest performer) to 10 (lowest performer). While this approach has the advantage of being fairly easy and quick to conduct, there are a number of serious disadvantages. The negative features include the problem of reducing performance to a single index, the inability to distinguish between different levels of performance (is the difference in performance between the third and fourth best performers the same as the difference between the seventh and eighth?), and concern about the method's legality (performance evaluation methods that are not based on a job analysis may be open to discrimination claims).

Trait-based rating scales are probably the oldest and most frequently used methods for evaluating employee performance. They are distinguished from ranking scales by at least three factors: (1) job performance is recognized as consisting of different dimensions, such as quality, dependability, cooperativeness, knowledge of work, and initiative; (2) each dimension is broken down by different levels of performance, usually on a five-point scale, or poor to outstanding; and (3) the meaning of the dimensions and the level of evaluation is clear to the rater and ratee, making feedback much easier. Some examples of different ratings scales are shown in exhibit 16-2. Rating scales are generally preferred over rankings; however, there still are a number of weaknesses, two in particular. First, the meaning of the dimensions must be clear and unidimensional. Second, some of the performance dimensions may not have applicability to the specific job and person being evaluated.

The critical incidents method attempts to use illustrations of actual behaviors to determine an evaluative rating.[7] For example, one of the assistant store managers in our department store may have prepared an excellent quarterly sales report for the store's different departments. The store manager may make a written note of this behavior and place it in a file maintained on each subordinate, to refer to at the time of the yearly performance review. While managers who use the critical incidents method like its behavior-specific and good feedback qualities, the time-consuming nature of the method, particularly for the manager who has many subordinates, has been a significant deterrent to its use.

Behaviorally anchored rating scales (BARS) have been gaining in popularity. They are called behaviorally based measures of job performance because they focus on detailed evaluation of *specific* acts or behaviors, rather than global aspects.[8] The development of a behaviorally anchored rating scale depends upon the judgment of those employees and managers who are closest to the job itself—those individuals who will be the ones using the final instrument or receiving feedback from it. The development of one of these scales involves at least the following steps:

Exhibit 16-2
Examples of Rating Scale Items

A.

Consider employee's efforts since the last review dated _____ and show by a check (X) any changes in each of the categories.

REVIEW CAREFULLY AND CHECK ☒ ONE BLOCK AS APPROPRIATE

						HAS IMPROVED	LITTLE OR NO CHANGE	HAS GONE BACK
1. SAFETY PERFORMANCE Consider all facets of safety in connection with present job title, in carrying out company safety policies.	Careless of safety of self and others. (A) ☐	Occasionally causes mishaps. (B) ☐	Accepts safety as part of job.	Practices good safety habits and is considerate of others.	Exercises great care and foresees hazards to self and fellow employees.			
	During Past 2 Years No. Disabling Work Injuries ____ No. Medical Treatment Injuries ____ No. Motor Vehicle Accidents ____		(C) ☐	(D) ☐	(E) ☐	☐	☐	☐
2. ATTENDANCE and PUNCTUALITY Consider attendance on the job and reporting on time.	Undependable, absent or late without proper notice. (A) ☐	Frequently absent or late. (B) ☐	Some absence with good cause.	Occasionally absent or late. Notifies in advance.	Record is perfect.			
	During Past Year No. Days Incidental Absence ____ No. Days Benefit Absence ____ No. Times Tardy ____		(C) ☐	(D) ☐	(E) ☐	☐	☐	☐

B.

Has difficulty defining objectives. Sets objective levels which may be unrealistic. Has difficulty establishing priority of needs and may distribute resources inefficiently. Requires extensive supervision to accomplish objectives.	**1. Setting and Achieving Objectives** LOW ├─┼─┼─┼─┼─┼─┼─┼─┤ HIGH 1 5 9	Defines realistic objectives. Sets realistic objective levels. Ranks the objectives and distributes resources according to the needs of the company. Accomplishes objectives without the need for excessive supervision.

C.

	Extremely Low				Extremely High
1. Rate the quality of his/her job performance.	1	2	3	4	5
2. Rate the quantity of work performed in his/her job.	1	2	3	4	5

D.

☐ **Cooperativeness**
Cooperates well with others
Good teamworker

☐ **Judgment**
Ability to make sound decisions
Ability to solve and meet new problems
Judgment sought by others
Profit awareness shows good judgment

Check One   **Performance Key**

☐ A — Excellent-Outstanding
☐ B — Good-Superior
☐ C — Satisfactory-Average
☐ D — Unsatisfactory-Below Average
☐ E — Too new to appraise
☐ F — Does not apply

E.

Personal Relationships

├────────┴────────┴────────┴────────┤

| A fair weather operator. Often antagonizes other staff members. | Sometimes irritates other staff members. Somewhat prone to anger, moodiness or nervousness. | Generally friendly and effective in personal relationships. Satisfactory self control. | Stable personality, even temperament, good spirits. | Inspires friendly respect and confidence of others. Exceptional self control. |

- Expert judges—those closest and most familiar with the job—are asked to make two kinds of judgments about the job. First, they are asked to identify the basic task dimensions of the job (e.g., setting and achieving goals, developing subordinates). Second, they are asked to relate specific illustrative behaviors of either effective or ineffective activities with respect to each dimension.

- Several other groups of expert judges are asked to evaluate the illustrations generated by the initial group. They are asked first to assign each illustration to a particular task dimension. Second, they are requested to rate the employee's behavior in terms of how effective or ineffective it is in accomplishing the task dimension.

- Based upon the judgments of the second step, items or behavioral illustrations are retained only if there is substantial agreement among the judges as to how the behavior is defined and how effectively it relates to the success of the job. Items on which there is disagreement are thrown out.

The result of an analysis carried out according to these three steps is a pool of every job-specific item describing effective and ineffective behavior in the language of those closest to the job—raters and ratees. Exhibit 16-3 presents one of ten behaviorally anchored performance dimensions for the job of a design engineer. Note that the evaluator does not have to rely on general adjectives such as "outstanding" or "poor" in evaluating an engineer's performance. Instead, the evaluator can concentrate on specific job behaviors on the right side of the scale in deciding how effective the engineer was during the review period.

The behaviorally anchored scale is clearly a superior method of evaluating employee performance. Not only does this development process identify important job dimensions, but since many employees are involved in developing the scale, they may become more committed to its use. On the other hand, this method is time- and resource-consuming. Being job specific, a scale developed for design engineers may not be totally transferable to the job of construction engineer. Thus, the development process must be conducted for each different job or job classification.

Effectiveness-based measures depend heavily on objective measures of performance. MBO (see chapter 6) can be an effectiveness-based measure in which there is an emphasis on such quantitative or objective measures as time, costs, and sales.

Exhibit 16-4 presents an evaluation of the five methods according to the degree to which they accomplish the main goals of the performance evaluation process, along with the amount of resources (time, human, and administrative) needed to develop the method and the degree to which the method is job specific. As the exhibit indicates, behaviorally anchored scales and effectiveness-based measures (MBO) achieve the goals of the performance evaluation process better than the other measures because they are more job specific. But these methods do consume a large amount of organizational resources, which deters many managers from using them often.

Elements of the Evaluation Interview

Even when managers use the most appropriate approach and the most valid method, the entire performance evaluation process can prove disastrous if the actual evaluation interview is conducted poorly. Many reasons can be given for this problem.[9] The

Exhibit 16-3
A BARS Performance Dimension for a Design Engineer

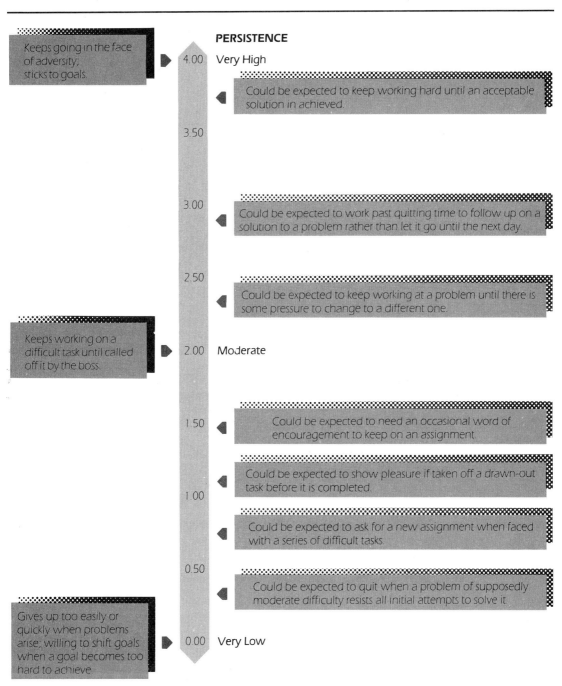

Keeps going in the face of adversity; sticks to goals.

PERSISTENCE

4.00 Very High

Could be expected to keep working hard until an acceptable solution in achieved.

3.50

3.00 Could be expected to work past quitting time to follow up on a solution to a problem rather than let it go until the next day.

2.50 Could be expected to keep working at a problem until there is some pressure to change to a different one.

Keeps working on a difficult task until called off it by the boss.

2.00 Moderate

1.50 Could be expected to need an occasional word of encouragement to keep on an assignment.

Could be expected to show pleasure if taken off a drawn-out task before it is completed.

1.00

Could be expected to ask for a new assignment when faced with a series of difficult tasks.

0.50

Could be expected to quit when a problem of supposedly moderate difficulty resists all initial attempts to solve it.

Gives up too easily or quickly when problems arise; willing to shift goals when a goal becomes too hard to achieve.

0.00 Very Low

Exhibit 16-4
Evaluation of Performance Evaluation Methods

	Performance Evaluation Purposes						
Method	Feedback/ Development	Promotion, Separation, Transfer Decision	Reward Allocation	Selection, Placement Decision	Assessing Training Needs	Resources Needed to Develop	Degree of Job Specificity
1. Global Ranking	Poor	Poor	Poor	Poor	Poor	Low	Low
2. Trait-Based Rating Scales	Fair	Poor to Fair	Fair	Poor to Fair	Fair	Low	Low to Moderate
3. Critical Incidents	Fair to Good	Fair	Fair	Poor to Fair	Fair	Moderate	Moderate
4. BARS	Good to Very Good	Very Good	Very Good	Very Good to Outstanding	Very Good	High	High
5. Effectiveness-Based Measures	Fair to Good	Good	Very Good to Outstanding	Good to Very Good	Good	High	High

Adapted from R.W. Beatty and C.E. Schneier, *Personnel Administration,* 2nd. ed.
(Reading, Mass.: Addison-Wesley, 1981), pp. 106-107.

manager may not be prepared or may not understand the important performance-related data for a particular subordinate; the manager may not be properly trained to conduct a performance evaluation interview; or the manager may not do well in one-on-one interactions and, as a result, either offers undeserved praise, focuses too much on the negatives of the individual's performance rather than equally on the positives, or tries to finish the interview as quickly as possible.

While describing the proper way to conduct an evaluation interview can take up an entire chapter, we have selected three broad areas for discussion: what to do before the interview, what to stress during the interview, and what to do after the interview.[10]

Preparing for the Evaluation Interview   At least three factors concern the manager preparing for an evaluation interview. First, he or she must decide how often to make the appraisal. Most organizations make a choice between either a standard review cycle, such as every twelve months, or an evaluation at "natural" points, such as the completion of a project. In some rare situations, the employee requests the appraisal. Which alternatives are appropriate depends upon the nature of the work and the skills of the employee. For example, if the tasks are relatively simple and standard (e.g., janitors or clerical personnel) and/or the subordinates have minimal job-related skills, a standard review cycle is usually preferred. If subordinates are highly skilled professionals, and/or tasks do not follow standard cycles (e.g., accountants, scientists, or engineers), it probably would be better if the review followed shortly after the completion of a unit of work. For example, an accountant may work on three major

Faced with time constraints and pressures, some managers have a tendency to ignore employee performance evaluation or place it low on their list of priorities. Few managers have had training in school or on the job in conducting an accurate performance evaluation. The result is that, although we pay lip service to the importance of employee evaluation, in practice evaluation frequently gets done in a haphazard and last-minute fashion.

The end product of such a practice is predictable: poor morale, ineffective pay/performance programs, management development failures, and many legal problems. However, General Telephone and Electronics (GTE) may be an exception.

In the late 1970s, GTE began a program in which managers are trained in performance evaluation methods and approaches. Each GTE manager takes a two-day course in how to make evaluations in which extensive use of videotaping sessions are used. The unique feature of this program is that, at the end of the training, the manager's own performance is rated by his or her subordinates.

In the training program itself, managers are exposed to procedures that combine evaluation with coaching and counseling. They learn how their implicit styles (correct and incorrect) have a direct impact on how well their subordinates perform, and that this in the aggregate has an impact on the financial and operating health of the firm.

The capstone of the program is a management practices survey that gathers information about how the manager communicates goals, organizes and stresses teamwork, and rewards behavior. Both the manager and his or her employees respond to the survey. Comparing the self-report responses of the managers with the observations of the subordinates can be shocking. More frequently, the results are better reviews, more attention paid to instances of outstanding performance, and improved morale.

Adapted from "Training Managers to Rate Their Employees," *Business Week* (March 17, 1980).

projects during a twelve-month period—a performance appraisal, therefore, may occur after each project has been completed. Many organizations are moving toward the "natural" point review because of its motivational value—that is, according to reinforcement theory, if the appraisal and rewards follow the actual performance closely, the chance that desired behavior will continue is enhanced.

Second, the manager should spend some time and *prepare* for each subordinate's review. This means gathering and reviewing all the important information and identifying the major points of discussion.

Finally, the manager should *set aside enough uninterrupted time* for the interview to cover all the key points. This means holding phone calls and other visitors until later. The subordinate must feel that this is his or her time, not to be shared with other people.

The Evaluation Interview   If the actual performance evaluation interview could be reduced to its simplest components, it would answer these two questions for the subordinate: *How well am I doing?* and *Where do I go from here?* (see exhibit 16-5). The first question generally covers the issues of maintaining or improving successful performance or correcting unsuccessful performance. In the case of a subordinate who is performing at or above acceptable standards, it makes sense to discuss why performance is at that level, to help the person "keep up the good work."[11]

With a low-performance subordinate, the process of identifying the contributing factors becomes more important. At least four factors apply: (1) Does the person have sufficient job-related knowledge and skills to perform effectively? (2) Has the person been equitably rewarded in the past for his performance? (3) Does the present job satisfy his job-related needs? and (4) Are there certain extraneous factors, such as poor co-worker relationships or inadequate working conditions, that are adversely affecting his performance?

The second question *(Where do I go from here?)* involves discussing career interests and developmental needs. This topic relates to our discussion of training and development activities in chapter 10 and the subject of managerial career development, which we will discuss in detail in chapter 20.

The success of the evaluation interview hinges on the environment the manager establishes. Exhibit 16-6 lists a set of points to *avoid* and to *try*.

After the Evaluation Interview   Shortly after the evaluation interview, there are at least three things the manager needs to do. First, the subordinate's file should be updated with all the information regarding the present period's performance. It may be helpful to write a brief report that summarizes all the activities, including the discussion in the appraisal interview. Second, the manager should begin the next period's evaluation profile with a summary of the present report and any goals and/or plans for the period. This would also be a good time to begin using the critical incidents method. Finally, in an informal way, the manager should let the employee know from time to time that he is interested in frequent progress reports on the person's performance, particularly if new data or changes are noted. The key point is not to appear to be nagging, but to let the subordinate be the one to initiate such informal progress reviews. In this manner, the two-way exchange of ideas and feelings is enhanced.[12]

Exhibit 16-5
Format for the
Evaluation
Interview

1. Open-ended discussion and exploration of problems, in which the subordinate leads and the supervisor listens and adds.
2. Problem-solving discussion, in which the subordinate leads, but the supervisor takes a stronger role.
3. Agreement between supervisor and subordinate on performance strengths and weaknesses and a plan for action.
4. Discussion of development, training, and career opportunities.
5. Closing evaluation in which the supervisor summarizes the interview and outlines future activities.

Adapted from M. Beer, "Performance Appraisal: Dilemmas and Possibilities," *Organizational Dynamics* (Winter 1981): 33.

Exhibit 16-6
General Guidelines for Performance Evaluation Interviews

Avoid	Try
Focus on the person and personalities.	Focus on the behavior.
Be judgmental.	Be descriptive.
Use negative words or too many criticisms.	Reassure the subordinate by building on strengths, giving confidence.
Use a ''you vs. me'' attitude.	Use a ''we'' attitude when discussing problems.
Give insincere or undeserved praise.	Be specific when discussing the positive and negative features of the performance.
Dominate the interview.	Draw employees out by asking questions, listening, and then reflecting on their responses.
Be a nit-picker.	Counsel, don't advise.
Appear bored or hurried.	Summarize, plan for improvement, write down results, close properly.

Legal Considerations of Performance Evaluation

Hiring, promotion, transfer, and termination decisions are among the most difficult and most important managers face in their work. The results of these decisions have an impact on the careers of the individual employees and the success and even survival of the organization.

While these decisions have always been difficult, they now are becoming more important, due to the increased attention and scrutiny by governmental agencies such as the Equal Employment Opportunity Commission (EEOC), the Office of Federal Contract Compliance Programs (OFCCP), and the courts. This interest by governmental agencies has, in the past few years, begun to affect performance evaluation activities.[13]

The need for a legal look at performance evaluation is not new—its beginnings can be found in the Constitution and the Civil Rights Acts of 1866 and 1871. The Civil Rights Act of 1964 has kindled current interest (particularly Title VII of that act as amended by the Equal Opportunity Act of 1972), as has the Equal Pay Act, the Civil Service Reform Act of 1978, and numerous court decisions.

From all this information, what should the manager know about the legal implications of performance evaluation? The following are some keys to consider:[14]

Is there a written company policy covering performance evaluation? It is important that such a policy statement exists that defines the goals of the program, the period covered and the frequency of evaluation, and the special circumstances.

Have evaluators been trained? The extent of evaluator training, how the training approaches the different methods and procedures to be used, and the documentation as to who attended and what material was covered are of interest.

On what foundation are evaluations based? It is becoming clearer with each passing year that the courts will look adversely on any evaluation system that does not use job analysis as its base for developing the content of the evaluations.

What is the focus of the evaluations? Similar to the importance of job analysis, the courts are leaning toward evaluations that are behavior based rather than trait based. The key is to be job specific, not focus on some unrelated performance trait.

How are the results of the evaluation communicated? It has been strongly suggested that the reviewed employees actually see their evaluation forms (some firms ask for the employee's signature), and are apprised of the stated policy, the standards upon which they are evaluated, and the availability of promotion opportunities. Documentation of how the evaluation was communicated is highly recommended.

Reward Systems

Each day, week, month, or year, organizations distribute a variety of rewards to employees. These rewards may be as simple as a verbal ''thank you'' for a job well done, or as complex as a promotion program; they may be closely tied to performance, such as pay systems, or generally unrelated to performance, such as employee benefits; they may have special meaning to a few individuals, as status symbols do, or have a meaning and value to all employees, as does a profit-sharing program. Whatever the focus, rewards can have both a short- and a long-term impact on the organization's performance and survival.

Rewards serve a variety of purposes and have different requirements, depending on whether they are seen from an individual viewpoint or an organizational viewpoint.[15] Individual employees generally seek rewards that satisfy their basic needs *(reward level)*, are given to them in line with their level of performance *(internal equity)*, are comparable to those of similar jobs in other organizations *(external equity)*, and offer a variety of rewards to satisfy the complex needs of the individual *(individuality)*.

Organizations, on the other hand, want the reward system to facilitate the process of people joining the organization *(membership)*, to enhance the probability of employees coming to work *(attendance or absenteeism)*, to relate rewards to performance *(motivation)*, and to vary the distribution of rewards to reinforce the differences in managerial levels and in the importance of different jobs *(structure)*.

Our discussion of organizational reward systems will cover three major points. First, a basic rewards system model will be presented which links the previous discussions on motivation (chapter 12) and performance evaluations. Second, because of their importance and frequency of use, pay systems, promotions, and employee benefits will be discussed separately. Finally, we will offer certain keys to success with rewards in organizations.

A Basic Reward System Model

Exhibit 16-7 shows a basic model of an organization's reward system. At least four important points can be derived from an analysis of this model. First, the exhibit represents an expansion of our basic motivation model (see chapter 12). That is, it links the concepts of motivation, performance, performance evaluation, rewards, and satisfaction. Second, it highlights again the centrality of the performance evaluation process. In other words, the absence of a valid and accurate evaluation system will not only hamper the equitable distribution of rewards, but later motivation may be adversely influenced.

Third, we have once more made a distinction between intrinsic and extrinsic rewards. Recall from chapter 12 that *intrinsic* rewards are those rewards that the individual receives from doing the job (e.g., achievement, pride, autonomy, and personal growth and development). *Extrinsic* rewards are those rewards that are given to the individual by someone else. Included are pay increases and bonuses, promotion, recognition and praise, and employee benefits. Since we covered the topic of intrinsic rewards in the job design discussion in chapter 12, we will concentrate on an analysis of extrinsic rewards in the remainder of this chapter.

Finally, the feedback loop from performance and satisfaction to motivation again emphasizes the importance of rewards to motivation. In essence, managers need to recognize that administering rewards is a continuous process.

Exhibit 16-7
A Basic Reward System Model

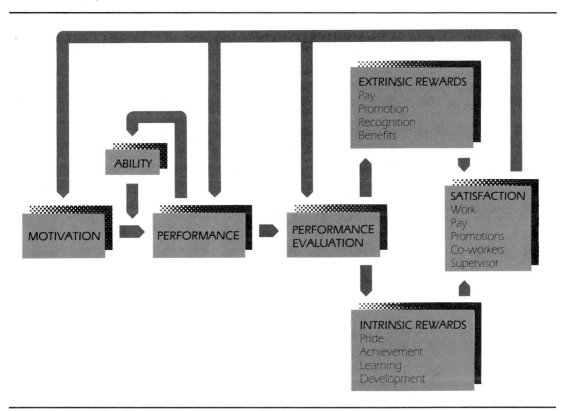

Approaches to Pay as a Reward

An organization can take many approaches to using pay as a reward. Most of these approaches can be categorized as base pay, increases in base pay, and supplemental or incentive pay systems.[16]

Base Pay   Base pay is the level of compensation that serves as the foundation of the employee's wage or salary level. Four major approaches can be taken: job evaluation, skill evaluation, piece-rate or commission, or the all-salaried work force.

Job evaluation as a base pay approach consists of describing the job and then assessing its characteristics. This flows from a job analysis and makes distinctions of organizational level and the amount of authority, responsibility, and accountability. Once a job has been evaluated, it is compared to what other organizations pay for similar jobs and pay is set at a level that is in line with the outside market and internal characteristics.

Skill evaluation pays employees according to what they *can do* rather than what they *actually do*—that is, in terms of their abilities rather than their level of performance. This type of pay program first came into prominence in Norway and has since spread to such organizations as Procter & Gamble and General Foods. While the idea of stressing learning new skills is a popular one, there is the problem of an employee "topping out"—that is, learning all the jobs with no place to go from there. As a result, the skill evaluation plan is more appropriate for newer plants than older plants, because in new plants there is an emphasis on the acquisition of new skills.

Piece-rate or commission is based on the amount of work that a person does. Examples include paying a certain rate for each unit produced or a commission for a sales representative. Because this approach depends on identifying a particular unit of work, its applicability has been limited.

The *all-salaried work force* attempts to eliminate some distinctions between managerial/professional and nonsupervisory employees. The idea is that by paying everyone the same way, improved loyalty, teamwork, and commitment and a decrease in administrative costs can result. IBM and Gillette have certain units on the all-salaried plan. In addition, the United Auto Workers (UAW) has raised the issue of all-salary

plans in negotiating with the big-three auto makers. Opponents of the plan claim that absenteeism and tardiness will increase with this plan because no time clock is used. Unfortunately, no solid research exists to support either the benefits or problems of the all-salary plan.

Increases in Base Pay   In most organizations, employees rarely stay at their base pay for an extended period of time. Because of an employee's level of performance, changes in the nature of the job, or external conditions (e.g., inflation), organizations have developed methods of increasing the pay level of employees. Four of the most popular approaches to increasing pay are merit increases, lump-sum payments, cost of living increases, and bargaining.

Merit increases is a performance-based approach—that is, the higher the performance, the greater the pay increase. This is the most popular approach in organizations for salaried personnel. It assumes, however, that a valid and accurate performance evaluation system exists. Since the use of a merit pay system not only rewards past performance but seeks to maintain or improve future performance, organizations attempt to tie performance and rewards as closely as possible.

Lump-sum payments attempt to make the manner in which the pay increase is given more flexible. For example, consider a media relations specialist working in the public affairs department of a large organization. If the person is making $24,000 per year and receives a 10 percent merit increase ($2,400), the traditional method is to increase the employee's salary check by $200 per month. In a lump-sum program, the employee is given the $2,400 in total at the first of the year (or anniversary date of employment). Employees, and some organizations, like the lump-sum plan because it gives the employee a large amount of money at one time (for possible purchases of large goods or services), it gives visibility to the organization's merit pay program, and it generally involves little or no cost to the organization. What happens if the person leaves the organization before the year has passed? In these cases, the lump-sum is treated as a loan and any excess is paid back.

Cost of living increases entail the adjustment in pay due to changes in external conditions, such as inflation or increases in pay levels for a comparable job in other organizations. Cost of living increases due to inflation are given so that the employee's basic financial needs are covered, while adjustments due to changes in the external job market are made to keep the organization competitive for skilled people.

Bargaining is the process whereby a group of employees negotiate for wage increases. This happens most frequently between management and labor groups.

Supplemental or Incentive Pay   A popular approach, supplemental or incentive pay is usually based on the level of the individual's performance, or in some cases, on the level of performance of the group or organization. Typically, such compensation is given as a one-time award, but the person is eligible for the supplement during the next period. We will discuss two broad supplemental approaches, bonuses and profit sharing.

A bonus is a form of supplemental pay that is given to employees for meeting or exceeding a particular goal set by the organization. In many organizations, higher level executives are frequently eligible for bonuses based on their unit's performance.

Profit sharing is quite popular with many workers because they can share in the successes of their organizations. A number of forms of profit sharing exist, but usually they are related to the distribution of income over a certain after-tax profit. In addition, the amount of money received by the employee is based on that person's level in the organization and on his particular level of performance. A popular approach is the Scanlon Plan, developed in the 1930s.[17] It can take the form of straight profit sharing, or be based on labor/cost efficiency. In the latter case, a base rate is established at the beginning of a period with respect to the ratio of total sales volume to total payroll expenses. At the end of the period, any money savings resulting from improvements over the base rate are shared equally by all workers. See exhibit 16-8 for a comparison of typical compensation packages for executives.

There are two practices in many organizations that may act to reduce the impact of compensation. First, many organizations prefer to review an employee's performance once per year, resulting in a yearly pay increase. Under such a system, it is difficult for the employee to make the connection between pay and performance, since the year is made up of many performance-related activities. In essence, the individual is rewarded on the basis of an *average* performance level.

Second, another way for the employee to make the connection between pay and performance is to have some knowledge of what other employees have received. Yet, most organizations function with a secret pay program; that is, there is a lack of knowledge among employees (non-union) about their respective pay levels.

Managers in favor of an open pay system claim that employees engage in a comparison process with other employees no matter what type of pay system exists. Research has shown that in a secret pay system, employees tend to overestimate the pay of individuals at their same organizational levels and those below them, but underestimate the pay of people above them. With an open system, a person can make accurate comparisons, which may lead to clearer performance-reward beliefs. An open system also communicates to employees that the organization has nothing to hide.

Managers favoring a secret pay plan point out that the secrecy gives pay administrators more freedom in administering pay, because they do not have to explain their actions. They suggest that certain pay inequities will always exist in most organizations because of differences in such aspects as demand for jobs and experience and expertise levels of employees. For example, in such professional occupations as accounting, finance, and engineering, the demand for these jobs may put the recent graduate and the organization in a difficult position. The young accountant may join a firm with a salary of $18,000 per year. After one year, good performance yields a 10 percent merit increase to $19,800. That same year, the tight market for accountants forces the firm to increase starting salaries to $19,500. If an open pay system existed in this firm, consider the morale problems among accountants as described above when they realize that after a year of good performance they are making only $300 per year more than the newly hired, inexperienced accountant.

Exhibit 16-8

Changes In Executive Compensation

1971			1981		
Industry	Largest Company	Chief Executive's Compensation	Largest Company	Chief Executive's Compensation	Increase (Decrease)
Aerospace	Boeing	$80,000	Boeing	$957,551	1,096.9%
Food	Swift	$68,053	Dart & Kraft	$748,647	1,000.1%
Pharmaceuticals	American Home Products	$240,000	Johnson & Johnson	$968,542	303.6%
Publishing	Time Inc.	$203,025	Time Inc.	$633,367	212.0%
Metal Manufacturing	U.S. Steel	$300,000	U.S. Steel	$821,322	173.8%
Retailing	Sears Roebuck	$386,800	Sears Roebuck	$1,010,137	161.2%
Utility	AT&T	$360,500	AT&T	$894,400	148.1%
Office Equipment	IBM	$394,331	IBM	$940,000	138.4%
Commercial Banking	Bankamerica	$171,543	Bankamerica	$390,325	127.5%
Petroleum Refining	Standard Oil (N.J.)	$505,100	Exxon	$1,105,412	118.9%
Brokerage	Merrill Lynch	$296,501	Merrill Lynch	$642,524	116.7%
Advertising	J. Walter Thompson	$191,587	JWT Group	$372,881	94.6%
Mutual Life Insurance	Prudential	$300,000	Prudential	$582,744	94.2%
Conglomerates	General Electric	$500,000	General Electric	$853,976	70.8%
Automotive	General Motors	$838,750	General Motors	$489,250	(41.7%)

. . . As Compared With

	Compensation		Compensation	Increase
Major-League Baseball Player (average)	$31,543		$196,500	523.0%
Starting Lawyer in a Wall Street Law Firm	$15,500		$43,300	179.4%
Harvard MBA Graduate Entering Consulting (median)	$18,000		$46,100	156.1%
Auto Worker (average hourly wage)	$4.72		$11.01	133.3%
Airline Pilot (average for union members)	$28,390		$60,280	112.3%
President of AFL-CIO	$70,000		$110,000	57.1%
U.S. Senator	$42,500		$60,663	42.7%
President of the U.S.	$200,000		$200,000	0.0%
Consumer Price Index (1967=100)	121.3		272.4	124.6%
Minimum Wage	$1.60		$3.35	109.4%
Standard & Poor's 500 Stock Index (year-end)	102.09		122.55	20.0%

Source: C. J. Loomis, "The Madness of Executive Compensation," *Fortune* (July 12, 1982); 45.

In addition, secret pay proponents not only claim that it would be extremely difficult to communicate to employees all the details of a pay plan, but also that in reality there is no great demand by employees that pay raises be made public. This, however, is a questionable assumption. The debate over secret versus open pay plans will no doubt continue for some time to come. It seems that most organizations will adopt a system that best fits their particular climate.

Promotions

Promotions, because of their impact on the development of the individual and the organization, are some of the most important long-range decisions that managers make in the human resource area. Ideally, one would like to see a promotion program that is fair, free from bias and discrimination, and performance- or merit-based. In some organizations, these objectives are met; in others, they are not.

Promotion programs in organizations can take many forms and involve different processes. We will discuss two promotion programs—Plan A and Plan B—that may be considered at the extremes of existing programs.

Plan A is characterized by both openness and an emphasis on an analysis of the needs of the organization and the abilities and skills of the person. Among the most frequently used techniques in Plan A are human resource planning and assessment centers (see chapter 10), MBO (see chapter 6), career pathing (see chapter 20), and a comprehensive performance evaluation system. The result is a fairly steady stream of capable, skilled, and high-performance managers who are available for frequent movement throughout the organization.

Plan B, at the other extreme, is based on secrecy and a minimum understanding by the employee of the ongoing process. Because promotions are regarded as so important to the organization, the decisions about who will be moved where and when are made by managers who are at least one managerial level above the position that is being filled. The whole process is kept secret; often even the people being considered for a position are not aware of the fact. Sometimes they are not even aware that a position is open, or about to be open. It is not uncommon, for example, to find that top management has a secret staffing chart (i.e., human resource plan) that shows the back-up people for all positions in the organization. The use of this type of promotion plan sometimes results in a lack of understanding about the kinds of career paths and plans that are available to managers, and a decrease in morale when managers feel bypassed for promotions.

While most organizations have adopted a promotion program that is somewhat between the Plan A and Plan B extremes, it appears that the movement is more toward the acceptance of a Plan A approach. The clarity and openness not only improves motivation, but the emphasis on analysis helps identify and select the managers with the greatest potential to handle complex situations.

Job posting is a move toward more openness. It is a common practice in many government organizations and such companies as Xerox, Texas Instruments, Tenneco, and Procter & Gamble.

Open posting often entails some additional administrative work; on the other hand, it may lead to better promotion decisions. For one thing, open posting helps ensure that all qualified applicants who want to be considered are considered. Often when jobs are being filled, the individuals who make promotion decisions are not aware of who is available or who can do the job, especially in large organizations. A possible negative feature of the open posting system is that by publicly declaring interest in a different job, people may unknowingly be sending a signal to their superiors that they are dissatisfied. Depending on individual superior-subordinate relationships, if the promotion is not received, repercussions may occur.

Employee Benefits

Compensation and promotion make up the major reward systems in organizations. However, these components do not represent the total cost to the organization for services performed by the employee. Today a variety of benefits, referred to in the past as fringe benefits, supplement the wages that are paid directly to employees. These benefits include vacations, holidays, retirement pensions, unemployment benefits, social security, and a variety of insurance benefits. We will look at two employee benefit trends that may have a significant impact on managers—cafeteria plans and executive perquisites.

Cafeteria Plans   Employee benefits are not only one of the most costly employee-related activities for organizations, but these costs have increased dramatically over the last two decades. In 1955 organizations on the average devoted approximately

---

The Manager's Job

John Sculley of Apple Computer Inc.

As president of Pepsi-Cola Company, PepsiCo's U.S. soft drink unit, John Sculley not only had a challenging job (he was overseeing the introduction of Pepsi Free, Pepsi's caffeine-free cola), but he and his family were living comfortably in Greenwich, Connecticut. He clearly had a good shot at the chairmanship of the parent company when the current chairman retired in three years. This led him to turn down a number of chances to go elsewhere. So why did he move across the country and become Apple Computer's new president?

To get Sculley to move, Steven Jobs, chairman of Apple Computer, had to reckon with the usual considerations in any high-level executive search—money, prestige, family and lifestyle—as well as Sculley's fast-track status. Such campaigns can be stressful and can take nearly a year to finalize. In Sculley's case, intangibles—Sunday afternoon strolls through Manhattan's Central Park and the Metropolitan Museum—carried as much weight as cash compensation. So, too, was the organization's philosophy and internal climate. In Apple's situation, Sculley was impressed with the firm's openness and the dedication of all employees to their work.

To lure Sculley away from PepsiCo, Apple offered $2 million in salary and a bonus the first year, $1 million guaranteed severance pay, and help in buying a house. Another important factor was the offer of options on 350,000 shares of Apple stock, which would give Sculley a share in the growth of the firm he was to manage and a chance to become wealthy.

Mr. Sculley kept his wife up-to-date on the entire process, and they evaluated all options. It helped significantly when they found a home in Woodside, California, with gardens similar to those of their Connecticut home. About his wife, Mr. Sculley says, "She knew I had turned down an earlier Apple offer, and I had moped around the office all week. She knew I wanted to be at Apple." After they both evaluated the latest offer, he called Apple and told them he was accepting.

Adapted from J. Guyon, "Apple Lured President from Pepsi with Patient Persuasion and Cash," *The Wall Street Journal* (April 15, 1983): 24.

$1,000 per employee for benefits, which equated to 25 percent of total payroll costs. In 1982, these figures increased to nearly $6,000 per employee and over 40 percent of total payroll costs.[18]

Even with these impressive figures, research has clearly shown that there is wide variation in benefit satisfaction among employees; a benefit that is valued by one employee sometimes is not valued by another. These programs end up costing an organization a great deal of money for benefits that are not valued by many employees and, therefore, do not contribute to either their satisfaction or their motivation.

One way that organizations have attempted to overcome this problem is through the use of a cafeteria plan.[19] This plan involves telling employees just how much the organization is willing to spend on their total pay package and then giving them the opportunity to spend this money as they wish. A younger employee, for example, can take the major part of the money in cash, another employee may decide to devote more money to medical insurance to cover family expenses, while an older employee may choose to emphasize retirement benefits. This type of plan makes it clear to employees how much the organization is spending to compensate them, and it assures that the money will be spent on the benefits the employees really want.

Executive "Perks"   Throughout the world, in all types of organizations, executives receive special perquisites because of their positions. Known as "perks," they tend to be used more in Europe than in the United States because such extras are frequently taxed as income in this country. Examples include the following (see exhibit 16-9):

Income or Insured Benefits—Income deferral, supplemental retirement benefits, supplemental life insurance and disability insurance, liability insurance, profit sharing, and stock purchase plans.

Special Privileges—Financial counseling services, company loans for stock option exercise, home purchase, education, or personal investment, company cars, paid memberships to clubs, liberal expense accounts, company housing, first-class airfare and hotel suites, employment contracts, second office in home, executive medical examinations, and a special office decorating allowance.

Expense Privileges—Tuition assistance and scholarships for children, discounts on company products, services and facilities, and uncovered family medical expenses.

The popularity of perks is increasing in organizations; however, their exact meaning and contribution to organizational effectiveness has not been defined. One thing is clear—the use of perks will continue to spread in all types of organizations. The competition for proven management talent across organizations almost requires the use of perks to acquire, reward, and retain this talent. The growth in the use of perks, however, may decline as more and more of them become taxable.[20]

Conflict

In 28 years, John Brooks Fuqua has outfoxed many an adversary while transforming his business holdings from a lone tv station in Augusta, Georgia, into Fuqua Industries, a $16 billion-a-year conglomerate, one of the largest corporations in the South.

Exhibit 16-9
Typical Compensation and Benefits Packages

	Top Management	Middle Management	Lower Management
Title	Chief Operating Officer ($1½ bil. sales manufacturer)	Division Manager	Division Controller
Base Salary	$400,000	$150,000	$80,000
Initial Bonus (To make up for benefits lost by changing jobs)	1 year's salary	25%-50% of one year's salary if giving up equity plan or deferred compensation	$10,000 maximum (usually for relocation expenses only)
Annual Bonus (expected/maximum)	50% of base salary 100% of base salary	40% of base salary 80% of base salary	25% of base salary 50% of base salary
Capital Accumulation	25,000 non-qualified stock options plus 50,000 performance units	7,500 non-qualified stock options	2,000 non-qualified stock options
Retirement Benefits	company pension plan plus other benefits to equal 65% of final average 5-year gross pay (salary plus bonus)	40%-50% of final average 5-year gross pay	40%-50% of final average 5-year gross pay
Life Insurance	3 times base salary	1½ times base salary	1½ times base salary
Major Medical/Dental	company group plan plus other benefits	company group plan	company group plan
Perks	car, luncheon club, country club, personal tax and financial planning advice	possibly car, a luncheon club or a country club	none

Adapted from J. Bettner, "Executive Pay Raises: Bonuses and Perks Keyed to Job Performance," *The Wall Street Journal* (November 17, 1980): 42.

Late in 1980, Fuqua Industries quietly announced another transformation. Mr. Fuqua planned to make the company private by buying back all the company's stock.

The drama began calmly enough when Fuqua Industries made a bid to buy all its stock—12.9 million shares—at $20 a share, or $258 million. The stock was then selling on the New York Stock Exchange at about $15. But less than two weeks later, Forstmann Little, a small investment firm in New York, surfaced with a $25-a-share bid, worth $322.5 million.

Without consulting their boss, four of Fuqua's top executives brought the Forstmann bid to the attention of the board of directors. For their presumption, Mr. Fuqua promptly fired them all. As one of the fired executives told an Atlanta media representative, "He just sat there and told us we were fired 'because you aren't acting in the best interests of management.' "[21]

This short illustration is just one example of a frequently occurring behavior in organizations—conflict. Because an organization is complex and dynamic, the various subunits and groups that people manage develop different and sometimes highly specialized ways of doing their work. When individuals, groups, and units interact, these differences can lead to conflict. For our purposes, we will define conflict as the disagreement between two or more parties concerning the activities used to achieve certain organizational goals.

The ways in which organizations view and resolve conflict have changed greatly during the last two decades. Two major views are most prominent—traditional and contemporary. The traditional approach views conflict as something to be avoided, caused by personality differences or a failure of leadership, and resolved by physically separating the parties or by direct managerial intervention. The contemporary approach, on the other hand, views conflict as an inevitable consequence of everyday life at work, caused primarily by the complexities of internal systems, and resolved through the use of various mechanisms. The essence of the contemporary approach is that conflict is not always bad or always good. It does, however, need to be controlled, which is the subject of this section.

Types of Conflict

At least five types of conflict are found in organizations. First, *conflict within the individual* is a special form of conflict that does not exactly fit our definition. It is basically a situation where a person feels uncertain about himself, his ability to perform, and the demands put on him by the organization. The individual who questions his or her capability to handle a difficult project and the person who questions whether what the organization wants him or her to do is ethically right are people who have this type of conflict.

Conflict between individuals is the most frequent form in organizations. It concerns the quality of interactions between two organizational members. In the past, many managers felt that it was caused by severe personality differences between the parties. However, as we discussed earlier (and will expand on in the next section), most of these problems are role related.

Conflict between individuals and groups typically occurs when a member resists the influences of the group to conform to certain practices. As we discussed in chapter 14, acceptance into a group implies that the individual accepts the norms of the group. Lack of acceptance can lead to conflict.

Conflict between groups, or intergroup conflict, is a frequently occurring problem facing managers in diverse and complex organizations. As presented in the next section, this type of conflict is related to such factors as groups fighting for scarce resources, differences of opinion about the way a unit should be managed, and the dependence of one group on another. For instance, in building a new manufacturing facility, the production group may want a plant that permits long manufacturing runs that can provide greater cost efficiencies, while the marketing group would like a plant that is flexible to customer needs and can be changed quickly to produce a different product.

Conflict between organizations is built into many economic systems through the competitive motive. Such conflicts result in new products, services, technologies, and innovations. On the other hand, organization-to-organization conflict can occur when, for example, there is a disagreement on procedures and practices. Illustrations include the interaction between federal regulatory agencies and business on safety, investment issues, prices, and employment discrimination.

In the following sections, our focus will be on conflicts between individuals, conflicts between individuals and groups, and intergroup conflict.

Sources of Conflict

To illustrate the potential sources of conflict, let us consider a high-level policy-making task force in a large domestic airline. The task force consists of managers from operations, maintenance, scheduling, engineering, finance, and flight services and is charged with recommending to top management which new wide-bodied aircraft to purchase for their fleet—the European Airbus A-300 or the Boeing 757/767. The task force is given six months to make its choice.

There are at least four major sources of conflict among and between groups: (1) goal incompatibility; (2) availability of resources; (3) performance expectations and (4) organization structure.[22] These sources are shown in exhibit 16-10.

Goal Incompatibility   Goal incompatibility, which is defined as lack of agreement concerning the direction of group activity and the criteria for evaluating task accomplishment, is probably the most frequently identified source of conflict. Two elements

Exhibit 16-10
Sources and
Resolution
of Conflict

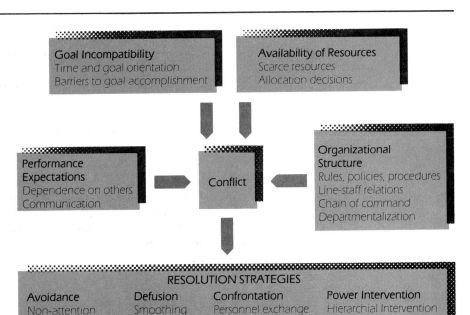

contribute to goal incompatibility. First, as discussed in chapter 8, individual members bring with them different time and goal orientations, which creates a state of high differentiation. Deliberations in the airline task force may become conflictful when the maintenance and operating representatives evaluate the alternative aircraft from a short-term, cost, and efficiency orientation, while the engineering member believes the two planes should be looked upon from the more long-term point of view of technical superiority.

Another source of goal incompatibility or barrier to goal accomplishment is the case in which one person or group's goal attainment stands in the way of others'. In our illustration, the scheduling and operations representatives may lean toward the Airbus because its immediate availability will enable them to put the plane on routes where competition already is using wide-body aircraft. On the other hand, maintenance may prefer the Boeing plane because it is less costly to operate and maintain, even though the plane's delivery time is twice as long as the Airbus.

Availability of Resources   Another frequent contributor to conflict concerns the availability of resources, particularly when the resources are limited. Managers must divide financial, physical, and human resources in what they believe is the most efficient and equitable manner. However, what is perceived as equitable by one group may not be perceived in a similar manner by other groups. A group that believes it is not receiving a fair share of organizational resources often becomes antagonistic toward the organization and toward other groups. This conflict can result in withholding of information, disruptive behavior, and similar actions.

In our airline example, the finance representative may push for the Airbus because he knows that, it being a European-made plane, the company can receive better long-term financing for the purchase of a fleet of planes from European banks. The flight-service representative, however, recognizes that the Airbus will cost more per plane than the Boeing counterpart. Because of this added cost, he believes that the organization would not look favorably on his future request for capital to build a new flight-training facility.

Performance Expectations   The third source of conflict is activity or performance of one group or member that affects the performance of other groups. For example, in examining the differences between the two planes, the finance member is charged with putting together a cost analysis on each plane. To do this, he asks the maintenance representative to provide cost information on the repair frequencies and parts costs of each plane; similarly, the representative from operations is requested to collect comparative operating efficiency (fuel) data on each plane. When one or both members are late in providing this information to the finance representative, a conflict can arise.

Organizational Structure   In many organizations, the structure is a potential source of conflict. There can be function-to-function conflict in a functional structure, division-to-division conflict in a product structure, and function-to-division conflict in a matrix structure.

The most visible conflict here is the relationship between line and staff.[23] The heart of the conflict lies in the line and staff members' different viewpoints of each other and their roles in the organization. In essence, these viewpoints have their foundation in the aforementioned causes of conflict—that is, line and staff members have different time and goal orientations, they compete for the same resources, and so on. Because of these multiple sources, this type of conflict can become heated and be detrimental to the overall performance of the organization.

How does line and staff conflict develop? Consider the relationship between the manufacturing (line) group and the personnel department (staff) in a plant producing heavy industrial equipment. The manufacturing manager may view the personnel department this way:

Staff members interfere with normal operations. The activities of the personnel department are an intrusion into the daily operations of the manufacturing area. When manufacturing wants to promote an hourly worker to a salaried supervisory position, they want it done as soon as possible, but the personnel department takes three weeks to approve the promotion.

Staff members don't understand what is going on in line functions. Because they are not involved in the everyday activities in the manufacturing area, line managers may claim that the ideas and decisions made by the personnel function are not realistic. The manufacturing manager requests the hiring of six new maintenance workers for an additional maintenance crew. Personnel, however, only authorizes four new hires, not knowing that six people make up a crew.

Staff members rarely take the blame for their mistakes. "When they make a suggestion that proves to be successful, personnel tries to grab all the glory. When one of their ideas results in a failure, all personnel does is hide behind their staff doors and claim that they had no control over what manufacturing does."

On the other hand, the manager of personnel may make the following statements about the manufacturing function:

Line managers don't use staff functions properly. Because of conflict, line managers are reluctant to contact staff experts on an issue. In promoting a particular hourly worker to a supervisory position, personnel did some checking and found that not only would the person's benefits be different, but there was a stipulation in the latest union contract which stated that the worker with the greatest seniority must be offered the job first.

Line managers resist the ideas of staff members. While they may not be knowledgeable in the total expertise of the line positions, staff members are experts in their own areas. The approval to hire only four new maintenance workers may have originated from human-resource budget considerations, but the latest industry data also suggest a four-person maintenance crew can perform as effectively as a larger crew.

Line managers think of staff positions as being "excess baggage." Line managers frequently develop the view that anything or anyone not directly involved with the product or service is not contributing to the overall performance of the organization. Personnel managers, for instance, can point out that every manufacturing manager and supervisor could not become totally expert in the growing body of legislative and judicial acts and positions on the handling of human resource problems. A specialized staff position is needed to handle this issue.

These four major sources of conflict are not all-inclusive. They are, however, the most frequently reported and most serious situations. In the next section, we will discuss the effects of conflict in the special case of the relationship between two or more groups.

Conflict Resolution Strategies

The ability to minimize and resolve conflict successfully is an important skill for managers to develop. The various strategies for minimizing and resolving conflict can be classified into four categories: (1) avoidance; (2) defusion; (3) power intervention; and (4) confrontation.[24]

Avoidance   Avoidance strategy generally involves disregarding the causes of the conflict but enabling the conflict to continue only under certain controlled conditions. Three separate methods prevail under an avoidance strategy: (1) nonattention; (2) physical separation; and (3) limited interaction.

Nonattention involves the manager totally avoiding or ignoring the dysfunctional situation. Individuals tend to "look the other way" or disregard hostile actions in hopes that the situation will resolve itself in time. Because the sources of conflict are not identified by this method, it is likely that the situation will continue or worsen with time.

Physical separation involves actually moving conflicting groups physically apart from each other. The rationale for this strategy is that if the groups cannot interact, conflict will diminish. The disadvantages of this strategy are that not only have the sources of conflict not been identified, but if the groups are highly interdependent, physical separation will adversely affect the overall effectiveness of the organization. It is at best only a stopgap measure and may eventually require more organizational resources for continuous surveillance to keep the groups separate.

Limited interaction is not an all-inclusive strategy, as is physical separation, because conflicting parties are permitted to interact on a limited basis. Interactions are permitted generally under only formal situations, such as a meeting at which a strict agenda is followed. The same disadvantages caused by physical separation (i.e., still-present sources of conflict, problems of high interdependency, and future dysfunctional consequences) can result from a limited interaction strategy.

Defusion   Defusion strategy attempts to buy time until the conflict between two groups becomes less emotional or less crucial. It involves solving minor points of disagreement, but allows the major points to linger or diminish in importance with time. Two particular methods are classified as defusion strategies: (1) smoothing; and (2) compromise.

Smoothing involves a process of playing down the differences between two groups while accentuating their similarities and common interests, in the hope that the groups eventually realize they are not as far apart (e.g., goal incompatibility) as they initially believed. Although building on a common viewpoint is preferable to an avoidance philosophy, the sources of conflict have not been fully confronted and remain under the surface. Sooner or later, the central conflict issues will surface, possibly creating a more severe situation in the future.

Compromise is a ''give-and-take'' exchange, resulting in neither a clear winner nor loser. Compromise can be used when the object, goal, or resource in conflict can be divided up in some way between the competing groups. In other cases, one group may yield on one point if it can gain something in exchange from the other group. Some types of management-labor negotiations can be viewed as compromise. For example, management will agree to a cost-of-living pay increase if labor will guarantee productivity level increases. Compromise is generally effective when the conflicting groups are relatively equal in strength. However, in situations where one of the groups is significantly stronger or in a better position than the second group, a compromise strategy would probably not work because the stronger group would hold out for a one-sided solution.

The important point to remember about using a compromise strategy is that because each group gives up some position, neither group may be totally satisfied with the outcome. Because of this, a compromise solution is usually only temporary, and the sources of conflict that initiated the situation may occur again in the future.

Power Intervention A frequently used resolution approach, power intervention, involves the use of power to end the conflict. The sources of the conflict may or may not be identified; the objective, however, is to resolve the situation as soon as possible. These may include: (1) hierarchial intervention; or (2) politics.

Hierarchial intervention involves the entry into the conflict situation of a higher level, many times more powerful, executive. The conflict is resolved by a simple, ''Let's end it here, or else,'' or by removing the parties from the situation into new jobs (or worse!).

Politics, like hierarchial intervention, is a fact of life in organizations that must be recognized. Political conflict resolution generally involves the distribution of power between the conflicting parties. If one party can accumulate sufficient power (through resource accumulation or the formation of a coalition), that party can exert considerable influence over the outcome of the decision or solution to the problem. Like avoidance and defusion, with politics the problem may well reoccur unless the sources of power have been identified.

Confrontation This final conflict resolution strategy, confrontation, differs from avoidance and defusion approaches in that the sources of conflict are generally identified and discussed, during which process the attainment of the common interests of the conflicting groups is emphasized. Three techniques are categorized as confrontation methods: (1) mutual personnel exchange; (2) emphasis on a superordinate goal; and (3) problem-solving or confrontation meetings.

Mutual personnel exchange involves increasing the communication and understanding between groups by exchanging personnel for a period of time. The basic assumption underlying this strategy is that the exchanged personnel can learn about the other group and communicate their impressions back to their original group. For example, a common practice among manufacturing firms is to have shipping supervisors and sales representatives exchange roles. During the short exchange period (usually three to six weeks), it is hoped that each will gain an appreciation of the other's job. This approach is limited because it is only a temporary solution mechanism. In addition, on their return to their permanent group, the exchanged personnel may be treated as outsiders, which may result in their knowledge and opinions not being fully considered.

Superordinate goals are common, more important goals on which the conflicting parties are asked to focus their attention.[25] Such goals are unattainable by one group alone and generally supersede all other goals of each group. A common superordinate goal could be the survival of the organization. Petty differences are considered unimportant when the survival of the overall organization is in question.

A number preconditions are required for this technique to be successful. First, mutual dependency of the groups is required. Second, the superordinate goal must be desired by each group and have a high degree of value attached to it. Finally, there must be some form of reward for accomplishing the goal. By identifying and working toward a common interest, superordinate goals provide a realistic strategy for resolving intergroup conflict.

Problem-solving involves bringing together conflicting groups in order to conduct a formal confrontation meeting. The objective of this approach is to have the groups present their views and opinions to each other and work through the differences in attitudes and perceptions. Issues regarding who is right or wrong are not allowed; only the discussion of the identification of problems and possible solution alternatives is permitted. This technique is most effective when a thorough analysis of the problem and identification of points of mutual interest can be made and alternatives can be suggested. However, a problem-solving approach requires a great deal of time and commitment and usually is ineffective when the source of conflict originates from value-laden issues.

Employee Terminations

As we are all aware, employees do separate from organizations. These *terminations* result from at least four circumstances: (1) termination by the employer with due cause (theft, incompetence, wrongdoing, etc.); (2) termination by the employer without due cause (layoff, plant closing, and so on); (3) voluntary termination by the employee (resignation or turnover); and (4) termination in the event of death, disability, or retirement. For our purposes, we will focus only on termination by the organization.

Termination by the Organization

Throughout this book, we have stressed methods of improving or maintaining high performance levels among all employees. In many cases, however, an employee can continually prove to be ineffective. At least four options are available to organizations under these circumstances. First, the person can be *transferred* to another position in which there is a better match between the requirements of the job and the skills and abilities of the person. This strategy, however, requires careful selection and a willingness by the employee to make the move.

Second, the employee can be *re-trained* through extensive training and development programs. This can be a costly process that assumes both that the person can be re-trained and that it would benefit the organization. Third, an infrequently used strategy is to *demote* the person to a less responsible position. With a demotion, the employee may find it hard to maintain relationships with former superiors, peers, and subordinates. Sometimes a demotion can take the form of a lateral transfer or the creation of an impressively titled job, but one with much less responsibility.

Finally, the employee may be *fired*. In terminating an employee the organization must be careful not to leave itself open for claims of discrimination. It is wise to back up a termination with a file on the person's performance, or economic and resource justifications for the termination. Out-placement counseling is gaining popularity. Through this service, the organization helps the terminated employee find another job or pays to have the person re-trained. This "easing out" process may limit the shock of losing a job.

Terminating a number of employees to control or reduce costs can have its drawbacks. Consider the case of Ed Hennessy who, in 1979, became president of the financially troubled Allied Chemical Company (now Allied Corporation):

> The painful job of making [personnel] cuts fell to Hennessy himself. The corporate staff was hardest hit, the census declining from 1600 to 450. Many people were fired and others were transferred to jobs in the operating companies. . . . One result will be a $30 million annual savings in overhead. . . . Hennessy made at least one serious tactical mistake. When the pink slips were handed out in mid-September, he was on a long-scheduled visit to Allied's operations in the North Sea. He acknowledged that he should have been on the firing line in Morristown. When he returned to the office, he was accompanied for a week, on the advice of his "out-placement" consultants, by a bodyguard.[26]

As we can see, the process of termination—whether of one manager or a large group—should be carefully planned and carefully implemented.

Termination Costs

Rarely is a manager or nonmanager terminated by an organization without being given some form of severance pay. This extra pay can range from less than a month's to more than a year's salary. As shown in exhibit 16-11, the amounts vary by reason and by country. In Venezuela, severance pay is provided for all terminations, while in Australia, no severance pay is ever given.

Termination by the organization is an emotionally difficult, but many times necessary, decision. Termination does not always equate to employee incompetence. A personality conflict with one's superior, the phasing out of a product line or plant, or the merger with another company can result in the elimination of a job, even though the employee has performed effectively. The literature is full of instances where managers have been terminated by one organization, only to become a success in another. Consider the case of W. Michael Blumenthal, whose success as chairman of

Exhibit 16-11
Severance Pay by Termination Reason for Different Countries

Country	Termination With Cause	Termination Without Cause	Voluntary Termination	Retirement	Death	Disability
Latin America						
Argentina	–	×	–	–	–	–
Mexico	–	×	×	×	×	×
Puerto Rico	–	×	–	–	–	–
Venezuela	×	×	×	×	×	×
Europe						
Austria	–	×	–	×	×	×
Denmark	–	×	–	–	–	–
Italy	×	×	×	×	×	×
England	–	×	–	–	–	–
Middle East/ North Africa						
Egypt	–	×	×	–	–	–
Israel	–	×	–	×	–	–
Saudi Arabia	–	×	×	×	–	–
Asia/Pacific						
Australia	–	–	–	–	–	–
India	–	×	×	×	×	×
Japan	–	×	×	×	×	×
Singapore	–	–	–	–	–	–
Taiwan	–	×	–	–	–	–

Adapted from J. C. Roberts, "Termination Indemnities Around the World," *The Personnel Administrator* (June 1979): 75-80.

Bendix Corporation led to his appointment as treasury secretary in President Carter's cabinet. Unfortunately, his corporate successes did not carry over into governmental activities—he was one of a number of cabinet members who abruptly left (or were fired?) during 1979. Since leaving government, Blumenthal has once again achieved success, this time as president of Burroughs Corporation.[27]

POINTS TO CONSIDER
An Emphasis on Managerial Skills

1. **Performance evaluation should focus on the behavior, not the person.**
   The issue at hand is what the person did, not who he or she is. By focusing on the worker's behavior, confusing and potentially conflictual personality differences can remain out of the evaluation process.

2. **Seek out multiple sources of employee performance data.**
   Even though an organization may use a rating scale for performance evaluation, the manager should feel free to seek other information. More information may help the manager to conduct a more accurate evaluation.

3. **Performance evaluation is an ongoing process.**
   Performance evaluation is more than a once-a-year activity. If only informally, the manager should be involved continually with evaluation. If the employee is doing well (or poorly), tell him or her now—don't wait until review time. In this way, good performance is reinforced, poor performance can be corrected—all in a timely fashion.

4. **Maintain flexibility in a reward system.**
   An effective reward system for an organization is one that covers all employees equally but allows enough flexibility to meet the differences in employee needs, performance levels, and changing external conditions.

5. **Reward and performance evaluation systems go hand-in-hand.**
   A reward system is only as good as the accuracy and validity of the performance evaluation system. As we discussed in chapter 12, linking the appropriate reward with its equivalent performance level can have a significant impact on employee motivation.

6. **Conflict is not always bad for the organization.**
   Taking the view that conflict is inevitable for most organizations, managers should approach its occurrence as an opportunity to learn about certain problems. The key is that when attempting to resolve it, the manager should get at the cause—if not, chances are that it will occur again.

7. **Managerial roles and skills are directly involved with performance evaluation and rewards.**
   From a managerial role perspective, performance evaluation and rewards involve all three roles: interpersonal (providing guidance and direction); informational (receiving, aggregating, and communicating information on performance); and decisional (making judgments on performance and future activities). Managerial skills are also involved, particularly human skills (conducting the evaluation review), and diagnostic skills (identifying the causes of good and poor performance).

 # SUMMARY FOR THE MANAGER

1. An integral part of a control system is the process of performance evaluation. The manager should recognize that performance evaluation serves many purposes: appraising employee performance, identifying training needs, providing information for selection, placement, and termination decisions, and providing information for allocating rewards.

2. Performance evaluations in organizations can vary by approach and method. While the manager can use a number of different approaches to evaluate an employee's performance (superior, peer, subordinate, or self-evaluation), it is best to seek multiple inputs, as opposed to a single source of information, for validity and accuracy.

3. Performance evaluation methods, such as global ranking, trait-based rating scales, critical incidents, BARS, and effectiveness-based measures can be used to evaluate a subordinate's

performance. It is crucial for the manager to understand the strengths and weaknesses of each of these methods. For example, rankings are quick, but can be inaccurate; BARS and effectiveness-based measures are job specific, but extremely time consuming.

4. The appraisal interview can make or break the performance evaluation process. It is important that the manager understands the employee's performance data, establishes a positive climate for the interview, focuses on the behavior, not the person, and ends the interview so that the employee knows how well he or she has done and what to do next.

5. Managers are giving increased attention to the legal implications of performance evaluations. From a legal standpoint, a policy statement covering performance evaluation is developed, evaluators are trained, job analysis and job-specific criteria are used, and the results of the evaluation are communicated to the employee.

6. Pay is one of an organization's most powerful reward components. Forms of pay include base pay, increases in base pay, and supplemental pay. Whatever the organization chooses, it is important that the employees connect the level of their performance and the amount of their pay.

7. Promotion and employee benefits are two other reward system components. In promotion programs the manager should consider the openness of the program. This includes job postings and open knowledge of career paths and how promotion decisions are made. In employee benefit plans, the manager should be aware of cafeteria plans and the selective use of executive perks.

8. To retain competent and capable managers, organizations are turning more and more to the use of executive "perks." Involved are, for example, income deferral, insured benefits, stock options, expense privileges, and special services.

9. Organizational conflict can originate from many sources. Among the most prevalent are goal incompatibility, decision-making requirements, and performance expectations. The actual conflict/resolution strategies can be categorized into four major classes: avoidance, defusion, power intervention, and confrontation.

10. A control system also includes the process of terminating employees. Termination can occur as a result of due cause, organizational reasons, voluntary termination, death, retirement, or disability. The key factor is that effort should be given not only to justifying the termination, but if the plan involves more than one employee, it must be well planned and implemented.

 # REVIEW AND DISCUSSION QUESTIONS

1. Why is it recommended that a manager use multiple sources of information in evaluating the performance of employees?
2. What are the major differences between trait-based rating scales and BARS?
3. Why is it important for the manager to establish a good climate in the performance evaluation interview?
4. What role should the subordinate play in the performance evaluation interview?
5. What are the advantages and disadvantages of having more than one performance evaluation during the year?
6. What are the differences between defusion and confrontation conflict resolution strategies?

7. If you had a choice between working for an organization with a secret pay program and one where there was more openness, which would you choose and why?
8. Why have the courts stressed the use of job analysis and job-specific performance criteria in performance evaluation?
9. Why are executive perks becoming so popular and important to many organizations?
10. Under what conditions would termination of an employee benefit the organization?

NOTES

1. See R. N. Anthony and J. Dearden, *Management Control Systems*, 3rd. ed. (Homewood, Ill.: Irwin, 1976); M. Beer, "Performance Appraisal: Dilemmas and Possibilities," *Organizational Dynamics* (Winter 1981), pp. 24-36; and J. Todd, "Management Control Systems: A Key Link Between Strategy, Structure, and Employee Performance," *Organizational Dynamics* (Spring 1977): 65-78.
2. C. E. Schneier and R. W. Beatty, "Integrating Behaviorally Based and Effectiveness-Based Methods," *The Personnel Administrator* (July 1979): 65-76.
3. See R. L. Sayles and G. Strauss, *Managing Human Resources* (Englewood Cliffs, N.J.: Prentice-Hall, 1981), pp. 325-43.
4. J. M. McFillen and P. G. Decker, "Building Meaning into Appraisal," *The Personnel Administrator* (June 1978): 75-84.
5. See S. J. Motowidlo, "Relationship Between Self-Rated Performance and Pay Satisfaction Among Sales Representatives," *Journal of Applied Psychology* (April 1982): 209-13; and K. R. Murphy, M. Garcia, S. Kerkar, C. Martin, and W. K. Balzer, "Relationship Between Observational Accuracy and Accuracy in Evaluating Performance," *Journal of Applied Psychology* (June 1982): 320-25.
6. R. M. Guion, *Personnel Testing* (New York: McGraw-Hill, 1965), pp. 90-95.
7. H. Levinson, "Appraisal of What Performance?" *Harvard Business Review* (July-August 1976): 30-48.
8. See J. P. Campbell, M. D. Dunnette, R. D. Arvey, and L. W. Hellervik, "The Development and Evaluation of Behaviorally Based Rating Scales," *Journal of Applied Psychology* (February 1973): 15-22; P. W. Hom, A. S. DeNisi, A. J. Kinicki, and B. D. Bannister, "Effectiveness of Performance Feedback From Behaviorally Anchored Rating Scales," *Journal of Applied Psychology* (October 1982): 568-76; and D. P. Schwab, H. G. Henneman III, and T. A. DeCotiis, "Behaviorally Anchored Rating Scales: A Review of the Literature," *Personnel Psychology* (Winter 1975): 549-62.
9. D. Cederblom, "The Performance Appraisal Interview: A Review, Implications, and Suggestions," *Academy of Management Review* (April 1982): 219-27.
10. R. Henderson, *Performance Appraisal: Theory and Practice* (Reston, Va.: Reston, 1980).
11. S. Zedeck, "Performance Appraisal Decisions as a Function of Rater Training and Purpose of the Appraisal," *Journal of Applied Psychology* (December 1982): 752-58.
12. J. M. Ivancevich, "Subordinate's Reactions to Performance Appraisal Interviews: A Test of Feedback and Goal-Setting Techniques," *Journal of Applied Psychology* (October 1982): 581-87.
13. D. E. Thompson and D. Moskowitz, "A Legal Look at Performance Appraisal," *Wharton Magazine* (Winter 1982): 66-70.
14. W. H. Holley and H. S. Feild, "Will Your Performance Appraisal System Hold Up in Court?" *Personnel* (January-February 1982): 59-63.
15. See M. H. Birnbaum, "Perceived Equity of Salary Policies," *Journal of Applied Psychology* (February 1983): 49-59; and E. E. Lawler III, *Pay and Organizational Effectiveness* (New York: McGraw-Hill, 1971).
16. This section draws heavily from E. E. Lawler III, "Reward Systems," in J. R. Hackman and J. L. Suttle, *Improving Life at Work* (Glenview, Ill.: Scott, Foresman, 1977), pp. 163-226.

17. R. J. Schulhof, "Five Years with a Scanlon Plan," *The Personnel Administrator* (June 1979): pp. 55-62.

18. W. F. Glueck, *Personnel* (Dallas: Business Publications, 1978), p. 456.

19. G. T. Milkovich and M. J. Delaney, "A Note on Cafeteria Pay Plans," *Industrial Relations* (June 1975): 112-16; and "A Varied Menu of Benefits," *Time* (June 27, 1983):54

20. See "Executive Compensation: Looking to the Long-Term Again," *Business Week* (May 9, 1983): 80-83; J. Main, "Hard Times Catch Up with Executives," *Fortune* (September 20, 1982): 50-54; and A. M. Morrison, "Those Executive Bail-Out Deals," *Fortune* (December 13, 1982): 82-87.

21. E. J. Tracy, "The Soap Opera at Fuqua Industries," *Fortune* (November 16, 1981): 143-51.

22. S. M. Schmidt and T. A. Kochan, "Conflict: Towards Conceptual Clarity," *Administrative Science Quarterly* (July 1972): 359-70.

23. M. Dalton, "Conflict Between Staff and Line Managerial Officers," *American Sociological Review* (June 1950): 243-51.

24. R. R. Blake and J. S. Mouton, *Managing Intergroup Conflict in Industry* (Houston: Gulf Publishing, 1964).

25. M. Sherif and C. W. Sherif, *Social Psychology* (New York: Harper & Row, 1969): 228-62.

26. P. W. Bernstein, "The Hennessy Hurricane Whips Through Allied Chemical," *Fortune* (December 17, 1979): 101.

27. See P. Cathey, "How to Hang On to the Right Employee," *Iron Age* (September 17, 1979): 35-38; R. Coulson, "The Way it is—The Rules of the Game—How to Fire," *Across the Board* (February 1982): 30-48; D. L. Nye, "Fire at Will—Careful, Now, Careful," *Across the Board* (November 1982): 37-40; and "A Fight over the Freedom to Fire," *Business Week* (September 20, 1982): 116.

A CASE FOR ANALYSIS

The Orange Computer Company

In these days of turbulent environments, changing human needs, and radical revisions in organizational structures, many managers are searching for more effective ways of evaluating and rewarding employees. Nowhere is this issue more of a concern than in the high technology microcomputer industry.

Consider the case of the Orange Computer Company. Founded in the late 1970s by former engineers of a major electronics firm, this California-based organization has seen its revenues grow from less than $1 million the first year to over $300 million in 1982. The firm's main product line includes four small computers: two models for use in companies, and two models designed as personal computers. Modifications to computer hardware and new software programs are added each year.

The company's innovative approach to management goes beyond high technology manufacturing to a concern for its human resources. Current human resource policies include flextime, shared jobs, frequent job rotations, a complete health and physical fitness center, and three months off for engineers every five years for personal development activities.

In 1982, company executives implemented a new compensation policy for its engineers. Faced with frequent and growing employee turnover and "raids" from competing firms, the firm's management decided to offer company engineers a choice in the form of merit increases: the typical raise, which would be spread out over twelve months, or the up-front raise, both based on the person's performance. The unique feature of the up-front raise is that the engineer is offered the money in cash during the performance evaluation meeting. No strings were attached to the up-front raise.

Industry critics scoffed at the new plan, predicting one or all of the following problems will occur:

- Engineers will take the money and run to a new job with another company.
- The new plan would have little or no effect on employee motivation or productivity.

- Less than 50 percent of the engineers will opt for the new plan.
- Pay satisfaction for those selecting the up-front raise will decline rapidly. The engineers will spend or waste the money rather quickly, causing them to come back and ask for more.

After one year of operation, none of the above concerns was noticed. The initial results showed that over 90 percent of the engineers opted for the up-front raise, turnover significantly dropped, productivity increased, and less than 10 percent of the engineers wanted to return to the traditional merit increase plan.

Suggested from "The Coming Squeeze on White Collar Pay," *Business Week* (September 12, 1980); and J. W. Annas, "The Up-Front Carat," *Compensation Review* (Fall 1982): 45-49.

Questions for Discussion

1. Why did most of the engineers select the up-front raise plan?
2. Why do you think the new pay raise plan worked after one year, proving the critics wrong? Do you think the plan will continue

to be as successful two years or three years from the date of implementation?
3. Can you think of a situation, or group of employees, in which such a pay plan might not work?

EXPERIENTIAL EXERCISE
Merit Pay Increases

Purpose

1. To examine the application and problems of merit pay increases

2. To consider the impact of multiple performance criteria in managerial decision making.

Required Understanding
The student should understand the different methods in performance evaluation.

How to Set Up the Exercise
Set up groups of four to eight students for the forty-five to sixty-minute exercise. The groups should be separated from each other and asked to converse only with members of their own group. The participants should then read the following:

Coastal Instrument Corporation is a small manufacturing company located in San Jose, California. The company is nonunionized and manufactures laboratory analysis equipment for hospitals.

Approximately one year ago, the manager of the assembly department established three manufacturing goals for the department. The goals were: (1) reduce raw material storage costs by 15 percent; (2) reduce variable labor costs (i.e., overtime) by 20 percent; and (3) decrease the number of quality rejects by 15 percent. The department manager stated to the six unit supervisors that the degree to which each supervisor met or exceeded these goals would be one of the major inputs into his or her merit pay increases for the year. In previous years, merit increases were based on seniority.

The six department supervisors worked on separate but similar production lines. A profile of each supervisor is as follows:

Jim Owens: black, age twenty-four; married with no children; one year with the company after graduating from a local college. First full-time job since graduation from college. He is well liked by all employees and has exhibited a high level of enthusiasm for his work.

Mary Beck: white, age twenty-eight; single; three years with the company after receiving her degree from the state university. Has a job offer from another company for a similar job that provides a substantial pay increase over her present salary (15 percent). Coastal does not want to lose Mary because her overall performance has been excellent. The job offer would require her to move to another state, which she views unfavorably. Coastal can keep her if it can come close to matching her salary offer.

Jack Turner: white; age thirty-two; married with three children; three years with the company; high school education. One of the most stable and steady supervisors. However, he supervises a group of workers who are known to be unfriendly and uncooperative with him and other employees.

Joseph Koch: white; age thirty-four; married with four children; high school equivalent learning; one year with the company. Immigrated to this country ten years ago and has recently become a U.S. citizen. A steady worker, well liked by his co-workers, but has had difficulty learning the English language. As a result, certain problems of communication within his group and with other groups have developed in the past.

Maria Juarez: Hispanic; age twenty-nine; divorced with three children; two years with the company; high school education. Since her divorce one year ago, her performance has begun to improve. Prior to that, her performance was very erratic, with frequent absences. She is the sole support for her three children.

Frank Wedman: white; age twenty-seven; single; two years with the company; college graduate. One of the best-liked employees at Coastal. However, has shown a lack of initiative and ambition on the job. Appears to be preoccupied with his outside social life.

Exhibit 16-12 presents summary data on the performance of the six supervisors during the past year. The data include current annual salary, performance level on the three goals, and an overall evaluation by the department manager.

The new budget for the upcoming year has allocated a total of $114,400 for supervisory salaries in the assembly department, a $10,400 (or 10 percent) increase from last year. Top management has indicated that salary increases should range from 4 percent to 12 percent and should be tied as closely as possible to performance.

In making the merit pay increase decisions, consider the following:

1. The decisions will likely set a precedent for future salary and merit increase considerations.

2. Salary increases should not be excessive, but should be representative of the supervisor's performance during the past year.

3. The decisions should be concerned with internal equity; that is, they ought to be consistent with each other.

4. The company does not want to lose these experienced supervisors to other firms. Management not only wants the supervisors to be satisfied with their salary increases, but also to further develop the feeling that Coastal Manufacturing is a good company for advancement, growth, and career development.

Instructions for the Exercise

1. Each student should individually determine the dollar amount and percentage increase in salary (4 percent, 8 percent, or 12 percent) for each supervisor. Individual decisions should be justified by a rational or decision rule.

2. After each individual has reached a decision, the group will convene and make the same decision as in (1) above.

3. After each group has reached a decision, a spokesperson for each group will present the following information to the class:
   a. The group's decision concerning merit pay increases for each supervisor (percentage)
   b. The high, low, and average individual decisions in the group
   c. A rationale for the group's decision

Exhibit 16-12

Individual Performance for the Six Supervisors During the Past Year

| Supervisor | Current Salary (000s Omitted) | Goal Attainment[a] | | | Manager's Evaluation[b] | | | |
		Storage Costs (15%)	Labor Costs (20%)	Quality Rejects (15%)	Effort	Dependability	Ability to Work Independently	Knowledge of Job
Owens	$16.5	18%	19%	17%	Excellent	Excellent	Good	Good
Beck	$18.0	18%	21%	16%	Excellent	Excellent	Excellent	Excellent
Turner	$18.0	12%	8%	3%	Good	Excellent	Good	Good
Koch	$16.5	10%	10%	12%	Excellent	Good	Fair	Fair
Juarez	$17.5	16%	15%	10%	Good	Fair	Fair	Good
Wedman	$17.5	12%	16%	3%	Fair	Fair	Fair	Fair

[a]Numbers designate actual cost and quality reject reduction [b]The possible ratings are poor, fair, good, and excellent

Management Information Systems

Chapter Outline

Key Points

1. The complex management task, availability of decision-making tools, and increased computer knowledge and usage are factors influencing the information revolution.
2. MIS is an organized approach to providing management with information related to internal operations and external intelligence.
3. Analyzing early warning signals, aiding decision making and planning, and exercising control are some of the purposes of MIS.
4. MIS emerged in at least four stages: initiation, growth, moratorium, and integration.
5. MIS applications can be found across organization functions and in different types of organizations.
6. A decision support system involves a data base, management science models, and a skilled manager operating from an interactive computer terminal.
7. Distributive processing involves decentralizing MIS activities.
8. User involvement, accurately estimating project timing and costs, training, and an awareness of possible behavioral dysfunctions are among the important issues in MIS implementation.

The Dallas Cowboys

Nearly one dozen and a half winning seasons, two Super Bowl championships, and 17 opening-day victories have been some of the highlights of the Dallas Cowboys' history, making it one of the most successful football franchises in the history of the National Football League. One reason for its consistent success is the use of computerized scouting to evaluate and rank collegiate talent in preparation for the annual draft.

As a result, the Cowboys have gained a reputation as a cold and impersonal organization that somehow uses computers to judge talent above and beyond what is possible with manual methods—a reputation reinforced by the cool, imperturbable presence of coach Tom Landry, the very picture of computer precision and dispassionate competence. Yet, as any data processing manager can tell you, computers cannot do more than they are told, and their value is subject to the quality of the input their masters provide. "The biggest fallacy in the minds of the fan on the street is that the computer can do something magical. But the old 'garbage in, garbage out' theory still applies," says "Tex" Schramm, president and general manager.

What the computer can do and does do, however, is provide a useful tool to save enormous amounts of time and provide protection against the possibly misleading tendencies of the human mind. The Cowboys use their computerized Player Evaluation and Selection System to gain an added measure of accuracy in predicting which players will prove to be good performers.

In 1960, when the Cowboys were formed, Schramm approached a friend who put him in touch with information systems experts within IBM. A long and difficult project ensued, in which the primary task was to define those qualities that made a good football player, and to develop a language that could describe these qualities.

"We had to start from scratch, because coaches used different terms that meant different things when they are describing players," Schramm says. For instance, the term *character* had meanings that ranged from "someone who would knock your head off," to "a real leader." It took four years of research and viewing countless films to let coaches decide exactly what such terms meant and how they could be used consistently. To check the developed model, the Cowboys fed back results; later they were able to make predictions in particular situations.

Commenting on the impersonal nature of the information system, Schramm states, "It is very humiliating for a player to be picked high in the draft and then not make a team. . . it is better for those who may not make the grade to know early. We are trying to use every means possible to evaluate a human being, and in the long run it is in the best interest of the individual."

Adapted from W. P. Martorelli, "The Dallas Cowboys Information Selection System," *Information Systems News* (November 16, 1981).

17

Throughout this book we have emphasized the importance of information as a resource in organizations. Information is important to managers in analyzing the external and internal environment; developing and implementing plans; communication; leadership and decision making; coordinating the work of departments and units; controlling resources, and so on.

In more recent times, we have seen the importance of information underlined with the emergence of *information systems*. Beginning with accounting and financial information, applications to other areas have developed at a rapid pace in all types of organizations. The Dallas Cowboys' system, revealed in our *Practice of Management* section, is just one example.

We have identified five major points of discussion in this third chapter on the control function. First, we will look at the background behind the emergence of management information systems, particularly, the information revolution. This will be followed by a discussion of the elements of management information systems (MIS). Selected applications of MIS in organizations will be highlighted in the third part, followed by an analysis of contemporary developments in MIS (e.g., decision support systems, distributive processing). We will conclude the chapter with a discussion of MIS implementation and evaluation—key organizational issues in the success of management information systems.

The Information Revolution

It is generally accepted that we are experiencing a knowledge explosion; some experts, in fact, claim that U.S. industries are now based more on knowledge and information than on manufacturing.[1] Researchers and managers in all fields continue to study our world, producing an ever-expanding mass of data, facts, theories, statistics, and laws to help us better understand and cope with our environment. This explosion of knowledge has been dramatic—50 years elapsed before the amount of knowledge available in 1800 doubled; in 1950 it doubled in ten years, and in 1970, in only five.

This growing body of knowledge is but one information-related factor affecting the modern organization and its economic-social-political-technological environment. Why are organizations becoming so dependent on the ability to process information? While many factors are important, we have chosen three to briefly discuss: the increasing complexity of the management task, the availability of decision tools, and increased computer understanding and usage.[2]

The Complex Management Task

The job of a manager has always been a difficult task, and it is more so today than ever before. One reason among many is the increasing size of organizations. Not only are we seeing an increase in the number of organizations, but the existing ones are getting bigger. According to *Fortune* magazine, the number of employees in the country's

500 largest industrial firms rose from 11.3 million in 1965 to 14.4 million in 1982, and assets increased from $252 billion to $1,309 billion.

Another reason is the greater complexity and usage of new technology. To be competitive, organizations must make an effort to keep pace with technology. The impact of technology so far has been significant—the electronic office, robotics, the automated factory, and much more.

Time frame is also a factor. Fewer and fewer managers are blessed with an excess amount of time to make decisions. Jet travel, satellite communications, and other electronics have quickened information flow and placed increased pressure on managers from suppliers, consumers, and competitors.

Finally, as we discussed in chapter 4, managers are faced with more social pressures today. Decisions, once based almost solely on economic considerations, must now evaluate non-economic concerns. Plant expansions, new products, financial decisions, and the like affecting local and national communities must all be weighed in terms of their short- and long-term impact.

Availability of Decision-Making Tools

The information revolution has also had an impact on the tools managers use to make decisions. New quantitative approaches, along with the application of electronic devices, are widening the arena of increased effectiveness in decision making.

The need for more information processing in the manager's job can be seen in many of the topics we have already discussed, including forecasting, strategic planning, telecommunications, and financial analyses. In the next chapter, we will add to this base with discussion of operations research and management sciences approaches.

Increased Computer Knowledge and Usage

No one thing has had as much of an impact on the information revolution as the computer. Its impact has been two-fold. First, by today's standards, the early computers were primitive. Exhibit 17-1 shows how the combined influence of technology,

Exhibit 17-1 Cost and Performance of Computer Electronics		1958	1965	1972	1980
	Technology	Vacuum tube	Transistor	Integrated circuit	Large-scale integrated circuit
	Cost per unit	$8	$0.25	$0.02	$0.001
	Cost per logic	$160	$12	$200	$.05
	Operation time (in seconds)	16×10^{-3}	4×10^{-6}	40×10^{-9}	200×10^{-12}

Source: W. D. Fraser, "Potential Technology Implications for Computers and Telecommunications in the 1980s," *IBM System Journal* (Vol. 18, No. 2, 1979): 33.

costs, and operating time have resulted in advances in capacity and convenience. Since most organizations today can afford small and powerful computers, maybe the question is whether organizations can afford *not* to have a computer!

The second issue is computer understanding and usage. For years, managers were quite happy to relegate computer activities to ''computer jocks.'' Only specialists who mastered mysterious computer languages and devoted all their time to the effort really understood computers.

Now the situation is changing dramatically. Computer courses, the simplifying of computer languages, and the development of personal computers have meant a wide variety of hardware and software designed for greater applications to management. Computer technology is simply more readily available. The lack of a computer with sufficient capacity, or a management populace ignorant of its potential applications, is no longer a problem.

The information revolution has had a significant impact on organizations. One of the major developments to come from this revolution is *management information systems,* the subject of this chapter.

Elements of Management Information Systems

For our purposes, we will define management information systems as:

> An organized system of providing past, present, and projection information relating to internal operations and external intelligence. It supports the planning, control and operational functions of an organization by furnishing uniform information in the proper time frame to assist the decision making process.[3]

Key to this definition is the word system, which identifies a group of elements or parts that are integrated through the common purpose of achieving a stated goal. As shown in exhibit 17-2, a system consists of four major elements: input, transformation, output, and control. In an auto assembly plant, raw materials (input) are assem-

Exhibit 17-2
A Basic Systems Model

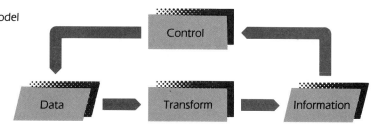

Source: R. McLeod, *Management Information Systems* (Chicago: SRA, 1983), p. 14.

bled by workers (transform) into a completed automobile (output). Management performs the control activity.

With this as a foundation, a MIS model consists of the following (see exhibit 17-3):[4]

- Data about the physical system of the firm—the workers and all the facilities and equipment used to produce the firm's products and services—are entered.

- Internal and external data about the system (input) are gathered.

- Data is directed to the information processing resources, which include the computer and the information services staff.

- The software library (or collection of programs) and the data base are used to convert data into information (transform).

- Information is used by management to make decisions to improve operations (output).

Exhibit 17-3
MIS Model

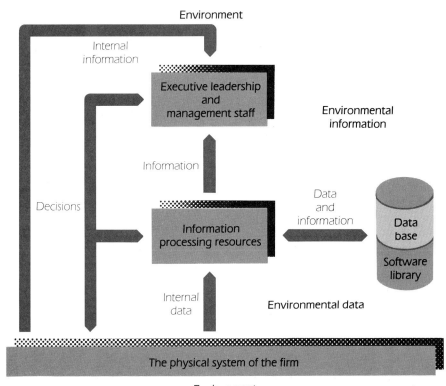

Source: R. McLeod, *Management Information Systems* (Chicago: SRA, 1983), p. 18.

Purposes of MIS

MIS in organizations has four main purposes.[5] First, MIS provides a basis for analyzing *early warning signals* that can originate both externally and internally. Proper information to managers prevents a long-term gap between plant capacity and the demand for the firm's products, averts surprises due to technological breakthroughs affecting the firm's products and services, and maintains an awareness of top-management succession problems.

Second, MIS is an important aid in *managerial decision making*. A way for managers to identify their specific information requirements is to isolate the nature, frequency, and interrelationships of the major decisions. This requires analysis of responses to the following questions:

- What decisions are made and/or need to be made?
- What factors are important in making these decisions?
- How and when should these decisions be made?
- What information is useful in making these decisions?

Examples include supplying financial trends and ratios, inventory reports, market share information, and providing models and computer hardware that will answer questions on profits, costs, and combinations of products and services.

Third, MIS can assist managers in making *programmed decisions*. As explained in chapter 7, relatively simple decisions that are made on a routine basis are programmed decisions. Assigning orders to machines, scheduling orders or services, allocating advertising expenditures to different media sources, and ordering supplies and raw materials are straightforward decisions, and MIS can do much of the detailed work.

Finally, MIS can be used to *automate* routine clerical operations. Preparing payrolls, inventory reports, and transportation system records are quite adaptable to automation. Automation can save the organization a great deal of money because less personnel are needed and turnaround time is much quicker.

As shown in exhibit 17-4, the purposes of MIS are related to the different types of information found in organizations. The information types include planning, management control, and operational control.[6]

Planning information concerns the process of formulating goals, strategies, and plans, the necessary resources for the goals and the policies that direct their use (see chapter 6). Because this information forms the input to top management for these nonprogrammed decisions, there is great emphasis on the early warning capability of an MIS.

Management control information aids managers in making decisions that are consistent with the efficient use of organizational resources. Used primarily by middle-level managers, the information is usually internal and concerns budgets, financial analysis, and so on.

Finally, *operational control information* is normally used by first-line managers for highly programmed decisions—the manager can build a program that identifies the time at which a decision is needed, the alternatives available, and the criteria for selecting the best alternative under different conditions.

While the "paperless society" remains a futurist's fantasy, Paine Webber Inc., had to bring much of that dream into reality for its securities processing operations—and fast! The large Wall Street brokerage firm found itself in the middle of a paper-induced nightmare. The company teetered on the brink of disaster as automated systems failed to keep up with an unprecedented trading volume increase in 1980.

According to Donald Brown, head of the Computer and Communications Department, the problem was caused by the soaring volume levels and the company's existing systems. "What we found out is that each off-line system didn't have enough automation." So, while the computers in place were technically capable of handling high volumes, the manual preparation that preceded the automated processing of the various transactions made the task impossible. It got so bad that, for example, the information processing for a Tuesday's transactions were not completed by the opening bell of Wednesday on Wall Street. Needless to say, by the end of the week, there was much catching up to do.

To resolve the problem, Brown planned and implemented a recovery project that included three "waves" of action:

- Wave One—purchase of a new, larger computer that could handle an increase in automated systems. It was installed in record time.

- Wave Two—thirty-three new MIS projects were begun in an effort to get manual handling down to an absolute minimum. The objective was to complete the information transfer of all transactions by midnight of the same day.

- Wave Three—long-term plans and improvements over the next three years to insure that Paine Webber "never loses control again, no matter what." Communications improvements are part of this plan, Brown says, but will not elaborate except to say that satellites will have an important role.

Adapted from *Information Systems News* (November 17, 1980).

Using this framework as a base, an analysis of an organization's decision-making patterns in strategy, managerial control, and operational control draws out the specific information requirements for the critical areas of the organization. Some examples of the information needs for an airline, a department store, and a savings and loan are also shown in exhibit 17-4.

Emergence of MIS

As we have noted, the information revolution has been a major influence in the emergence of MIS in organizations.[7] At least four distinct stages of development can be identified.[8] Exhibit 17-5 shows these.

Stage one, *initiation*, generally involves accounting applications of the operational and management control type. Top management first sees the goal of MIS as a

Exhibit 17-4
MIS Purposes and Example Information Needs

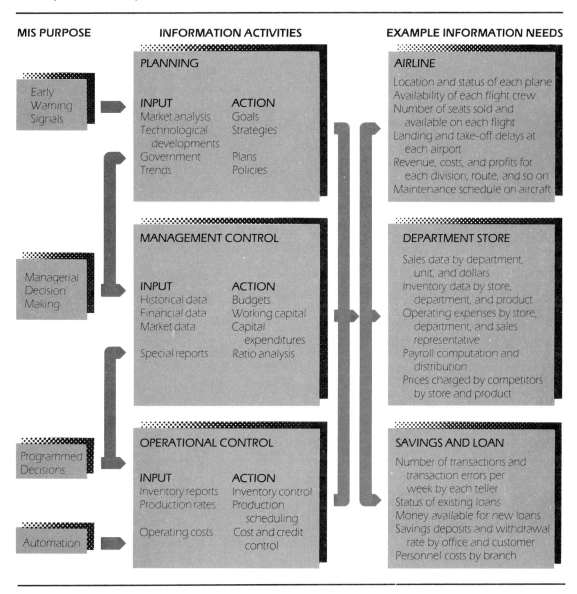

MIS PURPOSE	INFORMATION ACTIVITIES	EXAMPLE INFORMATION NEEDS
Early Warning Signals	**PLANNING** INPUT / ACTION Market analysis / Goals Technological developments / Strategies Government / Plans Trends / Policies	**AIRLINE** Location and status of each plane Availability of each flight crew Number of seats sold and available on each flight Landing and take-off delays at each airport Revenue, costs, and profits for each division, route, and so on Maintenance schedule on aircraft
Managerial Decision Making	**MANAGEMENT CONTROL** INPUT / ACTION Historical data / Budgets Financial data / Working capital Market data / Capital expenditures Special reports / Ratio analysis	**DEPARTMENT STORE** Sales data by department, unit, and dollars Inventory data by store, department, and product Operating expenses by store, department, and sales representative Payroll computation and distribution Prices charged by competitors by store and product
Programmed Decisions Automation	**OPERATIONAL CONTROL** INPUT / ACTION Inventory reports / Inventory control Production rates / Production scheduling Operating costs / Cost and credit control	**SAVINGS AND LOAN** Number of transactions and transaction errors per week by each teller Status of existing loans Money available for new loans Savings deposits and withdrawal rate by office and customer Personnel costs by branch

Exhibit 17-5
Emergence of MIS in Organizations

	STAGE ONE Initiation	STAGE TWO Growth	STAGE THREE Moratorium	STAGE FOUR Integration
Application focus	Accounting and cost reduction	Expansion of applications in many functional areas	Halt on new applications; emphasis on control	Integrating existing systems into the organization; decision support systems
Example applications	Accounts payable, accounts receivable, payroll, billing	*Stage one plus:* cash flow, budgeting, forecasting, personnel inventory, sales, inventory control	*Stage two plus:* purchasing control, production scheduling	*Stage three plus:* simulation models, financial planning models, on-line personnel query system
MIS staffing	Primarily computer experts and other skilled professionals	User-oriented system analysts and programmers	Entry of functional managers into MIS unit	Balance of technical and management specialists
Location of MIS in structure	Embedded in accounting department	Growth in size of staff; still in accounting area	Separate MIS unit reporting to head financial officer	Same as stage three, or decentralization into divisions
What top management wants from MIS	Speed computations with a reduction in clerical staff	Broader applications into operational areas	Concern over MIS costs and usefulness	Acceptance as a major organizational function; involved in planning and control
User attitudes	Uncertainty; hands-off approach; anxiety over applications	Somewhat enthusiastic; minimum involvement in system design	Frustration and dissatisfaction over developed systems; concern over costs of developing and operating systems	Acceptance of MIS in their work; involvement in system design, implementation, and operation

Adapted from Richard L. Nolan, "Controlling the Costs of Data Services," *Harvard Business Review* (July-August 1977): 114-24.

decrease in costs associated with personnel and computation time. The MIS unit is usually staffed by technical personnel and embedded in the accounting department. To most managers, MIS initially is an unknown area involving a "black box." This uncertainty develops into a hands-off philosophy by managers who do not have extensive computer knowledge.

As the use and value of MIS increases, stage two, the *growth* stage emerges. MIS applications expand significantly beyond accounting into production and marketing. It still involves the main use of operational and managerial control information. MIS personnel become highly specialized in their skills and the entire unit is able to separate from accounting, usually reporting to the controller. Stage three emphasizes a *moratorium* on the growth in use of MIS. Top management becomes concerned that the purpose of MIS and its integration into the total organization is clouded by a proliferation of larger computers and a lack of user awareness of the potential of MIS.[9]

Exhibit 17-6
MIS Structure in Kraft, Inc.

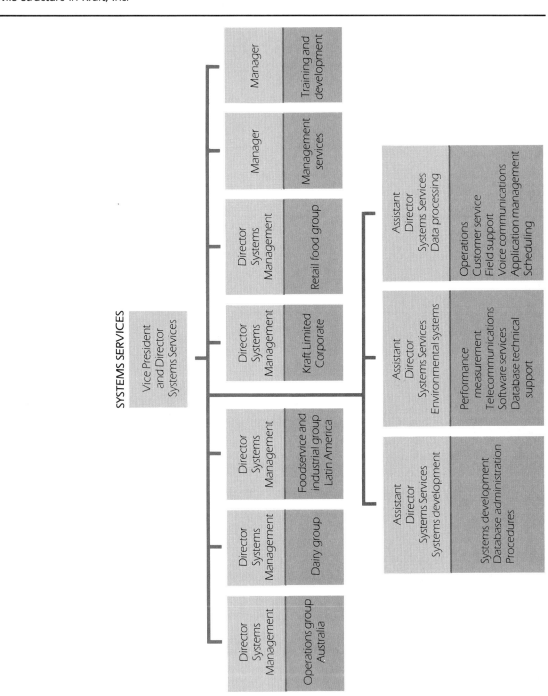

The fourth stage, *integration,* stresses the acceptance of MIS as a major management activity that must be integrated into the total organization. MIS is now used with all types of information (strategic, management control, and operational control), and with a new generation of computers. In addition, the use of portable, interactive terminals enables managers to have better access and, hence, more involvement in the system. The MIS unit is staffed not only with highly skilled technical people, but management specialists from other areas begin working their way into operating the unit. At this point, the combination of technical and management functional specialists allows MIS to be applied in everyday activities.

Integrating MIS into management activities can occur *across* organizations as well as within. Travel agents have long eyed the computer as a way to link up with airlines, hotels, and the rest of the travel business to improve their productivity and sales. A system developed by American Express appears to satisfy this need. It will do everything from booking a flight, hotel room, and rental car to giving video presentations of resorts and hotel rooms to prospective travelers.[10]

In stages three and four of our MIS development scheme, management information systems has in many cases evolved into a separate unit. Exhibit 17-6 shows the MIS unit for Kraft, Inc. Note the various activities depicted in the exhibit, from computer systems development and applications to telecommunications.

MIS Applications

MIS applications can be found in a variety of organizations (profit and not-for-profit) and organizational functions (manufacturing, marketing, accounting, personnel). Our discussion will follow MIS through two applications—personnel and patient billing in a hospital.

MIS in a Personnel Function

The personnel function is a natural for MIS. Consider the activity shown in exhibit 17-7, which depicts a portion of the human resource process. The diagram shows three major subprocesses: (1) determining human resource needs; (2) interviewing and hiring new employees to meet these needs; and (3) preparing and distributing detailed data on the state of human resources in the organization.

Application of the systems approach to MIS design and implementation is the exhibit's focus. The systems approach views ongoing operations or functions within a transformation framework; that is, inputs are transformed by a process (or processes) into outputs.

Three major *inputs* are shown. First, the human resource plan originating from the goals and strategies of the organization serves as the main input to the process of determining human resource needs. Second, area employment data act as inputs and also feed information to the human resource inventory file. Finally, wage and salary structure data are major inputs into the employee interviewing and hiring process.

Exhibit 17-7
Information Systems Flow Chart for Personnel MIS

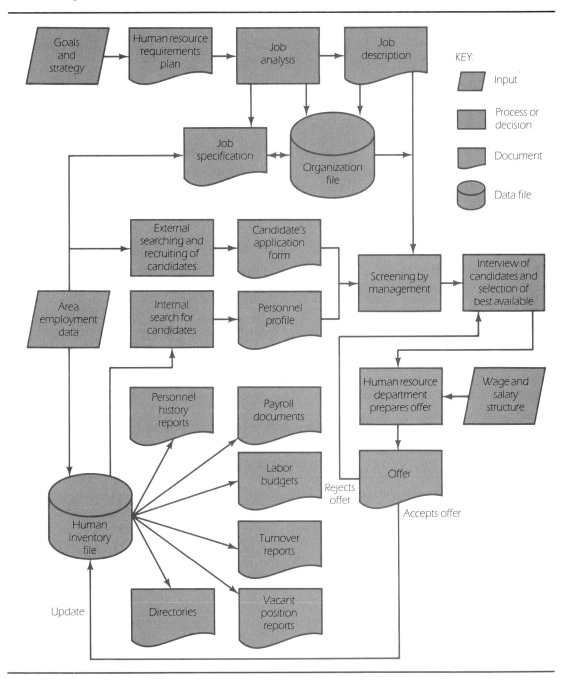

Adapted from Robert G. Murdick, *MIS: Concepts and Design* (Englewood Cliffs, N.J.: Prentice Hall, 1980). Reprinted by permission.

Transforming inputs into outputs is the role performed by *process* activities. In the illustration, the process is really a collection of decision-making activities. In hiring a new employee, management takes information from the human resource plan, data on area employment activities, and the organization's wage and salary structure and makes such decisions as searching for qualified employees, screening candidates, and making the offer.

There are two kinds of *outputs,* or end products of the process. First, an output can be in the form of a statement such as a written offer for employment or a set of job descriptions. Second, it can take the form of a series of reports given to managers for analysis such as reports on payroll, turnover, and position openings that are provided by the human resource inventory file.

An important part of our human resource system illustration is the two files that maintain organizational and human resource inventory information. These two files collect and distribute to management data on various jobs and personnel. In the past, these files were cumbersome and costly to maintain. Computer usage significantly increases the value of the file system.

MIS in Hospital Patient Billing

An application of MIS for patient billing in a hospital (shown in exhibit 17-8) provides a number of similarities and differences with the personnel system. *Inputs* are represented by admissions information, fee or charge structure, and the like. *Process* (or transformation) is accomplished by the billing system in which the inputs are converted to a patient account according to some formula or calculation. Finally, *outputs* are shown as patient bills, insurance claims, revenue and activity reports.

Three interesting elements distinguish this system. First, there are six different data bases (i.e., files) that store data on rates, individual patient charges, and so on. Second, the Hospital Financial Management System (HFMS) data base is an important tie-in between the billing system and the general accounting (budget) activities of the hospital. Finally, the terminal provides both an instantaneous readout of patient charges and a budget report. Needless to say, such quick information is valuable to the patient and the hospital.

Contemporary Developments in MIS

Because we can expect the use of MIS in organizations to flourish, we have selected two contemporary issues to examine more closely—decision support systems and distributive processing.

Decision Support Systems

Consider the case of Mr. Charles Fry, manager of material analysis and planning for Shaklee Corporation, a large California producer of food supplements, cosmetics, and household cleaners.[11] While sales had increased to $350 million in 1979—more than

Exhibit 17-8
MIS for Hospital Patient Billing

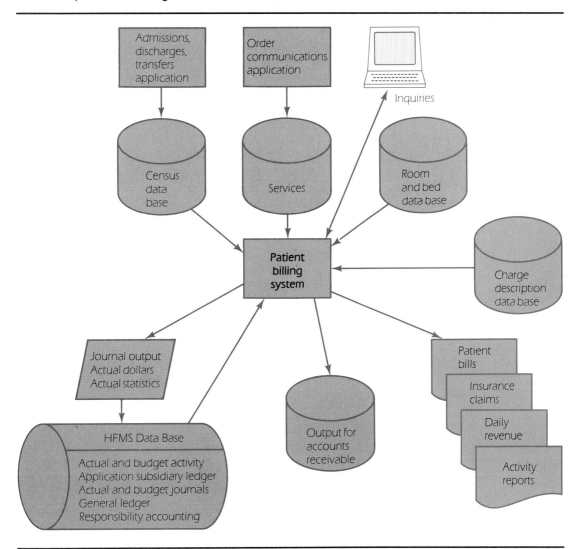

Source: *Hospital Financial Management Systems* Concepts, IBM 1975. Courtesy of IBM.

a thirtyfold increase in just ten years—Fry was concerned that top management was making many strategic and policy decisions less on objective information and more on a subjective and political basis.

To improve this situation, Fry's unit fed data on plant locations, products made, costs per unit, and production capacity for its three facilities and twenty contract manufacturers. It also stored details on more than 500 line items, 360 customers, and its 100 distribution centers. The first task was finding the best way to reduce delivery times to customers without increasing production or distribution costs. The newly developed decision support system calculated the impact that various delivery requirements would have on transportation costs, the cost of operating distribution centers, and the cost of carrying inventories. In the end, Shaklee found a way to speed up deliveries to customers and save money at the same time. The new system also allowed the company to develop a comprehensive information and data base that it could use to analyze other operating problems.

This illustrates a special type of information system that has begun to appear in many organizations—a *decision support system* (DSS), considered by many managers to be a highly advanced MIS.

A number of factors characterize a DSS in an organization. Its foundation is a MIS that has been in operation for some time. Sufficient computer hardware, software packages, and experienced personnel are already operating and can be "built up on." Second, the salient design feature of a DSS is the integration of management science models (see chapter 7), a comprehensive data base, and a skilled decision-maker usually working from an interactive computer terminal. Finally, rather than a series of scheduled reports, a DSS supplies analyses as the manager demands. In operation, the manager identifies a problem, enters information usually with the use of the terminal, and interacts with the information and the system's management science models until the desired results are obtained.

The nature of the DSS depends on the type of problem and the complexity of the models needed. The approach can range from straightforward problems, such as the use of simple statistical analysis models, to "what if . . ." contingency-type problems. For example, National Airlines (now part of PanAm) kept its flights on schedule during fuel shortages, while compensating for fluctuating supplies and rising costs, with a DSS.[12] The airline's system stores data on fuel prices and availability, along with storage costs and fuel capacity at each of the thirty cities it serves. The performance and tentative monthly itinerary are also included for each of its fifty-six aircraft. In just fifteen minutes the DSS produces a list of the best fueling stations and vendors for each flight, something that usually took a month to compute manually. Management runs the system three times a week, resulting in a fuel cost savings of 2 cents a gallon. Since the airline uses 25 million gallons per month, the savings is $500,000.

On the other hand, American Can Company faced a contingency-type problem when it recently planned to install a $50 million production system at one of its plants in the Pacific Northwest. When management used its DSS to investigate thirty-two alternative locations, they decided instead to locate the new system in a Southeastern plant.[13] If manufacturing had had its way, it would have cost the company an additional $7 million a year in distribution costs.

"We need the order-entry tracking system by the 1st. The budget consolidation in two weeks. The sales forecast next week. And the seating arrangement for my daughter's wedding by tomorrow."

Courtesy of General Electric Information Services Co.

A DSS is not something management can plug in and start running. Designing and implementing a DSS can be time consuming and costly. The Shaklee system, for example, took six months and $250,000 to develop, plus approximately $50,000 a year to operate. If the wrong model or inaccurate information is used, the result can be the phenomenon well known to computer users called GI-GO—garbage in, garbage out. Collecting appropriate and accurate data is the biggest obstacle to developing a sound DSS.

Even with these problems, development and use of DSS is expected to continue at a growing rate. The main reason is that DSS fits well into the integration stage of MIS development. Integrating computer technology and management science models and providing the functional manager with "hands-on" experience can result in improved managerial decison-making and performance.[14]

Distributive Processing

In MIS-user organizations during the 1970s, a mature MIS usually involved a large centralized computer supported by a substantial professional staff (the growth and moratorium stages of the emergence of MIS). On the plus side, the organization can maintain efficiencies of scale (i.e., cost control) and acquire the latest and most advanced large computer system. On the other hand, the use of centralized computers often leads to data input bottlenecks and lengthy delays in feedback information.

For the user-manager, the problems of a centralized system are particularly troublesome. You usually want information and analysis reports returned quickly, accurately, and at minimum costs. What can happen is that your problem is only one of many to be solved by the MIS unit, resulting in lengthy delays. In addition, the MIS specialist must be aware of the manager's needs to generate the appropriate output. Finally, the manager must pay for MIS services, not only in direct costs, but in incremental costs to cover overhead charges as well.

In order to eliminate some of these problems, many organizations are moving to a distributive processing approach to MIS.[15] Distributive processing is a decentralized approach that involves the use of smaller, self-contained MIS units that can be found within the divisional structures of the organization. With this approach, the user-manager is brought closer to the actual computations, and hence to greater involvement in the analysis. Several technological developments have contributed to the adoption of distributive processing:

Superchip. This remarkable development in computer processing, which can put the computer's heart and brains on a slice of silicon no bigger than a pencil eraser, is a key to processing at an extremely low cost. Products using the computer-on-a-chip include digital watches, postage scales that compute postage rates when zip codes are keyed in, and mobile telephones that can store up to ten numbers and automatically dial any one of them.

Advanced teleprocessing. New communication networks and technology are now capable of moving data at high speed and diminishing costs.

Improved hardware and software. New programming philosophies, translated into widely applicable systems, can effectively handle the complexities of data transmission, dispersed files, and the interconnection of units. In addition, a wide variety of terminals is available for data collection, report printing, visual display, and direct translation of data into information that can be easily interpreted by the user-manager.

The ability of user-managers to get closer to their analyses is an important benefit to the use of distributive processing. A major problem organizations wishing to go this route face is what to do with the large centralized computer systems and associated personnel. Management must solve the problem of selling the large computers and relocating personnel to the decentralized sites before distributive processing can reach its full potential. Exhibit 17-9 compares the benefits of centralized and distributive processing systems.

Exhibit 17-9 Centralization vs. Distributive MIS Processing		**For centralization**	**For distribution**
	Management control	More professional operation Flexible backup Efficient use of personnel	Better user control and response Simpler control Improved local reliability
	Technology	Large-scale capacity Efficient use of capacity	Efficient size Reduced telecommunications costs
	Data related	Multiple access to common data Assurance of data standards Better security	Easier access Better fit with field needs Data relevance
	Professional service	Specialized staff Reduced vulnerability to turnover Richer DP career paths	Stability of work force Better user career paths
	Organizational fit	Corporate style is centralized or functional	Decentralized corporate style

Adapted from J. L. McKenney and F. W. McFarlan, "The Information Archipelago—Maps and Bridges," *Harvard Business Review* (September-October 1982): 116.

MIS Implementation

The sequence of activities managers traditionally follow in implementing MIS is shown in exhibit 17-10. The eleven different activities can be divided into three broad categories: planning, testing, and operation. In a management information system for the personnel function, for example, planning activities would include: determining whether such a system can be developed (feasibility study), what information personnel managers want from such a system (requirements analysis), initial design of the system (system design), and estimating the costs and time associated with program development and/or purchase.[16]

Testing activities concern the actual development of certain software programs (system development), pilot testing with existing data (system testing), and review by the user to insure the quality and accuracy of the information. Operation entails putting the system to work (conversion) and evaluating the information produced.

Exhibit 17-10
MIS Implementation Activities

	Implementation Activity	Description
Planning	Feasibility study	Analysis to generate information to determine whether or not to commit organization resources and implement the MIS product
	Requirements analysis	Determination of the input, processing, and output attributes of the MIS product so it meets organizational needs
	System design	Configuration of hardware, software, and human components that enable a set of MIS requirements to be achieved
	System acquisition	Effort to develop proposals and solicit and evaluate bids when hardware or software must be acquired from vendors
Testing	System development	Internal programming effort to provide a software product
	System testing	Assurance of the correctness of an internally developed software product
	Acceptance testing	Evaluation of a MIS product, acquired externally or developed internally, by the product's sponsors (users) prior to accepting ''ownership'' of the product
Operation	Conversion	Introduction of the MIS product into the sponsoring organization
	Quality assurance	Continual evaluation of the organizational ''fit'' of the MIS product (and subsequent maintenance) after its introduction
	Training	Provision of necessary skills, knowledge, and understanding to facilitate the implementation effort
	Documentation	Description of the evolving MIS product and creation of a history of the implementation effort

Adapted from R. W. Zmud, *Information Systems in Organizations* (Glenview, Ill.: Scott, Foresman, 1983), p. 253.

Training and documentation, while noted as operation activities, actually occur throughout the entire process.

Certain key implementation activities can make or break a MIS project. First and foremost, it is crucial to *involve the user* in the system's development. Analogous to our discussion of strategic planning in chapter 5, functional managers who must implement and operate a system that has been developed by staff experts are going to have trouble. User participation throughout the process will not only help gain their support and commitment, but certainly their ideas about the functioning of the MIS will add a needed degree of relevancy.

A second key is to make clear estimates at the start on *timing and cost* factors of the project. Nothing is more frustrating or damaging to the future of MIS projects than to have a project come in late and considerably over budget. Closely related to this is the setting of clear and attainable *MIS performance goals*. All personnel using the system should understand what information it is to provide.

Training and documentation deserve mention. Here, the emphasis is developing and providing training programs for user-managers early in the project, supplemented with manuals (documentation) that are written for the user, not the data processing expert. Managers without computer experience will resist enough as it is; it is best not to compound the problem with manuals that are written in overly technical language.

Attention also should be given to certain *behavioral* aspects in MIS implementation.[17] As we will discuss in chapter 19, the process can be considered a change in the organization. As the system gains acceptance by user-managers, it is highly likely that established social networks, group norms, and authority/responsibility relations may alter. For example, a personnel MIS was recently developed by a major energy company. Since the system contained information on all company managers, a number of functional managers began accessing the system's data to seek out replacements for transferred or promoted employees. To advert potential problems of direct contact between the inquiring manager and the potential employee, a policy was instituted that limited direct access to the system to personnel representatives.

Finally, managers must not overlook the international aspects of MIS. Information in today's multinational companies must cross a number of country boundaries. Yet, the experiences of many managers tell us that critical reports and other data sources frequently reach the receiver late and in nonstandard form.

Why is this? A number of reasons can be given.[18] First, the systems may be different—some set up by the company, others set up by vendors, and so on. Second, the information requirements in the particular country may not be the same as that in the host country (see chapter 15). Finally, from the point of view of organizational structure, there may be no centralized development or control. Alleviating these problems in implementation usually involves standardizing systems and information requirements along with altering relationships of authority and responsibility. The key is that someone, or some unit, should be given responsibility for international information flow.

The information revolution, increased computer applications, accelerating information needs, and just the general direction of technology today all point to the importance of MIS in organizations. Accepting, understanding, and using management information systems effectively in today's competitive environment requires managers to develop key skills and roles.

 POINTS TO CONSIDER
An Emphasis on Managerial Skills

1. **A well-designed MIS doesn't automatically mean better decisions will be made.**
    Decision making is a matter of judgment and choice. Two managers given the same information may come up with completely different decisions. MIS must, therefore, be considered an input into the managerial decision-making process. Managers make decisions—MIS does not.

2. **Proper staffing of the MIS unit is important.**

   Since MIS involves highly technical work, organizations have tended to staff MIS units with technical personnel. Unfortunately, sometimes these experts cannot understand the information needs of functional managers. Because of this situation, many successful MIS units are staffed with people whose backgrounds are a blend of technical and functional, or applied, management skills.

3. **More information is not necessarily better information.**

   Too much information for the user-manager—information overload—can only confuse and impede the process of sorting important information from a mass of data and statistics. Managers need information they can use, not what they *might* eventually use.

4. **Some MIS-generated information should be considered confidential.**

   Even though it can be readily generated, most MIS information and data should be carefully distributed. As our example on use of MIS for personnel records shows, some information should be made available only on a ''need to know'' basis.

5. **Knowledge of MIS activities involves important managerial skills.**

   MIS presents at least two challenges to management. On one hand, use of MIS information will certainly sharpen the manager's diagnostic skills—he or she is given more information on which to study a problem. On the other hand, it is almost becoming a basic technical skill for the manager to understand how to use the computer, especially the computer terminal or the personal computer.

 # SUMMARY FOR THE MANAGER

1. Organizations are facing an information revolution that is changing the way work is done. Behind the revolution are the increasing complexity of the management task, the availability of decision-making tools, and growing computer understanding and usage.

2. Management information systems (MIS) is an organized approach to providing past, present, and projection information relating to internal operations and external intelligence.

3. MIS has four main purposes: to analyze early warning signals, to aid in managerial decision making, to automate clerical operations, and to use in the control function.

4. MIS emerged in many organizations in four stages: initiation (accounts payable), growth (budgeting), moratorium (purchasing control), and integration (planning models).

5. MIS applications can be found in a variety of organizations (profit and not-for-profit) and organizational functions (manufacturing, marketing, accounting, and personnel).

6. A Decision Support System can be considered an advanced MIS form. Included within a DSS are a comprehensive data base, management science models, and a skilled manager generally operating from an interactive computer terminal.

7. Whether to centralize or decentralize (distributive processing) MIS activities is a major issue among many for today's managers. The decision depends on a number of factors including the size of the firm, the physical dispersion of operations, and the turbulence of the organization's environment.

8. Implementing MIS projects involves consideration of many factors. One of the most important deals with human behavior and how a new system can change tasks, reporting relationships, and group activities.

REVIEW AND DISCUSSION QUESTIONS

1. Increased computer knowledge and usage was identified as a major influence in the information revolution. Why is this?
2. Identify the basic elements of MIS.
3. How may MIS be used for managerial control?
4. How would MIS work as an "early warning signal"? Can you provide any examples?
5. Why is the moratorium stage of MIS development important for the future of MIS usage?
6. What are the basic elements of a Decision Support System?
7. Why would a large, geographically dispersed retail company want to move from centralized to distributive processing?
8. What organizational structure (or structures) would be best for a distributive processing approach?
9. Why is it important for managers to accurately estimate the costs and completion time for MIS projects?
10. Why is the development and use of effective human skills important for successful MIS implementation?

NOTES

1. See J. Naisbitt, *Megatrends* (New York: Warner, 1982); and P. Nulty, "The Computer Comes to Main Street," *Fortune* (September 6, 1982): 78-86.
2. R. W. Zmud, *Information Systems in Organizations* (Glenview, Ill.: Scott, Foresman, 1983), pp. 6-7; and R. McLeod, *Management Information Systems* (Chicago: SRA, 1983), pp. 4-7.
3. W. J. Kennevan, "MIS Universe," *Data Management* (September 1970): 63.
4. McLeod, *Management Information Systems,* pp. 17-23.
5. R. G. Murdick, *MIS: Concepts and Design* (Englewood Cliffs, N.J.: Prentice-Hall, 1980), p. 253.
6. See W. M. Zani, "Blueprint for MIS," *Harvard Business Review* (November-December 1970): 100; and P. Nulty, "The Bar-Coding of America," *Fortune* (December 27, 1982): 98-106.
7. F. G. Withington, "Five Generations of Computers," *Harvard Business Review* (September-October 1972): 105; and "Insurance Agents Go Electric," *Business Week* (November 19, 1979): 142-43.
8. R. L. Nolan, "Controlling the Costs of Data Services," *Harvard Business Review* (July-August 1977): 117.
9. J. F. Rockart, "Chief Executives Define Their Own Data Needs," *Harvard Business Review* (March-April 1979): 81-93.
10. "Computer Rescue for Travel Agents," *Business Week* (April 7, 1980): 81-82.
11. "What If Help for Management," *Business Week* (January 21, 1980): 73-74.
12. "Helping Decision Makers Get at Data," *Business Week* (September 13, 1982): 118.
13. "How Computers Remake the Manager's Job," *Business Week* (April 25, 1983): 68.
14. See S. L. Atler, "How Effective Managers Use Information Systems," *Harvard Business Review* (November-December 1976): 97-104; and M. Gerstein and H. Reisman, "Creating Competitive Advantage with Computer Technology," *Journal of Business Strategy* (Summer 1982): 53-60.
15. F. Kaufman, *Distributive Processing* (New York: Coopers & Lybrand, 1977).
16. Zmud, *Information Systems in Organizations,* pp. 251-59.
17. R. Nolan, "Managing Information Systems by Committee," *Harvard Business Review* (July-August 1982): 72-79.
18. M. D. J. Buss, "Managing International Information Systems," *Harvard Business Review* (September-October, 1982): 153-62.

Great Lakes Boat and Marine Company

Your career is progressing nicely—six successful years with one of the Big Eight accounting firms in its management services division. Your performance as a computer consultant was so outstanding that you got a job offer from one of your clients. You managed the conversion from a batch to an online data processing system for Great Lakes Boat and Marine so well that the company offered you the position of vice-president of information services. Sue Rankin, the president, told you that the next step was to develop an MIS and she needed someone to implement it. The system you installed earlier does all the essential data processing tasks—order entry, inventory, billing, accounts receivable, purchasing, and receiving. You know that Great Lakes has a sound internal accounting system, which should make it possible to achieve an excellent MIS. During your first day on the job, you meet with Rankin to learn more about her expectations. She tells you she has formed an MIS committee consisting of Rick Guenther (vice-president of manufacturing), Don Lehnert (vice-president of marketing), Cheryl Mitchell (vice-president of finance), and you. Rankin wants you to call on each member, introduce yourself, and set a date and time for the first planning meeting.

You already know Mitchell, having worked with her on the installation of the data processing system. You know she is extremely computer literate and anxious to expand the scope of the computer applications. You have heard of Guenther and Lehnert but haven't met them. As you leave, you remember to ask Rankin, "Aren't you going to be on the MIS committee?"

"No," Rankin replies, "I'm too busy planning our entry into the New England market area next year. I just don't have time. That's why I hired you."

Your first stop is Guenther's office. You find him extremely likeable—a warm handshake, boundless energy, contagious optimism, and a great sense of humor. You spend two hours in his office, getting to know him and talking about the computer. Guenther wants to get started immediately.

"We've just been waiting for someone like you," he says. "We've known about MIS and how it can help us in manufacturing, but we haven't had anyone to pick up the ball and run with it. I want data collection terminals in every work area. We should be able to implement attendance reporting immediately, and I would like to be reporting all production activities within three months. I need good data to establish some good production standards. I want all manufacturing managers to have terminals in their offices, and I want each to attend a course on how to use the computer. I've seen what a good MIS can do in manufacturing, and I can't wait to get started."

Neither can you. You are so excited after talking with Guenther that you almost run down the hall to Lehnert's office. When his secretary ushers you into his office and his greeting is, "Well, what do *you* want?" you suspect rough sailing. You introduce yourself and explain your purpose. You feel uncomfortable when Lehnert nervously jingles coins in his pocket as you talk. When you pause to catch your breath, he says, "Listen, I don't have time to get involved with Sue's MIS. We're planning to expand our market area and I have to find eight new distributors by the end of the month. I can't do that sitting around talking about computer programs. If I can't get my marketing job done, there won't be any company to put an MIS in.

"Now, I have to go. Why don't you talk with my manager of marketing administration,

Willie Campbell. The MIS would really be in Willie's area. He'll get you fixed up. Just a minute, and I'll have my secretary take you to his office.

"I've appreciated meeting you, and I wish you all the luck in the world. I'm sure you'll give us a good MIS."

Source: R. McLeod, *Management Information Systems* (Chicago: SRA, 1983), pp. 404-405.

Questions for Discussion

1. From the information you have in the case, how would you rate the chances of Great Lakes' achieving a "good MIS"? What is the problem?
2. Assuming Lehnert won't cooperate, should you go ahead with work in Guenther's and Mitchell's areas? Why?
3. If Rankin insists that Lehnert must get involved, how might his cooperation be gained?

18

Production and Operations Control

Chapter Outline

Key Points

1. The elements of production and operations control involve consideration of selection, production design, production planning, and production evaluation.
2. Facilities layout, a component of production design, concerns the overall arrangement of equipment, people, materials, storage, and service operations.
3. Material requirements planning is a computer-based approach to production planning that is gaining in popularity among production managers.
4. Quality control is involved in the total production process—from input to output control. Acceptance sampling and process control charts are statistical approaches to quality control.
5. To be successful, production and operations control must be integrated into the total organizational system.
6. EOQ, PERT, linear programming, and queuing models are four of the many quantitative aids available to managers.
7. Production and operations in foreign countries require a careful analysis of the differences in the control elements.
8. Managerial skills, and the use of these skills in managerial roles, are found throughout the production and operations control system.

Pasta and the Airline Industry

To the casual observer, there is probably little relationship between pasta making and the function of production and operations control. If your name is Marcella Vitalini Aitken, the relationship is significant. Thanks to Mrs. Aitken, passengers on major U.S. airlines are saying arrivederci to meat and potatoes and benvenuto to some tasty lasagne, cannelloni, and fettuccine. With an efficient production plant, Mrs. Aitken has turned a small operation into a $6 million per year enterprise.

Vivacious, talkative, and as Italian as pasta itself, Mrs. Aitken is best known for her Miami, Florida restaurants, Marcella's and Cucino Mia. A few years ago, Marcella—as everyone calls her—sold Eastern Air Lines on the idea of serving pasta prepared according to her own recipes. Since then she has signed on with Pan Am, Western, and Ozark and is negotiating with nine other airlines, including Continental and US Air. Soon she will be feeding airline passengers as many as 25,000 meals per day.

The basis of pasta power is cost. It costs Marcella a mere 33 cents to prepare a meal of, say, crêpes Florentine. The airlines, which normally pay about $1.50 for a steak dinner, are more than willing to pay that much for a pasta meal. In just two years, Eastern's purchases have gone from 15,000 trial servings to over 150,000 per month.

Marcella had to enlist the help of her entire family to produce pasta. As the Eastern business increased, she decided to automate. Putting up $400,000 herself, and borrowing the rest from local banks, she invested $1 million in new equipment.

Her four-room factory, which is housed in a one-story building that connects with both her restaurants, turns out 25,000 meals every day—lasagne, Swiss crêpes, ravioli, cannelloni, and fettuccine alfredo. In one room, dough is turned into various kinds of pasta. In another, sauces bubble in huge vats. In a third room it all comes together, as sauces and pasta move along a production line. Each serving is then flash-frozen with liquid nitrogen in a fourth room, boxed, and sent off in refrigerated trucks.

Marcella recently took delivery on a $55,000 versatile Italian pasta-making machine from Milan. The only one of its kind in the U.S., it mixes the ingredients, kneads the dough, and turns out everything from fettuccine to macaroni. The machine then cooks the pasta, dries it, stuffs it with meat, cheese, or vegetables, and cuts it into portions. The new pasta maker will double capacity and reduce labor costs by two-thirds.

Marcella says that management success is just like cooking. She claims that you have got to have a good factory, a good product, good people, and good customers. Couple this with a management style that involves tenacity, patience, and a "never give up" attitude, and you have all the ingredients for success.

Adapted from Susie G. Nazem, "Mamma Marcella Takes to the Air with Pasta Power," *Fortune* (August 27, 1979): 118-19.

18 In this last chapter on the control function of management, we will focus on those activities directed toward production and operations. The basic principles of production and operations control can apply to a variety of organizations (as *The Practice of Management* section illustrates) and deal primarily with physical resources. As we will show, however, controlling physical resources involves consideration of human, information, and financial resources.

The chapter has been divided into four major sections. The first discusses the key elements of production and operations control, introducing the reader to selection, production design, production planning, and production evaluation. Second, three of these elements—production design, production planning, and production evaluation—are singled out for a separate discussion. The third section highlights some of the issues managers face in international production. The fourth section presents certain quantitative aids in production and operations control. These aids include economic order quantity (EOQ), linear programming, program evaluation and review technique (PERT), and queuing models.

Elements of Production and Operations Control

Production and operations control is a subset of a larger and growing area of study termed production and operations management (POM), production and logistics management (PLM), or just operations management (OPS Management). Whatever terminology, the concern is a variety of concepts and approaches to improve an organization's overall operating performance. The most frequently studied topics include the management of materials, products, equipment, and work force used in producing products and services.

Exhibit 18-1 depicts a production and operations system for a typical manufacturing organization. As the exhibit suggests, a discussion of production and operations control should consider the elements of selection, production design, production planning, and production evaluation.[1]

Selection identifies those factors necessary to establish the foundation of the production and operations control system. The system begins, as in most other organizational activities, with a statement of *goals and strategies*. This identifies what the organization wants to produce, where, and with what type of process and work force. This is translated into decisions on *products and processes,* the *site* of the producing facility, and the selection of a *work force*. Work force was discussed in detail in chapter 10.

Production design concerns the design of products, processes, services, jobs, wage and salary structure, and control systems. As we discussed in chapter 16, the major focus is *input controls*. The main functions include *product design, plant design engineering* (i.e., layout) and *training* the work force to use the newly developed *work methods* and procedures properly. Chapters 8 and 10 have covered this last topic.

Production planning involves those activities related to the actual production of the product or service. The important functions of *production scheduling,* material and equipment *purchases,* raw materials *inventory,* and *maintenance* procedures are considered. Later in this chapter, we will detail master production scheduling and material requirements planning. The main focus will be on *process controls,* as discussed in chapter 16.

Production evaluation concerns possible revisions to the production and operating system in light of the discovery of new products and services and technological breakthroughs. It also concerns work force control and problems with existing products and services. *Quality control,* finished product *inventories,* and employee *performance evaluation* are of particular concern (see chapter 16). We defined these earlier as *output controls.*

An Illustration   Many of the production and control elements presented for a manufacturing company are closely related to those found in banks, government offices, restaurants, and other service organizations. Consider the case of a county hospital commission in a large, growing urban area. The commission is responsible for the construction, operation, and maintenance of tax-supported health care institutions in the surrounding area. After analyzing data on population trends and movements, citizen needs, and the area's tax base, commission members have decided to build a new county hospital in one of the fastest growing parts of the county. From a production and operations viewpoint, what elements should the members consider?

In terms of *selection,* the decision to build the hospital is in response to the goals and strategies of the commission. This is followed by a concern for the site of the hospital, including evaluation of land according to cost, accessibility, and availability of utilities. Product and process selection involves decisions on the size of the hospital, the types of services (such as the comprehensiveness of the emergency room), and the degree of emphasis given to such specialties as surgery, pediatrics, and outpatient care. This leads to the selection of a work force that will fit the choices on products and services.

The initial decision on *production design* involves planning the physical layout of the hospital production system to achieve the most efficient flow of materials and people. Management chooses the specific work methods with regard to the type of work force hired and the nature of the hospital's physical layout.

Reprinted by permission.
© 1980 NEA, Inc.

Exhibit 18-1
An Example Production and Operations System

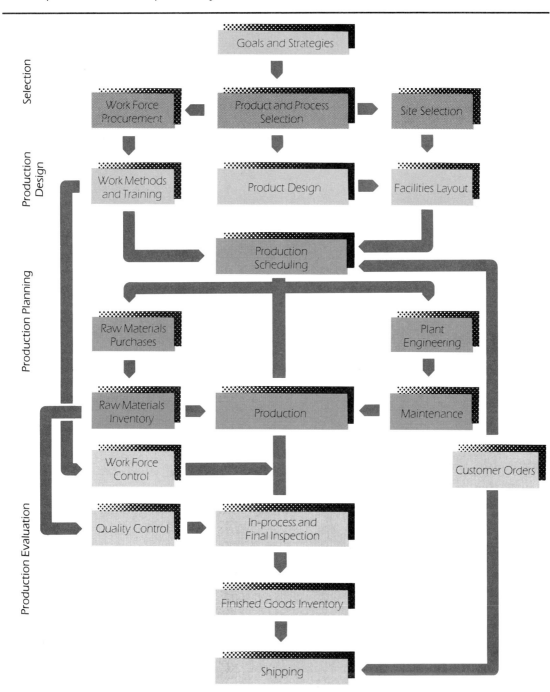

In *production planning,* hospital administrators are concerned with purchasing fixed equipment such as x-ray machines, equipping the pathology laboratory and surgical ward, and periodically purchasing supplies. In addition, emphasis must be given to scheduling employees to tasks and maintaining an efficient inventory of needed materials. Managers must develop an effective balance between material and product availability and the significant costs of having these inventories on hand.

The final element, *production evaluation,* concerns the development of accurate employee performance evaluation and reward systems so that the most effective work force is retained (see chapter 16). A second concern, which we will discuss later in this chapter, is quality control. The hospital management must give attention to the accuracy of laboratory tests, the quality of x-rays, the control of unit costs, and so on.

As this example illustrates, production and operations control is an integral part of the manager's job. It is not only a function that translates goals and strategies into action, it is clearly the place where the manager is "on the firing line" for the performance of the organization.

In the following sections, we will discuss three elements of production and operations control in greater detail—production design, production planning, and production evaluation (quality control).

 # Production Design

Production design, or facilities layout, is the overall arrangement of equipment, people, materials handling, storage, and service operations required for efficient operation of the production system. The way an organization's facilities, machines, and personnel are physically arranged can have a significant impact on overall performance, affecting time and money.

Goals of Facilities Layout

Production and operations specialists suggest the following production system:

- Materials handling and internal transportation requirements are designed to reduce the costs and time needed to move materials through the production process.
- Floor space requirements should eliminate congestion and bottlenecks, resulting in a maximum return on the fixed investment in facilities.
- The distance workers move to obtain materials, tools, and supplies, resulting in improved labor efficiency must be minimized.
- Employee convenience, safety, and comfort is provided for.
- Flexibility for expansion caused by growth, new products, and/or new processes is built into the system.

As an example, consider the Burger King division of Pillsbury.[2] Like many other organizations, this fast-food restaurant chain is faced with rising costs from land, labor, and raw materials that can adversely affect the division's profitability. To

Nowhere is automation making a larger impact than on the factory floor. Take the case of Yamazaki Machinery Works Ltd., one of Japan's biggest machine tool manufacturers. According to Tsunehiko "Tony" Yamazaki, the firm's senior executive managing director, the new plant's 65 computer-controlled machine tools and 34 robots will be linked via a fiber-optic cable with the computerized design center at the Nagoya headquarters, some 40 miles away.

From the design center, the automated factory can be directed to manufacture the company's products. The process is accomplished by entering into the computer's memory names of various machine tool models scheduled to be produced and pressing a few buttons to get production operating. The computer also can be programmed to direct production on parts and fixtures to make the models.

The plant is not totally automated, since 215 people are employed. A conventional factory of this size, however, would employ 2,500 workers. At maximum capacity the plant can turn out over $200 million of machine tools a year. But production is so organized and automated that sales can decline to less than 50 percent of capacity without laying off workers. This is an important feature of automated factories that is attractive to managers everywhere; a manufacturer can economically shrink production capacity to match lower market demand without severe disruptions in the human resource function.

Adapted from G. Bylinsky, "The Race to the Automated Factory," *Fortune* (February 21, 1983): 57.

counter this trend, Burger King's management started a productivity improvement program, part of which is aimed at better facilities layout. Time is money to Burger King; if ways can be found to reduce the time between the customer's order and when they receive the food, while maintaining high food quality, performance should improve.

Burger King's work on facilities layout involves both major and minor improvements. For example, the bell hose that rings when a car is in the drive-in lane was moved back ten feet from the remote order entry device. This distance allows workers to be ready to take the customer's order immediately after the car brakes for a stop. The time savings permits an extra thirty cars per hour to be handled. Similarly, to keep burgers hot without warming the iced drinks stationed next to them, the company installed a sheet metal plate between the products.

On the major improvement side, the company is experimenting with a new cash register that, besides calculating the customer's bill, electronically transfers food orders to cooks on a computerized readout terminal. The cooks make fewer mistakes and as a result don't waste as much food. The new cash registers have also been adapted to activate a machine that mixes, pours, and caps soft drinks automatically. In a further improvement, management studied traffic flow in its restaurants with a computer simulation program. The analysis resulted in a reduction in the number of floor plans from five to two—one for small towns and one for larger volume stores.

Layout Patterns

In visiting a number of factories, hospitals, or department stores, a manager can identify a great variety of production layouts. Most layouts, however, are based on three distinct patterns. As shown in exhibit 18-2, the three basic patterns are process, product, and fixed position.[3]

A *process* layout is one that groups similar processing components and equipment together in one area on the basis of the function they perform, without regard to the product. This pattern works best when the number of products is many and high flexibility is desired. Department stores, hospitals, and manufacturing job shops use process layouts.

When production components are arranged according to the steps required in producing a product, this is termed a *product* pattern. Product layouts are used in continuous production systems where the number of different products is small, the volume is high, and the parts are highly standardized and interchangeable. Automobile assembly lines, food processing plants, and appliance manufacturers are examples.

A *fixed-position* layout keeps the product in one position because of its bulk and weight, and workers, materials, and tools are brought to it. This pattern is normally used in producing ships, airplanes, locomotives, and large pieces of equipment.

Layout Pattern Comparisons

Each of the layout patterns offers distinct benefits and limitations. For the process layout, flexibility allows work to be shifted between machines when one breaks down. In a similar manner, since sequencing of operations is not a problem, equipment that is noisy or gives off irritating fumes can be located in another area. Since the pace of the work is determined by the person, not the machine, incentive pay systems can be used. However, complex production planning is required to control materials flow, inventory storage, and scheduling. Materials handling is the main key to success with the process layout.

With the product layout, materials handling is simplified by means of conveyor systems. Production control and employee training are easier; less inspection is required on the final product; and since there is less work in process and smaller aisles and storage are required, the useful floor area is more productive. Conversely, production equipment usually requires a higher capital investment; there are greater problems when work stoppages occur; the highly repetitive nature of the workers' jobs creates motivation and morale problems; and the inflexibility of the layout makes it costly when product or process design changes are implemented. Above all, the key to success with the product layout is balancing the production steps—each step in the process must be provided with enough capacity so that material flow will be uninterrupted. This is *line balancing*.

The fixed-position layout eliminates costly and space-consuming materials-handling equipment. This layout pattern is also popular with workers because they can move about freely and are not restricted to a particular area. On the other hand, fixed-position layouts require large and costly working areas, especially if more than one unit, such as at a GM locomotive assembly plant, is being worked on at the same

Exhibit 18-2
Layout Patterns

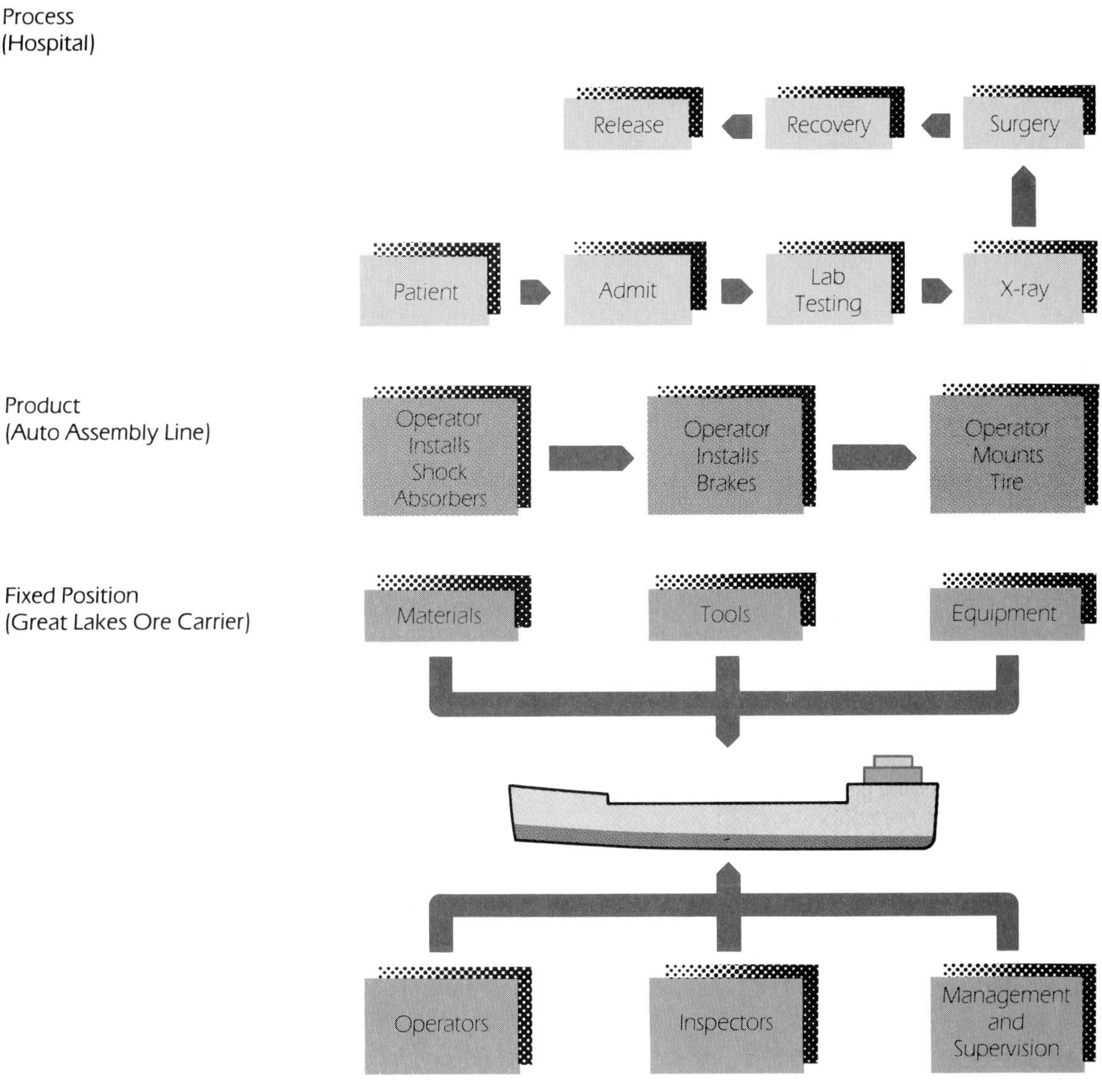

Process
(Hospital)

Release ◀ Recovery ◀ Surgery

▲

Patient ▶ Admit ▶ Lab Testing ▶ X-ray

Product
(Auto Assembly Line)

Operator Installs Shock Absorbers ➡ Operator Installs Brakes ➡ Operator Mounts Tire

Fixed Position
(Great Lakes Ore Carrier)

Materials   Tools   Equipment

Operators   Inspectors   Management and Supervision

time. In addition, highly skilled workers are needed to perform the jobs. This places a great deal of emphasis on the hiring and placement process. (For example, in gearing up to design and produce its 757 and 767 aircraft, Boeing was forced to advertise for skilled workers across the entire U.S.) One of the major keys to success with this layout is material availability. Parts must be stored close to the product, to reduce the travel and idle time. This often requires large and space-consuming storage areas.

In actual operations, most organizations combine layouts to produce a product. For example, automobile parts are manufactured with a process layout, while auto assembly uses a product layout.

The crucial factor in production layout is cost—fixed and variable. With a high-volume product, product and process layouts are preferred; a low-volume, high-cost product is amenable to a fixed-position format. Volvo and Saab can afford to use a combination of product and fixed-position layouts (low-volume, high-priced product).

Production Planning

One of the most difficult problems facing production and operations managers over the years is how to plan and control production and materials flow effectively. In essence, the manager must be able to juggle product design changes, purchasing needs, production rates and schedules, and inventories so costs are controlled and the customer receives the right product at the right time.

Until recently, managers have attacked this problem with an assortment of tools and techniques. However, a number of organizations, beginning with Black and Decker, Xerox, Steelcase, Hewlett-Packard, and Abbott Laboratories have begun to apply computer technology to the problem of production planning.[4] Use of the computer in production planning was favored by cost balance—computer computation costs were decreasing (see chapter 17), while production costs, especially raw materials and inventories, were rising. What has evolved is a new approach to production planning, material requirements planning (MRP) systems.

Material requirements planning is a computer-based system that develops schedules for the specific parts and materials required to produce a product, the particular numbers that are needed, and the dates when orders for these materials should be processed and received.[5] In application, the purposes of an MRP are to *control:* (1) inventory levels (order the right part, in the right quantity, at the right time), (2) priorities for materials (order with a valid due date), and (3) capacity planning (plan for complete and accurate production rates).[6]

The logic of MRP is that demand for materials and parts and fluctuations in inventories are a direct function of demand for the end product. This logic is described in exhibit 18-3, which illustrates the five core components in an MRP system: the master production schedule, the bill of materials file, the inventory file, the MRP computer program, and the various output reports.

Master Production Schedule   The master production schedule is the major input into the MRP system. Three elements make up the schedule. First are firm orders for products by customers—orders of known quantity and delivery time. For example, an electric utility company may have a long-term contract with a coal company to purchase a minimum number of tons of coal per year. The second element is forecasts of consumer demand (see chapter 3), including demand for both regular and replacement products. For instance, a producer of automobile spark plugs should forecast demand for installation in new cars as well as replacements.

Exhibit 18-3
Material Requirements Planning

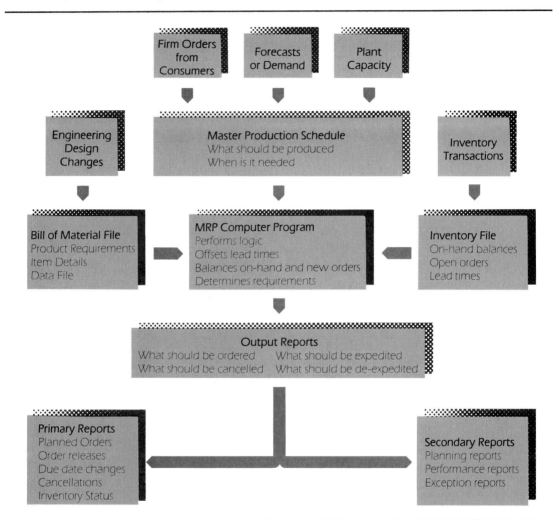

Adapted from Jeffrey G. Miller and Linda Sprague, ''Behind the Growth in Material Requirements Planning,'' *Harvard Business Review* (September-October 1975): 84

The final element is data on the production capacity of the unit. It is important for the manager to know if the demand will exceed or be less than existing capacity. Such information will show when idle capacity exists or when an increase in capacity is needed. For example, during the late 1970s and early 1980s the demand for small, fuel-efficient cars exceeded the plant capacities of General Motors and Chrysler to produce these cars. At the same time, the plants assembling the large-sized cars for each of these companies lay partially idle.[7]

A master production schedule, which evaluates demand for products and available capacity of the production unit, means that many decisions can be faced in planning rather than in a crisis. Instead of waiting (or hoping) for all production elements to fall together in the right order, managers can make sure these elements indeed fall together correctly. Budgets and other organizational plans can be more accurately developed and related to end products.

Bill of Materials   The bill of materials file (B/M) is usually developed by design engineers from product specifications. It lists all items, including quantities of each, required to produce one unit of finished product. Bills of materials can vary greatly by product. For example, one for a nonrefillable pen lists three pieces (plastic barrel, ink cartridge, and plastic cap with a clip) while one for a 747 requires thousands of pages.

Inventory File   The inventory file contains information on at least two factors. First, there is information on the three major types of inventories: raw materials and supplies, in-process, and finished products. Second, the lead times required between submission of the order for a raw material and date of receipt are needed. For Paper Mate, for example, it is important to know that the lead time for plastic pen barrels is ten days, but twenty-five days for ink cartridges.

Without inventories, organizations could not produce goods (raw materials), maintain stable production rates (in-process), or sell to customers (finished products). If they were not costly, most organizations would keep very large inventories on hand to maintain a smooth-running operation. However, inventories quite often represent a significant percentage of an organization's current assets, as much as 20 to 30 percent. Inventory cost categories include storage costs, insurance, inventory and property taxes, spoilage, obsolescence, and opportunity costs. Since these costs can be significant, managers need to develop techniques to balance smooth-running production runs with inventory costs. One approach to this problem, the economic order quantity (EOQ), will be discussed later in this chapter.

MRP Computer Program   The heart of the material requirements planning system is a computer program that operates on the inventory file, the bill of materials file, and the master production schedule. Most programs that are available commercially or can be developed by the organization operate in the following manner. First, information from the master production schedule (list of items needed by time period), the bill of materials file (description of the materials and parts needed to make each item), and the inventory file (number of units of each item and material currently on hand and on order) is placed in the system. Second, the program manipulates the inventory file while frequently referring to the bill of materials file to calculate the quantity of each item. Third, the number of units of each item required is corrected for on-hand amounts and net requirements are recomputed to allow for the lead time needed to obtain the material. Finally, the manager operating the program feeds in the different components of the master production schedule in an iterative manner. Each time the program is run, the output is compared with the production capacity of product demand characteristics of the production schedule. The master schedule is adjusted to try to correct for any imbalances and then the program is executed again. This process is repeated until a satisfactory output is obtained.

Output Reports   The various data that flow from the MRP system are combined into reports that focus on these questions: (1) What items should be ordered and when? (2) what items should be expedited? (3) what orders can be cancelled? (4) when can deliveries be stretched out? and (5) when can the customer be realistically told the product will be received? As shown in exhibit 18-3, the reports from an MRP system can be classified as either primary or secondary.[8]

Primary reports are the main reports used for production, operations, and inventory control. The most frequently developed primary reports are:

- *Planned orders* to be released at a future time
- *Order release* forms to execute the planned orders
- *Changes in due dates* of open orders due to rescheduling
- *Cancellations or suspensions* of open orders
- *Inventory status* data.

Secondary or optional reports that can be generated by an MRP system include:

- *Planning reports* that can be used in forecasting inventory and specifying requirements over a particular time frame
- *Performance reports* to identify the existence of inactive items and determine the agreement between actual and programmed lead times and between actual and programmed usage and costs
- *Exceptions reports,* which identify serious errors such as late or overdue orders, excess scrap, or out-of-range operations.

Production and purchasing managers are the main beneficiaries of the output reports. The MRP does the detailed scheduling and monitoring to ensure that work is being completed on time. Priorities for purchases are maintained and can be used for changing due dates or quantities. Feedback from these two functions is important because it can be used to revise inputs into the MRP system.

Production Evaluation

Organizations frequently advertise product quality. We are confronted daily with claims of 99 and 44/100 percent pure Ivory Soap, seemingly indestructible Maytag products, the perpetual life of Volvo automobiles, and the "100 percent pure beef" used in hamburgers by many fast-food chains. Quality also has been one of the major rallying cries of environmental and consumer interest groups. These groups point to quality problems such as flammable clothing and harmful toys for children, cars that fall apart after only a few thousand miles, and manufacturing plants that pollute.

To the consumer, quality means that a product or service performs according to manufacturing claims or to the consumer's expectations. On the other hand, the production and quality control managers speak of quality in terms of the manner in which product specifications are met within certain cost constraints. For our purposes, quality is a characteristic of a product or service that determines its value in the market and how well it performs the function for which it was designed.

In most organizations, quality of a product is usually expressed in terms of a standard; therefore, the role of quality control is to ensure that there is an acceptable degree of conformity to the standards set for the product or service. Our discussion of quality control will be presented in three parts: the dimensions of quality control, types of quality control, and statistical quality control methods.

Dimensions of Quality Control

Product quality is viewed by most organizations as multidimensional. The frequently used dimensions of quality include the following:[9]

- *Function* refers to whether the product or service actually performed its purpose when put into use. Does a lightbulb work when placed in a socket? Does a new car achieve its designated MPG? Does the automatic-erasing capability of a typewriter function correctly?

- *Reliability and durability* refer to the length of time the product will perform its function. Will a new auto tire actually wear for over 50,000 miles? Will a spotlight last for 1000 hours of continual use? Even though the odometer of a Mercedes-Benz automobile can register to 999,999 miles, will the car last that long?

- *Aesthetic characteristics* concern the physical appearance of the product. Is the dining room table free of scratches and chips? Is the new dress in style? Does the shape and color of the new refrigerator fit with the decor of the kitchen?

- *Safety* refers to whether the product will perform its function without unnecessarily endangering the user. Does the microwave oven emit dangerous radiation? Does the new roofing material resist fire? Does the food product contain foreign material?

In responding to these quality dimensions, one of the most important parts of a manager's job is to balance the marketability of high-quality products with the costs of achieving this high quality. Contrary to certain claims, it is rare that a company can "produce the highest quality product at the lowest possible cost." High quality usually entails greater costs. For example, the average television set has an approximately eight-year service life. If a manufacturer offers a set that lasts twenty years but costs nearly 200 percent more, how many customers would be interested in buying? The price, which incorporates the extra costs for higher quality, may not only be out of the expected price range of the typical buyer, but in twenty years the technology used in the set may be obsolete.

Types of Quality Control

As an illustration, consider a brewing company such as Coors, Miller, or Anheuser-Busch. In producing a particular beer, the quality control manager at each of these companies is concerned with at least three different types of quality control.

First is concern for the quality of the input materials, sometimes called *feedforward* control. This type of quality control focuses on the quality of purchased materials (hops, grain, and so forth) and other raw materials (water). The objective is to inspect before costly operations have been conducted with materials that are defective.

The second type of quality control, also *feedforward,* is evaluation of the *work in process*. In a brewery, the quality of the product is checked before and after each of the ingredients is placed in the batch reactor. In the auto industry, the metal finish of new cars is checked for foreign matter or rough surfaces. Before clothing products are sent to branch stores, the distribution operation of department stores quality checks goods for defects. In hospital pathology laboratories, a standard blood, urine, or tissue sample is placed in the sample flow from time to time to check the accuracy of the equipment and techniques.

Finally, a quality check is made on the final product. Termed *output* quality control or *feedback* control, this type of quality control insures that the product satisfies the original design specifications. Brewers not only check the product as it is placed in barrels for storage, but from time to time the products are checked in storage to insure that the quality is maintained. In some organizations, another form of feedback quality control involves investigating and responding to customer quality complaints. A poor quality product can invite bad publicity and possibly lower sales. For example, recent surveys indicate that one reason U.S. customers purchase Japanese cars is the perception that they are better quality cars than their American counterparts. The problem for U.S. automakers is that while these perceptions may develop quickly, they can take a long time to change.

Statistical Quality Control

Since quality control implies the existence of a standard, that standard must be stated in some measurable terms if it is to be enforced. Measurement can be by variables or by certain attributes. *Variable* measurement usually involves some form of physical measurement—height, weight, diameter, tensile strength, and so on. For example, automobile tires are checked for tread width, tread depth, diameter, circumference, and weight.

An *attribute* approach ascertains whether some characteristic does or does not apply to a product. Examples include whether or not flights arrive within ten minutes of the scheduled arrival for airlines, all buttons are on each shirt for a clothing manufacturer, and digital watches perform correctly for Timex.

Variable and attribute measures can be used with a variety of statistical quality control procedures. Two of the most frequently used are acceptable sampling procedures and process control procedures.

Acceptance Sampling Procedures   Acceptance sampling is a quality control procedure used to predict the quality of a batch, stream, or large number of products by an inspection of a sample or samples from the larger production run. Many organizations prefer this procedure because: (1) from a cost perspective, it would be unrealistic to test each unit; (2) inspection of each unit may result in the destruction of that unit (one cannot take a bite out of each Big Mac, or test each G.E. flashbulb or each

The Manager's Job

William Lord of Crompton Company

To Bill Lord, head of Crompton Company, a New York-based manufacturer of corduroy and velveteen, success—and even survival—in the textile industry depends greatly on the efficiency of the production plant. With this emphasis on efficiency, coupled with an aggressive exporting strategy, Crompton is one textile company that has not been beaten to death by inexpensive imports.

Crompton's keys to success are three major strategies. First, to push the efficiency of its weaving equipment as far as possible, the company keeps the machines running 24 hours a day, 350 days a year. New export markets provide the customers who buy the extra output produced by the nonstop operations. Over one-third of Crompton's sales in the last three years came from overseas markets. In the textile industry, a plant running at 88 percent of capacity is considered inefficient—Crompton consistently operates over 92 percent.

Second, Lord determined that rising quality defects was more a people problem than a machine problem. Low pay and erratic work schedules created morale, absenteeism, and turnover problems which were themselves related to quality rejects approaching 10 percent of total production. To counter this trend, Crompton instituted a three-day, twelve-hour work schedule that gives the mill hands a full week off once every eight weeks. In addition, not only were pay rates increased, but to decrease absenteeism Lord paid a bonus for employees who stay on the job; they are paid for forty hours if they complete the required thirty-six. Labor turnover at Crompton is only 9 percent, an impressively low figure in an industry where the average rate is over 50 percent.

Third, Lord promotes the use of engineering—sometimes of the bubblegum and paper clip variety—to improve the efficiency of his equipment. Some of the results haven't been worth the effort. For instance, Crompton tried out a complicated new piece of equipment to replace the workers who change the bobbins on spinning machines; but, Lord noticed that the contraption had to be constantly attended by three engineers, so he got rid of it. On the positive side, Crompton's engineers were dissatisfied with a spring-steel blade machine used to cut the tiny grooves that give velveteen its plushness. The unit didn't keep a sharp edge, so the engineers substituted ordinary razor blades and got a 60 percent boost in efficiency.

Company-wide, the emphasis on productivity has yielded an annual increase of 8 percent in output per labor-hour since 1974. This is well above the average for the textile industry and more than five times the average for the U.S. labor force as a whole.

Adapted from Edward Meadows, "How Three Companies Increased Their Productivity," *Fortune* (March 10, 1980): 92-101.

match from the Diamond Match Company); and (3) sampling allows management to check the product's quality more quickly than if each unit were tested.

Different forms of acceptance sampling can occur within the same department. For example, at one of GM's four-cylinder engine plants, 400 engines are assembled per day. Acceptance sampling involves three stages: (1) each engine is visually inspected to see that all parts have been assembled; (2) approximately one-fourth of the engines are "hot tested"—actually started and allowed to run for a period of time; and (3) twice a day, an engine is totally disassembled by a quality control technician and checked for proper assembling and operating characteristics.

In nonmanufacturing, acceptance sampling is also used, but less widely than in manufacturing enterprises. Earlier, we mentioned how hospital laboratories use standard samples to check for equipment and operator accuracy. Many labs augment this with frequent double checking on a patient's sample. For example, the lab supervisor may ask a second technologist to perform the same blood analysis on a sample that was performed earlier. At insurance companies such as Prudential or State Farm, samples of newly written policies are checked by a quality control unit for accuracy. In retail stores, control managers frequently check random customer accounts for proper credit calculations and balances. In many of these organizations, the unit performing the acceptance sampling is within the internal audit department (see chapter 15).

Process Control Procedures Acceptance sampling can be used in feedforward and feedback types of quality control. Process control, on the other hand, focuses almost exclusively on testing products in process so that adjustments can be made to the production process itself before poor quality items are produced.

For example, consider a dinnerware manufacturing plant of Corning Glass. One of the many variable measures of quality control is the diameter of the plates as they leave the forming oven. Sampling is an integral part of process control here. Process control occurs as follows:

> Right in the center of the plant are three big sets of traffic lights hanging from the ceiling. A green light means a production line is running smoothly; amber advertises the fact that a line needs close supervision because defects (diameter of plates) were found in some of its dinnerware. Red is shutdown. The signals are regulated by quality inspectors, who used to check each plate, but who now take a sampling. The new method has led to better quality control. It is also much faster.[10]

The major tool of process control is a process control chart. An example for a Corning Ware dinner plate is shown in exhibit 18-4. The first step in using the chart is to establish quality standard for comparison. For a dinner plate, the diameter standard is set at 10.0 inches ± 0.05 inches. Next, the frequency of sampling is determined. If the oven produces 1000 plates per hour, a sample every fifteen minutes, or after each 250-plate unit has passed, would be an example. Finally, the results of the quality control checks are plotted on the control chart and analyzed. In the example chart, samples 4 and 7 would necessitate an amber warning light; sample 16 would result in a red light. All other samples would cause a green light to be shown.

Exhibit 18-4
Process Control
Chart for
Monitoring
Corning Dinner
Plates

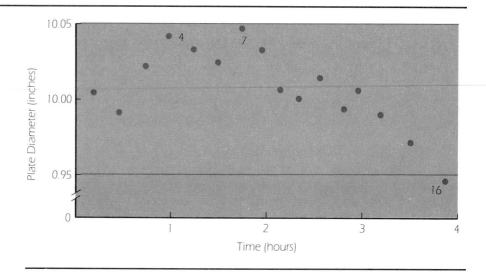

An Emphasis on Quality

American businesses, after years of relative inactivity, are reemphasizing the quality of their products and services to close the gap between American and Japanese companies that has existed for a number of years. American managers have come to see the direct relationship between product quality and profitability.

This emphasis on quality is taking many forms. Consider the following examples:[11]

▪ B. F. Goodrich Chemicals and United Technologies offer seminars in quality production and control to all managers, from the president on down.

▪ To combat Japanese inroads in the copier-duplicator market, Xerox began evaluating all facets of its production process, including the materials produced by suppliers. When suppliers could guarantee defect-free parts, they were awarded contracts. As a result, Xerox has reduced its vendors from 3000 to 500.

▪ Texas Instruments ranks its top 100 line executives by the quality of the products their operations turn out. This information is used to award pay increases and bonuses. Similarly, CBS Records uses product-quality data in its managerial promotion process.

▪ Many firms, including Carrier (maker of air conditioners), are using multifunctional teams to study and solve quality problems.

▪ By emphasizing quality production, National Semiconductor Corporation reduced the defect rate for computer chips forty times over.

▪ Statistical quality control methods have had an impact in the automobile industry. Ford reduced the number of defects per car by nearly 50 percent, while GM's Pontiac Division reduced scrap rate in engine manufacturing from 2 percent to 0.3 percent.

The drive for quality is aimed at restoring the prestige of U.S.-made products. From this, customer loyalty, effective competition against foreign firms, and sustained earnings and growth may result.

 # International Issues

With the growing importance of international trade and business, many organizations are taking a serious look at operating production facilities in other countries. This includes U.S. firms operating overseas and foreign organizations producing in the U.S. This chapter will discuss three major issues: plant acquisition or construction, site selection, and production design.

Plant Acquisition or Construction   If an organization decides to market products and services in another country, the decision of whether to construct a new production facility or to purchase an existing production plant must be made. For example, how important is it to acquire management, a labor force, or access to otherwise closed channels of distribution? As we have discussed, the availability of key managers and skilled labor is a significant problem in many countries. In addition, will acquisition allow early market entry? Will acquisition preempt purchase of facilities by a competing firm? Will construction allow the organization to build in the latest technological advances?[12]

The political factor is, in most cases, the most important. Past experience has shown that the acquisition of locally owned firms and their physical resources can generate more political problems than a decision to construct a new facility. Such countries as Canada, Japan, Australia, France, and the United Kingdom have exhibited opposition to takeovers by U.S. firms. The reverse is also true. If a foreign firm is a member of a cartel, U.S. antitrust laws may become a factor. Restraint of trade must also be considered. For example, when British Petroleum acquired a significant interest in Sohio, the U.S. Justice Department looked carefully at whether the acquisition would adversely affect competition in this country.

Beyond government resistance to foreign takeovers, an equally important factor is the price set by the owner for the organization. The demand for the foreign operation coupled with the nontaxation of capital gains in some countries has created an inflated price for acquisition. Because of these and other issues, the movement is more toward construction of new facilities rather than acquisition. However, construction is fraught with problems.

Site Selection   Once the decision has been made to construct production or service facilities in another country, management can concern itself with site selection. One of the first issues that must be confronted is the slowness of governmental bureaucracies. Since most land acquisitions require governmental approval—especially if the land is owned by the state, as it often is—the organization may be in for a long wait. For example, it may take as long as a year to acquire a site in Indonesia. Rarely can this process be speeded up, so management must build this time into their plans.

The actual selection process varies by organization and country. Exhibit 18-5 gives a simple evaluation scheme, which presents a weighting scheme for seven important variables. Of the six sites analyzed, A, E, and F would be worth investigating further for legal, engineering, and economic feasibility.

One of the major drawbacks of such an analysis is that in many countries markets can change rapidly. Power, resources, community development, and environmental issues can develop at a rate much faster than in the U.S. For example, the recent concern over the pollution of the Mediterranean Sea has forced many countries to revise their environmental regulations for facilities that border the sea or are located on rivers that discharge into it.

The key for managers is to consider site evaluation and selection as a *dynamic* as opposed to a *static* process. Evaluation must be conducted continuously, so sensitive issues can be identified early.

Production Design   The production design decision in foreign operations must consider the type of equipment and the local labor environment and determine the desired balance between machine skill and labor skill, given relative capital and labor costs. In other words, if only low-skilled labor is available, should the organization invest in highly automated equipment? Or, if skilled labor can be hired, is it better to use multipurpose equipment that requires this type of labor? Managers must recognize that automated equipment generally requires long production runs to bring down unit costs, while multipurpose equipment requires closer quality control, which in many developing countries is hard to come by.

To illustrate the need to adapt to the local environment, consider the following two examples. In the oil-producing Middle Eastern countries, there is a high percentage of low-skilled labor. Because of this, many of the oil companies have opted for highly specialized, narrowly defined jobs, thereby simplifying employee training. With a

Exhibit 18-5
Site Selection for an International Facility

Criteria	Maximum Value Assigned	Sites					
		A	B	C	D	E	F
Living conditions	100	70	40	45	50	60	60
Accessibility	75	55	35	20	60	70	70
Industrialization	60	40	50	55	35	35	30
Labor availability	35	30	10	10	30	35	35
Economics	35	15	15	15	15	25	25
Community capability and attitude	30	25	20	10	15	25	15
Effect on company reputation	35	25	20	10	15	25	15
Total	370	260	180	165	225	280	265

Source: E. S. Groo, "Choosing Foreign Locations: One Company's Experience," *Columbia Journal of World Business* (September-October 1971): 77.

few highly skilled troubleshooters, automated equipment can be used effectively. In Western Europe, on the other hand, Gillette decided to use multipurpose equipment with the available skilled work force.[13]

Success in international business requires a careful balance between volume, labor, and capital equipment costs. This further emphasizes the importance of an effective link between an organization's planning and control systems.

Aids in Production and Operations Control

Four techniques, based on the foundations of the management science school (see chapters 2, 6, and 7), have been successfully applied in many production and operations control activities. These are economic order quantity models (EOQ), program evaluation and review technique (PERT), linear programming, and queuing models.

A detailed discussion of each decision-aid technique is beyond the scope of this book. We have, however, selected one well-used technique for each of the four application areas.

Economic Order Quantity (EOQ)

Managers in all types of organizations are often faced with the problem of maintaining adequate inventories. A hospital is concerned with supplies of blood plasma, a clothing store with sweaters and pants, a grain elevator with wheat, or an Internal Revenue office with forms. Managers must minimize the costs of maintaining the inventory without jeopardizing service to the customer, client, or patient.

The inventory decision problem involves at least two fundamental issues—the size of the order and the point at which this order should be placed.[14] The main factors that determine the responses to these issues are two cost calculations, order cost and carrying cost.

Order cost refers to all the costs of procuring the material for the inventory. These costs, incurred each time an order is placed, include expenses for time needed to prepare bids and evaluate cost estimates, clerical expenses, telephone costs, and transportation expenses.

Carrying costs of an item include physical storage, interest, taxes, insurance, spoilage, and internal handling. An exact figure for carrying costs is difficult to determine. Since these costs generally vary in direct proportion to the price paid for the item, most organizations express carrying costs as a percentage of the total price paid during some period.

Consider the case of Robinson Machine Company, a manufacturer of commercial business machines. For its large business calculator, the company purchases a total of 20,000 keyboards per year to be used in the final assembly of the product. The cost for each order is $1000, while the purchase price for the keyboards is $40 per unit. The

Exhibit 18-6
Inventory Cost
Analysis

No. Orders Placed	Order Quantity	Order Costs ($1000)	Carrying Costs (25 Percent)	Total Costs
1	20,000	$ 1,000	$100,000	$100,000
2	10,000	2,000	50,000	52,000
4	5,000	4,000	25,000	29,000
8	2,500	8,000	12,500	20,500
16	1,250	16,000	6,250	22,250
20	1,000	20,000	5,000	25,000

inventory manager has determined that the inventory carrying cost for the keyboards is 25 percent of the inventory value. Exhibit 18-6 presents an analysis relating orders, quantities per order, and the various costs.

To minimize inventory costs, the manager must minimize both ordering and carrying costs by ordering the keyboards in just the right balance—the *economic order quantity* (EOQ). However, as the number of orders increases, ordering costs increase while carrying costs decrease. This relationship is shown in exhibit 18-7.

To calculate the order quantity that will minimize inventory costs, managers can use two methods. First, they can use the information shown in exhibit 18-7 to determine that the economic order quantity is somewhere between 2500 and 1250 units and 9 and 12 orders per year. The visual method is acceptable in simple cases; however, when inventory costs run into the hundreds of thousands of dollars, a more precise method of determining EOQ is desirable.

Exhibit 18-7
Inventory Cost
Relationships

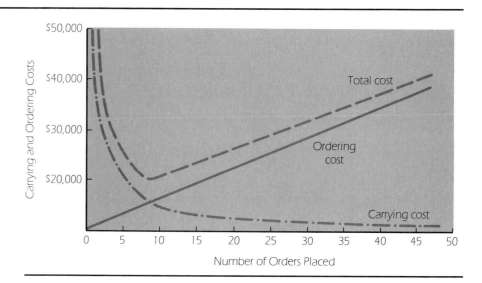

A more precise means of determining the EOQ is to derive it algebraically. To begin with, we can describe the various factors in the calculation as follows:

D = total annual demand for the keyboards = 20,000 units
Q = quantity per order
O = ordering costs = $1000 per unit
V = value of the item = $40 per unit
C = carrying costs, expressed as a percentage of average inventory
      value = 25 percent

If we assume a constant rate of inventory usage, then the average quantity in inventory at any one time is half the order quantity, or $Q/2$. If we also note that the relationships are linear, then setting carrying costs equal to ordering costs, we get:

$$\frac{Q}{2}(V)(C) = \frac{D}{Q}\ (O)$$

Solving for Q yields:

$$Q = \sqrt{\frac{2DO}{(VC)}}$$

This final equation is commonly known as the EOQ formula and can be used to solve our business machine keyboard problem. Using the collected data, we get:

$$Q = \sqrt{\frac{2(20,000)\ (\$1000)}{(\$40)\ (0.25)}} = \sqrt{\frac{\$40,000,000}{\$10}} = \sqrt{4,000,000} = 2000 \text{ units}$$

By using formula, we can see that with an EOQ of 2000 units, the optimum number of orders per year is ten, which is a more precise calculation.

Although the simplicity of this method is attractive, note that two of the most important inputs into the equation are *estimates*—demand and carrying costs. A slight variation in either variable can dramatically change the calculation. Shortages, seasonal variations, transportation problems, and cost changes all must be monitored carefully.

Program Evaluation and Review Technique (PERT)

During the late 1950s the U.S. Navy was faced with the crucial task of developing and deploying the Polaris ballistic missile program for our submarine fleet. This was no small task, since time and coordination were of prime concern. On one hand was the need to make the missile fleet operational as soon as possible. On the other hand, completion of the program would require coordination among 250 prime contractors, over 9000 subcontractors, and many thousands of individuals. To accomplish this task, the Navy developed a network planning technique known as Program Evaluation and Review Technique—PERT for short.[15] Not only did PERT help the Navy put the Polaris missile fleet into operation two years ahead of schedule, but since then many other projects, both within and outside the armed services, have adopted PERT in their planning programs.

PERT is termed a network planning model because it deals with a series of inter-related steps and activities. The key objective of the technique is to complete a project with a high degree of coordination. PERT facilitates the planning function through controlling the element of time, and, in some cases, cost.

Consider the problem of introducing a new consumer product into the market. Past experience has shown that such a venture requires the planning and coordination of at least the organization's manufacturing and marketing functions. The PERT analysis of this problem is shown in exhibits 18-8 and 18-9. The process elements of PERT are as follows:

Define events and activities. An activity is defined in terms of the time and resources required to complete a specific task. An event is the actual completion of that task. As shown in exhibit 18-8, activity 1—modifying the manufacturing plant—results in event A—completion of plant modifications.

Develop the PERT network. The activities and events are ordered in terms of occurrence—that is, G must happen before H. Wherever possible, two or more activities can occur at the same time. For example, while quality control procedures are being developed (activity 4), the plant work force can be trained (activity 5). As noted in exhibit 18-8, the result is a network of activities and events.

Exhibit 18-8
Activities, Events, and Expected Time of PERT

Activity		Event		Optimistic	Most Likely	Pessimistic	t_e
						Time	
1	Modify plant	A	Plant complete	18	24	30	24
2	Design packaging	B	Packaging design complete	5	8	11	8
3	Acquire raw materials	C	Raw materials received	2	3	4	3
4	Develop quality controls	D	Quality control complete	1	3	5	3
5	Train work force	E	Work force trained	3	4	6	4
6	Study price	F	Price set	1	2	3	2
7	Production trials	G	Plant ready	3	6	9	6
8	Study product specs	H	Set product specs	1	1	1	1
9	Develop promotion plan	I	Promotion set	3	4	6	4
10	Finalize packaging	J	Package set	1	2	3	2
11	Produce inventory	K	Inventory ready	1	3	6	3
12	Train sales force	L	Sales force ready	4	8	12	8
13	Study transportation	M	Transportation ready	1	1	1	1
14	Seek customer orders	N	Customer orders ready	2	4	6	4
15	Prepare shipments	O	Shipments prepared	1	2	3	2
16	Finalize shipments	P	Ship	1	1	1	1

Exhibit 18-9
PERT Network for Introducing a New Product

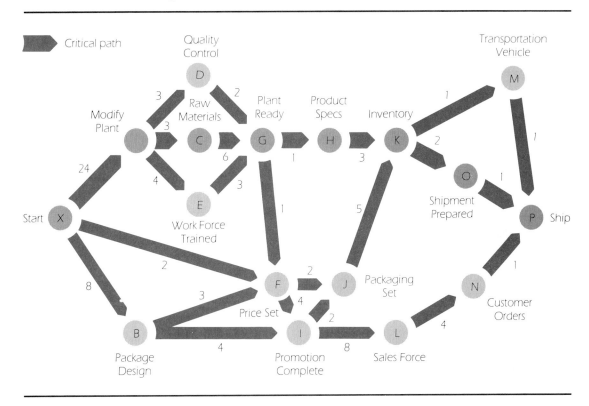

Estimate the time required between events. The third step is to estimate the time required to perform an activity, resulting in the occurrence of an event. Three time estimates are prepared: (a) *optimistic* or minimum time for completion, (b) *most likely* time for completion, and (c) *pessimistic* or maximum time for completion. The three time estimates are combined to compute the expected time *(t_e)*, which is a more realistic time estimate since it is based on three estimations, not one. Expected time is computed with the following equation, which is based on a Beta distribution:

$$\frac{\text{Optimistic} + 4 \text{ (Most likely)} + \text{Pessimistic}}{6} = t_e$$

Exhibit 18-8 shows the optimistic, most likely, pessimistic, and expected time for each activity.

Identify the critical path. The critical path in a PERT network is the series of activities and events that results in the *longest* time to complete the project. It is termed the critical path because a delay in completing any of the activities will result in a delay of the entire project. For our example, the critical path is the following:

A-C-G-H-K-O-P, which requires forty weeks for completion. In other words, this path is the most appropriate time network in which the project can be completed.

Slack time. The slack time in a particular network is the amount of *extra* time that can be spent without delaying the entire project. For example, the slack times for three of the many networks in exhibit 18-9 are:

A-D-G-H-K-O-P	(40 weeks − 36 weeks = 4 weeks slack time)
B-I-L-N-P	(40 weeks − 25 weeks = 15 weeks slack time)
F-J-K-O-P	(40 weeks − 12 weeks = 28 weeks slack time)

Slack time allows management to "fine tune" particular activities until they are at their optimum value.

Evaluation of PERT   Since its introduction about twenty-five years ago, applications of PERT have grown significantly. Uses can be found not only in plant construction and new product development, but in research and development programs, maintenance projects, development of new processes, or other complex projects with many interrelated and interdependent activities. In some cases, certain federal agencies doing business with contractors require them to plan with PERT.

PERT has several advantages. First, it draws attention to ways of preventing delays in projects. The manager must think in terms of time, cost, and interrelationships of events. Second, slack time allows the manager to divert resources to critical areas without endangering the project's progress. Finally, PERT has proven to be an excellent communications tool among managers. It provides a way of better communicating the roles of managers and subordinates involved in a project. And there is the intangible benefit of being able to provide a clear and easily understood picture of the entire project to everyone involved.

Three points of caution should be made regarding PERT. First, PERT is only as good as the information used to develop the network. Thus, managers should evaluate their estimates of time, the interrelationships among events, and so on. Second, any reallocation of resources from slack time adjustments may actually change the critical path. Finally, many of the PERT networks being developed today are far more complicated than our example. Computer usage may become a necessity, as such complex networks are beyond the skills of one person to develop or manipulate.

Linear Programming

Consider a problem faced by your author when he worked as a manufacturing manager in a chemical plant. One area of his responsibility was the production of two pigment-type products, one used in the manufacture of paper products (X_1), and the other in the manufacture of paints (X_2). The two products, which are silica based, are essentially the same, except the product used in the manufacture of paper contains less water.

Three production stages are required for each product—chemical reaction, drying, and packaging. The chemical reaction time for each 100 pounds of product is identical for X_1 and X_2; however, X_1 takes longer in the drying stage and requires slightly more time to package. Because of limited production capacities at the three stages, the

Exhibit 18-10 Manufacturing Data	**Minutes Required Per 100-Pound Units**		
Manufacturing Process Stages	**Product X_1**	**Product X_2**	**Total Minutes Available/Day**
Chemical reaction	6	6	960
Drying	8	4	720
Packaging	5	4	600

products are given only a certain number of minutes per day in each stage. Product X_1 contributes \$40 profit per 100 pounds sold, while X_2 contributes \$30 per 100 pounds. These data are shown in exhibit 18-10. The problem for the manufacturing manager is to allocate the production equipment within the production time constraints, such that profit is maximized.

This problem can be solved using a *linear programming model*.[16] Linear programming is a method that has the purpose of maximizing a goal such as profits, or minimizing a goal such as costs, within certain constraints. The model is termed *linear* because the variables under study are directly and precisely proportional to each other. The linear programming model is particularly useful when the manager must find an optimal way to allocate scarce or limited resources to achieve a goal.

In developing a linear programming model to solve our manufacturing example, two factors need to be discussed:

Objective function. The objective or goal of our example is to maximize profits for the two products within the time constraints of the production equipment. Mathematically, this can be expressed as:

$$\text{Maximize Profit } (P) = \$40 \ (X_1) + \$30 \ (X_2)$$

In other words, we need to determine what combination of production of products X_1 and X_2 (in 100-pound units) will yield the highest profits.

Constraining functions. As expressed in the example, there are a number of constraining factors. First, there are time constraints associated with each production stage—chemical reaction, drying, and packaging. Mathematically, these constraints can be shown as follows (note: $\leq$ means "less than or equal to"):

$$6X_1 + 6X_1 \leq 960 \text{ minutes (chemical reaction stage)}$$
$$8X_1 + 4X_2 \leq 720 \text{ minutes (drying stage)}$$
$$5X_1 + 4X_2 \leq 600 \text{ minutes (packaging stage)}$$

where X_1 and X_2 stand for the amount of product—in 100-pound units—that can be manufactured.

Since it is required that an amount of each product must be produced, this acts as another constraining function. This can be expressed as follows (note: $>$ means "greater than"): $X_1 > 0, X_2 > 0$.

An easy way of solving simple problems is with graphs. The solution is shown in exhibit 18-11. The graphical solution to the problem requires two steps:

Exhibit 18-11
Linear
Programming
Graphical Solution

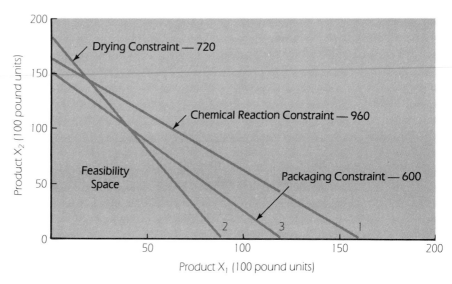

Graph constraining functions. Each of the first three constraining functions can be graphed through a simple process. For example, if we take the drying stage function, the process is as follows:

$$8X_1 + 4X_2 = 720$$

Setting X_1 equal to 0, we get:

$$8(0) + 4X_2 = 720$$

or X_2 equals 180 100-pound production units. Similarly, setting X_2 equal to 0, we get:

$$8X_1 + 4(0) = 720$$

or, X_1 equals ninety 100-pound units. This result is then plotted on the graph shown in exhibit 18-11.

Using a similar methodology we can solve and plot the linear relationships for the other two constraint functions.

Solve for maximum point. The possible solutions to this production problem are contained within the shaded area bounded by the linear constraining functions. This is called the "feasibility space or polygon." The maximum profit will occur at the extreme point of the feasibility space. Visually, this point is located at $X_1 = 40$ and $X_2 = 100$.

We can also solve the problem mathematically without a graph. Since the first constraining function does not enter into the solution, we can solve the remaining equations simultaneously by (a) multiplying the third function by -1 and adding the functions together:

$$(8X_1 + 4X_2 = 720) = 8X_1 + 4X_2 = 720 \quad \text{Drying function}$$

$$-1(5X_1 + 4X_2 = 600) = \underline{5X_1 + 4X_2 = 600} \quad \text{Packaging function}$$

$$3X_1 \qquad = 120 \quad \text{or } \underline{X_1 = 40}$$

(b) substituting 40 for X_1 in the third function

$$5(40) + 4X_2 = 600$$

$$4X_2 = 400 \quad \text{or} \quad \underline{X_2 = 100}$$

(c) returning to the objective function and substituting the values for X_1 and X_2

$$\text{Maximum Profit} = \$40(40) + \$30(100) = \$4600$$

The net result is if we produce 4000 pounds of product X_1 (or 40 100-pound units) and 10,000 pounds of product X_2 (or 100 100-pound units), the company can make a total of $4600 profit per day on production.

These graphical and mathematical solutions are special cases of the *general* simplex method of linear programming. For more complicated problems involving more than four constraints, it is necessary to use the *iterative* simplex method. This mathematical method begins with identifying an initial solution that satisfies all the constraints. Modifications are made to the initial solution and incorporated into a second feasible solution. This is repeated until the maximum solution is found. In other words, each step or iteration brings us closer to the final solution.

Uses of Linear Programming   Linear programming can be used in most situations where limited resources must be allocated to optimize some objective function. The objective functions can maximize profits, minimize costs, and so on. Uses of linear programming include product mix problems, minimizing transportation costs of shipping products from warehouses to customers, assigning personnel to projects, and allocating limited advertising funds to different products.

Queuing Models

Consider an airline reservations desk with several ticket agents, a bank with a number of teller positions, an automobile service station with several gas pumps, or a supermarket with a number of checkout counters. What these facilities have in common is that each provides service to a customer who demands the service at random times. When customers arrive to find all the service activities busy, they join a waiting line, or *queue*. For the manager, these situations involve two opposing costs—the cost of providing service and the cost of waiting for service. The decision to be made is how to minimize these costs while providing effective service.

Queuing problems have different levels of complexity. Exhibit 18-12 shows four examples of structural configurations of queuing systems, as defined by the type of service facility. Beyond the structural complexity of the servicing unit, queuing systems can vary along several dimensions. The most important include the following:[17]

■ *Population source.* The servicing population can be *finite*, such as employees using an elevator in a large building, or *infinite*, such as people attending a concert.

Exhibit 18-12
Different Queuing Model Structures

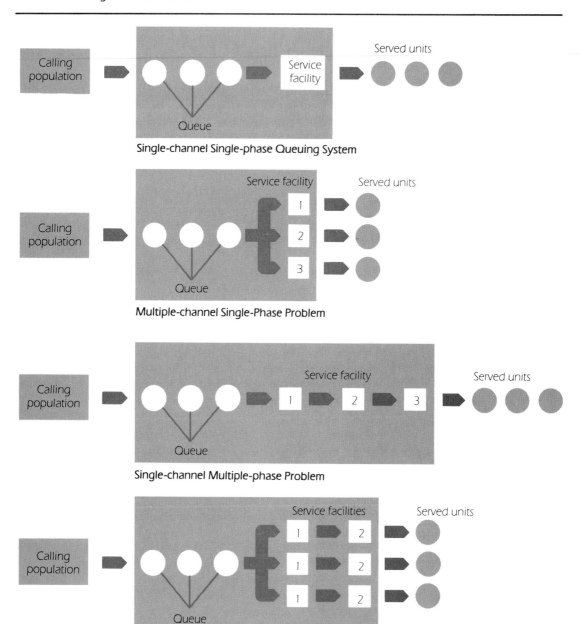

Single-channel Single-phase Queuing System

Multiple-channel Single-Phase Problem

Single-channel Multiple-phase Problem

Multiple-channel Multiple-phase Problem

Source: Herbert L. Lyon, John M. Ivancevich, and James H. Donnelley, *Management Science in Organizations* (Glenview, Ill.: Scott, Foresman, 1976), pp. 286-87.

▪ *Arrival characteristics.* Variations of arrival characteristics can include *pattern* (controllable, such as students going to lunch in an elementary school, or uncontrollable, such as the use of a refreshment stand at a football game), *size of arrival* (single, as cars through a car wash, or batch, such as passengers walking onto an airplane), *time of arrival* (constant, as on an assembly line, or random, such people entering an emergency room), and *degree of patience* (patient, such as trucks waiting to be unloaded, or impatient, as in waiting to cash a check during lunch hour).

▪ *Physical features of the queue.* The features of the queue can vary by *length* (infinite, as in waiting for gas for a car, or finite, such as patients in a physician's office) and *number* (single lines, such as golfers waiting to tee off at the first tee, or multiple, such as placing an order at McDonald's).

▪ *Selection from the queue.* A number of possibilities exist, including *first come, first serve* (checkout counter in a supermarket) or reservations and emergencies first (a restaurant or a hospital emergency room).

▪ *Service rate.* The service rate can vary at a *constant* rate, as in a car wash, or by some *mathematical* function, such as customers leaving cars off for repair.

▪ *Exit characteristics.* Once a customer or unit is serviced, it can have a low probability of *reservice,* as in a toll station on a turnpike, or a certain frequency of reservice, such as an aircraft scheduled for maintenance.

As one might discern, the development and analysis of queuing systems can become a complex activity. Consider the truck unloading dock in a large manufacturing firm. One crew of four employees is responsible for unloading incoming trucks, which are bringing in raw materials to be used in production. As shown in exhibit 18-12, this system may be considered a single-channel, single-phase queuing system. Assume that members of the unloading crew are each paid $6 per hour, with an overtime rate of one and one-half the normal pay scale. The truck drivers earn $10 per hour. During the normal day shift (8 a.m. to 4 p.m.), trucks can be unloaded at a constant rate of thirty minutes per truck, but the trucks are arriving at a constant rate of one every twenty minutes.

The manager of shipping and receiving is concerned with the costs of this arrangement. This is apparent since sixteen trucks can be unloaded per eight-hour shift, but a total of twenty-four trucks have arrived, and to service the trucks, a considerable amount of overtime has been paid.

An analysis of this problem using queuing models can proceed as follows. Assume that the first truck arrives at 8 a.m. and is unloaded by 8:30 a.m. with no excess wait time. The second truck arrives at 8:20 a.m. and is unloaded by 9 a.m., with thirty minutes of unloading time and ten minutes of waiting in the queue. Continuing, the sixteenth truck arrives at 1 p.m. but is not unloaded until 4 p.m., resulting in a thirty-minute unloading time, but a three-and-one-half-hour wait (assume that unloading continues through the lunch hour with a replacement unloading crew). Finally, the twenty-fourth truck arrives at 3:40 p.m., but does not leave until 8 p.m. The unloading time is still thirty minutes, but the queue wait is three hours and forty minutes, plus overtime for the unloading crew.

Exhibit 18-13
Queuing Cost Analysis

Unloading Crews	Regular Unloading Costs ($6/Hr × 4 Persons)	Overtime Unloading Costs ($9/Hr × 4 Persons)	Regular Truckers Costs ($10/Hr)	Excess Trucker Wait Costs ($10/Hr)	Total Costs
One crew	$192	$144	$120	$455	$911
One-and-one-half crews	$288	$0	$120	$0	$408

Mathematically, the manager can calculate the amount of time in minutes that the truck drivers spend in the queue as:

$$\sum_{i = 2,24}^{N} [(n_1 - 2)10 + 40]$$

where n_i is the arrival number of the truck.

Since the first truck has no time in the queue, twenty-three trucks incur an amount of waiting time during the regular shift plus overtime. The calculation reveals a total of 3450 minutes, or 57.5 hours total time in the queue for the truck drivers. Since 12 hours (24 trucks times 30 minutes) is allocated for unloading, a total of 45.5 accumulated hours are incurred by the drivers in waiting to be unloaded. A cost analysis of this problem, shown in exhibit 18-13, indicates that $911 is paid out by the organization in wages for the unloading crew and truck drivers. Of this amount, $599 or 65 percent is spent for problems due to queue time and overtime for the unloading crew.

As shown in exhibit 18-13, a solution to the cost problem is to use a second unloading crew to work half-time on the loading dock and the other half on the unloading side. With a second crew, the costs are $408, a significant reduction from the original situation.

The example, while simple, is not unlike many queuing problems experienced by managers in organizations. In more complicated situations, the use of complex equations may be necessary. More elaborate queuing models become fairly cumbersome and difficult to develop and understand. In such cases, a different aid, such as simulation, may provide better information.

 POINTS TO CONSIDER
An Emphasis on Managerial Skills

1. **Production and operations control is most effective when it has been integrated into the other organizational systems.**
   As is the case for MIS, production and operations control needs to be fully integrated into the organization to be fully effective. A "tacked-on" production and operations control system will make it seem not much more than a "police" function. Managers in this area need to be consulted frequently throughout the entire management process.

2. **Production criteria should be broad in scope.**

   Many production and operations managers believe that their main objective is to produce a product or service at the lowest possible cost. This may be fine, but managers must remember that such a product or service may have characteristics that are not desired by the consumer. A much more appropriate objective is to produce a product that satisfies the needs of the consumer and can be produced within an acceptable cost range.

3. **International environments require careful planning.**

   It is important to bear in mind that an organization cannot totally transfer production equipment, technology, and knowledge to an operation in another country without significant adjustments. Countries differ not only in cultures, but in size of markets, governmental processes and laws, availability of labor, and so on. Successful production and operations control clearly requires an emphasis on front-end planning to adjust to these national differences.

4. **Quality products and services generally improve competitiveness.**

   Many foreign manufacturers, particularly the Japanese, gained a strong foothold in the U.S. market during the last two decades through the sale of high quality products. American managers, recognizing the value of quality to their overall productivity, are again making efforts into improving quality, and the initial results are encouraging.

5. **Use diagnostic skills in analyzing production activities.**

   Identifying production problems involves a number of different methods, including simple observation. Observing with an eye to correct idle or broken-down equipment, parts and materials stored in aisles, lack of cleanliness throughout the plant, slow repair by maintenance crews, or excessive absenteeism can be just as effective as using the most sophisticated computer program or management science model.

6. **The production manager's job involves key decisional roles.**

   While each managerial role is important to the production manager's job, none is more central to performance than decisional roles. As a resource allocator, the manager must allocate scarce physical and human resources to crucial production activities. He or she must be a negotiator in representing management in labor interactions, act as a disturbance handler when transmitting control data to other functional managers, and frequently, perform an entrepreneurial function when attempting to improve the various stages of the production process.

 # SUMMARY FOR THE MANAGER

1. Production and operations control, sometimes referred to as production and operations management (POM) is the point at which planning, organizing, leading, and control come together. The four major elements of production and operations control are selection, production design, production planning, and production evaluation.

2. One of the major components of production design is facility layout—the overall arrangement of equipment, people, materials, storage, and service operations required to produce a product or service. The three main layout patterns—process, product, and fixed position—differ in their keys to success. The process layout is a flexible pattern that requires complex materials flow, storage, and production scheduling, along with a high percentage of highly skilled workers. Because of the sequential nature of a product layout, the balancing of production systems is of prime importance. Finally, the fixed-position layout requires a large work area that places a high degree of emphasis on material flow and availability.

3. One of the fastest-growing approaches to production planning is material requirements planning (MRP). It is a computer-based approach to scheduling that integrates information forecasts of demand, product specifications, and inventory data to produce output reports that can help in material purchases, inventories, and capacity planning, along with a stream of important control data.

4. Quality control is one of the main functions of production evaluation. Quality control pervades the entire production process in manufacturing and nonmanufacturing organizations alike. Quality control involves all three types of management controls: input (inspecting incoming raw materials and equipment); process (evaluating work-in-process); and output (checking the quality of the final product).

5. The measurement of quality can involve evaluation by variable or by attribute. The former concerns some form of physical measurement and the latter involves the presence or absence of some characteristic. Acceptance sampling and process control charts are two of the most frequently used statistical control methods.

6. Four popular quantitative aids in production and operations control were presented. EOQ attempts to minimize inventory costs by investigating the size and cost of an order along with what time an order should be placed. PERT is a technique that has been extensively used in both planning and control functions. As a network model, it develops the best approach to project completion by analyzing the time needed at each stage of the project. Linear programming has been frequently used in resource allocation decisions where knowledge of certain constraints is critical. Finally, queuing models focus on scheduling and sequencing decisions that concern how the waiting times of units, equipment, or people are managed in the production process.

7. Production and operations in foreign countries requires an analysis of the potential differences that may exist in such areas as site selection, production design, and construction versus acquisition. Careful and detailed planning is needed before operating and control decisions are made.

 # REVIEW AND DISCUSSION QUESTIONS

1. What is the difference between production design and production planning?
2. Why do managers and economists look at aggregate inventory figures as a sign of an upcoming recession?
3. What is the difference between PERT and MRP?
4. What elements should the manager be concerned with in international site selection?
5. Identify the keys to success for each of the three facility layout patterns.
6. What is the relationship between master production scheduling and MRP?
7. What are the differences between feedforward and feedback control?
8. List some products for which you would insist on a 100-percent quality inspection.
9. How can an airline company use production and operations control to select a particular aircraft—757 or DC-9— for a route?
10. In a bank, where is inventory control important? In a hospital?

NOTES

1. See R. B. Chase and N. J. Acquilano, *Production and Operations Management* (Homewood, Ill.: Irwin, 1977), p. 31; and R. Stobaugh and P. Telesio, "Match Manufacturing Policies and Product Strategy," *Harvard Business Review* (March-April 1983): 113-20.

2. E. Meadows, "How Three Companies Increased Their Productivity," *Fortune* (March 10, 1980): 92-101.

3. Chase and Acquilano, *Production and Operations Management*, pp. 157-58; and R. L. Francis and J. A. White, *Facility Layout and Location: An Analytical Approach* (Englewood Cliffs, N. J.: Prentice-Hall, 1974).

4. See E. W. Davis, ed., *Case Studies in Materials Requirements Planning* (Washington, D.C.: APICS, 1978); and J. Orlicky, *Material Requirements Planning* (New York: McGraw-Hill, 1975).

5. See D. Gervin, "Do's and Don'ts of Computerized Manufacturing," *Harvard Business Review* (March-April 1982): 107-16; and J. G. Miller and L. G. Sprague, "Behind the Growth in Materials Requirements Planning," *Harvard Business Review* (September-October 1975): 83-91.

6. See R. W. Hall and T. E. Vollmann, "Planning Your Material Requirements," *Harvard Business Review* (September-October 1978): 115-21; and J. D. W. Morecroft, "A Systems Perspective on Material Requirements Planning," *Decision Sciences* (January 1983): 1-18.

7. "An Unemployment Wallop," *Time* (May 12, 1980): 54-55.

8. Chase and Acquilano, *Production and Operations Management,* p. 425; and J. G. Miller, "Fit Production Systems to the Task," *Harvard Business Review* (January-February 1981): 145-54.

9. See W. L. Berry, T. E. Vollmann, and D. C. Whybark, *Master Production Scheduling* (Washington, D.C.: APICS, 1979); and H. E. Fearon, W. A. Ruch, P. G. Decker, V. G. Reuter, and C. D. Wieters, *Fundamentals of Production/Operations Management* (St. Paul, Minn.: West, 1979), p. 141.

10. Meadows, "How Three Companies Increased Their Productivity," p. 94.

11. "Quality: The U.S. Drives To Catch-Up," *Business Week* (November 1, 1982): 66-80.

12. See S. Mosca, "Changing Approaches to Plant Location in Europe," *Worldwide P&I Planning* (September-October 1967); and R. D. Robinson, *International Business Management* (Hinsdale, Ill.: Dryden, 1973), p. 143.

13. J. Baranson, "Automated Manufacturing in Developing Economies," *Finance and Development,* vol. 8, no. 4 (1971): 12-17.

14. See R. G. Brown, *Decision Rules for Inventory Management* (New York: Holt, Rinehart & Winston, 1967).

15. R. E. Schellenberger, *Managerial Analysis* (Homewood, Ill.: Irwin, 1969), p. 313.

16. See R. I. Lewin and R. Lamone, *Linear Programming for Management Decisions* (Homewood, Ill.: Irwin, 1969); and H. M. Wagner, *Principles of Operations Research* (Englewood Cliffs, N.J.: Prentice-Hall, 1975).

17. H. L. Lyon, J. M. Ivancevich, and J. H. Donnelly, *Management Science in Organizations* (Glenview, Ill.: Scott, Foresman, 1976), ch. 12.

A CASE FOR ANALYSIS

Production and Operations Control
Maytag

Mention the name Maytag to a group of people and most times the word "quality" comes to mind first. A growing number of consumers clearly believe in the superiority of Maytag appliances, which have won wider market shares in recent years. The most complicated product, the automatic clothes washer, commands a premium of roughly $70 at retail. Its sales are only one-fourth as large as Whirlpool, the major competitor. However, Maytag's return on equity of over 25 percent is nearly 50 percent more than Whirlpool.

Many people deserve laurels for Maytag's performance, not least its management team who exalts quality and abhors wasteful model changes, and a research department that quietly goes on modifying product designs "under the hood" to lessen vibration, wear, and breakdown. The chief defender of Maytag's reputation, however, is the man in charge of turning laboratory prototypes and books of specifications into gleaming appliances mass-produced at a rate of hundreds per hour. Appliances that will perform so well in millions of homes that at least some Maytag repairmen will really lead the lonely lives celebrated in television commercials. That crucial person is Maytag's vice president for manufacturing, Sterling Swanger.

Swanger puts on no airs and sits in a windowless office with desk drawers full of gears and other appliance innards that looks like that of someone two levels further down in the organization. He is a manager of great staying power who can gently monitor, decide, or put the pressure on, if necessary.

Swanger has held the line on quality in an era of widespread temptation to do otherwise. Like many appliance makers, in fact, Maytag is producing a more reliable machine than ever. In the mid-1950s, when the company's late president, Fred Maytag II, laid down a standard of ten years' trouble-free operation, the company's average automatic clothes washer was three years short of the target. Today, grueling "lifetime" tests show a typical machine leaving the loading platform should run fourteen years without serious trouble.

At the same time, the manufacturing division has chipped away at production costs. The plastic top of the water pump in a clothes washer, for example, was formerly put in place with thirteen screws, now it is quickly sealed with the application of heat. In 1979, the division beat its goal of $4 million worth of money-saving changes in methods and materials. Such savings, of course, cannot make up for the ever-rising prices of purchased materials or for increases in wages. Along with Frigidaire, Maytag has the highest wages in the industry.

Maytag's Newton, Iowa production plant, with extensive automation and twenty-five miles of overhead conveyors, is awesomely intricate and vulnerable to stoppage at dozens of points. But Swanger has the plant running with the dependability of—well, a Maytag washer. The worst production loss in the past three years occurred when a freak accident in a big press forced a brief four-hour shutdown of the clothes washer line.

The Iowa location is fertile soil in which someone like Swanger can thrive. The whole organization, most of it right in Newton, has the sort of productive attitude that the founders of work teams dream about. The top people are obsessed with the patient, painstaking pursuit of better products and production methods.

The new products come forth only when Maytag is good and ready. The company's first automatic clothes washer did not appear until 1949, a decade behind the nation's first "home laundry." Since then Maytag washers have gone on to outsell every competing make except Whirlpool (whose sales include the

Kenmore line produced for Sears) and General Electric. Maytag has slowly brought out other appliances, but only when it was sure that they could win a place at the top of the market. Since the product mix is limited and model changes are rare, the manufacturing people can concentrate on honing the production process.

As Swanger moved higher with successive promotions, his time-consuming involvement in projects like these came to an end. Today he functions mainly as a maestro, coaxing the best possible performances out of seven department heads who report to him. One of them, Gene Nicol, runs the actual assembly lines and operates largely on his own; on a typical day he spends only a half hour with Swanger, going over production reports. Swanger spends far more time on the other aspects of manufacturing, each of which has some special Maytag touches.

Quality control, for example, is strongly based on the premise that reliability cannot be "inspected" into a product. There's inspection aplenty, of course. Every Maytag appliance is operated just before it is packed for shipment. Clothes washers are hooked up on a slowly revolving "merry-go-round" and run through every function in a fifteen-minute test. Machines that don't work perfectly go to the "boneyard" for repair or dismantlement. (Whirlpool and G.E. also make a final test of every function on each machine and say that their tests, while shorter, are just as good as Maytag's.)

Long before the machines reach the final testing stage, inspectors from the 177-person quality-control department have watched them take shape at critical points on the assembly lines, and before that have sampled and tested the purchased materials and parts that went into them. Maytag is very fussy with suppliers, and in recent years has been working with them to improve the quality of such potentially troublesome components as motors and timers. Thanks to this effort, Swanger says, Maytag repairmen are sending back fewer defective motors and timers than ever.

The real key to quality control, however, is the attitude of the individual Maytag worker. The main role of inspectors, Swanger says, is to "audit" a quality control job that must be done by everybody. Pride helps.

His mission, Swanger observes, is to get people enthusiastic about keeping costs down and quality up, right down to the assembly line. Like any top executive, Swanger must also spend a good deal of his time preparing for Maytag's future. Promising young executives must be groomed for higher posts, and Maytag must be kept informed of new manufacturing technology.

Maytag is unique among manufacturers, particularly in this era of rising costs and the influx of cheap imports. Whether the company can retain its small-company atmosphere, high-quality products, and increasing market shares is a point that only time will decide.

Adapted from Edmund Faltermayer, "The Man Who Keeps Those Maytag Repairmen Lonely," *Fortune* (November 1977): 192-97.

Questions for Discussion

1. Discuss the key points of Maytag's quality control philosophy and process.
2. What important managerial skills does Swanger exhibit in the case? Do they work for him?
3. What internal and external threats should Swanger carefully consider that may adversely affect the company's high level of success? Do you think Maytag can survive in its present form in the future without major changes?
4. How important is the rural Iowa site and the type of people who live there, to the quality control function?

PART SIX

INTERVIEW

J.W. Streidl

*Director of Management
Development and
Education
Tenneco, Inc.
Houston, Texas*

Q: What important forces for change are currently facing your organization?

A: All large organizations are faced with the forces for change that are affecting society as a whole. The effects of these forces vary in frequency and intensity throughout our organization because we are diverse and geographically widespread. However, an effective organization will develop coping mechanisms to assure that it will continue to utilize its resources to achieve organization objectives even while it is responding to change.

It's difficult and perhaps impossible to list all forces for change in a short interview. Consumerism, government regulations, shifts from labor to knowledge work, concerns for equity on the part of various minorities, two-career families, changing work ethics, changing work values, the union movement—all of these have an effect on an organization's operations. These in turn all have an impact on how an organization can effectively manage human resources, materials, and money to achieve its objectives.

Q: Are there any that concern you more than others?

A: The human factor is the one factor that is most variable to management and is most affected by the forces of change. I believe that our major concern is to provide an organization that can somehow continue to effectively cope with and manage all the various forces that impinge on it while remaining concerned with the legitimate needs of both individual employees and groups of employees.

This is a relatively new phenomenon in organizations. In the past, organizations were mainly concerned with achieving their own objectives without regard to the human factor. We've learned that we cannot perform effectively unless we are fully aware of the impact the human factor has upon our goals.

Q: What does Tenneco do to monitor the state of organization for possible changes?

A: Tenneco has an "environmental scanning" effort that is used to monitor the forces for change that are most likely to affect our organization. The information gained through monitoring activities is used in developing human resource plans. Human resource plans in turn are part of and a supplement to the overall business plans of the organization. We recognize that plans are only valuable to the extent that they can be effectively implemented and their stated objectives achieved. However, we believe that our analysis of outside forces enables us to better build in the "coping mechanisms" mentioned above, particularly in the human resource area.

Q: How widely is this information distributed to management?

A: In general, the information obtained through such activities is distributed on a need-to-know basis to those managers who must develop and implement appropriate human resource and business plans.

The Adaptive Organization and Manager: Change

Q: What are some of the major sources of resistance to change that you have found in organizations?

A: Change is most strongly resisted when it is suddenly "sprung on" the people who are expected to implement it or who will be affected by the change. This is more likely to occur when changes are poorly planned and poorly communicated. An effective communications plan regarding change is probably even more important than the change itself.

Q: How do you overcome this resistance?

A: Wherever possible, changes should be handled through the active participation on the part of the person or persons who will be affected by the change. Functional resistance occurs when such communication steps are ignored.

Q: What elements make up Tenneco's career planning system? What is the relationship between career planning and Tenneco's human resource planning system?

A: Human resource planning is something an organization does to assure that it has the right number of people with the right skills and abilities at the right place and at the right time. Career planning is something an individual employee does to assure that he or she is able to achieve specific career objectives consistent with his or her interests, aspirations, skills, and abilities. In cases where it is possible to integrate these two distinct areas, the organization may achieve a serendipitous result. However, it is not always possible to do so.

For example, an organization may need a sales manager who can speak Chinese, who is willing to relocate on two weeks' notice to staff a Singapore office, and is willing to remain out of the country for at least three years. If a person with those qualifications who also sees such a move as congruent with his or her career interests can be found, a positive result can occur. However, that person may not exist within the organization and may have to be sought from another company. It seems to us that the best method for assuring that career plans can tie into human resource plans is to provide open communication systems regarding opportunities within the company. The more individual employees are aware of such opportunities, the better they can respond to specific openings that relate to their own career interests and aspirations.

Q: What important skills should future managers develop to become effective managers?

A: Those of us in the management education and development business have for years indicated that most management jobs require an appropriate combination of technical, conceptual, and human skills. As people progress from entry-level management to higher levels of management responsibility, the proportion of technical and conceptual skills needed to be effective are reduced, and human skills requirements become greater. Managers who want to progress in an organization therefore should be concerned with polishing all their human skills (e.g., communications, confronting conflict, negotiating, interpersonal relationships, etc.), even while they are maintaining an effective skill level in the technical and conceptual areas. Most managers fail not because of a lack of technical or conceptual skills but rather because they lack the appropriate combination of human skills.

CHAPTER

19

Challenges to Organizations

Chapter Outline

Key Points

1. Change can be proactive in nature (initiated by the organization) or responsive in nature (the organization adapts to change).
2. Increased international competition, population shifts, marketplace changes, increased business-government interaction, and technology are major external forces for change.
3. Internal forces for change include work-force changes, need for improved productivity, the quality of working life concept, and the availability of resources.
4. The planned change process includes diagnosis, establishing program goals, identifying constraints, selecting a change strategy, implementation, and evaluation.
5. Improved environmental monitoring, increased scope of organizational goals, new strategies and plans, and different approaches to decision making are some planning function changes.
6. Major changes now taking place in the organizing function include the office of the president, continued use of the group manager concept and temporary teams, and selection, training, compensation, and benefit plans.
7. The need for better productivity measurement, more flexible leadership styles, the ability to adapt to the growing numbers of knowledgeable workers, and the emphasis on a generalistic orientation are some leading function changes.
8. The control function is seeing an increased emphasis on budgetary procedures, the continued use of computers in all operations, and the growth of production sharing in international operations.

Cincinnati Milacron

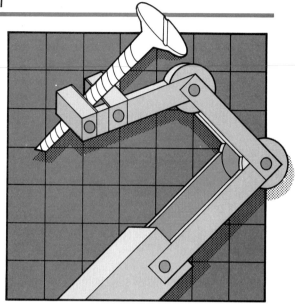

Change has been a prominent feature in the existence of Cincinnati Milacron Inc. In a meeting room on the top floor of its headquarters, the firm displays its past. A cobblestone walk leads to a replica of the company's first shop, where century-old machines hum away as they did back in 1884, when Cincinnati Screw and Tap Company opened for business.

Downstairs in the first-floor reception hall, the company displays its future. One of the T3 robots it produces stands amid pictures showing it inspecting an automobile body, lifting refrigerator parts, and even welding the arm of another robot.

In the 100 years that Milacron has been making manufacturing machinery, its machines have progressed far beyond the drills that put the same hole in the same place in identical pieces of metal. Now, according to *The Wall Street Journal,* its computer-controlled machine tools change their cutting tools and tasks automatically. The company's plastics-processing machines similarly can be programmed to mold different products, without help from a human operator. The T3 robots, management explains, can track, stack, and pack, search, feel, find, and react.

Such machines are winning Milacron a solid position in what the company is calling the new age of manufacturing, characterized more by the computer than by smokestacks. With the use of various automated devices, companies that make products ranging from cars to dishwashers will produce different models and designs simply by feeding new instructions to the computers that control the machines.

Milacron's move into high technology has been marked by a willingness to enter areas unlikely to pay off for years down the road. In the late 1960s, the company formed a new corporate research and development group and told its members they could work on anything but machine tools—which was the only thing they knew. There have been stumbles along the way. The company worked on a small office computer for eight years before it gave up. Similarly, it took nearly ten years for the robotics business to make a profit.

Milacron's recent history shows that even for a well-run, innovative concern, the process of change from life as a metal-bender to a supplier of new technology can be rugged. According to James Geier, the company's chairman and grandson of the firm's founder, "The joke around here is that our corporate motto, Find a Better Way, really means, Better Find a Way. Ranking as the number two robot maker in the U.S., Milacron's challenges are just ahead. Among the new makers of robots are IBM, General Motors, General Electric, and Westinghouse.

Adapted from P. Ingrassia and D. Darlin, "Cincinnati Milacron, Mainly a Metal-Bender, Now is a Robot Maker," *The Wall Street Journal* (April 7, 1983): 1.

19

In his thought-provoking book, Alvin Toffler argues that the environment is, and will continue to be, so dynamic and complex that it threatens people and organizations with *Future Shock*.[1] Future shock occurs when the nature, types, and speed of change overpower the individual's and organization's ability to adapt. Toffler dramatically illustrates this situation by pointing out that much of what we use daily has developed within our own lifetime.

No one can escape change, and *The Practice of Management* section about Cincinnati Milacron is a good illustration. This is why we stress that, for the survival of organizations, managers must be skilled in ways to respond to change. Confronting this challenge to organizations can be approached in a number of different ways. We prefer a planned change approach, because it is a deliberate attempt to modify or change certain operations, functions, and processes. Planned change can fall into two categories: *proactive,* in which the change is initiated by the organization, and *reactive,* in which policies and programs (such as contingency planning) are developed to respond quickly and effectively to unplanned change.

This chapter begins a two-chapter sequence on today's challenges to organizations and managers. This first chapter, which focuses on challenges to organizations, is divided into three major sections. First, we will identify some of the major forces for change, including those with external and internal origins. Second, the process of planned change will be discussed. Finally, we will conclude with a presentation of the impact of change on the management process.

Elements of Organizational Change

Change can affect all types of organizations, from IBM and the Mayo Clinic to a small machine-tool manufacturer and a social service agency. Even the neighborhood drugstore is not immune to the effects of change. For instance, the snowballing demands from insurance companies and government legislation have created a paper blizzard so fierce that the very survival of many drugstores is at stake. Pharmacists are spending nearly 40 percent of their time on paperwork, and the resulting squeeze on profitability has helped drop profit margins for the average store by 30 percent over the past decade.[2]

In response to these problems, many pharmacists are turning to time-sharing computers, whose main advantage is that they can store a great deal of information as well as quickly calculate many different transactions. Users of time-share computers in drugstores report that the benefits include an increase in filled prescriptions from twenty to fifty per hour, more accurate files on customer needs, increased knowledge of the availability of generic drugs, better control of drug prices, and significant clerical savings. The computer is not without drawbacks: new skills are required of the pharmacist in operating the system, and computer systems can cost as much as $30,000 per store to install.

This example illustrates the main elements of change in organizations. As shown in exhibit 19-1, three major elements have been identified. First is the recognition of certain forces for change. These forces can be external—such as insurance company and governmental requirements affecting drugstores—or internal—such as the drugstores' increase in paperwork and lower profitability. Second, in response to the forces of change, managers are required to diagnose the situation and choose strategies to control change's effects. Finally, the process of change can influence the way managers perform their functions. In the case of a drugstore, not only are new skills required, but a totally new operating system of files and clerical support is created. In the following discussion, we will look at each of these change elements.

External and Internal Forces for Change

In chapter 3, we pointed out important trends and developments that can influence management and performance. This section will extend that theme by highlighting some of the more important forces for change, both external and internal forces.

External Forces for Change

The list of forces in the external environment influencing organizations and managers is large and complex. Their effect varies across industries; forces that affect the airline industry are quite different from those that affect the health-care industry. While not all-inclusive, the following paragraphs describe a number of external factors that are affecting or will soon affect a wide variety of organizations.

Exhibit 19-1
Elements of
Organizational
Change

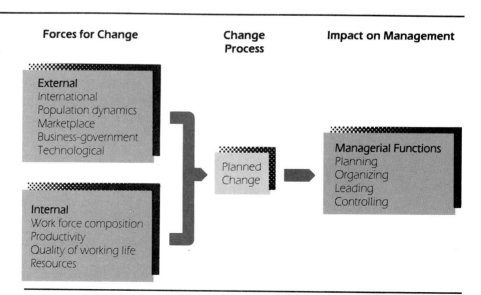

International   Among the most important external forces for change are the effects of managing in the *international* arena. As we have seen, organizations face as many differences as they do similarities when operating in other countries. Organizations must contend with and adapt to differences in culture, communication patterns, work ethics, and operating procedures before achieving desired levels of performance. There is also the increasing occurrence of foreign companies operating in the U.S. While this recognizes the stability and growth potential of the U.S. market, it adds to the already heavy competition across many product lines and services.

One movement within the international environment is the growth of *transnational organizations*.[3] The 1960s and 1970s saw the emergence of organizations with operations (production, sales, and/or distribution) in a number of countries—the multinational company. In the 1980s, the notion of a more integrated world economy is already beginning to take hold. This means not only more specialization of operations within a country, but these operations are being given more autonomy in developing and implementing strategies. With the Ford Escort car, the British-French Concorde plane, and Massey-Fergusson tractors we see products that have major parts manufactured in a variety of countries and assembled in another. We will cover this issue in more detail later in this chapter when we introduce the concept of production sharing.

Population Dynamics   A second important external force for change is the changing nature of *population dynamics*. Managers must consider at least three important factors. First, as we discussed in Chapter 10, the decline in the birth rate in developed countries is resulting in a definite shift in the age distribution of the population. This will mean not only visible shortages of skilled and capable people in many professions, but also that we will have to manage with a number of labor forces rather than a single labor force in mind. Second, the changing age distribution of the population will accentuate different lifestyles. Finally, geographic movement of people, particularly in the U.S., will force managers to re-think their marketing strategies and plans. The movement of individuals and families from the Northeast to Sunbelt cities, for example, is already forcing organizations to change the nature of their job offerings, products, and services.

The Marketplace   For a variety of reasons—some noted above—the *marketplace* in the latter part of this century will be in a dynamic state. Among other things, competitors will introduce new products, improve advertising, reduce prices, or improve services more frequently than in the past. The introduction of light beers and caffeine-free soft drinks, Pepsi's mass advertising campaign against Coke's dominant market position, "super saver" fares on airlines, and the growth of international competition are some examples.

A second point related to the marketplace is the effects of greater complexity in the nature of consumer markets. In the automobile industry, for example, segmentation of markets was initially accomplished by responding to differences in socioeconomic class. Different income groups wanted different cars—hence the popularity of the distinctions between Chevrolet, Pontiac, Oldsmobile, Buick, and Cadillac, which are all made by General Motors. Later came the emergence of segmentation by lifestyles. Car and price or status were no longer closely correlated, but car and lifestyle were. The Mustang, Corvette, and Thunderbird reflected the buyer's lifestyle, not his or her income. Finally, in the 1970s, came market segmentation by population dynamics. The emergence and popularity of such cars as the Eldorado, Volvo, Monte Carlo, and various pickup trucks and vans reflect a more complex distinction among consumers. Young professionals want a particular kind of car, recreation-oriented families want another type, older families and couples desire another model, and so on. A close observation of other products reveals the same type of segmentation. Examples are fast-food and other restaurants, travel, transportation, home preferences (e.g., condominium, apartment, patio home, or single-family dwelling), choice of higher-education institutions, and the like.

Business and Government   The continuing and growing relationship between *business and government* is another important external force for change. At issue are not only aspects of regulation-deregulation and the increasing number of employee-related legislative acts, but also concerns over the complex relationships between foreign governments.

The importance of business-government relations has given rise, at least in part, to a new type of manager in the 1980s. Characterized by executives at Du Pont, GE, Exxon, GM, AT&T, and Citicorp, these managers have become activists in society and politics.[4] The main reason is that they recognize that no organization can survive as an island; none can be totally successful without a sound economy and a good relationship between government, business and society. Irving Shapiro, recently retired chairman of Du Pont, stated:

> In the past, businessmen wore blinders. After hours, they would run to their club, play golf with other businessmen, have a martini—and that was about it. They did not see their role as being concerned with public policy issues. In a world where government simply took taxes from you and did not interfere with your operations, maybe that was sensible. In today's world, it is not. I'm more interested in what a U.S. Senator thinks than what some businessmen think.
>
> Most of the new executives understand the outside world, and they can deal with policy issues in America and abroad. If I were choosing a chief executive, I would not be overly concerned with his/her education or specific background. I would ask if he/she relates to the larger world as opposed to knowing how to produce widgets and nothing else.[5]

Such a description of the need for an integrated view of business-government-society is clearly an important concept for future managers to understand.

Technological   Finally, there is the issue of rapid *technological* change, involving change in the tools, equipment, processes, and knowledge used to produce a product or service. The main impact of technological change has been to shorten the life of many products and services to the point where nearly 60 percent of the products used today were not even available ten years ago. Developing new technologies is a high-

After years of significant growth in sales and earnings, giant Kodak Company is feeling the pressure for change. Kodak is being forced to change because the competition, primarily from Japan, is slowly gaining on it, while the worldwide recession of the early 1980s has hurt the demand for Kodak's products abroad. One of the company's major concerns is that sales of its much-heralded disk camera have not met expectations because of the competition from pocket-size 35mm cameras.

These problems faced Colby H. Chandler when he took over as chairman of the Rochester, New York company in 1983. Not one to waste time, Chandler initiated some immediate changes. Among these are:

- Not content to allow Japan's Fuji Film to make significant gains as the "Official Film of the 1984 Olympics," Chandler has purchased millions of dollars of tv time to advertise Kodak's product during Olympic broadcasts.

- To maintain its 65 percent worldwide share of amateur film, Chandler endorsed an aggressive marketing program centered around a large cost-cutting campaign.

- The structure of the consumer product sales unit has been streamlined by consolidating a number of United States offices in the hope that improved response time to market changes will evolve.

- To cut costs, Chandler pared nearly 5 percent of its work force through furloughs and early retirement.

- R&D funds have been poured into developing new technologies in order to become a world leader in solid-state computer chip-based electronic cameras.

An aroused Kodak is the last thing its competitors want. But with Kodak's resources to fuel growth and a new "lean and mean" organization, this is exactly what the company's competitors may find.

Adapted from "Kodak's New Lean and Hungry Look," *Business Week* (May 30, 1983): 33.

cost, high-risk activity for organizations; ignoring technological development is even more risky, often putting the survival of the organization at stake.

A discussion of technological forces for change would not be complete without a serious look at automation. After many years of development, manufacturers in the U.S. and other industrialized countries are beginning to make stunning leaps forward in the field. Even today, automated facilities have made important inroads in industry. At Chrysler, for example, robot welders have been installed to weld stamped steel panels into K-car bodies. Lockheed Corporation is using robots for painting and processing aircraft.[6]

The driving forces behind the automation movement are many, but they are not difficult to understand or appreciate. The development of the computer chip, management's desire for improved quality, and the need to remain competitive in the international marketplace are among the most significant.

Internal Forces for Change

Organizations and managers must also contend with internal sources of change. These forces can originate primarily from internal operations, or they can be the result of the impact of external changes. For example, changes in the *composition of the work force* are, in part, the result of changes in population characteristics of the external environment.

Work Force Composition A number of factors are involved in the anticipated changes in an organization's work force. First, as pointed out earlier, the age distribution in the U.S. population is beginning to create some interesting problems for the organization. As shown in exhibit 19-2, a dramatic increase in the number of managers in the 30-to-40-year-old age group has been projected, and signs are that it is taking place. This, coupled with a decrease in the number of older executives, means that not only will there be a large group of individuals competing for a few high management posts, but there will be a shortage of older executives to train these younger, career-minded managers.[7] A major project for management will be to develop methods to identify the young men and women with the greatest potential and then place them in an accelerated career path.

Major cultural and economic changes are re-forming the country's work force as numbers of women entering the ranks of management increases significantly. Stricter enforcement and adoption of antidiscrimination practices by organizations, increased educational achievement, women's greater emphasis on growth and self-development, and more acceptance in a formerly male-oriented work environment all contribute to an irreversible situation.

Additional changes in the work force include such issues as hiring the handicapped and the hardcore unemployed, the movement toward temporary employment, dual-career couples, and the increase in the number of white-collar, professional, or knowledge workers.

As Drucker states, the growth in knowledge workers creates the problem for management of the "double-headed monster." Illustrated by the saying "one cannot run a hospital with doctors, and one cannot run one without them," this situation applies to

Exhibit 19-2 Age Group Trends— 1976–1985		Percent Increase or Decrease	
1976 Age Group	**1976 Total Population (In Millions)**	**To 1980**	**To 1985**
30–34	13.8	+26	+42
35–39	11.6	+20	+49
40–44	11.1	+ 4	+23
45–49	11.8	− 8	− 3
50–54	11.8	− 3	−10
55–59	10.6	+ 6	+ 3

nearly all modern organizations. The "double-headed monster" is the situation in which the organization depends on the performance of professionals—such as doctors, lawyers, engineers, and technologists—who are as strongly dedicated to their discipline as they are to the organization. In other words, professional employees seek both acceptance by their profession and high performance levels in their position—the problem, as in the case of some university professors, is that these two roles may compete against each other.[8]

Productivity Another important force for change—which is both external and internal in origin—is increased emphasis on improving the *productivity* of the worker. Productivity is usually defined as the amount of goods or services produced per worker or per dollar invested. By most measurements, productivity in the U.S. is significantly lagging behind the rest of the world. Government statistics have revealed that productivity of the American worker has risen one percent or less per year over the last five years. This is a problem for the organization and the country for at least two reasons. First, if productivity rises as fast as wages, there will be enough goods around to soak up the extra money; but if wages rise faster, then there is more money chasing fewer goods—the classic definition of inflation. Second, America's ability to compete in the world market is measured by the unit costs of its goods—how much each unit costs to make. If wages and other costs rise faster than output, American goods will be more expensive abroad.

For example, Japanese productivity increased by 8 percent in 1978, while wages rose 6.1 percent. That gave Japan a 1.9 percent decrease in unit costs. In the U.S., wages outstripped productivity by nearly 8 percent during the same period. The message to managers is clear: U.S. goods and services will become less competitive unless productivity of workers improves. This problem is becoming acute for such American industries as autos, steel, televisions, and textiles.

Although productivity rates are growing faster in other countries, the U.S. still leads overall. On the average, each American still produces more than the individual Japanese or German worker, for example. The gap is narrowing, but as these nations become more service-minded, a slowing down of their productivity increases could result.[9]

Quality of Working Life A third major force for change—also one that has both internal and external origins—is the growing popularity of the *quality of working life* concept. For years, people have been concerned about work as a means for earning a living, but also as an outlet for creativity, a framework for group interaction, a means of attaining profits, and a contribution to a viable society. These broad factors include the many facets of the needs, ambitions, and goals of people, organizations, and different cultures and societies.

Because people spend a high proportion of their time on activities associated with their work, it is not surprising that management scholars and practitioners have become increasingly interested in the conditions of the workplace. Given the broad title of the "quality of working life," the focus of interest has centered on such questions as:[10]

Al, do whatever you have to do to increase productivity. Threaten, cajole, fire at will. Have fun.

© Valen Associates

■ What are the major elements and causes of employee dissatisfaction?

■ What are an individual's important needs? How do they change with increased material well-being and with personal development? How are they affected by changes in the work environment and changes in the external environment?

■ To what extent are the conditions of work determined by the technology of production and the organization's structure?

■ How can the quality of work affect organizational performance and societal benefits?

■ Is there a conflict between economic performance of an organization and the quality of working life of the individual worker?

These and other questions have been studied by organizations including GM, Shell Oil, Xerox, Nabisco, and Cummins Engine over the last few years. The key feature of this movement is strongly related to the concern over worker productivity; that is, can organizations improve the conditions under which most people work so an improvement in productivity results?

Resources   Finally, a major concern for managers is the changing nature and availability of needed *resources* to produce products and services. As we have already seen, the changing nature of the work force relates to the issue of human resources. Other resources will also change the management environment in the future.

For example, during the last two decades, world fuel consumption has tripled, oil and gas consumption quintupled, and electricity use increased nearly sevenfold. Worldwide energy shortages have become an almost yearly occurrence, which has affected our daily lives. The availability of gasoline, for instance, has altered significantly the travel and recreational patterns of many Americans. In a similar vein, many knowledgeable people are predicting that during the latter part of this century, water for human and manufacturing consumption will become scarce.

The process of managing limited natural resources is an important responsibility for all of us in the future, especially managers. It will take the best management to minimize productivity losses, keep up product lines, insure supplies, and build or maintain a reasonable standard of living for people worldwide.

These external and internal forces for change are just some of the many factors that will influence the practice of management in the future. The important key to managerial success is learning how to adapt and live with change. A crucial part of this way of life is understanding and practicing the process of planned change.

The Process of Planned Change

The process of planned change involves a number of distinct steps or subprocesses. Exhibit 19-3 is a model consisting of six basic steps linked in a logical sequence.[11] The process begins with the identification of the forces for change, which were presented in the previous section. The remaining steps are discussed below.

Recognition of Problem Areas: Diagnosis and Program Goals

Managers depend on the flow of accurate information from outside and inside an organization to stay aware of problems that require some form of change. Internally, an organization generates reports on resource utilization, human resource development, morale, absenteeism, and other areas of interest. The external data base includes information on competitive actions, customer or client demand, governmental regulations, and the public's attitude toward or impression of the organization. By combining internal and external information, managers are able to detect actual or potential problems. The more accurate the information, the more knowledge the manager has to assess the need for change.

Exhibit 19-3
Process of
Planned Change

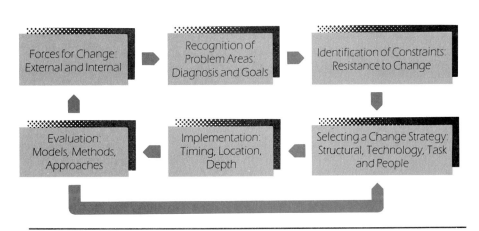

A need for change is obvious when key personnel are quitting in alarming numbers, or market share is rapidly declining, or executives are indicted for price collusion. Less catastrophic problems still demand managerial attention, for instance, information systems must be carefully monitored and diagnostic procedures kept at hand.

In essence, the job of a manager *always* involves diagnosis, whether the focus is on motivation, job design, leadership, or any other managerial topic; it involves diagnosis or study of the important properties in a systematic and valid manner. Performing a diagnosis of potential problem areas to facilitate change requires that a manager focus on a number of issues. Some of these are:

- Determining the specific problems that require correction
- Verifying or considering the potential determinants or forces causing these problems
- Deciding what needs to be changed and when to change it to resolve the problems
- Determining what the goals are for the change and how to measure goal accomplishment.

Answers to these crucial issues are difficult to generate because managers are typically overextended in their workload and do not have time to perform the necessary diagnostic work.

A variety of diagnostic techniques can be applied to help solve the questions brought up by these four issues. Organizations use committees, reports, consultants, task forces, interviews, questionnaire surveys, informal discussion groups, and other information-generating techniques. The central issue is not which technique or combination of them to employ rather, it is the gathering of reasonably valid information. Without good representative information, a change strategy is virtually worthless because it is blindly based. Thus, a thorough diagnosis is important to the success of organizational change efforts.

Consideration of the overall effects of change on the organization is also a key question that diagnosis can help answer. For example, is the organization interested in high production at any cost, or does it want a happy work force? The amount of performance that will be sacrificed for morale is basically a goal decision. The goals of organizational change can be made specific enough so that a decision can be reached about whether or not they are being achieved. Therefore, a desired result of the diagnosis and evaluation steps in our model are specifications that consider operationalization, constraints, costs, and consequences.

The Constraints

Numerous constraints to change must be considered. These constraints, which affect any type of change, include leadership climate, formal organization, and individual characteristics.[12]

Leadership climate is the atmosphere in the work environment that results from the leadership style and administrative practices of superiors. The climate is set by the leaders, who can influence subordinates to accept or reject changes implemented from the top executive group. The leader's values, attitudes, and perceptions are all constraining forces.

The *formal organization design* must have some compatibility with the proposed change. For example, attempting to implement a goal-setting program or participative decision-making practices in a rigid and bureaucratic organization is somewhat unrealistic and displays a lack of understanding. There must be some congruence between the program of change and the design of the system if the change is to be effective.

The *individual characteristics* that are important to change programs include learning abilities, attitudes, personality, and expectations. For example, highly sophisticated and expensive computer technology only makes sense when the employees making use of it are computer literate. Managers need to continually consider individual characteristics when analyzing potential constraints of a particular change strategy.

Although change is a recurring feature of organizational life, people tend to resist it. Resistance in the form of sabotaging performance standards, absenteeism, filing unfounded grievances, and reducing productivity regularly occurs in organizations. The resistance may be overt, such as slowing down production, or implicit, such as feigning illness so a new machine does not have to be faced on a particular day.[13]

Employees typically like to have some control over their work environments, the pace of their work, and the manner in which the job is accomplished. When management suddenly announces a change in work design, personnel, equipment, or work flow, there are usually some people who want to participate in these decisions. In addition, some changes are of such magnitude that they frighten employees because of the uncertainties associated with them. To understand why people resist, we need to focus on some of the causes from individual and group sources.

Fear of Economic Loss   Any change that creates the feeling that some positions will be eliminated and employees laid off or terminated is likely to meet with resistance, because of the serious fear of loss of earning power. Management would have a difficult time minimizing this fear and would need to make employees believe that job reductions will not follow a change. This requires communication to the work force on why the change is necessary. If employees need to be terminated, the rationale and procedures should be explained. This is not to say that the reduction will be accepted, but better understanding affords a chance of less disruption in the work process.

Potential Social Descriptions   Through working with each other, employees develop comfortable patterns of communication and interaction. This makes work more enjoyable and permits friendships to develop. Almost any change in structure, technology, or personnel has the potential to disrupt these comfortable interaction patterns or ties.

Inconvenience   The introduction of a new procedure for handling a job or a new machine to produce units more efficiently may disrupt the normal routine of performing a job. Employees generally resist any change that interferes with the normal patterns of their work.

The
Manager's
Job

Dr. Au Wang of
Wang
Laboratories

In 1951, a Chinese immigrant named Dr. Au Wang founded Wang Laboratories in Lowell, Mass. From a shaky beginning, "The Doctor," as he is called in the company, used his physics background along with an iron-willed entrepreneurial flair to make a mark in the world of high technology. Because of his uncanny timing in the marketplace and street-wise application of technology, the company holds first place in sales of word processing equipment.

But Dr. Wang, still chairman and chief executive officer, has identified a critical shortcoming that could trip the company in the future: management has not kept pace with the company's growth. Faced with rapidly changing technologies and a need to extend its product line downward into personal computers and executive work stations, change is required. But changing will not be easy, for it will test the company's management skills, financial resources, and technical abilities.

Not one to be overwhelmed by a major challenge, Dr. Wang has begun the change process. For example:

- A sweeping reorganization has hit the company. Besides restructuring divisions and setting more innovative corporate goals, decision making has been decentralized and a new management team has been put in place. Ironically, it was Dr. Wang's centralized and highly personal management style that contributed to the firm's current successes.

- To clean up its balance sheet, the company has instituted new controls to bring receivables and inventories into line. Lax controls had allowed a cash flow problem to develop, and Wang had to solve it by selling convertible debentures.

- The research and development operation, which had run out of control, has been put under strict supervision. A more focused approach to product development is a goal.

- Management is turning around the service function, which had been a problem for years.

Dr. Wang is confident that these changes will have a significant impact on the company's future. Anticipating continued success, he is devoting nearly 40 percent of his time to educational activities, including advisory positions at three colleges and directing the Wang Institute of Graduate Studies, an accredited school awarding degrees in software engineering.

Adapted from "Wang Labs' Run For a Second Billion," *Business Week* (May 17, 1982): 100-104.

Fear of Uncertainties By establishing a normal routine in performing a job, employees learn what their range of responsibilities are and what the supervisor's reaction to their behavior will be in certain situations. Any change creates some potential unknowns. Employees, before and after changes, speculate about what their modified roles will be and how their supervisors will respond to them and the changes. This speculation focuses on uncertainties that did not exist prior to the change and results in some resistance to the change.

Resistance from Groups   Groups establish norms of behavior and performance that are communicated to members. This communication establishes the boundaries of expected behaviors. Failure to comply with such norms can result in ostracism, lack of respect, or restriction of desirable rewards such as praise and recognition. The more attractive or cohesive the group is to its members, the greater the influence the group can exert on the membership. A group is attractive to the extent it satisfies the needs of its members. If management initiates changes that are viewed as threatening to a group's norms, the changes are likely to meet with resistance. The more cohesive the group, the greater its resistance to change.

Any change program needs to pay attention to the needs of both the organization and the individual in order to reduce resistance to change. The individual must be able to perceive personal benefits to be gained by the change. A good system of communication, involving group participation and feedback, creates an atmosphere of trust and helps employees perceive the changes as beneficial.

Strategies for Change

The next step in the planned change process is the identification and choice of change strategies. Exhibit 19-4 identifies four major change strategies—structure, technology, task, and people—while Exhibit 19-5 provides some examples of individual change approaches.

Structural change involves, among other aspects, the three dimensions of organizations—grouping, influence, and coordination—discussed in chapter 8. Examples include a large, centralized organization that decentralizes decision making, a change from a functional to a product structure, revising lines of authority and responsibility, and setting up a number of task forces to assist in coordinating the organization's activities.

Exhibit 19-4
Organizational
Change Strategies

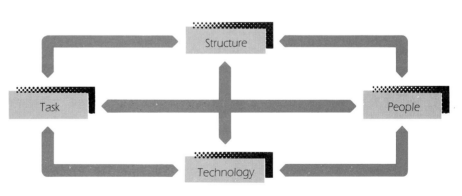

Source: Harold Levitt, "Applied Organizational Changes in Industry: Structural, Technological, and Humanistic Approaches," in *Handbook of Organizations*, ed. James G. March (Chicago: Rand McNally, 1965).

Exhibit 19-5
Examples of Change Strategies

Strategy	Examples	Strategy	Examples
Structure	Matrix organizational designs Decentralization Task forces and teams Socio-technical systems	People	Managerial grid Career planning Training and development Coaching and counseling Survey feedback Confrontation meetings Conflict resolution Management by objectives
Task	Job rotation Job enlargement Job enrichment Job redesign	Technology	Computer systems Production designs Automation Production tools, equipment, and methods

Technology changes concern the impact of new work methods, processes of production, and improved work flow and information systems. In the automobile industry, the increased use by U.S. manufacturers of automated equipment and the modular assembly revisions instituted by Volvo are some examples of technology change.

Task changes are some of the most frequently used change strategies by managers because of their ease of implementation. Job enlargement, job enrichment, and job redesign, along with an emphasis on team development, fall within the task change category.

Finally, *people changes* attempt to modify the attitudes, values, behavior, interpersonal skills, and potential for advancement of employees. Classroom and on-the-job training programs, external management development programs, behavior modeling approaches, career planning, and behavior modification efforts are aimed at people changes.

One of the most important aspects illustrated by exhibit 19-4 is the interrelated nature of the change strategies. That is, the implementation of any one change strategy can cause a change in one or more of the others. A movement toward decentralization, for example, will not only result in a change in the way work is performed, but may also change the attitudes of employees toward their work. Identifying potential side effects of change is an important management diagnostic skill.

Implementation

The implementation of any attempt at organizational change has three important dimensions: timing, location, and depth. *Timing* refers to the when of the effort—when is the best time to begin implementation? Two important issues are the organization's operating cycle and the completion of necessary preparation. Both need to be well coordinated. If the operating cycle is at its peak and if preparation (such as informing those to be affected) has not been completed, timing has not been properly handled. Of course, an organization's survival takes precedence over any timing consideration.

Managers involved in implementing change must decide where (i.e., *location*) to initiate the change. Many organizational change scholars believe change should be initiated from the top-management level to the lower-management or operating-employee level.[14] This is based on the belief that top management must display active support for the program for change efforts to accomplish their goals. If top management does not show support and commitment, there is a tendency for others in the organization to essentially "go through the motions," but the support of top management seems to generate more enthusiasm and interest among subordinates.

There is, however, some support for bottom-up or middle-level initiation of programs. Changes in work design through a job enrichment technique are usually initiated lower in the organization. Top management may allow these changes to occur, but they are not necessarily involved in them. Thus, for some change efforts, top-management commitment would be displayed through active involvement; in others, it would entail just allowing middle- and lower-level managers and nonmanagers to work out the details and follow through for change. The three locations for implementing organizational change are illustrated in exhibit 19-6.

The *depth* of the implementation involves the issue of target groups. Should the change program be directed at the total organization, units, groups, or individuals? In general, target growth involves not only the particular change strategy that is chosen, but the anticipated side effects of change.

Evaluation

The final segment of our model in exhibit 19-3 is evaluation. Only recently have scientifically based studies evaluated the effectiveness of change efforts. Much of the

Exhibit 19-6
Three Potential
Locations for
Implementing
Organizational
Change

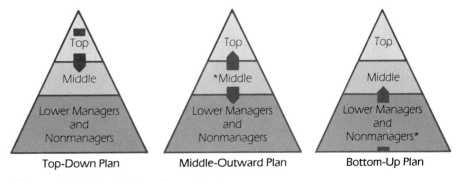

Top-Down Plan   Middle-Outward Plan   Bottom-Up Plan

*Change initiated in direction of arrowheads

literature on the evaluation of organizational change is based on enthusiastic testimonies by advocates of a particular technique, approach, or model. Fads have resulted in extravagant claims of the superiority of a particular program. The reasons for the abundance of testimonial support and the dearth of scientifically based studies of organizational change and development are clear.

First, it is difficult to conduct field studies over a period of time without the occurrence of major and uncontrollable changes, which contaminate the results of the planned change program and discourage many researchers from becoming involved in the necessary longitudinal studies. Second, it is difficult for skilled researchers to gain entree into organizations to perform sound evaluations. Practitioners are concerned about the disruption of normal operations when their organizations are intruded upon by researchers, who sometimes refuse to discuss problems in terms that are understandable and application oriented. Finally, many practitioners are not certain about the intent of a particular change effort because the objectives of the effort are not clearly stated.

Despite these problems, there are signs that more refined and valid research on organizational change is taking place. The literature is beginning to indicate that practitioners and researchers are starting to work together more intensely to improve the organizational change programs in progress. Only through evaluation can feedback be provided that can result in needed improvements.

Evaluation involves the use of interviews, self-report questionnaires, observation, records, or reports of critical incidents. If at all possible, it seems that a combination of these methods needs to be used to acquire a valid picture of the results of the efforts. The feedback received from the evaluation is returned to the forces-for-change stage and to the change strategy phase in our model. This link is essential for assessing any changes that have occurred in an organization, group, or individual. It aids the manager in reaching a conclusion about whether the change was effective in accomplishing desirable goals.

 ## Changes in the Managerial Process

Some of the major changes or situations that will affect the organization and its managers in the future were pointed out earlier in this chapter. The effects of these changes, along with the adequacy of the planned change program, are likely to vary from organization to organization. For example, the effects of changing population dynamics and the emphasis being placed on productivity are applicable to most organizations. On the other hand, the growing complexity of the marketplace may be of more concern to an IBM or a General Foods than it would be to a small-town hospital. This is another instance in which the contingency approach to management would apply (see chapter 2).

In a general sense, however, we may speculate what the manager of the future will face. Our discussion will focus on some of the changes one might expect to find in the functions of planning, organizing, leading, and controlling.

Changes in Planning

Part Two of this book, *Developing the Framework for Performance: Planning*, concerns the managerial activities of analyzing the external and internal environments, organizational goals, strategies and plans, and decision making. These planning activities can be expected to undergo significant changes in the future.

First, one can expect that the dynamic external environment will force many organizations into more extensive and formal *environmental monitoring* and *scanning activities*. While existing market and economic monitoring procedures will be strengthened, the most significant growth will be in monitoring and scanning political activities. A variety of approaches are already being used, including formal committees, paid consultants, and computer simulations.

For example Bechtel Corporation, a large construction company, lost a significant amount of money and assets as a result of the Iranian revolution in 1979. Since then, the company has used consultants, such as Richard Helms, former director of the Central Intelligence Agency, to check out political climates in foreign countries. Some major manufacturers such as Caterpillar and General Motors have formed advisory councils of prominent foreign managers and retired governmental officials. Henry Kissinger, for instance, serves as a paid advisor to Merck, the pharmaceutical company, and Goldman-Sachs and Chase Manhattan Bank in the financial sector. On the other hand, Gulf Oil uses an internal four-person international-studies unit to analyze foreign activities, while American Can, General Telephone and Telegraph (GT&E), and United Technologies have developed computer programs to study international situations. The computer analysis, made up of economic, financial, and questionnaire data from overseas managers, provides executives with an assessment by a large number of knowledgeable people.[15]

Managers can also expect to see the *goals* of their organizations change in the future. One of the major changes in organizational goals will be their broadening in scope. In manufacturing firms, for example, one may expect to find goals that reflect entry and expansion in international markets and a growing concern for the social responsibilities of the organization. A change in the scope of goals for hospitals is already seen. The early goals of taking care of the sick and injured have been transformed by today's growing emphasis on preventative medicine. In the future, the emergence of specialized clinics and health-care facilities may force the large community hospital into a further refinement of goals.

The area where the most significant changes will occur is *strategies and plans*. From a strategic point of view, at least two developments will have a major impact. First, many management scholars and practicing managers are forecasting a knowledge and innovation expansion similar to what happened during the 1950s and 1960s. New or totally revamped industries dealing with communications and more technologically oriented health care, manufacturing, and banking are expected to develop.

Due in part to technological change, the second major strategic issue in the future is the definition of "market leadership." In the past, an organization could be expected to survive and be successful if it was one of the top two or three in market share or profitability in the particular industry. Now, many managers are looking to a twofold redefinition of market leadership: being a market leader in a *broad* market such as food products, or a leader in a *narrow* market such as specialized medical diagnostic equipment.[16] These changes are already visible. For example, the number of profitable heavy equipment manufacturers had declined dramatically in the past two decades to the point where such well-known companies as International Harvester and Caterpillar are in danger of frequently operating at a loss, or being taken over by a larger organization. On the other hand, while the major domestic airlines are fighting for fewer and fewer long-distance travelers, the regional, intercity, or intrastate airlines are in a boom cycle.

Translating new strategies into action—planning—will require new approaches and skills from managers. The dynamic nature of the external environment will probably require managers to use contingency planning more frequently than in the past. In addition, a new type of planning—entrepreneurial planning—may become more important. The major function of entrepreneurial planning is to search out new opportunities that will enhance the growth of the organization. Venture groups, as discussed in chapter 14, are a preliminary form of this type of planning. As more and more organizations seek to take advantage of new technologies and/or achieve a market leadership position, entrepreneurial planning can be expected to grow in importance.

Finally, one of the consequences of revised goals, strategies, and plans will be a change in the way *decisions* are made. In particular, new technologies in the computer systems, electronic communication, and management information systems areas will enable managers to convert many decisions from nonprogrammed to routine-programmed decisions. The complexity and dynamic nature of the environment will also see a rise in different types of nonprogrammed decisions, particularly in the strategy formulation and contingency planning functions.

Future managers will probably face the same number of programmed and nonprogrammed decisions as their current counterparts; however, the types of each decision will change dramatically. For example, the availability of computer software and time-sharing packages have already converted some nonroutine decisions to programmed decisions. Stock investment decisions, medical diagnoses, and store locations for retailers are now at least partially programmed in some organizations.[17]

Changes in Organizing

A wide variety of structural arrangements will be available to organizations in the future. No one structure will dominate as bureaucracy did earlier in this century. Functional, product, mixed, and matrix designs will be just as prevalent tomorrow as they are today. This situation is due, in part, to managers' recognition that the most appropriate structure is the one that evolves from an analysis of the goals, strategies, and technology of the organization.

At least three major trends in organizational *structure* should become more widely adopted in the future. First, the single chief executive notion is being replaced by a concept known as the "office of the president." The volume of work and numbers of new and complex problems, coupled with the demand for different talents and skills, are issues that are almost impossible for one person to handle. As shown in exhibit

19-7, the duties of the president can be divided among a group of managers, including the president and four executive vice presidents. Each of these individuals is given specific responsibilities for a segment of the operations; thus, the typical hierarchy is replaced with a peer group or coalition of executives.

Exhibit 19-7 also shows the second major trend; that is, the continued movement toward the use of group managers under the office of the president. As discussed in chapter 14, group managers are responsible for particular segments or product lines of the organization. The major change in this concept is that the use of computers and other sophisticated information systems will permit a greater centralization of certain functions. For example, the centralization of such activities as purchasing, personnel,

Exhibit 19-7
Office of the President

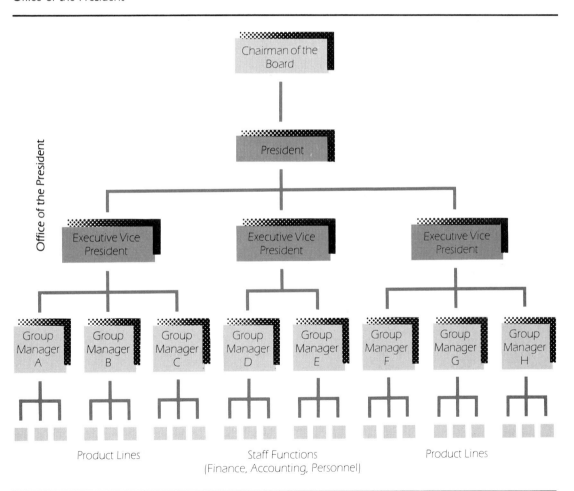

budgeting, planning, and transportation will enable the group manager to maintain greater control, and hence, provide more time to lower-level managers for innovative activities.

The third development in the organizing function will be more frequent use of temporary groups such as task forces or venture groups to do much of the opportunity finding, contingency planning, and innovative problem-solving which, in the past, were infrequently delegated to individual managers.

The combination of changing population dynamics and complex employee needs will have a major impact on the *human resource* policies of organizations. Selection procedures, for example, must adapt to the changing population mix. In addition to the typical high school and college graduate, the labor force (or labor forces) will contain a significant number of people who seek second careers, women who return to work or seek new jobs after raising their children, and individuals who choose to work instead of retire. All of these people will be competing for similar jobs.

Given this diversity in the labor force, managers will need to take a second look at training programs. Instead of throwing these people into a training program geared for the unskilled worker, for example, managers must take a more personalized approach. Mature workers bring with them expertise that the organization needs to recognize. The post-retirement-age worker knows *how* to work, and women who enter the work force after years of raising children have really been the "chief executives" of their homes. Organizations must account for this knowledge, maturity, and experience.

Compensation and employee benefit programs will also undergo many changes. The movement toward individuality in these programs will continue. Included will be the greater use of merit pay systems, modified workweeks, and cafeteria benefit plans in which each employee is given a set of options from which he or she can choose the package that gives him or her the most for the money available. As Peter Drucker states:

> The employer of tomorrow will have to learn to use full-time people and part-time people, men and women, people past retirement age and people who are interested only in working in one functional or technical skill (such as computer specialists) and who move on to a different employer once they have finished their particular assignment. Whether university, hospital, or business, the employer will have to move from managing personnel to managing people.[18]

Changes in Leading

The growing emphasis on productivity and productivity improvements will affect the leading function in a number of ways. First, there will be an increased effort to develop better ways of *defining and measuring productivity*. Before managers can successfully influence others to perform, they must have a clear understanding of what it is they are to achieve. In many cases, managers will be faced with more complex goals and productivity standards (e.g., quantity, quality, morale, employee retention, employee welfare).

Second, because of major changes in the organization's strategies, managers will need to carefully evaluate the *allocation and use of resources*. For example, a strategy of market leadership through specialization will require high concentration of resources in a particular area. In essence, this is what has happened to Chrysler and, to some extent, Ford: Chrysler's financial troubles in the late 1970s forced it to adopt a strategy of concentrating on a particular model of car (small, gas efficient) for a more specialized market. Throughout the entire management hierarchy, managers must make important decisions regarding where the physical, financial, and human resources of the organization will be allocated. Some of these decisions will result in layoffs, plant closings, and product-line eliminations. When the survival of the organization is at stake, the manager must take the lead and the responsibility.

The diversity of the work force will require managers to be more *flexible* in their styles of leadership. Besides leading a work force made up of many older workers, women, and part-time and temporary employees, one of the more interesting leadership issues will be directing the work of the professional or "knowledge" worker. The ranks of such knowledge workers as accountants, engineers, systems analysts, health-care technologists, and service personnel will increase significantly during the latter part of this century (see exhibit 19-8).

This situation will create at least two problems for managers. First, because knowledge workers are potentially the most productive, but also the most expensive, managers need to know the types of tasks best suited for the worker's skills. In other words, management must learn to assign the right people to a task where the potential for improved productivity is greatest. As the complexity of professions increases, this will become an increasingly demanding part of the manager's job.

Second, managers need to understand that the knowledge worker is likely to be more knowledgeable about how to perform a task than the manager. This means that the manager must be willing to ask employees about the task and the best way to perform it and, most importantly, listen to what they say. Practically as well as theoretically, this means that a portion of the manager's ability to influence is taken away.

We can see this situation today. For example, most laboratory technologists in hospitals have achieved an education level equivalent to a master's degree. The lab supervisor does not have to tell the technologist how to analyze a patient's blood sample. What the supervisor can do to insure high performance is to make sure that the right person is on the task, all the equipment is functioning well, and working conditions and procedures do not interfere with the successful completion of the work. For future success, managers must recognize that as the number of knowledge workers increases, so will the number of "substitutes for leadership" in the form of rules, higher education and training, and peer groups. Adapting to this situation is another important part of managing.[19]

The final change in the leading function is a paradox. On one hand, we anticipate that the number of professionals, specialists, and knowledge workers will increase. On the other hand, the people who manage these workers will increasingly need to be *generalists*. Improved productivity in groups, departments, divisions, or organizations will require managers who are able to *integrate* the various specialized tasks into

Exhibit 19-8
The Shifting Job
Market (By 1990)

Some Jobs Are Going. . . .

Occupation	Percent Decline in Employment
Shoemaking-machine operators	− 19.2
Farm laborers	19.0
Railroad-car repairers	17.9
Farm managers	17.7
Graduate assistants	16.7
Housekeepers, private household	14.9
Child-care workers, private household	14.8
Maids and servants, private household	14.7
Farm supervisors	14.3
Farmers, owners and tenants	13.7
Timber-cutting and logging workers	13.6
Secondary-school teachers	13.1

Others Are Growing. . . .

Occupation	Percent Increase in Employment
Data-processing-machine mechanics	+ 157.1
Paralegal personnel	143.0
Computer-systems analysts	112.4
Computer operators	91.7
Office-machine servicers	86.7
Tax preparers	77.9
Computer programmers	77.2
Aero-astronautic engineers	74.8
Employment interviewers	72.0
Fast-food restaurant workers	69.4
Child-care attendants	66.5
Veterinarians	66.1

But the Future Is Here.

Occupation	Estimate Employment
Industrial-robot production	800,000
Geriatric social work	700,000
Energy technicians	650,000
Industrial-laser processing	600,000
Housing rehabilitation	500,000
Handling new synthetic materials	400,000
On-line emergency medical	400,000
Hazardous-waste management	300,000
Genetic engineering	250,000
Bionic medical electronics	200,000
Laser, holographic and optical fiber maintenance	200,000

Source: U.S. Department of Labor, 1982.

a unified whole. In other words, the manager is not expected to actually perform the specialized task, but he or she must be able to pull the different tasks together into a smooth-running unit. This means that a premium will be placed on the development of important conceptual skills. We will discuss this issue further in the next chapter.

Changes in Controlling

Various aspects of the control function will also undergo changes in the future. For instance, with the increased attention expected to be given to the allocation of scarce resources to more specialized strategies, managers can also anticipate greater emphasis on control through budgetary procedures.

In addition to operational budgets, a second type of budget will require the time and attention of managers—the opportunities budget. Whereas the operational budget concerns acquisition and allocation of resources over a particular period of time, the opportunities budget looks at what resources will be needed in the long-term to take advantage of an anticipated opportunity. Many organizations such as Xerox, IBM, Gulf Oil, and John Deere are already building opportunities budgets into their long-range, entrepreneurial, and contingency planning processes.

Advanced computer systems can also be expected to make further inroads into the manager's job. This will not only include the use of the computer to solve complex problems, but also interactive terminals, which will increasingly be found in the manager's office. Through these devices, managers will tie directly into the organization's information systems for instant data analysis and information. As we noted earlier, increased use of the computer to handle routine and nonroutine decisions will enable managers to devote more time to long-range planning, innovative activities, and the like.

Finally, developments in the international area will provide both opportunities and constraints for management. In the developed countries of the West, the costs of traditional manufacturing activities will rise because of labor costs and labor shortages. In other words, those industries that are heavily labor intensive (e.g., automobiles, construction, and so on) will become increasingly noncompetitive. The opposite will occur in the developing countries, where the important industries are ones that will provide work for their surplus of labor.

One response to this problem and to the development of the transnational organization is *production sharing*. In production sharing, manufacturing a product can involve operations in more than one country.[20] The capital intensive part of the production process may occur in one of the developed countries, while the labor intensive portion will move to one of the developing countries.

Some examples can even be found today. Men's shoes, for instance, begin with the hide of an American cow; the hide is tanned in Brazil; the soles are made in Haiti; the uppers are put together in the British Virgin Islands; and, finally, the uppers and soles are sent to Puerto Rico or Jamaica for assembly and sent back to the U.S. as a finished shoe. Similarly, Japanese pocket calculators begin with an electronic chip manufactured in the U.S.; the chips are shipped to Singapore, Malaya, or Nigeria where they are assembled with steel components that were made in India. The finished unit is then sent to Japan where the "Made in Japan" label is applied.

Production sharing will place different demands on management. Not only will there be an increased emphasis on production design, quality control, and marketing, but managers must learn how to sharpen their managerial skills in these areas. More importantly, managers will be faced with decentralized control that will require the development of new integrating and coordinating methods and techniques. Unless new methods are developed, consumers will be faced with frequent product quality problems, costs will rise, and productivity will suffer.

Megatrends

More than a decade ago, John Naisbitt, a social scientist, began publishing a subscription report titled *The Trend Report*. Published three times each year, the purpose of the report was to inform subscribers of certain identifiable trends that could influence daily life in the not-too-distance future.

The interesting aspect of Naisbitt's report is that it involves little star gazing, use of the crystal ball, or excessive pontificating. Instead, his group scanned a massive amount of the available literature—magazines, newspapers, corporate reports, and the like—looking for threads and trends. He reviewed and analyzed the information and categorized it with the use of content analysis, a technique for counting the occurrence of information bits and topics.

In his popular book, *Megatrends*, Naisbitt identified ten important trends he believes are already reshaping our world.[21] According to Naisbitt, you cannot stop these trends, but you can think about them and apply what you learn, perhaps, to help yourself better adapt to change.

As shown in exhibit 19-9, these trends have a familiar ring. The information revolution, the use of temporal groups, the potential successes of high technology, and

Exhibit 19-9
Megatrends

---

1. We are in a megashift from an industrialized to an information-based economy.
2. For every high technology action, there is a high-touch reaction, or the technology will be rejected. (You cannot force technology on an unwilling population—it must satisfy a need.)
3. Our economy is becoming part of a global structure, moving away from isolation and national self-sufficiency. As a result, the U.S. will no longer be the world's dominant force.
4. U.S. corporate managers are beginning to think about the long-term rather than the next quarter.
5. Our centralized structures are crumbling. We are decentralizing and growing stronger from the bottom up.
6. We are reclaiming our traditional sense of self-reliance, after four decades of looking to institutions for help. (Among other things, this trend recognizes the strength of the entrepreneurial movement.)
7. Citizens, workers, and consumers are demanding and getting a greater voice in government, business, and the marketplace.
8. We are moving from hierarchies to networking; the computer is smashing the organizational pyramid.
9. The North-South shift in the United States is real and irreversible for the foreseeable future.
10. We no longer live in an either/or, chocolate or vanilla world; people have demanded and are getting a multitude of choices. (Recognized in this trend are the changes in the family, the desire for quality goods, new work schedules and so on.)

Adapted from T. Richman, "Peering into Tomorrow," *INC* (October 1982): 45-48.

Exhibit 19-10
Impact of Change on the Manager's Job: Summary

Change Element	Impact on the Manager's Job
Planning	
Increase in Environmental Monitoring and Scanning	New methods and approaches, both formal and informal, need to be developed. Strengthening of technical and diagnostic skill required. Informational roles will be emphasized.
Revised Organizational Goals	Broadening scope of goals will require improved knowledge of internal and external affairs. Conceptual skills will be stressed.
New Strategies and Plans	Ability to understand market leadership concept. Redefinition of keys to success for performance. Capacity to conduct both entrepreneurial and contingency planning. Strong emphasis on technical and diagnostic skills and decisional roles.
New Approaches to Decision Making	Ability to convert nonprogrammed decisions to programmed decisions with computer technology. Recognition of the emergence of new types of nonprogrammed decisions. Technical and conceptual skills stressed along with informational and decisional roles.
Organizing	
Different Structural Arrangements	Teamwork and cooperation required by the Office of the President concept. Wider range of skills and roles required to perform in a group manager's position. Increased use of temporary groups and task forces. Strengthening of human and conceptual skills along with interpersonal and decisional roles.
New Human Resource Requirements	Changing population characteristics will require new approaches to selection, placement, and training. Compensation and benefit programs need to be developed around the merit and individuality concepts. Further emphasis on human and diagnostic skills in addition to interpersonal roles.
Leading	
Revised Leadership Approaches	Changing measures of performance will require new ways of influencing others. More flexible leadership styles will be required. Human skills and interpersonal roles stressed.
Growth in the Number of Knowledge Workers	Improved mechanisms to integrate the professional needs of the individual with the performance requirements of the organization. Better understanding of the influence of leadership substitutes for knowledge workers. Human and conceptual skills required along with an emphasis on interpersonal roles.
Need for Generalists	Greater emphasis on managing people rather than being an expert in a field. Strengthening of all skills and roles.
Controlling	
New Control Approaches	Increased emphasis on resource allocation procedures. Development of more accurate performance evaluation methods. Improved knowledge and understanding of computers. Technical human and diagnostic skills and decisional roles stressed.
Production Sharing	Development of new plant location and design approaches. Increased knowledge of international operations. Improved management of decentralized operations. All skills and roles will be emphasized.

the need for managers to think about the long-term are certainly factors we have stressed throughout this book. There are also interesting and possibly controversial trends (e.g., global structure) that are generating a great deal of discussion in the field of management.

Summary

The points discussed in this section are some of the many potential changes that managers are expected to face in the future. They are not all-inclusive, nor are they guaranteed to occur. Some are anticipated, while others are already visible. Overall, the most important factor is that changes will occur in one form or another. The job of the manager will involve not only diagnosing what these changes are, but also what the appropriate responses should be to insure continued or improved performance. These changes and their suggested impact on the manager's job are shown in exhibit 19-10 on the previous page.

 SUMMARY FOR THE MANAGER

1. Change is an inevitable consequence of operating in a dynamic environment. For managers, it is important to recognize that change can be initiated by the organization (proactive) or be a reaction by the organization (responsive).

2. The major external forces for change include increased international competition, population characteristic changes, marketplace shifts, increased business-government interaction, and continued technological change. A major key to success with external change forces is the ability to identify its elements and develop programs in such a way that disruption is minimized.

3. Internal forces for change can originate within the organization, or be caused by external forces. Among the most important forces are changes in the composition of the work force, increased emphasis on improving productivity, the development of the quality of working life concept, and the availability of needed resources.

4. Whether change is proactive or responsive in nature, it is most successful when the organization adapts with a planned approach. The important elements of a planned change process include diagnosis and program goals, identification of constraints, selection of the proper change strategy, consideration of timing, location, and depth during implementation, and use of proven evaluation mechanisms.

5. Change can be expected to alter the managerial process. In planning, increased emphasis will be placed on improving environmental monitoring and scanning approaches, revising the scope of organizational goals, developing new strategies and plans, and changing the way decisions are made.

6. Changes in organizing will see new structures, including the office of the president, increased use of group managers and temporary teams and task forces, and new approaches to human resource management.

7.   The leading function in the future will see greater concern over productivity measurement, better ways of allocating resources, more flexible leadership styles, concern over the growing number of knowledge workers, and need for a generalist orientation.

8.   Changes in the control function will be significant. For example, budgetary procedures will be strengthened, use of computers in control will increase, and new production designs and systems will be needed if the concept of international production sharing continues to grow.

 REVIEW AND DISCUSSION QUESTIONS

1.   What major forces for change operate on a state university? A medical clinic?
2.   Why is improved productivity such an important issue for all types of organizations?
3.   What is the difference between proactive change and responsive change?
4.   Discuss the differences between task and technology change strategies. How can one affect the other?
5.   What methods can managers use to evaluate a change program?
6.   In what ways will the computer affect the manager's job in the future?
7.   Why is it important for managers to develop conceptual and diagnostic skills in coping with change?
8.   Why does the increase in the number of knowledge workers pose a problem for future managers?

NOTES

1.   A. Toffler, *Future Shock* (New York: Random House, 1970).
2.   "Saving Druggists in a Paper Storm," *Business Week* (June 2, 1980); 84.
3.   P. F. Drucker, *Managing in Turbulent Times* (New York: Harper & Row, 1980), pp. 103-10; and P. F. Drucker, "The Shape of Industry to Come," *Industry Week* (January 11, 1982): 55-59.
4.   W. Guzzardi, Jr., "A New Public Face for Business," *Fortune* (June 30, 1980): 48-52.
5.   M. Loeb, "The Corporate Chief's New Class," *Time* (April 14, 1980): 87.
6.   See D. D. Buss, "Retraining of Workers for Automated Plants Gets Off to Slow Start," *The Wall Street Journal* (April 13, 1983):1; and G. Bylinsky, "The Race to the Automated Factory," *Fortune* (February 21, 1983): 52-64.
7.   See E. C. Gottschalk, "Promotions Grow Few as Baby Boom Group Eyes Managers' Jobs," *The Wall Street Journal* (October 22, 1981); and J. Main, "Work Won't Be the Same Again," *Fortune* (June 28, 1982): 58-65.
8.   Drucker, *Managing in Turbulent Times,* pp. 130-34.
9.   See "How to Promote Productivity," *Business Week* (July 24, 1978): 146-51; C. R. Day, "Solving the Mystery of Productivity Measurement," *Industry Week* (January 26, 1981): 24-39; and R. S. Greenberger, "Work-Rule Changes Quietly Spread as Firms Try to Raise Productivity," *The Wall Street Journal* (January 25, 1983): 33.
10. See J. R. Hackman and J. L. Suttle, *Improving Life at Work* (Glenview, Ill.: Scott, Foresman, 1977).
11. See L. A. Girifalco, "The Dynamics of Technological Change," *The Wharton Magazine* (Fall 1982): 31-37; S. R. Michael, "Organizational Change Techniques: Their Present, Their Future," *Organizational Dynamics* (Summer 1982): 67-80; and N. Tichy, "Managing Change Strategically: The Technical, Political, and Cultural Keys," *Organizational Dynamics* (Autumn 1982): 59-80.

12. N. M. Tichy, "Agents for Planned Social Change: Congruence of Values, Cognitions, and Actions," *Administrative Science Quarterly* (March 1974): 164-82.

13. E. F. Huse, *Organizational Development and Change* (St. Paul, Minn.: West, 1975), p. 113.

14. See W. G. Bennis, *Organizational Development: Its Nature, Origins, and Prospects* (Reading, Mass.: Addison-Wesley, 1969); and R. Beckhard, *Organizational Development: Strategies and Models* (Reading, Mass.: Addison-Wesley, 1969).

15. L. Kraar, "The Multinationals Get Smarter About Political Risks," *Fortune* (March 24, 1980): 85-100.

16. Drucker, *Managing in Turbulent Times,* pp. 62-64.

17. W. Liechel, lll, "Everything You Always Wanted to Know May Soon Be On-Line," Fortune (May 5, 1980): 226-40.

18. Drucker, *Managing in Turbulent Times,* p. 130.

19. S. Kerr, "Toward a Contingency Theory of Leadership Based Upon the Consideration and Initiating Structure Literature," *Organizational Behavior and Performance* (October 1974): 62-82.

20. Drucker, *Managing in Turbulent Times,* p. 95.

21. See J. Naisbitt, *Megatrends* (New York: Warner Books, 1982); and T. Richman, "Peering into Tomorrow," *INC.* (October 1982): 45-48.

A CASE FOR ANALYSIS

Challenges to Organizations
General Motors

There have been and always will be many opportunities to fail in the automobile industry. The circumstances of the ever-changing market and ever-changing product are capable of breaking any business organization if that organization is unprepared for change—indeed, in my opinion, if it has not provided procedures for anticipating change.

Alfred P. Sloan, Jr.
My Years With General Motors

Alfred P. Sloan, Jr., whose icy intelligence shaped and presided over GM's awesome growth for more than three decades, died in 1966 at age 90. He imposed a management structure based on "decentralized planning with centralized financial controls" that enabled the company to handle anything that came along.

For more than half a century, Sloan's system of management worked beautifully. General Motors became the wonder of the industrialized world, a leader not only in finance and efficient production, but in masterful marketing as well. Sloan's machine was a wonderous thing in a world growing steadily more affluent, where fuel was cheap and the automobile removed restrictions of time and space for millions of people. Indeed, the automobile shaped the modern world and GM shaped the automobile.

Sloan's successors followed the blueprint closely, except for one important factor: the "procedures for anticipating change." They reacted rather than anticipated change. On more than one occasion since the energy crisis began in the 1970s, GM stumbled, reacting to events rather than anticipating them. For example:

- In response to foreign competition, GM introduced three new car lines (X, A, and J Cars) which were coolly received by the public. The cars were either overpriced, underpowered, or technologically outdated.
- To fund these new car lines, GM went heavily into debt, raising the concern of many in the investment community.
- On the very day in 1981 the United Auto Workers and GM announced some $2.5 billion in long-term wage concessions, a new bonus plan for GM executives was proposed for shareholder approval. That unfortunate timing set off an uproar.
- GM has failed to capitalize on the world market for automobiles. Both Toyota and Ford are bigger overseas. GM, in fact, loses money on its overseas operations.
- Management has allowed the corporation's five product lines (Cadillac, Buick, Oldsmobile, Pontiac, and Chevrolet) to grow and expand to the point that there is little distinction between the cars. As a result, confusion reigns in the marketplace.

Under current Chairman Roger Smith, GM's instinctive response to the new challenges of fuel economy, foreign competition, changing consumer tastes, and rising prices seems to be: Spend more money, speed up new product introductions, build more cars, cut costs here and there.

Why is GM in this situation? Many automobile industry experts point to the company's management development and succession program as a key factor. Since the late 1950s, the company's chairman has come up through the ranks of the finance division, while the president was frequently picked from the manufacturing area. With little marketing expertise in the executive suite, there was little doubt that finance and manufacturing were stressed. This was the hallmark of Sloan's decentralized planning/centralized control philosophy.

Few experts doubt the ability of GM to survive; many believe that automobile demand will increase, allowing its manufacturing and financial strengths to come to the forefront. The ultimate question is: Can GM adapt to a different world and adapt well enough to become consistently profitable again?

Adapted from T. O'Donnell and J. Andresky, "Are GM's Troubles Deeper Than They Look?," *Forbes* (September 27, 1982): 131-35.

Questions for Discussion

1. Identify the external and internal forces for change affecting GM.
2. Is there a relationship between GM's management development and succession program and the concept of resistance to change?
3. Commenting on Sloan's management system, one industry expert has stated, "The very system that once seemed to have institutionalized success may now be institutionalizing failure." Do you agree or disagree with this statement? If you agree, how would you change the system?

EXPERIENTIAL EXERCISE
Forces for Change

Purpose
To discuss certain forces for change in organizations and their implications for management.

Required Understanding
The student should have a basic understanding of the process of organizational change.

How to Set Up the Exercise
Groups of between four to eight persons should be established for the 30-45 minute exercise. The groups should be physically separated and members asked to converse only with their own group members.

Instructions
Presented here are three situations describing an identified force for change. Depending on the guidelines set by your instructor, each group should discuss and analyze one or more of the situations and answer the assigned questions. Each group's analysis should be presented to the total class.

A.   Demographers have over the past few years been predicting radical changes in organizations due to shifts in the population. For example, the Bureau of the Census and the Bureau of Labor Statistics are predicting the following demographic changes between 1980 and 1990:

    a. The number of persons 35 to 44 years old will increase to 36.1 million from 25.4 million, a 42 percent rise.

    b. The number of persons 45 to 54 years old will decrease slightly, from 21.3 million to 20.3 million.

    c. The number of jobs for managers and administrators at the middle-management level will increase to 10.5 million from 8.8 million, only a 19.1 percent gain.

Questions
1. What impact, if any, will these trends have on manpower planning?
2. What impact, if any, will these trends have on the design of jobs?

B.   We are fast moving from strict hierarchies to networking in organizations; the computer is smashing the organizational pyramid. As a result, the organization of the future will consist of:

    a. Small, task force units or teams (10 to 20 persons maximum). Members will have "functional homes" (i.e., sales, engineering, etc). However, the vast majority of their time will be spent in task force/team activities.

    b. Each unit will have economic and managerial control over its activities.

    c. Each unit in the organization will be connected with the executive structure through computer and telecommunication links.

    d. The popular organization chart will become a thing of the past.

This will be called the "atomized" structure to emphasize the small size and flexibility of its basic units in relation to their present counterparts. Its key objective will be to establish small units that can quickly adapt to an ever-changing environment.

Questions

1. What impact, if any, will this situation have on existing authority and control systems?
2. What impact, if any, will this situation have on employee training, development, and reward systems?

C. The Labor Department predicts that by the year 2000, nearly one-half of all U.S. jobs will be influenced or radically changed by some form of automation (e.g., robots, advanced word processing, telecommunication, and the like). A growing group of experts, however, predict that increased automation will result in a fundamental change in many workplaces that may require painful adjustments for organizations and workers alike. Among the expected problems identified by these experts are increased training costs for job-skills upgrading, a growing number of dead-end jobs (i.e., "baby-sitting" equipment), health and job pressure problems, and resistance from unions. As stated by *Business Week* (August 3, 1981):

> The new wave of factory and office automation in the U.S. will raise the productivity of American workers, improve the quality of the products they make, and increase the ability of domestic industries to compete with the imports that have eaten away at America's industrial strength. But these gains will be realized only if workers are convinced that the new machines are tools for improving their working lives rather than extremely efficient means of controlling behavior on the job. The challenge that faces management is to make the transition a smooth one.

Questions

1. Assuming the above to be true, what should management do to prepare for such changes?
2. Assuming the above to be true, to what degree should employees be involved in this change?

20

Challenges to Managers

Chapter Outline

Key Points

1. A bias for action, simple form-lean staff, closeness to the customer, and an emphasis on a key business value are just three of eight attributes identified as important characteristics of successful companies.
2. Profiles of successful executives show a tendency for them to be highly educated, have parents who were professionals, and have worked for less than three organizations throughout their careers.
3. A concern for results and people and a desire for achievement and responsibility are keys to successful managerial careers.
4. One's first job teaches lessons about unrealistic expectations, the first supervisor, confronting politics, and anxiety and stress.
5. Career planning has at least two elements: organizational career planning and individual career planning.
6. Career pathing involves vertical, lateral, and downward moves.
7. Individual career planning concerns resource analysis, a preference analysis, and a series of career goals.
8. Dual career couples and the mid-career plateau are two of the many current issues in managerial careers.

Success in the Computer Industry

Armed with degrees in math and engineering, Sandra Kurtzig went into business for herself in the early 1970s. She operated out of a room in her house and filed all her business funds in a shoe box. If there was more money in the box at the end of the month than the beginning, her small company had made a profit.

"I had no management experience," she recalls. "My long-range plans were figuring out where to go for lunch." Her business was simple enough: She developed computer software that let weekly newspapers keep track of their newspaper carriers. Apparently she learned how to be a manager, because the company became a success.

Slowing down a little, Sandra raised a family and then embarked on a new project. This time she recruited several bright young computer and engineering graduates and formed a company called ASK. They developed 10 software programs for other business applications. Executives at the nearby California Hewlett-Packard plant allowed the group to use one of the company's minicomputers at night to try to develop a management inventory control program. After many nights in sleeping bags on the floor, the company met with success.

The new programs were a big breakthrough for users. Manufacturing companies could now buy a 3000 minicomputer and the ASK program and use it to help run a plant. Kurtzig's small company has grown to $22 million a year in sales, 200 employees, $2.3 million of profits and a reputation as one of the most successful computer software companies.

Kurtzig's management career was highlighted by a number of important factors. First, she learned by doing—rolling up her sleeves and getting to know the ins and outs of the business. Second, as one industry expert pointed out, she didn't make the mistake many

computer software companies have made—she didn't try to become all things to all people. Instead, she concentrated on what she and her organization could do best—developing specialized computer software for manufacturing operations, emphasizing sales and service. Finally, she recognized that one of her most important resources were her employees. As a result, she stressed a good working environment, a competitive reward system, and an open, participative style.

Success stories like those of Ms. Kurtzig still happen, especially in the computer industry of California. What is new about these managerial careers is that more and more concern entrepreneurial women. In the past, a few women have gained prominence as entrepreneurs in such businesses as cosmetics and apparel but rarely in mainstream industries. Now, this is changing, as women are becoming owners of companies in widely varied fields such as construction, finance, and computer manufacturing and software.

Adapted from E. C. Gottschalk, Jr., "More Women Start Up Their Own Businesses, With Major Successes," *The Wall Street Journal* (May 17, 1983): 1.

20

In recent years, management scholars and practicing managers have given increased attention to assisting organizations and individuals develop career paths and career planning programs. This interest originates from a number of sources, including the dynamic environment, changing population demographics, changes in business patterns, and the emergence of international management. Most important is the fact that many people are seeking the challenge of a management career. The chapter's introductory *Practice of Management* section is a good illustration of this situation.

In this chapter, we will explore the challenges of a managerial career. There are two main sections. First, we will examine certain success keys, including profiles of successful organizations and managers. The second section will concentrate on career planning. This will involve discussions of organizational career planning programs, individual career planning activities, and select current issues such as dual careers.

 # Organizational Success Profiles

Throughout this book, we have suggested that there is no "one best way" of managing. There are too many factors and elements—such as differing environments, technologies, markets and products, and employee characteristics—that would support a single, universal approach to management. In essence, this is the contingency approach.

In absence of a universal approach to study, we may look at successful organizations and attempt to note any similar characteristics. Two recent studies that have reported such investigations are cited here.

In Search of Excellence

What makes for excellence in the management of a company? This was the question addressed by the management consulting firm of McKinsey & Company.[1] They studied the practices of 37 companies that are often used as examples of well-run organizations. Among the studied companies were IBM, McDonald's, Hewlett-Packard, Digital Equipment, 3M, Procter & Gamble, Johnson & Johnson, and Emerson Electric. Their findings identified eight attributes common to all the companies.

A Bias Toward Action The companies generally avoid analyzing and questioning products to death in search of the perfect plan. Instead, the key words are "do it, fix it, try it." The emphasis is on constant adjustments to change and doing the regular things well. Ideas, such as at 3M, are solicited regularly and tested quickly. Other characteristics include the existence of well-defined goals and an orientation toward focusing quickly on problems, generally with the use of task forces.

Simple Form and Lean Staff Even though all the companies studied have sales exceeding $1 billion, large, formalized structures are absent. Instead, most are organized around small entrepreneurial units where ideas could be given due consideration and the company was kept close to the market. Staffs are also kept small to avoid bureaucratic behavior.

Closeness to the Customer   The companies are customer driven, not technology or product driven. Constant contact with the customer provides insights that help direct the firm's plans. For example, at IBM and Digital Equipment, top management spends at least 30 days a year conferring with key customers.

Productivity Improvement via People   Rather than attempt to improve productivity by installing new capital equipment, a common attribute is to improve productivity through stimulating and motivating employees. This involves giving employees greater autonomy, allowing them to set their own targets, and implementing an extensive reward program with an emphasis on recognition awards.

Encouraging Entrepreneurship Through Autonomy   Almost all the companies strive to place new products in separate start-up divisions. This autonomy encourages managers to seek the highest performance and potential from the product, as well as encourage their own best effort. When problems or new ideas come to the surface at Texas Instruments, for example, managers in these new divisions can seek the help from a group of senior technical people called "individual contributors."

Stress on a Key Business Value   Rather than be all things to all people, the companies were found to generally follow a single-minded performance focus. At IBM, the focus is the customer; Texas Instruments stresses research and development; new product themes are emphasized at 3M and Hewlett-Packard; employee training is key at McDonald's, and so on.

Sticking to What They Know Best   All these successful companies have been able to define their strengths—marketing, low-cost manufacturing, new products—and then build on them. They have resisted the temptation to move into new businesses that look attractive but require organizational skills they do not have.

Simultaneous Loose-Tight Controls   Finally, the studied companies control a few key variables tightly but allow managers flexibility and looseness in others. 3M uses return on sales as a yardstick, but gives management a great deal of freedom in day-to-day operations; at Dana Corporation, the operations manual was thrown out and replaced with a simple one-page philosophy statement and control system that emphasizes the daily reporting of revenues and costs.

It should be pointed out that not only is a small sample of companies represented in this study, but the results do not necessarily suggest the right way to manage. Instead, it reports some common—and interesting—attributes that have been successful for some well-known firms. Whether these factors will work for many more companies remains an unanswered question.

Managers Evaluate Other Companies

Academicians, consultants, research institutes, and governmental agencies have all conducted evaluations of organizations, and the results have been published. The findings have been the subject of much discussion and comment.

Exhibit 20-1
Ranking of Corporate Strengths by Corporate Peers

Rank	Company	Industry group	Reason
1	IBM	Office equipment, computers	Quality of management, financial soundness, talented people
2	Hewlett-Packard	Precision instruments	Innovativeness, employee relations, management, products
3	Johnson & Johnson	Pharmaceuticals	Management, community relations, financial soundness
4	Eastman Kodak	Precision instruments	Product quality, community relations
5	Merck	Pharmaceuticals	Innovativeness, employee relations
6	AT&T	Utilities	Service quality, innovativeness, quality of management
7	Digital Equipment	Office equipment, computers	Innovativeness, quality of management, product quality
8	Smith Kline Beckman	Pharmaceuticals	Financial soundness, use of corporate assets
9	General Electric	Electronics, appliances	Quality of management, financial soundness, innovativeness
10	General Mills	Food	Financial soundness, product quality, asset use

Adapted from C. Makin, "Ranking Corporate Reputations," *Fortune* (January 10, 1983): 34-39.

Fortune magazine recently reported on a study with a different sample: nearly 6000 managers across 20 industries. Using a scale of 0 (poor) to 10 (excellent), these managers were asked to evaluate the companies in their own industries along eight key variables: quality of management, quality of products or services, innovativeness, value as a long-term investment, financial soundness, ability to attract, develop, and keep talented people, community and environmental responsibility, and use of corporate assets.

The results, shown in exhibit 20-1, reveal the top ten companies across all industries from the managerial sample. Interestingly, many of the successful companies examined in the McKinsey study turn up again in this sample.

 **Managerial Profiles**

In discussing a future managerial career, it may be helpful to look at elements of careers of working managers. We may be able to identify key factors that have led to managerial success. In this section, we will summarize recent studies investigating characteristics of managers.

We should caution the reader on two points. First, the majority of the data were

Exhibit 20-2
Managerial Profile: Career Factors

Work Week

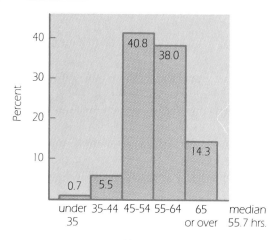

Hours

Years Employed by Present Company

Number of Years	Times Mentioned	Percent
Under 3	81	4.7
3-5	167	9.8
6-10	267	15.6
11-15	212	12.4
16-20	204	11.9
21-25	232	13.6
26-30	262	15.3
31-35	128	7.5
36 and over	133	7.8
No response	22	1.3
TOTAL	1708	100.0

Average: 19 years

Primary Career Emphasis of CEO's

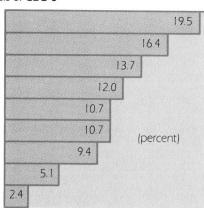

Financial — 19.5
Administrative/General Management — 16.4
Marketing — 13.7
Legal — 12.0
Production/Operations — 10.7
Technical — 10.7
Banking — 9.4
Founder — 5.1
Other — 2.4

(percent)

Number of Companies Worked for During Career

Number of Companies	Times Mentioned	Percent
1	445	26.0
2	426	24.9
3	413	24.2
4	215	12.6
5	80	4.7
6 and over	81	4.7
No Response	48	2.8
TOTAL	1708	100.0

Average: 3 companies

Source: Charles G. Burck, "A Group Profile of the Fortune 500 Chief Executive," *Fortune* (May 1976); "How Much Does Your Boss Make?" *Forbes* (June 11, 1979); John A. Sussman, "Making It to the Top: A Career Profile of the Senior Executive, *Management Review* (July 1979); and J.F. Veiga, "Do Managers on the Move Get Anywhere? *Harvard Business Review* (March-April 1981).

collected from middle and executive management levels. Thus, it is difficult to apply the data to lower management levels without some caution. Second, having these characteristics does not necessarily mean that the individual will be a successful manager. Similar to the trait theories of leadership (see chapter 13), success as a manager involves a number of factors, including individual characteristics, the nature of the task, the characteristics of the subordinates, and situational factors.

Background Factors

Fortune magazine recently surveyed top management in the 500 largest industrial companies and the 50 biggest commercial banking companies, insurance firms, retailers, transportation companies, and utilities. Among the most interesting findings were responses to questions on the executives' personal backgrounds. A number of important points can be derived from this information:

- Confirming recent trends, the data indicate that executives have high levels of educational achievement. Not only are more than 86 percent college graduates, but nearly 40 percent have received graduate degrees.

- The number of high-level executives who come from middle-class backgrounds has swelled, while the proportion from rich families has declined significantly. More executives than ever before grew up in blue-collar households. Yet, it is still striking that nearly 10 percent run large corporations previously headed by their fathers.

- The Midwest is the breeding ground for high-level executives. Even though it accounts for only 27 percent of the U. S. population, fully 40 percent were born there. It is interesting to note that in the thirty years that *Fortune* has been conducting this type of survey, the number of executives from the Midwest, Far West, and South have all increased, while the number from the Northeast has declined. This reflects, in part, the movement of the population to the Sunbelt states.

Career Factors

In addition to the *Fortune* study, a number of other investigations have been conducted on the managerial profile. A more recent study of nearly 2000 top executives revealed interesting findings concerning managerial career activities.[2] These results, shown in exhibit 20-2, include:

- Concurrent with the view of many people, executives devote a great deal of their time to work-related concerns. The executives' median workweek of 55.7 hours can be translated into over 11 hours per day for a five-day workweek, or over 9 hours if Saturdays are included.

- What is the path to the executive suite? Nearly one in five executives came from a primary career in finance, followed closely by general management and marketing. Yet, aspiring corporate executives should be cautioned against choosing a financial specialization solely because it is the leading background of today's executives. Twenty years ago the dominant career areas were production and operations, while in the mid-1970s, it was marketing. Current thinking suggests that by the late 1980s, a general management career emphasis will be dominant, followed by legal, which reflects the growing concerns over federal, state, and local legislative and regulatory activities.

▪ Frequent job hopping is not a characteristic of top-level managers. Over three-fourths of the sampled executives have been with three or less companies during their careers. These data are interesting, given the widely held view that the senior-level executive can be easily drawn away from a present employer if opportunities for advancement are not available.

Career Success Factors

What factors do successful managers believe were most important to their achievement? The opinions of executives are shown in exhibit 20-3.

From these results, a profile of the successful manager looks as follows: he or she is concerned with achieving high performance levels (the theme of this book!) and accomplishes this through integrity, responsibility, seeking behaviors, creativity, and concern for other people. At the other end, general appearance, intelligence level, and being in the right place at the right time are of lesser importance than some may believe.

Do these findings fit both male and female managers? Other studies suggest that they do.[3] While women managers are only now reaching the executive suite, recent findings suggest that they have reached the higher management levels through hard work, persistence, and concern for performance. Data on whether these same qualities apply to women managers who reach the top will become available as more do so. The major point, however, is that an emphasis on seeking high performance levels through drive, hard work, and persistence is a key to managerial advancement.

Exhibit 20-3 Managerial Profile: Career Success Factors	Factor	Percent Mentioned	Percent Mentioned As Most Important
	Aggressiveness	36.2%	3.6%
	Ambition, desire to achieve	38.1	9.4
	Appearance	14.8	2.1
	Concern for people	49.2	9.0
	Concern for results	73.7	17.5
	Creativity	44.7	2.8
	Desire for responsibility	57.8	14.3
	Integrity, honesty	66.3	3.6
	Intelligence	19.5	2.8
	Education	30.5	3.3
	Loyalty	23.4	3.2
	Professional or technical competence	34.3	2.5
	Timing—being in the right place at the right time	22.4	4.5

Adapted from John A. Sussman, "A Career Profile of the Senior Executive," *Management Review* (July 1979): 19.

 # Lessons from the First Job

A manager's career begins with the first job out of school. Usually, this initial position makes a deep and lasting impression. It can be a rapid learning experience in the ways of organizations, especially when the reward system and personal relationships are different from those experienced in school.

Because those first few years in an organization are so important to future success, it is worthwhile to discuss what you can expect to find. Expectations, initial job experiences, political processes, and coping with anxiety and stress will be discussed in this section.

Expectations

Many young managers enter their first job with the expectations that they will immediately take on significant responsibilities, be challenged daily with new experiences, have subordinates reporting to them, and earn a substantial salary. Unfortunately, these same young managers become disillusioned in the first few weeks or months on the job. Their first job is usually routine and boring, they supervise no one, and they find that the first paycheck—after taxes, social security, and other deductions—will not cover payments on a new car, an expensive apartment, or a new wardrobe. We are talking about a frequent phenomenon—unrealistic expectations.[4]

These unrealistic expectations have multiple origins. The most formative one is the college education process itself. In school, students become accustomed to studying large organizations and high-level managers who encounter problems or issues that demand the integration of many functional areas. The problems are interesting, challenging, and thought provoking. Unfortunately, students are led to believe that all problems that they will face in years to come will be of the same caliber. The education process has thus prepared the student to perform effectively in *later* positions, but not for the initial assignment out of school.

A second source of unrealistic expectations was discussed in chapter 10—the recruiting process. Company recruiters frequently overstate the attractiveness of the job and of the organization to secure a sufficient number of candidates. The candidates also create inaccuracies when they inflate their abilities or understate their needs in order to improve the chances of being selected. The result is a mismatch between the individual and the job.

Finally, the young manager's family can be a source of unrealistic expectations. The percentage of managers whose parents are professional or managerial is increasing. The young manager may hear about situations faced by a high-level manager, not the person on the first rung of the managerial career ladder. He or she may be thus ill-prepared for on-the-job experiences.

What can be done to reduce unrealistic expectations? First, the young recruit should find out what the organization expects of him or her.[5] These expectations are often some of the following:

- *Competence to get a job done*—to identify the problem and see it through to solution.

- *Ability to accept organizational "realities"*—to grasp organizational goals, recognition of group loyalties, internal power arrangements, office politics, and the like.

- *Ability to generate and sell ideas*—including translating technical solutions into practical terms, diagnosing and overcoming resistance to change, patience and perseverance in gaining acceptance of new ideas.

- *Loyalty and commitment*—to place the goals of the organization ahead of individual motives.

- *Personal integrity and strength*—to stick to one's point of view without being a rebel.

- *Capacity to grow*—to learn from experience and to demonstrate ability to take on increasing responsibility and maturity in the handling of interpersonal relationships.

Second, beyond participating in realistic job interviews and being honest about one's abilities and needs, it would help the new manager to seek out as much information as possible about the company and the job. This can be done by reading current literature and reports on the organization (e.g., *Business Week, Fortune,* and annual reports) and talking to people who are employed by the firm. If this is accomplished *before* the recruiting process begins, the young manager can be in a much better position to discuss important issues.

Initial Job Experiences

During the first few months in the new job, new managers are confronted with many different experiences and activities, all of which contribute to their learning. Among the most important concern the first supervisor, the performance evaluation process, and the challenge of the initial job.

The First Supervisor   The first supervisor can significantly influence your subsequent performance as a manager. This person is your first contact with the mentoring process.

Two general types of first supervisors are encountered. First, the supervisor can act with patience, understanding, and insight in directing new managers. He or she can insure that you do the right things at the right time and, if not, that you learn from mistakes. Consider the case of Russell Banks, founder of Metropolitan Telecommunications Corporation and later president of Grow Chemical Company. According to Banks, the first gap in his education turned out to be that he had not been taught much about analysis of financial statements. But his boss was sympathetic and helpful.

He gave me a great deal of authority in the beginning and therefore I got into the analysis and preparation of financial statements to a degree most young people couldn't. I became very inquisitive and he responded to every question so that I was able to understand the various systems people would be using and why. . . . He also taught me something about accuracy. When I reconciled a bank's annual statement to within 10 cents, I was proud. But my boss was not. "Russ," he said, "it's not 99 percent correct here, as it is in school. It's either 100 percent or nothing."[6]

On the other hand, the first supervisor can perceive the new recruit as a threat to his or her own position. It is possible that you may be coming to your job with more up-to-date technical skills and techniques than others, maybe even more than your supervisor. You also may be entering at a salary comparable to your peers' who have been working longer or even comparable to your supervisors'. Because of this, the relationship between you and your first supervisor may become strained and never develop its full potential.

Performance Evaluations   In chapter 16, we discussed the performance evaluation process. While we described how the process *should be* done, frequently just the opposite occurs. New managers often expect that feedback on their performance will be frequent and developmental. What can occur is that the performance review must be asked for and, when given, is done poorly. You are left in a state of confusion not only about how well you are doing, but also about what you can do to improve.

Job Challenge   We stated earlier that new managers usually find that their first job lacks challenge. Yet, there are ways you can make your jobs more challenging. For example, you can ask the supervisor for more to do or actually develop new ways of doing the job. New managers may be too accustomed to having everything presented to them, as happens in school. You need to take the initiative by taking a more active role in defining the job. Remember a credo: a job is *what you make it,* not something defined by a job description or the previous jobholder.

Confronting Organizational Politics

One of the most difficult lessons a college graduate must learn is that there are behind-the-scenes activities in organizations that often supersede more rational processes. New managers cannot understand, for example, why hard work and long hours haven't paid off in a promotion, why a seemingly straightforward decision took so long to make, or why a supposedly innovative idea was flatly turned down by higher management. These behind-the-scenes activities are well known to experienced managers as *organizational politics*.

As discussed in chapter 13, a manager's ability to influence others is closely connected to his or her power base. Managers will usually try to improve their power bases in as many ways as possible. This power-seeking behavior can focus on improving one's position (legitimate power), gaining control over important reward system components (reward and coercive power), and becoming skilled in a particular area (expert power).

Another important base is created when managers form political alliances with other managers—that is, when they gain the cooperation of peers and superiors. Such alliances can be used to resolve an issue more quickly than when more formal mechanisms are used. It is a give-and-take process among managers that can have short- and long-term effects on the organization.

What is difficult for the new manager to understand is that a new idea, for example, should be considered not only on its own merits, but also for the impact it has on other systems. For instance, an inexperienced sales representative may suggest the use of an

The career of Henry Porter is an example of the changing fortunes of the corporate world. When he graduated from college, ranking third in his class, Mr. Porter was inundated with job offers from major companies. He chose General Mills because he saw a vacuum in the financial area that, with proper training, he could partially fill in the future.

He guessed correctly, because in seven years he had risen to financial vice president. Even though success was followed with greater successes, Porter's sharp business senses told him that the top managers of General Mills in the future would be marketing and consumer executives, not financial types like himself.

So after fourteen years with General Mills, Porter moved to Louisville to take on another great opportunity—that of senior vice president of the U.S. subsidiary of British-American Tobacco Company. This time, his senses proved him wrong. The expected support from corporate headquarters for Porter's strategy of diversification out of the tobacco industry did not materialize.

With his discouragement growing, Porter quit his job and became an independent management consultant. Again successful and facing a new challenge, Porter muses about luck as a factor in managerial careers, "Most people who are successful have had fortuitous breaks. A lot of success is being in the right place when there's an opportunity and you're the easy choice. It happened to me at General Mills."

Adapted from E. C. Gottschalk, Jr., "Most Do Well Financially, But Few Lead Big Firms: The Importance of Luck," *The Wall Street Journal* (December 20, 1982): 1.

improved packaging design for a product. This person may only see the merits of the new packaging design from the view of consumer response. The sales representative's superior, however, may recognize that the new design will disrupt the production process overseen by the manufacturing manager. When the idea is turned down, the sales representative may fail to look beyond the packaging design itself to the more important elements of the "big picture." In other words, the sales manager and manufacturing manager had developed a political alliance over time that had resulted in a smooth-running operation for both.

Organizational politics has a number of important features. One, discussed in chapter 9, is position protection. That is, managers seek power through political processes for no other reason than to protect their jobs. They can influence others without exercising that power—just having the power is enough to get what they want. For example, an office manager of a large building complex may have obtained control over the budget for office equipment and must approve all office moves. Other managers may recognize this power base and how important it is for their own expansion plans. Therefore, in order to get what they want (new offices, new furniture, or an increase in word-processing equipment), they quickly form a cooperative alliance with the office manager. In this way, all get what they want—the functional manager receives the needed equipment and the office manager has protected his or her job. As an executive acquaintance of your author once said: "He who controls the gold, makes the rules."

Anxiety and Stress

All managers face anxiety and stress in their careers. The new manager is anxious over whether he or she will be able to adapt to organizational practices and perform effectively. Experienced managers will question your ability as assignments grow more challenging and demanding. Similarly, mature managers grow more concerned about demands of the job, competition from young, better-educated managers, and possible conflicts between the job and the family as their careers progress.

Anxiety and stress are part of every manager's job. On the positive side, stress can motivate, stimulate, and challenge the manager. Some people believe that too little stress on the job can be harmful, since the individual loses his or her mental acuity and can become open to other ailments. On the other side, excessive stress, especially when coupled with smoking and poor diet, can result in elevated blood pressure and the increased probability of heart disease.

If stress is excessive, what can the manager do to reduce it?[7] A number of techniques currently are used in organizations. Both the organization *and* the individual can take action to prevent or alleviate stress.

Interviews with top executives show that many of them know how to take stress in stride. Many executives believe that a person cannot reach the top unless he or she knows how to handle stress. Perhaps John Zimmerman, vice president of employee relations for Firestone Tire and Rubber, said it best: "Stress is what you make of it, and that can be the difference between coping and collapsing."[8]

Career Planning

Increasingly, management scholars and practitioners are turning their attention to assisting employees plan their careers in a manner that copes with today's changes. This process helps fill a need at a time when career development is central to many people's lives. It is also another way an organization can function effectively for its employees.

Our coverage of this process, known as career planning, will focus on career stages: organizational career planning, individual career planning, and current issues in career planning.

Career Stages

Most management scholars define a career as a sequence of jobs that unfolds over time. In addition to moving from one job to the next, an individual moves through identifiable occupational and life stages. As shown in exhibit 20-4, there are four distinct career stages.

Exhibit 20-4
Managerial Career Stages

			Career Stages	
	I	**II**	**III**	**IV**
Position	Trainee, novice	Manager	Middle manager	Senior manager or Executive
Primary Relationships	Apprentice	Colleague	Mentor	Sponsor
Major Activities	Helping, learning, following directions	Independent contributor	Training, interfacing with others	Shaping the direction of the organization
Focus of Task	Dependence, varied job activities, self-exploration and settling down, initial job choices	Independence, developing competence in an area, creativity and innovation, job rotation	Assuming responsibility, developing skills in training and coaching others, rotating into new jobs requiring new skills	Exercising power, identifying successors, long-range planning, increased outside activities
Organizational Processes	Training, indoctrination, socialization, acceptance as a group member, conferring of status	First testing of capacity to function, granting of real responsibility, preparation for bigger jobs, further education	Increased leadership activities, movement across functional boundaries	Key communication link, respected member, expert power, preparation for exit

Adapted from E. Schein, "The Individual, the Organization, and the Career," *Journal of Applied Behavioral Science* (1971); D. T. Hall and M. Morgan, "Career Development and Planning," in W. C. Hamner and F. Schmidt, eds., *Contemporary Problems in Personnel*, rev. ed. (Chicago: St. Clair Press, 1977); and G. W. Dalton, P. H. Thompson, and R. L. Price, "The Four Stages of Professional Careers," *Organizational Dynamics* (Summer 1977).

Stage I concerns the individual's first job in the organization. The main role is one of a trainee who seeks assistance and direction. Socialization and group acceptance processes are strong, and the individual concentrates on settling down and learning.

In *Stage II,* the first real managerial position is accepted. The individual begins to make his or her initial contribution to the organization. Job rotation is frequent, as are learning and skills development activities.

Stage III finds the manager at mid-career, where he or she has taken on more responsibility. Leadership roles include not only directional activities, but also mentorship and the training of others. Frequent job changes, sometimes cross-functional, add to the manager's skills.

Finally, in *Stage IV,* managers find themselves with at least two major job responsibilities. First, now at the higher-management levels, they are responsible for setting the future direction of the organization. They are in their most powerful position, where there is a high degree of control over important organizational resources. Managers in this career stage find that contact with people and organizations outside their own has increased significantly. The second major responsibility of Stage IV is the preparation for exit. This includes not only identifying and grooming possible successors, but preparing for retirement and the major adjustments that must be made. With recent changes in retirement laws, however, many executives are staying on beyond age sixty-five, either as executives or in an important advisory capacity.

A second way of looking at career stages is to recognize that some careers may be independent of the person's age. One way of depicting this situation is shown in exhibit 20-5, where the two major dimensions correspond to the manager's performance and advancement potential or promotability.[9] The *learner* is a manager who exhibits high promotability, but is performing at a low level. This can be the new management recruit or the person who has recently taken a new position, but has not had time to master it. The *star* is an individual who is doing outstanding work and has the potential to advance further in the organization. *Rocks* are managers who are consistent high performers, but may have plateaued in advancement. These managers provide the solid foundation for the organization's activities and may very well be chosen as mentors. Finally, *deadwood* applies to the manager whose performance and promotability are low. He or she is making little or no contribution to the organization and could be let go, moved to an unimportant job, or retrained.

The key feature of this approach to describing career stages is that a manager can move *between* the stages, unlike approaches that emphasize the manager's age and the sequential development of the stages. For example, a manager in a high-level manufacturing position may be considered a rock by the organization. Because the manager is a consistently high performer, top management may laterally move him or her to a newly created position in personnel in an important subsidiary. The transfer essentially moves the manager from the rock category to that of a learner. The hope is for the manager to learn and grow again to be a star. Similarly, organizations frequently use extensive training programs to move managers from the deadwood stage into the learner position.

Exhibit 20-5
Career Stress: Performance and Promotability

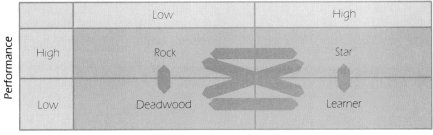

Adapted from T.P. Ference, J.A.F. Stoner, and E.K. Warren, "Managing the Career Plateau," *Academy of Management Review* (October 1977).

Elements of Career Planning

Even with the growing popularity of the concept, there is great confusion concerning the focus and definition of career planning. The literature is full of such terms as manpower planning, career counseling, career pathing, achievement programs, and career development. We believe that a better approach is to look at career planning as consisting of two major elements, as shown in exhibit 20-6: organizational career planning and individual career planning.[10]

Organizational career planning integrates human resource needs and a number of career activities, emphasizing career ladders or paths. Human resource needs are an important component of the human resource planning process, while career paths are sets of connecting job families within the organization.

As shown in exhibit 20-7, available career activities or programs are numerous, including career counseling, career pathing, human resource inventories and information systems, and training. Various organizations stress different components or programs.[11] For example:

Exhibit 20-6
Career Planning
Elements

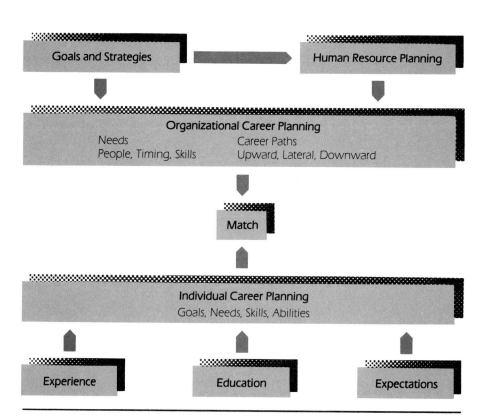

Exhibit 20-7
Specific Career Activities

Career Counseling
Career counseling during the employment interview.
Career counseling during the performance appraisal session.
Psychological assessment and career alternative planning.
Career counseling as part of the day-to-day supervisor/subordinate relationship.
Special career counseling for high-potential employees.
Counseling for downward transfers.

Career Pathing
Planning job progression for new employees.
Career pathing to help managers acquire the necessary experience for future jobs.
Committee performs an annual review of management personnel's strengths and weaknesses and then develops a five-year career plan for each.
Plan job moves for high-potential employees to place them in a particular target job.
Rotate first-level supervisors through various departments to prepare them for upper-management positions.

Human Resources
Computerized inventory of backgrounds and skills to help identify replacements.
Succession planning or replacement charts at all levels of management.

Career Information Systems
Job posting for all nonofficer positions; individual can bid to be considered.
Job posting for hourly employees and career counseling for salaried employees.

Management or Supervisory Development
Special program for those moving from hourly employment to management.
Responsibility of the department head to develop managers.
Management development committee to look after the career development of management groups.
In-house advanced management program.

Training
In-house supervisory training.
Technical skills training for lower levels.
Outside management seminars.
Formalized job rotation programs.
Intern programs.
Responsibility for manager for on-the-job training.
Tuition reimbursement program.

Special Groups
Outplacement programs.
Minority indoctrination training program.
Career management seminar for women.
Preretirement counseling.
Career counseling and job rotation for women and minorities.
Refresher course for midcareer managers.
Presupervisory training program for women and minorities.

Source: M. A. Morgan, D. T. Hall, and A. Martier, "Career Development Strategies in Industry: Where Are We and Where Should We Be?" *Personnel*, March-April 1979, (New York: AMACOM, a division of American Management Associations, 1979).

- General Electric begins with an extensive set of manuals. They include: (a) *Career Dimensions I*—a workbook for the employee's initial exploration of life issues that affect career decisions; (b) *Career Dimensions II*—a career-planning workbook for the employee; (c) *Career Dimensions III*—a guide to help the manager have effective career conversations with employees; and (d) *Career Dimensions IV*—a handbook for those who design and conduct career planning workshops and seminars. These manuals and workshops provide a background for career planning and career management.

- Syntex's interest in career planning evolved from a need to improve management selection and development. Their system uses three elements: an assessment center, a career planning workbook for all employees, and a series of regularly scheduled seminars designed for different level employees.

- Crocker Bank developed a career planning program that emphasizes career counseling, workshops, workbooks, job posting, and integration of career planning with the bank's human resource planning system.

- At IBM, the focus of career planning is the interaction between superior and subordinate. The employee, through descriptive brochures and cassettes, is encouraged to do some precounseling planning by preparing answers to a series of questions. These questions are analyzed with the superior, and a career plan is developed.

As the reader may have surmised, there is no one best approach to career planning. Organizations select these approaches that work best for them and refine them over time.

Individual career planning differs philosophically and procedurally from organizational career planning. This type of career planning focuses on individuals and their needs, skills, and desires. Most importantly, individual career planning involves procedures and diagnostic exercises to assist the person determine "who am I?" in abilities and potential. These procedures involve a "reality check" to help the individual toward a meaningful identification of his or her strengths and weaknesses, and encouragement to lead from strength and to correct weaknesses. This self-assessment aspect will be developed later in this chapter.

The key to career planning is the match between organizational career planning and individual career planning. The organization has as much to gain as the individual in identifying resource needs and creating and maintaining career paths that move people through talent-challenging experiences.

Organizational Career Planning: Career Pathing

Career pathing, an important component of organizational career planning, has its origins in the writings of many management scholars. One approach that has had a major impact is the work of Edgar Schein.[12] His model focuses on the career as a set of attributes and experiences of the individual who joins, moves through various jobs, and finally leaves the system. The appropriate career path is defined by the organization after consideration of whom to move, when, how, and how often.

The Cone Model

Schein's *cone model* (exhibit 20-8) indicates that career paths can proceed in at least three directions:

- *Vertically,* which involves increasing or decreasing one's role in the organizational hierarchy. We have come to know this as moving from first-line management, to middle-management, to the executive level.

Exhibit 20-8
Schein's Cone Model of Career Development

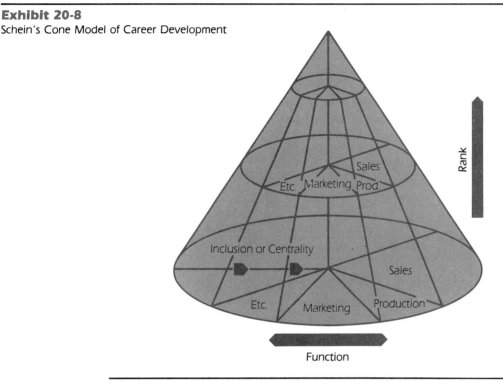

Source: Reproduced by special permission from *The Journal of Applied Behavioral Science*, "The Individual, the Organization, and the Career: A Conceptual Scheme," by Edgar Schein, vol. 7, no. 4, p. 404. Copyright 1971, NTL Institute.

- *Radially,* which is increasing or decreasing one's importance or centrality in the organization. This can mean moving from line to staff positions, or movement toward or away from the organization's "inner circle."

- *Circumferentially,* which involves moving from one functional area to another in the organization. In other words, managers may be moved from production to marketing, from marketing to personnel, and so on.

    Schein suggests that with each move, or combination of moves, the organization will attempt to influence the individual, and the individual will attempt to influence the organization in return. The influence of the organization on the individual can occur in two ways. First, in moving vertically or radially, the manager is subjected to different *socialization* attempts by members of the new unit. This is considered an important concept because acquiring new attitudes and values is necessary for high performance. For example, it must be made clear to a manager that in moving from the middle-management to the executive level, not only are different managerial functions emphasized, but new ways of thinking—as in going from short-range to long-range planning—are needed.

Second, a circumferential move will require additional *training* for the manager. For instance, if a manager moves from a job in production to one in personnel, there will be a need to acquire new skills and knowledge of the different roles that must be performed. The combination of socialization and training prepares the manager to not only perform effectively in the new position, but new attitudes, values, and skills are added to the manager's qualifications for future moves.

The way the individual influences the organization is through the *innovation* process. While vertical, radial, and circumferential movements force managers into new learning situations, managers also have ideas and approaches of their own. As we have all experienced, sometimes it takes a "new face" in our group to cause change, leading to improved effectiveness. Before a new manager can innovate, he or she must be accepted into the group and be recognized for some expert skill or valuable experience.

Schein suggests that socialization and training activities are most prevalent for the younger manager—that is, one who has not yet been fully acclimated to the organization. Innovation occurs most often later in a manager's career, when he or she has acquired more status and experience.

Career Pathing at Sears

Sears, Roebuck and Company has developed an approach to career pathing that uses a potent but very common training and development technique: the job. Sears has a long history of using job assignments for management development.[13] For example, for years college recruits started on the back dock and rotated through six or eight other job assignments during the first twelve to eighteen months. At the end of this period, the individual was assigned to his or her first supervisory position as a department manager. During ensuing years, if the individual was still considered promotable, he or she was assigned to a variety of store staff positions—perhaps as many as seven—ending with the assistant store manager and store manager positions.

Career Pathing Fundamentals   Career pathing at Sears is based on the following principles:

- The most important influences on career development occur *on the job*. Everyday job challenges and demands are important socializing and skill-building mechanisms. The job itself probably has more influence on development than formal classroom training programs.

- Different jobs demand the development of different skills. A first-line manager's job, for example, stimulates the development of improved human relations skills, while a position in finance may add to the individual's technical skills.

- Each new job requires the development of new skills. Very little is learned if a person is put into another job that demands skills the person has already mastered. A job in a career path should stretch the person to learn new skills or improve existing ones.

- With a systematic career pathing program, the time required to develop the necessary skills for a target job can be reduced. Without such a program, job assignments often overlap. Some promotions within the same functional area, for example, do not

The Manager's Job

Lewis Lehr of 3M Company

Lewis W. Lehr started his career at Minnesota Mining and Manufacturing (3M) shortly after World War II, testing competitor's tapes in the laboratory. He claimed it was one of the dullest jobs around, but stuck it out and recently was named chairman of the company.

The comings and goings of top executives spin tales of corporate intrigue at CBS, RCA, and Pillsbury—but not at 3M. Its management is one of the most inbred in the U.S., and it has long turned its back on job jumpers—executives who frequently move from one company to another.

According to Lehr, the foundation of this philosophy is an extensive career planning system. The key elements are as follows:

- A strong belief in promotion from within.

- An overall communication program featuring meetings, informal referrals, and communication to increase the awareness of career opportunities.

- A career information center with information about company jobs and career paths, current literature on career planning, and self-development programs.

- An extensive career counseling program.

- Career growth workshops to aid in assessing oneself and one's current job as a base for growth.

- Assistance in making job transfers.

Lehr believes that 3M's approach is to provide support services that make one's current job a continuing base for growth, increase personal satisfaction, and offer the opportunity for increased effectiveness.

Adapted from Lawrence Ingrassia, "3M Uses Promote-From-Within Policy to Breed Managers Like Chairman Lehr," *Wall Street Journal* (July 7, 1980): 13.

---

encourage skills development. A systematic approach, on the other hand, minimizes overlap in job demands, and thus enhances the development of skills.

Implementing the Approach The Sears approach begins with an evaluation of each job along three basic dimensions: know-how, problem-solving requirements, and accountability. Each of these dimensions itself has subdimensions. For example, know-how is broken down into job knowledge associated with technical, managerial, and human skills. Scores, or points, for each subdimension are assigned to each job, and a total value for each job is then computed.

With the use of this evaluation system, effective developmental career paths can be constructed. Each manager's career path is structured around three experience elements: (1) an increase in at least one skill area (e.g., know-how) on each new assignment; (2) an increase of at least 10 percent in total points on each new assignment; and (3) job moves, which can be upward, downward, or cross-functional.

To illustrate the steps managers' careers can take, consider the example in exhibit 20-9. The exhibit shows possible career paths for four managers. Manager 1 begins as a department sales manager with a career path that leads to the position of vice president of operations; manager 2 also begins as a department sales manager, but is career pathed to the vice president of merchandising position; manager 3's career path begins and ends the same as manager 1, but the path is different; finally, manager 4 stays within the personnel function, eventually achieving the vice president's job.

The exhibit also shows many of the possible combinations of experiences available to managers in this system. For example, the move by manager 3 from group manager of personnel to store manager entails an increase in at least one skill area. Manager 2's promotion from merchandise manager to vice president of merchandising involves more than a 10 percent increase in total points. Each manager experiences an upward

Exhibit 20-9
Career Pathing
Example in a
Retail Organization

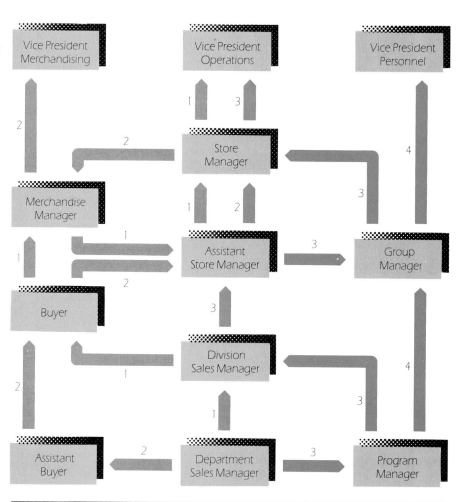

job move more than once. All managers, with the exception of manager 4, also experienced at least one lateral, or cross-functional move. A downward move is shown for manager 1 in the transfer from merchandise manager to assistant store manager.

Before this type of career pathing approach can work effectively, a number of issues need to be confronted. First, managers at all levels must be committed to the new system. As pointed out in the last chapter, moving from a strict vertical ladder approach to one with multiple moves can be met with considerable resistance. Second, managers must not view lateral, cross-functional or downward moves as being blots on their records. It must be clear that these moves are necessary for skills improvement. Downward moves in some organizations, in fact, are made with an agreement similar to academic tenure—that is, the manager accepting a downward move will not be terminated within the near future. Finally, one must be concerned with the accuracy of the job evaluation system. An inaccurate system will identify improper moves and prevent acceptable moves.

Individual Career Planning

Individual career planning consists of a number of important elements. The most crucial are a personal resource analysis, a career preference analysis, and career goals.[14]

Personal Resource Analysis

One of the first things a young manager should do in planning his or her career is a personal resource analysis, sometimes referred to as self-assessment.

We may take a lesson from our analysis of organizations, their goals, and their strategies when we develop a personal resource profile. First, the individual should identify various facets that make up his or her important characteristics. Included are needs, skills, experiences, abilities, aptitudes, and so on. Second, evaluate each of these characteristics as being a strength or weakness. For example, an individual can identify "I like to work on challenging tasks" and "I have a number of years as a manager in a high technology industry experience" as certain strengths. On the other hand, this same person can state that "I get bored very quickly if faced with routine job duties" and "I need a graduate degree to progress further in this organization and industry" are weaknesses. If available, a university testing center may be a good start in developing a resource analysis.

Several points should be made about this type of analysis. First, it is helpful to ask other people what they think your strengths and weaknesses are, especially for such hard-to-self-evaluate factors as interpersonal relations and ability to communicate. Second, it is important to consider your perspective when the analysis is developed. For example, if a promotion is your goal, then an evaluation such as this would be helpful. Conversely, if you are looking for long-term tenure in the present job, then some of the strengths and weaknesses could be revised or even switched. Last, this

analysis is only as good as the degree of honesty that goes into it. Throwing too many flowers on one's accomplishments or being too critical won't do anything but confuse the issue.

A personal resource analysis is not an end in itself. It is a good start and provides a foundation for further planning.

Career Preference Analysis

The personal resource analysis responds to the issue of "who am I?" The next step is to answer the question, "what do I want from a job and career?" Because this subject deals with preferences, there are no specific guidelines that fit everyone. What may be of assistance are a series of questions that each young manager should answer carefully. The first concerns *general issues.* For example:

- *Do I have a geographic preference for where I would like to work? Do I want to be near home? near recreations areas? in warmer climates? ski areas? How mobile am I willing to be? How important is the area to my lifestyle?* We all have certain preferences as to where we would like to live, but we must also recognize that the more detailed and demanding our preference, the more limited will be the job opportunities.

- *In what type of organization do I want to work (profit, not-for-profit, public sector)? What types of industries within these sectors appeal to me (manufacturing, insurance, health care, and so on)? Do I have a preference concerning the size of the organization (large, medium, or small)?* The choices available to the new manager are innumerable. There are opportunities in just about all types of organizations. In recent years there has been a significant movement of managers *across* industries; e.g., engineers working in hospitals, or personnel specialists in social service agencies moving to manufacturing firms. This trend offers greater opportunities for the manager.

▪ *Do I want to work for a growth organization or one that stresses stability? Would I like to work for a young organization or one that is an established concern?* These are some of the most difficult questions for the new manager. Many people initially want the challenge of working for a young and growing organization, yet few understand that such organizations are more risky to a career. On the other hand, though the established, stable firm may offer less risk, one can expect slower career growth than in the younger organization.

Beyond these general issues, the new manager should consider the following specific *job-related* questions:

▪ *What kind of job do I want? Do I want a fast track or one where I begin at the bottom and learn all facets of the business? Am I willing to accept a lower starting salary because the job is interesting or promises fast career movement after a few years?* The fast track may get the individual to a higher level quicker, but slower movements may provide him or her with a better understanding of the various functions of the organization. A lower starting salary is used by some organizations, especially in retailing, as a screening mechanism for young recruits. If the person is willing to pay his or her "dues" for a few years, the upper managerial ranks offer substantial increases in salary.

▪ *Do I prefer to work alone? in small groups? or in large groups? Do I like many committee and task-force assignments?* Understand your preferences and then investigate the policies of the organization. Remember that as one advances up the management ladder and as the external environment grows more complex, group-related activities will probably increase.

▪ *With what type of supervisor do I work best? Do I want someone who directs my work closely or someone who leaves me alone? Do I prefer one who gives me frequent feedback or one who communicates my good and bad points at infrequent intervals?* No two supervisors are the same. Like you, they have their own preferences and needs, so spend time understanding what motivates them. Whatever type of supervisors you work with during your career, remember a key point: learn from them, no matter if it is how to do something correct or how not to do something. Constantly observe, investigate, study, and ask—learn what it takes to be effective in various situations.

Setting Career Goals

Setting career goals is a natural result of the personal resource analysis and career preference analysis. In general, career goals consist of two components: time frame and criteria.

Time frame is important because too many young managers set career goals in terms of the highest level in the organization they wish to achieve, without considering how they are going to get there. To counter this, many career planning specialists suggest that at least three time frames be considered. The first is the *immediate* period after graduation from college through the first year of employment. Second, career goals should be set for a period *three to five years* after the immediate period. These are probably the most realistic goals to be set because they concern a time where some degree of forecast accuracy can be achieved. Finally, career goals for a period of *ten years* from the present time should be established. Normally, these ten-year goals are quite ambiguous because much can happen in ten years that cannot be forecast. Nevertheless, such goals serve a purpose if for no other reason than they force the manager to think carefully about what he or she wants to accomplish.

Career *goal criteria* consist of the particular work-related factors the manager wishes to achieve. The key factors include:

- Specific job titles
- Target salary
- Number of different jobs held during a period
- Number of people you would like to supervise
- Level of educational achievement (MBA, CPA, and so on)
- Type of lifestyle you want
- Level of responsibility
- Type, size, and growth of employing organization.

It may also be helpful for you to select priorities among the criteria within each time frame.

Career goals should be frequently analyzed and revised. Far too often, job-related and/or family-related situations can totally revamp your career planning. Career goals should be examined at least once a year to insure their accuracy with respect to current events.

Current Issues in Managerial Careers

Managerial careers can be exciting, challenging, but increasingly complex. We have chosen two important current issues for discussion—dual-career couples and the mid-career plateau.

Dual-Career Couples

An ever-increasing problem faced by individuals and organizations is the managing of dual careers. *Dual careers* describes the husband and wife who both have full-time careers, whether in similar or different fields, in the same or different organizations. There has been a rapid increase in the number of married women who have joined the work force on a full-time basis. More than one-half of all mothers with children under the age of three are in the work force. In addition, nearly 58 percent of all working women are married and living with employed spouses. This means that more than 46 million men and women—out of 98 million people in the American work force—are two-career couples.

At least two factors are possible causes for the growth in dual-career families.[15] First, pure economic reasons are behind a large number of married women seeking full-time employment. High inflation has put a crunch on many family budgets, forcing major adjustments. Also, particularly for young couples, two incomes provide for establishing the "good life" much earlier than their parents could. They have the opportunity to buy homes, take vacations, and purchase luxury items usually *before* children are added to the family. Their parents usually tried to attain this type of lifestyle only *after* the children left the nest. The second reason is simply women's needs, like men's, for professional growth, development, and recognition.

Whether the dual-career couple is motivated by economic need or professional development, it presents unique opportunities *and* adjustment problems for both the organization and the couple.[16] For example, if one is offered a significant promotion in another city that has limited job opportunities for the spouse, how should the couple react? What if the husband and wife work for two different organizations in a situation of potential conflict of interests? Also, a household still must be maintained, and in many cases there are children who must be raised. Some dual-career couples may believe that some of these problems are insurmountable; others look at it as an opportunity for a new start and a chance to give careers an added commitment. For the organization, there are a number of issues that must be faced: for example, how to manage recruitment if both are desirable employees for the firm; how to handle problems of travel, transfers, or promotions; whether the organization should get involved in dual-career planning.

When dual-career couples first appeared in organizations, neither the couple nor the organization knew how to handle the conflicts that invariably developed. Over time, however, a number of keys to success have been noted. For the couple, a successful dual career usually results from an emphasis on four factors. First, there must be a *mutual commitment* by the couple to *both* careers. This means that one member does not take precedence over the other on all career matters. Second, there should be *flexibility*—personal *and* job related—on the part of both members. There must be a willingness to change plans, shift gears, and try new ways of doing things. Third, successful dual-career couples have developed *coping mechanisms* to resolve job- and family-related conflicts. Finally, similar to the first two points, an emphasis should be placed on *keeping up to date* in one's career. To be flexible and adaptable, each member of the dual-career family should spend considerable time and effort on self-assessment and continuing education.

Organizations, too, must be able to adapt to dual-career couples. Initially, this can involve providing flexible career tracks, possibly involving cross-functional moves, instead of a rigid career path. Second, some internal policies may need to be revised; e.g., less rigid transfer policies (so that turning down a transfer does not exclude future promotions) and special recruiting techniques. Third, dual-career support services, which could help an unemployed spouse find a new job, for example, locate daycare centers or childcare arrangements, assist in buying and selling homes, revise fringe-benefit policies, or provide couple career counseling.[17]

In summary, it is important for managers and organizations to recognize that the dual-career phenomenon is here to stay. It is a reflection of changing societal and cultural norms on one hand, and on the other hand a recognition that a career is shaped more by the individual than by the organization. Because the individual's career may be redirected from time to time to meet the needs of the person, it is crucial for organizations to develop programs to accommodate people's talents more effectively.

Mid-Career Plateau

Once a manager has become established in his or her career (stage III or the "rock" in our earlier discussion), he or she enters what has been called the mid-career plateau. In contrast to the fierce strivings and achievement of the earlier stages, most of what managers do in this stage is oriented to holding their own and maintaining what they have already achieved. In other words, it is generally not a time for breaking new ground. Yet this is not a tranquil period, one of reaping the fruits of earlier labors and achievements. It can be a time for decline or for embarking on a new career. Research suggests that there are physiological, attitudinal, occupational, and family-related changes that occur at this stage.[18] For example:

- An awareness of advancing age, mentally and physically
- A recognition of what career goals have been accomplished and those that cannot be achieved
- A growing search for a change in lifestyle
- Observable changes in work-related relationships
- A growing sense of obsolescence
- The person feels less mobile and attractive in the job market and therefore, more concerned about job security.

More than anything, the mid-career plateau is an identity crisis filled with concerns about goals and questions such as "Where am I headed?" and "What can I do next?"

The preceding points may sound gloomy for the forty-year-old manager. Our knowledge about this situation, however, has increased to the point where methods and approaches are available to help managers effectively cope with mid-career stress. First, the person should *learn more about the processes of mid-career change* to understand what is going on inside him or her. He or she should be encouraged to face up to feelings of restlessness and insecurity, to reexamine his or her values and life goals, and to set new ones or recommit to old ones. Life planning and career planning exercises have been devised that are extremely helpful in mid-career.

Second, the mid-career manager can be used effectively to *help develop younger employees*. In this mentor role, the manager can grow along with the younger person. Such contact with younger employees can keep a person up-to-date, fresh, and energetic. One of the most important psychological needs of mid-career managers is to build something lasting, something that will be a permanent contribution to one's organization or profession. The development of a future generation of managers and executives certainly could be a satisfying contribution.

A third approach is to *deal directly with the issue of obsolescence*. This can be done by going back to school for seminars, workshops, courses, and degree programs. The manager not only gains new knowledge, but a great deal of learning and self-assessment can occur by interacting with managers like him or her in other organizations. A better approach is to prevent obsolescence from occurring in the first place. An organization that gives managers assignments throughout their careers that force them to develop new skills and learn about new developments in their fields is acting on this principle. As we have suggested throughout this book, the job itself probably has more impact on the manager's development than most off-the-job activities. With job rotation, the manager is assigned to a job where he or she is working with recent graduates where mutual learning and a trading of experiences can occur. The new job may require the learning of new skills such as computer operations, employee affirmative action laws, manufacturing techniques, and so on. If transfers were expected to continue throughout the career, more use could be made of learning potential in new jobs and new people, and obsolescence could be reduced.

Whatever the approach, the mid-career plateau happens to managers in all types of organizations. Organizations are recognizing this factor and are building preventive measures into their career planning programs.

A Concluding Comment: Building A Managerial Career

Choosing a managerial career can be one of the most exciting, challenging, and rewarding decisions in a person's life. Successful managerial careers are the result of careful preparation, hard work, and continual planning.

Throughout this book, we have discussed and presented the experiences of practicing managers and the research of management scholars as they relate to the development of key managerial skills. We conclude this chapter with a short, but hopefully valuable, list of career activities that may lead to improved managerial skills.[19]

Work hard—do excellent work.   On a continuing basis, this is probably the most important key to success. Hard work that is well done will pay off in both short-term and long-term results. Isolated setbacks will no doubt occur, but in the long run it is the high performer who reaps the most benefits. Consistent high performance will identify you as a dependable person, one who can be counted on when the chips are down.

Learn how to control organizational resources.   Controlling resources brings power and the ability to influence others. One of the most important resources is information. When you have valued information, others need your assistance and your influence increases. This also increases your visibility and your centrality to the purposes of the organization.

Learn how to get along with a variety of people.   Current and future managers will increasingly be asked to be generalists. This means they must become skilled in interacting with a variety of technical specialists, peers, subordinates, superiors, and people outside the organization. These skills involve not only understanding what motivates others, but concern for your own ability to effectively communicate and cooperate in a number of situations, be they committee meetings or one-on-one interactions.

Help superiors succeed in their work.   Your superiors are the key people who will make decisions on your career movement. Try to not only develop good relations with them, but become a valued subordinate by keeping them informed and assisting them when it is clear you can help. This, however, can create a problem. A key subordinate to an upwardly mobile superior may be considered part of an advancement team—that is, when your superior moves, he or she will take you. On the other hand, being an indispensable subordinate to a "deadwood" superior may hinder your career movement—you make the superior look so good, he or she is reluctant to let you go.

Find a supportive mentor.   As we have suggested throughout this book, mentoring is one of the most important processes in developing managers. Even if the organization does not have a formal mentor-protegé program, become associated with people from whom you can learn, and in effect you may have more than one mentor. When mentoring is not sanctioned by the organization, choose and maintain your mentor relationships carefully. Remember, you need mentors more than they need you, and losing a mentor can be quite harmful to you. When your mentor is not your direct superior, be careful not to alienate your superior by appearing disloyal or snubbing his or her advice.

Develop your own self-improvement program.   Career planning is as much your responsibility as the organization's. Don't wait for the organization to suggest career improvement methods—show initiative. This can include nominating yourself for new jobs, projects, or positions and indicating interest in education and training programs. One of the most important things for self-improvement is to read current literature. Know what is going on around you in other organizations, what the important trends are, and what you need to be up-to-date. *The Wall Street Journal, Business Week, Fortune, Forbes, Harvard Business Review,* and *Management Review* are just some of the many sources to draw upon. Hopefully, your interest in these sources has been kindled by their use in this book.

 ## SUMMARY FOR THE MANAGER

1.   While there is no universally accepted best way to manage, recent studies offer some interesting suggestions. One of these studies in the book *In Search of Excellence* identifies such factors as a bias for action, closeness to the customer, simple form-lean staff, and emphasis on key business values, which have proven critical to the success of certain outstanding companies.

2. The career profiles of today's successful executives present some interesting points. For example, educational levels are increasing, most had parents who were professionals or executives, the Midwest has been a breeding ground for many, and most have worked for fewer than three organizations during their careers.

3. The dominant factors for career success include concern for results as well as people, a desire of responsibility, and a desire to achieve.

4. An understanding of one's expectations and the expectations of the organization is one of the most important lessons to be learned from a first job. Unrealistic expectations create problems that the new manager must eventually confront.

5. Other lessons to be learned concern the impact of the first supervisor, the realities of performance evaluation, and the inherent lack of job challenge on initial assignments.

6. Organizational politics are a way of life in many firms and institutions. Managers must learn that political alliances exist and are based on power and influence. Such political activities, however, can be a source of anxiety and stress. Future success comes, in part, from learning how to cope with this ever-present stress.

7. The career planning process consists of organizational career planning and individual career planning. The two must be integrated for an effective mix.

8. One of the key components of organizational career planning is career pathing. It consists of a series of positions—vertical, lateral, and downward—from the manager's current job. Movement through these jobs systematically provides the manager with the necessary experience and skills for future performance.

9. Individual career planning involves at least three elements: personal resource analysis, personal preference analysis, and a statement of career goals. Career goals should be formulated not only with respect to time, but also criteria, preferably prioritized. These goals should be continually analyzed and revised.

10. Among the most important current issues in managerial careers are dual careers and the mid-career plateau. Many families now have two wage earners. This creates promises and problems for both family members and the organization. The mid-career plateau occurs for many managers during middle age. Job rotation, training, and mentorship are some of the many methods organizations have adopted to counter this problem.

 # REVIEW AND DISCUSSION QUESTIONS

1. Why is the service sector identified as a promising managerial career area?
2. Managers are more highly educated today than their past counterparts were. Why is this?
3. What role does college play in creating unrealistic expectations?
4. Why are many new managers not prepared for the realities of organizational politics?
5. In what ways does the young recruit's first supervisor affect his or her career?
6. What is the difference between organizational career planning and individual career planning?
7. Some career pathing programs involve downward moves for managers. What must the organization do to keep the manager on a positive track?

8. What is a personal resource analysis?
9. Why is time an important factor in developing career goals?
10. What new problems have been created for organizations and individuals with the emergence of dual-career couples?

NOTES

1. T. J. Peters and R. H. Waterman, *In Search of Excellence.* (New York: Harper & Row, 1982).
2. J. A. Sussman, "A Career Profile of the Senior Executive," *Management Review* (July 1979): 14-21.
3. M. C. Johnson, "Mentors—The Key to Development and Growth," *Training and Development Journal* (July 1980): 55-57.
4. See D. T. Hall, "Potential for Career Growth," *Personnel Administration* (1971): 18-30; and E. H. Schein, "The First Job Dilemma," *Psychology Today* (March 1968): 22-37.
5. D. T. Hall, *Careers in Organizations* (Glenview, Ill.: Scott, Foresman, 1976), p. 66.
6. T. M. Rohan, "Lessons for that First Job," *Industry Week* (August 20, 1979): 94.
7. J. M. Ivancevich, M. T. Matteson, and C. Preston, "Occupational Stress, Type A Behavior, and Physical Well Being," *Academy of Management Journal* (June 1982): 373-391; and J. S. Mancuso, "Executive Stress Management," *Personnel Administrator* (November 1979): 23-26.
8. "Executive Stress May Not Be All Bad," *Business Week* (April 30, 1980): 96.
9. T. P. Ference, J. A. F. Stoner, and E. K. Warren, "Managing the Career Plateau," *Academy of Management Review* (October 1977); and J. F. Veiga, "Mobility Influences During Managerial Career Stages," *Academy of Management Review* (March 1983): 64-85.
10. E. H. Burack, "Why All the Confusion About Career Planning?" *Human Resource Management* (Summer 1977): 21-23.
11. M. Jelinek, ed., *Career Management* (Chicago: St. Clair, 1979), pp. 354-56.
12. E. H. Schein, "The Individual, the Organization, and the Career," *Journal of Applied Behavioral Science* (1971): 404-17.
13. H. L. Wellbank, D. T. Hall, M. A. Morgan, and W. C. Hamner, "Planning Job Progression for Effective Career Development and Human Resources Management," *Personnel* (March-April 1978): 54-64.
14. S. Gould, "Career Planning in the Organization," *Human Resource Management* (Spring 1978): 8-11; and M. A. Von Glinow, M. J. Driver, K. Brousseau, and J. B. Prince, "The Design of a Career Oriented Human Resource System," *Academy of Management Review* (January 1983): 23-32.
15. Hall, *Careers in Organizations*, p. 187.
16. D. T. Hall and F. Hall, "What's New in Career Management," *Organizational Dynamics* (Summer 1976): 17-33; and R. W. Scholl, "Career Lines and Employment Stability," *Academy of Management Journal* (March 1983): 86-103.
17. M. Bralove, "Problems of Two-Career Families Start Forcing Businesses to Adapt," *The Wall Street Journal* (July 15, 1981): 22.
18. See Hall, *Careers in Organizations*, p. 85; and D. J. Levinson, *The Seasons of a Man's Life* (New York: Knopf, 1978), pp. 191-200.
19. See M. A. Morgan, ed., *Managing Career Development* (New York: Van Nostrand, 1980); E. Jennings, "Success Chess," *Management of Personnel Quarterly* (Fall 1980): 2-8; and A. N. Schoonmaker, *Executive Career Strategy* (New York: American Management Associations, 1971).

Challenges to Managers

Fast Track at Bethlehem Steel Corporation

Attempting to convince bright, young college graduates to take jobs in the U.S. steel industry has not been an easy task during the past few years. Steel companies have a reputation for stodgy management, dirty pants, small profits, and big problems. The trend, however, seems to be shifting as more and more college graduates are investigating careers in the steel industry, particularly Bethlehem Steel. The reason apparently is the desire to participate in Loop, an unusual recruiting and training program that puts new graduates on the management track the day they join the company. Surprisingly, Bethlehem's program has existed since 1922.

Other big industrial companies woo college graduates with promises of challenging jobs and good salaries. But Bethlehem adds what its recruiters call "the third piece of the pie"—a guaranteed shot at management before the newly minted graduate even learns the first real job. This may sound risky, since most employees move into management at most companies only after they demonstrate they can handle subordinate jobs. But Bethlehem contends that the qualities that mark people as management material—leadership and personal integrity, for example—are evident by the time they are college seniors. Offering these students places in the Loop program often allows the company to overcome both the poor image of the steel industry and the higher salary offers made by other companies.

Bethlehem's three-phase program "loops" trainees through all of the company's operations, from steelmaking to accounting to public relations. The first phase is a two-week orientation session at headquarters that gives participants an overall look at the company and thorough exposure to the steelmaking process. Extensive movement through the recruit's assigned plant or office follows. Then there is on-the-job training for two years, with quarterly evaluations. The aim is to have participants rise at least as high as the department-head level during their careers.

Of Bethlehem's 270 top managers and executives, 56 percent were participants. At the middle-management levels and in some functions, the percentage is higher. For example, in steel operations, 78 percent of the managers went through the program while 61 percent of the firm's accounting managers took part. Loyalty also appears to be an outcome of the program. The company says that industrial firms typically lose an average of 50 percent of their new recruits during the first five years of employment. Since the program's inception, Bethlehem has retained 70 percent of its participants throught the first five years. Bethlehem executives indicate that employees do not have to go through the program to get ahead. The current chairman, in fact, was hired in 1975 from a large accounting firm. Other outside hirings of top executives have caused some concern among program participants.

Most current Loop classes nevertheless consider themselves to be among the chosen few, a feeling of being somebody special. That feeling breeds a mixture of comaraderie and competition among the class, numbering usually over 150 people. For example, during study sessions, engineers explain to accountants the technology of making steel, while accounting trainees show engineering trainees why it is better to use a faster depreciation method to offset inflation. On the other hand, during daily classes with top executives, the participants almost always vie for the attention with their work and even their appearance.

Adapted from Douglas Sease, "Grads Trained for Fast Track at Bethlehem," *The Wall Street Journal* (July 29, 1980): 31.

Questions for Discussion

1. What principles of career planning are used by Bethlehem?
2. Identify some of the positive features of the program. What are some possible negative features?

3. Why has the program been a success?
4. Would you want to be part of this type of program?

EXPERIENTIAL EXERCISE
Investigating Job and Career Opportunities

Purpose

1. To investigate job and career opportunities in organizations.

2. To develop an investigative framework that will enable the young recruit to minimize the effects of unrealistic job expectations.

Required Understanding

A basic understanding of the elements of career planning.

How to Set Up the Exercise

The instructor may assign this exercise to individual students or a team of students as an external project. The results can be handed in as a formal report, or discussed within the team or group.

Instructions for the Exercise

Students should contact an organization in the area—either in person or by telephone. A manager within the organization should be identified who can provide answers regarding job and career opportunities within the firm. An acquaintance employed by the organization or possibly someone within the personnel function can serve this purpose. After the manager has been identified, the following questions should be asked. Responses should be recorded for later presentation.

1. Nature of the work.
   a. What kind of job or career is being discussed?
   b. Is it an entry-level job or above?
   c. Briefly describe the kinds of things an employee is expected to do.
2. Conditions of work.
   a. What kinds of hours are you expected to work? (Watch for overtime, night work, regular hours, irregular hours, weekends, etc.) Are you paid for overtime?
   b. Does the job offer security? Is it seasonal or irregular? When people leave this job for another organization, what are the usual or prevalent reasons?
   c. What is the work environment like? Are there any hazards?
   d. Are there elements of the job that might be unpleasant to the employee, such as noise, heat, and so on?
   e. Can the job be challenging enough to hold your attention and motivate you?

3. Pay, training, and promotion.
   a. What are the maximum, average, and minimum wages for this job?
   b. What are the normal promotional steps for this job? How long do the steps take on the average? Does a formal career planning program exist? How does pay change with each step? Does the organization support a mentorship program, formal or informal?
4. Worker relationships.
   a. Do you work primarily alone or with other people in this job?
   b. Is there a lot of competition between fellow workers in this job, such as commissions or promotions?
   c. Are the relationships between employees on the job formal or informal?
   d. Given the nature of the work, are there opportunities for close personal relationships?
5. Worker qualifications.
   a. Is previous experience or training required? What is the source, nature, and length for such experience and training?
   b. Is there evidence of any preference given on the basis of age, sex, or race?
6. Physical qualifications.
   a. Are there any eyesight, height, strength, stamina, speech, or appearance requirements?
7. Educational requirements.
   a. Does entry into this job require a high school diploma, associate degree, bachelor's degree, master's degree, doctorate, or post-graduate work?
   b. Does advancement on the job require formal education, advanced degrees, special classes, or special training?
8. Psychological qualifications.
   a. What aptitudes, abilities, personality characteristics, and so on are needed to be successful at getting and mastering the job?
   b. Are there types of screening exams or psychological tests given? What is the nature of such exams?
9. Work experience.
   a. What experience, if any, is required for entry-level and higher-level jobs?
   b. What special skills must one possess to qualify for this job?
   c. Are there any skill tests given for this job?
10. Performance evaluation.
    a. When are employees evaluated on this job? Does it vary with length of service?
    b. Who is expected to conduct these evaluations? Are superiors trained in formal performance appraisal methods? Does a formal evaluation system exist? When and in what form can the employee expect to receive feedback on his or her performance?
    c. Are career planning and performance appraisals separate or simultaneous?
11. Equipment requirements.
    a. What items, such as tools or clothing, must be supplied by the employee?
    b. Is an automobile required?
12. Employment opportunities.
    a. To what extent are workers in demand today in this type of job?
    b. Where is the greatest demand, geographically or within the industry?
    c. Is employment likely to increase, decrease, or stay the same in the next three-to-five years?

Adapted from Edmond Billingsley, *Career Planning and Job Hunting for Today's Student* (Glenview, Ill.: Scott, Foresman, 1978), pp. 33-34.

List of Key Terms

Abilities   Potentials for carrying out specific acts or behaviors that are necessary but not complete conditions for behavior.

Accountability   A person's obligation to carry out responsibilities and be answerable for decisions and activities.

Achievement   A motive that causes a person to prefer tasks that involve only a moderate amount of risk and involve rather immediate and clear feedback on results.

Activity   The work necessary to complete a particular event in a PERT network. An activity consumes time, which is an important variable in a PERT system.

Activity ratios   Ratios used during ratio analysis that indicate how well an organization is selling its products in relation to its available resources.

Ad hoc committee   A temporary committee formed to serve a short-term, specific purpose.

Affirmative action programs   Programs whose basic purpose is to eliminate barriers and increase opportunities for underutilized and/or disadvantaged people.

Assessment center   A multidimensional approach to the measurement of performance and potential.

Assistant-to   A staff assistant to a line manager; though normally lacking line authority, this person often has considerable responsibility and influence.

Audit   An investigation of activities. An *internal audit* is conducted by an organization's own personnel; an *external audit* is conducted by an outside firm.

Authority   The power to issue commands, make decisions, take action, and enforce obedience.

Automation   The use of mechanical or computerized equipment in routine operations and/or decisions, replacing human activity.

Avoidance   The administration of a reinforcement that prevents an undesired behavior.

Avoidance conflict resolution   A strategy that generally disregards causes of a conflict by enabling the conflict to continue under controlled conditions.

Balance-sheet budget   A composite of all financial plans that reflect anticipated assets, liabilities, and owners' equity at a future time.

Behavior   The tangible acts or decisions of individuals, groups, or organizations.

Behavior modeling   A training or skills development technique that emphasizes role playing and videotape review to afford learning through experience.

Behavioral decision theory   Decision models that examine the influence of individual, group, and organization factors in decision making.

Behavior modification   An approach to motivation that uses operant conditioning. Operant behavior is learned through consequences. If a behavior causes a desired outcome, it is reinforced. Because of its consequences it is likely to be repeated. Thus, behavior is conditioned by adjusting its consequences.

Behavioral leadership theories   Approaches to leadership that seek to identify the leadership styles that are the most effective in various situations.

Behaviorally anchored rating scales (BARS)   Performance ratings that focus on specific behaviors or acts as indicators of effective and ineffective performance, rather than focusing on broad adjectives such as "average, above average, or below average."

Brainstorming   A technique for generating a solution to a problem that involves the following steps: a group of people is assembled; each person suggests a solution; no criticism is allowed from other members of the group; and the ideas are evaluated.

Break-even analysis   A method for determining the relationship between cost and revenue at various sales levels in order to show the point at which it is profitable to produce and sell a product.

Break-even point   The point at which income equals cost.

Budget   A control tool that outlines how funds in a given period will be spent, as well as how they will be obtained.

Bureaucracy   An organizational system that relies on specialization of labor, a specific authority hierarchy, a formal set of rules and procedures, and rigid promotion and selection criteria.

Capital expenditure budget   A projection of the amount of money that will be needed during a given period for the purchase of capital items.

Career   An individual's sequence of jobs and behaviors associated with work-related experiences and activities over the span of his or her life.

Career path   The sequence of jobs planned for or by a person, which leads to a career objective.

Career planning The process of systematically matching an individual's career aspirations with opportunities for achieving them.

Career stages Distinct, but interrelated, steps or phases of a career.

Carrying costs The cost incurred by carrying an inventory. These include taxes and insurance on the goods in inventory, interest on the money invested in inventory and storage space, and losses because of inventory obsolescence.

Cash budget A projection of cash receipts and cash disbursements for a given period.

Centralization That situation in which a minimal number of job activities and a minimal amount of authority are delegated to subordinates.

Central tendency An error often associated with traditional rating scales. It consists of a rater incorrectly assigning similar ratings to a group of employees and not accurately representing the true distribution of performance. All ratings tend to cluster at the middle of the scale.

Chain of command The route by which authority is transmitted from top to bottom of an organization.

Chief executive officer (CEO) The highest-ranking person of authority in a company.

Classical conditioning The learning or acquisition of a habit (stimulus-response connection) through associating an unconditioned stimulus (UCS) with a conditioned stimulus (CS).

Classical decision theory A normative approach to decision making that emphasizes achieving known objectives by choosing the alternative that maximizes expected returns.

Classical design theory The theoretical approach based on scientific management procedures and bureaucratic principles.

Coercive power An influence over others based on fear.

Cohesiveness Closeness and common attitudes, behaviors, and performance of group members.

Committee A task group charged with performing a specific activity.

Communication The process by which information is transmitted and exchanged.

Communication barriers Factors that interfere with the process of communication. They include the distortion of messages, selective perception, semantic problems, timing, and information overload.

Compensatory decision process A rule whereby a decision maker allows a high value on one decision criterion to offset a low value on another criterion.

Competence The ability to perform well.

Competitive position Represents an organization's internal position on a product or product line from the General Electric Stoplight Strategy model.

Conceptual skill The ability to coordinate and integrate ideas, concepts, and practices. Such skill is most important to top-level managers.

Conformity Compliance with rules or customs.

Confrontation conflict resolution A strategy that focuses on the sources of conflict and attempts to resolve them through such procedures as mutual exchange of personnel, use of superordinate goals, or problem solving.

Conjunctive decision rule A rule whereby the decision maker establishes minimally acceptable levels on each of several decision criteria. To decide in favor of an alternative, that alternative must achieve minimally acceptable levels of every criterion.

Consideration Behavior of the leader that emphasizes openness, friendliness, and concern for the welfare of subordinates.

Constraint The relationship between an external opportunity and an internal weakness.

Content motivation theories Theories that focus on the factors within the person that start, arouse, energize, or stop behavior.

Contingency design approach An attempt to understand the interrelationships within and among organizational subsystems as well as between the organizational system on the whole and its environments. It emphasizes the multivariate nature of organizations and attempts to interpret how they operate under varying conditions and in specific situations.

Contingency plan A plan that outlines how to handle a possible but not necessarily probable future event.

Controlling function Managerial activity undertaken to assure that actual operations go according to plan.

Coordination The orderly arrangement of group effort to provide unity of action in the pursuit of a common purpose.

Critical incident method A job analysis technique that attempts to study the job in terms of specific, identifiable behaviors or actions that are critical to success in carrying out a job.

Critical path That sequence of events and activities within a PERT network that requires the longest period of time to complete.

Current ratio A liquidity ratio that indicates the organization's ability to meet its financial obligations in the short run.

Decentralization   The pushing downward in a hierarchy of decision-making authority.

Decision making   A choice among several mutually exclusive and exhaustive alternatives. The choice is made after a consideration of all possible outcomes, the probabilities of such outcomes, and the conditions associated with each alternative and its outcome.

Decision tree   A planning tool that graphically shows the future effects of given courses of action.

Decoding   A mental procedure that the receiver uses to decipher a message.

Defusion conflict resolution   A strategy that attempts to buy time to resolve intergroup conflict at a later point, when it is less emotional or crucial.

Delegation   The process of assigning job activities and related authority to specific individuals within an organization.

Delphi technique   A group decision technique closely associated with the nominal group technique, except members are physically separated from each other.

Departmentalization   The combining of jobs into a specific unit or department.

Diagnostic activities   Fact-finding or data-collection that attempts to find what is occurring within a unit or organization.

Differentiation   Segmentation of an organization's subsystems, each of which contains members who form special attitudes and behavior and tend to become specialized experts.

Division of labor   The assignment of various portions of a particular task among a number of organization members.

Downward communication   Communication that flows from any point on an organization chart downward to another point on the chart.

Dual careers   Describes the couple who both have full-time careers.

Effort   The motivated aspect of behavior, or the amount of energy expended by the individual in a given act. Level of effort is influenced by the strength of the individual's motives or needs.

Emergent leader   An individual who has emerged from a group to assume a role as the informal leader.

Encoding   Converting a communication into an understandable message.

Environmental uncertainty   The state of the external environment of an organization as defined by the degree of complexity and the degree of change.

EOQ model   The economic order quantity model, used to resolve problems regarding the size of orders. A manager concerned with minimizing inventory costs could use this model to study the relationships between carrying costs, ordering costs, and usage.

Equal Employment Opportunity Commission (EEOC)   Agency established to enforce the laws regulating recruiting and other managerial practices.

Esteem needs   Maslow's fourth set of human needs—desire for self-respect and respect from others.

Event   An accomplishment at a particular point in time on a PERT network. Consumes no time.

Expectancy   The perceived probability that a particular act will be followed by a particular outcome.

Expectancy theory   States that an individual will select an outcome based on how this choice is related to second-order outcomes (rewards). The choice of behavior acts is based upon the strength or value of the outcome and the perceived probability between first- and second-level outcomes.

Expert power   The capacity to influence based upon some skill, expertise, or knowledge.

Extinction   The decrease in undesirable behavior because of nonreinforcement.

Expenditure forecast   An estimate of the money an organization will spend during a given time period.

External communication   Communication that goes beyond an organization.

Extrinsic rewards   Rewards a person receives from sources other than the job itself. These include compensation, supervision, promotions, vacations, and friendships.

Favorableness   The leadership situation, based upon group atmosphere, task structure, and the leader's position power, which contributes to the leader's ability to influence subordinates.

Feedback   Knowledge about job peformance obtained from the job itself or from other employees.

Feedback control   Control that takes place after some unit of work has been performed.

First-line management   The lowest level of the hierarchy. A manager at this level coordinates the work of nonmanagers but reports to a manager.

Fixed cost   An expenditure that is not affected by a short-run change in revenue.

Flat organization chart   An organization chart characterized by few levels and large spans of control.

Flextime   A job design that staggers working hours so that employees decide when to begin and end their days.

Forecast   A prediction based on study and analysis of pertinent data.

Formal group   A subgroup created by management within an organization; formal groups, such as divisions and departments, make up the organization as a whole.

Friendship group   A group that evolves because of some common characteristic, such as age, political sentiment, or background.

Fringe benefits   Rewards given to an employee over and above wage or salary. They include vacation benefits, pension plan contributions, employee discounts, and other nonsalary rewards.

Functional group   A group that is created and specified by the structure of the organization.

Game theory   The simulation of real situations to test the effects of certain possible decisions.

Gantt chart   A graph on which projected and completed phases of production are plotted in relation to specific times.

Geographic departmentalization   The grouping of an organization's activities by area or territory.

Goal orientation   The particular goals (technological, economic, market, or scientific) with which individuals or groups are primarily concerned.

Goal setting   A critical activity identified as having an impact on the effectiveness of an incentive plan. To motivate performance through incentives, employees must accept the goals established for a task and/or set goals themselves.

Goal succession   The change in goals as a result of conscious effort by management to shift the course of the organization's activities.

Goals   At the organizational level, desired states that the system is attempting to achieve by planning, organizing, and controlling. Goals are created by individuals or groups within the organization.

Grid training   A leadership development method proposed by Blake and Mouton that emphasizes the necessary balance between production orientation and person orientation.

Graicunas's formula   A mathematical formula that shows geometrically how the addition of subordinates increases the complexity of managing.

Grapevine   A term referring to informal communication networks that parallel formal networks within organizations.

Group   Two or more individuals who are interdependent and interact for the purpose of performing to achieve a common goal or objective.

Group composition   The relative homogeneity or heterogeneity of a group based on the individual characteristics of its members.

Group decision   A decision reached jointly by members of a group. Interactions among people affect the group decision process. In addition, group decision making allows for the possibility of conflict among goals to be considered.

Group development   A series of stages that most groups go through over time (orientation, internal problem solving, growth and productivity, and evaluation and control).

Group norms   Standards of behavior established by a group that describe acceptable behavior.

Groupthink   A group defense reaction that impairs the quality of group decisions.

Halo effect   The forming of impressions (positive or negative) about a person based on performance in only one area.

Hawthorne effect   The tendency of people who are being observed to react differently than they would otherwise.

Hawthorne studies   Management studies conducted at the Western Electric Hawthorne plant near Chicago by a group of Harvard University researchers. The most famous studies ever conducted in the field of management.

Hierarchy-of-needs theory   A theory of motivation, proposed by Maslow, based on the idea that human needs form a hierarchy; as one need is satisfied the need at the next higher level emerges as a motivator.

Horizontal communication   Communication that takes place when the communicator and the receiver are at the same level in an organization.

Human resource accounting   An attempt to compute the worth of personnel by assigning monetary values to their contributions or to their costs in terms of recruitment and training.

Human resource planning   Estimating the size and makeup of the future work force.

Human skills   The ability to work with, motivate, and counsel people. Most important to middle-level managers.

Hygiene (maintenance) factors   Items that influence job dissatisfaction.

Incentive   A type of motive that focuses on an event or outcome attractive to an individual; outcomes towards which behavior is directed.

Incentive plan   A reward scheme that attempts to tie pay directly to job performance.

Industry attractiveness   Represents an organization's external position on a product or product line from the General Electric Stoplight Strategy model.

Initiating structure   The behavior of the leader that emphasizes structuring the task, assigning work, and providing feedback.

Influencing The process of guiding the activities of organization members in appropriate directions.

Informal group A subgroup created by the members themselves within an organization; e.g., people who regularly meet to play sports or to share ideas.

Information overload A condition in which too much information flows through communication channels; leads to ignoring potentially critical pieces of information.

Instrumental conditioning (See *Operant conditioning*.)

Instrumentality The relationship between first- and second-level outcomes.

Integration The quality of collaboration among departments that are required to achieve unity of effort by the demands of the environment.

Interaction requirements The variety of individuals, frequency, and qualities necessary in intergroup activities.

Interdependence The degree to which two or more groups are dependent on one another for inputs or outputs.

Interest group Informal groups created because of common characteristics or interests. Generally, when the interest declines, the group disbands.

Intergroup conflict Conflict between two or more groups.

Interval reinforcement A schedule of rewards that ties reinforcements to time. Such a schedule can be *fixed* or *variable*.

Intrinsic rewards Rewards associated with the job itself, such as the opportunity to perform meaningful work, complete cycles of work, see finished products, experience variety, carry out highly visible cycles of activity, and receive feedback on work results.

Inventory model A type of production control model that answers two questions relating to inventory management: "How much?" and "When?" An inventory model tells the manager when goods should be reordered and in what quantity.

Job A homogeneous cluster of work tasks, the completion of which serves some enduring purpose for the organization.

Job analysis The systematic study of jobs that attempts to discover the major task dimensions of a job and what it calls for in terms of employee behaviors and qualifications.

Job content Factors that define the specific work activities or tasks.

Job dynamics Situational factors surrounding the tasks of a job that must be considered to adequately define the job.

Job enlargement A job design strategy that expands the range of the individual's job horizontally, giving him or her more things to do.

Job enrichment A job design strategy, based on the motivator-hygiene theory, that seeks to improve performance and satisfaction by providing more challenge, responsibility, authority, and recognition to jobs.

Job evaluation A method that attempts to determine the relative worth of each job to an organization in order to establish a basis for relative wage rates within the organization. It is a major method for establishing reward policy.

Job functions The general requirements of a job and the methods involved in performing it.

Job rotation A job design strategy that involves moving the worker from task to task over a period of time to reduce boredom.

Job satisfaction An attitude held by a person that reflects an evaluation of a particular component in the work place.

Job specialization Dividing the work or tasks of a job into specialized, standardized, and simple tasks.

Job stress An individual's internal frustration and anxiety over certain job-related situations.

Key result area An aspect of a company's operations that has direct bearing on profitability.

Leadership The ability to inspire people to perform duties competently and willingly.

Leadership style A behavioral pattern a leader establishes while guiding organization members in appropriate directions.

Learning A relatively permanent change in behavior that occurs as a result of experience. Learning is to be distinguished from other factors influencing changes in behavior, including fatigue and maturation.

Legitimate power A leader's capacity to influence based upon his or her position in the organization.

Leniency An error often associated with traditional rating methods. It consists of a rater incorrectly assigning similar ratings to a group of employees without accurately representing the true distribution of performance, so that all ratings tend to cluster towards the high end of the scale.

Leverage The relationship between an external opportunity and an internal strength.

Leverage ratios Ratios used in ratio analysis to indicate the relationship between organizational funds supplied by the owners of an organization and organizational funds supplied by creditors.

Liabilities What an enterprise owes.

Line-and-staff organization An organization that has, because of its size or the complexity of its functions or goals, an advisory support staff in addition to a line staff.

Linear programming A method for determining the optimum combination of resources to use in attaining a goal. Used when a change in one variable results in a proportionate change in another.

Line authority The responsibility for carrying out an enterprise's main functions.

Line manager A person involved in carrying out the primary activities of an organization.

Liquidity ratios Ratios used in ratio analysis to indicate an organization's ability to meet upcoming financial obligations.

Management The process by which people, technology, job tasks, and other resources are combined and coordinated to achieve organizational goals.

Management audit An evaluation of the overall operation of an enterprise.

Management by objectives A process in which a superior and a subordinate or a group of subordinates jointly identify and establish common goals.

Management development The process of educating and developing selected employees so they have the knowledge, skills, attitudes, and understanding needed to manage in future positions.

Management functions The activities a manager must perform as a result of his or her position in the organization. Planning, organizing, leading, and controlling are the management functions.

Management information systems A structured complex of individuals, machines, and procedures to provide management with pertinent information from both external and internal sources. Management information systems support the planning, control, and operations functions of an organization by providing uniform information that serves as the basis for decision making.

Management science approach A method of studying management that emphasizes developing mathematical models to test management hypotheses.

Managerial roles The organized sets of behavior that belong to the manager's job. The three main types of managerial roles outlined by such researchers as Mintzberg are interpersonal, informational, and decisional roles.

Managerial grid activities A total organizational program that is implemented in six phases to upgrade individual managers' skills and leadership abilities, teamwork, goal setting, and monitoring of events.

Manpower planning Input planning that involves obtaining the human resources necessary for the organization to achieve its objectives.

Material budget A forecast of how much material will be necessary to achieve a given result.

Matrix design A design that includes the control features of functional organizational design and the adaptive aspects of product design, usually found in organizations that include a number of projects, programs, or task forces. In this arrangement, the special program managers have authority to supervise and divert subordinates from line managers.

Mechanistic organizations Organizations with highly specialized job tasks, rigid authority systems, top-down flow of communications, and conflict resolution by the superior.

Message The information a message sender communicates.

Message feedback The response of a message receiver to a message.

Message sender Anyone who communicates something to someone else.

Midcareer plateau The stage of a career at which there is no opportunity for further advancement.

Middle management The middle level of an administrative hierarchy. Managers at this level coordinate the work of other managers and report to a higher-level manager.

Mission statement A formal statement by the organization describing basic philosophies, products or services, and intentions.

Motion study The process of analyzing work in order to determine the most efficient motions for performing tasks. Motion study, a major contribution of scientific management, was developed principally through the efforts of Frederick Taylor and Frank and Lillian Gilbreth.

Motivation The inner strivings that initiate a person's actions.

Motivator-hygiene theory The theory that identifies two basic kinds of factors: hygiene factors and motivators. Hygiene factors (e.g., challenging job, personal growth, recognition and so on) increase satisfaction and, hence, affect motivation.

Network analysis An analytical technique which breaks down the whole of a project into specific parts so that each part can be evaluated in relation to the other parts and to time.

Noise Interference in the flow of a message from a sender to a receiver.

Nominal group technique A group decision method in which individual member judgments are pooled in a systematic fashion in making decisions. (See *Delphi technique.*)

Nonprogrammed decisions Decisions for novel and unstructured problems or for complex or extremely important problems. Nonprogrammed decisions deserve special attention by management.

Nonverbal communication The sharing of ideas without the use of words.

Operant conditioning A motivation approach that focuses on the relationship between stimulus, response, and reward.

Operating management Management which provides for the implementation of programs and projects in each area of performance, measures and evaluates results, and compares results with objectives.

Operational planning Organizational activities directed toward implementing strategic plans; concerned with establishing policies, procedures, and allocation of resources.

Operations manager A manager who converts strategic management's input into routine output for an organization.

Operations research (OR) A scientific approach to forecasting that uses mathematical models to predict which course of action from among the available alternatives will produce the best result.

Opportunity Term used to identify an external area where the organization may capitalize on certain positive factors.

Ordering cost An element in inventory control models that comprises clerical, administrative, and labor costs; a major cost component that is considered in inventory control decisions. Costs are incurred each time a firm orders items for inventory, as some clerical and administrative work is usually required to place the order and some labor is required to put the items in inventory.

Organic system An organizational design with a behavioral orientation, participation from all employees, and communication flowing in all directions.

Organization A system that coordinates people, jobs, financial resources, and managerial practices to achieve performance goals.

Organization structure The formally defined framework of task and authority relationships. The organi-

zation structure is analogous to the biological function of the skeleton.

Organizational change The intentional attempt by management to improve the overall performance of individuals, groups, and the organization by altering the organization's structure, behavior, and technology.

Organizing function All managerial activities that result in the design of a formal structure of tasks and authority.

Orientation The process of introducing new employees to an organization and to their specific jobs. *Formal orientation* is under the direct control of management; *informal orientation* is given by peers.

Path-goal leadership theory A leadership theory that emphasizes the influence of the leadership on subordinate goals and the paths to these goals.

Pay secrecy A management policy of maintaining silence or secrecy about individual employee salaries.

People change approaches Processes that modify attitudes, motivation, and behavioral skills through such techniques as training programs, selection techniques, and performance appraisal techniques.

Perception A process by which individuals (1) attend to incoming stimuli; and (2) translate such stimuli into a message indicating the appropriate response.

Performance The key dependent or predicted measure in our framework. It serves as the vehicle for judging the effectiveness of individuals, groups, and organizations.

Performance dimensions The basis for making appraisal judgments, consisting of the specific aspects, tasks, and outcomes upon which the performance of individuals and groups are judged.

Performance evaluation The process by which an organization obtains feedback about the effectiveness of individual employees and groups. It serves an auditing and control function in organizations.

PERT (Program Evaluation Review Technique) A form of network analysis used to determine time requirements for untried projects. Estimates are made of the best possible time, the most likely time, and the least desirable time in which the project will be completed.

Physiological (basic) needs Needs of the human body, such as food, water, and sex.

Planning function All managerial activities that lead to the definition of goals and to the determination of appropriate means to achieve those goals.

Policies Guidelines for managerial action that must be adhered to at all times. Policy making is an important management tool for assuring that action is oriented toward objectives. The purpose of policies is to achieve consistency and direction and to protect the reputation of the organization.

Position power A factor in the Fiedler contingency model of leadership that refers to the power inherent in the leadership position.

Positive reinforcement The administration of positive rewards, contingent on good performance, that strengthens desired behavior in the future.

Power The ability to influence another person's behavior.

Private sector organizations Profit-making organizations in the U.S. economy.

Problem The relationship between an external threat and an internal weakness.

Process motivation theories Theories that describe how behavior is energized, aroused, or stopped.

Profit sharing A plan by which a predetermined share of profits is paid to qualified personnel. Under *cash profit sharing,* a person's share of profits is distributed at regular intervals; under *deferred profit sharing,* a person's share of profits is invested in a fund and held until he or she reaches a certain age or leaves the company.

Profitability measures Measurement of the ratio of net profit to capital, to total assets, and to sales.

Program budgeting An extension and refinement of cost-effectiveness analysis whose purpose is to evaluate each organizational activity according to what it accomplishes for a given expenditure; that is, to relate objectives to resource allocation. Used by both private and public organizations.

Programmed decisions Responses to repetitive and routine problems, handled by a standard procedure that has been developed by management.

Project organizational design A design in which a project manager temporarily directs a group of employees who have been brought together from various functional units to complete a specific job.

Promotion from within A policy whereby management positions are filled by people who are already employees of the organization.

Public sector organizations Federal, state, and local governmental bodies.

Punishment The administration of negative rewards, contingent on poor performance, that acts to eliminate undesired behavior in the future.

Quality of working life A series of organizational interventions designed to improve the workplace for employees.

Queuing Scheduling people or items to minimize the cost of providing a service and the amount of time users of the service must wait.

Ranking An alternative method of performance appraisal in which a judge is asked to order a group of employees in terms of their performance from highest to lowest.

Rating A traditional method of performance appraisal that asks a judge to evaluate performance in terms of a value or index that is used in some standard way. Traditionally involves global rating scales.

Ratio analysis A performance-measuring device that uses ratios (percentages) to compare operating results of similar companies.

Ratio reinforcement A schedule of rewards that ties reinforcements directly to acts or behaviors. Can be *fixed* or *variable.*

Realistic job previews (RJP) The practice of providing realistic information to new employees, to avoid creating expectations that cannot be realized.

Recency of events error The tendency to make biased ratings because of the excessive influence of recent events.

Recruitment The initial screening of the total supply of prospective employees available to fill a position.

Referent power The capacity to influence based on identification with another powerful individual.

Reinforcement schedule The timing or scheduling of rewards.

Reinforcement theory A motivation approach that examines factors that energize, direct, and sustain behavior.

Reinforcer or reward A stimulus that follows an act and (1) reduces the need motivating the act; and (2) strengthens the habit that led to the act in the first place.

Responsibility The requirement imposed on an individual to take charge of and to answer to superiors for the performance of specific obligations.

Return on investment (ROI) The ratio of net income (earnings) to invested capital (stockholders' equity).

Revenue and expense (operating) budget A monetary plan that details anticipated revenues and predicted expenditures for a given period.

Revenue (sales) forecast An estimate of the amount of money that will be brought into an organization over a given period of time.

Reward bases The various methods for distributing rewards in organizations. Equity, equality, power, and need have served as bases for distributing rewards. A problem arises for management when bases conflict in reward policy.

Reward policy   An organizational policy concerning the type, amount, and way in which rewards are distributed in organizations.

Reward power   The capacity to influence based on the leader's ability to reward good performance.

Rewards   Outcomes or events in the organization that satisfy work-related needs.

Risk   The element of uncertainty involved in making decisions.

Risk propensity   A personality characteristic involving a person's like or dislike for taking chances.

Role   The expected-perceived-enacted behavior patterns attributed to a particular job or position.

Role ambiguity   Lack of clarity regarding job duties, authority, and responsibilities resulting in uncertainty and dissatisfaction.

Role analysis team building   Designed to clarify role expectations and responsibilities of team members. This clarification can be brought about by group meetings and discussion.

Role conflict   A state of tension created by multiple demands and conflicting directions from two or more individuals in performance of one's role, resulting in anxiety.

Rule   A statement that details what is and what is not to be done in a specific situation.

Scalar (chain-of-command) principle   Authority should flow directly and clearly from the top executive to each subordinate at successively lower levels.

Scientific management   A body of literature that emerged during 1890–1930 that reports the theories of engineers concerned with such aspects as job design, incentive systems, selection, and training.

Security needs   Maslow's second set of human needs, which reflect the desire to keep free from physical harm.

Selection   Choosing an individual to hire from all those who have been recruited.

Self-actualization   The need to fully realize one's potential.

Single-use plans   Plans used only once or on occasion because they focus on organizational situations that do not occur repeatedly.

Situational leadership theories   Approaches to the study of leadership that stress the importance of situational factors (leader and subordinate characteristics, the task, and organizational factors) on leader effectiveness.

Social density   A physical measure of the number of group members working within a certain walking distance of each other.

Societal environment   Forces external to an organization that influence what happens internally. Among these forces are political, regulatory, resource, economic, and technological factors.

Social responsibility   The responsibility to promote the overall welfare of society by refraining from harmful practices or by making an effort to help society.

Social responsiveness approach   An approach to meeting social obligations that considers business to have societal and economic goals as well as the obligation to anticipate upcoming social problems and work actively to prevent them.

Span of control   The number of subordinates who report directly to a supervisor.

Staffing   The management function of selecting, training, compensating, and evaluating people so that the work in an organization is performed according to established standards.

Staff manager   A person who serves as an adviser and is auxiliary to the organization in terms of helping it achieve goals.

Standard   A model level of performance to be attained.

Standing committee   A permanent committee that deals with specific, ongoing matters.

Status   A social ranking within a group assigned on the basis of position in the group or individual characteristics.

Status consequence   The agreement of group members about the relative status of members of the group.

Stereotyping   A perceptual error in which a person forms a judgment about another person based on ideas or impressions formed about that individual's group. Individual differences within the group are ignored.

Stimulus-response   The basic unit of learning (habit) in both the classical and instrumental conditioning models.

Strategic business unit (SBU)   The basic organizational unit for strategic planning. Usually is a division or department.

Strategic management   Develops the mission, objectives, and strategies of the entire organization; the top-level decision-makers in the organization.

Strategic planning   The activities that lead to the definition of objectives for the entire organization and to the determination of appropriate strategies for achieving those objectives.

Strategy   A comprehensive and integrated framework

that determines the nature, choices, and direction of an organization's activities toward goal achievement.

Strength Term used to identify a strong internal resource element.

Strictness An error often associated with traditional rating methods. It consists of a rater incorrectly assigning similar ratings to a group of employees without accurately representing the true distribution of performance, so that all ratings tend to cluster towards the low end of the scale.

Structural change approaches Changes brought about through new formal guidelines, procedures, policies, and organizational rearrangements.

Survey-feedback activities Activities that focus on collecting survey data and designing a plan of action based on the interpretation of the data.

Task force A temporary group formed to study a unique problem and offer a solution.

Tall organization chart An organization chart characterized by many levels and relatively small spans of management.

Task types A classification strategy that categorizes group tasks on the basis of one of three objectives: production, discussion, or problem solving.

Task uncertainty The extent to which internal or external events create a state of uncertainty with respect to job predictability.

Technical skill The skill of working with the resources and knowledge in a specific area. Such skill is most important to first-level managers.

Technical change approaches Changes that focus on rearrangements in work flow, new physical layouts, job descriptions, and work standards.

Technology People-machine activities carried out in the organizational system that utilize such technological inputs as capital goods, production techniques, and managerial and nonmanagerial knowledge.

Testing Examining human resources for qualities relevant to performing available jobs.

Theory X and theory Y McGregor's theory that behind every management decision are assumptions that a manager makes about human behavior. The theory X manager assumes that people are lazy, dislike work, want no responsibility, and prefer to be closely directed. The theory Y manager assumes that people seek responsibility, like to work, and are committed to doing good work if rewards are received for achievement.

Threat Term used to identify an external area where the organization may find problems or difficulties.

Time orientation The degree to which individuals or groups are oriented toward short-term or long-term results.

Time series analysis method A method of predicting future sales levels by analyzing the historical relationship within an organization between sales and time.

Top management The top level of an administrative hierarchy. Managers at this level coordinate the work of other managers but do not report to a manager.

Training The process of developing qualities in employees that ultimately will enable them to be more productive and, thus, contribute more to organizational goal attainment.

Trait leadership theories Approaches to the study of leadership that seek to identify a finite set of characteristics or traits that can distinguish effective from noneffective leaders.

Unity of command A management principle that states that each subordinate should report to only one superior.

Upward communication Communication from individuals at lower levels of an organization's structure to those at higher levels; e.g., suggestion boxes, group meetings, and appeal or grievance procedures.

Valence The strength or value placed by an individual on a particular reward.

Validity A measurement quality of any performance evaluation technique that demands information regarding performance effectiveness be gathered in a way that insures the relevance of the information to the purpose of the performance review.

Variable (flexible) budget A prediction intended to reflect changes in expenditures that will result from changes in revenue.

Variable cost An expenditure that is affected by a change in revenue.

Vertical integration The performance of a business at different levels in the same industry.

Verbal communication The sharing of ideas through words.

Vulnerability The relationship between a external threat and an internal strength.

Weakness Term used to identify a weak internal resource element.

Zero-base budgeting An accounting and planning tool that requires managers of organizational units to justify all planned expenditures and rank them in order of priority. Expenditures that recurred in prior budgets have to be rejustified. Originated in government but has also been utilized in the private sector.

Subject Index

Company/Product Index

Name Index

Photo Credits

Positions of photographs are shown in abbreviated form as follows: top (t), bottom (b). All photographs not credited are the property of Scott, Foresman.

vi(t) John Patsch/Hillstrom Stock Photo vi(b) Michal Herron/Woodfin Camp viii Charles Harbutt/Archive Pictures ix(t) Gould Inc. ix(b) Eric Kroll/Taurus Photos x, xi(t) Transamerica Corporation xi(b) FMC Corporation xii Santa Fe Railway Photo xiii(t) Warren Colman/Hillstrom Stock Photo xiii Shepard Sherbell/Picture Group xiii(b) Transamerica Corporation xiv(b) Photo courtesy of Travenol Laboratories, Inc. 4 Charles Harbutt/Archive Pictures 40 Jonathan Goell/Picture Cube 78 Ellis Herwig/Stock, Boston 112 David Powers/Stock, Boston 174 © 1982 Joel Gordon 208 Ken Robert Buck/Picture Cube 250 Jaye R. Phillips/Picture Cube 286 Jean-Claude Lejeune 318 Val Wilmer/Format 358 © 1980 Joel Gordon 428 Algimantas Kezys 464 FPG 504 © 1978 Joel Gordon 536 Charles Harbutt/Archive Pictures 578 © 1982 Joel Gordon 604 Peter Menzel/Stock, Boston 644 Ken Sexton/Hillstrom Stock Photo 679 Andrew Popper/Picture Cube

Exhibit Credits

The Practice of Management